Series Editors:
David R. Beukleman
Janice C. Light

Interventions for Individuals
with Autism Spectrum Disorder
and Complex Communication Needs

Also in the *Augmentative and Alternative Communication Series*:

Supporting Communication for Adults with Acute and Chronic Aphasia
edited by Nina Simmons-Mackie, Ph.D., BC-ANCDS,
Julia M. King, Ph.D.,
and David R. Beukelman, Ph.D.

Transition Strategies for Adolescents and Young Adults Who Use AAC
edited by David B. McNaughton, Ph.D.,
and David R. Beukelman, Ph.D.

*Practically Speaking: Language, Literacy, and
Academic Development for Students with AAC Needs*
edited by Gloria Soto, Ph.D.,
and Carole Zangari, Ph.D., CCC-SLP

AAC

Series

Interventions for Individuals with Autism Spectrum Disorder and Complex Communication Needs

edited by

Jennifer B. Ganz, Ph.D., BCBA-D
Texas A&M University
College Station

and

Richard L. Simpson, Ed.D.
University of Kansas
Lawrence

·P A U L·H·
BROOKES
PUBLISHING C⁰.®

Baltimore • London • Sydney

Paul H. Brookes Publishing Co.
Post Office Box 10624
Baltimore, Maryland 21285-0624
USA

www.brookespublishing.com

Typeset by BMWW, Baltimore, Maryland.
Manufactured in the United States of America by
Sheridan Books, Inc., Chelsea, Michigan.

The individuals described in this book are composites or real people whose situations are masked
and are based on the authors' experiences. In all instances, names and identifying details have been
changed to protect confidentiality.

Dedication image courtesy of Jennifer B. Ganz. The photograph shown in Figure 4.3 is courtesy of
Pat Mirenda. Figures 13.5, 13.6, 13.8, and 13.11 are courtesy of Tabi Jones-Whleber. Figure 13.2 is
courtesy of Mary Kotrady. Figure 13.3 is courtesy of Amanda Keilholtz. Figure 13.7 is courtesy of
Teresea Ismach.

Clip art © iStockphoto.com.

Library of Congress Cataloging-in-Publication Data

Names: Ganz, Jennifer B., editor. | Simpson, Richard L., 1945– editor.
Title: Interventions for individuals with autism spectrum disorder and complex communication
    needs / edited by Jennifer B. Ganz and Richard L. Simpson ; with invited contributors.
Description: Baltimore : Paul H. Brookes Publishing Co., 2019. | Series: Augmentative and
    alternative communication series | Includes bibliographical references and index.
Identifiers: LCCN 2018034678 (print) | LCCN 2018015195 (ebook) |
    ISBN 9781681252292 (pbk.) | ISBN 9781681253107 (epub) | ISBN 9781681253114 (pdf)
Subjects: LCSH: Autism spectrum disorders—Treatment. | Communicative disorders—Treatment. |
    Communicative disorders—Patients—Education.
Classification: LCC RC553.A88 I579 2019 (ebook) | LCC RC553.A88 (print) | DDC 616.85/882—dc23
LC record available at https://lccn.loc.gov/2018034678

British Library Cataloguing in Publication data are available from the British Library.

2022   2021   2020   2019   2018

10   9   8   7   6   5   4   3   2   1

Contents

Series Preface

The purpose of the *Augmentative and Alternative Communication Series* is to address advances in the field as they relate to issues experienced by individuals with complex communication needs across the life span. Each volume is research based and practical, providing up-to-date information on recent social, medical, and technical developments. Each chapter is designed to synthesize the research related to a specific issue or communication group and to consider implications for practice to improve outcomes for individuals that require augmentative and alternative communication (AAC). To help ensure a diverse examination of AAC issues, an editorial advisory board assists in selecting topics, volume editors, and authors. Prominent scholars, representing a range of perspectives, serve on the editorial board so that the most poignant advances in the study of AAC are sure to be explored.

There are many reasons for maintaining the AAC series, but foremost has been the number and diversity of people who experience complex communication needs and require AAC. AAC needs are not delineated by specific age parameters; people of all ages who have developmental and acquired disabilities rely on AAC. Appropriate interventions for individuals across a wide range of disabilities and levels of severity must be considered. The series is intended to advance research and improve practice in AAC, benefiting many stakeholders including individuals that use AAC and their families, speech-language pathologists, occupational therapists, physical therapists, early childhood educators, general and special educators, school psychologists, neurologists, and professionals in rehabilitative medicine and engineering.

Fundamentally, the field of AAC is problem driven. We, the members of the editorial advisory board, and all professionals in the field are dedicated to solving problems in order to improve the lives of people with complex communication needs. The inability to communicate effectively is devastating. As we chronicle the advances in the field of AAC, we hope to systematically dismantle the barriers that prevent effective communication for all individuals.

Series Editors

About the Editors

Jennifer B. Ganz, Ph.D., BCBA-D, Professor of Special Education, Educational Psychology, College of Education and Human Development, Texas A&M University, Mail Stop 4225, 801 Harrington Tower, College Station, TX 77843

Dr. Ganz is Professor of Special Education at Texas A&M University. She received her doctorate at the University of Kansas, with a concentration in autism spectrum disorder and behavioral disorders and is a Board Certified Behavior Analyst-Doctoral. Her research focuses on the use of technology to improve social-communication deficits in people with autism spectrum disorder (ASD) and other developmental disabilities. Dr. Ganz has worked in general and special education and as an educational consultant; she continues to consult and present in Texas to schools and parents on topics relating to ASD and other developmental disabilities. She has also been a speaker at regional, national, and international conferences on topics including interventions for behavior and ASD, including strategies to address social and communication skills. Dr. Ganz has received several grants to fund research and service projects involving students with ASD and intellectual disabilities and a personnel preparation project for professionals working with children with disabilities. In addition, Dr. Ganz has authored or co-authored numerous articles, books, and chapters.

Richard L. Simpson, Ed.D., Professor Emeritus, University of Kansas, Lawrence, KS

Dr. Simpson was Professor of Special Education at the University of Kansas, where he directed numerous University of Kansas and University of Kansas Medical Center demonstration programs for students with autism spectrum disorder (ASD) and other disabilities and coordinated a variety of federal grant programs related to students with ASD and other disabilities. Dr. Simpson also worked as a special education teacher, school psychologist, and coordinator of a community mental health outreach program. He authored numerous books, articles, and assessments on a variety of topics connected to students with disabilities. Dr. Simpson is the former senior editor of the professional journal *Focus on Autism and Other Developmental Disabilities*. His awards include the Council for Exceptional Children Research Award, Midwest Symposium for Leadership in Behavior Disorders Leadership Award, Autism Society of Kansas Leadership Award, and numerous University of Kansas awards and distinguished roles, including the Gene A. Budig Endowed Teaching Professorship of Special Education.

Contributors

Katherine J. Bateman, Ph.D., BCBA-D
Teaching Associate
University of Washington
Haring Center
Box 357925
Seattle, WA 98195

Wendy K. Berg, M.A.
Research Scientist
Center for Disabilities and
    Development
University of Iowa Stead Family
    Children's Hospital
100 Hawkins Drive, Room 251
Iowa City, IA 52242

Elizabeth E. Biggs, Ph.D.
Assistant Professor
Department of Special Education
College of Education
University of Illinois,
    Urbana-Champaign
Education Building, MC-708
1310 S. 6th Street
Champaign, IL 61820

Joanne M. Cafiero, Ed.S., Ph.D.
Executive Director
Cafiero Communications, LLC
Rockville, MD

Jessica G. Caron, Ph.D.
Assistant Professor
Communication Sciences and Disorders
The Pennsylvania State University
401G Ford Building
University Park, PA 16802

Erik W. Carter, Ph.D.
Professor
Department of Special Education
Vanderbilt University
PMB 228, Peabody College
Nashville, TN 37203

Ariane N. Gauvreau, Ph.D., BCBA-D
Field Director and Teaching
    Associate
Special Education
University of Washington
Miller Hall
Box 353600
Seattle, WA 98195-3600

Stephanie Gerow, Ph.D., BCBA-D
Assistant Professor of Educational
    Psychology
Baylor University
One Bear Place #97301
Waco, TX 76798

**Georgia Hambrecht, Ph.D.,
    CCC-SLP**
Professor
Department of Communication
    Sciences and Disorders
Western Carolina University
4121 Little Savannah Road, Office 103
Cullowhee, NC 28723

Christine Holyfield, Ph.D.
Assistant Professor
Department of Rehabilitation, Human
    Resources, and Communication
    Disorders
University of Arkansas
261 Epley Center
Fayetteville, AR 72701

Ee Rea Hong, Ph.D.
Assistant Professor
Faculty of Human Sciences,
    Disability Sciences
University of Tsukuba
1-1-1 Tennodai
Tsukuba, Ibaraki-ken 305-8572
Japan

**Tabitha Jones-Wohleber, M.S.,
    CCC-SLP**
Frederick County Public Schools
1799 Schifferstadt Boulevard
Frederick, MD 21701

Connie Kasari, Ph.D.
Professor
University of California, Los Angeles
68-268 Semel Institute for
    Neuroscience and Human Behavior
760 Westwood Plaza
Los Angeles, CA 90024

Ching-Yi Liao, M.Ed.
Texas A&M University
4225 TAMU
College Station, TX 77843

Rose A. Mason, Ph.D.
Assistant Professor
Department of Educational Studies
College of Education
Purdue University
100 N. University Street
West Lafayette, IN 47907

Jennifer J. McComas, Ph.D.
Professor
University of Minnesota
347 Education Sciences Building
Minneapolis, MN 55455

Pat Mirenda, Ph.D., BCBA-D
Professor
University of British Columbia
2125 Main Mall
Vancouver, BC V6T 1Z4
Canada

Billy T. Ogletree, Ph.D., CCC-SLP
Professor and Department Head
Department of Communication
    Sciences and Disorders
Western Carolina University
3971 Little Savannah Road
158 HHS Building
Cullowhee, NC 28723

Quannah E. Parker-McGowan, Ph.D.
Post-Doctorate Fellow, Teaching
    Specialist
CEHD Educational Psychology
University of Minnesota
56 E. River Parkway
Minneapolis, MN 55455

Christopher S. Prickett, M.A.
Department of Educational Psychology
Texas A&M University
4225 TAMU
College Station, TX 77843

Joe Reichle, Ph.D.
Professor
Department of Speech-Language-
    Hearing Sciences
University of Minnesota
115 Shevlin Hall
164 Pillsbury Drive S.E.
Minneapolis, MN 55455

Cynthia A. Riccio, Ph.D.
Department of Educational Psychology
Texas A&M University
4225 TAMU
College Station, TX 77843

Amy J. Rose, Ph.D.
Assistant Professor
Department of Communication
    Sciences and Disorders
Western Carolina University
3971 Little Savannah Road, Room 160
1 University Drive
Cullowhee, NC 28723

Kelly M. Schieltz, Ph.D.
Assistant Teaching Professor
Department of Educational, School &
    Counseling Psychology
University of Missouri
16 Hill Hall
Columbia, MO 65211

Ilene S. Schwartz, Ph.D.
Professor
University of Washington
Haring Center
Box 357925
Seattle, WA 98115

Jessica Simacek, Ph.D.
Research Associate
University of Minnesota
250 Education Sciences Building
56 East River Road
Minneapolis, MN 55455

Kyle Sterrett, B.A.
Graduate Student Researcher
University of California, Los Angeles
67-546 Semel Institute for Neuroscience
    and Human Behavior
760 Westwood Plaza
Los Angeles, CA 90024

David P. Wacker, Ph.D.
Professor Emeritus
Department of Pediatrics
The University of Iowa
140 Center for Disabilities and
    Development
Iowa City, IA 52242

Volume Preface

Meaningful and functional participation in the human experience requires the ability to communicate with others. Unquestionably, this is true for individuals with complex communication needs (CCN; this terminology is consistently used by all chapter authors to refer to individuals with severe language challenges, including those with minimal and no speech or capacity to use spoken words). In particular, this book focuses on individuals with autism spectrum disorder (ASD). Children, adolescents, and adults with CCN and ASD require specialized, multidisciplinary interventions and supports leading to development of functional communication assets and capacity. Outcomes of strategic and evidence-based communication-focused time and resource investment for individuals with CCN are noteworthy, including enhanced engagement with others, improved school and postschool experiences, increased opportunities for independence, and enhanced quality of life.

This book, an addition to Paul H. Brookes Publishing Co.'s Augmentative and Alternative Communication Series, was inspired and motivated by the need for widescale access to high quality and scientifically supported assessments and interventions for individuals with CCN. Both experienced and neophyte practitioners from multiple disciplines—including educators, speech-language pathologists, other related-service school professionals and staff members, and community professionals—require practitioner-friendly and up-to-date, evidence-supported information and methods they can use with students and clients with CCN. Professionals assigned the critical and demanding responsibility of designing, implementing, and monitoring first-rate programs for individuals with CCN can achieve positive assessment and intervention outcomes as a result of applying the most effective methods. We, as this book's editors and contributors, are hopeful this resource will contribute to the improvement of this significant challenge. We are certainly heartened by our experiences that have time and again demonstrated that individuals with CCN working with multidisciplinary professionals who are knowledgeable and skilled in using appropriate methods and intervention strategies demonstrate significant progress and enhanced positive outcomes.

Chapters included in this book were authored by experienced and internationally recognized authorities in speech-language pathology, behavior analysis, and special education. Each chapter contributes to improved understanding of individuals with ASD and CCN and addresses the current CCN "research-to-practice gap" by providing practitioner-friendly information and methods with potential to make positive differences in the lives of individuals with significant communication impairments. Chapter 1 overviews characteristics of children and adolescents with ASD who have CCN, therein creating a foundation for examining various elements of methods, supports, and interventions in subsequent chapters. Chapter 2 focuses on assessment, with emphasis on collection and analysis of multifaceted and multidisciplinary formal and informal data and related information that informs maximally effective instruction and intervention planning. Chapter 3 examines the state of the science related to the evidence for educational and behavioral interventions linked to improving outcomes for individuals diagnosed with ASD and CCN. Chapter 4 provides an overview of augmentative and alternative communication (AAC), including an examination of various tools and intervention options and their utility with learners with distinctive characteristics. Chapter 5 gives specific attention to "low-tech" AAC options; Chapter 6 concentrates on "high-tech" AAC modes and applications. Chapter 7 examines the communication–behavior connection, with a spotlight on functional communication training. Chapters 8, 9, and 10 address the needs and options for specific age groups: Chapter 8 focuses on early childhood populations, Chapter 9 addresses school-age groups, and Chapter 10 discusses evidence-based practices for older adolescents and adults. Chapter 11 is devoted to naturalistic interventions for individuals with ASD and CCN, in particular the role and capacity of Naturalistic Developmental Behavioral Interventions as elements of effective practice programming. Chapter 12 highlights the crucial role that parents/families and peers of individuals with CCN play in supporting and using communication-enhancement methods and interventions. Chapter 13 offers a comprehensive look at the visual and environmental methods that support the needs of individuals with CCN. Finally, Chapter 14 synthesizes salient content presented by chapter authors along with a research-focused pathway for advancing the capacity of the field to better serve the needs of children, adolescents, and adults with CCN.

Acknowledgments

This volume is the result of hundreds of hours of thought and work from a team of individuals dedicated to improving the lives of people with autism spectrum disorder (ASD) and complex communication needs (CCN) and their families.

Foremost, this book was the brainchild of the series editors, David Beukelman and Janice Light, who recognized the gap in collaboration and information sharing across several fields of service providers, family members, and researchers who develop and implement interventions with this population. We are thankful to David for his suggestions regarding real-life impacts of our words on the individuals we aim to serve. Janice, in particular, provided the vision, impetus, and long-term guidance that resulted in this book, which we hope lives up to Janice and David's vision of communicating effectively across and providing input to these fields and providers. The series editorial advisory board provided valuable insights as well.

The authors contributed stellar, comprehensive work that represents the state of the science in intervention research for individuals with ASD and CCN. These authors are researchers, authors, and service providers spanning at least 4 decades of contributions to this field and are affiliated with nationally recognized autism, applied behavior analysis, communication science, psychology, and special education research institutions. We are immensely grateful for their time and efforts, particularly given that the rewards for such tasks are typically low, although the benefits are great. We thank these authors for their dedication to this population and for fitting this work into their already busy work lives.

We thank the Brookes editorial team—including Stephanie Henderson, Astrid Zuckerman, and Melissa Solarz—for their unending patience, suggestions, and problem-solving.

Our students, former students, colleagues, mentors, and collaborators—too numerous to name—have provided support, literature, and inspiration from which we have drawn in the development of this book and our own chapters.

Our families have provided behind-the-scenes supports, including cheerleading, listening to ideas, picking up the slack at home, and providing forgiveness when we have struggled with deadlines and other hiccups along the way. Thank you, Janice, Michael, Eli, Hannah, and Bethany.

Finally, and most important, we would like to thank the families and individuals with ASD who are the impetus for this work and who, in countless numbers, have guided our development as researchers and authors with their practical input. This input has significantly increased the relevance and impact of our work, including the formation of this volume. We hope that this work at least partly returns the favor.

This volume is dedicated to Rich Simpson, the co-editor of this book and my first and best academic mentor. Rich was pivotal in my career as an autism researcher and in the careers of countless other academics, service providers, and policy makers. He was a pioneer in the field of special education and autism as an author and researcher; his body of work has helped shape the services provided to children and youth and has greatly advanced the evidence base in autism education research. This book is dedicated as a thank you to Rich for his steadfast support and guidance and enduring partnership. It was his hope, as it is mine, that this book improves the lives of individuals with autism spectrum disorder and their families. It is also my hope that this book extends rather than concludes Rich's legacy.

Rich, my dear friend and colleague, passed away during the final stages of this project. His fingerprints are on every page. He said, in reference to this book, "It is one we'll be proud to claim!" He was right.

—Jeni

Courtesy of Jennifer B. Ganz

I

Overview

1

Characteristics of Individuals With Autism Spectrum Disorder Who Have Complex Communication Needs

Richard L. Simpson

Children and youth with autism spectrum disorder (ASD) are having an ever-increasing presence and impact on the educational, clinical, and community landscapes. By any standard, worldwide and wide-ranging interest in autism is remarkable, including among various professional groups, parents and families, and the general public. The far-reaching interest in ASD is both understandable and warranted. Autism is an inimitable disability, characterized by myriad and perplexing challenges. For sure parents and families, educators, speech-language pathologists, and other related-service professionals, health care professionals, community and social service planners, and a host of other groups are directly and indirectly feeling the impact of individuals diagnosed with autism-related disorders.

One unmistakable reason for the extraordinary attention ASD are receiving is connected to its dramatic prevalence increase (Centers for Disease Control and Prevention [CDC], 2017). The CDC (2017) estimates approximately 1 in 68 individuals (and approximately 1 in 42 boys and 1 in 189 girls) fall on the autism spectrum. These remarkable frequency estimates, of course, mean that more and more schools, families, and communities are confronting challenges associated with autism. Autism-related disorders are currently more common than Down syndrome, juvenile diabetes, childhood cancer, and countless other diseases and disabilities (CDC, 2017). It is indisputable that ASD is having a profound impact on a wide sector of the world's population (Simpson & Myles, 2016).

Unsurprisingly, there have been countless attempts to identify and explain the cause or causes of the astonishing prevalence increase in ASD (Oller & Oller, 2010; Silberman, 2016; Young, Grier, & Grier, 2008), and these efforts continue. Personal statements and stories, viewpoints, myriad theories, and suppositions about why so many individuals are receiving autism diagnoses (LaCava, 2016) are ubiquitous. Despite unprecedented attention and research efforts, the clear-cut and precise cause or causes of ASD, along with countless other treatment and intervention issues, continue to be unsettled. The Interagency Autism Coordinating Committee (IACC) reported that between 2009 and 2014 over 11,000 studies about autism had been published, more than twice the number of studies from the preceding 5 years (IACC, 2014). Progress in gaining a better understanding of ASD continues; however, many issues, including cause, remain unresolved, and virtually every other matter of importance to ASD stakeholders requires extensive additional investigation.

Individuals diagnosed with ASD, including children and adolescents, have variable abilities and abilities that are often difficult to reliably gauge, including intellectual and cognitive assets. That some individuals with ASD have been known to demonstrate savant skills and gifted-level intellectual abilities is only one manifestation of this variability. Idiosyncratic, inconstant, and highly individualized language and communication abilities, behavior oddities and problems, and social interaction characteristics and patterns that define ASD also contribute to its seemingly mysterious image. These variable characteristics and diagnostic patterns, in combination with lack of clear and definitive explanations for the causes of ASD, have even further boosted the disorder's enigmatic persona.

Significant variability along fundamental fields of functioning and development among individuals with diagnoses of ASD has proven particularly challenging for educators, speech-language pathologists, and other professionals. Individuals with what was once officially diagnosed as Autistic Disorder and other classic forms of autism often have consequential cognitive and intellectual impairments, profound language and communication delays and problems, severe behavioral challenges such as self-stimulatory manifestations and related anomalies, and significant social abnormalities and social skill deficits (Heflin & Alaimo, 2007; Simpson & Myles, 2016; Thompson, 2007). The autism spectrum includes those who fall on the so-called "high end" of the continuum. These individuals share general features and characteristics with others who have ASD: language and communication concerns, atypical interpersonal features and quirks, social skill and social interaction challenges, and behavioral irregularities and problems (American Psychiatric Association [APA], 2013). Accordingly, educators, speech-language pathologists, and others involved in educating, treating, and supporting children and youth who fall on the autism spectrum must be prepared to address a wide variety of needs within multiple settings and circumstances. Unquestionably, a basic element of an effective program formula is multidisciplinary participation.

Augmentative and alternative communication (AAC): A system of communication that is intended to replace or supplement conventional speech in people with complex communication needs (CCN); also refers to the field of study of AAC.

Notwithstanding basic shared ASD features, individuals at the higher end of the ASD continuum characteristically appear quite dissimilar compared to those with classic forms of autism. These individuals, commonly identified as having high-functioning autism and Asperger syndrome, tend to have average to above-average intellectual and cognitive abilities, developmentally average speech and language abilities, and overall academic skills and capacity that typically allow them relatively routine access to standard grade-expected curricula and customary educational opportunities (Attwood, 2007; Simpson & Myles, 2011). In spite of these assets and qualities, these so-called "high functioning" children, youth, and adults routinely experience significant challenges connected to their ASD disability, especially social skill and social interaction problems (Simpson, Ganz, & Mason, 2012). Clearly it would be inaccurate to assume individuals who function at the high end of the autism spectrum have inconsequential and uncomplicated and undemanding needs.

The authors of this book, with full awareness of the far-reaching and substantial requirements of learners with high-functioning autism, focus on individuals with classic and severe forms of ASD. In particular, a range of chapters concentrate on individuals with significantly impaired language and communication skills, including individuals who have no speech or spoken words. Categorically and by definition and diagnostic characteristics, these learners have complex communication needs (CCN). The term CCN is used consistently throughout the book by chapter authors to refer to individuals with little or no speech or spoken word capacity and other significant communication impairments. These individuals require augmentative and alternative communication (AAC) supports and other evidence-based interventions implemented by qualified multidisciplinary professionals in order to communicate, and thus function. This introductory chapter sets the stage and creates a foundation for examining various elements of AAC methods and supports and interventions for learners with ASD and CCN in subsequent chapters. Relative to chapters in this book, AAC is an encompassing term that refers to a variety of communication methods used to supplement or replace speech for individuals with impairments in the production or comprehension of spoken language.

Complex communication needs (CCN): A person with complex communication needs is someone who does not use or understand speech, who uses speech that is difficult to comprehend, or who has difficulty understanding the speech of others. People may have lifelong or shorter term complex communication needs caused by disability or acquired illness or injury.

DEFINING ASD

A primary means of defining and diagnosing ASD is the *Diagnostic and Statistical Manual of Mental Disorders* (*DSM*). For years, this guidebook has been the primary source for diagnosticians and other professionals to define, classify, and diagnose a range of mental and mental health–related disorders and disabilities, including autism (APA, 2013). The *DSM*, as is the case with other reputable diagnostic guides, relies on behavioral observations. Such protocols are required because no valid medical or other tests or procedures currently exist.

Neither autism nor ASD were included in the two earliest editions of the *DSM* (APA, 1952; 1968). These omissions were related to the perceived infrequency of autism occurrences and because other diagnostic categories were used for autism-related disorders. Children who presented with what was at the time understood to represent "autistic traits" were judged to have a form of childhood schizophrenia.

It was not until 1980, as a part of the third edition (*DSM-III*), that autism was first introduced. In that edition, autism was termed *Pervasive Developmental Disability* (PDD). Within the *DSM-III*, PDD included three disability classifications: *Childhood Onset PDD, Infantile Autism*, and *Atypical Autism*. In 1987, as part of the APA's *DSM-III* text revision, the 1980 PDD diagnoses were replaced with two autism options: *Autistic Disorder* and *Pervasive Developmental Disorder Not Otherwise Specified* (PDD-NOS). The criteria used to make autism diagnoses were also revised to focus on three primary developmental domains: 1) qualitative impairments in reciprocal social interaction, 2) qualitative impairments in verbal and nonverbal communication and imaginative activity, and 3) significantly restricted activities, behaviors, and interests (APA, 1987). The PDD-NOS classification was designed to accommodate children with some autism characteristics, even though they did not demonstrate characteristics needed to qualify for a conventional and full autism diagnosis.

The *Diagnostic and Statistical Manual of Mental Disorders, Fourth Edition* (*DSM-IV*; APA, 1994) significantly revised and refined the PDD classification options to include three additional disorders: *Childhood Disintegrative Disorder, Asperger's Disorder*, and *Rett's Disorder*. In many ways Rett's Disorder was unlike other forms of autism. It was observed exclusively among girls, and it was thought to be the result of a specific genetic mutation (Amir et al., 1999). However, the condition did involve significant communication impairments, social interaction anomalies, and behavior abnormalities, thus explaining the rationale used to include Rett's Disorder within the autism umbrella. In 2000, the APA made minor amendments to the *DSM-IV*; however, those changes did not affect the PDD classifications.

The current fifth edition, or *DSM-5* (APA, 2013), significantly revised the ASD guidelines. The PDD term was dropped, and the five previous diagnostic options were replaced with a single classification: *Autism Spectrum Disorder*. The ASD terminology had widely been in place for years; thus, the APA decision brought *DSM* diagnostic terminology into line with existing lexicon. The *DSM-5* also created a severity scale with different levels. This system was used to gauge the extent and type of supports individuals with ASD would need for social interaction and communication and behavior problems. Supports were calibrated within three levels:

Level 3: Individuals who require very substantial support

Level 2: Individuals who require substantial support

Level 1: Individuals who require support

Foci of the *DSM-5* (APA, 2013) are two primary ASD components:

1. Deficits in social communication and social interaction (e.g., failure to initiate or respond to social interactions)

2. Restricted, repetitive patterns of behavior, interests, or activities (e.g., repetitive atypical motor movements, insistence on sameness, preoccupation with unusual objects)

The *DSM-5* thus consolidates the previously separate social interaction and communication categories. The *DSM-5* also relies on three additional important considerations:

1. Is there evidence the ASD symptoms were manifest during the developmental period (i.e., by age 3)?

2. Does the condition significantly impair social, occupational, or other important areas of functioning?

3. Does the individual being assessed have an intellectual disability or global developmental delay?

Relative to whether ASD symptoms were shown by age 3 and whether the ASD characteristics significantly impair functioning, there are three and four criteria, respectively. A child must meet all three criteria listed in the first area and at least two criteria in the second domain to meet the ASD diagnostic standards. Children and youth who are assessed for ASD are also evaluated for severity for the two aforementioned fields and whether an individual with ASD has an intellectual impairment, language impairment, and medical, genetic, or environmental conditions. Finally, the *DSM-5* clearly recognizes that ASD traits manifest early in life and the condition is a lifelong developmental disorder.

It is important to recognize that *DSM-5* provides guidelines for clinical professionals. It is almost universally used by clinical professionals (e.g., psychiatrists, clinical psychologists) within the United States and commonly is used worldwide. However, the *DSM-5* diagnostic criteria are not the primary ASD guide used by public school personnel within the United States. School psychologists and other school-based diagnostic professionals apply criteria outlined in the Individuals with Disabilities Education Improvement Act of 2004 (IDEA 2004; PL 108-446) to guide disability-related decisions, including whether a student is eligible for an ASD diagnosis. Nevertheless, school personnel, including speech-language pathologists and educators, commonly consider *DSM-5* criteria and reports as a part of conducting ASD evaluations. Furthermore, as shown next, the IDEA 2004 definition of autism generally aligns with the *DSM-5* criteria.

(c)(1)(i) Autism means a developmental disability significantly affecting verbal and nonverbal communication and social interaction, generally evident before age three, that adversely affects a child's educational performance. Other characteristics often associated with autism are engagement in repetitive activities and stereotyped movements, resistance to environmental change or change in daily routines, and unusual responses to sensory experiences.

THE SIGNIFICANCE OF LANGUAGE AND COMMUNICATION DEVELOPMENT FOR CHILDREN AND YOUTH WITH ASD

Language and communication play a particularly important role in diagnosing ASD. Even more important, language and communication domains are mandatory fields for concentrating intervention resources and supports. Indeed, development of functional language and communication assets are a primary determinant of education and posteducation achievement, independence, quality of life, and a host of other important outcome variables for individuals with autism-related disorders (Tager-Flusberg, Paul, Lord, et al., 2005). Without functional communication skills, the prognosis and opportunities for enhanced quality of life for individuals with ASD are significantly diminished (Levy & Perry, 2011; Wetherby, Prizant, & Rydell, 2000). Unquestionably, language and communication assets, capacity, and needs must be accurately identified at an early stage of life and suitable evidence-based interventions and supports designed and implemented in order for individuals with ASD to experience relative success in life.

It is particularly noteworthy when a child has difficulty learning to make appropriate gestures (pointing, waving) by 12 months, use meaningful single words by 16 months, or utter spontaneous two-word (nonechoic) phrases by 24 months; or loses previously acquired and functional language or social/communication skills at any age. ASD is considered to be a lifelong disability, and individuals with the disorder, especially those with classic and severe forms of autism, can be expected to need significant support during all phases of their life.

Notwithstanding these challenges and the need for supports, individuals diagnosed with autism who acquire the ability to functionally and competently communicate generally have significantly improved outcomes (Ogletree, 2016). Without doubt, the ability to communicate is a salient predictive variable for independence, general quality of life, and overall life success. Individuals with autism who can relatively effectively and functionally express their basic needs, initiate and respond to others in a mostly socially appropriate fashion, and interact in utilitarian fashion generally achieve the best outcomes (Gotham, Pickles, & Lord, 2008). Recognizing the lifelong impact of functional communication capacity and the need for purposeful and practical communication skills is an important first-step toward ensuring children and youth with ASD receive an appropriate education.

Noteworthy communication and social signs of ASD among young children, particularly those with more severe forms of autism, include the following:

- Limited gaze shifts and failure to consistently share visual attention with others

- Failure to share positive affect with others

- Failure to learn and use developmentally typical and symbolic gestures (e.g., wave "bye," say "hi")

- Reliance on unconventional means of communication (e.g., leading a parent's hand to a refrigerator as a sign of hunger, without recognizing the parent)

- Poor coordination of sounds, eye gaze, and communication gestures

- Failure to understand language and comprehend the communication attempts of others

- Delays or failure to make communication sounds (e.g., babble) and develop speech

- Atypical, unconventional, and aberrant use of objects and lack of pretend play

- Abnormal social behavior and development such as lack of interest or failure to orient and attend to others; difficulty recognizing and coordinating attention between people, objects, and events; and difficulty or lack of interest in understanding and sharing affect and emotional states.

These same items are also fundamental targets for intervention focus and resource allocation. For instance, highly successful programs with a variety of children with ASD have been implemented to shape age-appropriate communication gestures and functional nonverbal communication skills (e.g., handing a teacher or caregiver an icon of a desired item or activity; Ogletree, 2016). Individuals who are taught these basic skills are most apt to achieve the best outcomes and live relatively rewarding lives, both during their school years and as adults (Ogletree, 2016).

THE SOCIAL, BEHAVIOR, AND COMMUNICATION LINK

By definition, children and youth with ASD have communication and language impairments. Individuals with severe and classic forms of autism are particularly prone to significant communication deficits, including significant difficulty in developing expressive language and major functional communication skill deficits (Heflin & Alaimo, 2007; Prelock & McCauley, 2012).

Despite significant communication deficits, it is important to keep in mind that children and youth with autism who do not develop typical speech and language and who lack conventional nonverbal communication skill training almost always possess some form of communication system. These self-developed and improvised communication methods may be lacking in functionality, usefulness, and efficiency, and often they mostly rely on nonverbal behaviors, signals, and symbols. For example, children with severe autism who lack conventional communication training regularly make use of primitive and socially undeveloped gestures and actions (e.g., grabbing, hand-over-hand leading of a caretaker to a desired item, pounding the door of a refrigerator to indicate a desire to eat or drink), unconventional and unrecognizable verbal utterances and vocalizations (e.g., screaming, repeated consonant and vowel sounds), and atypical and aberrant behavior (e.g., odd, self-injurious or similar actions as signs of protest). Such communication attempts tend to be highly idiosyncratic and frequently involve a combination of actions, gestures, and vocalizations (Alpern, 2012; Wetherby et al., 2000). These self-developed nonverbal communication methods almost universally lack specific and precise intentionality and range (Machalicek, O'Reilly, Beretvas, Sigafoos, & Lanciono, 2007). That is, unlike young children with typical development, individuals with autism rely on a limited number of actions, responses, and gestures to represent a wide variety of wants and needs. For example, the same odd and unconventional verbal utterance or behavioral action may be used to express a wide variety of communicative functions ranging from hunger, thirst, desire for a particular item or activity, and objections and protests to countless other items. Along these lines, it is clear these individuals are depending on communication options with significantly limited utility, versatility, and functionality (Prelock & McCauley, 2012; Wetherby, Yonclas, & Bryan, 1989).

The same utility and functionality restrictions also apply to undeveloped and unskilled communication systems of children with autism related to regulating others and engaging in social activities such as participating in shared activities (i.e., joint attention). Children with severe autism who lack conventional communication assets and skills will have no communication alternative except to resort to rudimentary, unskilled, and primitive ways of requesting and protesting (e.g., screaming, hitting, uttering simple nonword sounds; Plumb, Wetherby, Oetting, & Craig, 2013). In addition, development of shared attention and joint attention skills, a common requisite among learners with severe and classic forms of autism, requires intervention and training. Shared attention, foundational for social and communication skill development, rarely occurs spontaneously and typically requires intervention. Thus, a basic building platform for development of even rudimentary social development will be dependent on children having a functional and shared communication system (Chiang, Soong, Lin, & Rogers, 2008; Maljaars, Noens, Jansen, Scholte, & van Berckelaer-Onnes, 2011; Paparella, Goods, Freeman, & Kasari, 2011).

Two major inferences can be clearly drawn regarding the connection between the communication assets and abilities of children with severe autism who lack conventional communication systems and social competence building assets. First, even if children lack expressive language and conventional nonverbal communication training and systems, they will almost always have ways of communicating and a communication repertoire. Understanding and accurately assessing a child's preintervention communication assets and system, such as motivating items (e.g., particular food) and regulatory strategies (e.g., tactics a child uses to request and protest), are essential. Carefully considering this information bodes well for designing and creating maximally effective and individually most appropriate AAC and related training methods and intervention programs.

A second clear conclusion regarding the link between a child's preintervention language and communication skills and ongoing development of social capacity is that children with severe autism will not develop improved functional skills and capacity without the assistance of others. These children require timely, evidence-based, and ongoing support and training from qualified multidisciplinary professionals in order to improve (Ogletree, 2016; Prelock & McCauley, 2012). Children who are permitted to continue to use their unconventional, unskilled, and undeveloped communication systems will not refine and naturally build on an existing system but rather continue to use the same nonfunctional strategies.

Many of the principles and themes regarding children with autism who lack expressive language also apply to individuals with limited and significantly delayed speech and spoken word use. Ogletree (2016) referred to these learners as *emergent verbal communicators*; emergent communicators with autism are likely to use some functional speech and spoken words in combination with various nonverbal communication strategies. The speech and spoken words of many of these individuals are likely to include immediate and delayed echolalia, and these verbalizations may be used to build and shape more conventional and functional verbal skills (Prizant, 1983; Roberts, 1989). At least some of these so-called *emergent verbal communicators* appear to gain speech and spoken word capacity boosts when taught with AAC methods (Ganz, Davis, Lund, Goodwyn, & Simpson, 2012).

It should be clear from this discussion that manifestations of behavior, including aberrant, aggressive, and other socially undesirable initiations and responses closely align and link to the communication domain. Indeed, "behavior is communication" is a common mantra of professionals who educate and offer related services to individuals with ASD. This is especially the case in understanding and addressing maladaptive and related unproductive behaviors of children and youth with ASD who have minimal or no speech and spoken words. In so many cases, these behaviors are the result of efforts to communicate wants, needs, and preferences; protest and manage situations, environments, and circumstances; make choices and voice independent thinking; and convey feelings such as frustration, anxiety, and fear (Carr & Durand, 1985; Durand & Carr, 1991). Individuals with typical development, as well as many high-functioning individuals with ASD, have the same need to communicate as do individuals with minimal or no speech, spoken words, or socially acceptable and shared communication options. However, individuals with shared and conventional language and communication assets have the capacity to interact with and manipulate their environments in a more advanced, shared, reciprocal, and effective manner. Individuals who lack functional communication skills often find themselves with few communication alternatives other than socially unacceptable and maladaptive behavioral manifestations.

A general starting point for understanding and planning for replacement of ineffective communication modes for individuals with no or minimal speech and spoken words is consideration and analysis of the context within which behavior occurs. Attempting to understand the purpose of a particular behavior, especially its communicative intent, is also fundamental to teaching an augmentative and alternative communication system. All behavior has a function, and behaviors vary in accordance with setting variables, environments, and circumstances. An often-experienced example of this principle is seen in the child with autism who consistently and effectively communicates at school using a speech-generating device. However, this same child relies exclusively on screaming and hitting at home to obtain desired objects and activities. Of course, this scenario may be reversed, wherein a child uses an improved communication system at home but not at school.

Especially for children with minimal or no speech or spoken words, the function of a behavior may not be readily apparent. Nevertheless, a guiding principle relative to assessing individuals for the purpose of designing an improved communication system is all behavior has both functional and adaptive qualities. (Chapter 7 of this book, "Functional Communication Training for Durable Behavior Change," by McComas et al., provides in-depth discussion of this topic.) Consider, for example, an elementary-age child with ASD who lacks conventional communication skills and who routinely screams to gain teacher and staff attention. School personnel may view this student's screaming behavior as maladaptive and socially inappropriate for a classroom. Yet, this student's screaming, within the context of this particular classroom setting, is adaptive in that it allows him to have teacher and staff attention. Thus, this socially immature and generally unacceptable behavior actually produces a functional outcome. For this reason, in the eyes of the student, screaming is neither ineffective, nor unpurposed or maladaptive because it serves as a relatively functional and effective communication tool. In order for this student to learn a more socially acceptable communication mode, the method will need to be systematically and consistently taught and reinforced, and his previously employed screaming mode will need to be ignored and replaced with the new method. Only when the new system proves to be more effective and efficient than the previous screaming strategy will it be accepted by the learner and consistently used.

LINKING CHARACTERISTICS OF INDIVIDUALS WITH ASD TO INTERVENTIONS AND EDUCATIONAL SUPPORTS AND PRACTICES

For a variety of reasons, ASD is a particularly notable and inimitable disability. Indeed, the disorder's designation as the quintessential enigma of disabilities is well deserved. This description and label is linked to both incomparable and highly variable and unique characteristics and unclear causal factors. The result of these exceptional and distinctive traits along with related factors (e.g., savant skills, unfounded causative explanations) has served as the foundation for a legacy of unusual (and at times bizarre) conceptions, discernments, and explanations of

ASD and a willingness to rely on out-of-the-ordinary and unproven interventions and treatments. This pattern has been particularly problematic for learners with minimal or no speech or spoken words.

Communication interventions and supports, as with other developmental domains germane to the needs of individuals with ASD, need to be scientifically supported. This logical and common-sense necessity has served as the underpinning for increased demand for identification, application, and ongoing evaluation of evidence-based practices and methods for individuals with ASD. Undeniably, there is a clear-cut connection between consistently and correctly using evidence-based interventions and supports and fostering the best school and postschool outcomes (Simpson & Crutchfield, 2013) Yet in spite of this clear fact, and supporting legislation such as The No Child Left Behind (NCLB) Act of 2001 (PL 107-110) that requires that educators and school professionals such as speech-language specialists base their programs and teaching on scientifically supported methods, there continues to be a willingness among some to rely on unproven and non-scientific methodology (Travers, Ayers, Simpson, & Crutchfield, 2016). Clearly, the effective practice initiative supporting individuals with ASD is in need of further development.

In general terms, evidence-based strategies and practices have been proven to yield positive outcomes. These methods have been validated based on high-quality research methodology, specifically scientifically valid research designs, appropriate procedures, and proven evaluation approaches (Cook, Tankersley & Landrum, 2016). Minor terminology distinctions have been made, including between scientifically supported methods, evidence-based practices, and research-validated strategies (Fixsen, Naoom, Blase, Friedman, & Wallace, 2005). However, each of these terms refer to interventions, strategies, and practices that have been shown to be effective and utilitarian based on objective empirical proof.

In spite of continued use of unproven methods by some practitioners, ever-growing agreement among ASD stakeholders indicates that educational and clinical programs serving individuals with ASD should base their programs on scientifically proved practices (National Professional Development Center on Autism Spectrum Disorders, 2010). This sentiment is far from full-bodied and universally supported, and it continues to compete with the tradition of some within the ASD community of tolerating and approving practices and strategies with little proven capacity to produce positive outcomes.

The history of systematically vetting interventions and supports purported to be useful for individuals with ASD is relatively recent, for the most part a 21st century phenomena. In 2001, the National Research Council identified and recommended basic effective practice components recommended for all educational programs serving young children with ASD, including structured early intervention experiences, intensive and active engagement instructional programs, individualized goals, and an emphasis on language and communication development.

Simpson and colleagues (2005) categorized and evaluated 33 commonly used interventions for students with ASD based on the following:

1. Outcomes and result

2. Qualifications of individuals using the methods

3. How, where, and when the methods were most appropriately used

4. Potential risks linked to the methods

5. Costs

6. Options for assessing a method's effectiveness

These factors were used to classify the 33 methods as one of the following:

1. *Scientifically based* (those with "significant and convincing empirical efficacy and support" [p. 9])

2. A *promising practice* (efficacy with persons with ASD, albeit additional verification was needed)

3. A practice that had *limited supporting data or information* (lacked scientific evidence, yet may have positive potential)

4. A *nonrecommended* method (interventions that failed to provide supporting scientific evidence)

In 2009, the National Autism Center (NAC) reported on their systematic evaluation of methods used with individuals with ASD. A panel of ASD experts used a structured protocol to review more than 700 intervention studies involving individuals with ASD. Interventions were reviewed using four major classifications: *established* (supported by strong empirical and scientifically valid evidence), *emerging* (some empirical and scientifically valid evidence, albeit further investigation needed), *unestablished* (little or no supporting empirical and scientifically valid evidence is available), and *ineffective/harmful* (method has been found to lack scientific support, and reports of harm exist). Although clearly important, the NAC's summary document has been challenged relative to its usefulness and practical worth for potential consumers. For example, many of the *established* methods were not clearly identified (e.g., "antecedent package"); the *emerging* methods included in equal status such well-established and proven methods as the Picture Exchange Communication System (PECS; Bondy & Frost, 2001) and relatively unconfirmed methods such as massage and touch therapy. In addition, no methods were judged to be *ineffective/harmful*. The widely discredited and potentially harmful facilitated communication method (Biklen, 1993; Wheeler, Jacobson, Paglieri, & Schwartz, 1993) was classified as an *unestablished* strategy rather than as an *ineffective/harmful* approach. The discredited facilitated communication technique involves another individual assisting a person with autism or another severe communication-related disability via use of an alphabet board or keyboard. The facilitator holds or touches the person's arm or hand during this process, thus purportedly assisting them to communicate by providing physical and emotional support for typing or pointing. Multiple research studies have revealed that the facilitator is responsible for the communication and the source of messages, not the person with the communication disability (Bebko, Perry, & Bryson, 1996; Hudson, Melita, & Arnold, 1993; Singer, Horner, Dunlap, & Wang, 2014).

Picture Exchange Communication System (PECS): PECS (Bondy & Frost, 2001) is a low-tech aided AAC protocol for teaching individuals with complex communication needs to communicate by selecting and handing pictures to another individual. The PECS protocol used strategies from applied behavior analysis and was developed for young children with autism spectrum disorder, although it is now used with individuals with other disabilities as well.

The National Professional Development Center on Autism Spectrum Disorders (2010) also significantly contributed to the understanding of effective practice methods for individuals with ASD. Experts identified 24 evidence-based practices after reviewing approximately 360 research studies published between 1997 and 2007: prompting, stimulus control/environmental modification, time delay, differential reinforcement, discrete trial training, extinction, functional behavior assessment, functional communication training, reinforcement, response interruption/redirection, task analysis and chaining, video modeling, naturalistic interventions, parent-implemented interventions, peer-mediated interventions, PECS, Pivotal Response Treatment (PRT; Koegel & Koegel, 2006), self-management, social narratives, social skills interventions, speech generating devices, structured work systems, computer-aided instruction, and visual supports. Arguably some of these so-called evidence-based methods lack clarity and thus potential utility for practitioners and other consumers (e.g., parent- and peer-implemented interventions). Notwithstanding this criticism, the National Professional Development Center on Autism Spectrum Disorders has significantly contributed to the ASD scientific credentialing process.

Wong and colleagues (2015) conducted a comprehensive computer search of methods and interventions for individuals with ASD. The initial search identified more than 29,000 articles. These findings were screened for inclusion and

---

TEXTBOX 1.1

Antecedent-based intervention (ABI)

Cognitive behavioral intervention (CBI)

Differential reinforcement of alternative, incompatible, or other behavior (DRA/I/O)

Discrete trial teaching (DTT)

Exercise (ECE)

Extinction (EXT)

Functional behavioral assessment (FBA)

Functional communication training (FCT)

- Replacement of interfering behavior that has a communication function with more appropriate communication that accomplishes the same function

Modeling (MD)

Naturalistic intervention (NI)

- Intervention strategies that occur within the typical setting/activities/routines in which the learner participates
- Teachers/service providers establish the learner's interest in a learning event through arrangement of the setting/activity/routine, provide

---

Textbox 1.1. Evidence-based methods for individuals with autism spectrum disorder. (From Wong, C., Odom, S., Hume, K., Cox, A., Fettig, A., Kucharczyk, S., Brock, M., Plavnick, J., Fleury, V., & Schulz, T. [2015]. Evidence-based practices for children, youth, and young adults with autism spectrum disorder: A comprehensive review. *Journal of Autism and Developmental Disorders, 45,* 1951–1966. https://doi.org/10.1007/s10803-014-2351-z. Adapted by permission.)

necessary support for the learner to engage in the targeted behavior, elaborate on the behavior when it occurs, and/or arrange natural consequences for the targeted behavior or skills

Parent-implemented intervention (PII)

Peer-mediated instruction and intervention (PMII)

Picture Exchange Communication System (PECS; Bondy &Frost, 2001)

Pivotal Response Treatment (PRT; Koegel & Koegel, 2006)

Prompting (PP)

Reinforcement (R)

Response interruption/redirection (RIR)

- Introduction of a prompt, comment, or other distracters when an interfering behavior is occurring that is designed to divert the learner's attention away from the interfering behavior and results in its reduction

Scripting (SC)

- A verbal and/or written description about a specific skill or situation that serves as a model for the learner. Scripts are usually practiced repeatedly before the skill is used in the actual situation

Self-management (SM)

Social narratives (SN)

- Narratives that describe social situations in some detail by highlighting relevant cues and offering examples of appropriate responding. Social narratives are individualized according to learner needs and typically are quite short, perhaps including pictures or other visual aids

Social skills training (SST)

Structured play groups (SPG)

- Small group activities characterized by their occurrences in a defined area and with a defined activity, the specific selection of typically developing peers to be in the group, a clear delineation of theme and roles by adult leading, and/or prompting or scaffolding as needed to support the students' performance related to the goals of the activity

Task analysis (TA)

Technology-aided instruction and intervention (TAII)

- Any electronic item/equipment/application or virtual network used to facilitate functioning

Time delay (TD)

- A brief delay occurring between the opportunity to use the skill and any additional instructions or prompts with the purpose of allowing the learner to respond without having to receive a prompt

Video modeling (VM)

Visual supports (VS)

methodological criteria and ultimately distilled to 456 studies. These research studies were used to identify 27 focused evidence-based intervention practices. These methods, shown in Textbox 1.1, have significantly contributed to advancing the use of evidence-based practices among professionals and other stakeholders involved in educating, supporting, and caring for individuals with ASD. It is also noteworthy that these methods have shown utility with individuals with minimal and no speech or spoken words. These methods are discussed by authors who contributed to this book as means for matching individual characteristics and needs of individuals with ASD with maximally appropriate AAC options.

Simply creating lists of so-called effective practice and scientifically supported methods is only a first step and insufficient if the goal is to ensure that practitioners correctly and consistently apply highly impactful strategies with individuals with ASD (Simpson, Mundschenk, & Heflin, 2011). Advancing this process, including crafting and implementing AAC interventions for individuals with minimal and no speech or spoken words, requires requisite actions. These foundational measures are discussed next.

The foremost basic building component is recognition and acceptance of the fact that effective practice implementation, including AAC methods, will only be successful if the methods are applied within structured and organized environments and in concert with appropriate and individualized curricula and instructional programs (Ganz, 2007). This basic element creates the conditions for permitting individuals to benefit from selected interventions. These fundamentals include clear performance and behavior expectations, visual and other environmental supports, routines and predictability, and so forth. Without these basic foundational elements, even the most effective methods will likely prove to be unsuccessful; data-based and objective assessment of the impact of selected methods and how they should be fine-tuned to make them maximally utilitarian will be impossible. For example, linking a student's speech-generating device with her daily activity schedule makes her aware that particular activities will be occurring and will assist in maximizing functional use of her voice output device.

A second foundational component for successfully implementing high-quality programs, including AAC instructional plans, involves striving to create an "evidence-friendly" culture among educators, speech-language specialists, and other related service professionals and additional stakeholders. Simply stated, this will require that practitioners and stakeholders commit to select, use with fidelity, and objectively evaluate evidence-based methods. As is the case with other standalone components, this factor in and of itself will be an insufficient step in the direction of full-scale adoption of evidence-based method usage, including AAC tools. Nevertheless, without such buy-in, advancement of the full potential of evidence-based method use will fall short. Forming a collective evidence-based mindset and culture must also involve recognition and acceptance of the fact that the ASD landscape has numerous professed interventions and methods that lack verification and that these unproven methods often have limited positive potential and in some cases the potential to do harm (Travers, Ayers, et al., 2016; Travers, Tincani, Thompson, & Simpson, 2016). Creation and regular gatherings of teams of stakeholders, including multidisciplinary professionals, family members, and when possible individuals with disabilities, is one illustration of this theme.

A third basic precondition for most productively using evidence-based methods will require professionals to put into practice thoughtful and purposeful consideration of the distinctive and individualized needs of learners with ASD. As discussed in this chapter, individuals with ASD have highly unique characteristics, and individuals with autism-related disorders manifest idiosyncratic traits that must be taken into account when crafting intervention programs. This is particularly the case with learners with limited and no speech or spoken words. Consider for example the case of Robert, an elementary-age boy with no spoken words who was hypersensitive to touch and highly resistant to anyone making physical contact with his hands. His teachers would likely be able to identify professional literature that would lead them to believe a child such as Robert would be a good candidate for learning sign language, specifically via hand-over-hand discrete trial training methodology. However, consideration of this student's strong aversion to being touched, and whether a signing instructional program would best match his needs, would likely redirect them to consider alternative communication options. Bluntly speaking, few universally applicable and all-purpose intervention tools are appropriate for all learners with ASD. Interventions and support methods must be individually designed and implemented to be suitable for the singular needs of individuals with CCN. It is simply not acceptable to attempt to implement interventions without considering their appropriateness for individuals and without individually designing these methods to best fit the characteristics of each person and their unique circumstances and environment.

Planning related to an individual's unique traits and nature is best accomplished via a collaborative, shared, and mutually respectful decision-making process. For example, para-educators and parents often know a school-age learner's distinctive communication characteristics the best and thus the adjustments and fine-tuning of AAC systems that will be needed for achievement of the best outcomes. In summary, it is essential that the perspectives of a range of multidisciplinary professionals as well as parents and family members who are familiar and involved with individuals with CCN be taken into account when determining AAC and other interventions and support methods. Whenever possible and appropriate, learners with ASD should also have input into this process.

The collaborative decision-making process regarding choice of AAC and other methods, and how these options fit with individuals' traits and qualities, can be facilitated via consideration of basic guiding questions: 1) Does a particular intervention being considered for use with an individual have objective and scientifically valid support; 2) How, when, and where will an individualized intervention, instructional method, or support be evaluated; and 3) How suited is an individualized method or intervention for an individual's unique characteristics and needs?

CONCLUSION

Overwhelming evidence indicates that communication development is an essential and salient developmental domain and that individuals with ASD who acquire functional language and communication skills have the best prognoses and quality of life outcomes (Levy & Perry, 2011). Understanding characteristics that define and distinguish autism and ASD is essential to the process of identifying, implementing, and evaluating AAC and other interventions and supports (Tager-Flusberg et al., 2005). Approved application of evidence-based AAC platforms, when individualized to address unique individual needs, is the most effective means of ensuring the most satisfactory school and postschool outcomes (Ogletree, 2016).

REFERENCES

Alpern, C. (2012). Enhancing language and communication development. In D. Zager, M. Wehmeyer, & R. Simpson, R. (Eds.), *Educating students with autism spectrum disorders: Research-based principles and practices* (pp. 287–310). New York, NY: Routledge.

American Psychiatric Association. (1952). *Diagnostic and statistical manual of mental disorders.* Washington, DC: Author.

American Psychiatric Association. (1968). *Diagnostic and statistical manual of mental disorders* (2nd ed.). Washington, DC: Author.

American Psychiatric Association. (1980). *Diagnostic and statistical manual of mental disorders* (3rd ed.). Washington, DC: Author.

American Psychiatric Association. (1987). *Diagnostic and statistical manual of mental disorders* (3rd ed., rev.). Washington, DC: Author.

American Psychiatric Association. (1994). *Diagnostic and statistical manual of mental disorders* (4th ed.). Washington, DC: Author.

American Psychiatric Association. (2000). *Diagnostic and statistical manual of mental disorders* (4th ed., text rev.). Washington, DC: Author.

American Psychiatric Association. (2013). *Diagnostic and statistical manual of mental disorders* (5th ed.). Washington, DC: Author.

Amir, R. E., Van Den Veyver, I. B., Wan, M., Tran, C. Q., Francke, U., & Zoghbi, H. Y. (1999). Rett syndrome is caused by mutations in x-linked mecp2, encoding methyl-cpg-binding protein 2. *Nature Genetics, 23,* 185–188.

Attwood, T. (2007). *The complete guide to Asperger syndrome.* Philadelphia, PA: Jessica Kingsley.

Bebko, J. M., Perry, A., & Bryson, S. (1996). Multiple method validation study of facilitated communication: II. Individual differences and subgroup results. *Journal of Autism & Developmental Disorders, 26,* 19–42.

Biklen, D. (1993). *Communication unbound: How facilitated communication is challenging traditional views of autism and ability/disability.* New York, NY: Teachers College Press.

Bondy, A. & Frost, L. (2001). Picture Exchange Communication System. *Behavior Modification, 25,* 725–744.

Carr, E. G., & Durand, V. M. (1985). Reducing behavior problems through functional communication training. *Journal of Applied Behavior Analysis, 18,* 111–126.

Centers for Disease Control and Prevention. (2017). *Autism spectrum disorder (ASD).* Retrieved from http://www.cdc.gov/ncbddd/autism

Chiang, C., Soong, W., Lin, T., & Rogers, S. J. (2008). Nonverbal communication skills in young children with autism. *Journal of Autism and Developmental Disorders, 38,* 1898–1906.

Cook, B., Tankersley, M., & Landrum, T. (2016). *Instructional practices with and without empirical validity.* Bingley, United Kingdom: Emerald.

Durand, V., & Carr, E. (1991). Functional communication training to reduce challenging behavior: Maintenance and application in new settings. *Journal of Applied Behavior Analysis, 24,* 251–264.

Fixsen, D. L., Naoom, S. F., Blase, K. A., Friedman, R. M., & Wallace, F. (2005). *Implementation research: A synthesis of the literature.* Tampa: University of South Florida.

Koegel, R., & Koegel, L. K. (2006). *Pivotal Response Treatments for autism: Communication, social, and academic development.* Baltimore, MD: Paul H. Brookes Publishing Co.

Louis de la Parte Florida Mental Health Institute, The National Implementation Research Network (FMHI Publication #231).

Ganz, J. (2007). Classroom structuring methods and strategies for children and youth with autism spectrum disorders. *Exceptionality, 15,* 249–260.

Ganz, J. B., Davis, J., Lund, E., Goodwyn, F., & Simpson, R. L. (2012). Meta-analysis of PECS with individuals with ASD: Investigation of targeted versus non-targeted outcomes, participant characteristics, and implementation phase. *Research in Developmental Disabilities, 33*(2), 406–418.

Gotham, K., Pickles, A., & Lord, C. (2008). Trajectories of autism severity using standardized ADOS scores. *Pediatrics, 130,* 1278–1284.

Heflin, J., & Alaimo, D. (2007). *Students with autism spectrum disorders: Effective instructional practices.* Upper Sadder River, NJ: Pearson/Merrill Prentice Hall.

Hudson, A., Melita, B., & Arnold, N. (1993). Brief report: A case study assessing the validity of facilitated communication. *Journal of Autism and Developmental Disorders, 23,* 165–173.

Individuals with Disabilities Education Improvement Act of 2004, PL 108-446, 20 U.S.C. §§ 1400 *et seq.*

Interagency Autism Coordinating Committee. (2014). *IACC strategic plan for autism spectrum disorder research: 2013 update.* Retrieved from the U.S. Department of Health and Human Services IACC website: http://iacc.hhs.gov/strategic-plan/2013/index.shtml

LaCava, P. (2016). Understanding and responding to the needs of children and youth with autism spectrum disorders. In R. L. Simpson & B. S. Myles (Eds.), *Educating children and youth with autism: Strategies for effective practice* (pp. 1–21). Austin, TX: Pro-Ed.

Levy, A., & Perry, A. (2011). Outcomes in adolescents and adults with autism: A review of the literature. *Research in Autism Spectrum Disorders, 5,* 1271–1282.

Machalicek, W., O'Reilly, M., Beretvas, N., Sigafoos, J., & Lanciono, G. (2007). A review of interventions to reduce challenging behavior in school settings for students with autism spectrum disorders. *Research in Autism Spectrum Disorders,1*(3), 229–246.

Maljaars, J., Noens, I., Jansen, R., Scholte, E., & van Berckelaer-Onnes, I. (2011). Intentional communication in nonverbal and verbal low-functioning children with autism. *Journal of Communication Disorders, 44,* 601–614.

National Autism Center. (2009). *National standards report.* Randolph, MA: Author.

National Professional Development Center on Autism Spectrum Disorders. (2010). *Evidence based practices.* Chapel Hill, NC: Author.

National Research Council. (2001). *Educating children with autism.* Washington, DC: National Academy Press.

No Child Left Behind Act of 2001, PL 107-110, 20 U.S.C. § 7801 (37).

Ogletree, B. (2016). In R. L. Simpson & B. S. Myles (Eds.), *Educating children and youth with autism: Strategies for effective practice* (pp. 83–120). Austin, TX: PRO-ED.

Oller, J., & Oller, S. (2010). *Autism: The diagnosis, treatment & etiology of the undeniable epidemic.* Sudbury, MA: James and Bartlett.

Paparella, T., Goods, K.S., Freeman, S., & Kasari, C. (2011). The emergence of nonverbal joint attention and requesting skills in young children with autism. *Journal of Communication Disorders, 44*(6), 569–583.

Plumb, A., Wetherby, A., Oetting, J., & Craig, E. (2013). Vocalization development in toddlers with autism spectrum disorders. *Journal of Speech, Language and Hearing Research, 56*(2), 721–734.

Prelock, P., & McCauley, R. (2012). *Treatment of autism spectrum disorders: Evidence-based intervention strategies for communication and social interaction.* Baltimore, MD: Paul H. Brookes Publishing Co.

Prizant, B. (1983). Language and communication in autism: Toward an understanding of the "whole" of it. *Journal of Speech and Hearing Disorders, 48,* 296–307.

Roberts, J. (1989). Echolalia and comprehension in autistic children. *Journal of Autism and Developmental Disorders, 19,* 271–282.

Silberman, S. (2016). *Neurotribes: The legacy of autism and the future of neurodiversity.* New York, NY: Avery.

Simpson, R., & Crutchfield, S. (2013). Effective educational practices for children and youth with autism spectrum disorders: Issues, recommendations for improving outcomes, and future trends. In B. Cook, M. Tankersley & T. Landrum (Eds.), *Advances in learning and behavioral disabilities* (pp. 197–220). San Diego, CA: Emerald.

Simpson, R., deBoer, S., Griswold, D., Myles, B., Byrd, S., Ganz, J., . . . Adams, L. (2005). *Autism spectrum disorders: Interventions and treatments for children and youth.* Thousand Oaks, CA: Corwin Press.

Simpson, R., Ganz, J., & Mason, R. (2012). Social skill interventions and programming for learners with autism spectrum disorders. In D. Zager, M. Wehmeyer, & R. Simpson (Eds.), *Educating students with autism spectrum disorders* (pp. 207–226). New York, NY: Routledge.

Simpson, R., Mundschenk, N., & Heflin, J. (2011). Issues, policies and recommendations for improving the education of learners with autism spectrum disorders. *Journal of Disability Policy Studies, 22*(1), 3–17.

Simpson, R., & Myles, B. (2011). *Asperger syndrome and high-functioning autism*. Austin, TX: PRO-ED.

Simpson, R., & Myles, B. (2016). *Educating children and youth with autism: Strategies for effective practice*. Austin, TX: PRO-ED.

Singer, G. H. S., Horner, R. H., Dunlap, G., & Wang, M. (2014). Standards of proof: TASH, Facilitated Communication, and the science-based practices movement. *Research and Practice for Persons with Severe Disabilities, 39*, 178–188.

Tager-Flusberg, H., Paul, R., Lord, C.E., et al. (2005). Language and communication in autism. In F. Volkmar, R. Paul & A. Klin (Eds.), *Handbook of autism and pervasive developmental disorder* (pp. 335–364). New York, NY: Wiley.

Thompson, T. (2007). *Making sense of autism*. Baltimore, MD: Paul H. Brookes Publishing Co.

Travers, J., Ayers, K., Simpson, R., & Crutchfield, S. (2016). Fad, controversial, and pseudo-scientific interventions. In R. Lang, T. Hancock, & N. Singh (Eds.), *Early intervention for young children with autism spectrum disorders* (pp. 257–292). New York,: Springer.

Travers, J., Tincani, M., Thompson, J., & Simpson, R. (2016). Picture Exchange Communication System and facilitated communication: Contrasting evidence-based practice with the most discredited method in the history of special education. In B. Cook, M. Tankersley, & T. Landrum (Eds.), *Advances in learning and behavioral disabilities* (pp. 85–110). United Kingdom: Emerald.

Wetherby, A., Prizant, B., & Rydell, B. (2000). Communication intervention issues for young children with autism spectrum disorders. In A. Wetherby & B. Prizant (Eds.), *Autism spectrum disorders: A transactional developmental perspective* (pp. 193–224). Baltimore, MD: Paul H. Brookes Publishing Co.

Wetherby, A., Yonclas, D., & Bryan, A. (1989). Communicative profiles of preschool children with handicaps: Implications for early identification. *Journal of Speech and Hearing Research, 54*, 148–159.

Wheeler, D., Jacobson, J., Paglieri, R., & Schwartz, A. (1993). An experimental assessment of facilitated communication. *Mental Retardation, 31*(1), 49–60.

Wong, C., Odom, S., Hume, K., Cox, A., Fettig, A., Kucharczyk, S., . . . Schulz, T. (2015). Evidence-based practices for children, youth, and young adults with autism spectrum disorder: A comprehensive review. *Journal of Autism and Developmental Disorders, 45*, 1951–1966.

Young, H., Grier, D., & Grier, M. (2008). Thimerosal exposure in infants and neurodevelopmental disorders: An assessment of computerized medical records in the Vaccine Safety Datalink. *Journal of Neurological Sciences, 27*, 110–118.

2

Autism-Focused Assessment and Program Planning

Cynthia A. Riccio and Christopher S. Prickett

The approach and focus of teaching and intervening for individuals with autism spectrum disorder (ASD) and complex communication needs (CCN) begin with reliable identification of each individual's strengths and weaknesses. A comprehensive assessment involves the collection of information across communication and behavioral domains, as well as making inferences (Riccio, 2008), not only for diagnostic purposes but to inform instruction and intervention. While often relying on formal standardized measures, the communication level of some children may preclude the use of some measures due to the test's verbal loading (Koegel, Koegel, & Smith, 1997; Schopler, Lansing, Reichler, & Marcus, 2005). That is, the limited speech and spoken-word abilities and assets of individuals with CCN makes verbally geared and loaded measures unfit for reliable use. In addition, those measures that are appropriate often do not meet the psychometric and related standards of measurement (Kasari, Brady, Lord, & Tager-Flusberg, 2013). In other words, the norming standards and metrics of many standardized measures simply do not extend to fit the responses of many individuals with CCN. Accordingly, alternative approaches to the identification of individuals' capabilities can be helpful and complement more formal approaches, especially for individuals with CCN.

For school-age children and youth with autism, the assessment process is ideally multidisciplinary (composed of a variety of professional specialties, speech-language pathologists, and special educators) due to the high rate of overlap with language impairment and adherence to best practice models of multi-source and multi-method assessment (Falkmer, Anderson, Falkmer, & Horlin, 2013). The potential overlap with other disorders (e.g., specific language impairment, intellectual impairment) needs to be considered in the process. For a diagnosis of ASD, the assessment needs to consider social communication as well as the hallmark restricted and repetitive behaviors (American Psychiatric Association [APA], 2013). For individuals with ASD and CCN, there may be, and frequently are, multiple challenging behaviors. As such, it is important to identify the salient behaviors so that removal of that behavior has the greatest likelihood of improving outcome across functional domains.

ASSESSMENT APPROACHES

There are an increasing number of measures and approaches to the assessment and diagnosis of autism (see Table 2.1). These include observation, interview, rating scales, and combinations of methods. With changes to the diagnostic criteria for ASD (APA, 2013), some assessment tools focus on autism and younger children, individuals with little or no speech and spoken word ability, or individuals with significant and pervasive delays. Other assessment options are more suited for individuals who may be on the spectrum but are older, verbally geared, and of average or even higher intellectual ability. With the emphasis of this book on individuals with CCN, the discussion is limited to those intended and appropriate for use with this population. Furthermore, the measures and methods most often utilized in the school setting are discussed in more detail (Klose, Potts, Kozenseki, & Skinner-Foster, 2012).

Diagnostic Assessment

The two most common assessment and diagnostic measures used, and often considered as the gold standard (Falkmer et al., 2013; Klose et al., 2012; Ozonoff, 2005), are the *Autism Diagnostic Observation Schedule, Second Edition* (ADOS-2; Lord, Rutter, et al., 2012) and the *Autism Diagnostic Interview, Revised* (ADI-R; Rutter, Le Couteur, & Lord, 2003). Together, these have the highest level of sensitivity and specificity based on extensive research evidence (Falkmer et al., 2013; Klose et al., 2012). Furthermore, taken together, they provide an observational evaluation as well as parent report of past and current behaviors.

Autism Diagnostic Observation Schedule, Second Edition   The original version of the *ADOS* was developed for children age 5 years and older through adulthood (Lord et al., 1989) and included a separate Pre-Linguistic version (*PL-ADOS*; DiLavore, Lord, & Rutter, 1995) for children who had a mental age of at least 3 years and some speech/spoken-word ability. These two versions were combined with revisions to accommodate a broad range of ages and for children who were nonverbal as well as verbal (Lord & Corsello, 2005; Lord et al., 2000). The latest revision (*ADOS-2*; Lord, Luyster, Gotham, & Guthrie, 2012) aligns with the changes in diagnostic criteria (APA, 2013), namely a spectrum classification configuration and a focus on deficits in social interaction and social communication and repetitive and restrictive behavioral patterns, activities, and interests. The *ADOS-2* measure is comprised of four modules, generally aligned with language development (i.e., Module 1 is for children who are nonverbal; Module 2 requires phrase speech; and so forth). With the second edition, the Toddler Module for children from ages 18–36 months (Lord, Luyster, et al., 2012) is added as well.

Regardless of the module, a prescribed number of opportunities for interaction or standardized interactions yield information on social and communication domains, while also providing opportunities to observe a range of behaviors. Parents or caregivers can be involved as needed and there is some flexibility in how the measure is applied. Despite this flexibility there are standardized prompts and hierarchies of behavior. The 30- to 40-minute observation period protocol provides information on current behavior and interaction styles. The algorithm yields a combined comparison score for social communication and restricted and repetitive

Table 2.1. Measures used in assessment of autism spectrum disorder (ASD)

Measure	General information	Rater(s)/informant(s)	Evidence base	Link to intervention/ progress monitoring
		Gold standard for diagnosis		
Autism Diagnostic Observation System (2nd ed.; ADOS-2; Lord, Rutter, et al., 2012)	Direct observation for individuals from 18 months to adult	Examiner/observer makes a judgment based on child behavior	High levels of sensitivity and specificity for ASD; strong inter-rater reliability; available in multiple languages but not Spanish (Lord, Rutter, et al., 2012); suitable for use with minimally verbal individuals (Kasari et al., 2013)	Functional strengths and weaknesses in social and communication functioning
Autism Diagnostic Interview-Revised (Rutter, LeCouteur, & Lord, 2003)	Interview format for use with individuals 18 months and older	Parent, guardian, caregiver	High levels of sensitivity and specificity for ASD; strong inter-rater reliability; available in multiple languages (Rutter et al., 2003); suitable for use with minimally verbal individuals (Kasari et al., 2013)	Functional strengths and weaknesses in communication, social relations, restrictive repetitive stereotyped behavior
		Other Measures Available for Assessment of Autism Spectrum Disorder		
Autism Screening Instrument for Educational Planning (ASIEP-3; Krug, Arick, & Almond, 2008)	2-13 years of age; observation as well as checklist	Parent, teacher complete checklist; examiner completes performance components	Evidence of general validity and reliability (Krug et al., 2008); multimodal model of assessment, but limited research and small normative sample	Functional strengths and weaknesses in vocal behavior, interaction, maladaptive behavior, educational areas, as well as symptom severity
Autism Spectrum Rating Scale (ASRS; Goldstein & Naglieri, 2009)	Rating scale 2-5 years and 6-18 years; can be administered on line or paper/pencil format	Parent/caregiver; teacher(s)	Available in Spanish; reliability and validity evidence is adequate and results obtained are consistent with other measures of ASD (Simek & Wahlberg, 2011)	Functioning levels are provided for social/ communication, behavioral rigidity, relationships, and other target areas for intervention; can be used for monitoring

(continued)

23

Table 2.1. *(continued)*

Measure	General information	Rater(s)/informant(s)	Evidence base	Link to intervention/ progress monitoring
Childhood Autism Rating Scale (2nd ed.; CARS-2 ST; Schopler, Van Bourgondien, Wellman, & Love, 2010)	Observation and interview with parent or teacher for children preschool to adult	Clinician makes the rating based on observation and information collected from others	Research support is available for the CARS (Schopler, Reichler, & Renner, 1988); minimal research is available on the CARS-2 ST (Dawkins, Meyer, & Van Bourgondien, 2016)	Functional strengths and weaknesses identified across 15 domains
Gilliam Autism Rating Scale (3rd ed.; GARS-3; Gilliam, 2014)	Rating scale, but can be used as structured interview for use with individuals 3–22 years	Parent/caregiver, teacher	Adequate evidence of reliability and validity; however, concerns raised with use when the informant has minimal knowledge of the individual and with normative sample (Karren, 2017)	Functional information on stereotyped problems, communication, and social interaction
PDD Behavior Inventory (PDDBI; Cohen & Sudhalter, 2005)	Rating scale for screening purposes of children ages 1.5–12.5 years	Parent/caregiver, teacher report forms	Yields two behavioral dimensions: Approach Withdrawal Problems and Receptive/Expressive Communication Abilities; evidence of reliability and validity (Cohen et al., 2016)	Functional information provided in multiple areas; initially intended to assess intervention outcome (Cohen, Schmidt-Lackner, Romanczyk, & Sudhalter, 2003)
Psychoeducational Profile (3rd ed.; PEP-3; Schopler, Lansing, Reichler, & Marcus, 2005)	Observation and parent/caregiver report for use with children ages 1–7 years	Examiner/observer completes the PEP-3 based on information from direct observation and parent/caregiver rating form	Normative data is somewhat dated; suitable for use with minimally verbal individuals (Kasari et al., 2013)	Functional strengths and weaknesses in cognitive, adaptive, affective, and social areas as well as maladaptive behaviors

behavior (RRB) based on age, as well as a cut-off score for diagnosis of autism or ASD. Across studies, results of the *ADOS* and *ADOS-2* have been found to be reliable and sensitive to behaviors that are specific to ASD (e.g., Klose et al., 2012; Lord, Rutter, et al., 2012). Although not necessarily providing adequate information on restricted and repetitive behavior, information is garnered for intervention planning in verbal and nonverbal communication as well as for social interaction (Klose et al., 2012). The *ADOS* and *ADOS-2* have been found to yield strong inter-rater reliability for trained examiners; however, less research is available on the Toddler Module (Lord, Luyster, et al., 2012; Luyster et al., 2009). An *Adapted ADOS* (*A-ADOS*) was developed for use with older individuals who do not have functional speech; however, this measure has not yet been validated (Plesa Skwerer, Jordan, Brukilacchio, & Tager-Flusberg, 2016).

Autism Diagnostic Interview, Revised   Neither the *ADOS-2* nor the previous versions provide information on age of onset, behavior in home or community settings, history of exposure and opportunity, or other information useful in diagnosis and intervention planning. Furthermore, for milder levels of autism, the RRB may not be observed in the relatively brief observation. For this reason, the gold standard of diagnostic and assessment practice includes both the *ADOS-2* and the *ADI-R*. The *ADI-R* is a very comprehensive interview beginning with basic history and global questions related to specific behavioral concerns parents might have about their child. Developmental history, specifically with regard to language development and any loss of skills, is queried in detail; other developmental milestones are noted, but to a lesser extent. Additional questions relate to interactions with family and others, friendships, and all levels of repetitive, restricted, and stereotypic interests (Rutter et al., 2003).

The *ADI-R* is a semi-structured interview with open-ended questions to the parent(s)/guardian(s). In most cases, there are follow-up questions related to the initial question to obtain clarification and more specific circumstances of the behavior. Notably, because the *ADI-R* is not only used for diagnostic purposes but also for follow-up, for children over age 5, parents are asked first to respond based on the child's current behavior and then to recall the behaviors from when the child was 4–5 years old. Furthermore, the informant(s) are asked initially when he/she/they first suspected a problem and the same question is asked at the end of the interview as a reliability check. There are two algorithms—one for diagnostic purposes and one for current level of functioning. The diagnostic algorithm includes the cutoff scores at which diagnosis of autism is likely in the three areas of reciprocal social interaction, abnormalities in communication, and restricted and repetitive behavior consistent with prior diagnostic criteria (APA, 2000), as well as consideration of age of onset of developmental concerns. The communication section includes consideration of children who are minimally or unable to use speech/spoken words so that language impairment is minimized as a confounding variable. Results of *ADI-R* provide robust information across domains of nonverbal and verbal language; social interaction; and repetitive, restrictive, and stereotypic behavior that is useful in intervention planning (Huerta, Bishop, Duncan, Hus, & Lord, 2012; Kent et al., 2013; Klose et al., 2012). Furthermore, the primary concerns of multiple stakeholders, including educators and other professionals, parents and caregivers, are identified, which is important for a variety of reasons, including prioritizing the target behaviors for intervention.

Communication Status and Developmental Level

Approximately 30% of children and adults with ASD have little or no spoken language (Tager-Flusberg & Kasari, 2013), and these deficits impact virtually all developmental areas, including play behavior and social interaction (Pierucci, Barber, Gilpin, Crisler, & Klinger, 2015). There is significant variability in language development of individuals with ASD. Assessment of language is critical, as communication has an impact on intervention needs, development, and treatment (Taylor, Mayberry, Grayndler, & Whitehouse, 2014). Thus, as part of the assessment process, it is important to consider communication skills. Both the *ADOS-2* and the *ADI-R* have items related to nonverbal communication (i.e., the use and understanding of gestures, how the child communicates his/her needs if not verbal). In particular, use of language and speech is noted on the *ADOS-2*; the *ADI-R* asks the parent/caregiver to estimate the number of words the child uses and understands. Albeit clearly useful, this information is not sufficient given the high overlap of specific language impairment and ASD; nor is it sufficient to address whether there is an accompanying language impairment in the diagnostic process (APA, 2013). The language level across children and adults with ASD varies considerably (Plesa Skwerer et al., 2016; Tager-Flusberg & Kasari, 2013; Taylor & Whitehouse, 2016). Some individuals may have receptive language but lack expressive language abilities, or receptive language may be limited to nouns (Gernsbacher et al., 2005). For some individuals with ASD, expressive language may be limited to repetition of songs, sentences, and so forth (i.e., echolalic rather than spontaneous or meaningful; Tager-Flusberg & Kasari, 2013). For others, language deficits may be evident across both receptive and expressive language (Rapin, Dunn, Allen, Stevens, & Fein, 2009).

The use of standardized language measures may be problematic, even for receptive language, due to attentional and other behavioral factors. Of the standardized receptive language measures, Kasari et al. (2013) suggested the use of the *Peabody Picture Vocabulary Test, Fourth Edition* (PPVT-4; Dunn & Dunn, 2007) for children and adults who are minimally able to use speech and spoken words. Alternatively, observation that includes documentation of language/communication (i.e., language samples) provides critical information and is well suited for individuals with minimal verbal ability (Kasari et al., 2013). For children ages 8–30 months, the *MacArthur-Bates Communicative Developmental Inventories* (CDIs; Fenson, 2007; Fenson et al., 1994) can be completed by the parent/caregiver to provide detailed information on children's communication abilities and status, but not without limitations (Luyster, Quiu, Lopez, & Lord, 2007; Plesa Skwerer et al., 2016).

An alternative assessment approach involves use of adaptive behavior measures that garner information from parent/caregiver, as well as teachers, across adaptive areas, including communication (Plesa Skwerer et al., 2016). The most commonly used of these are the *Vineland Adaptive Behavior Scales, Second Edition* (Vineland-II; Sparrow, Cicchetti, & Balla, 2005) and the *Adaptive Behavior Assessment System–Third Edition* (ABAS-3; Harrison & Oakland, 2015). These adaptive scales generate a standard score for communication based on developmental status norms and the individual's communication performance on a series of items. Including an adaptive behavior measure provides information on other significant domains and developmental areas as well, including motor skills and self-care.

It is limited, however, by responder perceptions and observations of behavior. For these reasons, Kasari et al. (2013) suggested that the *Vineland* scales be used with caution.

Most standardized measures of cognitive ability are verbally loaded and in the vast majority of cases inappropriate for individuals with CCN (Kasari et al., 2013; Koegel et al., 1997; Schopler et al., 2005). There are some nonverbal measures used in assessment of cognitive ability, including the *Leiter International Performance Scale, Third Edition* (Leiter-3; Roid & Miller, 2013), that have been used with individuals with autism and are well suited for persons with minimal verbal ability (Kasari et al., 2013). Although not a traditional performance-based measure of cognitively ability, De Giacomo et al. (2016) found significant positive correlations between the *Psychoeducational Profile, Third Edition* (PEP-3; Schopler et al., 2005), which can be administered by teachers, and the *Leiter-Revised* (Roid & Miller, 1997). Examination of general delays using a measure that does not require spoken language/speech, the *PEP-3,* or adaptive behavior may provide information to determine if there is co-occurring intellectual impairment (APA, 2013). Moreover, results can inform targets for intervention in natural environments.

Other Commonly Used Measures in Autism Assessment

Although the *ADOS-2* and *ADI-R* are the gold standard for diagnosis, a number of other measures are available and appropriate for informing both diagnosis and treatment. Some of these measures can be used effectively for progress monitoring as well. These may be screening measures, observation systems, interviews, rating scales, or a combination (see Table 2.1). Some measures focus more on communication, others on social interaction, whereas others are more comprehensive. Examples of different approaches are discussed in more detail.

The Psychoeducational Profile, Third Edition   The *Psychoeducational Profile, Third Edition* (PEP-3) uses both observation of skills through structured play and input from a parent(s)/caregiver(s) via a rating scale. As noted already, the *PEP-3* may provide information specific to developmental status including communication, visual motor, and motor skills. The *PEP-3* also provides information on affective expression, social reciprocity, and maladaptive behaviors, as well as self-care and general adaptive behavior when both the direct assessment and parent/caregiver information are used. Significant positive correlations have been found for *PEP-3* results with measures of cognitive and adaptive behavior as well as with results of the *ADOS* (Fu, Chen, Tseng, Chiang, & Hsieh, 2012; Fulton & D'Entremont, 2013). The *PEP-3* is one of few measures used predominantly for intervention planning rather than screening or diagnosis. Its strengths are in information gathered on verbal communication. Furthermore, it is helpful for intervention planning across areas of verbal and nonverbal communication, social interaction, repetitive and stereotypic movement, and unusual responses to sensory stimuli (Klose et al., 2012).

Childhood Autism Rating Scale, Second Edition   The *Childhood Autism Rating Scale, Second Edition* (CARS-2; Schopler, Van Bourgondien, Wellman, & Love, 2010) is described as a 15-item rating scale based on direct observation and subsequent interviews with caregivers. The Standard Version (CARS2-ST) is used for individuals younger than age 6 years and those with communication difficulties or below average estimated intellectual ability (Schopler et al., 2010). It is similar to the original version (Schopler, Reichler, & Renner, 1988) with updated field trials. There is also a version (High Functioning) for individuals who are verbally fluent, older than age 6, with estimated intelligence in the average or above-average range. Finally, there is a separate questionnaire for parent(s)/caregiver(s) to provide information on early development, social-emotional and communication status, RRB, as well as unusual sensory interests and responses.

The *CARS2-ST* is completed by a clinician for each of the 15 domains based on direct observation and interview with the parent(s)/caregiver(s), teacher(s), or others who work with the individual being evaluated. The clinician assigns ratings based on frequency, intensity, duration, and degree of atypicality of the behavior as observed or reported by others. Although the *CARS* has extensive research based on decades of use, there is less research specific to the *CARS-2*. Dawkins, Meyer, and Van Bourgondien (2016) found that children with language-based learning disability in combination with other behavioral concerns met the cutoff for ASD on the *CARS2-ST* but did not meet the criteria for ASD based on the *DSM-5* (false positives). Similarly, for the *CARS2-ST*, 13.3% met the criteria for the *DSM-5* for ASD diagnosis but had scores below the cutoff on the *CARS-2* (false negatives). In their review of commonly used measures in schools, Klose et al. (2012) concluded that the *CARS-2* was not useful in differential diagnosis with minimal information provided for identification and treatment planning related to verbal communication and social interaction. Furthermore, the factor structure is not consistent with the current or previous diagnostic criteria (APA, 2000; 2013); hence, its use for diagnostic purposes is not recommended. Despite these limitations, the manual includes guidelines for intervention planning and real-life examples that may be useful for program planning (Schopler et al., 2010).

Autism Spectrum Rating Scales   The *Autism Spectrum Rating Scales* (*ASRS*; Goldstein & Naglieri, 2010) were designed for use in the assessment of ASD via behavior frequency ratings by parent(s)/caregiver(s) and teachers for individuals 2–18 years of age. Unlike many rating scales for ASD, the *ASRS* standardization sample includes typically developing individuals, both males and females; fewer than 10% of the normative sample had a clinical diagnosis. Results are presented in *T*-scores, with higher scores indicative of higher levels of ASD behaviors than are typically reported for individuals of the same age. This measure can be completed online or using a pencil-paper format; there is a comprehensive form as well as a screener version, both in English and Spanish. A number of subscales are provided (e.g., Social/Communication, Behavioral Rigidity) as well as two composite scores—an *ASRS* Total Score and a diagnostic scale. Initially the diagnostic scale was labeled the *DSM-IV-TR* to align with the diagnostic criteria adopted by the APA (APA, 2000). The scoring norms have been updated to align with the new *DSM-5* diagnostic criteria (APA, 2013). There are options for a comparative report (i.e., to compare scores for up to five different ratings) as well as for progress monitoring to provide information on behavioral changes over time. The reliability and validity evidence suggests that the ASRS provides reliable and valid scores. The scale can be used to aid in intervention planning (Simek & Wahlberg, 2011) as well as program planning and monitoring.

LINKING ASSESSMENT TO INTERVENTION

As noted in the discussion of measures and information presented in Table 2.1, the domains of behavior assessed often are limited to social communication and restricted and repetitive behavior, with potentially more information collected about language level and adaptive functioning. While social deficits and restricted and repetitive behavior are core to ASD (APA, 2013), language and communication, motor, adaptive skills, play, executive function, social cognition, and academics also often are assessed due to frequent co-occurrence of impairment (Gould, Dixon, Najdowski, Smith, & Tarbox, 2011). Most important, communication status and identification of information and data needed for selection and implementation of evidence-based communicative approaches is critical for individuals with CCN. As such, it is important to consider augmentative and alternative communication (AAC) as part of the assessment process.

Augmentative and Alternative Communication Assessment

AAC assessment for individuals with CCN is a multifaceted process that considers numerous aspects of the individual's life, needs, and current functioning. One theoretical perspective often cited to guide what should be evaluated is the Participation Model (American Speech-Language-Hearing Association [ASHA], n.d.; Beukelman & Mirenda, 2013). This model first evaluates communication needs and capabilities as well as the communicative participation patterns of the individual with CCN before assessing the same areas in the learner's typical peers and identifying communication gaps between the two. Once gaps are identified, the evaluator looks for opportunity and access barriers affecting communication that may be leading to these gaps for the learner with CCN. Opportunity barriers lie within the learner's environment and refer to the lack of opportunities for the individual with CCN to communicate; access barriers lie within the individual and refer to his or her ability to access a communication system (ASHA, n.d.; Beukelman & Mirenda, 2013). Examples of measures used to assess language in conjunction with AAC assessment are provided in Table 2.2. Information important to the participation model, as well as assessment practices and methods, are discussed next and highlighted in Table 2.3.

Communication Competency and Contexts

Evaluators should consider other variables that relate to and may help in collecting information related to the participation model. Specifically, learner's communication competency (Light, 1989) and communication contexts (Light, 1997; Light & McNaughton, 2014) can provide information about the learner's present communication functioning and possible barriers. Communication competency refers to the ability to communicate in meaningful ways across settings to meet the demands of daily life, requiring appropriate skills, knowledge, and judgment across five domains: 1) linguistic competence (i.e., receptive and expressive language skills in the language(s) used in the home and larger community and the AAC system, syntax, grammar); 2) operational competence (i.e., mastery of skills to operate the AAC system); 3) social competence (i.e., pragmatic and relational aspects of

Table 2.2. Language and communication for augmentative and alternative communication (AAC) assessment

Measure	General information	Rater(s)/Informant(s)	Evidence base	Link to intervention/ progress monitoring
Clinical Evaluation of Language Fundamentals–Fifth Edition (CELF-5; Wiig, Semel, & Secord, 2013)	5–21 years Direct assessment with optional observation component	Examiner/observer completes CELF-5 based on observational and direct assessment data	Moderate to high levels of test-retest reliability, internal validity, and concurrent validity (Coret & McCrimmon, 2015)	Receptive/expressive language; verbal/nonverbal pragmatics; language recall; grammar and syntax; word class knowledge
Expressive Vocabulary Test, Second Edition (EVT-2; Williams, 2007)	Direct assessment for individuals 2.5–90 years	Examiner	Moderate to high reliability and validity (Williams, 2007)	Expressive language ability in several content areas, parts of speech, and setting needs
MacArthur-Bates Communicative Development Inventories (CDI; Fenson, 2007)	CDI: Words and Gestures: receptive/expressive language for use with children 8–18 months; CDI: Words and Sentences: expressive language for use with children 16–30 months	Parent/caregiver checklist	Evidence for reliability and validity in detection of language impairment (Makransky, Dale, Havmose, & Bleses, 2016)	Useful for intervention planning as well as monitoring of lexical and grammatical development (Makransky et al., 2016)
Peabody Picture Vocabulary Test, Fourth Edition (PPVT-4; Dunn & Dunn, 2007)	Direct assessment of one word heard (receptive) vocabulary for ages 2.5 years–90 years	Examiner administers to child; child points to correct response	Consistent evidence of reliability and validity	Two forms allow for use in progress monitoring
Test of Aided-Communication Symbol Performance (Bruno, 2010)	Direct assessment of symbol use and understanding for children and adults who can point functionally	Examiner administers items	Non-standardized measure intended to assist in selecting an appropriate AAC; yields scores in four different communication areas; no research or independent reviews found	Can be used to ensure necessary skills for intervention and to benchmark progress (e.g., Bruno & Trembath, 2009)

Table 2.3. Components of augmentative and alternative communication (AAC) assessment

Assessment Stage	Potential information obtained	Guiding variables/ considerations
Preassessment Case history Records review Interview(s) Plan direct assessment	*Types of Information* • Referral reason • Medical/developmental/ social function • Cognitive/sensory/motor function • Interests/motivation • Expressive/receptive language • Cognitive/sensory/motor • Symbol comprehension and use • Literacy • Multimodal communication • Child-system match • Device-related features	*Communication barriers* • Access • Opportunity *Communication competency* • Linguistic • Operational • Social • Strategic • Psychosocial *Communication contexts* • Physical • Functional • Language • Social • Cultural
Direct assessment Observation • Structured • Semi-structured • Naturalistic Formal testing • Norm-referenced • Criterion-referenced Informal testing Device trial(s)		

Sources: American Speech-Language Hearing Association (n.d.), Dietz, Quach, Lund, and McElvey (2012), Lund, Quach, Weissling, McKelvey, and Dietz (2017), and Visvader (2015).

social communication); 4) strategic competence (i.e., ability to communicate despite restrictions from AAC systems); and 5) psychosocial competence (i.e., motivation to communicate, attitude toward AAC use, communication confidence, resilience; Light, 1989; Light & McNaughton, 2014).

The learner's communication contexts are also important in order to provide an in-depth AAC evaluation. Communication context comprises the a) physical, b) functional, c) language, d) social, and e) cultural domains (Light, 1997). The physical context refers to the learner's physical environment, including the people, events, objects, and other aspects of the child's physical world. Experiences with the physical world provide chances to develop language and give conceptual basis to learn, hence a lack of access may stifle language development. The functional context reflects the time, place, and reason for language in the child's daily life (e.g., play). In this manner, assessment should focus on when language learning is already being elicited in the child's day and the times that are appropriate for increased language facilitation, times that are inappropriate, and times where the child is free from other demands. The language context refers to the linguistic code or codes of the child's world, including both the spoken language of the child's environment (e.g., school, home), as well as the codes (e.g., pictures, letters) of the specific AAC system the child uses or may use.

Evaluating the language context includes the child's receptive and expressive language skills, vocabulary, and symbol (e.g., letters, pictures) comprehension, as well as cognitive, sensory, and motor development that may influence the operation of and/or content within AAC systems. For instance, certain AAC systems require a certain level of fine-motor coordination to operate, whereas the visual scanning skills and cognitive development of the learner may guide the visual organization and complexity of certain systems and their displays. Consideration of all of these areas is important to the child's role in social communication (i.e., listener, communicator), as well as learning and using an AAC system.

The social context reflects interactions between the child and others in his or her environment, including the communication partners and content in these interactions. Understanding the child's social context may uncover opportunities and barriers to communication with others in the child's environment. Finally, the cultural context refers to the child's family, community, and societal values, expectations, and beliefs regarding language development, which may elucidate barriers to communication development and opportunity, depending on the expectations, customs, and routines of others (Light, 1997). Examining the communication competencies can elucidate the child's communication skills and needs, whereas evaluating the different contexts can help uncover potential and existing communication barriers.

Preassessment

The actual evaluation of AAC needs of individuals with CCN generally comprises preassessment activities, data acquisition, and analysis (Dietz, Quach, Lund, & McKelvey, 2012; Lund, Quach, Weissling, McKelvey, & Dietz, 2017; Orland, 2015; Visvader, 2015). Preassessment activities include gathering background information such as the reason for referral, possible communication competency, communication contexts, deficits, and potential barriers, as well as other relevant medical, social, developmental, motor, sensory-perceptual, and cognitive information through interviews or records review. Furthermore, this information helps inform the actual structure and content of the subsequent direct assessment, guiding what activities, materials, and assessment measures to include. For instance, understanding the child's interests may help choose reinforcing or motivating activities or vocabulary to include in the assessment and help to maintain engagement during the evaluations (Dietz et al., 2012; Lund et al., 2017; Visvader, 2015). Some, but not all, of this information can be obtained from the *ADI-R*, thus preassessment is often a crucial element of a good comprehensive evaluation. In addition, ASHA (n.d.) noted that exposing individuals with complex communication needs to AAC symbols or systems (e.g., through using visual language supports in the home or classroom) may improve evaluation accuracy.

Direct Assessment

Following the preassessment period, the evaluators can directly assess the child with CCN. During this step, evaluators observe and assess the child based on the needs identified during the first step (Dietz et al., 2012; Lund et al., 2017; Visvader, 2015). Visvader (2015) noted that assessment may need to span multiple sessions and settings because some individuals being evaluated may perform differentially based on contextual variables such as time and environment. In addition, recording of the sessions and/or having observers may be important so as not to miss important information. Having observers from multiple disciplines (e.g., physical therapist, occupational therapist) may help identify other areas for treatment or areas that might influence AAC use (Visvader, 2015).

Best-practice assessment importantly includes child observation during structured, semi-structured, and naturalistic settings (e.g., class or playtime; interactions with parents) to examine language and communication, as well as other aspects related to the communication competencies and contexts mentioned previously (Dietz et al., 2012; Lund et al., 2017; Visvader, 2015). In addition, the evaluator may set up tasks informally to elicit certain behaviors and preferences (see Visvader, 2015 for examples) or may use more formal measures (e.g., norm- and/or criterion-referenced standardized measures as noted previously) to assess the child's strengths and weaknesses in these and related areas (e.g., symbol comprehension and use, cognition, motor skills, literacy). Moreover, the evaluator should include tasks or situations involving the learner's use of different AAC systems to determine device-related features that may influence later AAC choices, implementation, and success such as choosing a speech-generating device versus a low-tech system (e.g., Picture Exchange Communication System; Bondy & Frost, 1994). Such considerations also should include the content and organization of the AAC system (e.g., vocabulary, display [e.g., grid versus visual scene display], array size), and the learner's and family's system preference. To do this, the evaluator may contrive situations to see how well the individual communicates with brief instruction on different systems, assess communication accuracy with different visual organizations and content, and perform a preference assessment (e.g., Hagopian, Long, & Rush, 2004) for two or more devices (ASHA, n.d.; Dietz et al., 2012; Lund et al., 2017; Visvader, 2015).

In addition, assessments such as the *Test of Aided-Communication Symbol Performance* (*TASP*; Bruno, 2010) can be helpful in examining skills necessary for optimal performance and communication with AAC systems. The *TASP* can be utilized from child- to adulthood and contains four sections related to symbol size and number, grammatical encoding, categorization, and syntactic performance. These areas uncover the optimal size and number of symbols from which a learner can select on a given AAC display page, the learner's current symbol understanding, the learner's ability to categorize word types, and the ability to form sentences by stringing symbols together (Bruno, 2010).

Fit between the individual user and AAC system is a vital area to assess because technology barriers (e.g., technology limitations, breakdowns, difficulty accessing the technology) are often-cited reasons for abandoning AAC systems (Lund & Light, 2007). Importantly, evaluators should assess for multimodal approaches to communication (e.g., low- or no-tech AAC systems in addition to high-tech systems) because those with CCN often may not have access to their AAC devices or certain devices are not always an efficient or appropriate communication method. For a given situation, because of the importance of fluency of communication, the mode and context need to match. This way, these individuals can learn to communicate effectively regardless of context. Finally, evaluators may implement a trial period wherein a learner spends an extended period with a device to assess the child–system match, as well as feedback from the parents or family who will have a role in implementing the AAC system (ASHA, n.d.; Dietz et al., 2012; Lund et al., 2017; Parrette & Angelo, 1996; Visvader, 2015). Results from the assessment can help guide subsequent treatment and AAC selection to build upon present strengths, meet communication needs, and reduce barriers to communication participation, as well as to monitor progress after intervention implementation.

Functional Behavioral Assessment

Beyond assessment for diagnosis and identification of the best approach for communication, it is important to consider the challenging behaviors that often are associated with ASD, especially those linked to communication and potentially interfere with interventions. Most concerning are aggressive, self-injurious, and disruptive behaviors. In addition, it is important to address stereotyped or repetitive movements, speech, or use of objects; an insistence on sameness and behavioral inflexibility; strong fixations or interests; and possible sensory issues (APA, 2013). Research suggests that the presence of those traits among individuals with ASD can negatively affects their learning (Koegel & Covert, 1972), social function (Loftin, Odom, & Lantz, 2007; Nadig, Lee, Singh, Bosshart, & Ozonoff, 2010), and family and home life (Bishop, Richler, Cain, & Lord, 2007; Greenberg, Seltzer, Hong, & Orsmond, 2006). Thus, decreasing restricted and repetitive behavior is important for the development of the individual with ASD.

Individuals with ASD are heterogeneous in the challenging behaviors they display; similarly, the stimuli that trigger the challenging behaviors vary from child to child. Functional behavioral assessments (FBAs) and analyses may prove useful in determining the functions of certain types of challenging behaviors and restricted and repetitive behavior, allowing for treatments that replace these behaviors with a more appropriate or useful behavior, when the behavior serves a discernible function (Boyd, McDonough, & Bodfish, 2012). Use of FBA and analysis methods also has been found to be helpful even when the events or triggers are not clearly identified or the function of the behavior is not fully understood (McLay, France, Blampied, Danna, & Hunter, 2017). There is a growing body of evidence for the use of these data-based methods to inform treatment planning for a range of behaviors and for individuals with ASD (Beavers, Iwata, & Lerman, 2013; Hanley, Jin, Vanselow, & Hanratty, 2014). Unquestionably, FBAs and analyses have been used to address a variety of challenging behaviors (e.g., Friedman & Luiselli, 2008; McLay et al., 2017). Readers will find additional information on this important topic in Chapter 7, "Functional Communication Training for Durable Behavior Change," by McComas et al.

Social Communication and Interaction

Social communication and interaction problems are core to ASD, comprising impaired social-emotional reciprocity and behaviors; social nonverbal communication (e.g., use of gestures, eye contact, emotional expressions); and ability to make, maintain, and understand social relationships and situations (APA, 2013). Research indicates that social deficits may play a role in anxiety in ASD (Bellini, 2006), as well as lower relationship quality and increased loneliness (Bauminger & Kasari, 2000). As noted, common ASD screening and diagnostic measures, as well as communication and language-specific measures can help inform subsequent treatment planning for individuals with ASD and CCN specific to symptomatology.

ASD assessment tools provide varying levels of intervention planning support (see Table 2.1). Specifically, assessments with interactive components (e.g., *ADOS-2* and *PEP-3*) provide the examiner direct information pertaining to social and communication interaction deficits, as well as which specific areas of functioning are impaired (e.g., responding to social interaction, nonverbal gestures, joint attention, requesting) and can thus be targeted for treatment to improve communication competencies via AAC implementation. Furthermore, the *CARS-2* allows observation in naturalistic settings, which may provide information regarding the when, where, why, and with whom the examinee may interact or need to interact and how successful the examinee is during these interactions. By doing so, current barriers to communication participation and needs can be gleaned and targeted. For instance, Light (1997) reviewed research indicating that adults and peers who interact with children with CCN often dominate interactions. Thus, training parents, teachers, and peers on how to interact with or create more communication opportunities for those with CCN and AAC systems may increase communication production and language development (Light, 1997; Sigafoos, 1999). Likewise, indirect measures such as the *ADI-R* and the various rating scales can help the examiner determine social and communication deficits and strengths, as well as communication settings that are not assessed or seen during more direct assessments, which can inform AAC needs and instruction related to communication competencies and contexts.

Language and communication-specific assessments or certain comprehensive measures can provide information regarding the examinee's current functioning in a number of areas important to choosing and implementing AAC technology. Information and data from these instruments also can be used to establish a starting point for language instruction and reducing barriers to participation. For example, language measures like the *PPVT-4*, the *Expressive Vocabulary Test, Second Edition* (*EVT-2*; Williams, 2007), the *Clinical Evaluation of Language Fundamentals—Fifth Edition* (*CELF-5*; Wiig, Semel, & Secord, 2013), and the *PEP-3* can provide current receptive and expressive language functioning compared to peers, thereby informing planning teams about language skills that can facilitate AAC instruction. For instance, receptive language is important for learning to operate AAC systems and can prove a launching point to increasing expressive language (Light, 1997). Similarly, the *TASP* (Bruno, 2010) is an important tool that systematically uncovers the examinee's use and comprehension of symbols to represent words and the most efficient display settings that can inform strengths and weaknesses to facilitate AAC device implementation and thereby increase communication.

Comprehensive assessments (e.g., *PEP-3*) also can provide important information that can inform treatment, indicating strengths and weaknesses in cognition, gross and fine motor skills, and social interaction, with each playing a role in AAC system recommendation, instruction, and design. For instance, impaired motor skills may preclude AAC learners from utilizing certain systems that require precise pointing, whereas cognitive deficits may make navigating certain AAC system organizations difficult (e.g., Lund & Light, 2007). In addition, FBA also may play a role in informing interventions to increase social interaction by identifying the function of interfering or challenging behaviors that impede social interaction (Koegel & Frea, 1993; Watkins, Kuhn, Ledbetter-Cho, Gevarter, & O'Reilly, 2017).

Additional Considerations to Intervention Planning

Including expertise from multiple disciplines is essential to appropriately and effectively integrating assessment results that lead to utilitarian and successful intervention and treatment plans (National Research Council [NRC], 2001; Wilkinson, 2017). This may include input from psychologists, speech-language pathologists, general and special educators, occupational and physical therapists, and when germane to situations, medical professionals (Wilkinson, 2017). Information from all aspects of assessment should inform target goals and behaviors for treatment. For instance, within a school setting, these goals should account for not only the individual's deficits but also his or her strengths, improve core ASD diagnostic symptoms, reduce challenging behaviors and RRB, increase the individual's access to academic content and achievement, address comorbid problems, and improve access to community services. Furthermore, due to the varied nature of ASD, intervention should be individualized and the goals should be relevant to the learner and setting, developmentally appropriate, realistic, and focused on increasing positive behaviors rather than simply eliminating inappropriate behaviors. Taken together, the multidisciplinary team, in conjunction with parents and family members, can create specific, observable, and measurable goals and treatment and intervention programs (NRC, 2001; Wilkinson, 2017).

Importantly, ASD and AAC evaluators should be cognizant of the demand that AAC places on families and the role family members play in assessment and effective and successful interventions (Angelo, 2000; Dietz et al., 2012; Lund et al., 2017; Schlosser & Raghavendra, 2004; Wilkinson, 2017). In a survey of more than 100 families of children with AAC systems, most parents reported increased roles, responsibilities, and time demands related to AAC devices (Angelo, 2000). Moreover, choosing and implementing a certain AAC system for an individual without parent and family input can lead to AAC underuse, abandonment (Parette & Angelo, 1996), and related poor outcomes. More specifically, AAC systems require varying levels of parental and family resources (e.g., time, money) to purchase, learn, and properly implement in addition to other demands already in place. Thus, when AAC professionals recommend an AAC system without considering the family's needs, capabilities, preferences, context, and goals, then potential AAC success decreases (Parette & Angelo, 1996).

In addition, the Individuals with Disabilities Education Act (IDEA, 2004) includes language pertaining to the delivery of supports and services that help ensure the child makes strides toward his or her annual goals, as well as the general education curriculum. These supports and services may come in the form of modifications, accommodations, and other services, which can be informed by ASD and AAC assessment. The National Dissemination Center for Children with Disabilities (NICHCY, 2010) identified modifications as changes to the curriculum or requirements of individuals with disabilities (e.g., less homework), whereas accommodations reflect student supports that help individuals with disabilities access the same material or partake in the curriculum (e.g., extended time on tests). Another service that also may be recommended is an extended school year to help mitigate possible loss of progress made due to school breaks. Regardless of what is provided, the specific supports provided should link to what was observed or reported during the assessment and be targeted for change.

Progress Monitoring   Monitoring the progress of learners, including the impact of interventions, is important to ensuring successful outcomes (Wilkinson, 2017) and ensuring that decision making is data based and prudently undertaken (Orland, 2015). Initial data collected during assessment provide a baseline with which to compare progress, and the presence or absence of change in behavior aids in determining whether to maintain, update, or change the current intervention. Progress monitoring is used to compare the individual's progress over time in relation to their own performance as well as in relation to some standard benchmark. Use of benchmarking and fluency-type curriculum-based measurement may be helpful in monitoring academic progress; however, formative assessment approaches that address core difficulties are often more informative for individuals with CCN and ASD (Witmer, Nasamran, Parikh, Schmitt, & Clinton, 2015). There are four identified approaches to progress monitoring (Riley-Tillman, Kalberer, & Chafouleas, 2005). These include review of permanent products, direct observation, rating scales, and daily behavior report cards or incident reports. Which of these is used should be determined by the target outcome or treatment goal. For instance, observational data collection is widely used with individuals with ASD, offering the ability to monitor the frequency, duration, or other characteristics of the target behavior (Wilkinson, 2017). Use of observational data allows for consideration of baseline data, change in behavior over time and in relation to changes in frequency, duration, or components of the intervention plan. Relative to using observational data, it is important for observers to be trained in the system being used and for some level of inter-observer agreement to be obtained (Witmer et al., 2015).

In addition to observational data, other types of measures can be used to assess change and progress (Wilkinson, 2017). McConachie and colleagues (2015) systematically reviewed 131 measurement tools used in research with children with ASD to determine which were useful in monitoring progress and outcomes. Although many tools are used in diagnosis and screening, McConachie et al. found that only a select few showed reliable potential for progress monitoring, depending on the behavior of interest. Two that emerged as having good potential were the *Vineland Screener* (Sparrow, Carter, & Cicchetti, 1993) and the *Autism Treatment Evaluation Checklist* (*ATEC*; Rimland & Edelson, 1999). The *Vineland Screener* consists of 45 parent-directed interview items, comprising communication, socialization, and daily living skills. It is a shorter (and older) version of the *Vineland Adaptive Behavior Scale–III* discussed previously. The *ATEC* is a 77-item parent and teacher checklist, designed specifically to monitor progress and treatment outcome in the areas of speech and language, social ability, sensory and cognitive awareness, and health, physical functioning, and behavior.

CONCLUSION

Kasari and colleagues (2013) pointed out the need for measures that effectively identify the strengths and weaknesses of individuals with minimal speech and spoken word ability. Many of the existing measures need to be revised to meet the changed diagnostic criteria with consideration of those with CCN and ASD. Assessment needs to be sufficiently comprehensive, and not solely for the purpose of diagnosis. Additional assessment (e.g., for AAC and FBA) is helpful in identifying the most salient behavioral and treatment considerations for a given individual. Furthermore, the role of such factors as context, family structure and history, and cultural linguistic difference needs to be considered. As noted, determination of current communication status and the most appropriate AAC, as well as identifying and addressing challenging behaviors that may interfere with outcomes, are additional considerations in intervention planning. Moreover, many published and standardized measures may not be sufficiently sensitive or specifically geared for individuals who are lower functioning or have CCN. Observational systems can be used; however, training is important for observers (e.g., parents/caregivers, teachers, therapists) to ensure reliability.

Professionals in the field of CCN and ASD have pointed to needs in future research in areas that increase navigation and more naturalistic, efficient organizational understanding. In particular, visual scene displays (VSD) provide a more schematic approach to communication, often reflecting the natural context of the child's worlds compared to traditional grid displays. More research is needed to fully explore the effects of VSD on individuals with ASD and CCN (see Light & Drager, 2007; Ganz, Hong, Gilliland, Morin, & Svenkerud, 2015). In addition, the rise of apps and mobile technologies linked to purportedly promoting communication abilities needs more research. Researchers have initiated transdisciplinary research (e.g., visual-cognitive science) to influence the design, efficiency, and learning of AAC systems for those with CCN.

Namely, eye-tracking has grown as a methodology to examine and improve the design and use of AAC systems (Dube & Wilkinson, 2014; Gillespie-Smith & Fletcher-Watson, 2014; Wilkinson, O'Neill, & McIlvane, 2014). For instance, eye-tracking has helped researchers understand how AAC users may overly attend to certain symbols or features of symbols rather than the specific meanings, which can lead to inaccurate symbol use and communication (Dube & Wilkinson, 2014). Importantly, these results can help inform certain interventions to improve visual scanning behavior to increase correct symbol use (Dube & Wilkinson, 2014). Similarly, eye-tracking has begun to help researchers and clinicians determine how organizational characteristics can promote more efficient and accurate visual scanning of AAC symbols (e.g., Wilkinson et al., 2014). Furthermore, eye-tracking may help determine characteristics of the symbols used within AAC systems that best facilitate communication by users with ASD or other disabilities, including the content, features, realism, and complexity of the symbols (for review, see Gillespie-Smith & Fletcher-Watson, 2014).

REFERENCES

American Psychiatric Association. (2000). *Diagnostic and statistical manual of mental disorders* (4th ed., text rev.). Washington, DC: Author.

American Psychiatric Association. (2013). *Diagnostic and statistical manual of mental disorders* (5th ed.). Washington, DC: Author.

American Speech-Language-Hearing Association. (n.d.). *Augmentative and alternative communication.* Retrieved from http://www.asha.org/PRPSpecificTopic.aspx?folderid=8589942 773&section=Key_Issues

Angelo, D. (2000). Impact of augmentative and alternative communication devices on families. *Augmentative and Alternative Communication, 16*(1), 37–47. doi:10.1080/074346100123312 78894

Bauminger, N., & Kasari, C. (2000). Loneliness and friendship in high-functioning children with autism. *Child Development, 71*(2), 447–456. doi:10.1111/1467-8624.00156

Beavers, G. A., Iwata, B. A., & Lerman, D. C. (2013). Thirty years of research on the functional analysis of problem behavior. *Journal of Applied Behavioral Analysis, 46,* 1–21.

Bellini, S. (2006). The development of social anxiety in adolescents with autism spectrum disorders. *Focus on Autism and Other Developmental Disabilities, 21*(3), 138–145. doi:10.1177/1 0883576060210030201

Beukelman, D. R., & Mirenda, P. (2013). *Augmentative and alternative communication: Supporting children and adults with complex communication needs.* Baltimore, MD: Paul H. Brookes Publishing Co.

Bishop, S. L., Richler, J., Cain, A. C., & Lord, C. (2007). Predictors of perceived negative impact in mothers of children with autism spectrum disorder. *American Journal on Mental Retardation, 112*(6), 450. doi:10.1352/0895-8017(2007)112[450:popnii]2.0.co;2

Bondy, A., & Frost, L. (1994). The picture exchange communication system. *Focus on Autistic Behavior, 9*(3), 1–19.

Boyd, B. A., McDonough, S. G., & Bodfish, J. W. (2012). Evidence-based behavioral interventions for repetitive behaviors in autism. *Journal of Autism and Developmental Disorders, 42*(6), 1236–1248. doi:10.1007/s10803-011-1284-z

Bruno, J. (2010). *Test of aided-communication symbol performance.* Pittsburgh, PA: DynaVox Mayer-Johnson.

Bruno, J., & Trembath, D. (2009). Use of aided language stimulation to improve syntactic performance during a weeklong intervention program. *Augmentative and Alternative Communication, 22,* 300–313.

Cohen, I. L., Liu, X., Hudson, M., Gillis, J., Cavalari, R. N. S., Roamanczyk, R. G., . . . Gardner, J. M. (2016). Using the PDD Behavior Inventory as a level 2 screener: A classification and regression trees analysis. *Journal of Autism and Developmental Disorders, 46,* 3006–3022. doi 10.1007/s10803-016-2843-0

Cohen, I. L., Schmidt-Lackner, S., Romanczyk, R., & Sudhalter, V. (2003). The PDD behavior inventory: A rating scale for assessing response to intervention in children with pervasive developmental disorder. *Journal of Autism and Developmental Disorders, 33,* 31–45.

Cohen, I. L., & Sudhalter, V. (2005). *The PDD behavior inventory.* Lutz, FL: Psychological Assessment Resources.

Coret, M. C., & McCrimmon, A. W. (2015). Test review: Wiig, E. H., Semel, E., & Secord, W. A. (2013). Clinical Evaluation of Language Fundamentals–Fifth Edition. *Journal of Psychoeducational Assessment, 33,* 495–500.

Dawkins, T., Meyer, A. T., Van Bourgondien, M. E. (2016). The relationship between the Child Autism Rating Scale: Second Edition and clinical diagnosis utilizing the DSM-IV-R and the DSM-5. *Journal of Autism and Developmental Disorders, 46,* 3361–3368.

De Giacomo, A., Craig, F., Cristella, A., Terenzio, V., Guttiglione, M., & Margari, L. (2016). Can PEP-3 provide a cognitive profile in children with ASD? A comparison between the developmental ages of PEP-3 and IQ of Leiter-R. *Journal of Applied Research in Intellectual Disabilities, 29,* 566–573.

Dietz, A., Quach, W., Lund, S. K., & McKelvey, M. (2012). AAC assessment and clinical-decision making: The impact of experience. *Augmentative and Alternative Communication, 28*(3), 148–159. doi:10.3109/07434618.2012.704521

DiLavore, P. C., Lord, C., & Rutter, M. (1995). The Pre-Linguistic Autism Diagnostic Observation Scale. *Journal of Autism and Developmental Disorders, 25,* 355–379.

Dube, W. V., & Wilkinson, K. M. (2014). The potential influence of stimulus overselectivity in AAC: Information from eye tracking and behavioral studies of attention with individuals with intellectual disabilities. *Augmentative and Alternative Communication, 30*(2), 172–185. doi:10.3109/07434618.2014.904924

Dunn, L., & Dunn, L. (2007). *Peabody Picture Vocabulary Test, fourth edition.* Circle Pines, MN: American Guidance Services.

Falkmer, T., Anderson, K., Falkmer, M., & Horlin, C. (2013). Diagnostic procedures in autism spectrum disorders: A systematic literature review. *European Child and Adolescent Psychiatry, 22,* 329–340. doi:10.1007/s00787-013-0375-0

Fenson, L. (2007). *MacArthur-Bates Communicative Development Inventories: User's guide and technical manual, second edition.* Baltimore, MD: Paul H. Brookes Publishing.

Fenson, L., Dale, P. S., Reznick, J. S., Bates, E., Thal, D. J., Pethick, S. J., . . . Stiles, J. (1994). Variability in early communicative development. *Monographs of the Society for Research in Child Development, 59*(5), 72–84. doi:10.2307/1166093

Friedman, A., & Luiselli, J. K. (2008). Excessive daytime sleep: Behavioral assessment and intervention with a child with autism. *Behavior Modification, 32,* 548–555.

Fu, C. P., Chen, K. L., Tseng, M. H., Chiang, F. M., & Hsieh, C. L. (2012). Reliability and validity of the Psychoeducational Profile third edition caregiver report in children with autism spectrum disorders. *Research in Autism Spectrum Disorders, 6,* 115–122.

Fulton, M. L., & D'Entremont, B. (2013). Utility of the Psychoeducational Profile-3 for assessing cognitive and language skills of the children with autism spectrum disorders. *Journal of Autism and Developmental Disorders, 43,* 2460–2471.

Ganz, J. B., Hong, E. R., Gilliland, W., Morin, K., & Svenkerud, N. (2015). Comparison between visual scene displays and exchange-based communication in augmentative and alternative communication for children with ASD. *Research in Autism Spectrum Disorders, 11,* 27–41.

Gernsbacher, M. A., Dissanayake, C., Goldsmith, H. H., Mundy, P. C., Rogers, S. J., & Sigman, M. (2005). Autism and attachment disorder. *Science, 307*(5713), 1201.

Gillespie-Smith, K., & Fletcher-Watson, S. (2014). Designing AAC systems for children with autism: Evidence from eye tracking research. *Augmentative and Alternative Communication, 30*(2), 160–171. doi:10.3109/07434618.2014.905635

Gilliam, J. E. (2014). *Gilliam Autism Rating Scale–Third Edition (GARS-3) manual.* Austin, TX: PRO-ED.

Goldstein, S., & Naglieri, J. A. (2010). *Autism spectrum rating scales.* North Tonawanda, NY: Multi Health Systems.

Gould, E., Dixon, D. R., Najdowski, A. C., Smith, M. N., & Tarbox, J. (2011). A review of assessments for determining the content of early intensive behavioral intervention programs for autism spectrum disorders. *Research in Autism Spectrum Disorders, 5*(3), 990–1002. doi:10.1016/j.rasd.2011.01.012

Greenberg, J. S., Seltzer, M. M., Hong, J., & Orsmond, G. I. (2006). Bidirectional effects of expressed emotion and behavior problems and symptoms in adolescents and adults with autism. *American Journal on Mental Retardation, 111*(4), 229. doi:10.1352/0895-8017(2006)111 [229:beoeea]2.0.co;2

Hagopian, L. P., Long, E. S., & Rush, K. S. (2004). Preference assessment procedures for individuals with developmental disabilities. *Behavior Modification, 28*(5), 668–677. doi:10.1177/0145445503259836

Hanley, G. P., Jin, C. S., Vanselow, N. R., & Hanratty, L. A. (2014). Producing meaningful improvements in problem behavior of children with autism via synthesized analyses and treatment. *Journal of Applied Behavior Analysis, 47,* 16–36.

Harrison, P., & Oakland, T. (2015). *Adaptive Behavior Assessment System—third edition* (ABAS-3). Torrance, CA: Western Psychological Services.

Huerta, M., Bishop, S. L., Duncan, A., Hus, V., & Lord, C. (2012). Application of DSM-5 criteria for autism spectrum disorder to three samples of children with DSM-IV diagnoses of pervasive developmental disorders. *American Journal of Psychiatry, 169*(10), 1056–1064. doi:10.1176/appi.ajp.2012.12020276

Individuals with Disabilities Education Improvement Act of 2004, PL 108-446, 20 U.S.C. §§ 1400 *et seq.*

Karren, B. C. (2017). Test review: Gilliam Autism Rating Scale—Third Edition. *Journal of Psychoeducational Assessment, 35,* 342–346. doi:10.1177/0734282916635465

Kasari, C., Brady, N., Lord, C., & Tager-Flusberg, H. (2013). Assessing the minimally verbal school-aged child with autism spectrum disorder. *Autism Research, 6,* 479–493.

Kent, R. G., Carrington, S. J., Couteur, A., Gould, J., Wing, L., Maljaars, J., & Leekam, S. R. (2013). Diagnosing autism spectrum disorder: Who will get a *DSM-5* diagnosis? *Journal of Child Psychology and Psychiatry, 4,* 1242–1250. doi:10.1111/jcpp.12085

Klose, L. M., Potts, C., Kozenseki, N., & Skinner-Foster, J. (2012). A review of assessment tools for diagnosis of autism spectrum disorders: Implications for school practice. *Assessment for Effective Intervention, 37,* 236–242.

Koegel, L. K., Koegel, R. L., & Smith, A. (1997). Variables related to differences in standardized test outcomes of children with autism. *Journal of Autism and Developmental Disorders, 27,* 233–243.

Koegel, R. L., & Covert, A. (1972). The relationship of self-stimulation to learning in autistic children. *Journal of Applied Behavior Analysis, 5*(4), 381–387. doi:10.1901/jaba.1972.5-381

Koegel, R. L., & Frea, W. D. (1993). Treatment of social behavior in autism through the modification of pivotal social skills. *Journal of Applied Behavior Analysis, 26,* 369–377.

Krug, D. A., Arick, J. R., & Almond, P. J. (2008). *Autism screening instrument for educational planning—third edition.* Austin, TX: PRO-ED.

Light, J. (1989). Toward a definition of communicative competence for individuals using augmentative and alternative communication systems. *Augmentative and Alternative Communication, 5*(2), 137–144. doi:10.1080/07434618912331275126

Light, J. (1997). "Let's go star fishing": Reflections on the contexts of language learning for children who use aided AAC. *Augmentative and Alternative Communication, 13*(3), 158–171. doi:10.1080/07434619712331277978

Light, J., & McNaughton, D. (2014). Communicative competence for individuals who require augmentative and alternative communication: A new definition for a new era of communication? *Augmentative and Alternative Communication, 30*(1), 1–18. doi:10.3109/0743 4618.2014.885080

Light, J. C., & Drager, K. D. R. (2007). AAC technologies for young children with complex communication needs: State of the science and future research directions. *Augmentative and Alternative Communication, 23,* 204–216. http://dx.doi.org/10.1080/07434610 701553635

Loftin, R. L., Odom, S. L., & Lantz, J. F. (2007). Social interaction and repetitive motor behaviors. *Journal of Autism and Developmental Disorders, 38*(6), 1124–1135. doi:10.1007/s10803-007-0499-5

Lord, C., & Corsello, C. (2005). *Autism Diagnostic Observation Schedule (ADOS): Manual.* Los Angeles, CA: Western Psychological Services.

Lord, C. Luyster, R. J., Gotham, K, & Guthrie, W. (2012). Autism diagnostic observation schedule: Second edition (ADOS-2) manual (Part II): Toddler module. Torrance, CA: Western Psychological Services.

Lord, C., Risi, S., Lambrecht, L., Cook, E. H., Leventhal, B. L., DiLavore, P. S., . . . Rutter, M. (2000). The Autism Diagnostic Observation Schedule–Generic: A standard measure of social and communication deficit associated with the spectrum of autism. *Journal of Autism and Developmental Disorders, 30,* 205–223.

Lord, C., Rutter, M., DiLavore, P., Risi, S., Gotham, K., & Bishop, S. L. (2012). *Autism diagnostic observation schedule* (2nd edition). Torrance, CA: Western Psychological Services.

Lord, C., Rutter, M., Goode, S., Heemsbergen, J., Jordan, H., Mawhood, L., & Schopler, E. (1989). The Autism Diagnostic Observation Schedule: A standardized observation of communicative and social behavior. *Journal of Autism and Developmental Disorders, 19,* 185–212.

Lund, S. K., & Light, J. (2007). Long-term outcomes for individuals who use augmentative and alternative communication: Part III—contributing factors. *Augmentative and Alternative Communication, 23*(4), 323–335. doi:10.1080/02656730701189123

Lund, S. K., Quach, W., Weissling, K., McKelvey, M., & Dietz, A. (2017). Assessment with children who need augmentative and alternative communication (AAC): Clinical decisions of AAC specialists. *Language Speech and Hearing Services in Schools, 48*(1), 56. doi:10.1044/2016_lshss-15-0086

Luyster, R. Gotham, W., Coffing, M., Petrak, R., Pierce, K., Bishop, S., . . . Lord, C. (2009). The autism diagnostic observation schedule–Toddler module: A new module of a standardized diagnostic measure for autism spectrum disorders. *Journal of Autism and Developmental Disorders, 39,* 1305–1320.

Luyster, R., Quiu, S., Lopez, K., & Lord, C. (2007). Predicting outcomes of children referred for autism using the MacArthur-Bates Communicative Development Inventory. *Journal of Speech, Language, and Hearing, 50,* 667–681.

Makransky, G., Dale, P. S., Havmose, P., & Bleses, D. (2016). An item-response theory-based computerized adaptive testing version of the MacArthur-Bates Communicative Development Inventory: Words and sentences. *Journal of Speech Language & Hearing Research, 59,* 281–289.

McLay, L., France, K., Blampied, N., Danna, K., & Hunter, J. (2017). Using functional behavioral analysis to develop a multicomponent treatment for sleep problems in a 3-year-old boy with autism. *Clinical Case Studies, 16,* 254–270. doi:10.1177/1534650116688558

Nadig, A., Lee, I., Singh, L., Bosshart, K., & Ozonoff, S. (2010). How does the topic of conversation affect verbal exchange and eye gaze? A comparison between typical development and high functioning autism. *Neuropsychologia, 48,* 2730–2739.

National Dissemination Center for Children with Disabilities. (2010). *Supports, Modifications, and Accommodations for Students*. Retrieved from http://www.parentcenterhub.org/accommodations/

National Research Council. (2001). *Educating children with autism*. Washington, DC: National Academies Press.

Orland, M. (2015). Research and policy perspectives on data-based decision making in education. *Teachers College Record, 117,* 04031.

Ozonoff, S. (2005). Evidence-based assessment of autism spectrum disorders in children and adolescents. *Journal of Clinical Child and Adolescent Psychology, 34,* 523–540.

Parette, H. P., & Angelo, D. H. (1996). Augmentative and alternative communication impact on families: Trends and future directions. *The Journal of Special Education, 30*(1), 77–98. doi:10.1177/002246699603000105

Pierucci, J. M., Barber, A. B., Gilpin, A. T., Crisler, M. E., & Klinger, L. G. (2015). Play assessments and developmental skills in young children with autism spectrum disorders. *Focus on Autism and Other Developmental Disabilities, 30,* 35–43.

Plesa Skwerer, D., Jordan, S. E., Brukilacchio, B. H., & Tager-Flusberg, H. (2016). Comparing methods for assessing receptive language skills in minimally verbal children and adolescents with autism spectrum disorders. *Autism, 20,* 591–604.

Rapin, I., Dunn, M. A., Allen, D. A., Stevens, M. C., & Fein, D. (2009). Subtypes of language disorders in school-age children with autism. *Developmental Neuropsychology, 34,* 66–84.

Riccio, C. A. (2008). A descriptive summary of essential neuropsychological tests. In R. C. D'Amato and L. C. Hartlage (Eds.), *Essentials of neuropsychological assessment: Treatment planning and for rehabilitation* (2nd ed., pp. 207–242). New York, NY: Springer.

Riley-Tillman, T. C., Kalberer, S., & Chafouleas, S. M. (2005). Selecting the right tool for the job: A review of behavior monitoring tools used to assess student response to intervention. *California School Psychologist, 10,* 81–92.

Rimland, B., & Edelson, M. (1999). *Autism Treatment Evaluation Checklist*. Retrieved from https://www.autism.com/ind_atec

Roid, G., & Miller, L. J. (1997). *Leiter international performance scale-revised*. Wood Dale, IL: Stoelting.

Roid, G., & Miller, L. J. (2013). *Leiter international performance scale (3rd edition)*. Wood Dale, IL: Stoelting.

Rutter, M., Le Couteur, A., Lord, C. (2003). *ADI-R: Autism Diagnostic Inventory Revised*. Torrance, CA: Western Psychological Services.

Schlosser, R. W., & Raghavendra, P. (2004). Evidence-based practice in augmentative and alternative communication. *Augmentative and Alternative Communication, 20*(1), 1–21. doi:10.1080/07434610310001621083

Schopler, E., Lansing, M., Reichler, R. J., & Marcus, L. M. (2005). *Psycho-educational profile: TEACCH individualized psychoeducational assessment for children with autism spectrum disorders* (3rd ed.; PEP-3). Austin, TX: PRO-ED.

Schopler, E., Reichler, J., & Renner, B. (1988). *The Childhood Autism Rating Scale (CARS)*. Torrance, CA: Western Psychological Services.

Schopler, E., Van Bourgondien, M. E., Wellman, G. J., & Love, S. R. (2010). *Childhood Autism Rating Scale, second edition*. Torrance, CA: Western Psychological Services.

Sigafoos, J. (1999). Creating opportunities for augmentative and alternative communication: Strategies for involving people with developmental disabilities. *Augmentative and Alternative Communication, 15*(3), 183–190. doi:10.1080/07434619912331278715

Simek, A. N., & Wahlberg, A. C. (2011). Test review: Autism spectrum rating scales. *Journal of Psychoeducational Assessment, 29,* 191–195.

Sparrow, S. S., Carter, A. S., & Cicchetti, D. V. (1993). *Vineland Screener: Overview, Reliability, Validity, Administration, and Scoring*. New Haven, CT: Yale University Child Study Center.

Sparrow, S., Cicchetti, D., & Balla, D. (2005). *Vineland Adaptive Behavior Scales, second edition*. Minneapolis, MN: Pearson Assessment.

Tager-Flusberg, H., & Kasari, C. (2013). Minimally verbal school-aged children with autism spectrum disorder: The neglected end of the spectrum. *Autism Research, 6,* 468–478.

Taylor, L. J., Mayberry, M. D., Grayndler, L., & Whitehouse, A. J. O. (2014). Evidence for distinct cognitive profiles in autism spectrum disorder and specific language impairments. *Journal of Autism and Developmental Disorders, 44,* 19–30.

Taylor, L. J., & Whitehouse, A. J. O. (2016). Autism spectrum disorder, language disorder, and social (pragmatic) communication disorder: Overlaps, distinguishing features, and clinical implications. *Australian Psychologist, 51,* 287–295. doi:10.1111/ap.12222

Visvader, P. (2015). *School-based AAC evaluation: Choosing effective assistive technology strategies for students with complex communication needs.* Boulder, CO: Author.

Watkins, L., Kuhn, M., Ledbetter-Cho, K., Gevarter, C., & O'Reilly, M. (2017). Evidence-based social communication interventions for children with autism spectrum disorder. *The Indian Journal of Pediatrics, 84*(1), 68–75. doi:10.1007/s12098-015-1938-5

Wiig, E. H., Semel, E. M., & Secord, W. (2013). *Clinical evaluation of language fundamentals—fifth edition.* San Antonio, TX: Pearson.

Wilkinson, K. M., O'Neill, T., & McIlvane, W. J. (2014). Eye-tracking measures reveal how changes in the design of aided AAC displays influence the efficiency of locating symbols by school-age children without disabilities. *Journal of Speech, Language, and Hearing Research, 57*(2), 455. doi:10.1044/2013_jslhr-l-12-0159

Wilkinson, L. A. (2017). *A best practice guide to assessment and intervention for autism spectrum disorder in schools* (2nd ed.). Philadelphia, PA: Jessica Kingsley Publishers.

Williams, K. T. (2007). *Expressive Vocabulary Test* (2nd ed.). San Antonio, TX: Pearson.

Witmer, S. E., Nasamran, A., Parikh, P. J., Schmitt, H. A., & Clinton, M. C. (2015). Using parents and teachers to monitor progress among children with ASD: A review of intervention research. *Focus on Autism and Other Developmental Disabilities, 30,* 67–85. doi:10.1177/1088357614525659

II

Overview of Evidence-Based Practices for Implementation With Individuals With Autism Spectrum Disorder and Complex Communication Needs

3

Overview of Evidence-Based Practices for Individuals With Autism Spectrum Disorder and Complex Communication Needs

Jennifer B. Ganz, Ee Rea Hong, and Ching-Yi Liao

Autism spectrum disorder (ASD) is one of the most common neurodevelopmental disorders, with an estimated prevalence of 1 in 45 children, ages 3–17 (Zablotsky, Black, Maenner, Schieve, & Blumberg, 2015). Although the term ASD refers to a group of neurodevelopmental disorders that have common areas of impairment and are encompassed under the umbrella term of ASD (Noterdaeme, Wriedt, & Höhne, 2010), individuals with ASD show a wide range of variability in the comorbidity and severity of their disorders and symptoms (de Bruin, Ferdinand, Meester, deNijs, & Verheij, 2007). The high rates of variability and concurrent condition in this population may exacerbate the core features of ASD and their impairments, especially in communication and language development (de Bruin et al., 2007).

UNIQUE CHARACTERISTICS AND NEEDS OF PEOPLE WITH ASD AND CCN

Among the characteristics of ASD are deficits in and atypical development of speech and language skills (American Psychiatric Association [APA], 2013). Recent studies suggest that approximately 80% of parents of children with ASD tend to recognize atypical development in their children by the age of 2 years (De Giacomo & Fombonne, 1998). More specifically, delays in speech and language development are among the most concerning and issues that those parents initially encounter (De Giacomo & Fombonne, 1998). Individuals on the autism spectrum vary in rate and sequence of language development (Smith, Mirenda, & Zaidman-Zait, 2007). Many individuals with ASD present either delayed or immediate echolalia, neologisms (i.e., made-up words), contact gestures (e.g., touching a photo to draw someone's attention to it), or lack of speech (APA, 2013). In severe cases, individuals with ASD produce unintelligible vocalizations but no functional speech (Taylor, Maybery, Grayndler, & Whitehouse, 2014). Some individuals with

ASD who have complex communication needs (CCN) do not develop any form of spoken language (Light & Drager, 2007), and this condition may last throughout the course of their lifetime (Tager-Flusberg & Kasari, 2013). Deficits and high variability in speech and language abilities of individuals with ASD result in complexity in diagnosis and intervention planning (Solomon et al., 2011). That is, this heterogeneity of language development in individuals with ASD may result in challenges for professionals and families to determine the best treatment for those individuals (Taylor et al., 2014).

During the infant preverbal stage, several skills precede spoken language and become a foundation for development of speech, including joint attention, behavior imitation, eye gaze, and toy play (Toth, Munson, Meltzoff, & Dawson, 2006). Since many of these preverbal skills are impaired in children with ASD and CCN (Toth et al., 2006), those children often use unconventional means of communication, such as tantrums, aggressive behaviors, or self-injurious behaviors, prior to the acquisition of speech and language (De Giacomo et al., 2016). Preverbal skills are considered predictive of future gains in expressive language skills (Bono, Daley, & Sigman, 2004); therefore, the skill deficits displayed by children with ASD may result in the failure of their later language outcomes. In addition, children with ASD and CCN show delay in pragmatic language development (Tager-Flusberg et al., 2009), leading to challenges in understanding how to communicate with and express their communicative intentions to others. Furthermore, children with ASD may have difficulty integrating information from different sensory modalities, which can result in difficulties with speech perception (Iarocci, Rombough, Yager, Weeks, & Chua, 2010). Furthermore, for successful speech production, both visual and auditory stimuli should be integrated (Massaro, 1998). Relatedly, individuals on the autism spectrum may have unusual responses to sensory stimuli; over 30% of individuals with ASD fit this description (Baranek, Foster, & Berkson, 1997). With respect to sensory inputs, many researchers have suggested that differences in sensory processing may contribute to language and speech impairments in ASD, given the findings that successful information integration across multiple senses can lead to better speech and language outcomes (Marco, Hinkley, Hill, & Nagarajan, 2011).

HISTORY OF SELECTION OF EVIDENCE-BASED PRACTICES FOR ASD

The first description of the syndrome of autism was reported by Leo Kanner in 1943. Since then, much attention has been given to this syndrome in the research literature and numerous treatments have been investigated to educate individuals with characteristics of ASD. For example, more than 100 behavioral intervention studies were published by 1970 (DeMyer, Hingtgen, & Jackson, 1981). In the early 1960s, researchers began examining the behavior of children with autism using the basic principles of behavior analysis (e.g., different schedule of reinforcement, stimulus control; see Ferster, 1961; Ferster & DeMyer, 1962). Since most of the earlier studies targeted nonfunctional behaviors (e.g., pulling levers, matching to sample for reinforcers), the interventions did not provide much benefit for the child participants in those studies (Lovaas, Koegel, Simmons, & Long, 1973). However, the results opened up possibilities for a relationship between the modification of environmental consequence and its effect on the behaviors of autistic children (Lovaas et al., 1973). Following this, there was an attempt to report cases that showed the effectiveness of the classic behavioral principles in mediating certain behavior symptoms of autistic children, such as functional communicative behaviors (Wolf, Risley, & Mees, 1964; Hart & Risley, 1975).

Contribution of Applied Behavior Analysis

As the treatment model that has its basis on behavior analysis and aims to make measurable changes in socially important behaviors (Baer, Wolf, & Risley, 1968), applied behavior analysis (ABA) has been considered to be a best practice supported by more evidence than most other interventions developed for individuals with ASD (Rogers & Vismara, 2008). ABA is an applied science and can be traced to laboratory experiments on animals and humans whose functioning levels were severely delayed (Snell, 1978). With its successful implementation of ABA techniques in clinical settings, this application was extended to a broader range of children. Lovaas and his colleagues first demonstrated positive outcomes in various skill domains of children with autism using ABA techniques, such as speech and behavior imitation skills and self-destructive and aggressive behaviors (e.g., Lovaas, 1961; Lovaas, Freitas, Nelson, & Whalen, 1967; Lovaas & Simmons, 1969).

With the emergence of research documenting significant improvements for autistic children following the work of Lovaas and his colleagues in the 1960s, ABA has since been recognized as an effective practice to build various areas of learning in individuals with ASD of all ages, including academic skills, daily living skills, language acquisition, and vocational skills. From the early 1980s, several models of ABA interventions involving home-based early treatments were found to have more evidence for use with individuals with ASD than any other approach (National Research Council, 2001). Among those, early intensive behavioral intervention has been considered the most thoroughly evaluated and well-established practice (Rogers & Vismara, 2008; Sallows & Graupner, 2005). Likewise, over the last few decades, it seems certain that the only practice that yields consistent evidence of improvements in outcome variables of individuals with ASD is ABA treatment (Jacobson, 2000). Accordingly, there has been much effort to disseminate the effectiveness of ABA treatment for individuals with ASD. Not only have many researchers and practitioners published their studies in peer-reviewed journals (Matson, Benavidez, Compton, Paclawskyj, & Bablio, 1996), governmental organizations also have endorsed the use of ABA techniques for children with ASD, such as the U.S. Surgeon General (U.S. Public Health Service, 1999). Furthermore, as more attention has been given to autism treatment and with the increasing prevalence of ASD, parents of children with ASD have become active advocates for their children and played an important role in the dissemination of the efficacy of ABA techniques (Jacobson, 2000). Eventually, these efforts resulted in increasing amount of autism research grants funded and the enactment of state legislation that mandates the coverage of health care for autism treatment developed based on ABA procedures (Singh, Illes, Lazzeroni, & Hallmayer, 2009).

Contribution of Speech-Language-Hearing Science

One of the most noticeable recent changes made in diagnostic criteria for ASD is that an individual may be given a diagnosis of ASD regardless of the presence of speech and language impairments (APA, 2013). Rather, an ASD diagnosis may be given if the child has impairments in two skill domains: social communication and restrictive behavior or activity (APA, 2013). With this change, it has become important for clinicians to be able to differentiate between ASD and social communication disorders, and speech-language pathologists (SLPs) are considered key personnel who play an instrumental role in determining differential diagnoses. Given the deficits and impairments of speech and language development in individuals with ASD, SLPs have also played a critical role in assisting those individuals and are key practitioners in the provision of high-quality communication interventions (Prizant & Rubin, 1999).

As can be seen, the scope of service in speech-language pathology is multifaceted, ranging from development of a multidisciplinary collaboration among professionals to promotion of overall health and education of individuals on the autism spectrum (American Speech-Language-Hearing Association [ASHA], 2016). Among these, providing a mode of functional communication, such as via augmentative and alternative communication (AAC) systems, is one of the central roles performed by SLPs and ensures individuals with ASD become independent self-advocates in social contexts (ASHA, 2016). For example, SLPs are responsible for development, selection, and prescription of AAC techniques (ASHA, 2016). AAC systems have been used to compensate for difficulties with auditory processing, receptive and expressive communication, and functional speech by augmenting and supplementing communication inputs and outputs with various types of aids (Ganz, Rispoli, Mason, & Hong, 2014). Both facilitation of an individual's ability to communicate effectively and teaching individuals with ASD to understand others' communication intentions are typically considered critical goals in the use of AAC systems (Wood, Lasker, Siegel-Causey, Beukelman, & Ball, 1998). AAC systems can be implemented with a wide variety of communication modes depending on targeted behaviors, including use of sign language, visual-graphic symbols, and speech-generating devices (SGD; Nunes, 2008). The research literature has evaluated effects of different types of AAC on various communicative skill domains (e.g., communicative input, output, mixed) with individuals with ASD (see Mirenda, 2001) and has found positive impacts on a range of targeted behaviors. Despite the increasing use and recognized benefits of AAC, some parents and practitioners have argued that AAC techniques may interfere with speech production in individuals with ASD (e.g., Beukelman, 1987), although this is untrue (Millar, Light, & Schlosser, 2006; Schlosser & Wendt, 2008). Such concern among the professionals and caregivers regarding the selection of the best treatment and type of instruction modality emphasizes the importance of involvement of experts including SLPs in evaluation of personal needs and each individual's ability to communicate as well as in development of appropriate techniques based on the evaluation.

STATE OF THE SCIENCE: EVIDENCE-BASED PRACTICES FOR INDIVIDUALS WITH ASD AND CCN

There is no single agreed-upon list of evidence-based practices for individuals with ASD, let alone for those with ASD and CCN. However, several autism-related research teams have conducted systematic literature reviews and meta-analyses to determine what interventions have evidence to improve outcomes for people with ASD. These include the National Autism Center (NAC), the National Professional

Development Center on Autism Spectrum Disorder, and What Works Clearing-house (WWC; web sites provided in the references), as well as a number of published literature reviews and meta-analyses. The following two sections of this book provide detailed information regarding the research support for specific evidence-based practices for people with ASD and CCN, with a particular focus on augmentative and alternative communication. In this chapter, the authors provide a broad overview, as an introduction to the state of the science. Figures 3.1–3.3 provide an illustration of recent meta-analyses and literature reviews that have found a number of practices to be supported by research for implementation with people with ASD. This information is broken down by age (Figure 3.1), general functioning level (Figure 3.2), and participant outcomes (Figure 3.3).

Established Practices for Individuals With ASD and CCN

There are a number of practices, including those that incorporate AAC use, that are considered to be evidence-based or established practices to improve outcomes in people with ASD. Several of these are based in applied behavior analysis (i.e., behavioral interventions.) In particular, interventions that involve evaluating the impact of and implementing appropriate antecedents or consequences have been thoroughly evaluated across individuals with a wide range of functioning levels and ages (NAC, 2015; Wong et al., 2014). The Lovaas method is an approach that relies heavily on applied behavior analysis, with a focus on early, intensive intervention and one-to-one instruction (Lovaas Institute, n.d.) and has at least some evidence for improvement of participants in cognitive skills (WWC, 2010). Applied behavior analysis, as a general approach, is the most thoroughly evaluated approach to educating individuals with ASD (Wong et al., 2014), including those with CCN (Brunner & Seung, 2009; Hong et al., 2016a). Specific to language training, behavioral approaches such as prompting and reinforcement are considered to be effective for this population, including those with CCN (Brunner & Seung, 2009; Camargo et al., 2014; Hong et al., 2016a), when paired with a selection of developmentally appropriate target outcomes (NAC, 2015). Other developmentally appropriate approaches, such as modeling in-vivo and video modeling (e.g., demonstrating targeted skills via video recordings), have been found to be effective with some individuals with ASD (NAC, 2015; Wong et al., 2014), including people with CCN (Brunner & Seung, 2009; Camargo et al., 2014; Hong et al., 2016a).

Functional communication training is considered an established treatment for use to improve challenging behavior in individuals with ASD by teaching communicative behaviors that serve the same function (Wong et al., 2014). While much of this literature base does not target people with CCN, some functional communication training has included the use of AAC, demonstrating its efficacy with this population (Brunner & Seung, 2009; Camargo et al., 2014; Heath, Ganz, Parker, Burke, & Ninci, 2015; Hong et al., 2016a). An upcoming chapter in this book, Chapter 7 ("Functional Communication Training for Durable Behavior Change," by McComas et al.), reviews the use of functional communication training with individuals with ASD, with a focus on its use with people with ASD and CCN.

Recent approaches to teaching individuals with ASD have focused on naturalistic teaching strategies (Hong, Ganz, Neely, Gerow, & Ninci, 2016b). Most of these involve strategies similar to incidental learning, which has also been referred

Figure 3.1. Matrix of evidence-based practices by age. A shaded cell means at least one study included the given age group. (Key: EBP, evidence-based practice; AAC, aided augmentative and alternative communication systems; ABI, behavioral interventions, antecedent and consequent interventions; LT, language training [production and understanding; selection of developmentally appropriate skills, prompting, or reinforcement]; MD, modeling; FCT, functional communication training; NT, natural teaching strategies [motivating activities, everyday materials, generalization instruction, natural consequences, training loosely]; PPMI, peer- or parent-mediated interventions.)

Resource	AAC 0-5	AAC 6-14	AAC 15-22	ABI 0-5	ABI 6-14	ABI 15-22	LT 0-5	LT 6-14	LT 15-22	MD 0-5	MD 6-14	MD 15-22	FCT 0-5	FCT 6-14	FCT 15-22	NT 0-5	NT 6-14	NT 15-22	PPMI 0-5	PPMI 6-14	PPMI 15-22
Bond et al. (2016)		X		X	X	X													X	X	X
Brunner and Seung (2009)		X						X		X											
Camargo et al. (2014)		X				X						X									
Ganz et al. (2012a)																					
Ganz et al. (2012b)																	X				
Ganz et al. (2014)		X																			
Heath et al. (2015)					X			X						X					X		
Hong et al. (2016a)					X			X			X										
Hong et al. (2016b)					X																
Law, Plunkett, & Stringer (2011)																					
Morgan et al. (2014)		X									X										
National Autism Center (2015)		X		X				X											X	X	X
Spain and Blainey (2015)																				X	
Wong et al. (2014)	X	X	X	X	X	X	X	X	X	X	X	X	X	X	X	X	X	X	X	X	X

EBP Resource	AAC			ABI			LT			MD			FCT			NT			PPMI		
	HF	CCN	NS	HF	CCN	NS	HF	CCN	NS	HF	CCN	NS	HF	CCN	NS	HF	CCN	NS	HF	CCN	NS
Bond et al. (2016)		▨									▨									▨	▨
Brunner and Seung (2009)		▨	▨			▨		▨	▨		▨	▨						▨		▨	▨
Camargo et al. (2014)		▨												▨							
Ganz et al. (2012a)		▨																			
Ganz et al. (2012b)																					
Ganz et al. (2014)																					
Heath et al. (2015)														▨							
Hong et al. (2016a)		▨						▨			▨			▨			▨				▨
Hong et al. (2016b)		▨				▨			▨			▨			▨			▨			▨
Law et al. (2011)																					▨
Morgan et al. (2014)		▨																▨			▨
National Autism Center (2015)				▨						▨											
Spain and Blainey (2015)																▨			▨		
Wong et al. (2014)	▨	▨									▨									▨	

Figure 3.2. Matrix of evidence-based practices by the levels of functioning. A shaded cell means at least one study included the given level of functioning. (*Key:* EBP, evidence-based practice; AAC, aided augmentative and alternative communication systems; ABI, behavioral interventions, antecedent and consequent interventions; LT, language training; MD, modeling; FCT, functional communication training; NT, natural teaching strategies; PPMI, peer- or parent-mediated interventions; HF, high-functioning/verbal; CCN, complex communication needs; NS, not specified [widely applicable].)

Figure 3.3. Matrix of evidence-based practices by outcomes related to core characteristics of autism. A shaded cell means at least one study included the given outcome. (*Key:* EBP, evidence-based practice; AAC, aided augmentative and alternative communication systems; ABI, behavioral interventions, antecedent and consequent interventions; LT, language training; MD, modeling; FCT, functional communication training; NT, natural teaching strategies; PPMI, peer- or parent-mediated interventions; SC, social and communication; BE, behavior; DLS, daily living skill.)

EBP Resource	AAC			ABI			LT			MD			FCT			NT			PPMI		
	SC	BE	DLS	SC	BE	DLS	SC	BE	DLS	SC	BE	DLS	SC	BE	DLS	SC	BE	DLS	SC	BE	DLS
Bond et al. (2016)	■	■		■	■	■	■	■	■		■								■	■	
Brunner and Seung (2009)	■	■		■	■								■			■					
Camargo et al. (2014)			■													■	■				
Ganz et al. (2012a)	■																■				
Ganz et al. (2012b)	■	■																			
Ganz et al. (2014)		■																			
Heath et al. (2015)														■	■						
Hong et al. (2016a)				■			■			■						■			■		
Hong et al. (2016b)	■															■	■				
Law et al. (2011)		■			■		■	■		■							■		■	■	
Morgan et al. (2014)																				■	
National Autism Center (2015)	■			■	■	■	■	■		■		■		■	■	■	■			■	
Spain and Blainey (2015)																					
Wong et al. (2014)	■			■	■	■	■			■						■	■		■	■	

54

to as milieu teaching and, when implemented with AAC, has been referred to as aided language stimulation, aided AAC modeling, the System for Augmenting Language (Ganz, 2015). These strategies involve 1) use of motivating activities and everyday materials, 2) instruction in socially valid and functional skills, 3) use of naturally available consequences and rewards, 4) training loosely to encourage broad responsiveness, and 5) instruction with a focus on generalization across contexts and people. Furthermore, these strategies often incorporate teaching peers and parents (i.e., peer- or parent-mediated interventions, to provide instruction or to respond in ways that encourage continued learning (NAC, 2015; Wong et al., 2014). Much of the research on these practices has demonstrated positive outcomes with individuals with ASD and CCN (Brunner & Seung, 2009; Hong et al., 2016a; Wong et al., 2014).

Emerging Practices for Individuals With ASD and CCN   A number of strategies have been determined to be promising or emerging practices for individuals with ASD, including some that were developed particularly for individuals with ASD and CCN (NAC, 2015). AAC devices have been determined to be promising; however, devices themselves are not practices (Ganz, 2015), although most practices for teaching the use of AAC devices to individuals with ASD are based in behavioral and naturalistic instructional practices. The Picture Exchange Communication System (PECS) is a protocol for teaching individuals with ASD and CCN to use pictures to communicate, primarily wants and needs. By design, AAC research, including on PECS, has included people with CCN, with positive results in social and communication skills and behavior (Ganz, Earles-Vollrath, et al., 2012b, Nunes, 2008). High- and low-tech AAC are reviewed in Chapters 5 and 6, respectively, including the research and descriptions of these communication modes (Chapter 5, "Considerations in Implementing Aided Low-Tech AAC Systems for Individuals With Autism Spectrum Disorder and Complex Communication Needs," by Reichle et al.; Chapter 6, "High-Tech Aided AAC for Individuals with Autism Spectrum Disorder and Complex Communication Needs," by Caron & Holifield).

Controversial Treatments for Individuals With ASD and CCN   Although there are a number of evidence-based and emerging practices for this population, this field is regularly prey to individuals marketing controversial or unproven approaches. People with ASD and CCN and their families are particularly at risk for being exposed to one such treatment: facilitated communication. Facilitated communication not only has no research to support it but also has been implicated in a number of cases of accusations of abuse and misuse. Facilitated communication, briefly, involves using full physical prompts to facilitate the communication of a person with CCN via an AAC mode. Unfortunately, this method has been repeatedly discounted as resulting in communication that originates from the facilitator and not the person with CCN. Although the data debunking this approach is decades old, the approach persists and thus is worth mentioning in this book. In short, facilitated communication has no research to support it and has been found to result in false communication (Ganz, 2014). Accordingly, a number of professional organizations have taken strong stances against the use of facilitated communication (American Psychological Association, 2003; American Speech-Language-Hearing Association, 1995; International Society for Augmentative and Alternative Communication, 2014).

Resources for Selecting Interventions for Individuals With ASD and CCN

The state of the science for interventions for this population is still emerging; thus, parents and practitioners are often uncertain about how to determine the best interventions for their clients or loved ones. Selection of interventions should balance the priorities of the family, the research in support of specific interventions, the knowledge of service providers, and data on the responsiveness of the individual to the intervention.

A team approach to program planning is ideal. Within a team, individuals from several fields are equipped to provide suggestions regarding best practices. School psychologists may conduct assessments of cognitive skills and consider the family's primary language to inform practitioners (Parette & Marr, 1997). Speech-language pathologists are well-informed regarding developmental appropriateness of communication targets and specific modes of communication to target, including AAC, and may conduct communication assessments (Beukelman, Ball, & Fager, 2008; Binger et al., 2012). Furthermore, speech-language pathologists are also trained to implement AAC in natural and classroom settings (Calculator & Black, 2009). Behavior analysts and educators are team members that may have primary responsibility for participating in assessments, implementing academic and other interventions, and collecting data to determine the effectiveness of approaches, including AAC interventions for individuals with ASD and CCN (Grether & Sickman, 2008). Coordination across team members is ideal as all of these professionals may provide valuable insight with regard to initial and ongoing assessment and evaluation of outcomes, designing and implementing interventions, and evaluating the effectiveness of interventions.

In addition to help from service providers, two primary online resources were developed specifically to identify evidence-based practices and translate this information for practitioners and family members. Both the National Autism Center (NAC, 2015) and the National Professional Development Center on Autism Spectrum Disorders (Wong et al., 2014) systematically review the literature evaluating potential evidence-based practices for people with ASD. While neither provides fine-grained detail to demonstrate whether particular interventions are effective for people with both ASD and CCN, the interventions they identify are a good starting point. Again, refer to Figures 3.1–3.3 for an overview of the literature sorted by participant characteristics, providing some guidance for practitioners in selecting tools appropriate for their clients or students.

CONCLUSION

Although there is a growing body of research on interventions for individuals with ASD, there is a significant amount of study that is needed that highlights the needs of those who have both ASD and CCN. That is, while there are a number of practices that have been deemed to be evidence-based practices for people with ASD in general, little research has focused on people with both ASD and CCN. Therefore, it is unlikely that many of the aforementioned interventions have been evaluated with this particular population. However, behavior-based interventions, such as prompting and providing reinforcement, are well-established, as are natural teaching strategies, with a wide range of individuals with ASD across functioning levels. Furthermore, AAC has been demonstrated to be at least emerging and at best moderately to highly effective. Given that AAC has been studied only with populations with CCN, it is safe to say that it is also an effective tool for use with individuals with ASD and CCN.

Techniques are available that allow finer-grained analyses of techniques for improving outcomes for particular populations. Systematic literature reviews require a thorough investigation of the available research on particular topics, such as the effects of interventions for individuals with ASD and CCN. This allows for a summary of the quality of the research and evidence for such interventions. Meta-analyses allow for further determination of the magnitude of effect for interventions and for determination of whether there are differentiated effects related to participant characteristics, types of interventions, and other variables. Furthermore, these analyses highlight the gaps in the literature, allowing for further research, via single-case studies or group research, to fill these gaps. Such a process should be conducted regarding the state of the science for interventions for individuals with ASD and CCN.

REFERENCES

American Psychiatric Association. (2013). *Diagnostic and statistical manual of mental disorders* (5th ed.). Washington, DC: Author.

American Psychological Association. (2003). *Facilitated communication: Sifting the psychological wheat from the chaff.* Retrieved from http://www.apa.org/research/action/facilitated.aspx

American Speech-Language-Hearing Association. (1995). *Facilitated communication* [Position statement]. Retrieved from https://www.asha.org/policy/PS1995-00089/

American Speech-Language-Hearing Association. (2016). *Scope of practice in speech-language pathology.* Retrieved from https://www.asha.org/policy/SP2016-00343

Baer, D. M., Wolf, M. M., & Risley, T. R. (1968). Some current dimensions of applied behavior analysis. *Journal of Applied Behavior Analysis, 1,* 91–97. doi:10.1901/jaba.1968.1-91

Baranek, G. T., Foster, L. G., & Berkson, G. (1997). Sensory defensiveness in persons with developmental disabilities. *OTJR: Occupation, Participation and Health, 17,* 173–185. doi:10.1177/153944929701700302

Beukelman, D. (1987). When you have a hammer, everything looks like a nail. *Augmentative and Alternative Communication, 3,* 94–96. doi:10.1080/07434618712331274329

Beukelman, D. R., Ball, L. J., & Fager, S. (2008). An AAC personnel framework: Adults with acquired complex communication needs. *Augmentative and Alternative Communication, 24,* 255–267. doi:10.1080/07434610802388477

Binger, C., Ball, L., Dietz, A., Kent-Walsh, J., Lasker, J., Lund, S., et al. (2012). Personnel roles in the AAC assessment process. *Augmentative and Alternative Communication, 28,* 278–288. doi:10.3109/07434618.2012.716079

Bond, C., Symes, W., Hebron, J., Humphrey, N., Morewood, G., & Woods, K. (2016). Educational interventions for children with ASD: A systematic literature review 2008–2013. *School Psychology International, 37*(3), 303–320.

Bono, M. A., Daley, T., & Sigman, M. (2004). Relations among joint attention, amount of intervention and language gain in autism. *Journal of Autism and Developmental Disorders, 34,* 495–505. doi:10.1007/s10803-004-2545-x

Brunner, D. L., & Seung, H. (2009). Evaluation of the efficacy of communication-based treatments for autism spectrum disorders: A literature review. *Communication Disorders Quarterly, 31*(1), 15–41.

Calculator, S. N., & Black, T. (2009). Validation of an inventory of best practices in the provision of augmentative and alternative communication services to students with severe disabilities in general education classrooms. *American Journal of Speech-Language Pathology, 18,* 329–342.

Camargo, S. P. H., Rispoli, M., Ganz, J., Hong, E., Davis, H., & Mason, R. (2014). A review of the quality of behaviorally-based intervention research to improve social interaction skills of children with ASD in inclusive settings. *Journal of Autism and Development Disorders, 44*, 2096–2116. doi:10.1007/s10803-014-2060-7.

de Bruin, E. I., Ferdinand, R. F., Meester, S., de Nijs, P. F., & Verheij, F. (2007). High rates of psychiatric co-morbidity in PDD-NOS. *Journal of Autism and Developmental Disorders, 37*, 877–886. doi:10.1007/s10803-006-0215-x

De Giacomo, A., Craig, F., Terenzio, V., Coppola, A., Campa, M. G., & Passeri, G. (2016). Aggressive behaviors and verbal communication skills in autism spectrum disorders. *Global Pediatric Health, 3*, 1–5. doi:10.1177/2333794x16644360

De Giacomo, A., & Fombonne, E. (1998). Parental recognition of developmental abnormalities in autism. *European Child & Adolescent Psychiatry, 7*, 131–136. doi:10.1007/s007870050058

DeMyer, M. K., Hingtgen, J. N., & Jackson, R. K. (1981). Infantile autism reviewed: A decade of research. *Schizophrenia Bulletin, 7*, 388–451. doi:10.1093/schbul/7.3.388

Ferster, C. B. (1961). Positive reinforcement and behavioral deficits of autistic children. *Child Development, 32*, 437–456. doi:10.2307/1126210

Ferster, C. B., & DeMyer, M. K. (1962). The development of performances in autistic children in an automatically controlled environment. *Journal of Chronic Disease, 13*, 312–345. doi:10.1016/b978-0-08-010054-8.50047-2

Ganz, J. B. (2014). *Aided augmentative and alternative communication for people with ASD*. In J. Matson (Ed.), Autism and Child Psychopathology Series. New York, NY: Springer. doi:10.1007/978-1-4939-0814-1

Ganz, J. B. (2015). AAC interventions for individuals with autism spectrum disorders: State of the science and future research directions. *Augmentative and Alternative Communication, 31*, 203–214. doi:10.3109/07434618.2015.1047532

Ganz, J. B., Davis, J. L., Lund, E. M., Goodwyn, F. D., & Simpson, R. L. (2012a). Meta-analysis of PECS with individuals with ASD: Investigation of targeted versus non-targeted outcomes, participant characteristics, and implementation phase. *Research in Developmental Disabilities, 33*, 406–418. doi:10.1016/j.ridd.2011.09.023

Ganz, J. B., Earles-Vollrath, T. L., Heath, A. K., Parker, R., Rispoli, M. J., & Duran, J. (2012b). A meta-analysis of single case research studies on aided augmentative and alternative communication systems with individuals with autism spectrum disorders. *Journal of Autism and Developmental Disorders, 42*(1), 60–74. doi:10.1007/s10803-011-1212-2

Ganz, J. B., Rispoli, M. J., Mason, R. A., & Hong, E. R. (2014). Moderation of effects of AAC based on setting and types of aided AAC on outcome variables: An aggregate study of single-case research with individuals with ASD. *Developmental Neurorehabilitation, 17*, 184–192. doi:10.3109/17518423.2012.748097

Grether, S. M., & Sickman, L. S. (2008). AAC and RTI: Building classroom-based strategies for every child in the classroom. *Seminars in Speech and Language, 29*, 155–163. doi:10.1055/s-2008-1079129

Hart, B., & Risley, T. R. (1975). Incidental teaching of language in the preschool. *Journal of Applied Behavior Analysis, 8*, 411–420. doi:10.1901/jaba.1975.8-411

Heath, A. K., Ganz, J. B., Parker, R., Burke, M., & Ninci, J. (2015). A meta-analytic review of functional communication training across mode of communication, age, and disability. *Review Journal of Autism and Developmental Disorders, 2*(2), 155–166. doi:10.1007/s40489-014-0044-3

Hong, E. R., Ganz, J. B., Neely, L., Boles, M., Gerow, S., & Davis, J. L. (2016a). A meta-analytic review of family implemented social and communication interventions for individuals with developmental disabilities. *Review Journal of Autism and Developmental Disabilities, 3*, 125–136. doi:10.1007/s40489-016-0071-3

Hong, E. R., Ganz, J. B., Neely, L., Gerow, S., & Ninci, J. (2016b). A review of the quality of primary caregiver-implemented communication intervention research for children with ASD. *Research in Autism Spectrum Disorders, 25*, 122–136. doi:10.1016/j.rasd.2016.02.005

Iarocci, G., Rombough, A., Yager, J., Weeks, D. J., & Chua, R. (2010). Visual influences on speech perception in children with autism. *Autism, 14*, 305–320. doi:10.1177/1362361309353615

International Society for Augmentative and Alternative Communication. (2014). ISAAC position statement on facilitated communication. *Augmentative and Alternative Communication, 30*, 357–358. doi:10.3109/07434618.2014.971492

Jacobson, J. W. (2000). Early intensive behavioral intervention: Emergence of a consumer-driven service model. *The Behavior Analyst, 23,* 149–171.

Law, J., Plunkett, C. C., & Stringer, H. (2011). Communication interventions and their impact on behaviour in the young child: A systematic review. *Child Language Teaching and Therapy, 28*(1), 7–23.

Light, J., & Drager, K. (2007). AAC technologies for young children with complex communication needs: State of the science and future research directions. *Augmentative and Alternative Communication, 23,* 204–216. doi:10.1080/07434610701553635

Lovaas Institute. (n.d.). *The Lovaas approach.* Retrieved from http://www.lovaas.com/approach-method.php

Lovaas, O. I. (1961). Effect of exposure to symbolic aggression on aggressive behavior. *Child Development,* 37–44. doi:10.2307/1126171

Lovaas, O. I., Freitas, L., Nelson, K., & Whalen, C. (1967). The establishment of imitation and its use for the development of complex behavior in schizophrenic children. *Behaviour Research and Therapy, 5,* 171–181. doi:10.1016/0005-7967(67)90032-0

Lovaas, O. I., Koegel, R., Simmons, J. Q., & Long, J. S. (1973). Some generalization and follow-up measures on autistic children in behavior therapy. *Journal of Applied Behavior Analysis, 6,* 131–165. doi:10.1901/jaba.1973.6-131

Lovaas, O. I., & Simmons, J. Q. (1969). Manipulation of self-destruction in three retarded children. *Journal of Applied Behavior Analysis, 2,* 143–157. doi:10.1901/jaba.1969.2-143

Marco, E. J., Hinkley, L. B., Hill, S. S., & Nagarajan, S. S. (2011). Sensory processing in autism: A review of neurophysiologic findings. *Pediatric Research, 69,* 48R–54R. doi:10.1203/pdr.0b013e3182130c54

Massaro, D. W. (1998). *Perceiving talking faces: From speech perception to a behavioral principle.* Cambridge, MA: MIT Press.

Matson, J. L., Benavidez, D. A., Compton, L. S., Paclawskyj, T., & Baglio, C. (1996). Behavioral treatment of autistic persons: A review of research from 1980 to the present. *Research in Developmental Disabilities, 17,* 433–465. doi:10.1016/s0891-4222(96)00030-3

Millar, D. C., Light, J. C., & Schlosser, R. W. (2006). The impact of augmentative and alternative communication intervention on the speech production of individuals with developmental disabilities: A research review. *Journal of Speech, Language, and Hearing Research, 49,* 248–264.

Mirenda, P. (2001). Autism, augmentative communication, and assistive technology: What do we really know? *Focus on Autism and Other Developmental Disabilities, 16,* 141–151. doi:10.1177/108835760101600302

Morgan, L. J., Rubin, E., Coleman, J. J., Frymark, T., Wang, B. P., & Cannon, L. J. (2014). Impact of social communication interventions on infants and toddlers with or at-risk for autism: A systematic review. *Focus on Autism and Other Developmental Disabilities, 29*(4), 246–256.

National Autism Center. (2015). *Findings and conclusions: National standards project, phase 2.* Randolph, MA: Author.

National Research Council. (2001). *Educating children with autism.* Washington, DC: National Academies Press.

Noterdaeme, M., Wriedt, E., & Höhne, C. (2010). Asperger's syndrome and high-functioning autism: Language, motor and cognitive profiles. *European Child and Adolescent Psychiatry, 19,* 475–481. doi:10.1007/s00787-009-0057-0

Nunes, D. R. (2008). AAC interventions for autism: A research summary. *International Journal of Special Education, 23,* 17–26.

Parette, H. P., & Marr, D. D. (1997). Assisting children and families who use augmentative and alternative communication (AAC) devices: Best practices for school psychologists. *Psychology in the Schools, 34,* 337–346.

Prizant, B. M., & Rubin, E. (1999). Contemporary issues in interventions for autism spectrum disorders: A commentary. *Journal of the Association for Persons with Severe Handicaps, 24,* 199–208.

Rogers, S. J., & Vismara, L. A. (2008). Evidence-based comprehensive treatments for early autism. *Journal of Clinical Child & Adolescent Psychology, 37,* 8–38. doi:10.1080/15374410701817808

Sallows, G. O., & Graupner, T. D. (2005). Intensive behavioral treatment for children with autism: Four-year outcome and predictors. *American Journal on Mental Retardation, 110,* 417–438. doi:10.1352/0895-8017(2005)110[417:ibtfcw]2.0.co;2

Schlosser, R. W., & Wendt, O. (2008). Effects of augmentative and alternative communication intervention on speech production in children with autism: A systematic review. *American Journal of Speech-Language Pathology, 17,* 212–230.

Singh, J., Illes, J., Lazzeroni, L., & Hallmayer, J. (2009). Trends in U.S. autism research funding. *Journal of Autism and Developmental Disorders, 39,* 788–795. doi:10.1007/s10803-008-0685-0

Smith, V., Mirenda, P., & Zaidman-Zait, A. (2007). Predictors of expressive vocabulary growth in children with autism. *Journal of Speech, Language, and Hearing Research, 50,* 149–160. doi:10.1044/1092-4388(2007/013)

Snell, M. E. (1978). *Systematic instruction of the moderately and severely handicapped.* Columbus, OH: Merrill.

Solomon, M., Olsen, E., Niendam, T., Ragland, J. D., Yoon, J., Minzenberg, M., & Carter, C. S. (2011). From lumping to splitting and back again: Atypical social and language development in individuals with clinical-high-risk for psychosis, first episode schizophrenia, and autism spectrum disorders. *Schizophrenia Research, 131,* 146–151. doi:10.1016/j.schres.2011.03.005

Spain, D., & Blainey, S. H. (2015). Group social skills interventions for adults with high-functioning autism spectrum disorders: A systematic review. *Autism: The International Journal of Research and Practice, 19*(7), 874–886.

Tager-Flusberg, H., & Kasari, C. (2013). Minimally verbal school-aged children with autism spectrum disorder: The neglected end of the spectrum. *Autism Research, 6,* 468–478.

Tager-Flusberg, H., Rogers, S., Cooper, J., Landa, R., Lord, C., Paul, R., et al. (2009). Defining spoken language benchmarks and selecting measures of expressive language development for young children with autism. *Journal of Speech, Language, & Hearing Research, 52,* 643–652. doi:10.1037/e515072009-001

Taylor, L. J., Maybery, M. T., Grayndler, L., & Whitehouse, A. J. (2014). Evidence for distinct cognitive profiles in autism spectrum disorders and specific language impairment. *Journal of Autism and Developmental Disorders, 44,* 19–30. doi:10.1007/s10803-013-1847-2

Toth, K., Munson, J., Meltzoff, A. N., & Dawson, G. (2006). Early predictors of communication development in young children with autism spectrum disorder: Joint attention, imitation, and toy play. *Journal of Autism and Developmental Disorders, 36,* 993–1005. doi:10.1007/s10803-006-0137-7

U.S. Public Health Service. (1999). *Mental health: A report of the surgeon general.* Rockville, MD: Author.

What Works Clearinghouse, Institute of Education Sciences, U.S. Department of Education. (2010). *Lovaas Model of Applied Behavior Analysis. WWC Intervention Report.* Retrieved from http://ies.ed.gov/ncee/wwc/EvidenceSnapshot/295

Wolf, M., Risley, T., & Mees, H. (1964). Application of operant conditioning procedures to the behaviour problems of an autistic child. *Behaviour Research and Therapy, 1,* 305–312. doi:10.1016/0005-7967(63)90045-7

Wong, C., Odom, S. L., Hume, K., Cox, A. W., Fettig, A., Kucharczyk, S., . . . Schultz, T. R. (2014). *Evidence-based practices for children, youth, and young adults with autism spectrum disorder.* Chapel Hill, NC: The University of North Carolina, Frank Porter Graham Child Development Institute, Autism Evidence-based Practice Review Group.

Wood, L., Lasker, J., Siegel-Causey, E., Beukelman, D., & Ball, L. (1998). Input framework for augmentative and alternative communication. *Augmentative and Alternative Communication, 14,* 261–267. doi:10.1080/07434619812331278436

Zablotsky, B., Black, L. I., Maenner, M. J., Schieve, L. A., Blumberg, S. J. (2015). Estimated prevalence of autism and other developmental disabilities following questionnaire changes in the 2014 National Health Interview Survey. *National Health Statistics Reports, 13*(87), 1–20.

4

Overview of AAC for Individuals With Autism Spectrum Disorder and Complex Communication Needs

Pat Mirenda

Manisha is a 12-year-old girl who has autism spectrum disorder (ASD) and limited speech. Despite these challenges, she is a successful communicator both at school and at home. When she wants something that is visible to her, she leads a family member, classmate, or teacher to it and vocalizes and gestures. When she wants something that is out of sight, she points to pictorial symbols in a communication book. When she wants a break from work or needs help with an activity, she uses the manual signs for break and help, respectively. Manisha also uses pictorial symbols for her daily schedule and as a component of her reading curriculum. During recess and lunchtime, she and her friends enjoy using her iPad with an AAC app that allows her to "talk" to her classmates while they look at photos of Manisha and her family engaged in fun activities (like their recent trip to Disneyland). During activities in her classroom, Manisha uses a computer with adapted software for writing because she has difficulty holding and using a pencil. Last but not least, Manisha uses speech to say "hi" when she meets someone, to say "no" when she doesn't like what is happening, and to ask for help ("hep") when necessary.

Because a single AAC technique will *never* meet all of an individual's communication needs, Manisha uses a combination of approaches, depending on the message and context. It is clear that she has been supported by family members and school personnel who understand that her inability to speak does not mean she has nothing to communicate and who have made systematic efforts to provide her with an individualized, multimodal augmentative and alternative communication (AAC) system. In this chapter, the combination of all of the symbols and devices used by an individual is referred to as his or her AAC system.

WHAT IS AAC?

The term augmentative and alternative communication (AAC) refers to interventions designed to compensate for impairments of both speech comprehension and production (Beukelman & Mirenda, 2013). The word *augmentative* suggests that these interventions can be used to improve upon the effectiveness of communication through existing means (including speech and gestures), whereas *alternative* implies that a person uses systems that temporarily or permanently replace speech.

Why AAC?

Several rationales underlie the use of AAC by individuals with ASD. First, some individuals with ASD have difficulty producing complex motor movements such as those required for speech (Tierney et al., 2015). However, the motor movements required to produce a manual sign or point to/exchange a pictorial symbol are less complex and thus easier to teach than those required for speech. Second, learning to associate a symbol such as a manual sign or picture with a referent may be less demanding than speech in terms of verbal memory and abstract understanding. This may be especially true with regard to pictorial symbols, which require recognition rather than recall memory for accurate production. Recall memory requires a search of one's memory for potential symbols (e.g., manual signs) that convey a particular message, while recognition memory does not require this search because the symbols used (e.g., pictorial symbols on a communication display) are readily visible. Cognitive scientists would argue that discriminations that require recognition rather than recall memory are easier to achieve because fewer cognitive resources are involved (Cabeza et al., 1997). Third, many individuals with ASD show evidence of both auditory processing deficits, particularly for nonspeech stimuli (O'Connor, 2012) and relatively strong visual-spatial skills (Mitchell & Ropar, 2004), the latter of which may facilitate the learning and use of pictorial or text symbols such as photographs or line drawings. In addition, the results of recent research suggest a possible advantage of pictures over spoken words in access to semantics for individuals with ASD (Kamio & Toichi, 2000). Finally, AAC may help to overcome the negative learning history associated with speech production that many individuals with ASD experience as a result of prolonged lack of progress. AAC provides an alternative learning path that can support language, literacy, and sometimes even speech development at the same time as providing a means of functional communication (Beukelman & Mirenda, 2013).

AAC strategies and techniques can be used with individuals with ASD across the range of age and ability. AAC can play an important role in early communication intervention because it provides young children with an immediate way to communicate with their parents and other communication partners until they develop speech. AAC may also decrease the likelihood that problem behaviors will emerge early in life by providing young children with socially appropriate strategies for requesting desired items or activities, escaping or avoiding undesired interactions or events, sharing information, and engaging in enjoyable social interactions and routines (Romski et al., 2009). If functional speech fails to develop,

AAC can be used for ongoing communication interactions by school-age children, adolescents, and/or adults. It can also be used to support language learning and comprehension in individuals with ASD of all ages (Drager et al., 2006; Mirenda & Brown, 2009).

AAC and Speech Development   One of the most common concerns expressed by parents and teachers regarding the use of AAC techniques with individuals with ASD is how it is likely to affect speech development. In 2006, researchers reviewed six studies in which AAC intervention involved the use of manual signs (Millar, Light, & Schlosser, 2006). Of the 72 children exposed to manual signs, none showed a decrease in speech production; in fact, those children with good verbal imitation skills showed improved speech production secondary to the introduction of manual signs. These researchers also reviewed 10 studies that involved the use of low-tech AAC systems, such as the Picture Exchange Communication System (PECS; Frost & Bondy, 2002). All of the 167 children involved in these studies showed improvements in either verbal approximations or speech production. Finally, the same authors reviewed two studies in which the AAC intervention involved the use of a speech generating device (SGD; a digital device that "speaks" a message when an individual presses one or more buttons on a display). All nine of the children involved in the SGD studies demonstrated improvements in speech production. In 2009, one of the authors of this review (Millar) updated it with additional studies that involved individuals with ASD. These studies also showed that AAC does not appear to interfere with speech development and, for some individuals, can support speech production.

When considering the potential problems that can develop when children with ASD do not have a means with which to communicate (e.g., problem behavior, loss of learning and social opportunities), it is clear that a wait-and-see approach to AAC intervention can be detrimental (Schwartz & Davis, 2014). Based on current information, it is better to introduce AAC early. Some children may develop sufficient speech and no longer require AAC, some may continue to use AAC along with speech, and some may continue to rely on AAC entirely (Hanson, Beukelman, & Yorkston, 2013). Withholding AAC intervention while waiting for the possibility of speech to develop may result in the child developing additional problems such as problem behavior. Instead, it makes more sense to provide AAC early. This will help the child to communicate with greater ease, thereby reducing frustration.

MESSAGES

Perhaps the most important decision to be made in the selection and design of a multimodal AAC system involves the messages an individual needs to communicate in various contexts. Communicative messages can be divided into four main categories, according to their functions (Light, 1988):

- Wants and needs
- Information sharing
- Social closeness
- Social etiquette

Wants and Needs

Messages that enable a person to communicate about his or her wants and needs are among the easiest to teach and acquire. Young children first communicate about wants and needs when they learn to say, for example, "I want _____"; "Give me _____"; "No"; and "I don't want _____." An AAC system should contain symbols that a person can use to make requests for food, activities, desired items, and people. There should also be symbols that can be used to say "no," ask for a break, ask for help, and ask to be left alone.

Information Sharing

Messages that can be used to share information with classmates, teachers, family members, and others are also important. For example, most parents ask their children, "What did you do at school today?" when they come home after school and then expect a response. In addition, students often have a need to exchange more complicated information, such as when they want to ask or answer questions in class. Symbols that correspond to the vocabulary of academic lessons (e.g., Halloween symbols in October, symbols for animals when learning about mammals) can help children share information and allow them to participate in these types of interactions.

Social Closeness

Often, the purpose of communication is simply to connect with other people for the sake of social interaction. For individuals with ASD, social closeness interactions include those that get the attention of other people; facilitate back-and-forth, conversational interactions; ask partner-focused questions, and allow them to use humor to connect to other people. At least some of the symbols in their communication systems should be related to messages for social closeness (e.g., "Let's go play!" "That was great!" "I like that").

Social Etiquette

Finally, a fourth purpose of communication has to do with the routines for social etiquette that are customary in specific cultures. In North America, for example, people are expected to say "please," "thank you," and "excuse me" in certain situations. It is also considered polite to say "hello" or "goodbye" when meeting or leaving someone and to shake someone's hand if it is offered. Students who rely on AAC need to be provided with symbols that enable them to interact with others in ways that are culturally acceptable and respectful.

Determining which messages of the four types should be included in a communication system for an individual with ASD display can involve a number of simple questions. First, what messages will be used on a regular basis (i.e., daily) or frequently (i.e., several times in a day)? Some examples might include greetings, requests for help, "yes," "no," requests related to basic wants and needs (e.g., bathroom, water, food), and social etiquette messages. Second, what messages will facilitate participation (e.g., information sharing) in family, community, medical, and/or school activities? For example, a student might tell his mother what he did at school today by showing her remnant symbols that are associated with various activities, such as paper scraps from his art project or the flyer he got at the school assembly. Third, what messages will enable the person to participate in social interactions? For example, a high school student at a pep rally might need a message in his single-switch device that says "Go, team, go!" Individuals of any age might want to talk about their family members, a recent vacation, or favorite topics using a speech-output "app" with photographs on a tablet device. From these examples, it should be evident that AAC communication is a multi-modal endeavor—no single technique or device is likely to meet all of any individual's ongoing, daily communication needs. It might be appropriate to begin by teaching an individual to communicate wants and needs, as these messages are likely to be among the most motivating. However, an AAC communication system must be able to accommodate a sufficiently large number of messages to meet students' social, learning, and other needs as well.

TYPES OF AAC SYMBOLS

Communicating without speech requires the use of symbols that represent messages. A symbol is something that stands for something else; the "something else" is referred to as a referent (Beukelman & Mirenda, 2013). There are two main types of AAC symbols: unaided and aided. Unaided symbols do not require any equipment to produce and include natural gestures, body language, vocalizations, and manual signs (among others). Aided symbols require a device that is external to the individual who uses it, such as a communication book, SGD (including a tablet device such as the iPad), and computer. The following section reviews the most commonly used *unaided AAC* symbols and discusses some of the primary advantages and disadvantages of each.

Unaided AAC: Natural Gestures and Body Language

Before children learn to use speech, they engage in a wide array of communicative gestures. Some of these gestures appear to be natural extensions of other actions. For example, pointing is very similar in form to reaching for something. Others seem to develop as an extension or a pantomime of actions. For example, a child may stop talking when he sees someone place a finger to their lips because he has learned to associate this gesture with the "shhh" sound that means "be quiet." Still other gestures are more formal and, like spoken words, have meanings only within a given culture. For example, in North America, most people know that the "thumbs up" gesture means "that's right," "that's good," or another positive affirmation. Although many gestures involve hand motions, people also use other parts of their bodies to convey messages. In North America, many people shrug their shoulders in doubt, frown in puzzlement, or fold their arms in front of them to indicate displeasure. Perhaps the most familiar gesture involves nodding and shaking the head to mean "yes" or "no."

People use gestures to communicate many types of messages. Perhaps the most obvious is communication about wants and needs. For example, a parent may hold out two toys to a child, say, "Which one do you want to play with?", and expect the child to point to or simply reach toward the desired toy. Similarly, before they are 2 years old, typically developing children learn that they can get help from adults by bringing objects to them. They also learn that they can get people to look at objects or events of interest by pointing to them. Other gestures, such as waving hi or bye, blowing a kiss, and playing Peekaboo, are used for purely social reasons. Still, they are very important for developing smooth social interactions between friends or between children and adults.

Unaided AAC: AAC systems that do not require external equipment; unaided AAC includes manual sign languages, gestures, and other formal or informal approaches to nonverbal communication.

Why Are Gestures Important?   A common mistake in teaching communication skills to children with ASD is neglecting the importance of natural gestures as components of a communication system. This mistake often occurs because many parents and teachers tend to view communication as an "either-or" skill: either the child communicates this way (e.g., with pictures, with an iPad) *or* the child communicates that way (e.g., with gestures)—which, of course, is not the case! Because children with ASD have difficulty learning what communication is all about, it is important to respond to and encourage them to use *all* forms of communication, as long as those forms are understandable and socially acceptable. For example, when Jonathan leads his father to the cupboard to ask for a treat, or when Penny cries after she falls down and skins her knee, they are communicating messages ("I want something" and "Ow! That hurt!") that should be respected and acknowledged.

Encouraging Gestural Production   Most children with ASD have difficulty learning to communicate through gestures, at least in part because of their known difficulty with imitation (Rogers, Hepburn, Stackhouse, & Wehner, 2003). However, young children with ASD are likely to benefit from naturalistic interactions that encourage them to use gestures to communicate in the context of motivating routines. An example is the Pat-a-cake game that Jon's dad plays with him every evening before bedtime. Jon and his father sit on the floor facing each other and dad moves Jon's hands through the corresponding motions as he voices the Pat-a-cake rhyme. After he has done this a few times, Jon's dad pauses in the rhyme and waits for Jon to move his hands or indicate with his voice that he wants Dad to continue. When they first started playing this game, Jon did not know what to do and would often just sit there when his dad paused. But little by little, Jon started to use body language and vocalizations during the pauses, and his dad responded right away by continuing the chant. By responding to Jon's behaviors, his dad taught Jon to ask for "more!" Soon, Jon began to pull on people's hands and to vocalize in other situations as well when he wanted "more." This example shows how easy it is to practice using gestures in the context of playful interactions and routines.

Teaching Gestural Comprehension   It is important to teach children with ASD to understand gestures as well as to use them. Otherwise, it is difficult to communicate messages efficiently and rapidly in many situations. For example, one important gesture for a child to understand is what we, as interventionists, mean when pointing to something. Usually, we want the child to look at what we are pointing to, at a minimum. Sometimes, we also want the child to retrieve the item that is pointed out ("Get that"), to put something in the direction we point ("Put it there"), or to remain in the place we point to ("Wait right here"). We usually accompany pointing with verbal directions to clarify the exact message, but the pointing itself is a critical part of the interaction. Similarly, gestures that involve social routines, such as waving goodbye, giving a "high five," or clapping to show approval, are important for the child to understand if communication is to be effective and efficient.

As with gestural production, it is important to teach gestural understanding in situations in which the meaning of a gesture is motivating to the child. For example, Peter likes to stack blocks and knock over the resulting tower and thus enjoys getting each block to complete this task. His mother decides to put all of the blocks in a box except for the first few, to provide a motivating context for teaching Peter to understand what she means when she points. When Peter begins to look for the next block, she points to the box and then immediately taps it with her finger. Peter looks at the box when he hears the tap, lifts the lid, and takes out a block. Over the next several pieces, instead of immediately tapping after pointing, mom gradually increases the delay between the two actions. Over time, Peter learns to respond to her point as a signal to get the next block. This technique can be adapted to teach children to understand other types of gestures as well.

Unaided AAC: Manual Signs

Most people are familiar with the manual sign language systems that are used by people who are deaf. Individuals with ASD who are able to hear but have difficulty understanding and/or producing speech may also use manual signs for both language input (i.e., to support comprehension) and output (i.e., to support production). Manual sign *input* occurs when communication partners use signs in addition to speech to communicate to an individual with ASD. For example, Felicia's teacher speaks at the same time she signs the key words in her message. So, when it is time for lunch, she tells Felicia to "Get your lunch and eat it" while signing GET, LUNCH, and EAT. She does this because Felicia seems to pay attention more readily and follow directions more accurately when she is provided with signed information in addition to speech. Manual sign *output* occurs when an individual with ASD uses manual signs to communicate to others. For example, when Felicia wants to use the computer in her classroom, she asks the teacher to turn it on by signing WANT COMPUTER.

Manual Sign Systems   There are several different manual sign systems, all of which involve the use of hand and finger movements (augmented by other body actions) to represent letters, words, or phrases. In the United States and most of Canada, American Sign Language (ASL) is used within the Deaf community for face-to-face interactions; Deaf communities in other countries have their own distinct languages (e.g., Auslan in Australia, Swedish Sign Language in Sweden). Signing Exact English, a manual sign system that codes English word order, syntax, and grammar, is sometimes used in North America as an alternative to ASL. For individuals with ASD, the most common approach involves using manual signs from one or more of these systems to produce short phrases concurrent with speech for the critical (i.e., "key") words in a sentence; this has been referred to as "total communication" (Casey, 1978). Thus, the spoken sentence "Go get the cup and put it on the table" might involve use of the signs GET, CUP, PUT, ON, and TABLE while the entire sentence is spoken. Interventions combining speech, manual signs, and other AAC techniques are also appropriate, in many cases.

Advantages and Disadvantages of Manual Signs   Manual signing was the most commonly used system of communication for people with ASD who relied on AAC in the 1970s and 1980s. A primary reason for this is that manual signs are totally portable and require no external devices to use. However, most parents, teachers, and classmates are not fluent in manual signing, and some individuals with ASD do not have the fine motor/finger dexterity skills that are needed to produce signs accurately. Thus, someone who is familiar with the (often idiosyncratic) manual signs made by a person with ASD has to be available at all times to translate their meanings to unfamiliar communicative partners. This is one of the reasons that manual signing has fallen out of favor as a primary mode of communication for people with ASD.

Another reason that manual signing is now used less than previously is that the extent to which it can be considered an evidence-based practice is a matter of some debate. In a 2006 systematic review, Schwartz and Nye concluded that "there is little compelling evidence that sign language provides substantial improvements in either oral or sign language communication" (p. 15) for individuals with ASD. In contrast, Wendt (2009) reached a different conclusion in his systematic review, stating that, for individuals ASD, "The available body of research on manual signs . . . reveals strong intervention effectiveness scores for symbol acquisition and production, as well as for related outcomes such as speech comprehension and production" (p. 93). Finally, a middle-ground conclusion was reached by the review panel of the National Standards Project (National Autism Center, 2015), who deemed manual signing as an "emerging" intervention that requires additional research before it can be considered evidence-based. At this point in time, there are no clear, empirically validated guidelines to use when making decisions the appropriateness of manual signing, either alone or in combination with other techniques. Regardless, the available evidence suggests that manual signing does not appear to reduce an individual's motivation to speak and may, in fact, enhance it (Millar, 2009).

Aided AAC

Aided symbols can be arranged on a continuum of iconicity, a term that refers to "any association that an individual forms between a symbol and its referent" (Schlosser, 2003, p. 350). At one end of the iconicity continuum are transparent symbols, in which "the shape, motion, or function of the referent is depicted to such an extent that meaning of the symbol can be readily guessed in the absence of the referent" (Fuller & Lloyd, 1991, p. 217). At the other end are opaque symbols, "in which no [symbol–referent] relationship is perceived even when the meaning of the symbol is known" (Fuller & Lloyd, 1991, p. 217). For example, a color photograph of a cup is transparent because it looks like a real cup, whereas the written word *cup* is opaque because it does not have any visual resemblance to its referent. Between the two extremes are translucent symbols, "in which the meaning of the referent may or may not be obvious but a relationship can be perceived between the symbol and the referent once the meaning is provided" (Fuller & Lloyd, 1991, p. 217). So, for example, a cup handle can be used as a symbol for *cup*, but its meaning may not be obvious without explanation. Many types of aided symbols are used to support individuals with ASD, including tangible symbols, pictorial symbols, and alphabetic symbols.

Aided AAC: AAC systems that require external equipment to be used, such as a picture board or an electronic communication device.

Aided AAC: Tangible Symbols

Tangible symbols are "permanent objects that can be touched or manipulated" (Roche et al., 2014a, p. 28). First described by Rowland and Schweigert (1996), they include real objects (e.g., a spoon to represent food/eating), miniature objects (e.g., a doll-size sock to represent dressing), and partial objects (e.g., a swatch of carpet to represent "circle time," when each student sits on a specific carpet square). Although tangible symbols are primarily used by individuals with severe intellectual disability in addition to blindness or a significant visual impairment (Roche et al., 2014a), they can also be used by individuals with ASD. For example, Terri uses tangible symbols to ask for what she wants and to share information with others. When she's thirsty, she brings her teacher a cup to ask for something to drink. When she wants to use the slide at her local park, she gives her mom a card with piece of shiny metal attached to it, similar to the metal of the slide. And, when she comes home from the park, she can tell her sister what she did by showing her the slide symbol and the Frisbee that she enjoys using there. For Terri, the cup, metal swatch, and Frisbee are symbols representing "I'm thirsty," "I want to go on the slide," and "I played Frisbee at the park." She has learned from experience to associate the symbols with the activities they represent.

Advantages and Disadvantages of Tangible Symbols   Some authors have suggested that "the three-dimensional aspect of [tangible] symbols could possibly facilitate learning" (Roche et al., 2014b, p. 250) because they place relatively low demands on memory and representational skills, compared to other types of symbols. A few examples from the research literature provide some support for this suggestion with regard to individuals with ASD. For example, Rowland and Schweigert (2000) taught nine students with ASD and additional disabilities to use a wide range of tangible symbols as part of a larger study with 41 participants. Other authors adapted the PECS protocol to teach students with ASD and blindness or severe visual impairments to use tangible symbols to request preferred objects (Ali, MacFarland, & Umbreit, 2011; Parker, Banda, Davidson, & Liu-Gitz, 2010). Most recently, Roche et al. (2014b) taught two boys with ASD to use tangible symbols, pictorial symbols, and an iPad to request preferred cartoons. Both boys learned to make requests using all three methods at comparable rates but preferred to use tangible symbols over the other two options.

Despite these reports, a systematic review by Roche et al. (2014a) concluded that because only a few studies of tangible symbol use employed rigorous experimental designs that provide conclusive evidence of an intervention effect, "the generally positive outcomes…must be interpreted with caution" (p. 38). Additional disadvantages of tangible symbols include their limited portability (which may be improved by use of miniature objects, in some cases), the related risk that they will be unavailable when needed, and the fact that they can be used solely to represent referents that can be symbolized readily. In addition, their meanings may not be transparent to unfamiliar communication partners; for example, a miniature shoe could be used to convey the literal message, "(I want the) shoe" or could be used to mean "Let's go for a walk."

Aided AAC: Pictorial Symbols

Pictorial symbols include both photographs and line drawing images and can be either black and white or colored.

Photographs   As part of an AAC system, photographs may be used to represent specific people, places, activities, or items. Photographs can be produced with a camera; downloaded online; or obtained from catalogs, magazines, coupons, product labels, or advertisements. For example, Tanisha uses photos of food items to ask for her lunch in the high school cafeteria. She can interact with her classmates about her family by showing photos of them on her iPad, and she can also tell her teachers that she went to San Diego over the holiday break by showing them postcards and photos of the places she visited.

The advantage of photographs is that they are easier to carry around than are tangible symbols. Their meanings are also transparent, in most cases, because they depict realistic images (e.g., digital pictures, color photographs) and/or people and objects in relation to one another, the natural environment, and the central action of an activity. The disadvantage is that they have to be collected in some way, so they can be somewhat time consuming to produce. On the other hand, anyone with a smartphone has easy access to a camera that can be used to produce high quality "in the moment" photos of virtually any activity. These photos can also be shared digitally and, if necessary, printed in hard copy format.

Pictorial (Line Drawing) Symbols   Many pictorial symbol sets are commercially available in a variety of sizes and forms. They all use simple line drawings (black and white, colored) to depict people, places, activities, objects, actions (e.g., eat, sit, sleep), feelings (e.g., happy, angry, bored), descriptors (e.g., hot, cold, big, little,), social etiquette messages (e.g., please, thank you), and other parts of speech. The symbol sets most often used with individuals with ASD are described in the next sections.

Pictorial Symbol Sets   One of the most commonly used symbol sets in North America is the Picture Communication Symbols set from Mayer-Johnson LLC (PCS; see Figure 4.1 for examples). The PCS library consists of over 11,000 pictorial graphics that represent words, phrases, and concepts on a range of topics. Both PC- and Macintosh-based versions of the Mayer-Johnson Boardmaker family of software and cloud-based products can be used to generate communication displays made of either black-and-white or color PCS in 44 languages. Animated PCS for many verbs (i.e., action words) are also available in several of the Boardmaker products.

Another pictorial symbol set in widespread use is Symbolstix. This set includes over 30,000 color line drawing symbols that depict activities and people as lively stick figures. Symbolstix are used in many tablet-based AAC applications ("apps"). Symbolstix Prime is a cloud-based symbol creation tool that can be used to create communication displays in either print or digital form. Figure 4.1 displays examples of Symbolstix.

Pics for PECS is a set of 3,200 color images that include vocabulary words for adolescents and adults as well as children (e.g., yoga, motor scooter). The set, available on a CD, was designed to be used in conjunction with PECS but can also be used more widely. Figure 4.1 displays examples of Pics for PECS.

Referent	Picture Communication Symbols	SymbolStix	Pics for PECS	Widgit Symbols
give				
eat				
think				
where				
friend				
television				
yesterday				
sad				

Figure 4.1. Examples of Picture Communication Symbols, Symbolstix, Pics for PECS, and Widgit Symbols. (The Picture Communication Symbols ©1981–2015 by Mayer-Johnson LLC a Tobii Dynavox company. All Rights Reserved Worldwide. Used with permission. Boardmaker® is a trademark of Mayer-Johnson LLC. Copyright Symbolstix, LLC. 2016. All rights reserved. Used with permission. Pics for PECS® images used with permission from Pyramid Educational Consultants (www.pecs.com). All rights reserved. Widgit Symbols © Widgit Software 2002–2018 www.widgit.com.)

Finally, the Widgit Symbols set has been developed over the past 30 years and contains more than 12,000 symbols that cover an English vocabulary of over 40,000 words. Widgit Symbols are available in 17 languages and are designed to conform to a set of standards and conventions (referred to as "schema") and can be used to support both communication and literacy development. Figure 4.1 displays examples of Widgit Symbols.

Aided AAC: Alphabet Symbols

The letters of the alphabet and the words that are spelled with them are also aided symbols. Even individuals who cannot read fluently might be able to recognize printed words to communicate some messages. For example, Alfredo can recognize the printed words for many of the foods and drinks he consumes regularly, such as *Cheerios* and *Coke*. He has several pages of printed food words in a communication book that he carries around with him. When he wants to ask for something he likes to eat, he simply points to the word in his book.

The advantages of printed words include the fact that many of them can be placed on a single page, and they are easily understood by communication partners who can read. On the other hand, it is important to be able to distinguish between word-calling—the ability to decode a written word—and comprehension—the ability to use that word appropriately or act on that word as equivalent to what it represents. People with ASD must have the latter skill in order to use alphabet symbols functionally.

AIDED AAC TECHNIQUES

Aided AAC symbols—including tangible, pictorial, and alphabet symbols—are the basic building blocks used to convey messages by many people with ASD. But aided symbols have to be provided in a way that makes them readily accessible to an individual with ASD at all times. Both nonelectronic (i.e., low-tech) and digital (i.e., high-tech) AAC techniques can be used with individuals with ASD to accomplish this successfully (Ganz, Earles-Vollrath, et al., 2012).

Low-Tech Aided AAC

Low-tech aided AAC techniques include pictorial symbol displays, letter displays, and picture exchange systems. The common feature of these AAC options is that they involve some type of aided symbol to represent messages, are portable, and do not rely on digital technologies. The most common form of low-tech AAC is a communication book that contains symbols to point to or symbols that are attached (e.g., with Velcro) and can be readily removed for exchange. Communication boards or wallets with laminated pictorial symbols (e.g., photographs, line drawings) are additional options for displaying aided symbols and facilitating portability.

There are both advantages and disadvantages to using low-tech aided techniques for communication. The advantages are that they are relatively inexpensive; can be designed so they are easy to transport or carry around; and can be used in flexible, individualized ways. For example, Harold has a few symbols representing outside play equipment attached to a loop that hangs on his belt so that he can use his hands freely on the equipment and also choose where he wanted to play next (e.g., on the swings, on the slide). The disadvantage is that someone must take responsibility for keeping the system updated with symbols representing messages that the individual needs to communicate. Of course, this is also the case with high-tech AAC options.

High-Tech Aided AAC

Numerous digital or high-tech communication devices that require some type of external power source (e.g., rechargeable batteries) are also available for use with individuals with ASD. The primary advantage of high-tech communication devices is that they produce speech or print output that can be readily understood by communication partners. Although many high-tech devices can be operated using alternative access methods in addition to simple touch, individuals with ASD are able to select items directly from a display by pointing, in most cases. For example, when Harriet touches a symbol on her AAC device, it speaks the message that was programmed for the symbol, and the printed word also appears on a display screen. Some high-tech devices are quite complex and expensive whereas others are relatively simple to program and operate. They range from single/serial message devices to those with static, dynamic, and/or visual scene displays (VSDs).

Single/Serial Message Devices   A number of battery-powered, microswitch-activated devices that can be programmed to speak single or serial messages can be used to support communication that is context specific. Some of these devices play a *single, recorded message* (usually, up to 2–3 minutes in length) when activated. Recording a message into the device takes only seconds, using the voice of whoever sets it up, and new messages can be recorded over old ones throughout the day. So, for example, with the assistance of an aide who is responsible for recording the messages, a student with ASD might use one of these devices to greet his teacher and classmates on arrival at school ("Hi, how are you today?"), then recite the *Pledge of Allegiance* with his classmates, and then participate in a language arts lesson by repeating the line of a story the teacher is reading (e.g., "I do not like green eggs and ham; I do not like them, Sam I am"; Seuss, 1960).

Serial message devices work in a similar way, except that a series of messages (for a total of 2–4 minutes of recording time, depending on the device) can be programmed to speak out loud *in the order they are programmed,* one message per successive activation. For example, most elementary school students in North America are familiar with the turn-taking routine of a "knock-knock" joke. Emilio, a student with ASD, uses his serial device to tell a "knock-knock" joke to a classmate as shown in Figure 4.2.

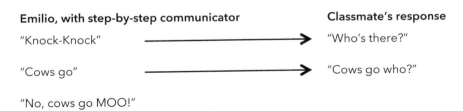

Figure 4.2.   How a student can use a serial device to tell a "knock-knock" joke to a classmate.

Finally, a series of spoken messages can be produced *in random order* using a device that features this option. These devices can be set such that once a random message is played, it is not played again. So, for example, Arthur uses his random-izer device to call out letter and number combinations when he and his friends play bingo at recess (e.g., "B-59," "N-4"). Because the device speaks the combinations in random order without repetitions, no two bingo games are ever the same. From these examples, it should be obvious that, while these simple devices require the support of a facilitator to program contextually relevant messages and are unlikely to meet all of an individual's communication needs, they can be used in creative ways to support active participation of individuals with ASD in a wide range of school- and community-based activities.

Static Display Devices   Static display devices employ aided symbols that are "fixed" in a particular location—that is, their positions on the device are static. Typically, the symbols are printed on laminated paper "overlays" that are affixed to the device by hand; when a symbol is activated (i.e., touched), a message that has been programmed in a corresponding location on the device is spoken out loud and/or appears on a small screen. Usually, static display devices are designed to accommodate messages that are programmed on multiple "levels," wherein each level corresponds to a different overlay of topical symbols.

The number of aided symbols available on a static display device is usu-ally dictated by a person's visual, tactile, cognitive, and motor capabilities. Many individuals with ASD who use static display devices are beginning communica-tors who have difficulty visually locating a desired symbol from a large array of options and/or have difficulty activating small symbols on more complex devices for other reasons (e.g., motor limitations). For example, Jackie is an adult with ASD who also has a visual impairment and thus needs large symbols to represent mes-sages. When Jackie and her dad go out for lunch at a fast-food restaurant, she uses the 12 symbols on Level 1 of her device to order food at the counter. After she has ordered, her dad changes the display to a paper overlay of 12 new symbols that depict Jackie's favorite activities and friends. He also switches her device to Level 2, which has messages that correspond to the new overlay and enable them to talk about what Jackie did last weekend. This example illustrates two of the major disadvantages of static display devices—namely, that the number of vocabu-lary items available at a time is limited and that facilitator assistance is required to change displays and levels to make additional vocabulary available. On the other hand, static display devices might be appropriate for beginning communicators like Jackie whose abilities constrain the number and/or size of messages that they can use in specific contexts.

Dynamic Display Devices   Dynamic display devices feature computer/digital screen displays with aided symbols that are programmed into the device itself and produce high-quality synthetic speech when activated. They include both dedi-cated AAC devices (i.e., those that are specifically designed for communication by people who require AAC) and iOS or Android tablet devices with one of the many AAC apps that provide dynamic display features (Lorah, Parnell, Whitby, & Hantula, 2015). There are usually at least two types of symbols in these devices—those that produce a spoken message and those that change the display itself when activated. When a *message* symbol is activated, the printed message appears on a small screen display and the device speaks the associated message out loud. When a *change* symbol is activated, the display screen automatically changes to a new set of programmed symbols. For example, on Ramon's device, his home screen displays symbols related to a number of topics, such as hockey, jokes, personal care, news, and family. When he touches the HOCKEY symbol, the screen changes to display symbols/messages related to hockey, which he then uses to interact with his friends while watching the game. When a break occurs at halftime, Ramon touches the HOME symbol to return to the initial screen and selects the FOOD symbol, which changes the screen to symbols of food options and enables him to order his own meal at the arena. After he eats, he can go back to the hockey symbols by touching HOCKEY again, or he might elect to change to the JOKES page to interact with his friends in this way.

The advantage of dynamic display devices is that they can contain many more messages and phrases than static display devices; with some iOS or Android apps, for example, thousands of messages are available. In addition, many dedicated dynamic display devices have other features as well, including print displays, calculators, large memory capacities for storing lengthy text and speeches, and the ability to interface with standard computers. The majority of modern dynamic display devices produce high-quality digitized speech that is available in both child and adult and both male and female voices across numerous languages. Virtually all such devices allow customization of symbol size, the number of symbols available a time, and many other features.

Aside from the cost (which can vary widely), one of the major disadvantages of dynamic display devices is that, because they are digital in nature, they are more complex to program and more vulnerable to simple wear and tear than are low-tech or static display options. They can break down, their batteries can run down or fail, and they require someone to program messages into them on a regular basis. In addition, it is important to emphasize that having an iPad or another type of digital device does not make a person a good communicator any more than having a piano makes someone Elton John! Digital AAC devices are *tools* for communication, and individuals with ASD will need to be taught how to use them in meaningful ways, just as they are taught to use other communication techniques.

Visual Scene Displays   A VSD is a picture, photograph, or virtual environment that depicts and represents a situation, place, or activity. Individual elements such as people, actions, and objects appear within the visual scene (Blackstone, 2004). For example, in a photograph of Max's birthday party, people, food, and gifts all appear in a single image. Spoken messages, such as the names of the birthday guests and the food items that were served at the party, can be accessed by touching "hot spots" associated with corresponding parts of the image. So, when the birthday cake is touched, the message "I love my birthday cake!" is spoken. When Max's picture is touched, the message "I'm 21 years old today" is activated. From these examples, it should be apparent that VSDs are quite different from the grid displays that are used in most high-tech AAC devices. The visual scene depicts a set of elements (people, actions, objects) within a coherent, integrated visual image, while a grid display arranges elements in separate boxes that are usually organized in rows and columns. Figure 4.3 depicts both a grid display and a VSD for a birthday party activity. VSDs are featured in a number of apps for tablet devices.

Figure 4.3.   Top: Grid display for a birthday party. (The Picture Communication Symbols ©1981–2015 by Mayer-Johnson LLC a Tobii Dynavox company. All Rights Reserved Worldwide. Used with permission. Boardmaker® is a trademark of Mayer-Johnson LLC.) Bottom: Visual scene display for a birthday party. Hot spots (rectangles) show areas that speak a related message when activated (e.g., from left to right: *mom, present, candle, cake, dad, balloon*); hot spots are invisible on the actual display. (Photo courtesy of Pat Mirenda.)

AAC INSTRUCTION

It is beyond the scope of this chapter to provide detailed information on the numerous instructional techniques that can be used to teach the use of AAC techniques. Readers are referred to the chapters in Parts III and IV of this book, and to both Beukelman and Mirenda (2013) and Johnston, Reichle, Feeley, and Jones (2012) for specific information in this regard. In the sections that follow, three of the most commonly used instructional approaches—PECS, naturalistic/milieu teaching, and aided language modeling—will be described briefly.

The Picture Exchange Communication System

The Picture Exchange Communication System is an AAC instructional approach (Frost & Bondy, 2002) that is based on research and practice in the area of applied behavior analysis. PECS instruction begins by teaching a learner to *exchange* graphic symbols to request desired items rather than point to them on a communication display. In PECS, an individual learns to communicate first with single pictures (or real objects; see Ganz, Cook, Corbin-Newsome, Bourgeois, & Flores, 2005), then to choose among two or more pictures, and finally to combine pictures to produce a variety of grammatical structures, semantic relationships, and communicative functions.

PECS instruction begins after an assessment of potential reinforcers (i.e., preferred items or activities) for the person who is learning to communicate. In Phase I of PECS, the person learns to pick up a single symbol (e.g., photograph, line drawing) and hand it to a communication partner (i.e., adult or child), who then gives the person the associated item (e.g., food, drink, toy). Initially, once the learner reaches toward the desired item or activity, an assistant to the partner provides only physical and gestural cues (i.e., no verbal cues to ask "What do you want?" or "Give me the picture") to prompt the learner to exchange the symbol. Over time, the assistant gradually fades the prompts until the symbol–item exchange is made unassisted. In Phase II, the assistant gradually moves away so that the person learns to find the symbol, take it to the partner from a distance, and exchange it for the desired item. In Phase III, the number of symbols available is increased from one to two (and eventually more) and procedures for teaching symbol discrimination are implemented. The next three phases extend instruction to teach the learner to construct simple sentences (e.g., "I WANT ____" in Phase IV and "I SEE ____" in Phase VI), respond to a partner's question "What do you want?" (Phase V), and employ descriptive symbols related to color, size, number, and so forth (see Frost & Bondy, 2002 and Bondy & Frost, 2009 for additional information).

Several systematic reviews and meta-analyses of the research on PECS have been conducted to examine efficacy and the variables that influence outcomes (e.g., Flippin, Reszka, & Watson, 2010; Ganz, Davis, Lund, Goodwyn, & Simpson, 2012). In some reviews, authors noted that, in the majority of research studies to date, participants have demonstrated mastery of PECS Phases I–III only; thus, empirical support for the efficacy of Phases IV–VI is lacking (Ganz, Davis, et al., 2012; Sulzer-Azaroff, Hoffman, Horton, Bondy, & Frost, 2009). Nonetheless, the general consensus across the reviews is reflected by Ganz, Davis, et al. (2012): "PECS appears to be a promising augmentative system that . . . has moderately positive effects on functional communication skills . . ." (p. 415). In addition, Yoder and Lieberman

(2010) provided evidence that PECS instruction can result in the ability to engage in picture exchanges under different conditions (i.e., novel contexts and with novel people) than those in which training occurred.

Naturalistic/Milieu Teaching

Jones and Feeley (2012) noted that naturalistic/milieu teaching "capitalizes on ongoing interactions about materials/activities within the learner's environment to prompt more sophisticated communicative acts . . ." (p. 163). These authors noted that the defining characteristics of this approach include the following: 1) instruction is provided in naturally occurring contexts by the communicative partners with whom the target skills are meant to be used (e.g., parents, teachers, peers), 2) communicative opportunities are either learner initiated or naturally occurring throughout the day (e.g., whenever a person has difficulty completing a task, she is provided with instruction aimed at teaching her to use her AAC system to ask for help), and 3) natural consequences are provided contingent on AAC use (e.g., when the person asks for help, assistance is provided). A variety of instructional techniques are employed in this regard, including incidental teaching, the mand-model procedure, a wide range of strategies for prompting and fading, time delay, behavior chain interruption, and embedded instruction (see Beukelman & Mirenda, 2013; Feeley & Jones, 2012).

Naturalistic/milieu teaching has been used in many studies with individuals with ASD, primarily to teach requesting. These studies have focused on the use of manual signs (e.g., Kouri, 1988), graphic symbols either on picture cards or in communication books (e.g., Hamilton & Snell, 1993), and SGDs (e.g., Olive et al., 2007). Interventionists include teachers, other direct care staff, or in some cases parents (Nunes & Hanline, 2003; Stiebel, 1999) or peers (Trembath, Balandin, Togher, & Stancliffe, 2009; Trottier, Kamp, & Mirenda, 2011). In general, these studies provide support for the use of naturalistic/milieu strategies to teach AAC use to individuals with ASD (Nunes, 2009), although additional research is required to examine the effectiveness for teaching communicative functions other than requesting.

Aided Language Modeling

Several language modeling techniques have been developed for AAC instruction and have been used successfully with children with ASD (Cafiero, 1998, 2001; Drager et al., 2006; Romski & Sevcik, 1996; Romski et al., 2009). The term *aided language modeling* (ALM) is used here to refer to the general approach, which is based on research describing how typically developing, speaking children acquire language by observing and interacting with communicative partners. ALM involves, at a minimum, a communicative partner who a) points to (i.e., models the use of) key pictorial symbols while speaking, in the context of motivating, interactive activities in natural contexts; and b) provides opportunities for the person with ASD to use the target symbols during the activity, make requests or comments, answer questions, and participate in other communicative routines. Because ALM techniques mimic the way natural speakers learn to comprehend language, they are intended to teach language in a very natural way that reduces the need for more explicit instruction.

In one of the empirical investigations with individuals with ASD, Drager et al. (2006) implemented ALM with two 4-year-old children who spoke between 10 and 20 words each. A clinician pointed to a target object in an interactive play activity and then simultaneously pointed to a corresponding line drawing symbol while saying its name. For example, when the clinician said, "It's time to feed the doll," she then pointed to a DOLL symbol while referring to the real doll. After repeated exposure to ALM, both children demonstrated increased comprehension and production of the target objects when provided with spoken labels alone (e.g., "Show me the doll"), suggesting that the pairing of symbols plus speech supported their language learning. Recently, Sennott, Light, and McNaughton (2016) summarized the existing ALM research in a systematic review and concluded that "AAC modeling-based intervention packages [have] had a positive impact across a range of language domains for young children who are beginning communicators" (p. 11).

CONCLUSION

The past 2 decades have seen an explosion of research related to strategies for supporting functional communication for individuals with ASD who rely on AAC (e.g., Beukelman & Mirenda, 2013; Johnston et al., 2012; Mirenda & Iacono, 2009). In particular, the AAC-RERC on Communication Enhancement (http://aac-rerc.psu.edu) includes a number of research and development projects that pertain directly to individuals with ASD across the age range. The Pennsylvania State University AAC website (http://aackids.psu.edu/index.php/page/show/id/1/index.html) is also a valuable resource for those working with young children with ASD and other complex communication needs. The future for individuals with ASD who experience severe communication challenges is promising, as researchers and clinicians continue to develop strategies for assessment and intervention that enable them to fully participate in home, school, and community life.

RESOURCES

Tobii Dynavox, 2100 Wharton Street, Suite 400, Pittsburgh, PA 15203; Phone: 1-800-588-4548; Fax: 1-866-585-6260; e-mail: mayer-johnson.usa@mayer-johnson.com; web site: www.mayer-johnson.com

REFERENCES

Ali, E., MacFarland, S. Z., & Umbreit, J. (2011). Effectiveness of combining tangible symbols with the Picture Exchange Communication System to teach requesting skills to children with multiple disabilities including visual impairment. *Education and Training in Autism and Developmental Disabilities, 46,* 425–435.
Beukelman, D. R., & Mirenda, P. (2013). *Augmentative and alternative communication: Supporting children and adults with complex communication needs* (4th ed.). Baltimore, MD: Paul H. Brookes Publishing Co.
Blackstone, S. (2004). Clinical news: Visual scene displays. *Augmentative Communication News, 16*(2), 1–8.
Bondy, A., & Frost, L. (2009). The Picture Exchange Communication System: Clinical and research applications. In P. Mirenda & T. Iacono (Eds.), *Autism spectrum disorders and AAC* (pp. 279–302). Baltimore, MD: Paul H. Brookes Publishing Co.

Cabeza, R., Kapur, S., Craik, F. I. M., McIntosh, A.R., Houle, S., and Tulving, E. (1997). Functional neuroanatomy of recall and recognition: A PET study of episodic memory. *Journal of Cognitive Neuroscience, 9,* 254–265.

Cafiero, J. (1998). Communication power for individuals with autism. *Focus on Autism and Other Developmental Disabilities, 13,* 113–121.

Cafiero, J. (2001). The effect of an augmentative communication intervention on the communication, behavior, and academic program of an adolescent with autism. *Focus on Autism and Other Developmental Disabilities, 16,* 179–189.

Casey, L. (1978). Development of communicative behavior in autistic children: A parent program using manual signs. *Journal of Autism and Childhood Schizophrenia, 8,* 45–59.

Drager, K., Postal, V., Carrolus, L., Castellano, M., Gagliano, C., & Glynn, J. (2006). The effect of aided language modeling on symbol comprehension and production in two preschoolers with autism. *American Journal of Speech-Language Pathology, 15,* 112–125.

Feeley, K. M., & Jones, E. (2012). Instructional strategies. In S. Johnston, J. Reichle, K. Feeley, & E. Jones (Eds.), *Augmentative and alternative communication strategies for individuals with severe disabilities* (pp. 119–154). Baltimore, MD: Paul H. Brookes Publishing Co.

Flippin, M., Reszka, S., & Watson, L. (2010). Effectiveness of the Picture Exchange Communication Systems (PECS) on communication and speech for children with autism spectrum disorders: A meta-analysis. *American Journal of Speech-Language Pathology, 19,* 178–195.

Frost, L., & Bondy, A. (2002). *Picture Exchange Communication System training manual* (2nd ed.). Newark, DE: Pyramid Education Products, Inc.

Fuller, D., & Lloyd, L. (1991). Toward a common usage of iconicity terminology. *Augmentative and Alternative Communication, 7,* 215–220.

Ganz, J., Cook, K., Corbin-Newsome, J., Bourgeois, B., & Flores, M. (2005). Variations on the use of a pictorial communication system with a child with autism and developmental delays. *TEACHING Exceptional Children Plus, 1*(6), Article 3.

Ganz, J., Davis, J., Lund, E., Goodwyn, F., & Simpson, R. (2012). Meta-analysis of PECS with individuals with ASD: Investigation of targeted vs. non-targeted outcomes, participants characteristics, and implementation phase. *Research in Developmental Disabilities, 33,* 406–418.

Ganz, J., Earles-Vollrath, T., Heath, A., Parker, R., Rispoli, M., & Duran, J. (2012). A meta-analysis of single case research studies on aided augmentative and alternative communication systems for individuals with autism spectrum disorders. *Journal of Autism and Developmental Disorders, 42,* 60–74.

Hamilton, B., & Snell, M. (1993). Using the milieu approach to increase spontaneous communication book use across environments by an adolescent with autism. *Augmentative and Alternative Communication, 9,* 259–272.

Hanson, E. K., Beukelman, D. R., & Yorkston, K. M. (2013). Communication support through multimodal supplementation: A scoping review. *Augmentative and Alternative Communication, 29,* 310–321. doi: 10.3109/07434618.2013.848934

Johnston, S., Reichle, J., Feeley, K., & Jones, E. (2012). *Augmentative and alternative communication strategies for individuals with severe disabilities.* Baltimore, MD: Paul H. Brookes Publishing Co.

Jones, E., & Feeley, K. M. (2012). Intervention intensity: Developing a context for instruction. In S. Johnston, J. Reichle, K. Feeley, & E. Jones (Eds.), *Augmentative and alternative communication strategies for individuals with severe disabilities* (pp. 155–181). Baltimore, MD: Paul H. Brookes Publishing Co.

Kamio, Y., & Toichi, M. (2000). Dual access to semantics in autism: Is pictorial access superior to verbal access? *Journal of Child Psychology and Psychiatry, 41,* 859–867.

Kouri, T. (1988). How manual sign acquisition relates to the development of spoken language: A case study. *Language, Speech, and Hearing Services in Schools, 20,* 50–62.

Light, J. (1988). Interaction involving individuals using augmentative and alternative communication systems: State of the art and future directions. *Augmentative and Alternative Communication, 4,* 66–82.

Lorah, E., Parnell, A., Whitby, P., & Hantula, D. (2015). A systematic review of tablet computers and portable media players as speech generating devices for individuals with autism spectrum disorder. *Journal of Autism and Developmental Disorders, 45,* 3792–3804.

Millar, D. C. (2009). Effects of AAC on the natural speech development of individuals with ASD spectrum disorders. In P. Mirenda & T. Iacono (Eds.), *Autism spectrum disorders and AAC* (pp. 171–192). Baltimore, MD: Paul H. Brookes Publishing Co.

Millar, D. C., Light, J. C., & Schlosser, R. W. (2006). The impact of augmentative and alternative communication intervention on the speech production of individuals with developmental disabilities: A research review. *Journal of Speech, Language, and Hearing Research, 49,* 248–264.

Mirenda, P., & Brown, K. (2009). A picture is worth a thousand words: Using visual supports for augmented input with individuals with autism spectrum disorders. In P. Mirenda & T. Iacono (Eds.), *Autism spectrum disorders and AAC* (pp. 303–332). Baltimore, MD: Paul H. Brookes Publishing Co.

Mirenda, P., & Iacono, T. (Eds.). (2009). *Autism spectrum disorders and AAC.* Baltimore, MD: Paul H. Brookes Publishing Co.

Mitchell, P., & Ropar, D. (2004). Visuo-spatial abilities in autism: A review. *Infant and Child Development, 13,* 185–198.

National Autism Center. (2015). *Findings and conclusions: National standards project, phase 2.* Randolph, MA: Author.

Nunes, D. (2009). AAC interventions for autism: Research summary. *International Journal of Special Education, 23,* 17–26.

Nunes, D., & Hanline, M. F. (2003). Enhancing the alternative and augmentative communication use of a child with autism through a parent-implemented naturalistic intervention. *International Journal of Disability, Development, and Education, 54,* 177–197.

O'Connor, K. (2012). Auditory processing in autism spectrum disorder: A review. *Neuroscience and Biobehavioral Reviews, 36,* 836–854.

Olive, M., de la Cruz, B., Davis, T., Chan, J., Lang, R., O'Reilly, M., & Dickson, S. M. (2007). The effects of enhanced milieu teaching and a voice output communication aid on the requesting of three children with autism. *Journal of Autism and Developmental Disorders, 37,* 1505–1513.

Parker, A. T., Banda, D. R., Davidson, R. C., & Liu-Gitz, L. (2010). Adapting the Picture Exchange Communication System for a student with visual impairment and autism: A case study. *Research and Practice in Visual Impairment and Blindness, 3,* 2–11.

Roche, L., Sigafoos, J., Lancioni, G., O'Reilly, M., Green, V., Sutherland, D., . . . Edrisinha, C. D. (2014a). Tangible symbols as an AAC option for individuals with developmental disabilities: A systematic review of intervention studies. *Augmentative and Alternative Communication, 30,* 28–39.

Roche, L., Sigafoos, J., Lancioni, G., O'Reilly, M., van der Meer, L., Achmadi, D., . . . Marschik, P. (2014b). Comparing tangible symbols, picture exchange, and direct selection response for enabling two boys with developmental disabilities to access preferred stimuli. *Journal of Developmental and Physical Disabilities, 26,* 249–261.

Rogers, S. J., Hepburn, S. L., Stackhouse, T., & Wehner, E. (2003). Imitation performance in toddlers with autism and those with other developmental disorders. *Journal of Child Psychology and Psychiatry, 44,* 763–781.

Romski, M. A., & Sevcik, R. A. (1996). *Breaking the speech barrier: Language development through augmented means.* Baltimore, MD: Paul H. Brookes Publishing Co.

Romski, M. A., Sevcik, R., Smith, A., Barker, R. M., Folan, S., & Barton-Hulsey, A. (2009). The system for augmenting language: Implications for young children with autism spectrum disorders. In P. Mirenda & T. Iacono (Eds.), *Autism spectrum disorders and AAC* (pp. 219–245). Baltimore, MD: Paul H. Brookes Publishing Co.

Rowland, C., & Schweigert, P. (1996). *Tangible symbol systems* (Rev. ed.) [Videotape]. San Antonio, TX: The Psychological Corporation.

Rowland, C., & Schweigert, P. (2000). Tangible symbols, tangible outcomes. *Augmentative and Alternative Communication, 16,* 61–78, 205.

Schlosser, R. (Ed.). (2003). Selecting graphic symbols for an initial request lexicon. In *The efficacy of augmentative and alternative communication: Toward evidence-based practice* (pp. 347–402). New York, NY: Elsevier.

Schwartz, I. S., & Davis, C. A. (2014). Best practices in early identification and early services for children with autism spectrum disorder. Best practices in school psychology.

In P. Harrison & A. Thomas (Eds.), *Best practices in school psychology VI*. Washington, DC: National Association of School Psychology.

Schwartz, J., & Nye, C. (2006). Improving communication for children with autism: Does sign language work? *EBP Briefs, 1*(2), 1–17.

Sennott, S., Light, J., & McNaughton, D. (2016). AAC modeling intervention research review. *Research and Practice for Persons with Severe Disabilities, 41*, 101–115.

Seuss, T. (1960). *Green eggs and ham*. New York, NY: Random House.

Stiebel, D. (1999). Promoting augmentative communication during daily routines: A parent problem-solving intervention. *Journal of Positive Behavior Interventions, 1*, 159–169.

Sulzer-Azaroff, B., Hoffman, A., Horton, C., Bondy, A., & Frost, L. (2009). The Picture Exchange Communication System: What do the data say? *Focus on Autism and Other Developmental Disabilities, 24*, 89–103.

Tierney, C., Mayes, S., Lohs, S., Black, A., Gisin, E., & Veglia, M. (2015). How valid is the Checklist for Autism Spectrum Disorder when a child has apraxia of speech? *Journal of Developmental and Behavioral Pediatrics, 36*, 569–574.

Trembath, D., Balandin, S., Togher, L., & Stancliffe, R. J. (2009). Peer-mediated teaching and augmentative and alternative communication for preschool-aged children with autism. *Journal of Intellectual & Developmental Disability, 34*, 173–186.

Trottier, N., Kamp, L., & Mirenda, P. (2011). Effects of peer-mediated instruction to teach use of speech-generating devices to students with autism in social game routines. *Augmentative and Alternative Communication, 27*, 26–39.

Wendt, O. (2009). Research on the use of manuals signs and graphic symbols in autism spectrum disorders: A systematic review. In P. Mirenda & T. Iacono (Eds.), *Autism spectrum disorders and AAC* (pp. 83–139). Baltimore, MD: Paul H. Brookes Publishing Co.

Yoder, P., & Lieberman, R. (2010). Brief report: Randomized test of the efficacy of the Picture Exchange Communication System on highly generalized picture exchanges in children with ASD. *Journal of Autism & Developmental Disorders, 40*, 629–632.

5

Considerations in Implementing Aided Low-Tech AAC Systems for Individuals With Autism Spectrum Disorder and Complex Communication Needs

Joe Reichle, Jessica Simacek, and Quannah E. Parker-McGowan

Augmentative and alternative communication (AAC) supplements or replaces conventional speech to provide support for an individual with a disability who has a permanent or temporary condition that has resulted in a complex communication need (CCN; Romski & Sevcik, 1997). There are two main categories of AAC: aided and unaided. Aided AAC includes systems that involve the use of equipment (Light, Roberts, Dimarco, & Greiner, 1998; Johnston, Reichle, Feeley, & Jones, 2012). Unaided communication involves the use of vocal/verbal or gestural mode communication (Johnston et al., 2012) where no additional materials/equipment is needed. Low-tech aided communication can successfully serve as an alternative or augmentation to speech production for a wide range of populations. These applications can be ideal for a beginning communicator who is very young and/or has a significant intellectual impairment in that low-tech AAC can accommodate a wide range of physical and instructional adaptations that can maximize the customization.

Low-tech aided communication represents an important topic for individuals with autism spectrum disorder (ASD), particularly for beginning communicators. By implementing low-tech AAC at early ages, an interventionist can generate an evidence base to support funding applications for a higher-tech device. Even if the learner should be provided with a higher-tech device, low-tech devices often provide a supplement in environments where a high-tech device may not be easily used (e.g., a sandy playground, very bright sunlight, a swimming pool, if a device runs out of charge or breaks). Low-tech devices may also avoid problems associated with high-tech devices, such as attending to a fixed position of a symbol rather than the symbol itself, which can be addressed by more easily repositioning symbols across learning opportunities (Johnston et al., 2012). In addition, although not the focus of this chapter, low-tech AAC applications can also better enable a learner's vocabulary comprehension skills by systematically pairing a spoken word with a graphic symbol chosen and/or by providing visual schedules (see Harris & Reichle, 2004; Johnston et al., 2012).

This chapter focuses primarily on low-tech aided AAC to produce communicative behavior. After differentiating lower- and higher-tech AAC options, the remainder of the chapter discusses features and the use of low-tech AAC applications.

GENERAL TYPES OF AIDED AAC APPLICATIONS

In addition to low-tech applications that do not involve the use of electronics and consequently do not result in speech output, mid- and high-tech speech generating devices (SGDs) do enable a learner to produce human-recorded, digitized speech and/or synthetic speech when activated (McNaughton & Light, 2013; Johnston et al., 2012). There is a continuum from mid- to high-tech AAC applications; some examples of mid-tech devices include the BIGmack and GoTalk series. These devices can range from one to approximately 128 messages or keys that each contains a different recorded message. Mid-tech devices tend to allow only human-recorded speech. Some provide the user with a specified number of seconds on which a message can be recorded on each symbol. Other devices allow a user to allocate the limited number of seconds of recording time available on the device to one or multiple symbol locations (for example one symbol could have one minute of recorded message while another might have only 2–3 seconds). Individualization of the number of seconds per message allows greater flexibility in participating in a greater range of communicative activities. Some mid-tech devices use paper overlays with each overlay corresponding to a different page of programmable symbols. Each of these levels can be selected by adjusting a switch to move across levels (electronic pages). Although this type of mid-tech communication device typically is less costly than high-tech AAC applications, it tends to require greater physical effort for the user to switch pages than using higher-tech devices that allow an automatic linking of one symbol to another across electronic pages (Johnston et al., 2012). On some mid-tech devices, the user's partner must switch from one level of recorded messages using a switch on the back of the device. On others, a row of symbols on the main page of the device can link to another page if the learner selects the symbol (Johnston et al., 2012). These features are apt to require more effort for the person using the device and that the learner's communicative partner be somewhat knowledgeable about changing page overlays and likely results in the need for their closer proximity to the user during at least some communicative exchanges.

High-tech AAC systems often combine digitized and synthesized speech output options so that sound effects and singing can be easily displayed via digitized recordings while text-to-speech and prediction applications can be readily utilized with synthesized speech affording the learner who has some literacy skills the capability of constructing his or her own messages. Many high-tech aided communicative options are tablet-size computers. Alternatively, an increasing number of software apps within multi-purpose mobile technology are available (McNaughton & Light, 2013; Shane, Blackstone, Vanderheiden, Williams, & DeRuyter, 2012). High-tech devices may also offer a variety of features such as prediction and e-mail access as described in other chapters.

As mentioned previously, low-tech options, the focus of this chapter, involve no electronics. Graphic symbols are housed in a communication wallet, communication board, or communication book containing multiple pages. In general, low-tech aided AAC devices have been considered to be moderately to very effective in increasing communication skills for individuals with ASD (Ganz, Earles-Vollrath, et al., 2012).

COMPARING LOW-TECH AIDED
AND UNAIDED COMMUNICATION SYSTEMS

Aided AAC may be beneficial for individuals who have challenges with recall memory (Martin, Reichle, Dimian, & Chen, 2013), abstract language, or fine motor control (Beukelman & Mirenda, 2005). Unaided AAC applications (including sign, gesture, and spoken word approximations), on the other hand, may work for individuals who have good recall memory, are able to more easily learn abstract symbols, have sufficient motor skills, and who have access to communicative partners who readily understand signs (Johnston et al., 2012; Rotholz, Berkowitz, & Burberry, 1989). In addition, unaided AAC can provide immediate access to unlimited vocabulary, improved portability, and speed of production (Johnston et al., 2012).

HOW DOES ONE DETERMINE WHETHER A LOW-TECH
AIDED AAC APPLICATION REPRESENTS A DESIRABLE OPTION?

Light and McNaughton (2013) cautioned that, "too often it is assumed that intervention begins and ends with the provision of a device" (p. 300). Unfortunately, to date, there are insufficient evidence-based guidelines that can be used to determine the most suitable communication modes for a given individual. One of the most basic decisions can be made by applying an assessment strategy that involves modality sampling (Reichle, York, & Sigafoos, 1991; Johnston et al., 2012). Modality sampling involves teaching different previously nonproduced symbols in each of three communicative modalities (verbal, gestural, and graphic). This strategy is replicated longitudinally along with generalization and maintenance probes for each symbol taught. Across replications, the interventionist can determine whether, in the short run, symbols in a particular mode appear to be more easily acquired, maintained, and generalized. In addition, interventionists and other stakeholders can examine learner and listener preference for a particular modality. Modality sampling can assist in determining which communication mode(s) to emphasize at the point of initial AAC implementation. It is important here to highlight the word "emphasize" as it is likely that many learners will benefit from using multiple communicative modes to achieve optimal efficiency even when one particular mode, overall, proves easier for a learner with respect to acquisition, maintenance, and/or generalization. For example, shaking one's head to indicate "yes" or "no" when one has a listener's attention can be faster than selecting a graphic symbol. However, if one's listener is not immediately present, there may be other more effective alternatives. Initially, the outcome of modality sampling is to select a communication option that will be worth the effort from the learner's perspective. Foundational or pivotal skills (e.g., Koegel & Frea, 1993) such as motor-imitation ability may predict the speed with which learners acquire certain communication modes (i.e., manual sign vs. picture exchange-based communication). However, the current evidence does not provide definitive guidance on the issue (Gregory, DeLeon, & Richman, 2009). Consequently, some have suggested that modality sampling using an alternating treatment single-case design can be beneficial. In an alternating treatment design, the interventionist on any given day implements each of two different augmentative communication strategies. Usually with individuals having significant developmental disabilities, each intervention is locked to a different set of symbols that have been matched and monitored for preference. Dependent measures include percent of opportunities in which symbols from each communicative mode are used during acquisition and maintenance. In addition, generalized use across individuals, activities, and settings also may represent areas examined (see Byiers, Reichle, & Symons, 2012 for additional information on alternating treatment designs; see Hyppa Martin, Reichle, Dimian, & Chen, 2013; Johnston et al., 2012 for further description of modality sampling procedures). Concurrently teaching graphic and gestural modes of communication can be challenging. For example, the behaviors being taught may not be totally independent from each other and as a result may be susceptible to multiple treatment interference (see Schlosser, 1999 for a discussion of this issue and methodological suggestions for addressing it). In addition, it may require greater short-term effort from the interventionist.

In summary, in the absence of a clear evidence base, a comparison strategy can determine the emphasis to place on a graphic compared to a gestural mode communication. Again, as mentioned at the outset of this discussion, it is important that the reader does not misinterpret the suggestion; this chapter's authors are *NOT* suggesting that only one mode or system be used as an outcome of comparisons. Implementing the described comparisons is not a one-time assessment. As environments and learners' skills change along with preferences, these comparisons must be repeated. Given our preceding discussion, it is reasonable to ask, when is it appropriate to implement a beginning AAC system?

Questions that Must Be Addressed When Beginning a Low-Tech Aided Communication System

Given the available evidence, implementing a low-tech AAC application at the earliest possible point in a learner's life has distinct advantages with no clearly identified disadvantages (Johnston et al., 2012; Millar, Light, & Schlosser, 2006; Wendt, 2009). However, there are many questions that must be addressed when arranging the implementation of a low-tech AAC application.

What Communicative Behaviors Does the Learner Direct to a Listener?   The term "intentional" addresses whether children who produce what might be interpreted as communicative acts do so with the preconceived plan of influencing a listener. Children with ASD who have not acquired communicative forms that are clearly intended for a listener have been reported to engage in *potential communicative acts* via idiosyncratic behaviors (Sigafoos et al., 2000, 2011). Many parents report that their children with significant developmental disabilities use nonverbal idiosyncratic behavior to communicate (Brady & Halle, 1997; Stephensen & Dowrick, 2005; Urbanowicz, Leonard, Girdler, Ciccone, & Downs, 2014). Forms that are often reported include eye gaze, eye pointing, facial expressions, vocalizations, pushing things away or reaching for things, leading someone by the hand, and challenging behavior. These behaviors sometimes are interpreted as communicating discomfort and happiness, making choices, requesting items, requesting activities, and requesting attention (Urbanowicz et al., 2014). In addition, the continued use of contact gestures in lieu of more sophisticated communicative forms also often occurs among individuals with moderate to more severe ASD (Johnston et al., 2012).

It is important to make a clearer distinction regarding how early communicative behaviors are used. Early forms may be either unintentional ("perlocutionary") or intentional ("illocutionary"). Perlocutionary forms occur when the learner did not intend their behavioral emission for the benefit of a communicative partner even though the partner may have interpreted the act as intentional and provided a relevant contingent response (see Reichle & Brady, 2012 for a detailed discussion). For example, when a parent sees a child struggling with a milk container, he or she may say "he's telling me that he needs help." Consequently, in this scenario, in response to the child's behavior, the parent may consistently provide access to the milk. While informative to the adult, the learner did not direct the action after referencing the parent in an overt communicative intent that was intended for the parent to see. An illocutionary response occurs when the learner is aware that he or she can influence the behavior of another individual by producing the act.

Interpreting the intentionality (illocutionary status) of idiosyncratic behaviors in beginning communicators with severe disabilities can be challenging. Several studies have examined communicative intent for children with severe disabilities (Byiers, Dimian, & Symons, 2014; Iacono, Carter, & Hook, 1998; Sigafoos et al., 2000). Results indicated many participants understood that their actions (even idiosyncratic) resulted in a predictable outcome. However, there is a lack of evidence that the acts were necessarily for the benefit of a listener. Given the preceding discussion, current literature offers an important starting point for interventionists. Exchange-based communication systems (described in the next section), alongside use of gestures, is one approach that can be considered for implementation for learners who may not yet realize that they need to direct their behavior to a listener.

Should Exchange- or Nonexchange-Based Picture-Photograph-Product Logo or Communication Systems Be Implemented?   Low-tech aided AAC options largely include nonexchange-based picture-photograph-product logo or exchange-based systems using the same types of symbols (Ganz, Rispoli, Mason, & Hong, 2014). Nonexchange-based systems provide a board or wallet containing pages of graphic symbols. In exchange-based systems, graphic symbols are proffered to a communicative partner to produce a communicative utterance (e.g. Picture Exchange Communication System [PECS]; Bondy & Frost, 1994). Exchange-based systems teach a learner to locate a communicative partner prior to producing a message. They are a particularly helpful approach for learners who are not yet proficient in engaging in initiated (sometimes referred to as *expressive* or *productive*) joint attention in which he or she independently calls a listener's attention to the referent of an utterance. During the early phases of intervention, these applications also allow the interventionist to randomize symbol choices presented across teaching opportunities to avoid the selection of a symbol based on its location rather than the symbol's visual features during the early phases of intervention (Reichle et al., 1991; Johnston et al., 2012). The PECS is an example of an exchange-based AAC instructional protocol (Frost & Bondy, 2002). Exchanged-based systems demonstrate marked impact on communication outcomes, particularly expressing wants and needs, for many beginning communicators with ASD, although it has been shown to be more effective with preschool children than those in elementary grades (Ganz, Davis, Lund, Goodwyn, & Simpson, 2012).

What Are Some Features that Should Be Considered in Designing a Low-Tech System?   Across the range of intervention methodologies that can be implemented with low-tech aided communication options, most make systematic instructional decisions based on closely monitoring performance data. A number of questions, which are discussed next, must be addressed in designing an optimal aided low-tech system. Although not a focus of this chapter, determining the dosage of intervention (see Warren, Fey, & Yoder, 2007) is a critical feature that requires careful evaluation.

What Symbol Type Should Be Chosen?   Earlier, the logic of modality sampling was discussed (see Reichle et al., 1991; Johnston et al., 2012). This strategy can be applied in selecting the type of symbols that would be easiest for a learner to discriminate. Options include both three-dimensional and two-dimensional symbols. For example, among three-dimensional symbols both miniature objects and parts of objects can be used. Remnants of actual objects may offer the opportunity of more closely conditioning the symbol with the referent. For example, each time one puts on a coat, one pulls a zipper. Consequently, *zipper* receives many pairing opportunities with *coat*. Subsequently, when an identical zipper swatch is placed on a communication board, the opportunity to establish the zipper as a symbol via conditioning has been enhanced. With respect to two-dimensional symbols, options include black and white or color photos, line drawings, product logos, and traditional orthography. By concurrently comparing the learner's ability to discriminate between symbols within each of these options, the interventionist can select a symbol type that is easiest for the learner.

How Should Symbol Specificity Be Addressed?   In addition to selection of a symbol type, it may also be important to consider the specificity of the symbols to be taught. General requests are context-dependent symbols that can apply across a variety of situations (Reichle & Sigafoos, 1991; Johnston et al., 2012). Examples of general symbols include asking for *more* across different situations (Laraway, Snycerski, Michael, & Poling, 2003; Michael, 1987). Alternatively, the comment *look* is a general vocabulary item often used to comment. There are limitations to relying only on general vocabulary items. For example, more general vocabulary items make a learner's communicative act more context-dependent. This, in turn, can limit the efficiency of a communicative production from the standpoint of a communicative partner. As a result, it may make it more likely that the learner will be more apt to communicate with more familiar individuals who better anticipate the child's needs. With more general vocabulary items, the risk of misinterpreting a communicative utterance could lead to frustration and a lack of autonomy and control for the learner. Once more general vocabulary is taught to a child with ASD, it may be difficult to teach more specific terms.

On the other hand, there are clear advantages associated with general vocabulary items. Often, general requests are recommended as an initial intervention target in that they are maximally generalizable to a number of contexts (Johnston et al., 2012; Reichle et al., 1991). More general items may be recommended when explicit requests would require a need to discriminate between greater numbers of symbol options representing a variety of explicit items. Furthermore, explicit vocabulary items may not be quickly enough established to adequately address a significant portion of different contexts in which the learner needs to communicate. For beginning communicators who tend to communicate about items and activities that are visible and nearby, general symbols may be a viable option.

Explicit vocabulary items and corresponding symbols involve a learner producing communicative acts that are less reliant on context (Mirenda, 2003). This provides potential benefits for communicating about items, events, or people that may not be in view. Discrimination between explicit symbols requires the following: 1) understanding the difference between how to ask for *cookie* or *chips*, 2) understanding when and where different items are available, and, particularly for aided AAC, 3) discriminating the features of a *cookie* or *chips* on a graphic symbol. Explicit vocabulary items and corresponding symbols are related to many benefits pertaining to quality of life (see Johnston et al., 2012).

What Type of Symbol Display Should Be Chosen?   Symbol display encompasses several variables. First, the display of symbols in general can be arranged in a grid or a visual scene display. In addition, within any given page, individual symbols can be arranged in a variety of ways that will also be discussed briefly.

In a grid display, vocabulary items are represented by separate symbols in "boxes" that are typically of equal size. A visual scene display (VSD), involves representing symbols in a naturalistic scene of a meaningful event within which specific symbols are embedded (Beukelman & Mirenda, 2005; Wilkinson, Light & Drager, 2012). For example, a photograph of a child playing on the swings at the park with his brother might constitute a visual scene display containing a series of relevant and meaningful people, objects, actions, and attributes, all related to this activity. In a VSD, the learner may have the advantage of a more representational display when compared to a traditional grid display. VSDs may have several advantages and disadvantages (see Beukelman & Mirenda, 2005) for young children or beginning communicators. As advantages, symbols are 1) arranged in context and 2) preserve conceptual and visual relationships between symbols that occur in life (e.g., the location, proportionality of concepts). Some potential disadvantages of VSDs can also be challenges with traditional grid displays, including that they 1) may be somewhat difficult to utilize in representing abstract concepts (although this is also true for grid displays) and 2) may create challenges in conveniently making vocabulary items such as *help* and *want* accessible across thematic activities without substantial redundancy in placing these symbols on each page of a display. There have been few investigations comparing these types of displays with individuals who have neurodevelopmental disabilities, although several studies have compared the two display types with typically developing children. For example, Drager, Light, Speltz, Fallon, and Jeffries (2003) reported that 2½-year-old children were more accurate finding vocabulary items using VSDs compared to performance using grid displays. However, Light, Drager, McCarthy, et al., (2004) reported that typically developing 4- and 5-year-old children demonstrated similar performances with nonpersonalized VSDs and grid layouts (see examples of displays in in Figure 5.1).

What Symbol Layout Should Be Chosen?   Another aspect of array arrangement is how to arrange symbols on any given page if one is using a traditional grid display (see Drager et al., 2003; Light et al., 2004). A variety of symbol arrangements

Figure 5.1. Visual scene displays (left) versus grid display (right) for playground vocabulary. (Created using The Picture Communication Symbols ©1981–2015 by Mayer-Johnson LLC a Tobii Dynavox company. All Rights Reserved Worldwide. Used with permission. Boardmaker® is a trademark of Mayer-Johnson LLC.)

have been described that include: a) *schematic* (groupings based on event experiences), b) *taxonomic* (categorically based; e.g., all fruits placed together), c) *semantic/grammatical ordering*, or d) *ease of access* (e.g., placing symbols representing more preferred items in the most difficult to access symbol locations while placing symbols representing less preferred events in easy to access locations). Unfortunately, these different arrangements have not been extensively compared among those with ASD who are utilizing low-tech AAC systems. This represents a potentially important area of future inquiry if initial applications of aided AAC are to be expanded.

Can the Learner Engage in "Matching to Sample" as Facilitating Skill Regardless of the Intervention Approach Selected?   Even though there is a lack of definitive evidence that matching to sample is a pivotal skill in aided communication, it is commonly assumed that it is a very helpful skill (Johnston et al., 2012). In using a beginning aided communication system, a communicative event often begins with a learner seeing an item or event about which he or she wishes to communicate and selecting a corresponding symbol from an array of symbols. By definition, this involves a matching to sample task. Thus, learning to use a graphic mode communication system may be facilitated by learning matching-to-sample skills. Matching-to-sample provides evidence that the learner can engage in a conditional discrimination (selecting a correct choice from an array is dependent or conditional on a given sample that is used as an instructional cue). For example, if a learner sees an apple that he wishes to eat (sample) the learner should choose a symbol (choice) representing *apple*. Alternatively, if he sees an actual banana in the kitchen that he would prefer (sample), then he would select a symbol choice representing *banana*. This topic is particularly important for learners with ASD because many intervention programs (particularly discrete trial formats) use formats based on a matching-to-sample procedure. Although not a primary focus of this chapter, conditional use involves differentially choosing and being able to match those symbols to a related referent; it also involves teaching a learner when it is and is not appropriate to emit a newly established symbol (e.g., it is appropriate to request a snack while watching TV but not appropriate during math time at school).

Prior to establishing conditional uses of newly taught communicative symbols, it is important to ensure that a learner can engage in simple discriminations. For example, a simple discrimination task can be established to demonstrate that a learner is able to discriminate between symbols. An interventionist might select three symbols that share similar colors (if color symbols are used). He or she places each in front of the learner and encourages him or her to select a symbol. As soon as a selection is made it is reinforced. Next, the position of the symbols is randomized, and another opportunity is offered. The symbol that was selected by the learner during the initial opportunity would be established as the criterion for a correct response. Across opportunities, if correct responses adhere to the learner's original choice (regardless of their position in the array); the interventionist would have an indication of a simple discrimination. Johnston et al. (2012) outlined procedures to teach simple discriminations when learners had difficulty engaging in the preceding task (given that vision acuity had been eliminated as a potential problem). These procedures were followed by strategies to transition from a simple to a conditional discrimination. Unfortunately, in many intervention studies, little attention has been given to determining whether learners can or cannot discriminate between different members of a symbol collection that will be used during intervention. This determination represents a critical skill. An example of an intervention that has systematically addressed conditional discriminations is the Picture Exchange Communication System, particularly Phase 3 (e.g., Charlop-Christy, Carpenter, Le, LeBlanc, & Kellet, 2002). In summary, learners who engage in simple and conditional discriminations may benefit from more diffuse and more natural teaching conditions because they have mastered the mechanics of what is done when one uses graphic symbols to communicate. These skills may be helpful in addressing more recent calls for not a single intervention approach but instead a combinatory use of different instructional formats.

What Are Some Approaches to Teach Low-Tech AAC?   Communication interventions for learners with ASD lay along a continuum—from behavioral approaches to social-pragmatic, more relationship-based approaches. Prizant and Wetherby (1998) characterized both behavioral and social-pragmatic developmental approaches to intervention. Table 5.1 compares some defining characteristics of the anchor points of this continuum (Prizant & Wetherby, 1998).

Each intervention approach has advantages and disadvantages. On one hand, advocates of discrete trial approaches cite experimental studies that have shown significant gains across a variety of skills (Eikeseth, Smith, Jahr, & Eldevik, 2002; Harris, Handleman, Gordon, Kristoff, & Fuentes, 1991; Howard, Sparkman, Cohen, Green, & Stainslaw, 2005; Romanczyk, Lockshin, & Matey, 2001; Smith, Groen, & Wynn, 2000). In addition, discrete trial approaches provide a task analysis of skills (i.e., a breakdown of a larger skill into manageable pieces and systematic data collection), this facilitates the interventionist's monitoring the learner's progress and programming changes as necessary.

Because a number of individuals with ASD engage in challenging behavior (Jang, Dixon, Tarbox, & Granpeesheh, 2011) and because it closely adheres to procedures consistent with the principles of applied behavior analysis, Functional

Table 5.1.   A comparison of discrete trial approaches to intervention and social-pragmatic developmental approaches

Discrete trial approaches to intervention	Social pragmatic developmental approach
Highly structured	*Flexibly structured*
Physical environment, teaching structure, reinforcement, and consequences are predetermined and prescribed.	Focus is on teaching communication skills within a flexible environment that emphasizes spontaneous communication.
Discrete behavior focus	*Less discrete behavior focus*
Predetermined focus on vocal imitation. Behaviors taught are on objectively defined behaviors and sequentially taught. Speech is the traditional mode of communication.	Behaviors taught may be focused on classes of behavior rather than discrete skills and taught in naturally occurring contexts. Multiple modes of communication are accepted.
Adult-driven context	*Child-driven context*
Sequenced curriculum is adult driven and administered in a 1:1 adult-to-child ratio.	The environment and activities within the environment are maximized for child engagement. Multiple social groupings are utilized.
Predetermined criteria	*Malleable criteria*
Correctness of response is predetermined. Each response is evaluated as "correct" or "incorrect."	Focus is on acknowledging a child's communicative bid (response) even if it is unconventional.
Focus on adult-initiated opportunities	*Focus on child-initiated opportunities*
Initial focus of teaching is on adult initiated teaching opportunities and child compliance.	Focus is on turn taking, reciprocity, and capitalizing on child's engagement.
Not necessarily congruent with typical child development	*Child development framework*
Curricula used is often not informed by child development literature.	Typical child development is used as the framework by which treatment planning and goals are created.
Reliance on oral language	*Reliance on contextual supports*
Interventionist relies minimally on contextual support and heavily on oral language.	Contextual supports such as visual and gestural cues are viewed as useful to help a learner navigate a social situation.

Source: Prizant and Wetherby (1998).

Communication Training (FCT), a discrete trial approach, is an intervention that is relevant to individuals with ASD (Derby et al., 1997; Tiger, Hanley, & Bruzek, 2008; Wacker et al., 1998; Wacker et al., 2013). In FCT, the communicative alternative typically has involved low- or mid-tech AAC applications. Ideally, the selection of intervention target(s) in FCT should be matched across dimensions that include 1) effort, 2) immediacy of reinforcement, and 3) magnitude of reinforcement (for a more detailed discussion, see Reichle & Wacker, 2017, and Chapter 7, "Functional Communication Training for Durable Behavior Change," by McComas et al.).

In contrast, advocates of social-pragmatic approaches cite increased generalization of skills across settings, people, and materials because of the focus of teaching opportunities embedded within naturally occurring contexts (Greenspan & Wieder, 1998; Prizant & Wetherby, 1998). In addition, other potential benefits of social-pragmatic approaches include naturally occurring reinforcement contingencies, a focus on social interactions (Snow, Midkiff-Borunda, Small, & Proctor, 1984), and a focus on relationships with prospective communicative partners.

The Blending of Discrete Trial to a Social-Pragmatic Instructional Approach

There seems to be general agreement that the more diffusely intervention can be embedded into the natural environment the better. Unfortunately, it is also clear that some learners struggle to acquire communicative skills when this is done at the outset of intervention. Within the past 15 years or so, the term "blended approach" increasingly has appeared in the literature. Blended approaches incorporate more discrete trial strategies within natural contexts (Hong, Ganz, Gilliland, & Ninci, 2014).

Naturalistic Developmental Behavioral Interventions (NBDIs) include those that blend applied behavior analysis (ABA) methodology with elements of developmental relevance for young learners (Schreibman et al., 2015). Therefore, the bases of many NBDIs rely on ABA behavioral principles and methods (e.g., systematic prompting and fading; Schreibman et al., 2015); however, interventions are also viewed through a more social-pragmatic lens. Strategies may include:

- Implementation within settings in which AAC skills would naturally be used, enabling generalization of skills into a range of settings (Light 1997; Ogletree, Davis, Hambrecht, & Phillips, 2012)

- Use of modeling instructional prompts in much the way that typically developing children learn to communicate by first hearing others modeling language (Binger & Light, 2007)

- Expansion of current communication skills (e.g., verbal, AAC, gestures)

- Implementation of behavioral techniques including time delay, positive reinforcement, and prompting (Reichle, Drager, & Davis, 2002) in natural contexts

- Inclusion of natural communication partners as key interventionists

Naturalistic Developmental Behavioral Interventions adhere to recommended early intervention practices of naturalized, routines-based, and family-centered interventions, as discussed by Schreibman and colleagues (2015). NBDIs may be easier for parents to implement and may promote child skill acquisition in a generalized and natural manner. However, there may be times when higher dose or more intensive interventions may be required.

The Early Start Denver Model (Early Start) is an example of a manualized NBDI protocol that combines elements of behavioral intervention models within a relationship-focused and developmental framework to improve social-communicative skills for young children with ASD (Dawson et al., 2010; Vismara, McCormick, Young, Nadhan, & Monlux, 2013; Vismara, Young, & Rogers, 2012). Considering the target age of children for whom Early Start programming would be appropriate (infants and toddlers with ASD), the protocol focuses on play-based and a large proportion of child-directed intervention. Learner-related skill areas that warrant consideration for the appropriate fit of Early Start are 1) the extent to which the learner can engage in child-directed instruction and 2) if challenging behavior is a significant concern. For learners with more complex communication needs such as these, Early Start programming may need to be supplemented with a more systematic and function-based approach.

In addition to the Early Start Denver Model, many interventions exist that blend naturalistic and traditional discrete trial interventions in that they require the interventionist to be responsive to a child's communicative bid, even if unconventional, and are often embedded within a naturally occurring context/routine. For example the pivotal response training addressed earlier is an intervention for children with ASD that targets pivotal behaviors in natural environments (Koegel, Bimbela, & Schreibman, 1996).

Milieu Language Teaching, an evidence-based intervention that integrates both behavioral and social-pragmatic developmental components has been successful with children with ASD (Kaiser, Yoder, & Keetz, 1992). Milieu Language Teaching blends behavioral and social interactionist perspectives and emphasizes parent implementation (Hancock & Kaiser, 2006). Hart and Risley (1975) proposed the original strategies for Milieu Language Teaching, including mand-model, time delay, and incidental teaching. Mand-model involves the interventionist first delivering a mand (e.g. "what do you want?"). If the learner fails to use this cue in producing a response approximation, the interventionist delivers a model (e.g. "What do you want—APPLE"). Once a learner is responding with some consistency to a mand, the interventionist fades the mand cue by delivering a delay between the initiation of an instructional opportunity and the delivery of a mand. Once the learner is consistently taking advantage of an instructional opportunity without requiring a mand, the interventionist shifts to incidental teaching. This aspect of milieu intervention involves the interventionist delivering additional instruction following the child's independent vocabulary production. For example, if a child said "doggie," then the interventionist might immediately follow with an expansion "doggie go" if the goal was to increase the combination of morphological units. Alternatively, if the goal of intervention was to establish new related vocabulary items, the interventionist might follow a child's production of "doggie" with "he's brown." Since its original implementation, Milieu Language Teaching has evolved to include prelinguistic communication (Prelinguistic Milieu Language Teaching) and conversational skills (Enhanced Milieu Language Teaching).

Often, during NDBI, planning priority is given to more diffuse intervention strategies in which fewer instructional opportunities may be generated than during a discrete trial approach. Learners may benefit from an exploratory model (a number of concurrently implemented symbols with fewer teaching opportunities per symbol).

One pivotal skill that may readily signal increasing reliance on a more diffuse model of intervention is "fast mapping." Mervis and Bertrand (1994) discussed the "Novel-Name Nameless Category" principle. This principle is believed instrumental in learners being able to acquire new symbols through inferential learning without direct instruction in the natural environment and is known as "fast mapping." Fast mapping occurs when a learner encounters a new word and it corresponds to an unfamiliar object for which they do not already have a name.

Fast mapping may be crucial to efficient symbol learning in that it permits learners to map new symbols to new objects after they have been labeled during a modest number of opportunities (Mervis & Bertrand, 1994). These investigators suggested a relationship between fast mapping and "vocabulary spurt." This is defined as acquiring 10 new words in a 14-day period. There is limited literature on the extent to which learners with ASD can learn to fast map and the extent to which their joint attention skill limitations may impact the ability to learn to fast map. The limitations on joint attention skills among learners with ASD may impede their skill in learning to fast map along with the propensity of some learners with ASD to engage in stimulus overselectivity (responding to, or fixating on, one of multiple cues or features of an item; Lovaas, Koegel, & Schreibman, 1979).

Generalization is also often a challenge for interventionists who heavily rely on discrete trial intervention approaches. Part of a learner's task is to increasingly identify situations where he or she can apply symbols that have been acquired. This requires an increasingly keen understanding of the stimulus characteristics that call for the emission of a particular symbol. This may be challenging for many individuals with ASD as a result of stimulus overselectivity.

For those who choose a more exclusively behavioral approach to intervention, minimizing the generalization challenges, a *general case* instructional framework may be required. This approach addresses both generalization and conditional use, which may require attention among those with more severe intellectual delay in addition to ASD.

MAXIMIZING THE CONDITIONAL USE OF NEWLY ESTABLISHED COMMUNICATIVE ALTERNATIVES

In part, conditional communication refers to generalizing communication to situations where its use should be extended (generalization), but simultaneously refraining from using a newly acquired behavior when it should not be used. Conditional communication is critically important for individuals acquiring a new conventional communicative repertoire (Johnston et al., 2012). Increasingly, translational research has placed the burden on communicators with developmental disabilities to optimize communicative behavior for one's listener rather than relying on a communicative partner to accommodate the speaker (see Johnston et al., 2012). For example, during acquisition, an individual may have learned to request preferred items. A large proportion of these requests may have been reinforced during acquisition. As a result, he or she may not have learned when it is inappropriate to request. For example, a) the item may not always be available, b) frequent consumption of the item may not be healthy or may interrupt other important daily living activities, c) the setting where the request occurs may be inappropriate (e.g., asking for food while in an area where no food is allowed), or d) the request may be inappropriate given the intended communicative partner (e.g., asking a stranger for money to operate a vending machine).

People with neurodevelopmental disabilities who experience significant communicative challenges often have difficulty using newly acquired communicative behavior conditionally (Horner & Albin, 1988; Johnston et al., 2012; Reichle, Rogers, & Barrett, 1984). In establishing conditional use, teaching exemplars must concurrently address both stimulus discrimination and stimulus generalization (Reichle & Wacker, 2017). *Discrimination* refers to responding differently when a relevant property is changed whereas *generalization* refers to responding in the same or a similar manner despite changes in irrelevant properties of a given stimulus (Cheng, Spetch, & Johnston, 1997). For example, when a child learns to ask for help after being asked to open a well-tightened jar (that he or she is not capable of opening), he or she must also continue to realize that no request is needed when he or she encounters a loosened container lid. In the latter context, he should act independently. It is likely important that the learner must see enough varying examples of each of these two conditions to make reasonable decisions about when to request help.

Together, discrimination and generalization skills serve as important building blocks in teaching a learner when to use a given vocabulary item and conversely when NOT to use it. To concurrently address the challenges of both appropriate discrimination and generalization, general-case instruction originated from Direct Instruction (Becker & Engelmann, 1978; Carnine & Becker, 1982). General-case instruction emphasizes the concurrent implementation of both multiple positive (where the new behavior being taught should be used) and negative (where the behavior being taught should not be used) teaching exemplars. When utilized to communication skills (e.g., Chadsey-Rusch, Drasgow, Reinoehl, Halle, & Collet-Klingenberg, 1993; Horner & Albin, 1988) general-case instruction has been more effective in producing generalized effects than single-instance instruction (e.g., Chadsey-Rusch et al., 1993). Unfortunately, general-case instructional strategies have not been studied or used extensively in the AAC community to date.

MAXIMIZING MAINTENANCE OF NEWLY ACQUIRED COMMUNICATION SKILLS

Although "loosening" instruction to include implementation in the most natural environments possible at the earliest possible point during intervention will help to facilitate generalization, explicit instructional frameworks can also be implemented to enhance maintenance among learners who have substantial learning challenges. Overtraining (i.e., training beyond the learner achieving mastery criteria) is a methodology to improve maintenance (Yeaton & Sechrest, 1981). However, limited experimental evidence exists related to establishing individualized maintenance criteria for learners. In fact, often maintenance has not been carefully scrutinized in communication intervention.

Unfortunately, examinations of the maintenance longevity of newly acquired AAC skills are reasonably limited. In a systematic review of social-communicative interventions for children with disabilities investigating fidelity (Parker-McGowan, 2016), the number of maintenance probes ranged from one to eight and were implemented from one week postintervention to several months postintervention. In a systematic review of parent-implemented FCT interventions for children (Simacek, 2016), maintenance was only measured for 37.5% of the participants. In other studies, maintenance probes ranged from 2 weeks (Rispoli, Camargo, Machalicek, Lang, & Sigafoos, 2014), 2 months (Moes & Frea, 2002), 6 to 9 months (Tait, Sigafoos, Woodyatt, O'Reilly, & Lancioni, 2004), and (although rare) as high as 17 to 20 months (Derby et al., 2007).

DESCRIBING COLLATERAL GAINS ASSOCIATED WITH LOW-TECH AAC

One concern that parents have is the fear that implementing AAC with their child will impede speech and/or language development. Existing evidence suggests that this is not the case (Johnston et al., 2012; Romski & Sevcik, 1997). To the contrary, for a number of research participants, expressive speech has been associated with

AAC instruction (Ganz, Earles-Vollrath, et al., 2012; Millar, Light, & Schlosser, 2006). In addition, some research has reported improvements in the comprehension of spoken vocabulary (e.g., Harris & Reichle, 2004), spontaneous speech (Mancil, 2006), and task completion (Schieltz et al., 2011) following the implementation of aided communication systems. In general, the study of collateral gains represents an important area for future scrutiny. Generally, collateral gains have been focused on learner outcomes. However, it is reasonable to believe that there might be collateral effects for the interventionist as well. Parent responsivity to prelinguistic emissions of their children has been shown to be an important component of language development for young children (Harwood, Warren, & Yoder, 2002; Yoder & Warren, 1998). Both with parents of typically developing and at-risk children who have acquired intelligible speech, responsivity has been associated with more rapid advances in communication acquisition (Hart & Risley, 1995). Parent affect (a variable related to the parent's responsivity) has been evaluated among parents of young children with ASD who were involved in a 1-week intensive training for pivotal response training (Koegel, Symon, & Koegel, 2002). Following pivotal response training, parental use of the strategies and children's spoken language improved; collateral ratings (a composite of parent–child interactions for perceived happiness, interest, and stress of the parent; Koegel et al., 2002) of parents' affect improved. Clearly, the potential for collateral gains in parent responsivity or affect would be an important area to study for parent–child interactions during AAC intervention.

CONCLUSION

This chapter has provided a summary of some areas to be considered in the implementation of a low-tech aided AAC system. Although mid- and high-tech AAC applications may provide distinct advantages for individuals with ASD, low-tech devices provide some immediate options to flexibly deliver well-organized intervention strategies for parents that help to ensure that learners fully acquire well-discriminated symbols. By focusing first on the instructional components of teaching, a family's task may be less effortful than when they must learn how to teach and the mechanics of programming and operating a more sophisticated system at the same time they are attempting to teach. In addition, the application of low-tech communication aids may provide an option for very early intervention to generate an evidence base for a strong funding application for families that have not yet purchased a device. Finally, a low-tech communication aid may provide a highly portable backup for an SGD (e.g., if a high-tech device runs out of charge, in bright sunlight where the display is compromised, on playground equipment requiring free hands, and in a swimming pool). For these reasons, despite advancing technology, low-tech aided communication is apt to play a continuing role in beginning a successful aided AAC application.

REFERENCES

American Academy of Pediatrics [AAP]. (2007). Management of children with autism spectrum disorder. *Pediatrics, 120,* 1162–1182.
Anderson, S. R., Avery, D. L., DiPietro, E. K., Edwards, G. L., & Christian, W. P. (1987). Intensive home-based early intervention with autistic children. *Education and Treatment of Children, 10,* 352–366.

Barton, E. E., & Fettig, A. (2013). Parent-implemented interventions for young children with disabilities. *Journal of Early Intervention, 35,* 194–219.

Becker, W. C., & Engelmann, S. (1978). Systems for basic instruction: Theory and applications. *Handbook of applied behavior analysis: Social and instructional processes,* 325–378.

Beukelman, D. R., & Mirenda, P. (2005). *Augmentative and alternative communication* (3rd ed.). Baltimore, MD: Paul H. Brookes Publishing Co.

Binger, C., & Light, J. (2007). The effect of aided AAC modeling on the expression of multi-symbol messages by preschoolers who use AAC. *Augmentative and Alternative Communication, 23,* 30–43.

Bondy, A. S., & Frost, L. A. (1994). The picture exchange communication system. *Focus on Autistic Behavior, 9,* 1–19.

Brady, N. C., & Halle, J. W. (1997). Functional analysis of communicative behaviors. *Focus on Autism and Other Developmental Disabilities, 12,* 95–104.

Byiers, B. J., Dimian, A. F., & Symons, F. J. (2014). Functional communication training in Rett syndrome: A preliminary study. *American Journal on Intellectual and Developmental Disabilities, 119,* 340–350.

Byiers, B. J., Reichle, J., & Symons, F. J. (2012). Single-subject experimental design for evidence-based practice. *American Journal of Speech-Language Pathology, 21,* 397–414.

Carnine, D. W., & Becker, W. C. (1982). Theory of instruction: Generalization issues. *Educational Psychology, 2,* 249–262.

Carr, E. G. (1988). Functional equivalence as a mechanism of response generalization. *Generalization and maintenance: Life-style changes in applied settings,* 221–241.

Carr, E. G., & Durand, V. M. (1985). Reducing behavior problems through functional communication training. *Journal of Applied Behavior Analysis, 18,* 111–126.

Chadsey-Rusch, J., Drasgow, E., Reinoehl, B., Halle, J., & Collet-Klingenberg, L. (1993). Using general-case instruction to teach spontaneous and generalized requests for assistance to learners with severe disabilities. *Research and Practice for Persons with Severe Disabilities, 18,* 177–187.

Charlop-Christy, M. H., Carpenter, M., Le, L., LeBlanc, L. A., & Kellet, K. (2002). Using the Picture Exchange Communication System (PECS) with children with autism: Assessment of PECS acquisition, speech, social-communicative behavior, and problem behavior. *Journal of Applied Behavior Analysis, 35,* 213–231.

Cheng, K., Spetch, M. L., & Johnston, M. (1997). Spatial peak shift and generalization in pigeons. *Journal of Experimental Psychology: Animal Behavior Processes, 23,* 469.

Committee on Educational Interventions for Children with Autism, Division of Behavioral and Social Sciences and Education, National Research Council. (2001). *Educating children with autism.* Washington, DC: National Academies Press.

Dawson, G., Rogers, S., Munson, J., Smith, M., Winter, J., Greenson, J., . . . Varley, J. (2010). Randomized, controlled trial of an intervention for toddlers with autism: The Early Start Denver Model. *Pediatrics, 125,* e17–e23.

Derby, K. M., Wacker, D. P., Berg, W., Deraad, A., Ulrich, S., Asmus, J., & Stoner, E. A. (1997). The long-term effects of functional communication training in home settings. *Journal of Applied Behavior Analysis, 30,* 507–531.

Drager, K. D., Light, J. C., Speltz, J. C., Fallon, K. A., & Jeffries, L. Z. (2003). The performance of typically developing 2 1/2-year-olds on dynamic display AAC technologies with different system layouts and language organizations. *Journal of Speech, Language, and Hearing Research, 46,* 298–312.

Eikeseth, S., Smith, T., Jahr, E., & Eldevik, S. (2002). Intensive behavioral treatment at school for 4–7-year-old children with autism: A 1-year comparison-controlled study. *Behavior Modification, 26,* 49–68.

Frost, L., & Bondy, A. (2002). *The picture exchange communication system training manual.* New Castle, DE: Pyramid Educational Consultants.

Ganz, J. B. (2015). AAC interventions for individuals with autism spectrum disorders: State of the science and future research directions. *Augmentative and Alternative Communication, 31,* 203–214.

Ganz, J. B., Davis, J. L., Lund, E. M., Goodwyn, F. D., & Simpson, R. L. (2012). Meta-analysis of PECS with individuals with ASD: Investigation of targeted versus non-targeted outcomes, participant characteristics, and implementation phase. *Research in Developmental Disabilities, 33,* 406–418.

Ganz, J. B., Earles-Vollrath, T. L., Heath, A. K., Parker, R. I., Rispoli, M. J., & Duran, J. B. (2012). A meta-analysis of single case research studies on aided augmentative and alternative communication systems with individuals with autism spectrum disorders. *Journal of Autism and Developmental Disorders, 42*, 60–74.

Ganz, J. B., Rispoli, M. J., Mason, R. A., & Hong, E. R. (2014). Moderation of effects of AAC based on setting and types of aided AAC on outcome variables: An aggregate study of single-case research with individuals with ASD. *Developmental Neurorehabilitation, 17*, 184–192.

Greenspan, S. I., & Wieder, S. (1998). *The child with special needs: Encouraging intellectual and emotional growth.* New York, NY: Addison-Wesley.

Gregory, M. K., DeLeon, I. G., & Richman, D. M. (2009). The influence of matching and motor-imitation abilities on rapid acquisition of manual signs and exchange-based communicative responses. *Journal of Applied Behavior Analysis, 42*, 399–404.

Hancock, T. B., & Kaiser, A. P. (2006). Enhanced milieu teaching. In R. J. McCauley & M. E. Fey (Eds.), *Treatment of language disorders in children* (pp. 203–236). Baltimore, MD: Paul H. Brookes Publishing Co.

Harris, M. D., & Reichle, J. (2004). The impact of aided language stimulation on symbol comprehension and production in children with moderate cognitive disabilities. *American Journal of Speech-Language Pathology, 13*, 155–167.

Harris, S. L., Handleman, J. S., Gordon, R., Kristoff, B., & Fuentes, F. (1991). Changes in cognitive and language functioning of preschool children with autism. *Journal of Autism and Developmental Disorders, 21*, 281–290.

Hart, B., & Risley, T. R. (1975). Incidental teaching of language in the preschool. *Journal of Applied Behavior Analysis, 8*(4), 411–420.

Hart, B., & Risley, T. R. (1995). *Meaningful differences in the everyday experience of young American children.* Baltimore, MD: Paul H. Brookes Publishing Co.

Harwood, K., Warren, S. F., & Yoder, P. (2002). The importance of responsivity in developing contingent exchanges with beginning communicators. *Exemplary Practices for Beginning Communicators: Implications for AAC*, 59–95.

Hong, E. R., Ganz, J. B., Gilliland, W., & Ninci, J. (2014). Teaching caregivers to implement an augmentative and alternative communication intervention to an adult with ASD. *Research in Autism Spectrum Disorders, 8*, 570–580.

Horn, E., Lieber, J., Sandall, S., Schwartz, I., & Worley, R. (2002). Supporting young children's IEP goals in inclusive settings through embedded learning opportunities. *Topics in Early Childhood Special Education, 20*, 208–223.

Horner, R. H., & Albin, R. W. (1988). Research on general-case procedures for learners with severe disabilities. *Education and Treatment of Children*, 375–388.

Horner, R. H., Jones, D. N., & Williams, J. A. (1985). A functional approach to teaching generalized street crossing. *Research and Practice for Persons with Severe Disabilities, 10*, 71–78.

Howard, J. S., Sparkman, C. R., Cohen, H. G., Green, G., & Stanislaw, H. (2005). A comparison of intensive behavior analytic and eclectic treatments for young children with autism. *Research in Developmental Disabilities, 26*, 359–383.

Hyppa Martin, J., Reichle, J., Dimian, A., & Chen, M. (2013). Communication modality sampling for a toddler with Angelman syndrome. *Language, Speech, and Hearing Services in Schools, 44*, 327–336.

Iacono, T., Carter, M., & Hook, J. (1998). Identification of intentional communication in students with severe and multiple disabilities. *Augmentative and Alternative Communication, 14*, 102–114.

Jang, J., Dixon, D. R., Tarbox, J., & Granpeesheh, D. (2011). Symptom severity and challenging behavior in children with ASD. *Research in Autism Spectrum Disorders, 5*, 1028–1032.

Johnston, S. S., Reichle, J., Feeley, K. M., & Jones, E. A. (2012). *AAC strategies for individuals with moderate to severe disabilities.* Baltimore, MD: Paul H. Brookes Publishing Co.

Kaiser, A. P., Yoder, P. J., & Keetz, A. (1992). Evaluating milieu teaching. In S. F. Warren & J. Reichle (Eds.), *Communication and language intervention series: Vol. 1. Causes and effects in communication and language intervention* (pp. 9–47). Baltimore, MD: Paul H. Brookes Publishing Co.

Koegel, R. L., Bimbela, A., & Schreibman, L. (1996). Collateral effects of parent training on family interactions. *Journal of Autism and Developmental Disorders, 26*, 347–359.

Koegel, R. L., & Frea, W. D. (1993). Treatment of social behavior in autism through the modification of pivotal social skills. *Journal of Applied Behavior Analysis, 26*(3), 369–377.

Koegel, R. L., Symon, J. B., & Koegel, L. K. (2002). Parent education for families of children
with autism living in geographically distant areas. *Journal of Positive Behavior Interventions,
4*, 88–103.

Laraway, S., Snycerski, S., Michael, J., & Poling, A. (2003). Motivating operations and terms to
describe them: Some further refinements. *Journal of Applied Behavior Analysis, 36*, 407–414.

Light, J. (1997). "Let's go star fishing": Reflections on the contexts of language learning for
children who use aided AAC. *Augmentative and Alternative Communication, 13*, 158–171.

Light, J., Drager, K., McCarthy, J., Mellott, S., Millar, D., Parrish, C., . . . Welliver, M. (2004).
Performance of typically developing four-and five-year-old children with AAC systems
using different language organization techniques. *Augmentative and Alternative Communication, 20*(2), 63–88.

Light, J., & McNaughton, D. (2013). Putting people first: Re-thinking the role of technology
in augmentative and alternative communication intervention. *Augmentative and Alternative Communication, 29*(4): 299–309. doi:10.3109/07434618.2013.848935

Light, J. C., Roberts, B., Dimarco, R., & Greiner, N. (1998). Augmentative and alternative
communication to support receptive and expressive communication for people with
autism. *Journal of Communication Disorders, 31*, 153–180.

Lovaas, O. I., Koegel, R. L., & Schreibman, L. (1979). Stimulus overselectivity in autism:
A review of research. *Psychological Bulletin, 86* 1236-1254

Mancil, G. R. (2006). Functional communication training: A review of literature related to
children with autism. *Education and Training in Developmental Disabilities, 41*, 213–224.

Martin, J. H., Reichle, J., Dimian, A., & Chen, M. (2013). Communication modality sampling
for a toddler with Angelman syndrome. *Language, Speech, and Hearing Services in Schools,
44*, 327–336.

Mervis, C. B., & Bertrand, J. (1994). Acquisition of the novel name-nameless category (N3C)
principle. *Child Development, 65*, 1646–1662.

McNaughton, D., & Light, J. (2013). The iPad and mobile technology revolution: Benefits and
challenges for individuals who require augmentative and alternative communication.
Augmentative and Alternative Communication, 29, 107–116.

Michael, J. (1987). Establishing operations and the mand. *The Analysis of Verbal Behavior, 6*,
3–9.

Millar, D. C., Light, J. C., & Schlosser, R. W. (2006). The impact of augmentative and alternative communication intervention on the speech production of individuals with developmental disabilities: A research review. *Journal of Speech, Language, and Hearing Research, 49*,
248–264.

Mirenda, P. (2003). Toward functional augmentative and alternative communication for students with autism manual signs, graphic symbols, and voice output communication aids.
Language, Speech, and Hearing Services in Schools, 34, 203–216.

Moes, D. R., & Frea, W. D. (2002). Contextualized behavioral support in early intervention
for children with autism and their families. *Journal of Autism and Developmental Disorders,
32*, 519–533.

Ogletree, B. T., Davis, P., Hambrecht, G., & Phillips, E. W. (2012). Using milieu training to
promote photograph exchange for a young child with autism. *Focus on Autism and Other
Developmental Disabilities, 27*, 93–101.

O'Neill, R. , & Reichle, J. (1993). Addressing socially motivated challenging behaviors by
establish communicative alternatives: Basics of a general-case approach. In J. Reichle &
D. P. Wacker (Eds.), *Communicative alternatives to challenging behavior: Integrating functional
assessment and intervention strategies* (pp. 205–237). Baltimore, MD: Paul H. Brookes Publishing Co.

Parker-McGowan, Q. E. (2016). *A comparison of fidelity of two parent-implemented vocabulary
interventions for young learners with autism spectrum disorder* (Doctoral dissertation, University of Minnesota).

Prizant, B. M., & Wetherby, A. M. (1998). Understanding the continuum of discrete-trial
traditional behavioral to social-pragmatic developmental approaches in communication
enhancement for young children with autism/PDD. *Seminars in Speech and Language, 19*,
329–353.

Reichle, J., & Brady, N. (2012) Teaching pragmatic skills to individuals with severe disabilities. In S. S. Johnston, J. Reichle, K. M. Feeley, & E. A. Jones (Eds.), *AAC strategies for individuals with moderate to severe disabilities* (pp. 3–23). Baltimore, MD: Paul H. Brookes Publishing.

Reichle, J., Drager, K., & Davis, C. (2002). Using requests for assistance to obtain desired items and to gain release from nonpreferred activities: Implications for assessment and intervention. *Education and Treatment of Children, 25*(1), 47–66.

Reichle, J., Rogers, N., & Barrett, C. (1984). Establishing pragmatic discriminations among the communicative functions of requesting, rejecting, and commenting in an adolescent. *Research and Practice for Persons with Severe Disabilities, 9*, 31–36.

Reichle, J., & Sigafoos, J. (1991). Establishing an initial repertoire of requesting. In J. Reichle & J. Sigafoos (Eds.), *Implementing augmentative and alternative communication: Strategies for learners with severe disabilities*, 89–114. Baltimore, MD: Paul H. Brookes Publishing Co.

Reichle, J., & Wacker, D. (2017). *Functional communication training for problem behavior.* New York, NY: Guilford Press.

Reichle, J., York, J., & Sigafoos, J. (1991). *Implementing augmentative and alternative communication: Strategies for learners with severe disabilities.* Baltimore, MD: Pau H. Brookes Publishing Co.

Rispoli, M., Camargo, S., Machalicek, W., Lang, R., & Sigafoos, J. (2014). Functional communication training in the treatment of problem behavior maintained by access to rituals. *Journal of Applied Behavior Analysis, 47*, 580–593.

Rogers-Warren, A., & Warren, S. F. (1980). Mands for verbalization facilitating the display of newly trained language in children. *Behavior Modification, 4*, 361–382.

Romanczyk, R. G., Lockshin, S., & Matey, L. (2001). The children's unit for treatment and evaluation. In J. S. Handleman & S. L. Harris (Eds.), *Preschool education programs for children with autism* (pp. 49–94). Austin, TX: Pro-Ed.

Romski, M. A., & Sevcik, R. A. (1997). Augmentative and alternative communication for children with developmental disabilities. *Mental Retardation and Developmental Disabilities Research Reviews, 3*, 363–368.

Rotholz, D. A., Berkowitz, S. F., & Burberry, J. (1989). Functionality of two modes of communication in the community by students with developmental disabilities: A comparison of signing and communication books. *Research and Practice for Persons with Severe Disabilities, 14*, 227–233.

Schieltz, K. M., Wacker, D. P., Harding, J. W., Berg, W. K., Lee, J. F., Dalmau, Y. C. P., . . . Ibrahimović, M. (2011). Indirect effects of functional communication training on non-targeted disruptive behavior. *Journal of Behavioral Education, 20*, 15–32.

Schlosser, R. (1999). Social validation of interventions in augmentative and alternative communication. *Augmentative and Alternative Communication, 15*(4), 234–247.

Schreibman, L., Dawson, G., Stahmer, A. C., Landa, R., Rogers, S. J., McGee, G. G., . . . McNerney, E. (2015). Naturalistic developmental behavioral interventions: Empirically validated treatments for autism spectrum disorder. *Journal of Autism and Developmental Disorders, 45*, 2411–2428.

Shane, H. C., Blackstone, S., Vanderheiden, G., Williams, M., & DeRuyter, F. (2012). Using AAC technology to access the world. *Assistive Technology, 24*, 3–13.

Sigafoos, J., Wermink, H., Didden, R., Green, V. A., Schlosser, R. W., O'Reilly, M. F., & Lancioni, G. E. (2011). Effects of varying lengths of synthetic speech output on augmented requesting and natural speech production in an adolescent with Klinefelter syndrome. *Augmentative and Alternative Communication, 27*, 163–171.

Sigafoos, J., Woodyatt, G., Keen, D., Tait, K., Tucker, M., Roberts-Pennell, D., & Pittendreigh, N. (2000). Identifying potential communicative acts in children with developmental and physical disabilities. *Communication Disorders Quarterly, 21*, 77–86.

Simacek, J. J. (2016). *Communication intervention for children with severe neurodevelopmental disabilities: An application of telehealth as a service delivery mechanism* (Doctoral dissertation, University of Minnesota).

Smith, T., Groen, A. D., & Wynn, J. W. (2000). Randomized trial of intensive early intervention for children with pervasive developmental disorder. *American Journal on Mental Retardation, 105*, 269–285.

Snow, C., Midkiff-Borunda, S., Small, A., & Proctor, A. (1984). Therapy as social interaction: Analyzing the context for language remediation. *Topics in Language Disorders, 3*, 72–85.

Stephenson, J., & Dowrick, M. (2005). Parents' perspectives on the communication skills of their children with severe disabilities. *Journal of Intellectual and Developmental Disability, 30*, 75–85.

Tait, K., Sigafoos, J., Woodyatt, G., O'Reilly, M., & Lancioni, G. (2004). Evaluating parent use of functional communication training to replace and enhance prelinguistic behaviours in six children with developmental and physical disabilities. *Disability and Rehabilitation, 26*, 1241–1254.

Tiger, J. H., Hanley, G. P., & Bruzek, J. (2008). Functional communication training: A review and practical guide. *Behavior Analysis in Practice, 1*, 16–23.

Urbanowicz, A., Leonard, H., Girdler, S., Ciccone, N., & Downs, J. (2014). Parental perspectives on the communication abilities of their daughters with Rett syndrome. *Developmental Neurorehabilitation, 19*(1),17–25.

Vismara, L. A., McCormick, C., Young, G. S., Nadhan, A., & Monlux, K. (2013). Preliminary findings of a telehealth approach to parent training in autism. *Journal of Autism and Developmental Disorders, 43*, 2953–2969.

Vismara, L. A., Young, G. S., & Rogers, S. J. (2012). Telehealth for expanding the reach of early autism training to parents. *Autism Research and Treatment, 2012*, 1–12. doi:10.1155/2012/121878

Wacker, D. P., Berg, W. K., Harding, J. W., Derby, K. M., Asmus, J. M., & Healy, A. (1998). Evaluation and long-term treatment of aberrant behavior displayed by young children with disabilities. *Journal of Developmental and Behavioral Pediatrics, 19*, 260–266. doi:10.1097/00004703-199808000-00004

Wacker, D. P., Lee, J. F., Padilla Dalmau, Y. C., Kopelman, T. G., Lindgren, S. D., Kuhle, J. . . . Waldron, D. B. (2013). Conducting functional communication training via telehealth to reduce the problem behavior of young children with autism. *Journal of Developmental and Physical Disabilities, 25*, 35–48. doi:10.1007/s10882-012-9314-0

Warren, S. F., Fey, M. E., & Yoder, P. J. (2007). Differential treatment intensity research: A missing link to creating optimally effective communication interventions. *Mental Retardation and Developmental Disabilities Research Reviews, 13*, 70–77.

Wendt, O. (2009). Research on the use of graphic symbols and manual signs. In P. Mirenda & T. Iacono (Eds.), *Autism Spectrum Disorders and AAC* (pp. 83–139). Baltimore, MD: Paul H, Brookes Publishing Co.

Wilkinson, K. M., Light, J., & Drager, K. (2012). Considerations for the composition of visual scene displays: Potential contributions of information from visual and cognitive sciences. *Augmentative and Alternative Communication, 28*, 137–147.

Yeaton, W. H., & Sechrest, L. (1981). Critical dimensions in the choice and maintenance of successful treatments: Strength, integrity, and effectiveness. *Journal of Consulting and Clinical Psychology, 49*, 156.

Yoder, P. J., & Layton, T. L. (1988). Speech following sign language training in autistic children with minimal verbal language. *Journal of Autism and Developmental Disorders, 18*, 217–229.

Yoder, P. J., & Warren, S. F. (1998). Maternal responsivity predicts the prelinguistic communication intervention that facilitates generalized intentional communication. *Journal of Speech, Language, and Hearing Research, 41*, 1207–1219.

6

High-Tech Aided AAC for Individuals With Autism Spectrum Disorder and Complex Communication Needs

Jessica G. Caron and Christine Holyfield

Individuals with autism spectrum disorder (ASD) contribute to the heterogeneous group of individuals with complex communication needs (CCN). Some individuals will develop speech that is adequate for communication, yet 30%–50% of learners with ASD never develop functional speech (Shane et al., 2015; Wodka, Mathy, & Kalb, 2013) and the majority of individuals with ASD demonstrate language delays (Shane et al., 2015). Difficulties in producing and/or comprehending language are likely to have serious implications for active participation in society. These individuals will require AAC, frequently high-tech aided AAC, to maximize interpersonal relationships, educational outcomes, employment opportunities, and leisure pursuits.

This chapter aims to provide practitioners and parents with recommendations for whom and under what circumstances high-tech aided AAC may be useful for individuals with ASD. This chapter is organized according to the progression from emerging communication to independent communication. The progression is discussed in three stages: 1) early symbolic communicators, 2) semantic-syntactic communicators, and 3) independent communicators. Per stage, the authors will outline language skills that occur, discuss considerations and needs in relation to those with ASD and CCN, and describe high-tech AAC supports that have potential to support the needs and skills of the communicator. Each of the three communication stages will be summarized with a case example, illustrating the linguistic skills, needs, and application of key high-tech AAC considerations for three different individuals with ASD and CCN.

WHAT IS HIGH-TECH AAC?

High-tech AAC includes electronic devices that generate speech and are used to supplement or replace conventional speech. These devices are often referred to as speech-generating devices (SGDs), or voice output communication aids (Reichle, Ganz, Drager, & Parker-McGowan, 2016). High-tech AAC includes dedicated AAC devices and mobile technology applications or "apps" (Shane et al., 2015). Dedicated devices and apps are dynamic high-tech AAC systems, wherein they respond by speaking or navigating to different vocabulary based upon activations of symbols by the communicator. Furthermore, many high-tech AAC systems include an onboard camera to support quick capture of personalized memories and images, in addition to the option to connect to the Internet to send e-mails, download additional images, and participate in social media (Light & McNaughton, 2012). High-tech AAC systems allow for certain benefits over low- and mid-tech counterparts that may be important to individuals with ASD (Ganz, 2015). Some of these benefits will be highlighted in the subsequent discussions of individuals across the continuum of communication development—from high-tech AAC considerations for those individuals with ASD who are at the earliest stages of communication (e.g., early symbolic communicators) to those individuals with ASD who are using AAC masterfully (e.g., independent communicators). Presently, aided, graphics-based AAC systems are used frequently and successfully with individuals with ASD who require AAC to increase social interaction (e.g., turn taking, social initiations), communicate (e.g., requesting, symbol comprehension), participate in academic activities (e.g., spelling), and decrease challenging behaviors (Ganz, 2015; Ganz et al., 2012; Mirenda & Erickson, 2000). In addition, individuals with ASD who require AAC often select high-tech devices when offered choices among SGDs, exchange-based systems, or manual sign language (Ganz, 2015).

Speech-generating device (SGD): SGDs are high-tech aided AAC systems. Examples include a single-switch communication buttons with voice-output, dedicated communication devices, and AAC mobile applications. Also known as a **voice-output communication aid.**

Despite the chapter focus on high-tech AAC solutions, AAC interventions must be based on the individual's skills and needs, with the goal of supporting a broad range of communication functions and activities (McNaughton & Light, 2013). This includes consideration of the individual as a multimodal communicator—using a combination of speech, signs, gestures, and low-tech and high-tech strategies, when appropriate, to communicate with a range of partners. As Hershberger (2011) stated, "The greatest pitfall is for us to focus too much on the technology. Providing an AAC solution is a complex process. An AAC device is only a tool, one of the many components of a solution" (p. 33). Simply providing access to AAC technology does not ensure success and effective communication (Caron, 2015; McNaughton & Light, 2013). AAC systems must be carefully selected based on the skills and needs of the individual with ASD and customized to meet these individualized skills and needs (Beukelman & Mirenda, 2013; Gosnell, Costello, & Shane, 2011).

As a starting point, practitioners should consider the current language skills and needs of the individual (see Table 6.1). The individual's language skills and needs have implications for AAC system components. For example, an individual

Table 6.1. Summary of language skills and augmentative and alternative communication (AAC) needs of three communication stages

	Language skills	Likely AAC needs			
		Representation	Vocabulary	Organization	Output
Early symbolic communicator	Lexicon of approximately 50 words or fewer Communication through single words Comment on the current context	Color photographs	Salient and meaningful People, objects, actions familiar to the individual "Grabbed" from the current context	Schematic Visual Scene Displays	Digitized speech
Semantic-syntactic communicator	Lexicon of approximately 50–300 words Emergence of syntax Telegraphic word combinations with words they have learned (e.g., action + object, agent + action)	Photographs Line drawings Text—Use of sight words for known words and concepts that are hard to represent with images	Access to a growing lexicon Access to basic syntax and morphology	Taxonomic (category driven) or schematic (event or experience driven) grids Access to message window Access to keyboard	Digitized or synthesized speech
Independent communicator	Lexicon of >300 words >2- to 3-word combinations Talk about a broad range of topics	Line drawings Text—Use of sight words for known words and concepts that are hard to represent with images	Access to a growing lexicon Access to basic syntax and morphology	Access to keyboard Text-based displays Left to right orientation of common sentence construction	Synthesized speech

who is communicating via approximately 20 single words through pointing at photographs has different skills and needs than an individual who is able to use a keyboard to communicate a range of simple sentences. More specifically, these individuals necessitate different features in representation, vocabulary, organization, and output in order to best meet their skills and needs (see examples in Table 6.1). Considerations in representation include knowledge of the individual's understanding and use of symbols (e.g., Picture Communication Symbols [PCS], Blissymbols, signs, photographs). Research indicates that over time, individuals who require AAC can learn to use a variety of AAC symbols; yet, reducing some of the learning demands of AAC technologies can be achieved through matching the skills and representation needs of an individual (Light & Drager, 2007). The language skills of an individual will also impact the range, type, and number of words selected for the AAC system. The organization and layout of representations can facilitate the accuracy and efficiency with which an individual is able to locate, select, and functionally use the representations (Light & Drager, 2007). Aspects critical for consideration of layout and organization include the groupings (e.g., context, category) and arrangements (e.g., visual scene, grid) of the representations on the AAC technology (Light & Drager, 2007). In addition, it is important to consider the output of the AAC technology, specifically digitized or synthesized speech, and find a close match between the voice and the individual using the AAC system. Examples of skills and needs of early symbolic, semantic-syntactic, and independent communicators, as well as considerations of representation, vocabulary, layout/organization, and output are provided in Table 6.1 and discussed in more details in throughout the chapter.

EARLY SYMBOLIC COMMUNICATORS

Zane is a 22-year-old man with ASD who lives at home with his parents and attends an employment training program during the day. He enjoys rock-and-roll "oldies," television, and spending time with his family. Zane enjoys scrapbooking with his mom and will often point to family members when asked, "Where is ___?" He currently communicates mostly through physical communication (e.g., grabbing a communication partner's hand and leading him or her to an object/activity of interest), facial expressions, and vocalizations (e.g., laughing); however, his mother recently purchased an iPad for Zane in hopes of expanding his communication and integrating highly preferred and motivating photographs.

Language Skills of Early Symbolic Communicators

Early symbolic communicators may demonstrate a range of communication profiles. However, all early symbolic communicators use fewer than 50 symbols expressively; that is, they use fewer than 50 words to speak, sign, or communicate through aided AAC (Romski, Sevcik, Hyatt, & Cheslock, 2002). Often, early symbolic communicators utilize a range of idiosyncratic communicative means in addition to communicating with traditional symbols (Iacono, Carter, & Hook, 1998). Also described by Tager-Flusberg and colleagues (2009) as the first word phase, early symbolic communicators use nonimitated, spontaneous single words referentially and symbolically. The words in their initial lexicon can be communicated symbolically through a variety of means: from spoken words, pointing to pictures, and gestures (Owens, 2012). Often, this initial lexicon contains the names of people or object especially meaningful to the communicator (e.g., *brother, car*). The nature of these first words usually promotes social closeness, one of the earliest developing communication functions (Light, 1988). In addition, the symbols in the early symbolic stage of communication are largely bound to the context in which the concepts the symbols represent occur (Light, 1997). For instance, an early symbolic communicator might label a dog that walks by her in the park with the word *dog*.

Considerations for Individuals With ASD Who Use AAC

AAC intervention is crucial to supporting early symbolic communication and language development for individuals who do not have access to functional speech (Beukelman & Mirenda, 2013). Early symbolic communicators are not limited to young children. Rather, individuals with ASD who require AAC may enter adulthood while still in the stage of early symbolic communication (Iacono et al., 1998). AAC intervention for these early symbolic communicators is critical and can work to build upon strengths and challenges most central to individuals with ASD in this stage of language. Several of these strengths and challenges are summarized through intrinsic and extrinsic factors and listed next.

Intrinsic Factors

- Consistent demonstration of intentional communication (e.g., leading dad by the hand to show a desire for him to open a cereal container), although often not symbolic, can be harnessed and shaped toward symbolic communication; Iacono et al., 1998).

- An established, albeit limited, corpus of symbols that form a lexicon may be ready to explode with new vocabulary (Light, 1997).

- Motor movements (fine and gross), although potentially impaired, often allow for successful and efficient direct selection of aided AAC and the production of a variety of signs and gestures.

- Working memory capacity may be restricted and limit the cognitive resources that can be devoted to communication (Thistle & Wilkinson, 2013).

- Disruptions in processing auditory language may be present (Drager et al., 2006).

- Difficulty with social communication (American Psychiatric Association, 2013) may be particularly impactful for early symbolic communicators with ASD as social closeness is the earliest developing communicative function for most communicators (Light, 1988).

- Visual processing may be an area of strength (Mirenda, 2008; Shane et al., 2015).

Extrinsic Factors

- Differences in AAC device features can have a major impact on communication (Gosnell et al., 2011; Holyfield, Caron, Drager, & Light, 2018; McNaughton & Light, 2013).

- Visual scene displays (described in the Organization and Output section) may be a powerful and accessible AAC organization option to maximize early communication (Drager et al., 2014; Holyfield et al., 2018; Light & Drager, 2007).

- Quick and easy high-tech programming allows for communication about objects and people of interest within the communicative context (Schlosser et al., 2015), supporting first words.

- Communication partners carry a heavy burden in recognizing and responding to sometimes subtle, idiosyncratic communication; therefore, the competence of the communication partner can have a large impact on communication (McNaughton & Light, 2013).

- Aided AAC with visual symbols (e.g., photographs) can tap into visual processing strengths (Mirenda, 2008; Shane et al., 2015).

- Aided AAC vocabulary may be mismatched with internal lexicon if unable to otherwise express those internal symbols (Smith & Grove, 2003).

- Lack of expertise from some communication partners could have led to a history of limited success with communication, potentially leading to limited motivation or the extinguishing of previously used communicative behaviors (Iacono et al., 1998).

- Individuals with ASD who are in the early symbolic stages of communication, despite being beyond the first year of life, may be wrongly evaluated by professionals as being too early in language development to utilize or benefit from high-tech AAC (Light & McNaughton, 2012; Romski & Sevcik, 2005).

- In contrast to the highly salient and social first words common in typical development (e.g., "sissy"), the first aided symbols afforded to early symbolic communicators with ASD who require AAC are often favorite foods or objects with limited social function (Ganz, 2015; Holyfield, Drager, Kremkow, & Light 2017).

- The organizational and operational linguistic, cognitive, and visual demands of some aided AAC options (e.g., grid displays with abstract, isolated symbols) may limit early language expression and communication (Light & Drager, 2007; Drager, Light, Speltz, Fallon, & Jeffries, 2003).

High-Tech AAC Needs and Supports for Early Symbolic Communicators

AAC is a beneficial support for early symbolic communicators with communication impairment but may be particularly impactful for individuals with ASD for whom visual processing is a strength (Mirenda, 2008; Shane et al., 2015). High-tech AAC, in particular, offers specific benefits to early symbolic communicators with ASD. One key component of AAC intervention that must be investigated is the AAC app/technology itself. In recent years, there has been increased consideration of the impact of AAC system design on communication and language learning (Light & McNaughton, 2012). This includes the representation, vocabulary, organization, and output features that will need to be customized to each individual's needs (Light & Drager, 2007; see Table 6.1).

Representation and Vocabulary   Color photographs are a transparent and alluring symbol representation (Mirenda & Locke, 1989). This transparency reduces cognitive-linguistic demands for early symbolic communicators to use AAC as they do not have to devote these resources to interpreting the meaning of more abstract symbols (e.g., line drawings; Mirenda & Locke, 1989). Also, color photos are appealing to people in general. In this way, using color photos as representations may help engage communication partners and support social communication, therefore providing a scaffold for the central deficit of ASD (American Psychiatric Association, 2013).

While representation can engage communication partners who are attending to an early symbolic communicator with ASD, the voice output feature that high-tech AAC offers can attract the attention of potential communication partners. When considering vocabulary to be programmed for voice output for early symbolic communicators, high-tech AAC should be programmed with words that are especially salient in the communicator's life (Light & Drager, 2007). Particularly salient vocabulary will represent contexts that are frequently occurring in the individual's life and are interesting and motivating to that individual.

Organization and Output   When considering organization, a less cognitively demanding option for organizing vocabulary than grid displays (symbols in the display occupy individual spaces at regular intervals) are visual scene displays (VSDs; Drager et al., 2003; Light & Drager, 2007). High-tech AAC allows VSDs to be quickly and easily created by taking advantage of the onboard camera afforded by most tablets (Caron, Light, & Drager, 2016). After a moment is captured on camera, vocabulary can be programmed onto an area of the visual scene display through the creation of a "hotspot," embedding vocabulary concepts within a naturalistic scene (see Figure 6.1). In studies investigating the organization and layout of representations with typically developing children, Drager, Light, and colleagues (2003) found that the youngest children (2½-year-olds) were more accurate in locating vocabulary within VSD than grid displays. Visual scene displays seem to have several important cognitive-linguistic processing advantages, as described by Light and McNaughton (2012):

- VSDs capture the social interactions that are the contexts in which early symbolic communicators learn language and communication skills; VSDs replicate these contexts within the AAC system, thus providing visual supports for the individual's language learning and use.

- VSDs concretely represent events actually experienced by the individual, thus supporting access to language concepts via episodic memory, not just semantic memory.

- VSDs preserve functional relationships, which minimizes working memory demands.

- VSDs present language concepts within familiar event schema, thus providing more contextual support for the individual's understanding of these representations.

- VSDs preserve the conceptual relationships as well as the visual relationships (i.e., proportional size, location) between people and objects as they are experienced in the real world, thus providing greater support for young individuals' comprehension and use.

- "VSDs exploit the human capacity for rapid visual processing of naturalistic scenes" (Light & McNaughton, 2012, p. 39).

The theoretical advantages of VSDs for early symbolic communicators are numerous (Light & Drager, 2007). In addition to their theoretical importance, the literature base in this area is emerging, suggesting the benefits of VSDs on high-tech AAC devices for early symbolic communicators with ASD. When provided access to VSDs within high-tech devices, participants with ASD and profiles of early symbolic communication have demonstrated the following: 1) the acquisition of undiscriminated requests (Gevarter et al., 2016), 2) improved comprehension of directives (Schlosser et al., 2013), 3) an increase in the frequency of symbolic turns during social interactions (Holyfield et al., 2018, and 4) the expression of a wider variety of vocabulary concepts (Holyfield et al., 2018).

Case Example: Zane

As previously described and outlined in Table 6.1, steps to support the communicator include: 1) determining the individuals' current stage of language development, 2) identifying communication goals that are meaningful to the individual and his or her family, and 3) identifying technology and design considerations to support success in reaching those goals. Because providing access to AAC technology does not ensure success and effective communication, it is therefore imperative that the support plan also includes: 4) identifying and providing opportunities and effective instruction, as well as teaching strategies to reach goals, and 5) evaluating progress toward goals. Additional information in regard to relevant instructional practices are discussed in chapters 7–13 of this book, and case examples throughout this chapter provide application of these steps. The following case example illustrates a possible plan of high-tech AAC support for Zane, the young man briefly described at the beginning of this section who is an early symbolic communicator.

Step 1: Identify Stage of Language and Communication Development
Despite being 22 years old, Zane is an early symbolic communicator. His communication is largely presymbolic (e.g., facial expressions, vocalizations). However, he appears to demonstrate beginning symbolic communication by pointing to people in family photographs. Thus, given his large repertoire of presymbolic communication behaviors and his emerging use of symbolic communication and interest in photographs as symbols, Zane fits within this stage.

Step 2: Identify Goals   In order to support Zane's communication, it is important to establish goals that take into account 1) his current communication profile and 2) the events and interactions that are meaningful to his life. Examples of high-tech AAC goals include the following:

- When Zane cannot complete a task without help, he will spontaneously request assistance from his job coach using a high-tech AAC support in 8 of 10 opportunities.

- Using a high-tech AAC support, Zane will label family members when reviewing family photographs spontaneously during three consecutive scrapbooking sessions.

- Using a high-tech AAC support, Zane will engage in a minimum of five symbolic turns during an interaction with a family member about a recent family vacation or activity.

- Using a high-tech AAC support, Zane will spontaneously greet his job coach upon entry into his vocational program in at least four of five daily opportunities for three weeks.

Step 3: Identify Technology and Important Design Considerations   As discussed previously, VSDs are a promising AAC feature for early symbolic communicators like Zane. High-tech AAC featuring VSDs may be particularly supportive because the onboard cameras that most mobile technology options offer would allow Zane's communication partners to capture photos of moments from Zane's life that can become VSDs. This technology addresses many of the extrinsic factors previously outlined by offering the linguistic, cognitive, and visual benefits identified previously. The use of color photographs as the VSDs would further increase the benefits for Zane by increasing the transparency of the representation (Mirenda & Locke, 1989). The almost-instantaneous programming of VSDs available within some AAC apps would enable Zane to communicate concepts from the immediate context as they become of interest to him, reflective of how language is typically developed. For example, if Zane and his cousin attended a baseball game together, different photos could be taken to represent events that occurred or will occur (e.g., a photo of a hotdog he wants to order or his two favorite players high-fiving after a great play). See Figure 6.1 for an example.

Figure 6.1.   An example of a custom, high-tech AAC display created to support an early symbolic communicator. Specifically, this is an example of a visual scene display for Zane, when watching baseball. The dashed circles represent hotspots with preprogrammed messages. For example, this visual scene could be programmed to say "Nice hit!" and "Strike."

Step 4: Identify and Provide Opportunities and Instruction   Providing access
to appropriate technology would not be sufficient in supporting Zane's early symbolic communication or transition to more sophisticated use of syntax and symbol
combinations (see Step 5). Zane will also require access to meaningful, systematic, evidence-based instruction to support his AAC use. To enhance effectiveness,
instruction should be 1) organized around a meaningful activity; 2) responsive to
developmental needs/interests of Zane, and 3) supportive of multiple and interesting opportunities to continue to expand knowledge and learning (Light &
McNaughton, 2013). An example of an activity that may be meaningful to Zane
would be scrapbooking that he enjoys participating in with his mother. High-tech
AAC intervention could be built responsively to Zane's limited working memory
and attentional demands, as an early symbolic communicator, by shifting the activity to digital "scrapbooking" on Zane's communication tablet. This way, the activity and the communication context would occur together as VSDs, therefore limiting attentional demands on Zane (Light & Drager, 2007). Finally, as this is activity
in which Zane and his mother regularly engage, he would have multiple opportunities to practice and grow his symbolic communication within this context.

Also, given the impact of communication partner skills and knowledge identified under extrinsic factors, intervention for Zane and other early symbolic communicators should focus largely on training and informing communication partners. In addition to learning communication support strategies, partners should
be familiarized with high-tech AAC and relevant instructional practices (see
Section III for additional discussions of instructional practices) so as to use it effectively in interactions with early symbolic communicators. As you can imagine, the
digital scrapbooking example could not be effective if Zane's mother does not feel
comfortable or confident using the technology.

Step 5: Evaluate Progress   Even with utilizing the most promising AAC technology and instruction, it is important for Zane's team to monitor his communication and receptive and expressive language to determine if the high-tech AAC
intervention implemented has the intended positive effects. Data should be systematically gathered for each goal. Progress should be communicated regularly with
the important individuals in Zane's life (e.g., his parents), and goals and intervention should be adjusted to respond to progress made so that Zane's progress does
not grow stagnant as the result of lack of increases in access and opportunities.
While addressing Zane's current communication strengths and needs, his AAC
team should consider future technology and instruction that may benefit Zane as
he transitions into the next stage of early language development (see the following
section on semantic-syntactic communicators). With these considerations, Zane's
team should lay foundations for the technology and opportunities that he will
require when these stages are reached.

SEMANTIC-SYNTACTIC COMMUNICATORS

Erica is 10 years old and has a diagnosis of ASD. She was first introduced to AAC
when she was 3 years old through early intervention. At the time, the interventionist provided recommendations to create a binder with removable graphic symbols
for things Erica likes. The family expressed that they experienced a lot of success
with this system, finally understanding what Erica wanted—from places she wanted

to go, to foods she wanted to eat, and toys she wanted. As she entered kindergarten, teachers added to the binder with new concepts represented as graphic symbols. The speech-language pathologist suggested adding a sentence strip on the front of the binder so Erica could create a sentence (e.g., "I want chips," "I want ball"). Over the years, Erica was making progress, acquiring and using over 70 graphic icons and occasionally spontaneously combining two words to request (e.g., red ball, more juice). However, the family expressed frustration with both management and a need for growing the current AAC support, so they purchased an iPad with an AAC application. They hope the iPad can support better management of all the graphic symbols the current binder contains and allow Erica to communicate more complex thoughts for a variety of functions more efficiently.

Language Skills of Semantic-Syntactic Communicators

Semantic-syntactic communicators have acquired a core lexicon of approximately 50 words and begin to experience a critical shift from expressing single- to multi-word messages (Nigam, Schlosser, & Lloyd, 2006; Owens, 2012). Described by Tager-Flusberg and colleagues (2009) as the word combination phase, this phase includes the emergence of syntax; the grammar, structure, or order of elements in a language statement; and the onset of generative language (Binger & Light, 2008). At first, telegraphic word combinations emerge, predominantly consisting of words that they have already learned. For example, the words *more* and *juice* become *more juice*. In addition, early word combinations are characterized by primarily two-term semantic relationships (i.e., the meaning and relationships between words—e.g., action + object for *drink + juice*). The early word combinations are often devoid of inflectional marking, like *daddy car* meaning *daddy's car*, or function words like *want cracker* meaning *I want a cracker*. Linguistic development for semantic-syntactic communicators continues at a rapid rate, with acquisition of a minimum core lexicon of 200–300 words (Owens, 2012) and regular use of basic morphology and syntactic structures in conversation.

Considerations for Individuals With ASD Who Use AAC

Individuals who use AAC, when provided with supports and intervention, can expand their lexicons and develop early syntactic structures (Cafiero, 2001; Drager et al., 2006; Romski, Sevcik, Robinson, Mervis, & Bertrand, 1996). The transition to use of words in combination and development of basic morphology and syntactic structures is important to all individuals, including those individuals with ASD who use AAC. The use of multi-symbol messages with basic morphology and syntax by individuals who use AAC will ultimately support the expansion of content and function of messages (Wilkinson, Romski, & Sevcik, 1994). This additional information will allow individuals to clearly convey increasingly more complex messages to partners (Binger & Light, 2008). Yet, the transition from single-symbol to multi-symbol utterances, and then use of basic grammar, is recognized as a difficult step for individuals who use graphic-based AAC systems (Binger & Light, 2008). A number of challenges have been documented in the literature for reasons that individuals who use AAC may be at a single-symbol message impasse despite seemingly being capable of much more sophisticated language. Several of these intrinsic and extrinsic factors are summarized and listed next.

Intrinsic Factors

- A quickly growing vocabulary can allow for the combination of words and the beginning of more complex syntax; limitations in expressive and receptive language can impact an individual's ability to combine graphic symbols (Binger, Kent-Walsh, Ewing, & Taylor, 2010; Sevcik, 2006).

- A more established language repertoire can support the use of such language in a wider range of interactions.

- As individuals produce longer and more complex AAC utterances, more effort and working memory is required (Lund & Light, 2003); consequently, individuals may prefer to communicate more telegraphically in order to maintain a conversational rate of communication (Lund & Light, 2003; Sutton, Soto, & Blockberger, 2002).

- Learning and using abstract words and morphemes required for syntactic communication may be less motivating than highly motivating early words (Light, 1997).

Extrinsic Factors

- Productive experiences, not just comprehension experiences, can support the transition from single to multiple words (Sutton et al., 2002).

- World experiences are important to the development and use of language (Light, 1997); shared reading about unfamiliar people and places, a valuable context for learning syntax, can supplement limitations in world experiences.

- AAC systems must represent abstract concepts, like possession and present progressive tense; the nonlinguistic and iconic nature of these concepts poses challenges for individuals who are to derive meaning from the representations in the AAC system (Smith, 2005).

- Elements of syntax are complicated and require understanding and use of more rules (Sutton et al., 2002).

- AAC symbols often represent many concepts and therefore require metalinguistic skills by the individual who uses AAC to use the concept flexibly; for example, Light (1997) discussed that the concept "more" is often represented by someone pouring more juice into a glass that contains some juice; yet, it is expected that the individual use the *more* symbol (represented by the individual pouring more juice) to also request *more cookies* or *more bouncing*, whereby the individual who uses AAC must dissociate the term (*more*) from the object represented (*juice*) (Light, 1997).

- An individual's AAC systems may not be programmed with supports to foster use of symbol combinations or correct grammar; for example, the AAC system may have a limited number of graphic symbols available to the individual, or the graphic symbols may primarily consist of nouns (Binger & Light, 2008; Sutton et al., 2002).

- An individual may need to be explicitly taught how to produce multi-symbol messages, yet intervention goals may not target multisymbol utterances or use of correct syntax and grammar (Nigam et al., 2006).

- The individual who uses AAC experiences input/output asymmetry, whereby the channel of input (provided by a communication partner) is spoken language, and the channel of output (messages by the individual who uses AAC) is multimodal communication; this results in a paucity of language models occurring within the modality used expressively by the individual who uses AAC (Smith & Grove, 2003).

- Communication partners may ask the individual who uses AAC questions requiring only a single-word response, take more conversational turns, and co-construct the AAC user's messages to fill in missing information; these behaviors by the partner ultimately preclude the need or opportunity to produce longer utterances (Binger & Light, 2008).

High-Tech AAC Supports for Semantic-Syntactic Communicators

Despite intrinsic and extrinsic factors impacting linguistic development, some evidence exists to support that individuals with ASD who use AAC can learn to communicate using multisymbol combinations using low- and high-tech aided AAC supports (e.g., Nigam et al., 2006; van der Meer et al., 2013). Yet, to date, research is limited in this area, with research primarily focusing on requesting (Holyfield et al., 2017; Mirenda, 2008) and symbol combinations involving a carrier phrase (e.g., *I want + request for specific item*) (Still, Rehfeldt, Whelan, May, & Dymond, 2014). For example, in a meta-analysis (24 articles) and a research synthesis (44 articles) of single-subject interventions with individuals with ASD who use AAC, the intervention studies reviewed overwhelmingly focused on teaching the individuals to make simple requests (Ganz et al. 2012; Wendt, Schlosser, & Lloyd, 2006). More recent papers have investigated the use of mobile technology with AAC applications with people with ASD (e.g., Flores et al., 2012; Ganz, Boles, Goodwyn, & Flores, 2014; Gevarter et al., 2016), yet these studies continue to focus on more early symbolic communication skills, like requesting or labeling objects using a single word or message. More research is urgently needed to advance the understanding of how high-tech AAC can be used to facilitate skills beyond communication for the function of requesting and the critical shift toward multiword utterances.

In addition to intervention components, continued research is necessary related to the design of high-tech systems. As Light and Drager (2007, p. 206) stated, "Although the positive benefits of a range of AAC systems have been documented, the full potential of AAC technologies has not yet been realized for young children with complex communication needs." Attention to the design of high-tech AAC systems, with a view to better matching the specific needs and strengths of individuals with ASD, is needed (Ganz, 2015; Gosnell et al., 2011). For example, research is needed to better understand features that may optimally support the transition from single-word utterances to multiword utterances for individuals with ASD. Specific components for individualized consideration can include the representation of language concepts, vocabulary, organization/layout, and output (Light & Drager, 2007); see Table 6.1.

Representation and Vocabulary   Graphic symbols like photographs and line drawings (e.g., PCS) capitalize on the visuospatial strengths commonly seen in people with ASD (Drager et al., 2006). Over time, individuals with ASD can learn to understand and use a variety of symbols (Shane et al., 2015). However, the area of representation often contributes negatively to linguistic development; potentially hindering instead of supporting the transition from single-word to multiword use and the use of basic syntax and morphology (Light, 1997). AAC symbols often represent many concepts and therefore require strong metalinguistic skills by the individual who uses AAC to use the graphic symbol flexibly (refer to the *more* example described previously).

When considering ways to support the transition from single-word to multiword utterances and basic syntax and morphology, at a minimum, the AAC system should provide access to a range of concepts (including descriptive, social, and relationship concepts) and continue to be programmed to develop a growing lexicon. Early semantic combinations should be targeted in intervention, initially with concepts that are familiar (e.g., agent + action; see Figure 6.2). Due to the inherent constraints within the AAC system that require reliance on graphic symbols, parallel instruction in literacy is recommended (Light & McNaughton, 2013; Mirenda, 2008). The morphologic markers, to indicate tense or plural forms, for example, can more explicitly be taught through decoding and sight words (Light & McNaughton, 2013), potentially reducing the learning demands that are currently required to acquire the same grammatical markers through abstract and nonlinguistic iconic representations.

Organization and Output   The organization, layout, and output of representations, either graphic or text, can serve to facilitate or impede the accuracy and efficiency with which an individual can locate, select, and functionally use AAC vocabulary concepts (Thistle & Wilkinson, 2015). SGDs have frequently organized representations in grid-array formats in which language concepts are represented by separate symbols in boxes organized in rows and columns (Wilkinson & McIlvane, 2013) with synthesized or digitized speech. The grid formats can be arranged in taxonomic (category driven), schematic (event or experience driven), or iconic encoding (combinations of semantic associations) layouts. Research by Light and colleagues (2004) found that children, by ages 4 and 5, were able to locate vocabulary accurately in VSDs and grid displays but continued to experience difficulty with iconic encoding. Limited research exists related to high-tech AAC system organization, and future research is needed to compare the demands of different layouts for individuals with ASD.

Case Example: Erica

The following case example illustrates a possible plan of high-tech AAC support for Erica; the girl briefly described at the beginning of this section who is a semantic-syntactic communicator. As with the case of Zane, five main steps are discussed in order to consider Erica's individuals needs in relation to linguistic development and system design.

Step 1: Identify Stage of Language and Communication Development   Erica is beyond the early symbolic stage, as she has been successfully using symbols to communicate since she was 3. She also has a lexicon of 50–75 words yet is not independently generating novel thoughts with necessary grammar and syntax in a conversation. Erica occasionally uses two graphic symbols together to request (e.g., *more juice*) and is experiencing the need for a critical shift from single-word messages to multiword messages; she can be described as entering the semantic-syntactic stage.

Step 2: Identify Goals   Erica's family and team are interested in supporting Erica in participating in a broad range of communication functions. In addition, intervention goals should support Erica to expand her utterances from single words to multiword messages. Examples of goals follow.

- Using a high-tech AAC support, Erica will spontaneously produce at least a 2- to 4-word utterance to request and comment, across 3 communication contexts, for 1 month.

- Using a high-tech AAC support, Erica will use morphological endings to denote past (-ed) and present (-ing) during a shared book-reading activity, with 90% accuracy.

- Using a high-tech AAC support, Erica will engage in a 3-minute interaction with a peer or family member about a recent activity taking at least 5 independent turns.

- Using a high-tech AAC support, Erica will ask and respond to partner-focused questions using appropriate syntax, in at least 4 of 5 daily opportunities for 3 weeks.

Step 3: Identify Technology and Important Design Considerations   A growing number of families are adopting and embracing the use of mobile technologies as high-tech AAC systems (Caron, Shane, & Costello, 2014). Although, in this case, the family has made a switch to use of technology, the underlying purposes of communication and the need for more opportunities remain the same. Since Erica can recognize and use a range of representations, from photographs to line drawings, graphic-based symbols from her low-tech support should be consistent and programmed to match these representations within the new high-tech support. In addition, new concepts need to be programmed and provided as Erica's current system primarily focuses on nouns. Early semantic combinations should be targeted in intervention, initially with concepts that are familiar (e.g., agent + action, descriptor + object). Displays programmed with voice output and organized in schematic (event or experience driven) grids could potentially foster this early word combination, with minimal navigation demands (see Figure 6.2). In parallel, literacy instruction should be provided. As words for highly motivating and commonly used graphic symbols are learned, text can replace the icons. As seen in Figure 6.2, Erica enjoys using electronic devices. The grid display supports access to combining words to comment, request, and ask simple questions. The words that she has learned are represented with orthography rather than the graphic symbol. These text-based displays support the development of basic syntax. With the addition of a keyboard, morphology can be addressed, supporting Erica's transition to the next linguistic stage.

Step 4: Identify and Provide Opportunities and Instruction   Instruction should be 1) organized around a meaningful activity, 2) responsive to the developmental needs/interests of Erica, and 3) supportive of multiple opportunities to continue to expand knowledge and learning (Light & McNaughton, 2009). Classroom activities may be a valuable opportunity to provide instruction for Erica and other school-age semantic-syntactic communicators. Erica's vocabulary, like everyone's, has room to grow and mature. Vocabulary appearing in school-required readings

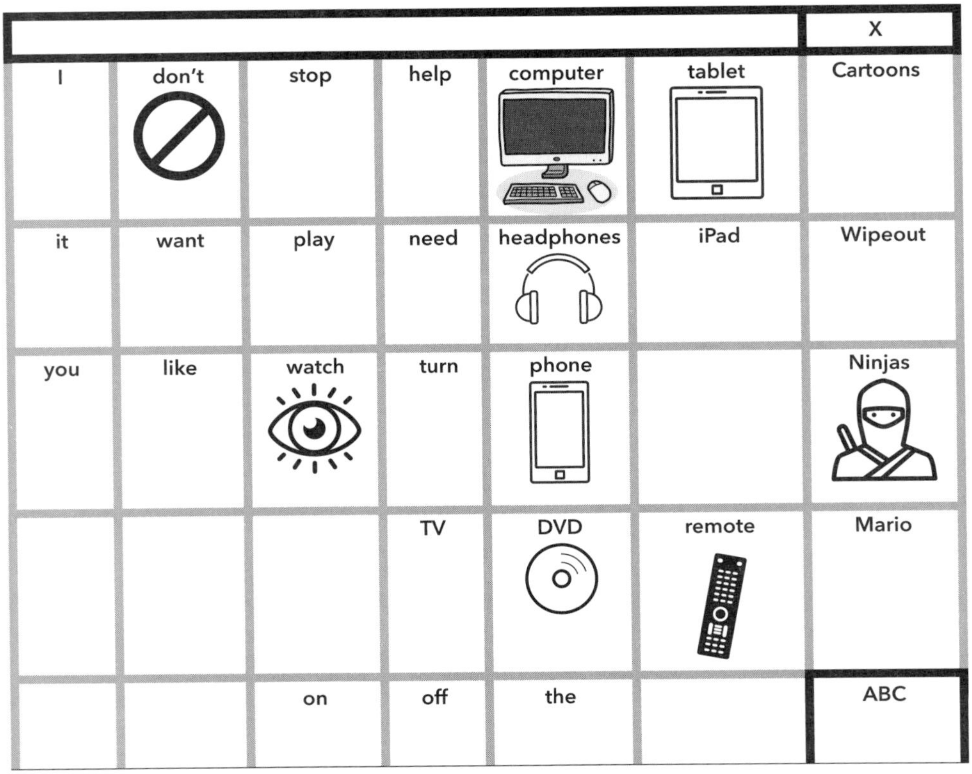

I	don't	stop	help	computer	tablet	X Cartoons
it	want	play	need	headphones	iPad	Wipeout
you	like	watch	turn	phone		Ninjas
			TV	DVD	remote	Mario
		on	off	the		ABC

Figure 6.2. An example of a custom, high-tech AAC display created to support a semantic-syntactic communicator. This display corresponds to the case of Erica, who uses a schematically organized grid display. The display expands from only use of the carrier phrase "I want" and supports the option to combine 2–4 symbols to request ("Turn on computer."), comment ("I like cartoons."), or ask a simple question ("Do you like Wipeout?") using simple syntax, but lacking morphology. *Note:* Graphic icons were removed once the sight words were acquired.

or frequently observed in the conversation of same-age peers would make for meaningful additions to her expressive repertoire. In addition, considering common instructional structures in Erica's classroom might help professionals prioritize syntactic structures to teach Erica (see Section III for relevant instructional strategies). For example, if students in Erica's classroom are expected to ask questions of each other and the teacher, teaching Erica a consistent question asking syntactic structure could be a priority. She could then use this familiar form to input newly learned classroom vocabulary to participate effectively in group instruction.

Step 5: Evaluate Progress   The team should continue to monitor Erica's progress, collecting data on her current goals, including her accuracy and use of multi-symbol combinations, basic syntax, and expansion of lexicon for a broad range of communicative functions. In parallel, the team should monitor words that Erica is acquiring during literacy instruction. As the data indicate acquisition of words, these words should replace graphic symbols, with text only, within the high-tech SGD. This representation transition will lay some foundations for progression to the next linguistic stage of independent communication.

INDEPENDENT COMMUNICATORS

Mateo was 6 years old when the practitioners first met him. He has a diagnosis of autism and uses a combination of behavioral and gestural communication in addition to aided AAC. For example, Mateo uses behavioral communication (e.g., gets up and walks away from the table) to refuse or protest. He also used his high-tech AAC system to answer wh- questions, request, and comment. Mateo has transitioned from using a four-button grid display within a mobile technology AAC app to request preferred items, to using a grid display that integrates graphic icons, text, and a keyboard within a 60-icon grid. Mateo's school speech-language pathologist said that in the past 2 years, Mateo has gone from being prompted to combine words to independently combining multiple words to communicating in full sentences, often with appropriate morphology (e.g., -ing, -ed, -s). In school, the teacher and SLP are currently working on using the AAC system with peers and supporting Mateo to develop and share simple narratives.

Profile of Independent Communicators

Independent communicators have increased their lexicon to well over 1,000 words (Owens, 2012); as they continue to combine words to indicate that they would like something to happen again (e.g., *more juice*) and to deny something (e.g., *no sleep*), their combinations gradually expand in function and utterance length (Owens, 2012). For example, independent communicators begin to include description of what something looks like or feels like (e.g., *big truck*) and use *and* to join two sentences (e.g., *I ate crackers and I played trains*). Caregiver's expansions and responses support this continued linguistic growth—demonstrating how to make a sentence longer, providing opportunities to learn new words, and modeling appropriate morphology (Yoder & Warren, 2002). Earlier conversations are often limited to present moments, yet independent communicators soon expand their contributions to incorporate information about the jointly remembered past events and make-believe stories (Soto, Hartmann, & Wilkins, 2006). Described by Tager-Flusberg and colleagues (2009) as the sentences and complex language phases, these phases include the development and ability of independent communicators to talk about a broad range of age-appropriate topics in flexible ways, accurately describe a sequence of events, and share narratives wherein they provide the information needed for listeners to make sense of a story (Owens, 2012).

Considerations for Individuals With ASD Who Use AAC

As with the previous stages of linguistic development, the transition to more advanced use of language is recognized as a difficult step. Intrinsic and extrinsic factors previously discussed continue to contribute to the level of competence in which individuals with ASD communicate. For example, by this point in linguistic development individuals with ASD may have access to a high-tech AAC system, yet the system may not include morphological or syntactic forms for more advanced communication (Sutton et al., 2002). This lack of access is often exacerbated by limited language models and limited opportunities to communicate and learn (Light, 1997). These factors combine to limit growth toward independent communication.

Intrinsic factors that create challenges in language development might slowly change over time, as individuals with ASD develop stronger expressive and receptive language or the motivation to communicate for a variety of functions, across partners and contexts. Yet extrinsic factors can potentially be a starting point to effect change in the limited outcomes that currently exist for individuals with ASD. Possibilities include starting with system design, changing expectations, or providing effective interventions.

Mirenda (2008) proposed a paradigm shift. The shift calls for the use of "back door approaches" (p. 220) to address many of the extrinsic factors that potentially limit outcomes for individuals with ASD who use AAC. More specifically, the conceptual shift calls for AAC clinicians and researchers to part ways from a traditional "front door view" (p. 221) of ASD, which commonly includes low expectations, limited access to instruction in literacy and other academics, and AAC interventions that place limits on long-term language and communication development (e.g., a preponderance of AAC interventions focusing on single-word requesting). The "back door approach," rather, provides interventions that capitalize on specific strengths and interests of individuals with ASD (e.g., visual memory, visual processing, attention to technology) and provides compensatory supports to address intrinsic factors (e.g., language comprehension; Mirenda, 2008). Furthermore, expectations are shifted to presume competence, technologies are redesigned to minimize learning demands, and interventions/instruction are provided without readiness models preventing individuals with ASD access to more vocabulary, literacy, or academics.

High-Tech AAC Supports for Independent Communicators

Research has emerged that has focused on extrinsic factors, specifically related to system design (e.g., Caron, Light, Holyfield, & McNaughton, 2018; Gillespie-Smith & Fletcher-Watson, 2014; Liang, Wilkinson, & Regiec, 2015). The results of these studies show promise and provide suggestions for design to support individuals with ASD. These results are just the beginning, and future research is needed in order to understand how to provide individuals with AAC supports that maximize language development. Like the previous stages, consideration of the representations of language concepts, vocabulary, organization/layout, and output (Light & Drager, 2007) are important to match the needs of an individual with ASD (see Table 6.1). These considerations, in this later stage, should focus on contributions to the development and implementation of robust and generative communication systems for individuals with ASD.

Representation and Vocabulary   The areas of representation and vocabulary often contribute negatively toward the area of linguistic development. AAC symbols often represent a heavy noun-based vocabulary (Light & Drager, 2007), using graphic symbols that represent objects in isolation and often with abstract pictorial conventions (e.g., arrows or wavy lines to denote implied movement). Graphic-based AAC systems often continue to be used, even when individuals have a robust sight word vocabulary and know many of the orthographic representations for the concepts within their AAC systems (Caron et al., 2018). Light, McNaughton, Jakobs, and Hershberger (2014) conceptualized and developed a potential solution to support the transition from graphic symbols to literacy through AAC system design. The changes to AAC design, specifically the Transition to Literacy (T2L) software features, are grounded in the state of the science in visual cognitive processing, literacy instruction, and instructional design (Light et al., 2014) and incorporate the following:

- Selection of a graphic symbol from a personalized AAC system by the individual who uses AAC to support learning driven by the individual's interests and needs (Light & McNaughton, 2009)

- Text dynamically presented on the AAC system's screen, utilizing movement or animation as an attractor of visual attention to increase the individual's attention to the text (Wilkinson & Jagaroo, 2004)

- Text paired with graphic symbol and speech output, allowing direct active pairing to support learning of the association between written word and referent (picture symbol and/or spoken word; Browder & Xin, 1998)

- Text eventually replacing the graphic symbol and consistently incorporated into communication, providing increased opportunities for learning and use throughout the day

Although the design changes are intended to complement, not replace, literacy instruction, emerging research supports that individuals with ASD and CCN can acquire words through system design changes alone (Caron et al., 2018). In a study with four individuals with diagnoses of severe ASD, CCN, and limited literacy skills (e.g., fewer than 25 sight words and no decoding skills), all four individuals (ages 9–19) made gains from baseline (range: +54% to +88%) after exposure to the T2L software features (a range of 60–288 exposures to each word) (Caron et al., 2018). Another study by Caron and colleagues (2018) used the same T2L software feature with five individuals with diagnoses of severe ASD, CCN, and some literacy skills (e.g., identification of all letter sounds, 150–300 sight words, and no decoding skills). All five individuals (ages 6–14) acquired a minimum of 10 single sight words and made gains from baseline (range: +45% to +69%) after only 20–32 exposures to each word (Caron et al., 2018). Although continued research is needed, this design change may be one way to support the transition away from graphic-based systems, with the future potential of using orthography to bootstrap syntactic development and support use of more advanced and independent communication (Light, McNaughton, & Caron, 2016).

Organization and Output   If the individual currently cannot rely on his or her decoding and encoding skills to operate orthographic-based systems, high-tech SGDs can continue to be arranged in a grid format with synthesized output. Layouts could transition from a common main page existing of categorical options to text-based displays supporting left to right orientation of common sentence construction order (e.g., pronouns in the left columns, verbs in the middle, and articles and conjunctions on the right; see Figure 6.3). Access and instruction to support combination of single words and spelling to complete sentences for novel messages will be an important focus of this linguistic stage as the individual continues to develop toward being an independent communicator. In addition, as the individual no longer requires the selection of whole words, a completely keyboard-based system could become the primary form of communication or an option to supplement a more traditional AAC system, such as the use of text-to-speech applications on smaller and portable mobile technologies.

Case Example: Mateo

The following case example illustrates a possible plan of high-tech AAC support for Mateo, the boy briefly described at the beginning of this section who is a later syntactic and emerging independent communicator. As with the previous cases, five main steps are discussed in order to consider Mateo's individual needs in relation to linguistic development and system design.

Step 1: Identify Stage of Language and Communication Development Mateo has been successfully using graphic icons and text to communicate for a range of functions. He is generating novel thoughts with basic grammar and syntax to take turns in a conversation. Thus, he can be described as a later syntactic communicator and on his way to becoming an independent communicator across partners and contexts.

Step 2: Identify Goals Mateo's team is interested in supporting him to continue to communicate with age-appropriate grammar and syntax as well as generate and share simple narratives. In addition, they would like to see more independent communication with a range of partners to expand his SGD use with less familiar people and peers. Use of the keyboard can also expand partners and contexts, as use of traditional orthography will allow his use of social media, e-mail, and texting in the future. Examples of goals to address the items previously discussed are as follows:

- Using a high-tech AAC support, Mateo will respond to questions or share information about past and current events, producing a short narrative of 2–5 sentences, across 3 communication partners, for 1 month.

- Using a high-tech AAC support, Mateo will use his keyboard to type 2–5 sentence short stories, to describe a photograph, with 90% accuracy.

- Using a high-tech AAC support, Mateo will spontaneously ask questions about the communication partner using correct syntax, across 3 different communication contexts, for 3 weeks.

Step 3: Identify Technology and Important Design Considerations Displays programmed with voice output and organized with text representing common sight words and personally relevant vocabulary, in addition to access to a keyboard, continue to foster his independent communication with minimal navigation demands. Text can continue to replace graphic icons as Mateo acquires more words, and a keyboard with prediction could potentially replace the current 60-grid layout (see Figure 6.3).

Step 4: Identify and Provide Opportunities and Instruction Instruction should be 1) organized around a meaningful activity within a range of communication contexts, 2) responsive to the developmental needs/interests of Mateo, and 3) supportive of multiple and interesting opportunities, with varied partners, to continue to expand his communicative competence (Light & McNaughton, 2009). Show-and-tell is part of 6-year-old Mateo's classroom routine. In that case, one meaningful way to work on Mateo's generation of text may be to have him choose his show-and-tell topic weeks beforehand and spend time each week working with him on writing about it. This writing could be programmed into his AAC app as

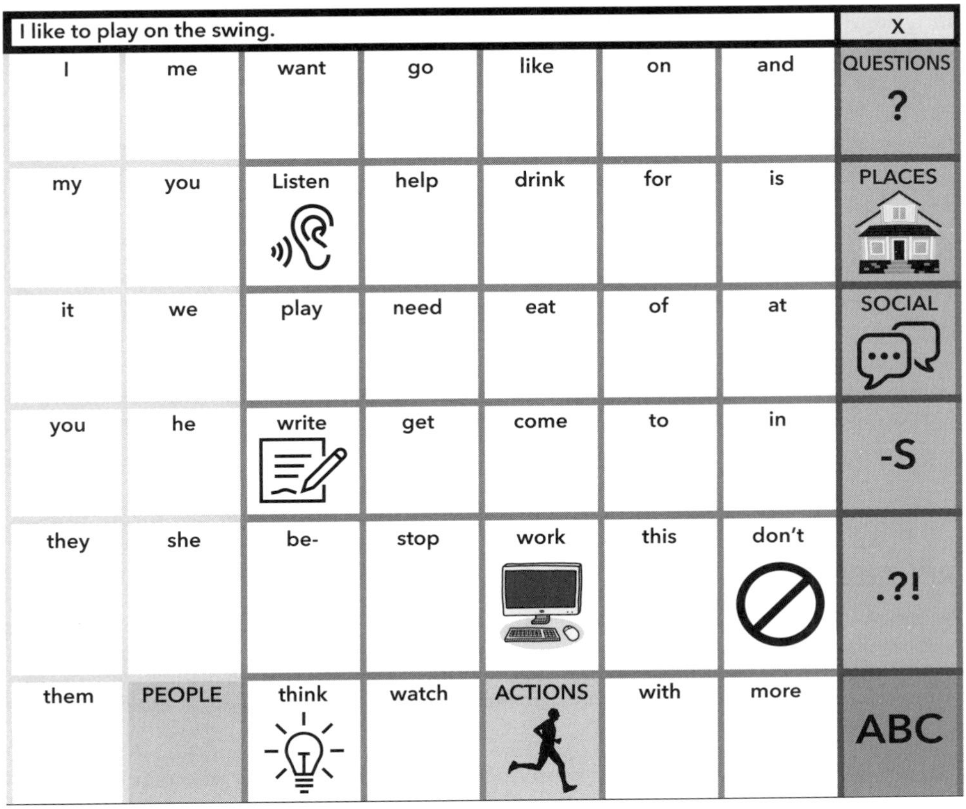

I like to play on the swing.							X
I	me	want	go	like	on	and	QUESTIONS ?
my	you	Listen	help	drink	for	is	PLACES
it	we	play	need	eat	of	at	SOCIAL
you	he	write	get	come	to	in	-S
they	she	be-	stop	work	this	don't	.?!
them	PEOPLE	think	watch	ACTIONS	with	more	ABC

Figure 6.3. An example of a custom, high-tech AAC display created to support a later syntactic or independent communicator. This display corresponds to the case of Mateo, who has the graphic icons removed once he can read the words. Upon selection of an item in the grid, the dynamic display shows a new set of relevant and related icons and words.

a sequence of buttons that he could then use to share with the class when it is his turn for show and tell. In this way, the activity could support both his orthographic and syntactic development as well as his classroom participation and interaction with peers. In addition, choosing storybooks with a repetitive syntactic structure that is new to Mateo, and modeling use of that structure with repeated readings of those books, could support Mateo's development of complex syntactic use of his text-based AAC grid.

Step 5: Evaluate Progress   The team should continue to monitor Mateo's progress, collecting data on his current goals. In parallel, the team should monitor Mateo's use of a keyboard and prediction. These features can continue to support Mateo's development of independent and generative communication across partners and communication contexts.

CONCLUSION

This chapter focused on high-tech AAC considerations through discussion of three linguistic stages: early symbolic communicators, semantic-syntactic communicators, and independent communicators. Promising high-tech supports can promote language development and communication in each of these stages—early symbolic communicators may benefit from photo VSDs on computer-based systems to promote social interaction and early expression; semantic-syntactic communicators can be provided with high-tech supports to promote the combination of words and the development of syntax; and later syntactic and independent communicators benefit from word prediction and other features offered by high-tech AAC. Still, research examining these issues has been somewhat sparse, with a preponderance of research focused on requesting, labeling, or matching icons. Additional investigation is necessary to fully understand intervention and design considerations that will best support the unique needs of individuals with ASD in each of the stages of linguistic development. As Mirenda stated in 2008, "In the immortal words of Mick Jagger, we 'can't get no satisfaction' until we have figured out how to provide every individual with ASD with a viable, robust, flexible, and generative communication system that will support long-term language development" (p. 225). Future research is urgently needed to advance understanding in the field in order to maximize language learning and development for individuals with ASD and CCN, including with the use of AAC and communication supports and interventions.

REFERENCES

American Psychiatric Association. (2013). *Diagnostic and statistical manual of mental disorders* (5th ed.). Arlington, VA: Author.

Beukelman, D., & Mirenda, P. (2013). *Augmentative and alternative communication: Supporting children and adults with complex communication needs* (4th ed.). Baltimore, MD: Paul H. Brookes Publishing Co.

Binger, C., Kent-Walsh, J., Ewing, C., & Taylor, S. (2010). Teaching educational assistants to facilitate the multisymbol message productions of young students who require augmentative and alternative communication. *American Journal of Speech-Language Pathology, 19,* 108–120. doi:10.1044/1058-0360

Binger, C., & Light, J. (2008). The morphology and syntax of individuals who use AAC: Research review and implications for effective practice. *Augmentative and Alternative Communication, 24,* 123–138.

Browder, D. M., & Xin, Y. P. (1998). A meta-analysis and review of sight word research and its implications for teaching functional reading to individuals with moderate and severe disabilities. *The Journal of Special Education, 32,* 130–153.

Cafiero, J. M. (2001). The effect of an augmentative communication intervention on the communication, behavior, and academic program of an adolescent with autism. *Focus on Autism and Other Developmental Disabilities, 16,* 179–189.

Caron, J. G. (2015). "We bought an iPad": Considering family priorities, needs, and preferences as an AAC support provider. *SIG 12 Perspectives on Augmentative and Alternative Communication, 24,* 5–11. doi:10.1044/aac24.15

Caron, J., Light, J., & Drager, K. (2016). Operational demands of AAC mobile technology applications on programming vocabulary and engagement during professional and child interactions. *Augmentative and Alternative Communication, 32,* 12–24. doi:10.3109/07434618.2015.1126636

Caron, J., Light, J., Holyfield, C. & McNaughton, D. (2018). Effects of dynamic text in an AAC app on sight word reading for individuals with autism spectrum disorder. *Augmentative and Alternative Communication.* Advanced online publication. doi:10.1080/07434618.2018.1457715.

Caron, J. G., Shane, H., & Costello, J. (2014, July 23) *Mobile device and app selection: Who's driving the decision?* Presentation at the 16th Biennial ISAAC Conference, Lisbon, Portugal.

Drager, K., Light, J., Currall, J., Muttiah, N., Smith, V., Kreis, D., . . . Wiscount, J. (2014, August). "Just in time" technologies and visual scene displays: Adolescents with severe disabilities. Presentation at the biennial conference of the International Society of Augmentative and Alternative Communication, Lisbon, Portugal.

Drager, K. D., Light, J., Speltz, J., Fallon, K., & Jeffries, L. (2003). The performance of typically developing 2 1/2-year-olds on dynamic display AAC technologies with different system layouts and language organizations. *Journal of Speech, Language, and Hearing Research, 46*, 298–312.

Drager, K. D., Postal, V., Carrolus, L., Castellano, M., Gagliano, C., & Glynn, J. (2006). The effect of aided language modeling on symbol comprehension and production in 2 preschoolers with autism. *American Journal of Speech-Language Pathology, 15*, 112–125.

Flores, M., Musgrove, K., Renner, S., Hinton, V., Strozier, S., Franklin, S., & Hil, D. (2012). A comparison of communication using the Apple iPad and a picture-based system. *Augmentative and Alternative Communication, 28*, 74–84. doi:10.3109/07434618.2011.644579

Ganz, J. (2015). AAC interventions for individuals with autism spectrum disorders: State of the science and future research directions. *Augmentative and Alternative Communication, 31*, 203–214. doi:10.3109/07434618.2015.1047532

Ganz, J. B., Boles, M. B., Goodwyn, F. D., & Flores, M. M. (2014). Efficacy of handheld electronic visual supports to enhance vocabulary in children with ASD. *Focus on Autism and Other Developmental Disabilities, 29*, 3–12. doi:10.1177/1088357613504991

Ganz, J. B., Earles-Vollrath, T. L., Heath, A. K., Parker, R. I., Rispoli, M. J., & Duran, J. B. (2012). A meta-analysis of single case research studies on aided augmentative and alternative communication systems with individuals with autism spectrum disorders. *Journal of Autism and Developmental Disorders, 42*, 60–74. doi:10.1007/s10803-011-1212-2

Gevarter, C., O'Reilly, M. F., Kuhn, M., Watkins, L., Ferguson, R., Sammarco, N., . . . Sigafoos, J. (2016). Assessing the acquisition of requesting a variety of preferred items using different speech generating device formats for children with autism spectrum disorder. *Assistive Technology.* Advance online publication. doi:10.1080/10400435.2016.1143411

Gillespie-Smith, K., & Fletcher-Watson, S. (2014). Designing AAC systems for children with autism: Evidence from eye tracking research. *Augmentative and Alternative Communication, 30*, 160–171. doi:10.3109/07434618.2014.905635

Gosnell, J., Costello, J., & Shane, H. (2011). Using a clinical approach to answer "What communication apps should we use?" *SIG 12 Perspectives on Augmentative and Alternative Communication, 20*, 87–96.

Hershberger, D. (2011). Mobile technology and AAC apps from an AAC developer's perspective. *SIG 12 Perspectives on Augmentative and Alternative Communication, 20*, 28–33.

Holyfield, C., Caron, J., Drager, K., & Light, J. (2018). Effects of mobile technology featuring visual scene displays and just in time programming on the communication turns by pre-adolescent and adolescent beginning communicators. *International Journal of Speech-Language Pathology.* Advance online publication. doi:10.1080/17549507.2018.1441440

Holyfield, C., Drager, K., Kremkow, J., & Light, J. (2017). Systematic review of AAC intervention research for adolescents and adults with autism spectrum disorder. *Augmentative and Alternative Communication, 33*, 201-212. doi:10.1080/07434618.2017.1370495

Iacono, T., Carter, M., & Hook, J. (1998). Identification of intentional communication in students with severe and multiple disabilities. *Augmentative and Alternative Communication, 14*, 102–114.

Liang, J., Wilkinson, K., & Regiec, C. (2015, November). Gaze toward social interactions in photographs by individuals with autism: Implications for AAC design. Poster presentation at the Annual Conference of the American Speech-Language and Hearing Association, Denver, Colorado.

Light, J. (1988). Interaction involving individuals using augmentative and alternative communication systems: State of the art and future directions. *Augmentative and Alternative Communication, 4*, 66–82.

Light, J. (1997). "Communication is the essence of human life": Reflections on communicative competence. *Augmentative and Alternative Communication, 13*, 61–70.

Light, J., & Drager, K. (2007). AAC technologies for young children with complex communication needs: State of the science and future research directions. *Augmentative and Alternative Communication, 23*, 204–216.

Light, J., Drager, K., McCarthy, J., Mellott, S., Millar, D., Parrish, C., . . . Welliver, M. (2004). Performance of typically developing four- and five-year-old children with AAC systems using different language organization techniques. *Augmentative and Alternative Communication, 20*, 63–88.

Light, J., & McNaughton, D. (2009). Addressing the literacy demands of the curriculum for conventional and more advanced readers and writers who require AAC. In G. Soto & C. Zangari (Eds.), *Practically speaking: Language, literacy, and academic development for students with AAC needs* (pp. 217–246). Baltimore, MD: Paul H. Brookes Publishing Co.

Light, J., & McNaughton, D. (2012). Supporting the communication, language, and literacy development of children with complex communication needs: State of the science and future research priorities. *Assistive Technology, 24*, 34–44. doi:10.1080/10400435.2011.648717

Light, J., & McNaughton, D. (2013). Putting people first: Re-thinking the role of technology in augmentative and alternative communication intervention. *Augmentative and Alternative Communication, 29*, 299–309. doi:10.3109/07434816.2013.848935

Light, J., McNaughton, D., & Caron, J. (2016, August 9). Evidence-based literacy intervention and apps for individuals who require AAC. Seminar at the International Society for Augmentative and Alternative Communication Conference, Toronto, Canada.

Light, J., McNaughton, D., Jakobs, T., & Hershberger, D. (2014). *The RERC on AAC. R2: Investigating AAC technologies to support the transition from graphic symbols to literacy.* Retrieved from https://rerc-aac.psu.edu/research/r2-investigating-aac-technologies-to-support-the-transition-from-graphic-symbols-to-literacy

Lund, S. K., & Light, J. (2003). The effectiveness of grammar instruction for individuals who use augmentative and alternative communication systems: A preliminary study. *Journal of Speech, Language, and Hearing Research, 46*, 1110–1123.

McNaughton, D., & Light, J. (2013). The iPad and mobile technology revolution: Benefits and challenges for individuals who require augmentative and alternative communication. *Augmentative and Alternative Communication, 29*, 107–116. doi:10.3109/07434618.2013.784930

Mirenda, P. (2008). A back door approach to autism and AAC. *Augmentative and Alternative Communication, 24*, 220–234.

Mirenda, P., & Erickson, K. A. (2000). Augmentative communication and literacy. *Autism spectrum disorders: A transactional developmental perspective, 9*, 333–367.

Mirenda, P., & Locke, P. (1989). A comparison of symbol transparency in nonspeaking persons with intellectual disabilities. *Journal of Speech and Hearing Disorders, 54*, 131–140.

Nigam, R., Schlosser, R. W., & Lloyd, L. L. (2006). Concomitant use of the matrix strategy and the mand-model procedure in teaching graphic symbol combinations. *Augmentative and Alternative Communication, 22*, 160–177.

Owens, R. (2012). *Language development: An introduction.* Upper Saddle River, NJ: Pearson Education.

Reichle, J., Ganz, J., Drager, K., & Parker-McGowan, Q. (2016). Augmentative and Alternative communication applications for persons with ASD and complex communication needs. In D. Keen, H. Meadan, N. Brady, & J. Halle (Eds.), *Prelinguistic and minimally verbal communicators on the autism spectrum* (pp. 179–213). Singapore: Springer. doi:10.1007/978-981-10-0713-2

Romski, M., & Sevcik, R. (2005) Augmentative communication and early intervention: Myths and realities. *Infants and Young Children, 18*,174–185.

Romski, M., Sevcik, R., Hyatt, A., & Cheslock, M. (2002). A continuum of AAC language intervention strategies for beginning communicators. In J. Reichle, D. Beukelman, & J. Light (Eds.), *Exemplary practices for beginning communicators: Implications for AAC* (pp. 1–24). Baltimore, MD: Paul H. Brookes Publishing Co.

Romski, M. A., Sevcik, R. A., Robinson, B. F., Mervis, C. B., & Bertrand, J. (1996). Mapping the meanings of novel visual symbols by youth with moderate or severe mental retardation. *American Journal of Mental Retardation, 100*, 391–402.

Schlosser, R., Laubscher, E., Sorce, J., Koul, R., Flynn, S., Hotz, L., . . . Shane, H. (2013). Implementing directives that involve prepositions with children with autism: A comparison of spoken cues with two types of augmented input. *Augmentative and Alternative Communication, 29*, 132–145. doi:10.310/07434618.2013.784928

Schlosser, R., Shane, H., Allen, A., Abramson, J., Laubscher, E., & Dimery, K. (2015). Just-in-time supports in augmentative and alternative communication. *Journal of Developmental and Physical Disabilities, 1–17.* doi:10.1007/s10882-015-9452-2

Sevcik, R. A. (2006). Comprehension: An overlooked component in augmented language development. *Disability and Rehabilitation, 28*, 159–167.

Shane, H., Laubscher, E., Schlosser, R., Fadie, H., Sorce, J., Abramson, J., . . . Corley, K. (2015). *Enhancing communication for individuals with autism: A guide to the visual immersion system.* Baltimore, MD: Paul H. Brookes Publishing Co.

Smith, M. (2005). The dual challenges of aided communication and adolescence. *Augmentative and Alternative Communication, 21,* 67–79.

Smith, M., & Grove, N. (2003). Asymmetry in input and output for individuals who use AAC. In J. Light, D. Beukelman, and J. Reichle (Eds.), *Communicative competence for individuals who use AAC: From research to effective practice* (pp. 163–195). Baltimore, MD: Paul H. Brookes Publishing Co.

Soto, G., Hartmann, E., & Wilkins, D. P. (2006). Exploring the elements of narrative that emerge in the interactions between an 8-year-old child who uses an AAC device and her teacher. *Augmentative and Alternative Communication, 22,* 231–241.

Still, K., Rehfeldt, R. A., Whelan, R., May, R., & Dymond, S. (2014). Facilitating requesting skills using high-tech augmentative and alternative communication devices with individuals with autism spectrum disorders: A systematic review. *Research in Autism Spectrum Disorders, 8,* 1184–1199. doi:10.1016/j.rasd.2014.06.003

Sutton, A., Soto, G., & Blockberger, S. (2002). Grammatical issues in graphic symbol communication. *Augmentative and Alternative Communication, 18,* 192–204.

Tager-Flusberg, H., Rogers, S., Cooper, J., Landa, R., Lord, C., Paul, R., . . . Yoder, P. (2009). Defining spoken language benchmarks and selecting measures of expressive language development for young children with autism spectrum disorders. *Journal of Speech, Language, and Hearing Research, 52,* 643–652. doi:10.1044/1092-4388(2009/08-0136)

Thistle, J., & Wilkinson, K. (2013). Working memory demands of aided augmentative and alternative communication for individuals with developmental disabilities. *Augmentative and Alternative Communication, 29,* 235–245. doi:10.3109/07434618.2015.815800

Thistle, J. J., & Wilkinson, K. M. (2015). Building evidence-based practice in AAC display design for young children: Current practices and future directions. *Augmentative and Alternative Communication, 31,* 124–136. doi:10.3109/07434618.2015.1035798

van der Meer, L., Kagohara, D., Roche, L., Sutherland, D., Balandin, S., Green, V. A., . . . Sigafoos, J. (2013). Teaching multi-step requesting and social communication to two children with autism spectrum disorders with three AAC options. *Augmentative and Alternative Communication, 29,* 222–234. doi:10.3109/07434618.2013.815801

Wendt, O., Schlosser, R., & Lloyd, L. (2006, August). *The effectiveness of AAC in autism spectrum disorders: A quantitative research synthesis.* Presented at the 12th biennial conference of the International Society for Augmentative and Alternative Communication, Düsseldorf, Germany.

Wilkinson, K., & Jagaroo, V. (2004). Contributions of principles of visual cognitive science to AAC system display design. *Augmentative and Alternative Communication, 20,* 123–136.

Wilkinson, K. M., & McIlvane, W. J. (2013). Perceptual factors influence visual search for meaningful symbols in individuals with intellectual disabilities and Down syndrome or autism spectrum disorders. *American Journal on Intellectual and Developmental Disabilities, 118,* 353–364. doi:10.1352/1944-7558-118.5.353

Wilkinson, K., Romski, M., & Sevcik, R. (1994). Emergence of visual-graphic symbol combinations by youth with moderate or severe mental retardation. *Journal of Speech, Language, and Hearing Research, 37,* 883–895.

Wodka, E., Mathy, P., & Kalb, L. (2013). Predictors of phrase and fluent speech in children with autism and severe language delay. *Pediatrics, 131,* 1128–1134. doi:10.1542/peds.2012-2221d

Yoder, P. J., & Warren, S. F. (2002). Effects of prelinguistic milieu teaching and parent responsivity education on dyads involving children with intellectual disabilities. *Journal of Speech, Language, and Hearing Research, 45,* 1158–1174.

7

Functional Communication Training for Durable Behavior Change

Jennifer J. McComas, Kelly M. Schieltz,
Jessica Simacek, Wendy K. Berg, and David P. Wacker

Challenging behavior, including aggression, tantrums, self-injury, and stereotypy has been reported in more than 90% of individuals with autism spectrum disorder (ASD; Jang, Dixon, Tarbox, & Granpeesheh, 2011). Furthermore, severe aggression and self-injurious behavior are reportedly the leading cause of emergency room visits among children with ASD (Kalb, Stuart, Freedman, Zablotsky, & Vasa, 2012). A U.S. population-based study of ASD over 3 surveillance years suggested the prevalence of self-injury averaged 27.7% (Soke et al., 2016). In this chapter, the authors discuss one intervention approach for challenging behavior. This chapter begins with a brief background on the early development and evolution of functional communication training (FCT), followed by a brief survey of FCT research from between 2007 and 2016. Next, it discusses considerations related to durability of intervention effects before going into some detail regarding assessment and intervention procedures. Finally, it provides case examples that illustrate the assessment and intervention process for developing durable treatment effects for challenging behavior of individuals with ASD.

For more than 3 decades, researchers and practitioners have successfully implemented FCT (Carr & Durand, 1985) to reduce the challenging behavior of individuals with intellectual and developmental disabilities including those with ASD (Tiger, Hanley, & Bruzek, 2008). FCT is a procedure in which an individual is taught to produce a communicative response, often a request. The request, referred to throughout this chapter as a mand, effectively competes with challenging behavior because care providers provide more reinforcement (e.g., more often, greater amount, more immediate, longer duration, higher quality reinforcement) than they provide for the challenging behavior. To illustrate, a child with an intellectual or developmental disability uses a mand, such as the manual sign, PLAY or BREAK, to make a request, such as for a tangible item or a break from demands. The care provider responds to the mand with the requested item/break and withholds or reduces reinforcement for challenging behavior.

Iwata, Dorsey, Slifer, Bauman, and Richman (1982/1994) provided the first methodology, known as functional analysis (FA), for systematically identifying the consequences that reinforce an individual's challenging behavior. The major applied benefit of conducting an FA is that the results specify the reinforcer(s) for an individual's challenging behavior, meaning that differential reinforcement procedures (i.e., withholding reinforcement for challenging behavior and delivering it contingent on appropriate behavior instead) such as FCT often can be used to successfully treat even the most severe forms of challenging behavior (Heath, Ganz, Parker, Burke, & Ninci, 2015; Pelios, Morren, Tesch, & Axelrod, 1999).

Carr and Durand (1985) published the seminal article that demonstrated that teaching a communicative alternative led to the successful replacement of challenging behavior when the communicative alternative (i.e., the mand) produced the same reinforcing consequences that were identified in the FA of challenging behavior. This treatment approach has been evaluated, replicated, and demonstrated to be a remarkably robust, effective, and popular applied behavior analysis (ABA) intervention for even the most severe challenging behavior of individuals with intellectual and developmental disabilities (Tiger et al., 2008). Most frequently, FCT is implemented within a two-step sequence that begins with an FA followed by teaching the mand under controlled training conditions. Tiger and colleagues (2008) conducted a literature review and summarized the effectiveness of FCT across 91 studies ($n = 204$) from 1985 to 2006. The reviewers concluded that there is a sizable database that demonstrates the effectiveness of FCT on acquisition of a functional mand and reduction of challenging behavior across disability categories, age ranges, and challenging behavior. Mancil (2006) conducted a similar review of the literature on FCT, specifically for children with ASD, which resulted in similar findings and conclusions.

Despite the effectiveness of FCT, there have been few demonstrations, and even fewer analyses, of generalization or maintenance of treatment effects (Mancil, 2006; Tiger et al., 2008). Falcomata and Wacker (2013) conducted a review of the literature on FCT as a function-based treatment for challenging behavior through 2012. They specifically sought studies that assessed generalization and maintenance and found only nine published FCT studies that used single-case designs to evaluate generalization and maintenance.

A BRIEF SURVEY OF FCT FROM 2007–2016

We, the chapter's authors, sampled peer-reviewed journal articles from the past 10 years of FCT research for children with ASD (2007–2016). Studies were considered if they included an analysis of the effects of FCT. Individual participants' data were extracted from studies if they met the following inclusion criteria: 1) the participant was younger than 18 years old, 2) the participant had a diagnosis of ASD, and 3) the function of the participant's challenging behavior was identified through an FA or other functional assessment. Fifty participants were included from 25 studies that met the inclusion criteria (see Literature Review Methodology section and Appendix 7.1).

Table 7.1 shows participant characteristics, including age, diagnosis, communication repertoire, and challenging behavior. The largest proportion of participants were younger than 5 years of age, followed closely by the group between the ages of 5 and 12 years. A large portion of studies did not include information about communication repertoire. For cases in which results of a communication assessment

Table 7.1. Participant characteristics

Code	N	Percentage of participant sample
Age		
Birth–5	23	46
5.1–12	22	44
12.1–18	5	10
Diagnosis		
Autism	40	80
PDD-NOS	9	18
Asperger syndrome	1	2
Communication repertoire		
Not described/unclear	17	34
Speaking/AAC in phrases	17	34
Limited vocal/AAC	13	26
Not vocal/no AAC	3	6
***Challenging behavior**		
Aggression	32	68
Tantrums	28	56
Self-injury	23	46
other	19	38

25 studies; *N* = 53.

* Indicates participants could be counted in multiple categories.

Key: PPD-NOS, pervasive developmental disorder not otherwise specified; AAC, augmentative and alternative communication.

were listed, few specific details about the results or communication repertoire were described. Based on the available information, 60% of the participants fell into the combined review categories of "speaking/AAC in phrases" and "limited vocal/AAC," which we defined as five or more vocal or AAC terms but not speaking in multiple phrases. The highest proportion of children engaged in aggressive behavior (multiple topographies of challenging behavior were common), followed by tantrums, and then self-injurious behavior; several participants engaged in other topographies including noncompliance, elopement, and repetitive behavior.

The types of assessments (i.e., descriptive assessment, FA, and preference assessments) conducted are shown in Table 7.2. Descriptive assessment procedures, which included interviewing parents, observing children prior to the FA,

Table 7.2. Assessment approach

Type of assessment conducted	N	Percentage of participant sample
Descriptive assessment		
Yes	38	76
No	12	24
Functional analysis		
Yes	50	100
No	0	0
Preference assessment		
Yes	37	74
No	13	26

25 studies; *N* = 53.

collecting ABC (i.e., data regarding the relevant antecedents, behaviors, and consequences) or similar observational data, and antecedent analyses were conducted with the majority of participants. However, aside from the suggested reinforcer for challenging behavior, little of the information obtained from the descriptive assessments was included in the articles. Descriptive assessment information appeared to be used in conjunction with subsequent consequence-based FAs for 76% of the participants, and preference assessments were conducted with 74% of the participants.

Intervention variables including location of intervention, primary interventionist, communicative modality selected, and use of reductive procedures (i.e., extinction or punishment) appear in Table 7.3. Half of the participants' analyses and interventions were conducted in settings in which the children lived or attended school; the remainder were conducted in inpatient or outpatient clinics, with one completed in the community near the participant's home. Twenty-four percent of the participants' interventions were conducted by a trained behavior therapist from a remote location using telehealth technology to coach a parent or other care provider to implement FCT. A parent or educator conducted the procedures with half of the participants, including those who participated via telehealth, with a researcher or clinical therapist conducting the others. Ninety-six percent of participants were taught to use a vocalization, manual sign, or low-tech device such as a picture exchange card or a simple electronic device such as a microswitch

Table 7.3.   Intervention variables

Code	N	Percentage of participant sample
Primary setting		
Clinic (outpatient)	19	38
Home	10	20
School	8	16
Telehealth: Home	6	12
Telehealth: Clinic	6	12
Community	1	2
Clinic (inpatient)	0	0
Telehealth: School	0	0
Primary interventionist		
Parent	20	40
Researcher	14	28
Educator	10	20
Clinician/therapist	6	12
Communication modality		
Vocal	21	40
Low tech	13	26
Combined topographies	12	23
Sign/gesture	2	4
High tech	2	4
Reductive procedure		
Yes	50	100
No	0	0

25 studies; N = 53.

Table 7.4. Postintervention evaluation

Type of postintervention evaluation	N	Percentage of participant sample
Schedule thinning/demand fading		
Yes	23	46
No	27	54
Generalization		
Yes	5	10
No	45	90
Maintenance		
Yes	3	6
No	47	94

25 studies; N = 53.

that contained a single vocal output message to mand; only 4% used a high-tech device (e.g., a vocal output device that requires discrimination among multiple messages). Finally, a reductive procedure, most commonly extinction (i.e., withholding the functional reinforcer following challenging behavior), was a treatment component for 100% of participants.

Participants' data were reviewed for the inclusion of postintervention analyses of FCT in the form of schedule thinning (e.g., intermittent reinforcement, demand fading), generalization, or maintenance (see Table 7.4). Results indicated that postintervention analyses were conducted with fewer than 50% of participants. Specifically, following acquisition of the mand, schedule thinning was implemented with 46% of participants. Notably, for the majority of participants for whom there was a generalization or maintenance evaluation, the authors reported that generalization or maintenance was observed but generally did not describe the procedures used for promoting generalization or maintenance. Generalization of treatment effects was demonstrated with 5% of participants across care providers, responses, or contexts using procedures such as training sufficient exemplars. Maintenance in the form of continued mands in the absence of continued training was documented with 6% of participants. By contrast, for the 46% of participants who experienced schedule thinning, the authors presented data on the continuation of mands under conditions of reduced reinforcement (e.g., increasing response requirements, increasing delay to reinforcement).

SECOND-GENERATION ISSUES WITH FCT: DURABILITY

The success of these FCT programs has led to a number of second generation issues, including the best way to signal when to use (and when not to use) the acquired mand (Greer, Fisher, Saini, Owen, & Jones, 2016), how to best train care providers to implement FCT (Suess et al., 2014), and how to deliver FCT to more families and schools (Lindgren et al., 2016; Machalicek et al., 2016; Suess, Wacker, Schwartz, Lustig, & Detrick, 2016; Wacker et al., 2013). This chapter focuses specifically on the durability of the effects of FCT over time. The term *durable* is based on Nevin and Wacker (2013), who proposed that maintenance of treatment effects is shown by its persistence in spite of challenges such as decrements in or delays to reinforcement, extinction, or increases in response requirements. In practical terms, the goal is an intervention that results in the individual producing the mand beyond a narrow set of training conditions that involves immediately reinforcing every mand under tightly controlled conditions. Durable treatment involves both generalization and maintenance. With respect to generalization, it is important to communicate with a variety of care providers and in a variety of settings. With maintenance, it is important to continue to produce the mand over time even though the stimulus conditions in the environment change constantly and the environment itself also changes. For both generalization and maintenance, it is important that the strength of the mand is sufficient such that it persists even when the first attempt to mand does not produce immediate reinforcement. To date, there is a relative lack of evidence demonstrating the durable effects of FCT.

Because generalization and maintenance are viewed as requirements for the long-term success of FCT, and both are active components of durable treatments, we use the term *durable* throughout the remainder of this chapter. Although the importance of generalization and maintenance has been widely discussed relative to FCT, there is very limited evidence of active programming for or probing the long-term durability of mands. The continued development of FCT would benefit from a three-step approach that involves assessment, intervention, and generalization/maintenance. Specifically, and especially for challenging behavior reinforced by social consequences, programming for generalization and maintenance should occur early in the training process and become a standard aspect of the training protocol. For challenging behavior that is reinforced by nonsocial consequences (e.g., escape from pain, access to visual stimulation), for which even less is known, the next step in the evolution of FCT is to document whether treatment effects are durable. By collecting specific descriptive information about the context in which challenging behavior occurs, assessment and FCT might be conducted and designed (respectively) in a way that actively and effectively promotes durability of the intervention effects. In this model, information collected during the descriptive assessment informs the particulars of the FA, FCT, and generalization and maintenance protocols.

As discussed by Wacker and colleagues (2011), maintenance has been defined as steady state behavior under conditions similar to training conditions, and yet the desired outcome is not continued responding under the same treatment conditions that were present during initial acquisition. Rather, FCT should be considered successful when durable results are achieved despite the ever-changing environment within which the participant is engaged. With respect to FCT, durability can be defined as the mand effectively competing with challenging behavior in a variety of natural situations with varied antecedent and consequent conditions, such as when reinforcement is intermittent, with novel communication partners, and in multiple settings (Nevin & Wacker, 2013).

LITERATURE REVIEW METHODOLOGY

We used a three-pronged search process for our literature review. First, we searched electronic databases (e.g., PsychINFO, ERIC, Academic Search Premier) for articles published between 2007–2016 using the terms *functional communication training + autism, functional communication training + developmental disabilities, functional equivalence training + autism, functional equivalence training + developmental disabilities,* and *FCT.* The authors examined the titles and abstracts of studies located in the search.

If at least one participant within a study potentially met inclusion criteria, the full manuscript was reviewed. Second, after identifying articles meeting inclusion criteria from the electronic search, we searched the following academic journals: *Journal of Applied Behavior Analysis, Journal of Behavioral Education*, and *Journal of Experimental Analysis of Behavior*. Third, we conducted an ancestral search of the included studies.

Participants who met the following inclusion criteria within studies were included; therefore, a study may have had some participants who met inclusion criteria and others who did not. Studies and participants were included if 1) the study was published in a peer-reviewed journal between 2007 and 2016; 2) the study was an experimental, single subject design that investigated the effects of FCT; and 3) the participant was diagnosed with autism (including PDD-NOS and Asperger syndrome to account for these disorders prior to the *DSM-5* diagnostic changes; APA, 2013).

Studies and participants were excluded that 1) were found in non–peer-reviewed journals, were dissertations, or were thesis papers; 2) did not demonstrate experimental control during FCT (e.g., instead depicted an AB design or case study) or did not provide graphic displays of participant data; 3) FA or functional assessment was not conducted prior to FCT; and 4) participants did not have a diagnosis of ASD, PDD-NOS, or Asperger syndrome, and/or were older than 18 years old.

The search procedure yielded 90 studies; of those, 25 studies had a least one participant who met the inclusion criteria. A total of 53 participants were included, for whom information in the following categories was extracted: 1) participant characteristics (the participant's age, diagnosis, communication level, and challenging behavior), 2) assessment procedures (whether the authors reported having conducted a descriptive assessment, FA, or preference assessment), 3) intervention variables (where FCT was conducted, who conducted FCT, what mand modality was taught, and whether the authors described using a reductive procedure [either extinction or punishment]), and 4) postintervention evaluation (whether data were presented demonstrating schedule thinning and/or demand fading; generalization across people, settings, or responses) or maintenance (continued demonstration of mand in the absence of continued training). See Appendix 7.1 for a list of studies with One or More Participant Included in the Review.

The remainder of this chapter is focused on FCT consisting of a comprehensive set of procedures involving assessment and intervention for producing durable treatment effects. To illustrate the process, a description of planning for generalization and maintenance beginning in the earliest part of the assessment process is provided (see Figure 7.1), followed by case examples of individuals who display challenging behavior that is maintained by both social (positive and negative reinforcement) and nonsocial (automatic reinforcement) reinforcers.

ASSESSMENT

The focus for assessment is on the specific environmental variables that must be considered when programming for durable treatment effects. One way to think about this is in terms of contextual fit. Contextual fit refers to consideration of the specific context in which the intervention is designed and has relevance for designing, choosing, implementing, and adjusting interventions to be effective

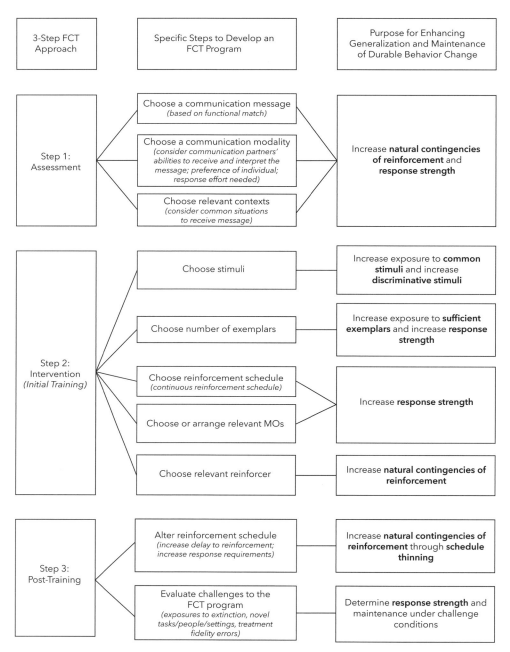

Figure 7.1. Three-step approach to designing durable functional communication. (*Key:* MO, motivating operation; FCT, functional communication training.)

as well as sustainable (Reichle & Wacker, 2017). It makes intuitive sense that if there is good contextual fit, then care providers will be more likely to continue to reinforce the mand because the behavior will be viewed as relevant and acceptable. Thus, one goal for a descriptive assessment is to determine what will be likely expected of a participant post treatment. This information establishes the goal for treatment. Should the participant be able to work without a break for 5 minutes, to play without attention for 10 minutes, to take turns with a sibling for a desired item? Each of these represent potential challenges to the treatment that can be identified prior to starting treatment and probed throughout treatment to determine the conditions under which the mand will be reinforced and thus generalization and maintenance will be more likely to occur. One way to improve the match between the treatment goal and intervention may be to pay increased attention to variables identified from the descriptive assessment that could influence contextual fit when designing FCT. For example, if grandparents or paid baby sitters will need to implement FCT in the home, with the materials available in the home, and in the presence of siblings, then intervention will need to include these variables.

Contexts

Contextual fit requires knowledge of the interventionists, functional conditions, and variety of situations in which the intervention is required. To better promote the durability of treatment effects, detailed descriptive assessment information for each individual will be needed to augment the information obtained from the FA. Specific information is gathered about variables such as what intervention will entail (which communicative messages, modalities, contexts), who will be implementing the intervention (communication partners), priorities of those implementing FCT (natural communities of reinforcement), and available resources (schedules of reinforcement by different providers and/or in different situations). Collecting specific descriptive information about the context in which challenging behavior occurs, like the results of the FA, may be necessary for FCT to achieve the goal of durable treatment effects.

Contextual features that have been reported to be correlated with occurrences of challenging behavior include the presence of specific people and specific types of toys. A case reported by Asmus, Derby, Wacker, Porter, and Ulrich (1993) illustrates the differential effect that the presence of a specific person (a younger sibling) can have on a young boy's challenging behavior. The researchers observed that when the boy was in a room with just his parents, he engaged in challenging behavior during play and escape conditions but not when his parents ignored him. However, when his 1-year-old sibling was present in the room, the boy engaged in appropriate behavior during play sessions and challenging behavior when his parents ignored him while they played with his sibling. The probability that FCT will produce durable effects is increased if the variables have been identified that will likely challenge the effectiveness of treatment over time or across various situations.

Communication Message

As mentioned previously, an FA informs subsequent FCT because the message for the mand is selected to match the function of challenging behavior identified during the FA. For challenging behavior maintained by escape (negative reinforcement was the most common function identified by Mancil, 2006), a mand for a work break is often taught. Messages requesting negative reinforcement can be stated in a variety of ways, such as "break," "break, please," or "I want to take a break," or can specify what the individual would prefer to do during the break (e.g., "play").

For behavior maintained by access to preferred tangible items, a mand containing the message "play" is often taught. It can also be a request for a very specific item or activity such as "toys" or "drink." In our own work with young children with ASD, we have most often identified escape and tangibles as the reinforcers maintaining problem behavior. For both functions, we often teach a mand for a preferred activity that the individual likes to do while on break. In our experience, very few children, and especially young children, want to simply sit and do nothing, and so a mand for a preferred item or activity is what we teach during FCT. For challenging behavior maintained by social attention, the mand can also be for a preferred activity or form of attention ("hug") or general, such as "Come here, please."

Regardless of whether the mand is general or specific and which specific mand is contained within the message, the selection of the mand should be identified from information gathered during descriptive observations of the individual; for example, while he or she is interacting with communication partners. Thus, the FA identifies the class of functional reinforcement, and the descriptive assessment identifies the specific message delivered to the provider. For example, asking grandma for a "break" may be functionally related to the challenging behavior but may not be understood by the care provider in all situations (e.g., wants to play instead of taking medications). Thus, the selection of the message can be very complex as it involves a potentially wide range of variables rarely analyzed in the existing literature. Identifying appropriate messages may be one variable that influences the durability of FCT.

Communication Modality

The modalities commonly used for FCT include vocal words, manual signs, gestures, picture cards, low-technology electronic devices such as microswitches, and high-technology devices such as speech-generating devices (SGDs). Each modality has advantages and disadvantages and needs to be selected to match the needs of the individual who will receive FCT and the acceptability of these devices to the care provider. Several guidelines that are based on research findings are available to inform those decisions (see Mancil & Boman, 2010).

One consideration is the ability of potential communication partners to accurately interpret the mand. For example, manual signs can be a very efficient response if the individual is fluent with manual signs. However, a manual sign will not be acknowledged if the communication partner does not recognize the sign. Spoken mands may be readily available to the communicator, but their effectiveness will depend on the individual's independence in producing the mand and the listener's comprehension of the mand. (Durand & Carr, 1991).

A second consideration is whether an individual is more likely to use a communicative response across contexts. Studies have shown that individuals with intellectual and developmental disabilities can learn multiple mand modalities that compete effectively with challenging behavior (Kahng, Hendrickson, & Vu, 2000), and individual preferences for a particular modality have been documented to emerge (Harding, et al., 2009; Winborn, Wacker, Richman, Asmus, & Geier, 2002; Winborn-Kemmerer, Ringdahl, Wacker, & Kitsukawa, 2009; Winborn-Kemmerer, et al., 2010). Multiple communication responses in an individual's repertoire may be beneficial because they may facilitate the use of what speech pathologists refer to as *communication repair strategies* (Reichle & Wacker, 2017). For example, if an individual attempts to communicate a message and the communication partner does not respond accordingly, the individual may attempt an alternative modality for communicating the same message if he or she has multiple communication responses.

The effort required to produce the mand is a third consideration. Mands that are less effortful have been shown to compete with challenging behavior more effectively than mands that require more physical effort or require more steps to complete (Buckley & Newchok, 2005; Horner & Day, 1991). Mand proficiency can refer to the person's ability or skill in using a mand modality, which would influence the level of effort required to perform the mand (Ringdahl et al., 2009).

Descriptive assessments can provide information regarding communication partners, the context in which mands will be used, the individual's preference for particular mand modalities, whether teaching multiple mands is an option, and the effort required to produce the mand. After gathering information about the context in which intervention will be implemented, the next consideration is how to implement FCT using procedures that have been shown to be related to improve durability.

Common Stimuli

Identifying salient stimuli that can be programmed as common stimuli (Stokes & Baer, 1977) across training and generalization settings is an important goal of a descriptive assessment. For example, it is often unclear if an individual is actually attending to a stimulus (e.g., a direction provided by a parent) and so the addition of salient visual stimuli to augment the spoken stimulus may be important for durable treatment results to occur. Visual stimuli can function to cue an individual to produce the desired response, in this case the mand, in nontraining contexts. Visual stimuli might include an object, picture cards, or other AAC equipment that are either a) portable and available in treatment and generalization settings or b) features of tasks, preferred activities, or the context that are directly relevant to generalization setting(s).

Shamlian and colleagues (2016) conducted a series of experiments to test for differential effects of naturally occurring discriminative stimuli (S^Ds; e.g., a therapist reading a newspaper, listening to music, watching television) and stimulus deltas (S^Δs; e.g., cooking, cleaning, and talking on the telephone) vs. arranged and potentially more salient discriminative stimuli (i.e., wearing different colored wristbands) on the occurrence of mands and challenging behavior. Their findings, consistent with previous studies (e.g., Kuhn, Chirighin, & Zelenka, 2010; Leon, Hausman, Kahng, & Becraft, 2010) suggested that it may be advisable to begin the training process with highly salient arranged discriminative stimuli and then to transfer control to naturally occurring discriminative stimuli.

REINFORCEMENT-BASED INTERVENTION

Differential reinforcement of alternative behavior is comprised of reinforcement for a target response (e.g., appropriate mand) with concurrent extinction for targeted challenging behavior and is the foundation of most FCT interventions. Response allocation, or making a choice between two or more concurrently available responses, such as appropriate communication and challenging behavior, shifts toward one response over the other(s) when one of those responses produces a relatively more favorable schedule in terms of reinforcement rate, amount, duration, or immediacy, than the other response(s). For example, a continuous schedule (fixed ratio schedule of reinforcement for each mand) of immediate reinforcement contingent on the mand is most often used during initial FCT to establish the mand in the individual's behavioral repertoire. Two options for decreasing a target challenging response involve 1) extinction or 2) arranging the reinforcement schedule to favor a desired, competing response (e.g., mand). As mentioned previously, the authors' review of the literature between 2007 and 2016 indicates that the vast majority of FCT interventions involve reductive procedures such as extinction for the targeted challenging behavior. For example, in the early part of virtually all FCT programs, reinforcement is provided immediately following each mand whereas reinforcement is withheld contingent on any occurrence of the challenging behavior. Similarly, if challenging behavior occurs during the reinforcement period, other reductive procedures such as response cost (e.g., restricted access to preferred items) may be used to further reduce the occurrence of challenging behavior. Another option is to provide an improved (e.g., a richer) schedule for the mand (Peck et al., 1996). For example, in cases in which it is dangerous or otherwise impractical to use extinction for the challenging behavior, reinforcement that is of relatively brief duration, of low quality, or both can be provided contingent on the challenging behavior whereas a mand results in reinforcement that is of longer duration, higher quality, or both.

Inextricably related to reinforcement are motivating operations (MOs; Laraway, Snycerski, Michael, & Poling, 2003; Michael, 1982). MOs are environmental events that affect an individuals' behavior by altering 1) the effectiveness of a reinforcing stimulus, and therefore 2) the likelihood of the behavior that produces that reinforcing stimulus. Thus, the effectiveness of a reinforcer tends to be somewhat dynamic and dependent on the momentary value of the reinforcer. To illustrate, for many people, the chain of responses that involves ordering a cup of coffee and paying for it is reinforced by the hot liquid caffeine that is produced by that chain of responses. However, after a third cup of coffee, the likelihood that a person will engage in that chain again in the near future is low because the value of caffeine as a reinforcer has decreased. In the case of challenging behavior and mands, if access to a preferred toy serves as a reinforcer for a child's challenging behavior, then restricting access to that toy will set the occasion for either challenging behavior or a mand that produces access to the toy. However, if the child receives a new toy, the child may become more interested in playing with that toy rather than the toy originally used as the reinforcer for appropriate behavior. In this case, the new toy creates a change in the MO for the original toy, and this change in MO needs to be considered when arranging the contingencies for the appropriate response (mand) to maintain the child's use of the mand. This is why frequent preference assessments need to be conducted so that the MOs related to the reinforcers for manding have been identified.

TRAINING FOR DURABILITY

As discussed previously in this chapter, factors such as the communication context, the mand modality, the natural communities of reinforcement, and the treatment challenges likely to be encountered should be identified during assessment and then probed throughout FCT. Furthermore, procedures should be considered in advance for effectively programming persistence of the desired behavior change when challenged by environmental changes such as increased response requirements or delays to reinforcement.

To date, although the reviews of FCT are mostly positive, and studies conducted with FCT often show generalization, very few studies have been conducted on durability and it is not clear what the best tactics are for obtaining durable outcomes. For example, Wacker and colleagues (2005) showed that generalization of treatment effects often occurred following FCT to different settings, people, and (less so) tasks. This is a positive outcome, but the study does not provide guidance regarding what to do when durability is not achieved. Thus, we suggest that programming for generalization and maintenance occur early in the training process and become standard aspects of the training protocol, just as FA/assessment is standard prior to implementation of a treatment strategy. The following sections provide some exemplars of procedures that should be considered for inclusion as components of FCT programs because they have been shown to be related to durable treatment results.

Schedule Thinning via Delayed Reinforcement

Schedule thinning can serve as a bridge from continuous reinforcement schedules used during initial FCT to the intermittent schedules likely to be encountered outside of treatment. One example of schedule thinning is to increase the delay between the mand and reinforcement delivery (Hagopian, Boelter, & Jarmolowicz, 2011). For example, during initial FCT for behavior maintained by attention, a mand for attention receives immediate reinforcement in the form of attention. When challenging behavior consistently remains low and mands continue to occur, the delay to reinforcement is incrementally increased (e.g., 5s). Schedule thinning continues in this way until the terminal goal is reached. In some cases, during the delay period, alternative activities or reinforcers are provided (Austin & Tiger, 2015), which may enhance the maintenance of responding.

Schedule Thinning via Increased Response Requirements

Response requirements should be increased so that more tasks are required to earn negative reinforcement. Initial treatment for escape-maintained behavior often involves requiring only one task or portion of a task (e.g., putting one block in a bucket or completing one math problem) before a mand for a break is required. After the individual establishes a pattern of successfully completing one task demand and then manding for a break, the number of task demands required to earn access to a requested break are systematically increased. Wacker et al. (2011) began FCT with a requirement that participants complete two task demands before a mand for break would be reinforced. After a stable decrease in challenging behavior was observed, demands were doubled to four and then doubled again to eight over the course of the study.

Signals to Promote Successful Schedule Thinning

One highly successful approach to schedule thinning involves the use of signals. Greer and colleagues (2016) summarized 25 applications of FCT schedule thinning in which a discriminative stimulus was used to signal the availability of reinforcement during conditions of reduced reinforcement. For example, if mands in the form of touching a picture card have been reinforced on a dense schedule during FCT, the presence of the picture card becomes an S^D because it signals the availability of reinforcement. Findings by Greer and colleagues suggest that the use of signals was effective for both 1) guiding the individual when a mand will be reinforced and 2) maintaining mands while minimizing the need for supplemental behavior reduction procedures during schedule thinning sessions. To illustrate, following FCT in which a fixed ratio 1 (FR1) schedule was used to establish a mand, Fisher, Greer, Fuhrman, and Querim (2015) used a green wristband worn by the therapist to signal the availability (S^D) and a red wristband worn by the therapist to signal the unavailability of reinforcement (S^Δ). In addition, the schedule that was signaled was described: "Scott, we are going to do some work. When the green bracelet is on, you can ask for a break by touching the card. When the red bracelet is on, you can touch the card, but you will not get a break." The participants responded accordingly; they manded in the presence of the green wristband and did not mand in the presence of the red wristband. Similar procedures used in other studies have produced the same effects and those effects maintained as the reinforcement schedules were thinned over time, both gradually (Hanley, Iwata, & Thompson, 2001) and abruptly (Betz, Fisher, Roane, Mintz, & Owen, 2013).

Natural Contingencies of Reinforcement and Response Strengthening

One tactic for promoting generalization involves making use of naturally existing opportunities for reinforcement (Stokes & Osnes, 1989). For example, one can arrange the generalization environment for the newly acquired behavior to contact natural consequences. Durand and Carr (1991) evaluated the persistence of trained mands with untrained therapists in two conditions designed to decrease attention-maintained challenging behavior: 1) FCT and 2) time-out. Results showed that for the group that received FCT, manding for attention persisted and challenging behavior remained low across therapists involved in the training sessions as well as with untrained therapists. Notably, the untrained therapists understood the mands and provided attention contingent on the mands. In contrast, for the group that received time-out contingent on challenging behavior, time-out reduced challenging behavior in the presence of the training therapists but not in the presence of untrained therapists. These results suggest that behavior is more likely to maintain or persist in untrained situations if the behavior trained is one that is more likely to contact natural reinforcement consequences (e.g., receiving attention contingent on requesting attention).

Previously, the importance of signals was discussed. In the ideal world, whenever the individual emits the mand, it would be reinforced because the initial goal is to strengthen the mand as much as possible, and this strengthening occurs through response-reinforcer pairings. Thus, providing more rather than fewer reinforcement trials or sessions should lead to more persistence of the mand. Conversely, when the mand produces extinction, the response is weakened. Thus, mands should not be emitted that are not reinforced, and yet there will be occasions in which the care provider either cannot or chooses not to provide reinforcement.

Signaling the individual regarding when a mand will be reinforced reduces the likelihood that mands will contact extinction.

Measuring Response Persistence During Extinction

It is important to measure both adaptive and challenging behavior during and postintervention because if only challenging behavior is measured, then one might conclude that FCT was a failure even though the acquired mands are showing maintenance. Volkert, Lerman, Call, and Trosclair-Lasserre (2009) examined responding during extinction and during intermittent reinforcement schedules that followed FCT. Following consistent reductions in challenging behavior and displays of the target mands during FCT, reinforcement for mands and challenging behavior were withheld during extinction conditions. Although challenging behavior increased quickly for four of the five participants, mands continued to occur for at least the initial extinction sessions for most of the participants. Similar results were reported by Wacker and colleagues (2011), showing that improved persistence in manding can occur even when there is not initially a correlated decrease in challenging behavior. This persistence suggests that over time, as reinforcement continues to be provided for manding but not for challenging behavior, one would expect reductions in challenging behavior to be obtained.

Summary of Highlighted Approaches

Table 7.5 lists the approaches to programming for durable effects of FCT that have been discussed in this chapter and that are illustrated in the case studies that follow.

Table 7.5. Highlighted approaches to programming durable effects of functional communication training (FCT)

Approach	Description	Illustrated in case example
Common stimuli	Incorporating physical stimuli to prompt the mand to occur in nontraining contexts; fitting contextual features to FCT	José, Ella, Andy
Sufficient exemplars	Training more than one mand or training in more than one context	José, Ella, Andy
Signals	Using signals to indicate the availability of reinforcement under intermittent or delayed reinforcement schedules	José, Andy
Schedule thinning	Moving from continuous immediate reinforcement to schedules that are intermittent, delayed, or both; For negative reinforcement, includes increasing response requirements	José, Andy
Natural contingencies of reinforcement	Arrange the generalization environment for the trained behavior to contact natural consequences	Ella, Andy
Response strengthening	Conducting the intervention until persistence is shown, via repeated exposures to extinction, or other challenges	José, Ella, Andy

CASE EXAMPLES

Escape Function: José

This case example shows how treatment is developed to improve durable effects. José (Wacker et al., 2011) was 4 years old and diagnosed with fragile X syndrome and moderate intellectual disability. He used a small number of single words and manual signs (e.g., "done"), and engaged in destructive behavior that included biting and hitting others, biting his own finger, and throwing toys. All assessment and intervention sessions were conducted by José's mother, with coaching from a behavior therapist, in the living room in José's home. Preference assessments were conducted to identify highly preferred activities and nonpreferred tasks. The results of the consequent-based FA revealed elevations in both the demand/escape from a nonpreferred task and restricted access/tangible conditions, suggesting that José's destructive behavior was maintained by both escape from nonpreferred tasks and access to preferred tangible items (see Wacker et al., 2011 for more specific details and FA data for this case example).

The behavior therapist provided a BIGmack microswitch and a 10.2 cm x 10.2 cm communication card, created with Boardmaker, as an augmentative communication device during FCT. The communication card, which was taped to the touch plate of the microswitch, had the word *Play* written and a black line-drawing of a child surrounded with toys on it. José's parents recorded the message, "Play, please," on the microswitch so that when José pressed the touch plate, the message played.

During FCT sessions, José's mother required him to complete two nonpreferred tasks during 5-minute sessions. Each session began with 20–30 seconds of parent attention and play with preferred toys. Then José's mother said, "Time to work" and directed him to sit in a chair at his desk. His mother provided a specific vocal direction (e.g., "Point to the picture of a _____") and modeled how to complete the task. Destructive behavior during work activities was blocked in a neutral fashion (i.e., escape extinction) and the prompt was repeated. Noncompliance resulted in hand-over-hand physical guidance to complete the task. Independent task completion resulted in his mother presenting the word card/microswitch and saying "Good job! More work or play?" or after several sessions, his mother often said, "What do you want to do?" when presenting him with the microswitch. Contingent on pressing the switch, José's mother allowed him to play with her and his preferred toys for 1–2 minutes. If he engaged in destructive behavior during break activities, the break ended and José's mother directed him back to work.

As training continued, José's mother thinned the reinforcement schedule by increasing the work requirements from one task to eight tasks before the microswitch was presented. As shown in the top panel of Figure 7.2, following the baseline condition that consisted of extinction for all responses, José's destructive behavior remained at low levels across FCT sessions, increased work requirements, and repeated extinction challenges to determine if the strength of adaptive behavior was greater than for challenging behavior. The data in the middle panel of Figure 7.2 demonstrate that under conditions of reinforcement (FCT), regardless of the amount of work required, José independently manded for play following task completion but that mands did not persist during repeated extinction challenges. Finally, the results in the bottom panel of Figure 7.2 indicate that José's task

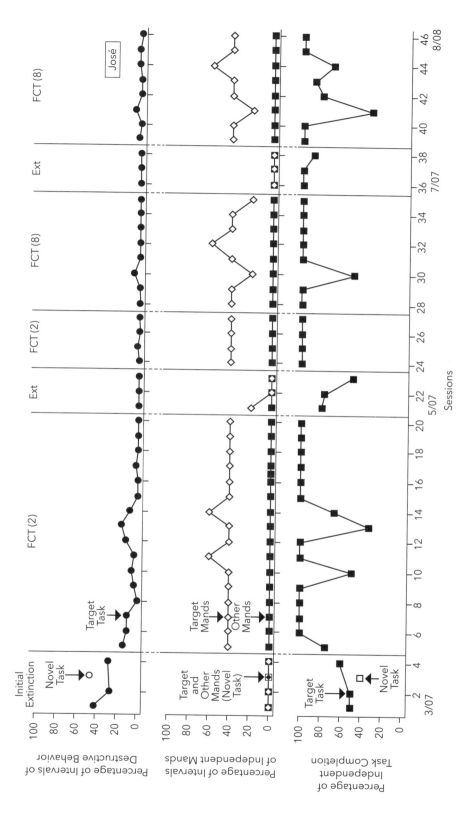

Figure 7.2. Percentage of intervals of destructive behavior (top panel), percentage of intervals of independent target manding and other manding (middle panel), and percentage of independent task completion (bottom panel) during FCT for José. FCT = functional communication training. Ext = extinction. (From Wacker, D. P., Harding, J. W., Berg, W. K., Lee, J. F., Schieltz, K. M., Padilla, Y. C., ... & Shahan, T. A. [2011]. An evaluation of persistence of treatment effects during long-term treatment of destructive behavior. *Journal of the Experimental Analysis of Behavior, 96,* 261–282. doi: 10.1901/jeab.2011.96-261. Reprinted by permission.)

completion was higher during FCT conditions compared to the first and second extinction conditions, but that task completion persisted during the final extinction condition, demonstrating durable treatment effects. To further assess durability, additional treatment challenges were conducted, again specifically testing for the strength of adaptive behavior versus challenging behavior. For example, one challenge involved an extended period of extinction to test José's persistence of mands, compliance, and decreased challenging behavior during sessions that lasted 15 mins rather than 5 mins. Results of all treatment challenges showed that the effects of treatment persisted and thus were durable.

Taken together, José's case illustrates how information gathered prior to implementing FCT is used in the design of FCT. For example, an S^D was used in the form of a card with the word "play" written on it that was attached to the microswitch to provide José with a signal for when reinforcement (work breaks with preferred activities) was available. More than one task was identified so that the therapist could implement FCT across sufficient exemplars. The therapist thinned the reinforcement schedule via demand fading in which the response requirements were increased from two to eight tasks. Response strengthening was assessed through repeated extinction probes and extended extinction sessions. Although mands did not persist during these sessions, near zero occurrences of challenging behavior were observed and task completion persisted.

Tangible Function: Ella

This case example demonstrates assessment and intervention for routines-based, parent-implemented FCT (see Simacek, Dimian, & McComas, 2016, for more specific details). Ella was a 4-year-old girl diagnosed with ASD. She did not engage in vocal communication, but occasionally signed MORE. Ella also engaged in a number of idiosyncratic communicative responses, such as leading her parents toward items and locations. Her parents reported that leading was the primary modality Ella used to gain access to preferred items and activities. Ella engaged in tantrum behavior (crying, yelling, dropping her body to the floor, attempted biting or hitting others, throwing items). Her parents reported that tantrums occurred frequently across environments, care providers, and activities, including restricted access to tangibles (e.g., food or kitchen area), task demands (e.g., puzzles at the table), and transitions. FCT, with coaching via telehealth, was conducted using a low-tech system (i.e., a picture card) embedded within natural routines and contexts.

Assessment was conducted in three phases: 1) functional assessment interview with parents (O'Neill et al., 1997), 2) structured descriptive assessment, and 3) functional assessment. First, the therapist gathered information via a functional assessment interview with Ella's parents on the target behaviors, potential antecedents, consequences, and MOs related to the challenging behavior. Next, the behavior therapist worked with Ella's parents to determine an appropriate mand modality to target during FCT. Ella had been exposed to a variety of AAC systems but did not use any independently and did not consistently use any one of them. At school, Ella's educators targeted a SGD that was comprised of a six-symbol array of digitized messages including requests and comments. In school and speech therapy, Ella was previously exposed to several manual signs (e.g., MORE) and the Picture Exchange Communication System (PECS; Bondy & Frost, 1994). At home,

Ella's parents used a combination of manual signs and vocal imitation prompts and although they had attempted to use the SGD, they reported it was unsuccessful and that Ella frequently threw the device. The behavior therapist and parents selected a picture exchange AAC system as the mand modality because 1) if Ella threw a card, no one would get hurt and no expensive equipment would get broken, 2) multiple printed and laminated copies of the cards were readily available for use in various locations around the home and in the community, and 3) the icons and messages on the picture cards could be transferred easily into Ella's SGD if desired following mastery of the picture exchange program. By having cards available for use in various locations and using icons and messages that could be transferred to Ella's SGD at a later time, common stimuli were naturally programmed into Ella's FCT program.

The second phase of assessment involved a structured descriptive assessment in which the behavior therapist observed the conditions reported in the functional assessment interview; free play, restricted access to tangibles (food/drink and videos), diverted parental attention, and demands (completing a puzzle at the table with a parent). The behavior therapist instructed Ella's parents to set up each of the above conditions and to respond to Ella's behavior as they typically would if they were not being observed. The behavior therapist then noted when challenging behavior occurred as well as other responses Ella independently displayed (i.e., leading a parent and approaching people/items). In addition, the behavior therapist noted natural arrangements in the routines the parents conducted within each condition. For example, her parents took turns caring for Ella's infant sibling, or if only one of them was available for a session, they placed the infant in the highchair with an activity. Similarly, the behavior therapist observed that Ella often watched the video on a tablet while either seated in her booster chair at the table or while in her parent's lap.

In the third phase of assessment, the behavior therapist coached the parents to set up and implement the FA conditions, including coaching to provide the appropriate contingencies for challenging behavior in a timely manner. The FA was conducted in which free play involved Ella playing with her parents on the living room floor, no consequences were provided for challenging behavior, and parents provided any items or activities to which she led them. During all other conditions, Ella and at least one parent were seated at the kitchen table. During the escape condition, the therapist instructed Ella's parents to prompt Ella to complete a puzzle that required her to match shapes. The therapist instructed Ella's parents to remove the task only contingent on challenging behavior. During the attention condition, Ella was seated at the kitchen table and at least one of her parents was seated next to her, paying attention to a sibling. The therapist instructed Ella's parents to only provide her with attention contingent on challenging behavior. During the tangible sessions, a preferred activity, identified during the structured descriptive assessment, was restricted (e.g., toys, videos, food). Contingent on challenging behavior, the therapist instructed Ella's parents to return the restricted item to Ella.

Results of the analyses indicated that tantrums occurred in the tangible condition. In the structured descriptive assessment, leading parents occurred most frequently during restricted access to tangibles. Ella's parents began FCT with the mand she had used occasionally in the past, "more," for preferred food and drinks during snack time and for preferred videos during playtime. Thus, the assessment results informed the routines-based FCT, which was tailored to fit in the natural routines of Ella and her family's day, allowed the therapists to program for natural contingencies of reinforcement, and capitalized on a mand she had previously used on occasion.

During FCT, Ella quickly acquired handing the picture exchange card (an example of AAC) to her parents (see Figure 7.3). Because she exhibited low levels of challenging behavior but high levels of leading (informal idiosyncratic communication), leading behavior was the target during FCT for preferred items. Leading was selected as the target because leading is not a communicative response that is likely to be acceptable or reinforced by someone who does not know her. Data from the analysis in the snack context are displayed in the top panel. The effects of FCT on mands and idiosyncratic behavior (leading) were analyzed in an ABAB design in which leading produced FR1 reinforcement during baseline conditions (mands did not produce reinforcement) and mands produced FR1 reinforcement during FCT conditions (leading did not produce reinforcement) to show that she would use whichever communicative response was reinforced. During both the initial baseline and return to baseline conditions, the frequency of leading behavior increased, whereas it occurred at lower levels during the FCT conditions, when it was on extinction. Similar results occurred for the video condition as shown in the bottom panel.

In summary, Ella's parents programmed common stimuli by providing multiple cards available for use in various locations and using icons and messages that could be transferred to Ella's SGD at a later time. FCT sessions were conducted during the natural routines of Ella and her family's day. For example, Ella's parents conducted FCT for food at the kitchen table during snack and meal time, during which she was given a small bite of food or drink. To gain additional bites or drinks, she was required to mand. This approach provided the opportunity for several response-reinforcer pairings to strengthen the mand, and multiple exemplars were trained in the form of various food and drink items that served as the reinforcers across several snacks and meals. Thus, the assessment results informed the routines-based FCT, which was tailored to fit within the natural routines of Ella and her family's day and allowed them to program for natural contingencies of reinforcement in the form of obtaining more food/drink when she manded.

Attention Function: Andy

Andy was a 12-year-old boy diagnosed with ASD. He had no spoken language and did not independently use any formal communication system. His special education team at school used an SGD with several themed pages that required him to use an index to locate the appropriate page and then to scan and identify the desired message from 16 or more messages on each page. Andy followed multiple-step directions and often took his parent's hand and put it on the device but did not use their hands to effectively navigate the device to generate a message. Occasionally, if the preferred items page was open, he would point to a snack item but would often refuse it when it was offered to him. He was referred for an evaluation and treatment of aggressive behavior toward his parents and 7-month-old sibling at home.

A functional assessment interview was conducted with Andy's mother. She reported that Andy had been aggressive with her on only a few occasions before

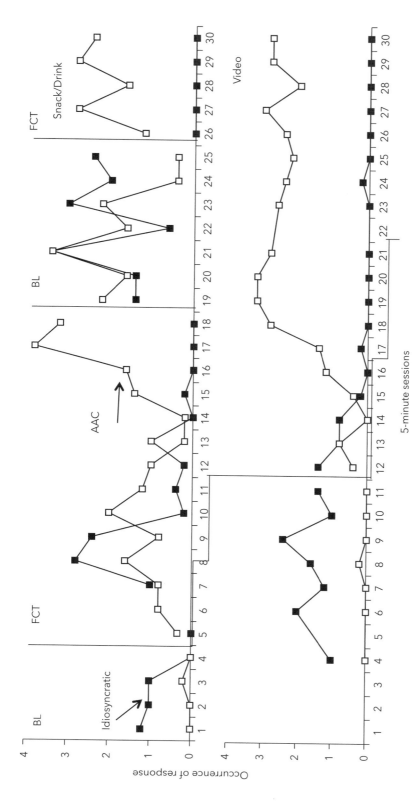

Figure 7.3. Ella's FCT data for two contexts: snack and video. Closed squares represent idiosyncratic responses and open squares represent mands for "more" using a picture exchange card with the word *more* and a black line drawing of two hands signing MORE on it. (From Simacek, J., Dimian, A.F., & McComas, J.J. [2016]. Communication intervention for young children with severe neurodevelopmental disabilities via telehealth. *Journal of Autism and Developmental Disabilities.* doi: 10.1007/s10803-016-3006-z. Adapted by permission.)

his sibling was born but that Andy's aggression had escalated to multiple times per day since the baby came home from the hospital. She reported that she never left the infant alone with Andy because she feared Andy would injure his sibling. She indicated that the aggression occurred most frequently when the three of them were together in the living room after school and after dinner and when she was feeding the infant. She was able to block most attempts at aggression toward the sibling by placing her body between Andy and the baby, which resulted in her being hit with sufficient force to be bruised on multiple occasions. She indicated that after Andy hit her, she talked to him about the fact that it was not okay to hit and that he had hurt her. She said that after those conversations, his aggression would not occur again for up to 30 minutes, but that after several minutes, "the effects seemed to wear off." She indicated that she did not require him to do any tasks except activities of daily living, during which she placed the baby in his crib with the door shut while she worked with Andy to dress, brush his teeth, bathe, and so forth. Andy's mother reported that Andy was compliant with those activities and that she did not recall him ever being aggressive during those activities.

Behavior therapists conducted descriptive assessment observations of Andy in his home with his mother and infant sibling during the after-school hours when aggression was reported to be most frequent. Andy was observed sitting on the floor in front of the television watching videos and when his mother was in the room, sitting on the couch on his mother's left side. The infant sibling was often strapped into a car seat or lying on the couch to the right side of Andy's mother so she was always between Andy and the baby. A free operant preference assessment (Roane, Vollmer, Ringdahl, & Marcus, 1998) was conducted that indicated Andy's two highly preferred activities were watching videos of his choosing and listening to music of his choosing. When Andy was offered a nonpreferred video, he took it to the shelf and exchanged it for a preferred video and when he was offered a particular album on the iPad, he effectively used the touch screen to change pages until he found a preferred album to play.

Andy's mother conducted the sessions of a structured descriptive assessment with coaching from a behavior therapist. Observations were conducted during free play that involved Andy, his mother, and his infant sibling in the living room watching one of Andy's preferred videos; a diverted attention condition, in which Andy was in the living room while his mother was in the kitchen with the infant; divided attention, while the three of them were at the dinner table but Andy's mother was feeding the infant who was seated in a highchair; and a task condition, in which Andy's mother instructed him to complete activities of daily living such as washing his face and brushing his teeth and hair. No restricted access to tangible condition was conducted because Andy was able to independently secure preferred items and the functional assessment interview did not indicate that access to tangibles was a viable hypothesis regarding Andy's aggression. The behavior therapist instructed Andy's mother to respond the way she normally would if she were alone at home with her children. Aggression was not observed during the task condition or divided attention condition when Andy's mother was in the kitchen with the infant. Attempts at aggression toward the infant and Andy's mother were observed during the free play condition and divided attention condition at the dinner table. Following each attempt or aggressive contact, Andy's mother shielded the infant, secured the infant in a car seat away from Andy, and had a brief conversation with

Andy about the aggression while stroking his hands to model gentle hands. The results suggested that aggression was most likely to occur in the presence of the infant sibling and that perhaps the presence of the sibling was an MO for attention-maintained aggression. An FA of aggression was not conducted because Andy's mother did not want to reinforce aggressive attempts toward the infant.

FCT was designed to provide attention from Andy's mother contingent on a mand rather than on aggressive behavior. During the descriptive assessment observations, behavior therapists noted that although Andy did not independently use the high-tech device, he would occasionally point to a preferred item on it if the correct page was open. The long-term goal was for Andy to independently use the device, beginning with touching the page. For this reason, the icon from the device for PLAY was used, which consisted of a black line-drawing of two hands making the manual sign PLAY within a picture exchange format. Several copies of the icon were printed and cut into 2" x 2" cards and separately laminated. Andy's mother gave him a card, placed a card next to him on the couch, and kept a card on the dinner table so that he could easily access a card in the places where aggression was likely to occur. FCT was conducted initially during 10-minute sessions in which the infant was secured in a car seat to the right of Andy's mother and Andy was seated to her left. She told him that if he wanted her to hold his hand, he should give her the card. Contingent on giving her the card, she stroked his hands, which was selected as the specific reinforcer based on the results of the structured descriptive assessment. During FCT sessions, a behavior therapist stood behind Andy in order to avoid eye contact or other forms of attention. Every 10 seconds, if he had not handed his mother the play card, the therapist tapped it. If Andy attempted to hit his mother, she turned her back on him and walked out of the room while the behavior therapist stood between Andy and the infant in the car seat, facing the infant. Within three sessions, Andy independently manded at least once per minute, sometimes as often as three times per minute, and by the fourth session, displayed no attempts at aggression.

Andy's mother then began changing the environmental arrangement by placing the infant on her left side instead of right side and by sitting in a chair instead of on the couch. These adjustments were designed to promote generalization via sufficient exemplars. Subsequent sessions were conducted at the dinner table while Andy's mother fed the baby. The behavior therapist stood behind Andy's chair at the table to prompt, if necessary. At the beginning of the first session at the table, Andy's mother slid the card toward Andy's plate and said, "If you want me to hold your hand, give me the card." He immediately handed her the card and she stopped feeding the baby and stroked Andy's hands for approximately 10 seconds, praising him for telling her what he wanted. During the rest of the meal, he manded several times and did not engage in aggressive behavior. Andy continued to mand approximately two times per minute and his mother now expressed frustration at being interrupted so frequently while trying to feed the baby. Therefore, a delay to reinforcement procedure was implemented during the subsequent sessions. Providing delayed reinforcement was important to make the intervention acceptable to his mother and also promoted maintenance through the use of intermittent reinforcement.

The behavior therapist and Andy's mother agreed that a flexible, varied approach to teaching Andy to tolerate a delay to reinforcement would work best in their home. Andy's mother signaled the delay by saying, "Just a minute, wait until I ____" and she filled in the blank with whatever she needed to finish at the moment. These signals were provided, from Andy's standpoint, in an unpredictable manner, and thus were indiscriminable. Although indiscriminable, they were signaled to show Andy that his mands would be reinforced. For example, if Andy manded for attention when the baby had just a small number of carrots left in the jar, his mother would say, "Just a minute, Andy, let me finish these carrots. Keep eating and I'll hold your hand in a minute." Then she would feed the baby no more than three additional bites before putting down the spoon and stroking Andy's hand. The first two times she said, "Just a minute," he handed her the card a second time. She repeated her statement and by the time she had repeated the statement, she had finished what she was doing and turned her attention to Andy. After the second time, she delivered delayed attention contingent on a mand. Andy never repeated the mand after hearing her vocal signal but, rather, kept eating until she stroked his hand. He did not display aggressive behavior during the delayed reinforcement sessions.

Delayed reinforcement was then introduced in the living room to continue with schedule thinning. Instead of securing the infant in the car seat at the beginning of the session, Andy's mother sat down with the infant in her arms to continue training using sufficient exemplars. As soon as Andy gave her the card, she said, "Just a minute, let me put the baby in the seat." Then after securing the baby in the seat, she held Andy's hand for approximately 10–20 seconds. Then she picked up the baby and repeated the procedure. These sessions continued without aggression.

In summary, descriptive assessment observations provided information about the context in which it would be necessary for Andy to continue to mand for attention postintervention and therefore informed the strategies used to actively program for generalization and maintenance during intervention. For example, Andy had a high-tech vocal output device but was not proficient in using it independently, so a picture exchange card was created with an icon that appeared on the device. This icon functioned as a way to program common stimuli and also provided a response that was more efficient and therefore effectively competed with aggression to obtain his mother's attention. Training sufficient exemplars was implemented by conducting the training in both the living room and at the dinner table where aggression was likely to occur. Furthermore, FCT sessions also eventually required Andy to produce a more effortful response (i.e., walk across the room to give his mother the card) so that manding would persist regardless of where his mother and sibling were seated. Finally, the reinforcement schedule was thinned with a natural delay signal by conducting training sessions in which Andy's mother said, "Just a minute until I finish _____." In this way, she acknowledged the mand and cued the duration of the delay but it was unknown to Andy whether attention following any particular mand would be immediate or delayed.

Automatic/Nonsocial Functions

In the preceding examples, the message selected for FCT consisted of a mand that matched the social function identified as maintaining challenging behavior during the FA. Falcomata, Roane, Feeney, and Stephenson (2010) used a similar approach to address a behavior maintained by automatic reinforcement. The participant in this study was a young boy with ASD who was referred for the assessment and treatment of elopement. The results of an FA showed that elopement occurred in an undifferentiated pattern across FA conditions. A subsequent evaluation showed that elopement was maintained by gaining access to a form of stereotypy (i.e., opening and closing doors in a hallway) that was maintained by automatic reinforcement. An FCT treatment that made access to the doors contingent on touching a communication card was effective in reducing elopement to near-zero levels.

Falcomata et al. (2010) selected touching a card as the mand modality for the FCT treatment because the researchers were able to control the participant's access to the card, making the card available when mands for door play would be honored and restricting the card when door play was not available. Repeated pairings of the card with the opportunity to mand for reinforcement should, over time, result in the presence of the card exerting stimulus control over manding. The communicative response, touching a card, was presumably less effortful than eloping, and the researchers reduced the effort even further by providing physical guidance if needed and presenting the card within close proximity to the participant, thus using differences in response effort to bias the participant's responses toward card touches over elopement. All card touches resulted in 30 seconds of access to door play and any instance of elopement resulted in extinction (i.e., access to door play was blocked).

The initial FCT treatment was conducted in an analogue hallway with the participant sitting in a chair prior to the opportunity to mand for door play. The second context for treatment (natural hallway) provided a closer match to the context associated with elopement; the child walked with the researcher through hallways in the building with the mand card available at the researcher's side. Delay to reinforcement was introduced to decrease the frequency of mands to a rate that was feasible for care providers. A timer was introduced to signal a delay to access the communication card and the opportunity to mand for door play. During the initial demand-fading sessions, the timer was set for a brief amount of time and held in view of the participant. When the timer sounded, the communication card was presented to the child and card touches resulted in access to door play. The length of the delay was increased across sessions until the participant reached the goal of a 10-minute delay to the opportunity to request access to door play.

Falcomata and colleagues (2010) were able to manipulate the child's access to automatic reinforcement (i.e., access to opening and closing doors) by locking or physically blocking the doors. In most examples, care providers are not able to directly observe or manipulate the specific stimuli assumed to function as automatic reinforcement. In these situations, one approach is to provide access to alternative stimuli, arbitrary and matched, that compete with the automatic reinforcers maintaining challenging behavior.

Arbitrary stimuli are not related to the function of challenging behavior (Fischer, Iwata, & Mazaleski, 1997) but may compete with automatic reinforcers if they are relatively more preferred. Numerous researchers have shown that providing access to items associated with low levels of challenging behavior and high levels of item engagement can be effective in reducing challenging behavior maintained by automatic reinforcement for some participants (Berg et al., 2016;

Groskreutz, Groskreutz, & Higbee, 2011; Ringdahl, Vollmer, Marcus, & Roane, 1997; Roscoe, Iwata, & Zhou, 2013). Other researchers have shown that items with sensory properties similar to those thought to maintain challenging behavior (i.e., matched stimuli) competed effectively with automatic reinforcement, even when the matched stimuli and access to automatic reinforcement via challenging behavior were both freely available (Piazza, Adelinis, Hanley, Goh, & Delia, 2000; Rapp, 2007). Hanley, Piazza, Keeney, Blakely-Smith, and Worsdell (1998) conducted communication training to teach a young boy with multiple disabilities to use a voice-output switch to mand for physical attention from a therapist (e.g., hugs, tickles, praise). The physical attention effectively competed with self-injurious behavior that was maintained by automatic reinforcement and instances of self-injury decreased to near-zero occurrences.

Studies such as Falcomata and colleagues (2010), Hanley and colleagues (1998), and Steege, Wacker, Berg, Cigrand, and Cooper (1989) show that treatments that include teaching participants to mand for preferred stimuli can be effective in reducing challenging behavior maintained by automatic reinforcement in the short term. Unfortunately, little information is available regarding the long-term effects of communication-based treatments for reducing behavior maintained by automatic reinforcement. Berg and colleagues (2016) evaluated the long-term effects of a communication-based treatment to reduce self-injury maintained by automatic reinforcement via monthly treatment probes conducted over a 12-month period. In this study, competing stimuli were identified within a choice (concurrent operants) assessment (Harding et al., 1999). A young woman with severe intellectual and developmental disabilities who engaged in multiple forms of self-injurious behavior was prompted to make the manual sign PLEASE to gain access to preferred toys that were identified as being more preferred than access to self-injurious behavior during a preceding concurrent operant assessment. The communication treatment included a response cost for instances of self-injury and resulted in a 75% reduction in challenging behavior from pretreatment levels. Berg and colleagues (2016) demonstrated long-term reductions in challenging behavior over a 1-year period. However, during reversals to a play condition with noncontingent access to play materials, self-injurious behavior resurged within minutes following the removal of both treatment components (mand to request the play items and response cost for self-injurious behavior), even following 10 months of treatment. These results demonstrate the need to identify approaches to increase the durability of treatment effects in the absence of the full treatment package for behavior maintained by automatic reinforcement. Long-term evaluations of the effects of procedures such as establishing stimulus control of opportunities for reinforcement of mands paired with demand fading (Falcomata et al., 2010; Roane, Fisher, Sgro, Falcomata, & Pabico, 2004) are needed to increase the long-term durability of treatment effects for behaviors maintained by automatic reinforcement.

CONCLUSION

More than 30 years after the demonstration by Carr and Durand (1985) that FCT is an effective treatment approach for decreasing challenging behavior and increasing appropriate requests (i.e., mands) for the functional reinforcer maintaining challenging behavior, scientists and practitioners should no longer be satisfied with demonstrations of initial behavior change that results from FCT. The initial effects of treatment should be considered as constituting necessary but not sufficient data for concluding that FCT was effective. Extensive literature on ABA shows that FCT is a robust intervention that is effective across behavior topographies, operant functions, disability categories, ages, and care providers with varied levels of training. Focus must now be on behavioral processes and applied procedures that produce durable behavior change. Rigorous examination of behavioral processes including but not limited to reinforcement schedules, extinction, stimulus control, and response generalization are essential for understanding the specific conditions under which durable behavior change can be expected. Information from these translational studies can, in turn, be used by applied behavior analysts to study how durability of treatment effects can be best programmed. To begin, FCT as an intervention to address challenging behavior is perhaps best considered as constituting a concurrent operants (choice) arrangement in which there are at least two response options: the challenging behavior and an appropriate alternative response (i.e., the mand). Intervention is then conducted to bias responding in favor of the mand.

The next generation of translational or applied researchers should consider building on the studies of Peck and colleagues (1996), Ringdahl and colleagues (2016), Simacek and colleagues (2016), and Winborn and colleagues (2002) to conduct the analyses within concurrent operants schedule designs that involve more than two response alternatives—for example, multiple mand modalities. This will lead to a number of additional second-generation questions. For example, if multiple mands are taught, does teaching them simultaneously or serially produce more durable behavior change in the form of suppressed recurrences of challenging behavior? As Falcomata and Wacker (2013) asked, do interventionists need to conduct sufficient exemplar training within response classes, or should they train across all relevant functional response classes simultaneously? What are the effects of the extinction component for challenging behavior in the differential reinforcement of alternative behavior arrangement for mands (Schieltz, Wacker, Ringdahl, & Berg, 2017)? Is behavior change more durable if mands emerge immediately in the early sessions of FCT and challenging behavior rarely, if ever, contacts extinction, or are numerous challenging behavior-extinction pairings necessary to enhance persistence of the mand and reduce the likelihood of resurgence of challenging behavior? Do procedures employed to enhance persistence of the mand also enhance persistence of the challenging behavior and if so, how can FCT be arranged to avoid enhancing persistence of challenging behavior? Designing FCT procedures based on understanding of basic behavioral processes is essential for promoting improved durability of FCT.

On a more applied level, we attempted to show in this chapter how descriptive assessment data can be used to design durable interventions. We also suggested the need to examine the effects of FCT on challenging behaviors that have proven to be resistant to other forms of treatment and/or have not been evaluated relative to FCT. In this chapter, we chose behavior maintained by automatic reinforcement as our case in point, and as shown in our case example, FCT may prove to be effective even for behaviors considered to be nonsocial.

REFERENCES

American Psychiatric Association. (2013). *Diagnostic and statistical manual of mental disorders, fifth edition* (DSM-5). Washington, DC: Author.

Asmus, J. M., Derby, K. M., Wacker, D. P., Porter, J., & Ulrich, S. (1993, May). The stimulus control effects of siblings during functional analyses conducted in home settings. In C. H. Kennedy (Chair), *Stimulus control of problem behavior*. Symposium presented at the annual meeting of the Association for Behavior Analysis International, Chicago, IL.

Asmus, J. M., Wacker, D. P., Richman, D., Cooper, L. J., Harding, J., Berg, W., & Andelman, M. (1996, May). The application of concurrent choices to behavior maintained by automatic reinforcement. In T. R. Vollmer (Chair), *Developing treatments based on functional analysis*. Symposium presented at the annual meeting of the Association for Behavior Analysis International, San Francisco, CA.

Austin, J. E., & Tiger, J. H. (2015). Providing alternative reinforcers to facilitate tolerance to delayed reinforcement following functional communication training. *Journal of Applied Behavior Analysis, 48,* 663–668. doi:10.1002/jaba.215

Berg, W. K., Wacker, D. P., Ringdahl, J. E., Stricker, J., Vinquist, K., Kumar Dutt, A. S., Dolezal, D., Luke, J., Kemmerer, L., & Mews, J. (2016). An integrated model for guiding the selection of treatment for components for problem behavior maintained by automatic reinforcement. *Journal of Applied Behavior Analysis, 49,* 617–638.

*Betz, A. M., Fisher, W. W., Roane, H. S., Mintz, J. C., & Owen, T. M. (2013). A component analysis of schedule thinning during functional communication training. *Journal of Applied Behavior Analysis, 46,* 219–241. doi:10.1002/jaba.23

Bondy, A. S., & Frost, L. A. (1994). The picture exchange communication system. *Focus on Autistic Behavior, 9,* 1–19.

Buckley, S. D., & Newchok, D. K. (2005). Differential impact of response effort within a response chain on use of mands in a student with autism. *Research in Developmental Disabilities, 26,* 77–85.

Carr, E. G., & Durand, V. M. (1985). Reducing behavior problems through functional communication training. *Journal of Applied Behavior Analysis, 18,* 111–126.

*Dalmau, Y. C. P., Wacker, D. P., Harding, J. W., Berg, W. K., Schieltz, K. M., Lee, J. F., . . . Kramer, A. R. (2011). A preliminary evaluation of functional communication training effectiveness and language preference when Spanish and English are manipulated. *Journal of Behavioral Education, 20,* 233–251.

*Danov, S. E., Hartman, E., McComas, J. J., & Symons, F. J. (2010). Evaluation of two communicative response modalities for a child with autism and self-injury. *The Journal of Speech and Language Pathology–Applied Behavior Analysis, 5,* 70–79.

*Davis, T. N., Fuentes, L., & Durand, S. (2014). Examination of systematic durations of presession reinforcer access on functional communication training. *Journal of Developmental and Physical Disabilities, 26,* 263–270. doi:10.1007/s10882-013-9360-2

Durand, V. M., & Carr, E. G. (1991). Functional communication training to reduce challenging behavior: Maintenance and application in new settings. *Journal of Applied Behavior Analysis, 24,* 251–264.

*Falcomata, T. S., Muething, C. S., Gainey, S., Hoffman, K., & Fragale, C. (2013). Further evaluations of functional communication training and chained schedules of reinforcement to treat multiple functions of challenging behavior. *Behavior Modification, 37,* 723–746. doi:10.1177/0145445513500785

*Falcomata, T. S., Muething, C. S., Roberts, G. J., Hamrick, J., & Shpall, C. (2016). Further evaluation of latency-based brief functional analysis methods: An evaluation of treatment utility. *Developmental Neurorehabilitation, 19,* 88–94. doi.org/10.3109/17518423.2014.910281

*Falcomata, T. S., Roane, H. S., Feeney, B. J., & Stephenson, K. M. (2010). Assessment and treatment of elopement maintained by access to stereotypy. *Journal of Applied Behavior Analysis, 43,* 513–517. doi:10.1901/jaba.2010.43-513

*Falcomata, T. S., Roane, H. S., Muething, C. S., Stephenson, K. M., & Ing, A. D. (2012). Functional communication training and chained schedules of reinforcement to treat

---

Papers included in the literature review are marked by an *.

challenging behavior maintained by terminations of activity interruptions. *Behavior Modification, 36,* 630–649. doi:10.1007/s10882-012-9287-z

Falcomata, T. S., & Wacker, D. P. (2013). On the use of strategies for programming generalization during functional communication training: A review of the literature. *Journal of Developmental and Physical Disabilities, 25,* 5–15. doi:10.1007/s10882-012-9311-3

*Falcomata, T. S., Wacker, D. P., Ringdahl, J. E., Vinquist, K., & Dutt, A. (2013). An evaluation of generalization of mands during functional communication training. *Journal of Applied Behavior Analysis, 46,* 444–454.

*Falcomata, T. S., White, P., Muething, C. S., & Fragale, C. (2012). A functional communication training and chained schedule procedure to treat challenging behavior with multiple functions. *Journal of Developmental and Physical Disabilities, 24,* 529–538. doi:10.1007/s10882-012-9287-z

Fischer, S. M., Iwata B. A., & Mazaleski, J. L. (1997). Noncontingent delivery of arbitrary reinforcers as treatment for self-injurious behavior. *Journal of Applied Behavior Analysis, 30,* 239–249.

Fisher, W. W., Greer, B. D., Fuhrman, A. M., & Querim, A. C. (2015). Using multiple schedules during functional communication training to promote rapid transfer of treatment effects. *Journal of Applied Behavior Analysis, 48,* 713–733.

*Flynn, S. D., & Lo, Y. Y. (2016). Teacher implementation of trial-based functional analysis and differential reinforcement of alternative behavior for students with challenging behavior. *Journal of Behavioral Education, 25,* 1–31. doi:10.1007/s10864-015-9231-2

Greer, B. D., Fisher, W. W., Saini, V., Owen, T. M., & Jones, J. K. (2016). Functional communication training during reinforcement schedule thinning: An analysis of 25 applications. *Journal of Applied Behavior Analysis, 49,* 105–121.

Groskreutz, M. P., Groskreutz, N. C., & Higbee, T. S. (2011) Response competition and stimulus preference in the treatment of automatically reinforced behavior: A comparison. *Journal of Applied Behavior Analysis, 44,* 211–215. doi:10.1016/j.rasd.2011.01.018

*Grow, L. L., Kelley, M. E., Roane, H. S., & Shillingsburg, M. A. (2008). Utility of extinction-induced response variability for the selection of mands. *Journal of Applied Behavior Analysis, 41,* 15–24. doi:10.1901/jaba.2008.41-15

Hagopian, L. P., Boelter, E. W., & Jarmolowicz, D. P. (2011). Reinforcement schedule thinning following functional communication training: Review and recommendations. *Behavior Analysis in Practice, 4,* 4–16.

Hanley, G. P., Iwata, B. A., & Thompson, R. H. (2001). Reinforcement schedule thinning following treatment with functional communication training. *Journal of Applied Behavior Analysis, 34,* 17–38. doi:10.1901/jaba.2001.34-17

Hanley, G. P., Piazza, C. C., Keeney, K. M., Blakeley-Smith, A. B., & Worsdell, A. S. (1998). Effects of wrist weights on self-injurious and adaptive behaviors. *Journal of Applied Behavior Analysis, 31,* 307–310.

Harding, J. W., Wacker, D. P., Berg, W. K., Cooper, L. J., Asmus, J., Mlela, K., & Muller, J. (1999). An analysis of choice making in the assessment of young children with severe behavior problems. *Journal of Applied Behavior Analysis, 32,* 63–82.

Harding, J. W., Wacker, D. P., Berg, W. K., Winborn-Kemmerer, L., Lee, J. F., & Ibrahimovic, M. (2009). Analysis of multiple manding topographies during functional communication training. *Education and Treatment of Children, 32,* 21–36.

Heath, A. K., Ganz, J. B., Parker, R., Burke, M., & Ninci, J. (2015). A meta-analytic review of functional communication training across mode of communication, age, and disability. *Review Journal of Autism and Developmental Disorders, 2,* 155–166. doi:10.1007/s40489-014-0044-3

Horner, R. H. & Day, H. M. (1991). The effects of response efficiency on functionally equivalent and competing mands. *Journal of Applied Behavior Analysis, 24,* 719–732.

Iwata, B. A., Dorsey, M. F., Slifer, K. J., Bauman, K. E., & Richman, G. S. (1994). Toward a functional analysis of self-injury. *Journal of Applied Behavior Analysis, 27,* 197–209. (Reprinted from *Analysis and Intervention in Developmental Disabilities, 2,* 3–20, 1982)

Jang, J., Dixon, D. R., Tarbox, J., & Granpeesheh, D. (2011). Symptom severity and challenging behavior in children with ASD. *Journal of Autism Spectrum Disorders, 5,* 1028–1032.

*Jarmolowicz, D. P., DeLeon, I. G., & Contrucci-Kuhn, S. A. (2009). Functional communication during signaled reinforcement and/or extinction. *Behavioral Interventions, 24,* 265–273.

Kahng, S., Hendrickson, D. J., & Vu, C. P. (2000). Comparison of single and multiple functional communication training responses for the treatment of problem behavior. *Journal of Applied Behavior Analysis, 33,* 321–324. doi:10.1901/jaba.2000.33-321

Kalb, L. G., Stuart, E., Freedman, B., Zablotsky, B., & Vasa, R. (2012). Psychiatric-related emergency department visits among children with an autism spectrum disorder. *Pediatric Emergency Care, 28,* 1269–1275.

Kuhn, D. E., Chirighin, A. E., & Zelenka, K. (2010). Discriminated functional communication: A procedural extension of functional communication training. Journal of Applied Behavior Analysis, 43, 249–264. doi:10.1901/jaba.2010.43-249

Laraway, S., Snycerski, S., Michael, J., & Poling, A. (2003). Motivating operations and terms to describe them: Some further refinements. *Journal of Applied Behavior Analysis, 36,* 407–414.

Leon, Y., Hausman, N. L., Kahng, S., & Becraft, J. L. (2010). Further examination of discriminated functional communication. Journal of Applied Behavior Analysis, 43, 525–530. doi:10.1901/jaba.2010.43-525

Lindgren, S., Wacker, D., Suess A., Schieltz, K., Pelzel, K., Kopelman, T., Lee, J., Romani, P., & Waldron, D. (2016). Telehealth and autism: Treating challenging behavior at lower cost. *Pediatrics, 137*(Suppl. 2), S167–S175. doi:10.1542/peds.2015-2851O

*Machalicek, W., Lequia, J., Pinkelman, S., Knowles, C., Raulston, T., Davis, T., & Alresheed, F. (2016). Behavioral telehealth consultation with families of children with autism spectrum disorder. *Behavioral Interventions, 31,* 223–250. doi:10.1002/bin.1450

Mancil, G. R. (2006). Functional communication training: A review of the literature related to children with autism. *Education and Treatment of Children, 41,* 213–224.

Mancil, G. R., & Boman, M. (2010). Functional communication training in the classroom: A guide for success. *Preventing School Failures, 54,* 238–246. doi:1080/10459881003745195

Michael, J. (1982). Distinguishing between discriminative and motivational functions of stimuli. *Journal of the Experimental Analysis of Behavior, 37,* 149–155.

Nevin, J. A., & Wacker, D. P. (2013). Response strength and persistence. In G. J. Madden (Ed.), *APA Handbook of Behavior Analysis* (Vol. 2, pp. 109–128). Washington, DC: APA Books.

*Olive, M. L., Lang, R. B., & Davis, T. N. (2008). An analysis of the effects of functional communication and a voice output communication aid for a child with autism spectrum disorder. *Research in Autism Spectrum Disorders, 2,* 223–236. doi:10.1016/j.rasd.2007.06.002

O'Neill, R. E., Horner, R. H., Albin, R. W., Sprague, J. R., Storey, K., & Newton, J. S. (1997). *Functional assessment and program development for problem behavior: A practical handbook.* Pacific Grove, CA: Brooks/Cole Publishing.

Peck, S. M., Wacker, D. P., Berg, W. K., Cooper, L. J., Brown, K. A., Richman, D., . . . Millard, T. (1996). Choice-making treatment of young children's severe behavior problems. *Journal of Applied Behavior Analysis, 29,* 263–290.

Pelios, L., Morren, J., Tesch, D., & Axelrod, S. (1999). The impact of functional analysis methodology on treatment choice for self-injurious and aggressive behavior. *Journal of Applied Behavior Analysis, 32,* 185–195.

Piazza, C. C., Adelinis, J. D., Hanley, G. P., Goh, H., & Delia, M. D. (2000). An evaluation of the effects of matched stimuli on behaviors maintained by automatic reinforcement. *Journal of Applied Behavior Analysis, 33,* 13–27. doi:10.1901/jaba 1998.31-165

Rapp, J. T. (2007). Further evaluation of methods to identify matched stimulation. *Journal of Applied Behavior Analysis, 40,* 73–88. doi:10.1901/jaba.2007.142-05

Reichle, J., & Wacker, D. P. (2017). *Communicative alternatives to problem behavior: Implementing functional communication training.* New York, NY: Guilford Press.

Ringdahl, J. E., Berg, W. K., Wacker, D. P., Ryan, S., Ryan, A., Crook, K., & Molony, M. (2016). Further demonstrations of individual preference among mand modalities during functional communication training. *Journal of Physical and Developmental Disabilities, 28,* 905–917: doi:10.1007/s10882-016-9518-9

Ringdahl, J. E., Falcomata, T. S., Christensen, T. J., Bass-Ringdahl, S. M., Lentz, A., Dutt, A., & Schuh-Claus, J. (2009). Evaluation of a pretreatment assessment to select mand topographies for functional communication training. *Research in Developmental Disabilities, 30,* 330–341. doi.org/10.1016/j.ridd.2008.06.002

Ringdahl, J. E., Vollmer, T. R., Marcus, B. A., & Roane, H. S. (1997). An analogue evaluation of environmental enrichment: The role of stimulus preference. *Journal of Applied Behavior Analysis, 30,* 203–216.

*Rispoli, M., Camargo, S., Machalicek, W., Lang, R., & Sigafoos, J. (2014). Functional communication training in the treatment of problem behavior maintained by access to rituals. *Journal of Applied Behavior Analysis, 47,* 580–593. doi:10.1002/jaba.130

Roane, H. S., Fisher, W. W., Sgro, G. M., Falcomata, T. S., & Pabico, R. R. (2004). An alternative method of thinning reinforcer delivery during differential reinforcement. *Journal of Applied Behavior Analysis, 37,* 213–218.

Roane, H. S., Vollmer, T. R., Ringdahl, J. E., & Marcus, B. A. (1998). Evaluation of a brief stimulus preference assessment. *Journal of Applied Behavior Analysis, 31,* 605–620.

Roscoe, E. M., Iwata, B. A., & Zhou, L. (2013). Assessment and treatment of chronic hand mouthing. *Journal of Applied Behavior Analysis, 46,* 181–189. doi:10.1002/jaba.14

*Santiago, J. L., Hanley, G. P., Moore, K., & Jin, C. S. (2016). The generality of interview-informed functional analyses: Systematic replications in school and home. *Journal of Autism and Developmental Disorders, 46,* 797–811. doi:10.1007/s10803-015-2617-0

*Schieltz, K. M., Wacker, D. P., Harding, J. W., Berg, W. K., Lee, J. F., Dalmau, Y. C. P., . . . Ibrahimović, M. (2011). Indirect effects of functional communication training on non-targeted disruptive behavior. *Journal of Behavioral Education, 20,* 15–32. doi:10.1007/s10864-011-9131-z

Schieltz, K. M., Wacker, D. P., Ringdahl, J. E., & Berg, W. K. (2017). Basing assessment and treatment of problem behavior on behavioral momentum theory: Analyses of behavioral persistence. *Behavioural Processes.141,* 75–84. doi:10.1016/j.beproc.2017.02.013

*Shamlian, K. D., Fisher, W. W., Steege, M. W., Cavanaugh, B. M., Samour, K., & Querim, A. C. (2016). Evaluation of multiple schedules with naturally occurring and therapist-arranged discriminative stimuli following functional communication training. *Journal of Applied Behavior Analysis, 29,* 228–250. doi:10.1002/jaba.293

Simacek, J., Dimian, A. F., & McComas, J. J. (2016). Communication intervention for young children with severe neurodevelopmental disabilities via telehealth. *Journal of Autism and Developmental Disabilities.* doi:10.1007/s10803-016-3006-z

Soke, G. N., Rosenberg, S. A., Hamman, R. F., Fingerlin, T., Robinson, C., Carpenter, L., Giarelli, E., Lee, L-C., Wiggins, L. D., Durkin, M. S., & DiGuiseppi, C. (2016). Brief report: Prevalence of self-injurious behaviors among children with Autism Spectrum Disorder—A population-based study. *Journal of Autism and Developmental Disorders, 46,* 3607–3614. doi:10.1007/s10803-016-2879-1

*Stevenson, M. T., Ghezzi, P. M., & Valenton, K. G. (2015). FCT and delay fading for elopement with a child with autism. *Behavior Analysis in Practice, 9,* 169–173. doi:10.1007/s40617-015-0089-5

Steege, M. W., Wacker, D. P., Berg, W. K., Cigrand, K. K., & Cooper, L. J. (1989). The use of behavioral assessment to prescribe and evaluate treatments for severely handicapped children. *Journal of Applied Behavior Analysis, 22,* 23–33.

Stokes, T. F., & Baer, D. M. (1977). An implicit technology of generalization. *Journal of Applied Behavior Analysis, 10,* 349–367. doi:10.1901/jaba.1977.10-349

Stokes, T. F., & Osnes, P. G. (1989). An operant pursuit of generalization. *Behavior Therapy, 20,* 337–355. doi:10.1016/S0005-7894(89)80054-1

*Suess, A. N., Romani, P. W., Wacker, D. P., Dyson, S. M., Kuhle, J. L., Lee, J. F., Lindgren, S. D., Kopelman, T. G., Pelzel, K. E., & Waldron, D. B. (2014). Evaluating the treatment fidelity of parents who conduct in-home functional communication training with coaching via telehealth. *Journal of Behavioral Education, 23,* 34–59.

Suess, A. N., Wacker, D. P., Schwartz, J. E., Lustig, N., & Detrick, J. (2016). Evidence on the use of telehealth in an outpatient behavior clinic. *Journal of Applied Behavior Analysis, 49,* 686–692.

Tiger, J. H., Hanley, G. P., & Bruzek, J. (2008). Functional communication training: A review and practical guide. *Behavior Analysis in Practice, 1,* 16–23.

*Torelli, J. N., Lambert, J. M., Da Fonte, M. A., Denham, K. N., Jedrzynski, T. M., & Houchins-Juarez, N. J. (2015). Assessing acquisition of and preference for mand topographies during functional communication training. *Behavior Analysis in Practice, 9,* 165–168. doi:10.1007/s40617-015-0083-y

Volkert, V. M., Lerman, D. C., Call, N. A., & Trosclair-Lasserre, N. (2009). An evaluation of resurgence during treatment with functional communication training. *Journal of Applied Behavior Analysis, 42,* 145–160.

Wacker, D. P., Berg, W. K., Harding, J. W., Barretto, A., Rankin, B., & Ganzer, J. (2005). Treatment effectiveness, stimulus generalization, and acceptability to parents of functional communication training. *Educational Psychology, 25,* 233–256. doi:10.1080/0144341042000301184

*Wacker, D. P., Harding, J. W., & Berg, W. K. (2008). Evaluation of mand-reinforcer relations following long-term functional communication training. *The Journal of Speech and Language Pathology–Applied Behavior Analysis, 3,* 25–35. doi:10.1901/jaba.2008.-25.

*Wacker, D. P., Harding, J. W., Berg, W. K., Lee, J. F., Schieltz, K. M., Padilla, Y. C., . . . Shahan, T. A. (2011). An evaluation of persistence of treatment effects during long-term treatment of destructive behavior. *Journal of the Experimental Analysis of Behavior, 96,* 261–282.

*Wacker, D. P., Lee, J. F., Dalmau, Y. C. P., Kopelman, T. G., Lindgren, S. D., Kuhle, J., . . . Waldron, D. B. (2013). Conducting functional communication training via telehealth to reduce the problem behavior of young children with autism. *Journal of Developmental and Physical Disabilities, 25,* 35–48. doi:10.1007/s10882-012-9314-0

Winborn, L., Wacker, D. P., Richman, D. M., Asmus, J., & Geier, D. (2002). Assessment of mand selection for functional communication training packages. *Journal of Applied Behavior Analysis, 35,* 295–298.

Winborn-Kemmerer, L., Ringdahl, J. E., Wacker, D. P., & Kitsukawa, K. (2009). A demonstration of individual preference for novel mands during functional communication training. *Journal of Applied Behavior Analysis, 42,* 185–189.

Winborn-Kemmerer, L., Wacker, D. P., Harding, J., Boelter, E., Berg, W., & Lee, J. (2010). Analysis of mand selection across different stimulus conditions. *Education and Treatment of Children, 33,* 49–64.

7.1

Studies with One or More Participant Included in the Review

Study	Participants (age; dx)	Target problem behavior	Targeted behavioral function	Target communicative response	AAC mode	Treatment results
Betz, Fisher, Roane, Mintz, & Owen (2013)	Casey Age: 5 Dx: PDD-NOS	Elopement	Tang	"May I have my _____ please?"	Vocal	*Exp 1:* FCT increased the FCR and decreased problem behavior *Exp 2:* FCR rates were high in the reinforcement component and low in the extinction component when signaled (multiple schedule) and undifferentiated when unsignaled (mixed schedule) *Exp 3:* Gradual schedule thinning was not necessary when the reinforcement component was signaled (i.e., FCR rate remained high and problem behavior low when the schedule quickly shifted from 60/60 to 60/240)
Dalmau et al. (2011)	Sofia Age: 5 Dx: PDD & spinal muscular atrophy	SIB, Agg, Dest	Esc	"Play"	Microswitch, vocal, or signing	FCT resulted in decreases in problem behavior and increases in the FCR across English and Spanish sessions
	Javier Age: 6 Dx: ASD & Mild ID	SIB, Agg, Dest	Esc	"Play"	Microswitch, Vocal, or Signing	No preference for manding or obtaining reinforcement in either English or Spanish was shown
Danov, Hartman, McComas, & Symons (2010)	John Age: 3 Dx: ASD	SIB	Tang	"(Name of item)" versus handing a picture card	Vocal versus picture exchange	Picture exchange resulted in increases in the FCR and decreases in problem behavior; vocal requests rarely occurred
Davis, Fuentes, & Durand (2014)	Amos Age: 6 Dx: ASD & ID	Disrup	Tang	"I want Barney"	Vocal	Varying levels of presession access to the relevant reinforcer resulted in decreases in problem behavior and increases in the FCR during FCT The FCR occurred more often during 25% presession access sessions when compared to 50% presession access sessions

Study	Participant	Problem behavior	Function	FCR	Modality	Outcome
Falcomata, Muething, Gainey, Hoffman, & Fragale (2013)	Alonzo Age: 7 Dx: ASD	Agg, Disrup	Esc, Tang, Att	Requests for S^D (i.e., "wristband please") or functional requests (i.e., "iPad please," "break please")	Vocal	FCT resulted in decreases in problem behavior and increases in the FCR for the S^D, which maintained during schedule thinning Specific functional requests rarely occurred
	Joe Age: 12 Dx: ASD	Agg, SIB	Esc, Tang, Att			
Falcomata, Muething, Roberts, Hamrick, & Shpall (2016)	Aaron Age: 4 Dx: ASD	Agg	Tang	"TV please"	Vocal	FCT resulted in decreases in problem behavior and increases in the FCR, which maintained during schedule thinning
	Vincent Age: 4 Dx: ASD	Disrup, Elopement	Tang	"Can I play with the computer?"		
Falcomata, Roane, Feeney, & Stephenson (2010)	John Age: 5 Dx: ASD	Elopement	Tang, Auto	Card touches	Card touches	FCT resulted in decreases in problem behavior and increases in the FCR across settings, which maintained during schedule thinning
Falcomata, Roane, Muething, Stephenson, & Ing (2012)	Steph Age: 8 Dx: Asperger syndrome	Agg, Disrup, Disrobing	Tang	"May I have the necklace?"	Vocal	FCT resulted in decreases in problem behavior and increases in the FCR, which maintained during schedule thinning
	Mike Age: 8 Dx: ASD	Agg, SIB, Dest	Tang	"May I have the star?"		
Falcomata, Wacker, Ringdahl, Vinquist, & Dutt (2013)	Lowell Age: 4 Dx: ASD	SIB, Disrup	Att, Esc, Tang	Card Touches and Signs (i.e., "want," "mom," "please," "finished," "break")	Card touches and manual signs	Stimulus control training procedures effectively taught manual signs and decreased problem behavior across functional contexts Generalization of trained mands was also observed
	Nick Age: 3 Dx: ASD	Agg, SIB, Disrup	Att, Esc, Tang			

(continued)

Study	Participants (age; dx)	Target problem behavior	Targeted behavioral function	Target communicative response	AAC mode	Treatment results
Falcomata, White, Muething, & Fragale (2012)	Danny Age: 8 Dx: ASD	Disrup	Att, Esc, Tang	"May I have the wristband?"	Vocal	FCT resulted in decreases in problem behavior and increases in the FCR, which maintained during demand fading
Flynn & Lo (2016)	1A Age: 12 Dx: ASD	Disrup, Elopement	Esc	"Break please"	Vocal	FCT resulted in decreases in problem behavior and increases in the FCR
	1B Age: 12 Dx: ASD	Disrup	Att	Raising hand	Gestural	
	2A Age: 11 Dx: ASD	Disrup	Att	Raising hand	Gestural	
	2B Age: 11 Dx: ASD	Giggling	Esc	Holding up picture card	Gestural	
Grow, Kelley, Roane, & Shillingsburg (2008)	Gus Age: 8 Dx: ASD	Disrup	Tang	"Don't" requests	Vocal	FCT resulted in decreases in problem behavior and increases in the FCR
	Curtis Age: 10 Dx: ASD	Agg, Disrup, Grabbing	Esc	Shaking head "no"	Gestural	
	Jason Age: 15 Dx: ASD	Agg	Tang	Reaching for an item	Gestural	
Jarmolowicz, DeLeon, & Contrucci-Kuhn (2009)	Rachel Age: 13 Dx: ASD, seizures, ID	Agg, Disrup	Tang	Picture exchange	Picture exchange	FCT resulted in decreases in problem behavior and increases in the FCR with the signaled FR1/EXT schedule obtaining better results during schedule thinning than other schedules assessed (signaled FR1 or signaled EXT)

Citation	Participant	Target behavior	Function	FCR	Mode	Results
Machalicek, et al. (2016)	Lily Age: 8 Dx: ASD	Agg, Disrup, SIB, Dest	Esc	"I need a break"	Vocal or gestural (i.e., pointing, handing card)	Decreases in problem behavior occurred across multiple treatment strategies (antecedent strategies, FCT, DRA) implemented by parents with behavioral consultation occurring via telehealth
	Logan Age: 9 Dx: ASD, Fragile X, seizure disorder	Agg, Disrup, SIB	Tang	"I want…"		
	Emma Age: 16 Dx: ASD	SIB, Disrup	Tang	"I want…"		
Olive, Lang, & Davis (2008)	Kerri Age: 4 Dx: ASD	Disrup	Att	Pressing button or "I want you to play with me"	VOCA or Vocal	FCT resulted in decreases in problem behavior and increases in the FCR across activities
Rispoli, Camargo, Machalicek, Lang, & Sigafoos (2014)	Timmy Age: 4 Dx: PDD-NOS	Disrup	Tang	"I don't want that"	Vocal	FCT resulted in decreases in problem behavior and increases in the FCR across routines, which maintained during schedule thinning
	John Age: 3 Dx: ASD	Agg, Disrup	Tang	Handing picture	Picture Exchange	
	Diego Age: 3 Dx: PDD-NOS	Agg, SIB, Disrup	Tang	Handing picture	Picture Exchange	
Santiago, Hanley, Moore, & Jin (2016)	Zeke Age: 14 Dx: ASD	SIB, Agg, Disrup	Esc/Tang/Att	"May I have my way please?"	AAC	FCT resulted in decreases in problem behavior and increases in simple and complex FCRs, which maintained during denial and delay tolerance training
	Karen Age: 11 Dx: ASD	Agg	Tang/Att, Esc/ Preferred conversation	"Can I have that?" and "Change topics"	Vocal	

(continued)

Study	Participants (age; dx)	Target problem behavior	Targeted behavioral function	Target communicative response	AAC mode	Treatment results
Schieltz et al. (2011)	Juan *Age:* 3 *Dx:* ASD	Agg, SIB, Dest, Disrup	Esc	"Play please"	Microswitch, Vocal, or Gestural	FCT resulted in decreases in targeted and nontargeted problem behavior and increases in the FCR, which maintained during demand fading
	Bud *Age:* 3 *Dx:* ASD, ID	Agg, SIB, Dest, Disrup	Esc			
Shamlian et al. (2016)	Maurice *Age:* 5 *Dx:* ASD	Disrup	Tang	"I want movie please"	Vocal	FCT resulted in decreases in problem behavior and increases in the FCR
	Bernard *Age:* 5 *Dx:* ASD	Disrup	Tang	"Movie please"	Vocal	FCR was obtained more rapidly with arranged S^Ds than with naturally occurring stimuli (2 of 3 participants)
	Keith *Age:* 10 *Dx:* ASD, cerebral palsy	Agg, SIB, Disrup	Tang	"I want the iPad please"	Vocal	Generalization to novel contexts occurred more with arranged stimuli than with naturally occurring stimuli (2 of 3 participants)
Stevenson, Ghezzi, & Valenton (2015)	Damon *Age:* 9 *Dx:* ASD	Elopement	Att, Tang	Requesting items or activities	Vocal	FCT resulted in decreases in problem behavior and increases in the FCR, which maintained during schedule thinning
Suess et al. (2014)	Lane *Age:* 2 *Dx:* PDD-NOS	SIB, Agg, Dest	Esc	"Play please"	Microswitch or Vocal	FCT resulted in decreases in problem behavior across coached and independent trials, which maintained during demand fading
	Jace *Age:* 2 *Dx:* PDD-NOS, ID	SIB, Agg, Dest	Esc		Microswitch	
	Jude *Age:* 3 *Dx:* PDD-NOS	SIB, Agg, Dest	Esc		Microswitch or Vocal	

Study	Participant	Agg	Esc, Tang	Pressing device or touching therapist with a picture card	iPad or GoTalk or Picture exchange	Results
Torelli et al. (2015)	Lucas *Age: 4* *Dx: ASD*	Agg	Esc, Tang			FCT resulted in decreases in problem behavior and increases in the FCR Preference for the iPad was shown across functional contexts
Wacker, Harding, & Berg (2008)	Susan *Age: 5* *Dx: ASD, DD*	SIB, Agg, Dest	Att	"Please" and "Mom"	Vocal	The FCR differentially occurred across conditions that provided different durations of attention contingent on appropriate mands
Wacker et al. (2011)	Tina *Age: 3* *Dx: ASD, DD*	Agg, Dest	Esc	"Play"	Vocal, Manual sign, or Microswitch	FCT resulted in decreases in problem behavior and increases in the FCR, which maintained during demand fading and in the absence of FCT following months of treatment
Wacker et al. (2013)	Jack *Age: 5* *Dx: ASD*	Agg, SIB, Dest, Disrup, Elopement, Repetitive Behavior, Dangerous Behavior	Esc	Functionally relevant request	Vocal, Manual Sign, or Microswitch	FCT, conducted via telehealth, resulted in decreases in problem behavior, which maintained during demand fading
	Jake *Age: 5* *Dx: ASD*		Esc			
	Jill *Age: 6* *Dx: ASD*		Esc			
	Mitt *Age: 2* *Dx: ASD*		Tang			
	Tad *Age: 5* *Dx: PDD-NOS*		Att			
	Zeke *Age: 5* *Dx: PDD-NOS*		Esc			

Key: Dx, diagnosis or diagnoses; PDD-NOS, pervasive developmental disorder not otherwise specified; ASD, autism spectrum disorder; ID, intellectual disability; DD, developmental disability; Agg, aggression; SIB, self-injurious behavior; Dest, property destruction; Disrup, disruptive behavior; Esc, escape; Att, attention; Tang, tangible; Auto, automatic; VOCA, voice output communication aid; AAC, augmentative and alternative communication; FCT, functional communication training; FCR, functional communication response; S^D, discriminative stimulus; EXT, extinction; DRA, differential reinforcement of alternative behavior; FR1, fixed ratio, 1 schedule of reinforcement.

167

III

Evidence-Based Practices to Address Communication

8

Effective Strategies for Working With Young Children With Autism Spectrum Disorder and Complex Communication Needs

Ilene S. Schwartz, Ariane N. Gauvreau, and Katherine Bateman

People use communication to control their environment. Babies lift their arms to get picked up by their loved ones. Toddlers point to an airplane in the sky to direct the attention of their caregiver, or to a bowl of blueberries on the breakfast table to request their favorite food. Preschoolers learn to ask for "one more minute" to avoid everything from going to bed to getting out of a swimming pool. This ability to use communication to control the environment, including the behavior of others, starts very early and motivates much of people's communication throughout the lifespan. Understanding the function of communication—that is, what motivates a communicator to find a partner and share a message—is an essential when planning intervention for children with complex communication needs (CCN) and related disabilities (e.g., autism spectrum disorder [ASD]).

The ability to control the environment is important to gain access to materials, activities, and information that a child may want or need. It also gives children the opportunity to protest appropriately. The goal is for all children to have a way to share experiences and learn, engage in social interactions leading to development of meaningful relationships with peers and adults, communicate their discomfort, and advocate for their needs. For example, children with CCN may need to tell people around them that they are done with a challenging activity, that they are uncomfortable sitting under a cold air-conditioning vent, or that a noise in the environment is too loud. Once you understand the power that communication plays in lives of all humans, it is easy to understand the relationship between communication delays and challenging behavior. One of the most important findings in special education and applied behavior analysis in the past 30 years is that behavior is communicative and that by teaching children an appropriate and functionally equivalent alternative, challenging behavior will decrease (e.g., Carr & Durand, 1985; Carr et al., 2002; Durand & Carr, 1991). It is interesting to note that educators often say that *challenging* behavior is communicative. It is important to remember that what motivates and maintains all communicative behavior is to somehow change the behavior of your communicative partner. So, when a young developmentally challenged child with a CCN throws a puzzle at the teacher who has asked her to complete the same four-piece wooden puzzle every day for the past 2 weeks, she is really saying, "No, thank you. I do not want to do that puzzle again." When the same child claps with delight when the teacher plays the piano, she is saying, "I love music and you play beautifully!" The interventionists' goal, in both situations, is to help the child with CCN find multiple, and hopefully more conventional, effective strategies to communicate. Interventionists want to teach children that they have the power to control their own environments through appropriate communicative behavior and teach the adults in the environment to listen and respond.

The purpose of this chapter is to provide guidance about how to incorporate augmentative and alternative communication (AAC) systems into a comprehensive program for a child with CCN and related disorders. As the evidence across disciplines tells us, children with more advanced communication skills demonstrate better outcomes. This finding has been replicated with typically developing children and children with a range of disabilities (e.g., Hart & Risley, 1995; Sandall et al., 2011; Sigman, & Ungerer, 1984). Communication skills, including the use of AAC, must be considered a crucial component of a comprehensive program for children with CCN and related disorders—not a related service provided by one member of the interdisciplinary educational team. This chapter addresses the instructional targets and strategies for teaching children how to use AAC effectively, fluently, and across settings (e.g., at home, with peers, in the community). In addition, evidence is embedded throughout the chapter supporting the use of AAC devices and specific instructional strategies to demonstrate they are effective and evidence-based.

COMMUNICATION IS CORE

Teaching children with CCN and related disorders to use AAC systems effectively is just *one* aspect of the comprehensive intervention needed for children to make meaningful education progress (e.g., Schwartz & Davis, 2014; Schwartz & McBride, 2014). In addition to systematic instruction on how to effectively and independently use AAC systems, young children with CCN require intensive and effective instruction in the domains of behavioral regulation, social interactions, independence, executive functioning, pre-academic or cognitive skills, and motor skills. Learning to use AAC to express one's wants and needs is just one component of comprehensive treatment that young children with autism and related disabilities may need to successfully access and participate in a variety of inclusive environments. The ability to be an effective communicator, however, is key to achieving many of these other valued outcomes (e.g., social interactions, emotional regulation, exchanging information). Therefore, planning, instruction, and support for the use of AAC systems must be integrated with instruction from different domains, provided across environments, and implemented by all members of the child's team.

EFFECTIVE INSTRUCTIONAL STRATEGIES FOR YOUNG CHILDREN WITH CCN AND RELATED DISORDERS

There is a wealth of research on different evidence-based instructional strategies to teach young children with CCN to use AAC systems (e.g., Calculator & Black, 2009; Downing & Eichinger, 2003; Mirenda, 2017; Wong et al., 2015). Some of the strategies with the most compelling research base include enhanced milieu teaching (e.g., Kaiser & Wright, 2013), least to most prompting (e.g., Sigafoos et al., 2004), peer-mediated strategies (e.g., Schwartz, Garfinkle, & Bauer, 1998; Thiemann-Bourque, 2012), and embedded explicit instruction (e.g., Bondy & Frost, 2002). (See Table 8.1 for a description of these and other instructional strategies.) Regardless of which instructional strategy is used, the *goal of instruction* remains the same—to support the child to be a confident, competent, and independent communicator using AAC. Light and Binger (1998) propose that competent communicators using AAC should demonstrate social skills such as these:

- Portray a positive self-image to their communicative partners

- Show interest in others and initiate interactions

- Actively participate and take equal turns in a conversation

- Be responsive to communication partners by making comments, asking questions, and discussing shared topics

Table 8.1.   Naturalistic instructional strategies

Strategy	Description	Example
Enhanced milieu teaching (e.g., Kaiser & Wright, 2013)	Conversation-based intervention method uses children's interests to promote more complex communicative behavior.	Child is playing with blocks and trucks. The child's favorite trucks are the firetrucks; the teacher places those materials in sight but out of reach. When the child says, "Trucks," the teacher says, "What trucks?" and the child responds, "Red fire trucks." The teacher says, "Here are three red fire trucks" and gives them to the child.
Least to most prompting (e.g., Sigafoos et al., 2004)	Teacher begins the prompting sequence by providing the least intrusive level of assistance. The level of prompting increases only as necessary to yield the correct child response.	The child is trying to open a jar with stickers in it. The teacher says, "What do you need?" The child continues to struggle. The teacher increases the intrusiveness of her prompt and says, "Say, 'Help me.'" The teacher says, "Thanks for asking" and opens the jar.
Peer-mediated strategies (e.g., Schwartz, Garfinkle, & Bauer, 1998; Thiemann-Bourque, 2012)	Children in the classroom are used as instructional agents to help other children learn targeted skills.	Children who use the Picture Exchange Communication System use their system to request desired materials from their peers who control access to those materials during small-group activities.
Embedded explicit instruction (e.g., Bondy & Frost, 2002; Schwartz, Ashmun, McBride, Scott, & Sandall, 2017)	Explicit instruction is embedded into ongoing classroom activities and routines.	The child's favorite art activity involves markers. The teacher controls access to the markers and requires the child to ask for them using their communication system. If the child does not ask independently, the teacher provides the amount of prompting needed to yield the correct response.

(continued)

Table 8.1. *(continued)*

Strategy	Description	Example
Expectant time delay (Halle, Marshall, & Spradlin, 1979; Kozleski, 1991; Sigafoos, 1999)	Preferred items are visible in the child's environment, but the child must request to access them. This can also be used to require children to ask for assistance when needed.	Teacher puts out construction stickers, a highly preferred item, at the art table to create an opportunity for a child to ask. Another option involves creating a situation where a child needs help, such as giving the child a granola bar that they need help opening.
Missing or out of reach item (Cipani, 1988; Sigafoos, 1999)	An item needed to complete an activity is placed out of reach.	All scoops and shovels are hung on hooks out of reach, above the same table, as a way to encourage children to ask for these.
Incomplete presentation (Duker, Kraaykamp, & Visser, 1994; Sigafoos, 1999)	After a child requests an item or activity, teachers deliberately leave out a necessary item or tool.	Yogurt (a preferred snack) is served at snack, but no spoons are provided.
Interrupted behavior chain (Goetz, Gee, & Sailor, 1985; Sigafoos & Mirenda, 2002).	An ongoing activity is interrupted to encourage a child to request.	Teacher begins singing a preferred song and stops in the middle of a verse, waiting for the child to request that she continue singing.
Wrong item format (Sigafoos, 1999; Sigafoos & Roberts-Pennell, 1999).	After requesting a specific item, a teacher intentionally gives the child something different, providing him with the opportunity to use a repair strategy to clarify the initial request.	A child requests to play with bubbles but is given a truck instead.
Incidental teaching (e.g., Charlop-Christy & Carpenter, 2000; Christensen-Sandfort & Whinnery, 2013; Hart & Risley, 1978)	After a child makes an initiation, the teacher requires the child to expand his utterance.	The child points to a car and says, "Car." The teacher blocks access to the car and says, "What color car do you want?"

- Put their partners at ease with their AAC system by using an accessible introduction, such as a card that reads, "Hi, I am Nicole. I use this device to communicate by touching pictures of what I want to say."

These guidelines help educators working with young children with CCN and their families address the various functions of AAC and the roles they play in the overall development of their users. AAC enables children to communicate in a variety of ways; therefore, it is essential to emphasize their *functionality*. In other words, is the child who uses AAC able to control her environment given the skills being taught? Is the AAC independent and intelligible with the method? Can they use the method in various settings? Do the skills being addressed help the child express his wants and needs effectively, independently, and appropriately? Does the system contribute to an increase in the child's (and their family's) quality of life?

Special considerations may be necessary when teaching young children with CCN and ASD. It is well documented that children with disabilities may require more opportunities to learn a new skill (Odom, Boyd, Hall, & Hume, 2010; Schreibman et al., 2015; Schwartz, Ashmun, McBride, Scott, & Sandall, 2017; Schwartz & Davis, 2014). These children benefit from explicit instruction and repeated opportunities to practice new skills, with systematic prompting to ensure they are learning, and planned opportunities for generalization (Schwartz et al., 2017).

It is important to note, however, that explicit and intensive instruction does not necessarily mean decontextualized or isolated instruction. Like all young learners, children with CCN and ASD learn best when they are active, motivated, and when the instruction involves materials and outcomes that are important for them (e.g., Schreibman et al., 2015). This picture of instruction differs from what many educators envision when they think about explicit, intensive, and effective instruction with children who have significant disabilities (e.g., discrete trial teaching). Schwartz and her colleagues (2017) address this potential instructional quagmire by emphasizing that educators focus on the context of instruction, not the specific instructional strategy. Effective instructional strategies must be used regardless of the context of instruction. Even the most seemingly intensive strategy, discrete trials, can be embedded into child selected, classroom-based activities. Rather than conceptualizing instruction as a dichotomy between intensive, isolated instruction and more naturalistic instruction, the DATA Model (a comprehensive, inclusive, and school-based approach for providing early intensive behavioral intervention to toddlers and preschoolers with ASD; Schwartz et al., 2017) makes the distinction by examining the context of the instruction and the materials used. Decontextualized instruction may take place sitting at a table, using reinforcers that are not related to the task, with a high degree of teacher direction. Embedded instruction may take place on the playground or during free choice within the context of a child-initiated activity using materials essential to that activity as the reinforcer. All instruction, regardless of where it takes place, is based on the instructional frame of a discrete trial. A discrete trial consists of five components:

1. Instruction (also called a Discriminative Stimulus—S^D)

2. Prompt (the only optional component of a discrete trial)

3. Child's response

4. Consequence

5. Inter-trial interval (see Table 8.2 for examples of an embedded and decontextualized discrete trials)

Although most educators and behavior analysts think of discrete trial teaching as a strategy that is used in isolated settings, context is not part of the definition. Rather, a discrete trial is merely a method to frame an instructional interaction. The context and materials can be modified to meet the needs of the learner at that specific moment in his or her learning career. For example, when beginning to teach a skill, instruction may be more heavily weighted toward the decontextualized side of the continuum. The instruction will be more teacher directed, the environment may look more like "work time," and there may be more frequent opportunities for a learner to respond in a short period of time. As the child begins

Table 8.2. Example of the components of a discrete trial

Components of a discrete trial	Embedded discrete trial	Decontextualized discrete trial
Instruction (also called a discriminative stimulus, or S^D)	Abigail, a 4-year-old with ASD, is playing at the water table. Her teacher holds up a green cup and a blue cup and says, "Show me the blue cup."	Abigail is now sitting at the table with pictures of three different items in front of her. Her teacher says, "Point to pants."
Prompt (the only optional component of a discrete trial)	No prompt was necessary.	Abigail makes no response. After 3 seconds, the teacher points to the correct picture.
Child's response	Abigail points to the blue cup and vocalizes, "Bu, Bu."	Abigail points to the picture of the pants.
Consequence	The teacher hands her the blue cup and says, "Great job, you showed me blue cup."	The teacher claps her hands and says, "You are right, you showed me pants. You earned a token" and places a token on Abigail's token board.
Intertrial interval	The teacher and Abigail take turns pouring water from their respective cups.	Abigail's teacher records data on her clipboard, changes the position of the cards on the table, and 3 seconds later delivers another instruction to begin a new trial.

to acquire the skill, instruction will be more embedded. It is more likely to occur as part of child-initiated activities using a wider variety of materials and occurring in a wider range of settings. Across the continuum of instruction, however, teachers plan the instruction, provide prompts as necessary, provide positive reinforcement or corrective feedback to close the instructional loop, and monitor child progress through data collection. Importantly, effective teachers move across points in this instructional continuum fluidly. Children will be receiving both decontextualized and embedded instruction every day. The type of instruction provided depends on the child's progress with that specific skill. If a child is not making adequate progress as demonstrated by the data, then the type of instruction (e.g., intensity, context) and/or the materials and systems will be modified. This approach to instruction assumes that child failure is instructional failure.

WHAT TO TEACH

Young children with ASD and CCN have unique needs with regard to what skills must be taught, suitable communication modes, and technology considerations.

Important Skills for Children who Use AACs

Beukelman and Mirenda (2013) posit that AAC users must have the vocabulary, technical, and social skills to use their system across settings. It is essential that these skills not be viewed as prerequisites but rather as issues to be addressed by the teachers, community, and child together to support the child's successful communication. Children must be able to

- Communicate using vocabulary aligned with their interests

- Communicate using a variety of words

- Have the technical skills to operate their devices by turning them on or off and navigating to the necessary page

- Possess the conversational skills necessary to have effective interactions with their communicative partners

- Use repair strategies or other methods of communication to ensure their needs and wants are met should the device malfunction

Proficiency in each of these areas ensures that AAC users can fully participate and communicate in various settings (Beukelman & Mirenda, 2013). These researchers suggest children must have competence in four areas: linguistic competence, operational competence, social competence, and strategic competence. Linguistic competence includes the required receptive and expressive vocabulary a child needs to communicate his or her wants and needs. Operational competence refers to the technical skills required to effectively operate an AAC system, such as turning it on and navigating pages to find a specific word or symbol. Social competence refers to social interaction skills such as initiating, maintaining, and ending a conversation or communicative interaction. Finally, strategic competence includes the compensatory strategies necessary for dealing with the limitations of a system, such as navigating through multiple pages or using a backup method to communicate should the method fail or malfunction (Light & McNaughton, 2014). This framework helps teachers consider the multiple functions an AAC device has for a child and the necessary skills needed to teach for children to use these devices independently and effectively.

Considerations for AAC Method Selection

Once the decision has been made to introduce AAC to a child with CCN and related disorders, the next step is deciding which AAC systems to use. Including family members in this selection process (Starble, Hutchins, Favro, Prelock, & Bitner, 2005) and taking into consideration the family's culture and home language (Kulkarni & Parmar, 2017) is imperative as the system must be acceptable and intelligible to the family if it is to be used across environments and people in the child's life.

When selecting AAC, teachers and parents should consider a system that matches the child's current abilities and immediate needs while also developing a wider plan for expanding the child's skills in preparation for future communication needs. Beukelman, Yorkston, and Dowden (1985) refer to this as AAC decisions aimed at "today" and those aimed at "tomorrow." The "today" decisions must consider the child's current communication abilities and, specifically for young children with CCN, his or her demonstration of understanding the social aspects of communication. The "tomorrow" decisions are based on future opportunities and needs as well as new skills learned from instruction with the current device or system. As with all materials designed to support young children with special needs, AAC methods can and will change over time as the child grows, gains new skills, and requires different vocabulary.

Low Tech vs. High Tech AAC: Considerations   A common pitfall of AAC selection is giving a child a device or method without teaching him or her the social nature of communication. In the authors' clinical practice, they worked with a team who selected an expensive, computerized system only to have the child, sitting in a room alone, press the "cookie" symbol repeatedly without getting anyone's attention or using a repair strategy to get their needs met. This obviously led to frustration and challenging behavior on the child's part. The instructional team determined the poor outcome and the child's unrewarded repeated "cookie" response was at least in part a function of poor instruction. In addition, the team concluded the technically advanced computer system was not the best choice for the child. Accordingly, the team ultimately decided to use a low-tech system, the Picture Exchange Communication System (PECS; Bondy & Frost, 2002), that systematically teaches the child how to find and engage a communicative partner. Once the child understood the function of communication and that another person is an essential component of communication, her ability to communicate dramatically improved. Research, and hundreds of examples in our own practice, demonstrate that PECS (Bondy & Frost, 2002) may be the best first system for young children with CCN. It is easier and faster for young children with CCN to learn, easier for families and providers to access, and easier to maintain compared to speech-generating devices (SGDs; Beck, Stoner, Bock, & Parton, 2008). Teams working with students who continue with AAC systems may want to consider SGDs or other systems as children get older and their communicative repertoire expands. Finally, the team members concluded that fundamental and salient features of an effective communication method would need to be clearly understood before any future AAC method, high or low tech, could be implemented in an effective manner for this child and his family.

Accurate, Efficient, and Nonfatiguing AAC Systems

Bailey, Stoner, Parette, and Angell (2006) identified ease of implementation of AAC systems as one of the major facilitators to successful and independent use across different environments and settings. When systems are cumbersome (i.e., they are hard to navigate, challenging to carry, or difficult to operate), children may find it difficult to engage in communication and the effectiveness of intervention is obviously threatened. For this reason, low-tech systems such as PECS are very attractive to young AAC users.

Regardless of the communicator's age, AAC systems are geared to permit children to express needs and wants, exchange information, and develop social relationships. In addition, all AAC systems must be accurate, efficient, and nonfatiguing (Light & McNaughton, 2014). An *accurate* system enables a child to communicate with a minimal number of communication breakdowns or errors. An *efficient* system allows a child to easily produce messages in a short amount of time without extensive training. A major contribution to the success of AAC systems is the amount of effort these systems require for a child to engage with the method. To ensure children are motivated to use their AAC system, effort level must be minimal. If children with CCN find it easier to use their current mode of communication (e.g., pointing and/or speech approximations, more challenging behavior such as yelling or hitting) the likelihood that children will use their AAC system to communicate decreases. Furthermore, when systems are challenging to navigate, or icons and words are difficult to find, AAC systems are less effective and harder for children to use. Finally, a *nonfatiguing* system lets a child communicate for as long as necessary without becoming tired. The concept of nonfatiguing methods for very young children is important because these children may struggle to carry a heavy or bulky device across environments, or struggle with the fine-motor skills necessary to activate certain buttons. Teachers will likely need to make modifications to AAC systems to ensure the child can move it around the environment as needed. Modification examples include a shoulder strap attached to a PECS book or voice output device that enables the child to carry it like a bag, or a plastic overlay that separates each button on an SGD limiting accidental presses for children with limited fine-motor control. Given the necessary implications of system use for younger children, selecting methods that are durable, inexpensive, and easily portable is crucial. One example would be using PECS as a "today" system (Buekelman, Yorkston, & Dowden, 1985), with the goal of moving the child to a more sophisticated SGD system as their vocabulary grows and their communication needs become more complex.

Navigation and Display

How the vocabulary in any AAC system is visually organized and displayed is another important consideration. Navigating through multiple pages or screens in an AAC system to reach a certain symbol can be challenging for all users, especially young children. Furthermore, systems are usually organized in a way that makes sense to adults without communication needs, not children with disabilities (Drager, Light, Speltz, Fallon, & Jefferies, 2003). AAC devices are commonly organized in three ways: a taxonomical grid layout, a schematic grid layout, or visual scene display (VSD). A grid display includes symbols organized in rows and columns, according to events or experiences. A taxonomical grid layout includes symbols organized in hierarchical categories and displayed in rows and columns. For example, the system for a young child might have one page with food items displayed in a grid, three pictures across and four pictures down, for a total of 12 different food items. Another page of the system might display toys, and another might display materials needed during small-group activities at school (e.g., scissors, crayons). A VSD illustrates a contextual scene with symbols embedded under hot spots in the scene. A system using this display might actually have a picture of the kitchen and different preferred food items might be displayed in the pantry, or the refrigerator, or the fruit bowl depending on where the family kept them. Regardless of the organization structure, in order to successfully navigate and access necessary vocabulary, children must recall the conceptual model of the hidden pages in any system, understand the relationship between the representations on the menu page and their categories, *and* remember the hidden pages of vocabulary (Light & Drager, 2007).

While most systems are organized with symbols arranged in a grid, with rows and columns, there is no evidence that suggests this format is best for young children (Light & Drager, 2007). Rather, displays where language concepts are embedded within a contextual scene are more salient. For example, a system could include a photo of the child's room, and the concept *play* would be accessible by selecting the toy box, or within a photo of the kitchen, *eat* could be accessible by selecting the pantry or refrigerator. Contextual displays such as these reduce the cognitive effort required to locate a certain word or concept and are easier and more utilitarian for young children to navigate (Drager et al., 2003). In addition, these schematic displays where words and concepts are organized around a specific schema are similar to the way children without disabilities organize information (Lucariello, Kyratzis, & Nelson, 1992). Researchers have found that screenshots of hidden pages within VSDs can be one way to support children's navigation. In one study, typically developing 3-year-olds were more accurate in locating vocabulary when screenshots of scenes were provided on the menu page (Drager et al., 2003). However, some studies have found that by age 4–5 years, typically developing children were able to use VSD and grid layouts with similar accuracy (Light et al., 2004). As previously mentioned, teams should consider the child's communication needs for "today" when first selecting a method, considering the possibility of moving to an alternative format as the child grows. This might include starting with a VSD and moving toward a taxonomical grid layout when the child is older and uses more complex vocabulary.

As with all interventions and support, AAC systems should be individualized to best meet the child's and family's needs. Given the unique needs of a young child, including durability, portability, and cost, selecting a low-tech system such as PECS can be a useful way to teach the child to communicate using AAC while planning to move to a computerized or other more multifaceted or complex system as the child grows.

Emerging Technologies and AAC

The range of technology available to AAC users, specifically when considering the use of mobile technologies such as tablets and smartphones, grows daily. Countless apps designed to support communication are now available, making high-tech communication options available at a fraction of the cost and many times more user friendly. Although these technological options may be very attractive to teachers and families, it is important to keep in mind that some children with autism learn the social function of communication as a process linked to learning to use these options. Of course, purchasing a tablet and installing an application does not ensure that a child will immediately be able to use this to communicate across environments. As these technologies continue to improve, they will provide AAC users with more options and accessibility. Access without instruction, however, will not produce competent communicators. Although it is beyond the scope of this chapter to predict what AAC systems will look like in even a few years, it is safe to say that without instruction on how to use the method, how to engage a communicator partner, and how to understand the power of communication, new technology alone will not improve the communication skills of children with CCN. The next section of this chapter discusses strategies to teach children to communicate using AAC systems.

SCOPE, SEQUENCE, AND METHODOLOGY FOR TEACHING CHILDREN WITH CCN TO USE AAC SYSTEMS

When teaching young children with ASD and CCN to communicate, it is critical that a multidisciplinary team provide input and scope, that sequence of skills taught are individualized based on the child's needs, and that instruction is embedded within natural contexts.

The Importance of Including all Members of a Child's Team

Incorporating professionals from different areas of expertise increases success of intervention, as professionals can each offer their expertise to ensure development of a highly effective plan for intervention. Researchers have identified collaboration as a critical contributing factor in effective implementation of intervention (i.e., Alant, Champion, & Peabody, 2013; Anderson, 2013; Division for Early Childhood [DEC], 2014; Paulsen, 2008).

Inclusion of primary stakeholders, including family members and caregivers identified by the family, in early intervention plays a critical role in the effectiveness of intervention (Dunlap & Fox, 2007; Fettig & Ostrosky, 2011). These stakeholders, such as parents, provide numerous additional opportunities for communication, highlighting the need for these members of a child's team to be included in the use and development of AAC systems for children with CCN. Because these additional members of a child's team are also involved in implementation of AAC interventions, it is important to include the priorities and goals of multiple participants in the development and design of intervention. In addition, as children begin to build their vocabulary with their AAC system, continuous updating and ongoing development of systems is needed. As consistent communicative partners, it is necessary that parents, and other primary stakeholders of a child's team, know how to alter and update their child's system in order to promote ongoing, consistent, and maximally utilitarian implementation of AAC systems across a child's daily life.

When the primary stakeholders of an intervention (i.e., parents) view an intervention in a positive manner, the intervention is much more effective (Bradshaw, Steiner, Gengoux, & Koegel, 2015). Simply put, parents who like any intervention are more likely to implement it. When parents see the value in their child's AAC device or system, they are more likely to consistently use it in the home or community. Furthermore, the acceptability and sustainability of interventions depends on how easily they align within the ongoing routines and beliefs of the implementer (Wainer & Ingersoll, 2011). Decreases and lapses in fidelity of implementation often occur when stakeholders are not fully invested in implementation of intervention (Callahan, Henson & Cowan, 2008; Carroll et al., 2007). This relationship between decreases in fidelity of implementation and low acceptability of intervention has shown to lead to negative treatment outcomes, emphasizing the need for development of interventions with high social validity (Forgatch, Patterson, & DeGarmo, 2005). Stakeholders who do not like a certain device or system, or are unsure how to use it, are unlikely to participate in consistently using an AAC intervention. Therefore, if practitioners want to ensure AAC interventions are implemented with fidelity and maintained over time, all members of the team must be involved.

Scope and Sequence of AAC Instruction

Once the team, including the speech-language pathologist, teachers, and family members, decides which system to use, the question remains how to best teach the child to use it. Teachers should consider teaching the following skills, ensuring that children can demonstrate independent use of each of these important skills:

- Communicative intent

- Vocabulary for highly preferred items and activities, as well as those items that will support social interaction and participation in valued activities and routines

- Appropriate protesting

- Conversational skills

Teaching Communicative Intent and Joint Attention   Before you can teach children how to communicate, there must be a reason *why* they want or need to communicate. Children must understand that communication is a social act and involves other people—this is often referred to as communicative intent. Communicative intent is the ability to understand that communication will have an effect on a listener and that the initiator will persist in communicative behavior until a request is met or denied (Bates, 2014; Prizant & Wetherby, 1987). When considering effective instruction on the use of AAC systems, specifically young children with ASD and CCN, teaching the social function of communication is the initial step. Given that autism is, by definition, a social and communication impairment, teaching young children how to appropriately engage in social interactions as well as gain the attention of a communicative partner are crucial initial steps of AAC instruction. By beginning instruction with this foundational skill, children learn that communication involves two people. In the PECS protocol (Frost & Bondy, 2002), all learners begin in Phase 1, where individuals learn to exchange a picture for a desired item. With this AAC method, requesting by getting the attention of another person is maintained by access to a desired item. For example, a child asks for a cracker by handing someone a picture of a cracker and receives the snack, or asks for a toy by exchanging a symbol, and is then handed the toy. This skill is likely to be learned quickly because the child *immediately* receives what is wanted (Bondy & Frost, 2002; Yoder & Lieberman, 2010). By understanding the concept of communicative intent, or that communication always involves another person, young children with CCN learn that they must always approach another person for what they want or need. Regardless of which AAC system a team chooses to use, teaching the child to find a communicative partner and demonstrate intent to communicate must be part of the instructional strategy. Demonstrating intentional communication is a foundation skill upon which all others are built. Once a child has demonstrated how to engage another person in a communicative interaction, teachers can move on to teaching new vocabulary words.

Teaching and Expanding Vocabulary   When considering vocabulary selection and AAC for young children with CCN, teachers must consider the items and activities that a child is motivated to discuss or request. Children must be motivated to use these methods across settings and activities, therefore vocabulary should be representative of the activities, items, toys, foods, beverages, and so forth that a child prefers. In addition, preferred social routines and social interaction items should be included. One common mistake witnessed in clinical and educational practice is to load communication systems with symbols related to the classroom curriculum, yet unrelated to anything motivating to the child. For example, including symbols for glue sticks and markers for a child who does not enjoy art activities is not going to increase spontaneous requesting or commenting…although it may provide an opportunity to practice appropriate protesting! Most children are not going to ask for materials that they do not want. Although at some point teachers may want children to answer questions about what tools they need or make comments about what supplies they are using, these types of utterances are not the same as learners exerting control over their environment to gain access to a favorite material using AAC. Thus, they should not be included in the preliminary intervention stages.

Rather, the beginning stages of vocabulary building should focus on preferred items and reinforcers. Teachers should complete a preference assessment (e.g., Pace, Ivancic, Edwards, Iwata, & Page, 1985; Schwartz et al., 2017) to determine which activities, materials, toys, and more are most preferred for the child throughout the day and to ensure these symbols are programmed or included in any AAC system. A preference assessment is a systematic way of determining the things about which the child is most interested. Essentially, child preferences drive symbol selection when first teaching the child how to use an AAC system.

Many children with CCN and related disorders have a limited range of preferred objects and activities. This may be due to lack of opportunity to interact with a wide variety of materials and activities. Part of a comprehensive intervention program is to increase children's experience and fluency with different materials and activities. You cannot enjoy a toy or activity if you have never seen it, tried it, or developed some competence in using it. As a child's range of experiences broadens, so does his or her list of potential reinforcers, topics for conversation, and overall vocabulary.

Once the child is able to use AAC to request highly preferred items, teachers can begin to include other vocabulary items. Buekelman and Mirenda (2013) note that preliterate individuals, such as young children with disabilities, require vocabulary that falls into two categories: 1) vocabulary that is necessary for communicating messages, and 2) vocabulary that is necessary for developing language skills. In addition, *coverage vocabulary* (Vanderheiden & Kelso, 1987) refers to messages that convey a child's basic needs in every environment he or she participate in. For example, the vocabulary necessary for block play is very different from the vocabulary needed at a friend's birthday party. When playing in the block area, a child with autism who enjoys this part of her preschool classroom may need symbols for vehicles, train tracks, and tools. The same child may have a hard time at gatherings with many people; therefore, the vocabulary necessary for a birthday party may include a symbol for cake and ice cream but also symbols that enable her to request a break or noise cancelling headphones. Coverage vocabulary is especially important when teaching functional communication (Carr & Durand, 1985). For children with CCN who engage in challenging behavior, all AAC systems must include a functional, appropriate way for them to get their needs met (Mirenda, 1997). This may include symbols for request help, a break, to be finished with an activity, a way to get an adult's attention, and so forth.

Teaching Appropriate Protesting   All children protest. Ask the parent of any 2-year-old and they will attest to the presence of generalized protesting skills. The challenge for everyone working with young children is to channel that appropriate function into an appropriate form. All young children, with and without disabilities, benefit from instruction and support in appropriately protesting, yet children with autism and related disabilities engage in higher rates of challenging behavior (Dunlap & Fox, 2007). Research and clinical experience has shown that as children's communicative skills increase, rates of challenging behavior increase. An essential skill for every competent communicator is to know how to protest in a socially appropriate manner. Part of instruction on effective and independent AAC use must include vocabulary necessary for children to protest appropriately. Words and phrases such as, "I need more time," "No, thank you," "I am all done," "I want more," and so forth are necessary to ensure children can successfully participate in a variety of environments while advocating for themselves in an appropriate manner.

Teaching protesting is similar to teaching requesting. In both it is important to know about a child's preferences. Requesting works on a positive reinforcement paradigm—the child is asking for preferred items. Protesting works on a negative reinforcement paradigm—this child is asking for something that he or she considers to be aversive (e.g., instructional demands) to be removed. Both positive and negative reinforcement increase the likelihood of a behavior happening again. Teaching protesting is often encompassed under the term FCT or the replacement of challenging behavior that has a communication function with more appropriate communication that accomplishes the same function (Wong et al., 2015). However, it is important to remember that *protesting is not a challenging behavior.* The form of behavior a child uses to protest (e.g., throwing materials) may be a challenging behavior, but the function of protest is important for every communicator to learn. Protesting must be taught systematically when the child is calm. Although often used in real time when a child is beginning to become agitated, children are not optimally prepared and available for instruction at that time. Children need to learn and practice appropriate strategies to ask for a break or request assistance during nonstressful times, and then be supported to use these new skills when difficult or aversive situations occur (e.g., the child cannot get the top off the container of bubbles). An example might include a teacher supporting a preschooler in using PECS to ask for a break from a nonpreferred activity. The teacher begins by creating a "break" symbol, showing the child the symbol, and explaining what it means. When the child is calm, the teacher can prompt the learner to request using the symbol, then immediately direct her to the break area of the classroom. After practicing a few times, the teacher explains to the child that it is time for snack (a nonpreferred activity) and that she can ask for a break using her "break" symbol. At the snack table, the teacher observes the child becoming agitated and immediately prompts her to initiate use of the BREAK symbol and thus gain access to the break area. By immediately prompting her to appropriately protest, the teacher has supported her vocabulary development and self-regulation and avoided a behavior problem.

Teaching Conversation Skills   Although requesting and protesting are effective strategies to control their environment, a child needs other skills to be considered a competent communicator. Once children are using a variety of vocabulary to get their needs met across environments with different people, teachers should begin providing instruction on social and conversation skills. A large part of this instruction involves teaching AAC users to direct initiations to their peers and teaching their peers (both with and without disabilities) to respond and initiate communication bids with children using AAC.

Peers can effectively be incorporated into the implementation of AAC systems (e.g., Barker, Akaba, Brady, & Thiemann-Bourque, 2013; Garfinkle & Schwartz, 2001; Thiemann-Bourque, 2012; Trembath, Balandin, Togher, & Stancliffe, 2009). In order for AAC to be truly functional, children must be able to use it to communicate with all of the people in their life—children and adults. Several effective strategies support children without disabilities in being effective communicators with their peers using AAC systems. Some of these strategies can be very straightforward, such as arranging the environment to ensure there are skilled communicators sitting close to children with CCN. Others may need more planning and more intentional instruction.

For example, Garfinkle and Schwartz (2001) taught children who communicated with PECS to use their system with peers. Their approach involved both instruction to the entire class about the AAC system and embedded instruction to dyads in which one of whom was communicating with PECS. One popular classroom activity for this instructional strategy was snack. Every child at the snack table was assigned to be in charge of a component of the snack (e.g., plates, cups, crackers, apples). When the child asked the teacher for something, she would say, "I don't have apples. Look around. Who has the apples?" The teacher would prompt the child, if necessary, to ask the appropriate child for the apples. This strategy facilitated every child in the group to make requests to peers and to respond to requests to peers. Garfinkle and Schwartz (2001) expanded the use of this strategy to other activities and observed an increased use of peer interaction across activities in the classroom.

Gauvreau (2017) developed a strategy called "snack talk" to facilitate conversation between children in inclusive classrooms. She created visual supports with ideas for conversation topics (e.g., What is your favorite movie? What is your favorite food?) and corresponding pictures. These snack-talk visuals were available during mealtimes in the classroom. The visuals enabled children of all abilities to initiate and respond in conversations with their peers, and the use of the snack-talk visuals also increased overall interaction and decreased challenging behavior in the classroom.

Another approach used to facilitate the social interaction skills of children with CCN and related disorders is to teach typically developing children to respond to communication bids from their peers with CCN. Kamps and her colleagues (2015) demonstrated the effectiveness of peer network interventions to enhance social skills. They defined peer network instruction as a strategy that combines adult facilitation, continuous opportunities for social interactions in natural contexts, and active peer mediation with children with disabilities. English, Shafer, Goldstein, and Kaczmarek (1997) demonstrated the effectiveness of a similar strategy they called "stay-play-talk." In this teaching strategy, typically developing peers are taught to stay with their peers and play with them while engaging in conversation. Visual supports are used to remind children with and without disabilities of expectations. Peer models are reinforced for talking with their friends, and children with complex communication needs are reinforced by ongoing communication with their peers.

Teaching peers how to respond to a child using an AAC system is critical to expanding a child's repertoire of communication to people across environments they encounter daily. If typically developing peers do not know how to respond to a child using an AAC system, communication bids initiated by children with CCN are not reinforced, decreasing the future likelihood that children will engage in communication bids with their peers. As children of all abilities learn the skills necessary to engage with their peers, regardless of their mode of communication, an inclusive environment is created and promoted. Research has identified vastly positive outcomes when including typically developing peers within intervention, highlighting the importance of this strategy to increase social and communication development among children with and without developmental disabilities (Kasari, Rotheram-Fuller, Locke, & Gulsrud, 2012; Thiemann-Bourque, 2012).

Where to Teach: Decontextualized and Embedded Instruction

Given that the very nature of communication is social, supporting children to develop spontaneous communication within and across natural environments is crucial. As previously mentioned, young children with CCN benefit from systematic instruction, with multiple opportunities to practice new skills (Odom et al., 2010; Schreibman et al., 2015; Schwartz et al., 2017). There are a number of advantages to initially teaching new skills, including communication in one-to-one settings, thus enabling a teacher to modify the environment to best meet individual learner needs. This format is also the preference of many early childhood educators. Once data demonstrate that the child is learning how to use AAC, practitioners must ensure the child has embedded opportunities to use it across settings, including the school, home, and community. Naturalistic strategies outlined in Table 8.1 are simple to embed within ongoing routines occurring in natural environments, ensuring that children can use their AAC system in various places and with different communicative partners. These strategies also align with the recommendation that intervention occurs within naturally occurring routines (DEC, 2014). Accordingly, all adults in the child's life must be trained to use AAC (Schwartz et al., 1998; Soto, Müller, Hunt, & Goetz, 2001).

Embedded Instruction   Embedded instructional strategies are especially useful when teaching children with CCN how to use AAC. Embedded or naturalistic instructional strategies are a set of strategies for teaching functional communication within ongoing routines that reflect the child's interests and take advantage of naturally occurring reinforcing consequences (Hepting & Goldstein, 1996; Kaiser & Hester, 1994; Schreibman et al., 2015). This instruction involves three steps:

1. Teacher arranges the environment to create communication opportunities.

2. Teacher prompts the child to communicate.

3. Teacher provides feedback, either by positively reinforcing the behavior or providing corrective feedback. (Beukelman & Mirenda, 2013)

An example would be a preschool teacher gathering a child's favorite snack item in a closed container, setting up a snack space in a quiet area of the classroom, and ensuring the child had multiple opportunities to successfully request this snack using a picture symbol. Another example might be a teacher collecting a child's favorite building materials and sitting with the child in the block area to teach her to create a sentence to request the pieces she would like to use to build a tower (e.g., "I want red Legos"), using an SGD. In both examples, the teachers planned ahead to determine what sort of materials would be most motivating for the child to request, arranged the environment to ensure the child would be successful, and provided multiple opportunities for the child to communicate and receive immediate reinforcement for this communication. Table 8.1 describes how teachers can implement these strategies to support children with CCN using AAC.

SUPPORTING ONGOING INTERVENTION IMPLEMENTATION: THE IMPORTANCE OF HIGH-QUALITY, ONGOING TRAINING

One of the most prevalent and commonly identified constraints to effective implementation of AAC systems across various settings and contexts is limited, low-quality training (i.e., Douglas, 2012; Douglas, Light, & McNaughton, 2013; McMillan, 2008). This barrier applies to everyone who is involved in supporting the use of a child's AAC system. Research supports implementation of high-quality, continuous training for numerous interventions. This applies not only within the area of communication but across multiple early childhood interventions (i.e., Love, Carr, Leblanc, & Kisamore, 2013; Rosales, Stone, & Rehfeldt, 2009). Positive outcomes are attributed to thorough training prior to the start of an intervention as well as repeated opportunities for continuous training and coaching throughout implementation (e.g., McMillian, 2008; Wenz-Gross & Upshur, 2012). Providing trainees with opportunities throughout development and implementation of intervention ensures participants have opportunities to perfect their skills, build confidence, and increase fidelity of implementation. This ultimately affects the success of intervention, as effectiveness of intervention is increased through reliable, consistent implementation.

PUTTING IT ALL TOGETHER: A MODEL FOR TEACHING COMMUNICATION SKILLS

The past 25 years has yielded a plethora of research about how to teach communication skills to children with a variety of disabilities (e.g., Goldstein, 2002; Kaiser & Roberts, 2011; Mirenda, 1997; Schreibman et al., 2015; Schwartz et al., 2017). This literature suggests a model with four primary components for teaching successful child communication (see Figure 8.1):

1. Children need effective strategies to share information and their wants and needs and socially engage with people in their environment.

2. Children need partners who are willing, responsive, and communicative.

3. Environments need to be arranged to facilitate communication.

4. Effective instruction must be available to support children's communicative attempts.

None of these components, in isolation, is enough to support communication development. It is only when they are all present that children will learn to be successful communicators.

CONCLUSION

Interventionists working with children with CCN and related disorders must ensure that children have access to interesting, inclusive, and developmentally appropriate environments. These are the environments that will provide children

Figure 8.1. Components of effective communication instruction.

with information and requests that they want to share with peers, parents, and teachers. The research literature has multiple examples of intervention programs that appear to work but that do not produce generalized or durable behavior change. That type of result is unacceptable. To make meaningful change in the lives of children with CCN and related disorders, interventionists must help them acquire, generalize, and maintain effective communication skills. Ensuring that these children have something to talk about, someone to talk to, an environment that supports their communication, and access to effective instruction as needed is essential to help them acquire those skills.

REFERENCES

Alant, E., Champion, A., & Peabody, E. C. (2013). Exploring interagency collaboration in AAC intervention. *Communication Disorders Quarterly, 34*(3), 172–183.

Anderson, E. M. (2013). Preparing the next generation of early childhood teachers: The emerging role of interprofessional education and collaboration in teacher education. *Journal of Early Childhood Teacher Education, 34*(1), 23–35.

Bailey, R. L., Stoner, J. B., Parette, Jr., H. P., & Angell, M. E. (2006). AAC team perceptions: Augmentative and alternative communication device use. *Education and Training in Developmental Disabilities,* 139–154.

Barker, R. M., Akaba, S., Brady, N. C., & Thiemann-Bourque, K. (2013). Support for AAC use in preschool, and growth in language skills, for young children with developmental disabilities. *Augmentative and Alternative Communication, 29*(4), 334–346.

Bates, E. (2014). *The emergence of symbols: Cognition and communication in infancy.* New York, NY: Academic Press.

Beck, A. R., Stoner, J. B., Bock, S. J., & Parton, T. (2008). Comparison of PECS and the use of a VOCA: A replication. *Education and Training in Developmental Disabilities,* 198–216.

Beukelman, D., & Mirenda, P. (2013). *Augmentative and Alternative Communication: Supporting children and adults with complex communication needs* (4th ed.). Baltimore, MD: Paul H. Brookes Publishing Co.

Beukelman, D. R., Yorkston, K. M., & Dowden, P. A. (1985). *Augmentative communication: A casebook of clinical management.* San Diego, CA: College-Hill Press.

Bondy, A., & Frost, L. (2002). *A picture's worth: PECS and other visual communication strategies in autism. Topics in autism.* Bethesda, MD: Woodbine House.

Bradshaw, J., Steiner, A. M., Gengoux, G., & Koegel, L. K. (2015). Feasibility and effectiveness of very early intervention for infants at-risk for autism spectrum disorder: A systematic review. *Journal of Autism and Developmental Disorders, 45*(3), 778–794.

Calculator, S. N., & Black, T. (2009). Validation of an inventory of best practices in the provision of augmentative and alternative communication services to students with severe disabilities in general education classrooms. *American Journal of Speech-Language Pathology, 18*(4), 329–342.

Callahan, K., Henson, R. K., & Cowan, A. K. (2008). Social validation of evidence-based practices in autism by parents, teachers, and administrators. *Journal of Autism and Developmental Disorders, 38*(4), 678–692.

Carr, E. G., Dunlap, G., Horner, R. H., Koegel, R. L., Turnbull, A. P., Sailor, W., . . . Fox, L. (2002). Positive behavior support: Evolution of an applied science. *Journal of Positive Behavior Interventions, 4*(1), 4–16.

Carr, E. G., & Durand, V. M. (1985). Reducing behavior problems through functional communication training. *Journal of Applied Behavior Analysis, 18*(2), 111–126.

Carroll, C., Patterson, M., Wood, S., Booth, A., Rick, J., & Balain, S. (2007). A conceptual framework for implementation fidelity. *Implementation Science, 2*(1), 1.

Charlop-Christy, M. H., & Carpenter, M. H. (2000). Modified incidental teaching sessions (MITS): A procedure for parents to increase spontaneous speech in their children with autism. *Journal of Positive Behavior Interventions, 2*, 98–112.

Christensen-Sandfort, R. J., & Whinnery, S. B. (2013). Impact of milieu teaching on communication skills of young children with autism spectrum disorder. *Topics in Early Childhood Special Education, 32*(4), 211–222.

Cipani, E. (1988). The missing item format. *Teaching Exceptional Children, 21*(1), 25–27.

Division for Early Childhood. (2014). DEC recommended practices in early intervention/early childhood special education 2014. Retrieved from http://www.dec-sped.org/recommendedpractices

Douglas, S. N. (2012). Teaching paraeducators to support the communication of individuals who use augmentative and alternative communication: A literature review. *Current Issues in Education, 15*(1).

Douglas, S. N., Light, J. C., & McNaughton, D. B. (2013). Teaching paraeducators to support the communication of young children with complex communication needs. *Topics in Early Childhood Special Education, 33*(2), 91–101.

Downing, J. E., & Eichinger, J. (2003). Creating learning opportunities for students with severe disabilities in inclusive classrooms. *Teaching Exceptional Children, 36*(1), 26.

Drager, K. D., Light, J. C., Speltz, J. C., Fallon, K. A., & Jeffries, L. Z. (2003). The performance of typically developing 2½-year-olds on dynamic display AAC technologies with different system layouts and language organizations. *Journal of Speech, Language, and Hearing Research, 46*(2), 298-312.

Duker, P., Kraaykamp, M., & Visser, E. (1994). A stimulus control procedure to increase requesting with individuals who are severely/profoundly intellectually disabled. *Journal of Intellectual Disability Research, 38*(2), 177–186.

Dunlap, G., & Fox, L. (2007). Parent–professional partnerships: A valuable context for addressing challenging behaviours. *International Journal of Disability, Development and Education, 54*(3), 273–285.

Durand, V. M., & Carr, E. G. (1991). Functional communication training to reduce challenging behavior: Maintenance and application in new settings. *Journal of Applied Behavior Analysis, 24*(2), 251–264.

English, K., Goldstein, H., Shafer, K., & Kaczmarek, L. (1997). Interaction among preschoolers with and without disabilities: Effects of across-the-day peer intervention. *Journal of Speech, Language, and Hearing Research, 40*(1), 33–48.

Fettig, A., & Ostrosky, M. M. (2011) Collaborating with parents in reducing children's challenging behaviors: Linking functional assessment to intervention. *Child Development Research*, 1–10, doi:10.1155/2011/835941

Forgatch, M. S., Patterson, G. R., & DeGarmo, D. S. (2005). Evaluating fidelity: Predictive validity for a measure of competent adherence to the Oregon model of parent management training. *Behavior therapy, 36*(1), 3–13.

Frost, L., & Bondy, A. (2002). *The picture exchange communication system training manual.* (2nd ed.). Newark, DE: Pyramid Educational Products.

Garfinkle, A. N., & Schwartz, I. S. (2001). "Hey! I'm talking to you": A naturalistic procedure to teach preschool children to use their AAC systems with peers. *Young Exceptional Children.* Monograph Series, 3, 47–48.

Gauvreau, A. (2017). Using 'snack talk' to support social communication in inclusive preschool classrooms. *Young Exceptional Children, 20*(4). DOI.org/10.1177/1096250617725503

Goetz, L., Gee, K., & Sailor, W. (1985). Using a behavior chain interruption strategy to teach communication skills to students with severe disabilities. *Journal of the Association for Persons with Severe Handicaps, 10*(1), 21–30.

Goldstein, H. (2002). Communication intervention for children with autism: A review of treatment efficacy. *Journal of autism and developmental disorders, 32*(5), 373–396.

Halle, J. W., Marshall, A. M., & Spradlin, J. E. (1979). Time delay: A technique to increase language use and facilitate generalization in retarded children. *Journal of Applied Behavior Analysis, 12,* 431–439.

Hart, B., & Risley, T. R. (1978). Promoting productive language through incidental teaching. *Education and Urban Society, 10,* 407–429.

Hart, B., & Risley, T. R. (1995). *Meaningful differences in the everyday experience of young American children.* Baltimore, MD: Paul H. Brookes Publishing Co.

Hepting, N. H., & Goldstein, H. (1996). What's natural about naturalistic language intervention? *Journal of Early Intervention, 20*(3), 249–264.

Kaiser, A. P., & Hester, P. P. (1994). Generalized effects of enhanced milieu teaching. *Journal of Speech, Language, and Hearing Research, 37*(6), 1320–1340.

Kaiser, A. P., & Roberts, M. Y. (2011). Advances in early communication and language intervention. *Journal of Early Intervention, 33*(4), 298–309.

Kaiser, A., & Wright, C. (2013). Enhanced milieu teaching: Incorporating AAC into naturalistic teaching with young children and their partners. *Perspectives on Augmentative and Alternative Communication, 22*(1), 37–50.

Kamps, D., Thiemann-Bourque, K., Heitzman-Powell, L., Schwartz, I., Rosenberg, N., Mason, R., & Cox, S. (2015). A comprehensive peer network intervention to improve social communication of children with Autism Spectrum Disorders: A randomized trial in kindergarten and first grade. *Journal of Autism and Developmental Disorders, 45*(6), 1809–1824.

Kasari, C., Rotheram-Fuller, E., Locke, J., & Gulsrud, A. (2012). Making the connection: Randomized controlled trial of social skills at school for children with autism spectrum disorders. *Journal of Child Psychology and Psychiatry, 53*(4), 431–439.

Kozleski, E. (1991). Expectant delay procedure for teaching requests. *Augmentative and Alternative Communication, 7*(1), 11–19.

Kulkarni, S. S., & Parmar, J. (2017). Culturally and linguistically diverse student and family perspectives of AAC. *Augmentative and Alternative Communication,* 1–11.

Light, J., & Binger, C. (1998). *Building communicative competence with individuals who use augmentative and alternative communication.* Baltimore, MD: Paul H. Brookes Publishing Co.

Light, J., & Drager, K. (2007). AAC technologies for young children with complex communication needs: State of the science and future research directions. *Augmentative and alternative communication, 23*(3), 204–216.

Light, J., Drager, K., McCarthy, J., Mellott, S., Millar, D., Parrish, C., . . . & Welliver, M. (2004). Performance of typically developing four-and five-year-old children with AAC systems using different language organization techniques. *Augmentative and Alternative Communication, 20*(2), 63–88.

Light, J. & McNaughton, D. (2014). Communicative competence for individuals who require augmentative and alternative communication: A new definition for a new era of communication? *Augmentative and Alternative Communication, 30*(1), 1–18, doi:10.3109/0743461 8.2014.885080

Love, J. R., Carr, J. E., LeBlanc, L. A., & Kisamore, A. N. (2013). Training behavioral research methods to staff in an early and intensive behavioral intervention setting: A program description and preliminary evaluation. *Education and Treatment of Children, 36*(1), 139–160.

Lucariello, J., Kyratzis, A., & Nelson, K. (1992). Taxonomic knowledge: What kind and when? *Child development, 63*(4), 978–998.

McMillan, J. M. (2008). Teachers make it happen: From professional development to integration of augmentative and alternative communication technologies in the classroom. *Australasian Journal of Special Education, 32*(2), 199–211.

Mirenda, P. (1997). Supporting individuals with challenging behavior through functional communication training and AAC: Research review. *Augmentative and Alternative Communication, 13*(4), 207–225.

Mirenda, P. (2017). Values, practice, science, and AAC. *Research and Practice for Persons with Severe Disabilities, 42*(1), 33–41.

Odom, S. L., Boyd, B. A., Hall, L. J., & Hume, K. (2010). Evaluation of comprehensive treatment models for individuals with autism spectrum disorders. *Journal of Autism and Developmental Disorders, 40*(4), 425–436.

Pace, G. M., Ivancic, M. T., Edwards, G. L., Iwata, B. A., & Page, T. J. (1985). Assessment of stimulus preference and reinforcer value with profoundly retarded individuals. *Journal of applied behavior analysis, 18*(3), 249–255.

Paulsen, K. J. (2008). School-based collaboration: An introduction to the collaboration column. *Intervention in School and Clinic, 43*(5), 313.

Prizant, B. M., & Wetherby, A. M. (1987). Communicative intent: A framework for understanding social-communicative behavior in autism. *Journal of the American Academy of Child & Adolescent Psychiatry, 26*(4), 472–479.

Rosales, R., Stone, K., & Rehfeldt, R. A. (2009). The effects of behavioral skills training on implementation of the picture exchange communication system. *Journal of Applied Behavior Analysis, 42*(3), 541–549.

Sandall, S. R., Ashmun, J. W., Schwartz, I. S., Davis, C. A., Williams, P., Leon-Guerrero, R., Boulware, G. L., & McBride, B. J. (2011). Differential responses to a school-based programs for young children with ASD. *Topics in Early Childhood Special Education, 33,* 166–177.

Schreibman, L., Dawson, G., Stahmer, A. C., Landa, R., Rogers, S. J., McGee, G. G., . . . McNerney, E. (2015). Naturalistic developmental behavioral interventions: Empirically validated treatments for autism spectrum disorder. *Journal of Autism and Developmental Disorders, 45*(8), 2411–2428.

Schwartz, I. S., Ashmun, J., McBride, B., Scott, C., & Sandall, S. R. (2017). *The DATA Model for teaching preschoolers with autism: Blending approaches to meet individual needs.* Baltimore, MD: Paul H. Brookes Publishing Co.

Schwartz, I. S., & Davis, C. A. (2014). Best practices in early identification and early services for children with autism spectrum disorder. Best practices in school psychology. In P. Harrison & A. Thomas (Eds.), *Best Practices in School Psychology VI.* Washington, DC: National Association of School Psychology.

Schwartz, I. S., Garfinkle, A. N., & Bauer, J. (1998). The picture exchange communication system communicative outcomes for young children with disabilities. *Topics in Early Childhood Special Education, 18*(3), 144–159.

Schwartz, I. S., & McBride, B. (2014). Getting a good start: Effective practices in early intervention. In K. D. Burton and P. Wolfberg (Eds.), *Educating learners on the autism spectrum: Preparing highly qualified educators and related practitioners* (2nd ed.; pp. 82–105). Kansas City, KS: AAPC Publishing.

Sigafoos, J. (1999). Creating opportunities for augmentative and alternative communication: Strategies for involving people with developmental disabilities. *Augmentative and Alternative Communication, 15*(3), 183–190.

Sigafoos, J., Drasgow, E., Reichle, J., O'Reilly, M., Green, V. A., & Tait, K. (2004). Tutorial: Teaching communicative rejecting to children with severe disabilities. *American Journal of Speech-Language Pathology, 13*(1), 31–42.

Sigafoos, J., & Mirenda, P. (2002). Strengthening communicative behaviors for gaining access to desired items and activities. In J. Reichle, D. R. Beukelman, J. C. Light (Eds.), *Exemplary practices for beginning communicators: Implications for AAC* (pp. 123–156). Baltimore, MD: Paul H. Brookes Publishing Co.

Sigafoss, J., & Roberts-Pennell, D. (1999). Wrong-item format: A promising intervention for teaching socially appropriate forms of rejecting to children with developmental disabilities? *Augmentative and Alternative Communication, 15*, 135–140.

Sigman, M., & Ungerer, J. A. (1984). Cognitive and language skills in autistic, mentally retarded, and normal children. *Developmental Psychology, 20*, 293–302.

Soto, G., Müller, E., Hunt, P., & Goetz, L. (2001). Critical issues in the inclusion of students who use augmentative and alternative communication: An educational team perspective. *Augmentative and Alternative Communication, 17*(2), 62–72.

Starble, A., Hutchins, T., Favro, M. A., Prelock, P., & Bitner, B. (2005). Family-centered intervention and satisfaction with AAC device training. *Communication Disorders Quarterly, 27*(1), 47–54.

Thiemann-Bourque, K. (2012). Peer-mediated AAC instruction for young children with autism and other developmental disabilities. *SIG 12 Perspectives on Augmentative and Alternative Communication, 21*(4), 159–166.

Trembath, D., Balandin, S., Togher, L., & Stancliffe, R. J. (2009). Peer-mediated teaching and augmentative and alternative communication for preschool-aged children with autism. *Journal of Intellectual and Developmental Disability, 34*(2), 173–186.

Vanderheiden, G., & Kelso, D. (1987). Comparative analysis of fixed-vocabulary communication acceleration techniques. *Augmentative and Alternative Communication, 3*(4), 196–206.

Wainer, A. L., & Ingersoll, B. R. (2011). The use of innovative computer technology for teaching social communication to individuals with autism spectrum disorders. *Research in Autism Spectrum Disorders, 5*(1), 96–107.

Wenz-Gross, M., & Upshur, C. (2012). Implementing a primary prevention social skills intervention in urban preschools: Factors associated with quality and fidelity. *Early Education & Development, 23*(4), 427–450.

Wong, C., Odom, S. L., Hume, K. A., Cox, A. W., Fettig, A., Kucharczyk, S., . . . Schultz, T. R. (2015). Evidence-based practices for children, youth, and young adults with autism spectrum disorder: A comprehensive review. *Journal of Autism and Developmental Disorders, 45*(7), 1951–1966.

Yoder, P. J., & Lieberman, R. G. (2010). Brief report: Randomized test of the efficacy of Picture Exchange Communication System on highly generalized picture exchanges in children with ASD. *Journal of Autism and Developmental Disorders, 40*(5), 629–632.

9

Evidence-Based Methods for Teaching School-Age Children and Youth With Autism Spectrum Disorder and Complex Communication Needs

Billy T. Ogletree, Amy Rose, and Georgia Hambrecht

In the 21st century, instructional practices for children with autism spectrum disorder (ASD) who have complex communication needs (CCN) have become both more prevalent and evidence based. Perhaps this trend follows society's burgeoning inclusion of individuals with disability and its increased effort to value all individuals. These and other variables have certainly contributed to the development and application of numerous teaching methods and strategies.

The purpose of this chapter is to review scientifically supported and practitioner-friendly instructional methods now available for children with limited functional speech. The chapter begins with the definitions of terms critical to this topic. The concept of minimal verbal abilities is presented and the notions of scientifically supported and practitioner-friendly practices are explored. A review of exemplar intervention approaches follows, with a critical eye to "supported" and "friendly" methodologies. The chapter concludes with examples of scientifically supported and practitioner-friendly treatments presented in two brief case studies. Throughout this chapter, interventions are described and discussed within the broad context of promoting communication gains. This said, most of the techniques and many of the approaches presented have broad applications with the instruction/facilitation of developmental, educational, and functional skills in children with disabilities.

CHILDREN WITH COMPLEX COMMUNICATION NEEDS WHO ARE MINIMALLY VERBAL

This chapter addresses children with CCN who use limited to no speech. More specifically, these children are minimally verbal in that they primarily communicate nonsymbolically yet may produce some nongenerative speech (speech not characterized by complex word order) or use other symbol forms in a nongenerative manner (symbol use not characterized by complex word order). In addition, children with CCN who are minimally verbal may communicate nonsymbolically using intentional or nonintentional signals. For example, they may move their body in a way interpreted by others as a request or protest or deliberately (intentionally) reach for or offer an object in an attempt to request or show. Aside from these nonsymbolic behaviors, children who are minimally verbal may use speech including single words or short phrases. Their speech may be perseverative or echolalic (i.e., a class of speech repetitions further discussed later in this chapter). Children with CCN who are minimally verbal may also use other symbol forms expressively (e.g., objects, photographs, line drawings, simple print) in single-symbol constructions or in simple-symbol combinations.

Clearly, there are several reasons why many children with CCN have only minimal verbal abilities. Of course, some are simply chronologically young. These children are not the focus of this chapter. Other children present intelligence within a normal range but may have severe sensory or motor planning deficits. Again, these children are not addressed here. Still others present intellectual disabilities that limit their functioning to developmental levels consistent with CCN and minimal verbal abilities. Children in this category may present with severe intellectual and other disabilities and often have concomitant diagnoses including health conditions, sensory impairments, and specific syndromes. Children with severe disabilities are addressed in the sections that follow. Finally, many children with minimal verbal abilities fall on the autism spectrum. According to Tager-Flusberg and Kasari (2013), these children may or may not have low nonverbal IQs.

Individuals with Autism, Complex Communication Needs, and Other Severe Disabilities

Initially, McLean and Snyder-Mclean (1988) and later Ogletree, Bruce, Finch, and Fahey (2011) used terms from speech act theory (Searle, 1969) to describe the communicative abilities of individuals with severe disabilities. These authors referred to perlocutionary communicators as those who communicate without intent. The child communicating at a perlocutionary level has nonsymbolic behaviors, expressions, movements, and vocalizations interpreted by others as purposeful. In contrast, an illocutionary communicator provides clear evidence of communicative intent, such as persistent signaling, repair of signaling, and termination of signals once goals are achieved. Finally, the locutionary child with severe disabilities uses symbols to communicate. This group may use and understand simple words and phrases as well as objects, signs, photographs and drawings, print, and other symbol forms. It should be noted that individuals can demonstrate communication from more than one of these levels. That is, a locutionary child may use some speech, reach with intent nonsymbolically, or even vocalize unintentionally in a manner interpreted by others.

When referring to children with autism and other severe disabilities, each of the three groups of communicators described here would fall into our broader category of children who have CCN and minimal verbal abilities. There is a considerable literature base describing the communication of children with autism and other severe disabilities, especially those with illocutionary and locutionary capabilities. In summary, these children are likely to use gestures, excess behaviors, vocalizations, words, and simple phrases to express themselves (Ogletree et al., 1992). Their communication may lack sophistication (gesturally, vocally, and verbally) and will primarily be used to achieve regulatory purposes (i.e., to request and protest; Ogletree et al., 1992). Of course, more social means of communication such as greeting, showing, labeling, and calling may be observed. Children who are minimally verbal and present with severe disabilities may also use a variety of unaided (e.g., sign language) and simple aided (e.g., communication boards and simple speech generating devices [SGDs]). Finally, it should be noted that children with severe disabilities, including autism, will present impairments of communication and language comprehension, although comprehension is often difficult to assess in this population (Ogletree, 2016a).

Individuals with Autism Spectrum Disorder and Complex Communication Needs

Ogletree (2016b) described the communication and language abilities of children with ASD using three groups of communicators. Two of these groups, nonverbal and emergent verbal communicators, consist of individuals with minimal verbal abilities. Ogletree's (2016b) nonverbal group typically uses gestures (intentional and otherwise) with limited sophistication (physical contact) and often presents with vocal immaturity (Wetherby, Prizant, & Hutchinson, 1998). According to Ogletree, gestures and vocal behaviors used by communicators lacking speech and spoken words typically express regulatory communicative functions like requesting and protesting. Aside from conventional gestural forms, this group has also been observed to communicate through problem behaviors (e.g., aggression) that may serve communicative purposes (Carr, 1977; Carr & Durand, 1985; Sigafoos et al., 2016).

In contrast, Ogletree's (2016b) emergent verbal communicators (i.e., beginning speech and spoken word use) use simple generative and echolalic speech in addition to other symbolic and nonsymbolic communicative means expressively. For example, they may use gestural forms described previously paired with generative single words and echolalic phrases. Echolalia in children who are minimally verbal on the autism spectrum may well be the result of a gestalt processing style in which language learning occurs through memorization and repetition (Ogletree, 2016b). If this is the case, children may progress from using larger rote phrases to smaller units of more generative speech (Prizant & Rydell, 1984). For some time, echolalia has been recognized as a means of expressing communicative functions (McEvoy, Loveland, & Landry, 1988; Prizant & Duchan, 1981; Prizant & Rydell, 1984) in children with autism and also noted to be a possible sign of limited comprehension (Peters, 1977). As with all children with severe disabilities, assessing comprehension in children with CCN, including emergent verbal abilities, is challenging.

One might wonder just how many children on the autism spectrum have CCN with minimal verbal abilities. Tager-Flusberg and Kasari (2013) reported that children with autism with minimal speech have received limited attention in the literature. This said, a recent report suggests that 25–40% of these young children present minimal verbal abilities even after early intervention (Rose, Trembath, Keen, & Paynter, 2016). Weismer and Kover (2015) noted greater postintervention verbal outcomes for children with autism, although their subjects entered treatment earlier (30 months as compared to 44 months in the Rose and colleagues study). Both studies suggest that large numbers of young children with ASD lack speech and spoken-word-use ability for protracted periods and many remain so even after treatment. This conclusion is consistent with recent estimates of adults with autism who have limited functional speech (25%) (Rowland, 2009).

With a definition for children with CCN and descriptions of children with severe disabilities and autism who fail to develop speech and spoken-word abilities in hand, attention can be turned to terms and concepts critical to effective communication practices for this group. As the chapter moves into the presentation of core practice ideals and methods, its focus narrows from a general discussion of all children to a more specific discussion of those receiving service in school settings (i.e., children and youth ages 5 to 18 years). The section that follows lays the groundwork for a review of methodologies used with school-age children by describing scientifically supported and practitioner-friendly practices.

SCIENTIFICALLY SUPPORTED AND PRACTITIONER-FRIENDLY: DEFINING TERMS

One focus of this chapter is to help identify practices that are scientifically supported and practitioner-friendly. Awareness and evaluation of scientific support for therapeutic practices has been a recent and well-defined focus in the field of communication sciences and disorders (Mayo et al., 2016; McCurtin & Roddam, 2012). The notion of practitioner friendly, however, is more nebulous, yet in the opinion of the chapter authors, an exceptionally relevant idea for stakeholders of children with CCN. This section examines these two concepts.

For the purpose of this chapter, *scientifically supported* interventions are those reported in published, reliable journals (i.e., journals produced through critical peer review conducted by individuals with exceptional content knowledge and/or experience as a researcher). Expert review helps ensure that research is well-designed and theoretically sound. While web sites may identify methods examined in published reports, they often lack sufficient quality control to be accepted as scientifically supported. Book chapters are also a valuable source of scientifically supported information that has typically appeared earlier in reliable journals. However, evaluators of research must remember that it is primary-source material, the published journal article, that has sufficient detail to allow for the following components of scientific support to be examined.

While knowing that a study was reviewed and accepted for publication is a good beginning step, it does not negate the need to evaluate an investigation's research design and implementation. Checklists have been developed to facilitate the evaluation of each section of a research article from the abstract through the discussion (Meline, 2006; Pyrczak, 2013). Recently, Snell and colleagues (2010) identified four quality indicators for use when evaluating published articles concerning communication interventions for individuals with severe intellectual and developmental disabilities. These included the completeness of participant descriptions in relation to the dependent measure of the study, replicability of study procedures and treatment fidelity, reliability of the data, and maintenance and generalization measures.

After a study's integrity has been evaluated, evidence needs to be viewed in relation to the research questions posed. Questions formulated in the PICO format examine Population, Intervention, Comparison, and Outcome (Aslam & Emmanuel, 2010; Justice, 2010; Lof, 2011). For this chapter, the population (P) is school-age children and youth with CCN; the intervention (I) is approaches to teaching communication and other functional skills; the comparison (C) is interventions to no intervention/baseline; and the outcome (O) is functional communication or other skills. The evidence itself is examined based on the level of the research design or the level of evidence. Increased issues with the reliability and validity of findings occur as the level of evidence descends. The reliability and validity measures are more stringent in a randomized control group design than an observational report where no controls were set.

Five levels of evidence (Levels 1A–4) have been established to allow readers to weigh the "persuasiveness" of research findings (Robey, 2004). The higher the level of evidence, the greater adherence to the rules of the scientific method is found within the structure of the experimental design. The highest level (Level 1A) is the meta-analysis that statistically combines results of controlled studies. The second highest level (Level 1) is the randomized controlled study where subjects in the experimental and control groups are selected at random. The third level (Level 2) is the controlled design without randomization. This type of quasi-experimental design assigns subjects to groups in a nonrandom manner. The next evidence level (Level 3) includes observational investigations with controls. These designs include retrospective studies, interrupted time-series, case-control studies, and cohort studies with controls. The lowest level (Level 4) is classified as observational studies without controls.

When all findings across reliable journal articles support the same outcome and clinical decision, the answer to the PICO question is clear. It is when evidence supports different conclusions that the level of evidence must be critiqued to make an informed, scientifically supported clinical decision.

The concept of *practitioner friendly* is associated with the clinical judgment arm of the evidence-based practices (EBP) model. Clinical judgment along with scientific evidence and patient/family preference represent the three components reflected in a strong clinical practice. For the purpose of this chapter, *practitioner* is defined very broadly and includes all individuals serving as intervention agents. This includes speech-language clinicians, teachers, aides, and family members who are in the role of providing remediation services that support the intervention method being utilized (Brady et al., 2016). *Friendly* implies an ease of usability of the method, consideration of resources expended, and value of results. *Friendly*, for the purpose of this chapter, will include factors of learnability, efficiency, and effectiveness. Learnability captures the concept of ease in mastering the role of interventionist. Learnability is enhanced when methods clearly establish steps of intervention and guidelines that promote fidelity or consistency of method implementation. A method can be considered learnable if a step-by-step plan of practice is included. Efficiency reflects an awareness of the time component and means needed to implement the method. A method that yields results in the shortest time frame at the least cost is deemed most efficient. Efficiency is increased when professionals work together and with carefully selected individual and/or group instruction formats. A method that involves a team approach, as well as considers use of individual and group practices, can be identified as efficient. Last, effectiveness focuses on the meaningfulness of the change pursued. As our focus is children, change across valued communication domains or other developmental/

Table 9.1.   Level of scientific support and degree of practitioner friendliness

		Level of scientific support	
		High	Low
Degree of practitioner friendliness	High	High scientific support High practitioner friendliness	Low scientific support High practitioner friendliness
	Low	High scientific support Low practitioner friendliness	Low scientific support Low practitioner friendliness

educational areas can be referred to as effective. For the purposes of this chapter, meaningfulness equates with social validity or the social importance of goals, procedures, and outcomes (Foster & Mash, 1999).

Combining the two aspects of scientifically supported and practitioner friendly can be best visualized in Table 9.1. The aim of this chapter is to highlight those methods that fall in the first quadrant—scientifically supported and practitioner friendly. With scientifically supported and practitioner friendly defined, the last important concept for this chapter is intervention.

INTERVENTION

Our goal is to define intervention as it relates to children and youth who have CCN and minimal verbal abilities. Intervention is a term generally used in the behavioral and educational literature to specify environmental adjustments that affect change on a student's performance or behavior (National Autism Center [NAC], 2015). Intervention approaches can be viewed in terms of comprehensive treatment models (CTMs) or focused intervention practices. Intervention can also be categorized along a continuum with traditional behavioral approaches at one end, developmental social-pragmatic approaches at the other end, and contemporary behavioral approaches falling in between (Prelock, 2006; Wetherby & Prizant, 2000; Wong et al., 2013).

CTMs are defined as "a set of practices designed to achieve a broader learning or developmental impact on core deficits" (Wong et al., 2013). Odom, Boyd, Hall, and Hume (2010) characterized these models in accordance with their conceptual framework, manualized procedures, intensity throughout the week, longevity, and multiple targeted outcomes. Focused intervention practices, on the other hand, typically address a single skill or goal, are operationally defined, address specific learner outcomes, and often occur over a brief period of time. Examples of CTMs and focused interventions are provided later in this chapter.

When conceptualizing intervention approaches along a continuum from traditional behavioral to developmental, Prizant and Wetherby (1998) described traditional approaches as placing significant emphasis on behavioral techniques with repetitive practice of isolated skills, and developmental approaches as relying on naturally occurring events with greater emphasis on social-communicative interaction and competence. "Contemporary" approaches fall between these two ends of the continuum and incorporate some of the traditional behavioral techniques along with using more natural and balanced social transactions initiated by the child (Prizant & Wetherby, 1998). Once again, examples of interventions across this continuum are provided as the chapter progresses.

What Do Interventions Have in Common and How are They Different?

Whether interventions are broad or focused, traditional or developmental, they share many commonalities. First, intervention targets typically focus on increasing developmentally/educationally appropriate skills and/or decreasing undesirable behaviors interfering with life functioning and inclusion (NAC, 2015; Prelock, 2006). Second, interventions are increasingly dependent upon a range of stakeholders as trainers. Finally, many techniques and tools employed within approaches are similar. What follows is a description of common intervention techniques followed by a discussion of how they are applied within more and less structured approaches. It should be noted that this list is not exhaustive.

Techniques and Tools   Two broadly used techniques are prompting and modeling. These can be applied in isolation but are more commonly used in conjunction with other instructional tools. Prompting involves directly assisting a child or youth with completion of a task through gestural, verbal, and/or positional cues (NAC, 2015; Ogletree & Oren, 2001; Sevcik & Romski, 2016). Although different hierarchies can be employed, a most-to-least prompt hierarchy is frequently used by practitioners, starting with a high level of prompting (more invasive), such as physical prompts with hand-over-hand assistance to complete a task, and fading down to lower levels of prompting (less invasive), such as the use of verbal directions or gestural assists, as skills are mastered (Ogletree & Oren, 2001; Sevcik & Romski, 2016).

Modeling involves the demonstration of a desired skill as a "model" for learners in training (NAC, 2015; Ogletree & Oren, 2001). Live and video are two different types of modeling often incorporated into intervention approaches. As can be inferred by the terms, live modeling involves a live demonstration of a skill whereas video modeling requires a child or youth to view a recording of a person performing a target behavior followed by an opportunity to imitate (LeBlanc, 2010).

Chaining, differential reinforcement, and extinction are techniques typically employed in behavioral intervention approaches. There are two types of chaining: forward and backward (Slocum & Tiger, 2011). In forward chaining, the initial step in a task analysis is taught to mastery and then additional steps are sequentially added with reinforcement provided only after all of the steps are completed accurately. Backward chaining involves teaching the final step of the task analysis first and then progressively teaching earlier steps with reinforcement provided only after all of the steps are completed correctly (Slocum & Tiger, 2011). Forward chaining is recommended if a child can complete more steps at the beginning of the chain, whereas backward chaining is preferred when a child is more successful with steps at the end of the behavior chain.

Differential reinforcement and extinction are techniques used to increase desirable behaviors and decrease undesirable behaviors. In differential reinforcement, reinforcement is applied to one member of a response class (desirable behavior) and not to other (less desirable) behaviors (Fiske et al., 2014; Ogletree & Oren, 2001). Extinction occurs when reinforcement is withheld for a previously reinforced behavior to reduce the occurrence of that behavior (Ogletree & Oren, 2001).

The techniques and tools just described in addition to others not mentioned are the cornerstones of intervention approaches used with children who are minimally verbal. Treatments are different, however, with respect to how techniques and tools are used.

Categorizing Interventions by Structure and Function

As noted previously, interventions typically employ similar techniques and tools yet apply these differently in the pursuit of treatment goals. Conceptualizing intervention according to the theoretical constructs of structure and functionality provides a window into how various interventions differ, especially with the use of specific treatment techniques and tools.

Ogletree and Oren (1998) describe structure as the degree to which trainers control stimuli, response acceptability, and response consequences. Functionality is described as the degree to which trainers use natural events, objects, and consequences in the pursuit of practical goals within typical routines. Structured, semi-structured, and limited structure categories are presented below as a framework for organizing interventions for children and youth with CCN and minimal verbal abilities. The reader will note that some of these interventions rely more heavily on the techniques and tools described above. In fact, some favor specific treatment strategies over others. It is our opinion that the structure/functionality dichotomy is useful as one parses intervention options.

Approaches that fall within the "structured" intervention category are usually trainer directed, utilize a planned set of resources, and occur in a relatively controlled environment. The techniques used within these approaches (e.g., prompting, chaining, reinforcement, extinction) are often specifically outlined with frequent occurrence and gradual fading to ensure response acceptability or consequence. The approaches that fall within this category are behavioral approaches including discrete trial training (DTT), applied behavior analysis (ABA), the Picture Exchange Communication System (PECS), and visual supports (refer to Table 9.2). These approaches are described more completely in sections that follow. Intervention in this category can present as highly structured but are variable in their functionality. Both DTT and APA have low functionality within the classroom setting as they are typically employed in a 1:1 setting with a high degree of intensity. The PECS is moderately functional within the classroom setting as it can be personalized to each student and can be used for a range of activities. Visual supports are highly functional within the classroom setting as a majority of the students can participate and benefit during educational activities containing visual instruction and visual schedules.

The "semi-structured" intervention category includes approaches that occur in more naturalistic settings, during social interactions, and within the context of the child's daily routines and activities. They typically employ some structure with

Table 9.2. Categorization of approaches by structure and function

	Structured intervention	Semi-structured intervention	Limited structure intervention
Low function	Discrete trial training Applied behavioral analysis		Developmental Individual-difference Relationship-based DIR) Floortime Model (Greenspan, 1979, 1989) Play therapy
Moderate function	Picture Exchange Communication System (Bondy & Frost, 1993, 1994)		
High function	Visual supports • Visual schedules • Visual instruction	Socially based approaches • Scripting • Social Stories (Gray & Garand, 1993) • Peer training Pivotal Response Treatment (PRT; Koegel, Koegel, Shoshan, & McNerney, 1999) Milieu teaching (Fey et al., 2006; Fey, Yoder, Warren, & Bredin-Oja, 2013)	

respect to the trainers' choice of treatment techniques and tools (e.g., prompting, modeling, reinforcement, stimuli, environmental manipulation), but flexibility is evident in the progression of activities, spontaneity opportunities, and the natural nature of reinforcement. Pivotal Response Treatment (PRT); Milieu Language Teaching; and socially based approaches such as scripting, Social Stories, and peer training are all examples of semi-structured interventions (again, these are described more fully later in this chapter). All approaches in the "semi-structured" category tend to be very functional due to their high degree of flexibility and ability to be modified dependent upon a student's progress and changing needs.

Interventions falling in the "limited structure" category include play-based therapies and the well-known Floortime Model by Stanley Greenspan (Greenspan & Wieder, 2005) (described later in this chapter). These approaches typically occur within the child's natural environment with practitioners following the child's lead and interests. The primary focus of play-based intervention approaches is increasing intention, interaction, and engagement. The degree of functionality of these approaches within the classroom setting is low due to student–teacher ratio and the challenge of following each child's lead throughout the school day. Typically, play-based approaches most frequently occur in preschool settings and/or can be used in combination with more structured approaches.

SCIENTIFICALLY SUPPORTED AND PRACTITIONER-FRIENDLY INTERVENTIONS FOR CHILDREN AND YOUTH WITH COMPLEX COMMUNICATION NEEDS AND MINIMAL VERBAL ABILITIES

The preceding section used structure and function as constructs to describe and categorize existing intervention approaches popular and suitable for use with children and youth with CCN. These approaches have been used to teach a variety of skills (e.g., self-help to academic) including expressive communication abilities. What follows is a discussion of each of the structured, semi-structured, and limited structure categories of intervention as to their scientific support and their ability to be conducted within practitioner-friendly frameworks. Structured interventions are those based on a high degree of clinician control. Semi-structured interventions rely less on clinician control than structured interventions, although they do involve the use of some preparation and direct instruction from the clinicians and operate best within natural routines or activities. Limited structure interventions build on child and youth-focused interests and actions through nondirective techniques. The ideas of scientific support and practitioner friendly have been developed prior to this review. This section ends with thoughts about interventions that do not fit neatly into the categorical structure used in this chapter.

Earlier, scientifically supported approaches were defined as those with a reliable evidence base. That is, evidence generated from research reflecting appropriate methodological rigor and appearing in credible scholarly outlets. In addition, there are descending levels of evidence that may occur in published research ranging from meta-analyses to observational studies. Consistent with our definition of scientifically supported, the National Professional Development Center on Autism Spectrum Disorders (Wong et al., 2014) created useful criteria for the evaluation of evidence bases supporting specific treatment approaches. This group noted the need for supportive published studies in peer-reviewed journals that utilized a) randomized or quasi-experimental designs, b) single-subject designs, or c) a combination of evidence defined as one high-quality randomized or quasi-experimental group design study and at least three high-quality single-subject design studies (Wong et al., 2014). The NAC (2015) uses similar guidelines to identify "established interventions" for school-age children and youth or those they suggest have a clear evidence base. The section that follows concludes discussions of structured, semi-structured, and limited structure interventions with National Professional Development Center on Autism Spectrum Disorders (NPDC) and NAC findings (NAC, 2015; Wong et al., 2014) specific to treatment approaches identified in Table 9.2.

Earlier, this chapter defined "practitioner" broadly to include all service providers and family members involved in a child's life. Furthermore, "friendly" as it relates to interventions was equated to the learnability, efficiency, effectiveness, and social validity of an approach. One could also consider naturalness or functionality as a critical feature of practitioner-friendly intervention approaches. These variables are all considered in the intervention reviews that follow.

Structured Interventions

Structured interventions, considered collectively, are those based on a high degree of clinician control. Marc Fey, in his seminal language-intervention text, referred to these as clinician-directed interventions (Fey, 1986). Clinician control is best described in relation to decisions about the goals of intervention, applications of specific strategies (including timing of delivery), and acceptability of target responses (including the management of reinforcement). With the clinician or teacher "in charge" of these variables, interventions are structured tightly. As suggested earlier in this chapter, structured interventions have not been primarily characterized by their functionality (i.e., their use of natural events, objects, and consequences within typical routines), yet they often yield high rates of skill practice for the learner (Ogletree & Oren, 1998; Ogletree & Oren, 2001).

A nonexhaustive list of structured interventions is listed in Table 9.2. Next, interventions in this list are summarized and considered as to their scientific support. This is followed by a collective discussion of how structured interventions are considered by the NAC and NPDC (NAC, 2015; Wong et al., 2014) reviews of evidence-based practices. Finally, a broad-based discussion of practitioner friendliness is offered as it applies to all structured interventions.

Applied Behavior Analysis   ABA is a framework for intervention that applies the principles of behaviorism to promote observable change in children or adults. ABA identifies and manipulates the antecedents and consequences of behaviors in an attempt to modify said behaviors. As a broad framework, ABA provides the theoretical basis for many more specific behavioral interventions. All individuals experience the impact of ABA when provided rewards or negative consequences to make behaviors more or less likely. In the world of children who are minimally verbal, ABA has been successfully used to teach self-help, academic, social, and communicative skills.

ABA methodologies have been considered some of the most evidence-based procedures for children and youth with developmental disabilities including ASD. This is particularly evident when one reviews recent well-controlled studies and meta-analyses (Eldevik et al., 2010; Makrygianni & Reed, 2010; Peters-Scheffer, Didden, Korzilius, & Sturmey, 2011; Virués-Ortega, 2010; Warren et al., 2011).

Applied behavior analysis (ABA): An approach to evaluating the variables that increase, maintain, or decrease socially important, observable behaviors and developing strategies to promote positive outcomes in applied settings. ABA has been implemented to instruct both human and nonhuman animals.

Discrete Trial Training   DTT is a specific form of ABA that emphasizes discrete trials in instruction. Based on this method, trials have five parts including 1) the cue, 2) the prompt, 3) the response, 4) the consequence, and 5) the response trial interval (Smith, 2001). The training sequence proceeds as follows: a) the cue or discriminative stimulus is provided (e.g., a command "Do this"), b) the cue is followed by or concurrently offered with a prompt to complete the task, c) the learner responds to the cue and prompt (successfully or not), d) the instructor responds to the learner with a reward or by indicating that the response was incorrect (e.g., averting gaze and removing stimulus materials), and e) a new trial is offered after a brief pause. As with ABA, DTT has been used to teach a variety of skills to children and youth with CCN, ranging from self-help to expressive language development.

Discrete trial training has a long history with minimally verbal children and youth (Blank & Milewski, 1981; Guess, Sailor, Rutherford, & Baer, 1968; Jeffree, Wheldall, & Mittler, 1973; Lovaas, 1987; Lovaas, Schreibman, & Koegel, 1974; McEachin, Smith, & Lovaas, 1993; Stevens-Long & Rasmussen, 1974). Although noted to facilitate communication and other skill acquisition, this method has been criticized for failing to result in gains generalizable across new training partners and contexts (Lovaas, Koegel, Simmons, & Stevens-Long, 1973). Ogletree, Saddler, and Bowers (1995) noted that DTT may lend itself to the instruction targeting specific language forms or more rote responding; however, it is likely less useful for the instruction of functional, generative communication skills.

The Picture Exchange Communication System   The PECS utilizes a training protocol (Bondy & Frost, 1993, 1994) based on the seminal work of B. F. Skinner (1957). The protocol encourages increasingly complex communication through the application of behavioral training techniques. In PECS, trainers offer reinforcement and support communication bids. The ultimate PECS treatment goal is increased spontaneous communication within social contexts.

In PECS Phase I, the learner is instructed to hand a single picture to another person in exchange for an object (requesting). Phase II expands exchanges by including additional pictures and increasing communicative partners and training environments. In Phase III, the learner discriminates between multiple picture choices when making requests. Phase IV emphasizes phrase construction for requests as the learner exchanges sentence strips. Phases V and VI expand instruction to include exchanges for nonregulatory purposes (e.g., questioning and commenting).

Several meta-analyses have considered the effectiveness of PECS with encouraging emergent communicative behaviors and reported generally positive findings, particularly in the area of requesting. For example, Sulzer-Azaroff, Hoffman, Horton, Bondy, and Frost (2009) reported positive results from 34 studies including increased requesting and describing, increased verbal behavior, expanded communication repertoires, and skill generalization. Flippin, Reszka, and Watson (2010) reviewed 54 studies and reported generally positive findings, although skill maintenance and generalization could not be determined. The best results were generated from studies in which subjects had progressed to phase IV of training. Finally, Ganz, Davis, Lund, Goodwyn, and Simpson (2012) evaluated 13 single-subject design studies and reported findings supportive of PECS as an intervention for young children with ASD. Like Flippin and colleagues (2010), Ganz and colleagues reported the best outcomes from studies in which subjects progressed farther into PECS training phases.

One surprising PECS outcome has been the emergence of spoken language among some participants at or beyond training phase IV (Charlop-Christy, Carpenter, Loc, LeBlanc, & Kellet, 2002; Ganz & Simpson, 2004). McCleery, Elliot, Sampanis, and Stefanidou (2013) attributed this phenomena to the introduction of time delay.

Visual Supports   Visual supports are included in Table 9.2 as a structured framework for intervention, although they can certainly be implemented across the spectrum of structured, semi-structured, and limited structure methodologies for children with minimal verbal abilities. The application of visual supports (i.e., visual schedules or visual-based structured teaching such as that provided in Treatment and Education of Autistic and related Communication-handicapped CHildren [TEACCH] [Mesibov, Shea, & Schopler, 2005]) is rooted in the assumption that many children, especially those on the autism spectrum, respond best to static rather than transient stimuli (Ogletree, 2016b; Quill, 1995). Visual supports often are used to assist with task completion (e.g., the sequential presentation of visual representations of task-sequence steps) or to develop expectancy and routine (e.g., the sequential presentation of "what's next" in a task or day). If used with maximal trainer control (as in clinician-directed interventions) visual supports are considered structured.

Empirical data backing the use of visuals has grown substantially over the past 2 decades, and these methodologies are now widely used with children who are minimally verbal (Dettmer, Simpson, Smith-Miles, & Ganz, 2000; Matson, Sevin, Box, Francis, & Sevin, 1993; Morrison, Sainato, Chaaban, & Endo, 2002).

The National Autism Center and National Professional Development Center on Autism Spectrum Disorders Structured Intervention Findings   In 2015, the NAC published results of its evidence-based review (2015). Likewise, in 2014 the NPDC, a Frank Porter Graham Project of the University of North Carolina at Chapel Hill, published a list of 27 evidence-based practices (Wong et al., 2014). As was stated previously, both groups-based findings on peer-reviewed published research emphasizing randomized or quasi-experimental-designed studies, single-subject studies, or combinations of both.

The subset of structured interventions reviewed in this section were evaluated, either in part or in whole, by the aforementioned organizations (NAC, 2015; Wong et al., 2014). All four (ABA, DTT, PECS, and visual supports/instruction) were designated as "established" and "evidence-based" practices by one or both reviews. PECS was described as an "emerging" intervention by the NAC. Given the strong endorsements of these prominent professional organizations, it can be assumed that these structured interventions meet the rigor of a scientifically supported approach as described in this chapter. Are they, however, practitioner friendly?

Structured Interventions and Practitioner Friendliness   Judging the practitioner friendliness of structured interventions is difficult. One must consider the potential use of these interventions across stakeholders in addition to evaluating their learnability and efficiency. In addition, structured interventions' contribution to socially valid change for children must also be evaluated.

The interventions reviewed in this section appear well-suited for use across all involved in an individual's life, assuming those in consistent contact with the child/youth are open to instruction by trainers knowledgeable about each method. One could argue, in fact, that such "cross stakeholder" training would promote skill generalization and maintenance, important outcomes for any treatment. The predictable and prescriptive nature of structured interventions would also support each approach's learnability. That is, structured interventions' clear instructional steps seem reasonably easy to master for the naive learner who might serve as an additional trainer. As is evident from the preceding review, structured interventions have a substantial literature base supporting their effectiveness in promoting skill acquisition, yet data about their comparative efficiency as approaches are lacking. More specifically, the relative efficiency of structured interventions when compared to other less-structured approaches has generally not been determined. One exception to this claim is preliminary data providing limited support for PECS instruction when compared to prelinguistic milieu training (PMT) with young children with autism (Yoder & Stone, 2006). One could argue that the prescriptive nature of structured interventions provides increased training trials and may result in a more efficient path to skill acquisition. The question remains, however, if these learned skills are generalizable and maintained over time.

The most troubling aspect of user-friendliness for structured interventions is their contribution, or lack thereof, to socially valid outcomes for learners. One considers social validity when questioning how treatments benefit the moment-to-moment aspects of an individual's daily life (Ogletree, Howell, & Carpenter, 2005). Do children/adolescents have more friends because of treatment, are they more independent or more well-liked by others? Some would argue that the ordered nature of structured instruction fails to mirror typical learning experiences for children and youth and, accordingly, lacks social validity. Furthermore, many studies reporting on the use of structured interventions have applied the methods to achieve measurable but narrow, well-defined outcomes. These have included the pursuit of specific self-help skills or the use of specific communication forms in restrictive contexts. One can certainly question whether these types of treatment goals result in socially valid outcomes for children. In addition, the overarching criticism of structured interventions has been their failure to result in skill generalization to new trainers and learning contexts (Lovaas, Koegel, Simmons, & Stevens-Long, 1973). Generalization failure suggests that learned skills are either not meaningful in new settings or are simply not evocable. Either way, a failure to generalize skills puts children at risk of limited socially valid change.

These concerns regarding structured interventions and socially valid outcomes are precautionary. That is, the authors of this chapter believe that structured interventions can result in socially valid outcomes if this is the intent of training. One can certainly envision a visual support system, for example, contributing to a child's more seamless participation in a group activity or the exchange of a picture opening meaningful opportunities for a child or youth to be more self-determinant.

In conclusion, though, scientifically supported, structured interventions may only be practitioner friendly with careful planning. Efforts toward this end require an engaged and informed network of trainers who are committed to modifying procedures, when needed, to reflect more naturally occurring interaction and selecting treatment goals with real-world value.

Semi-Structured Interventions

Semi-structured interventions for individuals with CCN and minimal verbal abilities, considered collectively, rely less on clinician control and operate best within natural routines or activities. Semi-structured methodologies have been referred to as milieu interventions in that they combine aspects of structured and unstructured interventions (Fey, 1986). They typically utilize the predictability of common routines to entice a student's participation. Within participation turns, a trainer can be more structured, frequently applying techniques and tools common to ABA such as prompting or shaping. In contrast to structured intervention, semi-structured interventions have been characterized by their functionality (i.e., their use of natural events, objects, and consequences within typical routines) (Ogletree & Oren, 1998; Ogletree & Oren 2001).

A nonexhaustive list of semi-structured interventions is in Table 9.2. They are then briefly summarized and considered as to their scientific support. This is followed by a collective discussion of how these interventions are considered by the NAC and the NPDC (NAC, 2015; Wong et al., 2014). Finally, a broad-based discussion of practitioner friendliness is offered as it applies to all semi-structured interventions.

Social Scripts and Social Stories   Social scripts and Social Stories typically describe situations, skills, or concepts using relevant social cues, including visual supports and text (Gray & Garand, 1993). A goal of scripts and stories is to share accurate, and often less perceptible, social information in a manner that reduces anxiety often associated with more novel social events.

One might question the use of social scripts and stories with students with CCN, especially those with limited comprehension. In fact, Kokina and Kern (2010) suggested that comprehension of stories is central to social scripting and story success. These authors also suggested that evidence for scripts and stories with children and youth lacking reading or verbal-comprehension abilities is limited. By doing so they endorse a perspective that assumes comprehension underlies students' success with these supports.

Although comprehension and reading ability would enhance the value of social scripts and stories, a cogent argument can be made for the use of less complex, sequential visual-social supports. This idea is particularly intriguing given the apparent preference for static stimuli (Ogletree, 2016b; Quill, 1995) among many students who lack speech and spoken words; and this group's frequent, though less obvious, reading proclivity (Erickson, Hanser, Hatch, & Sanders, 2009). A final related thought: Providing scripts and stories to children and youth who may not have mastered them completely has support in the literature (Crozier & Tincani, 2007; Sansosti, Powell-Smith, & Kincaid, 2004).

In general, overwhelming empirical support for social scripts and stories as a semi-structured intervention is lacking. In a meta-analysis of 18 investigations, Kokina and Kern (2010) reported that study findings were evenly distributed as either being strongly supportive or not supportive.

Peer Mediation   Peer-mediated interventions are those in which peers are instructed in social behaviors and techniques to assist students with disabilities. This type of intervention has primarily emphasized teaching peers to initiate with and respond to the communication of children/youth with impaired socio-communicative abilities including ASD (Day, Powell, Dy-Lin, & Stowitschek, 1982; Odom, Hoyson, Jamieson, & Strain, 1985). Peer interventions can be implemented in single dyads (e.g., through "buddy" systems) but are more commonly delivered within active group settings.

As with social scripts and stories, one could question the applicability of peer mediation relative to children and youth with CCN and minimal verbal abilities. If, however, appropriate skills are targeted (prelinguistic forms to emergent language and symbol use in social contexts), peer-mediated interaction would appear to have significant applications with this group. The successful use of peer-mediated intervention with children and youth with moderate to severe intellectual disabilities supports this contention (Haring & Breen, 1992).

Numerous communicative gains have been reported in children receiving peer-mediated intervention, including increased social responding, better comprehension, and improved participation in group social exchanges (Garfinkle & Schwartz, 2002; Kohler et al., 1995). Peers have also reported a positive sense of helping others after engaging in peer mediation (Jones, 2007).

Pivotal Response Treatment   PRT targets "pivotal" behaviors (e.g., motivation, responding to multiple cues, self-management, social initiations) rather than individual or discrete incremental skills (Koegel, Koegel, Shoshan, & McNerney, 1999). PRT occurs within play-based and child-initiated activities and can be used to facilitate socio-communicative skills and manage disruptive behaviors. Family involvement, natural reinforcement, child choice in activities, use of familiar tasks, and the introduction of novelty through routines are all features of PRT. Therapy sessions typically involve six segments during which skills are targeted in structured and unstructured formats using both behavioral and more incidental teaching strategies (Koegel et al., 1999).

PRT has a substantial evidence base including numerous reports of gains specific to speech, language, and play in young children (Koegel, Camarata, Valdez-Menchaca, & Koegel, 1997; Koegel, Koegel, & Surrat, 1992; Stahmer, 1995) and comparable reported successes with social and independence skills in children and youth who are older (Dunlap, Dunlap, Koegel, & Koegel, 1991; Koegel, Carter, & Koegel, 2003).

Milieu Teaching   Milieu teaching represents a broad grouping of instructional approaches that can be categorized into prelinguistic milieu teaching, responsivity education/prelinguistic milieu teaching, and milieu communication teaching (Fey et al., 2006; Fey, Yoder, Warren, & Bredin-Oja, 2013). Prelinguistic milieu teaching targets students' prelinguistic or nonverbal communication by directly teaching specific gestures, vocalizations, and coordinated eye gaze behavior in the context of social routines occurring in the individual's natural environment (Fey et al., 2006). The goal is to facilitate a solid foundation of nonverbal communication that supports the development and growth of more complex linguistic communication (Fey et al., 2013). Prelinguistic milieu teaching is a hybrid approach that supplements the base method with a parent-education component. During parent responsivity education, parents learn how to respond optimally to their child's communicative acts in both small-group and individual sessions (Yoder & Warren, 2002). Milieu teaching can follow prelinguistic milieu teaching once a student is using intentional communication frequently and/or there is emergence of conventional symbols (Fey et al., 2013).

Milieu teaching therapy sessions are characterized by the use of predictable routines. Once established, routines are interrupted, creating training opportunities. Training occurs through the application of training techniques and tools of varied directiveness (e.g., modeling, prompting, chaining). MT shares many features of PRT (reviewed above) including the use of structured instruction embedded within natural interactions, the application of techniques to elicit responses, and the acceptance and modification of response approximations (Delprato, 2001; Kaiser, Yoder, & Keetz, 1992).

Milieu teaching has been used successfully with many populations, including preschoolers with developmental delays (Fey et al., 2006), school-age children and youth with disabilities (Parker-McGowan et al., 2014), children and youth with autism (Franco, Davis, & Davis, 2013; Kaiser, Hancock, & Nietfeld, 2000; Mancil, Conroy, & Haydon, 2009; Ogletree, Davis, Hambrecht, & Wooten, 2012), and toddlers with intellectual disabilities (Fey et al., 2013). A student's communicative level has become a guidepost for the prescription of the various forms of milieu teaching. For students with one or two spontaneous, intentional nonsymbolic communicative acts per minute in social interaction, prelinguistic milieu teaching is recommended whereas milieu teaching is the frequent choice for children with 10 or more words or symbol forms (Warren et al., 2006).

National Autism Center and National Professional Development Center Semi-Structured Intervention Findings   The subset of semi-structured interventions reviewed in this section were evaluated, either in part or in whole, by the National Autism Center and National Professional Development Center (NAC, 2015; Wong et al., 2014). All four semi-structured interventions (social scripts and stories, peer-mediated intervention, Pivotal Response Treatment, and milieu teaching) were designated as either "established" or "evidence-based" practices by these reviews. It should be noted that milieu teaching and PRT were not mentioned specifically in either review but were subsumed under the broader category of "Naturalistic Interventions or Teaching Strategies." Several techniques (e.g., modeling, prompting, reinforcement, time delay) used in both milieu teaching and PRT were deemed "established" practices by the NPDC. Given the strong endorsements of these two groups, it can be assumed that these semi-structured interventions meet the rigor of a scientifically supported approach as described in this chapter. Once again, the question is—are they practitioner friendly?

Semi-Structured Interventions and Practitioner Friendliness   As with any treatment, determining the practitioner friendliness of semi-structured interventions requires the consideration of their potential use across stakeholders, their learnability, and their efficiency. In addition, semi-structured interventions' role in promoting socially valid change for children and adolescents must be evaluated.

Most semi-structured interventions depend on stakeholder and family involvement making their potential use across partners and environments likely. Prelinguistic milieu teaching and PRT are clear illustrations of treatments that emphasize prominent training roles for stakeholders. Compared to structured interventions, semi-structured approaches are somewhat less rigid and formulaic, possibly reducing their learnability. This said, studies have demonstrated the viability of parents and others as trainers in semi-structured intervention (Peterson, Carta, & Greenwood, 2005). Like structured interventions, the relative efficiency of semi-structured approaches has received little attention in the literature. From a clinical perspective, however, semi-structured interventions likely will generate fewer learning opportunities for children than their structured counterparts due to the less frequent use of elicitation procedures.

An evaluation of dependent variables in semi-structured interventions suggest that they lend themselves to the encouragement of socially valid outcomes for individuals with CCN. The frequent appearance of pragmatic targets (e.g., initiations; Franco et al., 2013) make this point. Of course, social validity is a concept unique to the child/youth and her circumstances. That is, meaningful change is in the eye of the beholder. It is at least fair to suggest that the natural formats of semi-structured interventions invite socially valid treatment targets. These same formats, and the many "trainers" who work within them, also promote gains that generalize and are maintainable over time.

To conclude, semi-structured interventions appear to have some advantages over structured interventions in terms of practitioner friendliness. These are most likely related to the more natural/functional nature of these approaches.

Limited Structure Interventions

The final category of interventions for children and youth with CCN minimal verbal abilities are those that employ limited structure. Using Fey's (1986) conceptualization of language interventions, approaches with limited structure are best described as "child directed." That is, they build on child/youth-focused interests and actions through nondirective techniques such as modeling or expansions rather than emphasizing trainer elicitations of target behaviors. The classic example of limited structure is language therapy within play, where growth is targeted by following a child's play lead while modeling expansive versions of the child's utterances (Fey, 1986).

Limited structure interventions are known for their functionality but typically do not have a strong empirical basis (Ogletree & Oren, 2001). However, the quality of research, especially that used in parent-mediated limited structured interventions, is improving (Nevill, Lecavalier, & Stratis, 2016).

Only one example of a limited structure intervention, the DIR (Developmental Individual-difference Relationship-based) Floortime Model, was identified in Table 9.2. Floortime is discussed below and its evidence base is considered using NAC and NPDC conclusions (NAC, 2015; Wong et al., 2014). Finally, a broad-based discussion of practitioner friendliness is offered as it applies to all limited structure interventions.

Developmental Individual-Difference Relationship-Based Model—Floortime
Floortime emerged from the Developmental Individual-difference Relationship-based (DIR) Model (Greenspan, 1979, 1989). It encourages play at the child's physical and developmental level and can be used in isolation or with other treatment approaches. In Floortime, the trainer engages in activities of the child's interest yet directs them to greater complexity by expanding actions and modeling more sophisticated behaviors. Sessions are characterized by reciprocal exchanges through which joint attention is established and problem-solving occurs. Floortime's emphasis is directed more to emotional growth than specific skill acquisition (Wieder & Greenspan, 2003).

An early report of Floortime's effectiveness came in the form of a case study (Wieder & Greenspan, 2003). Subsequent larger studies utilizing group designs have reported promising results (Casenhiser, Shanker, & Stieben, 2013; Pajareya & Nopmaneejumruslers, 2012; Solomon, Van Egeren, Mahoney, Quon Huber, & Zimmerman, 2014), although methodological issues limit their conclusions.

National Autism Center and National Professional Development Center Limited Structured Intervention Findings   Floortime is considered to be an unestablished intervention by the most recent NAC report (2015). This designation is

reserved for approaches that have no clear evidence of effectiveness. One can assume that the unestablished moniker for Floortime relates to a perceived lack of credible research findings. The NPDC does not consider Floortime in its evidence-based treatments (Wong et al., 2014).

Limited Structure Interventions and Practitioner Friendliness   As with the two previous intervention categories, several factors are central to limited structure treatments' practitioner friendliness. These include potential use across stakeholders and the learnability and efficiency of approaches. In addition, limited structure interventions' role in promoting socially valid change for children and youth must be evaluated.

It would appear that stakeholder inclusion in limited structured interventions is highly valued. In fact, as was noted with semi-structured approaches, limited structured interventions often rely in part or solely on stakeholders (often parents) rather than less familiar trainers (Nevill, Lecavalier, & Stratis, 2016). Again, like semi-structured interventions, limited structure treatments are less prescriptive and will likely provide fewer training moments, potentially making them less learnable and efficient than structured approaches.

Limited structure interventions would seem to share semi-structured advantages in the promotion of socially valid outcomes for children and youth with CCN. Their emphasis on a child-driven focus and their use of common daily activities provide a ripe setting for treatment outcomes meaningful in the daily lives of children and adolescents. Of course, as with all three of our categories of intervention, the promotion of socially valid outcomes requires a complete knowledge of the child/youth, her needs, and her communicative contexts. Pursuing socially valid treatments results from the trainer's careful consideration of these and other variables. Limited structure interventions, then, have the strong potential for practitioner friendliness, yet lack the empirical backing of structured and semi-structured treatments.

Final Treatment Considerations

Some treatments used with children and youth with CCN who are minimally verbal do not lend themselves to simple categorization. More specifically, they do not fit exclusively in any of the three intervention groupings described thus far. Two examples are the Social Communication, Emotional Regulation, Transactional Support (SCERTS®) Model (Prizant, Wetherby, Rubin, Laurent, & Rydell, 2006) and the broad-based application of Augmentative and Alternative Communication (AAC). The SCERTS model is designed for team-based intervention and is flexible enough to incorporate aspects of many of the approaches described thus far. Similarly, AAC is a defined interprofessional field of practice that can make use of training methodologies regardless of their emphasis, or lack thereof, with respect to structure and function. Both are considered below.

The Social Communication, Emotional Regulation, Transactional Support (SCERTS®) Model   The SCERTS® intervention is best described as a framework for addressing communication and social-emotional abilities in individuals with ASD (Prizant et al., 2006). The model has been used with children and youth of all ages and severity levels and addresses Social Communication (i.e., spontaneous communication to build relationships), Emotional Regulation (i.e., management of emotional arousal, thus supporting engagement and learning), and Transactional Support (i.e., support techniques and strategies critical to goal attainment).

SCERTS implementation includes the broad-based assessment of an individual's functioning, learning preferences, and motivations. Assessment data inform the selection of SCERTS goals, activities, and supports in a manner that respects family priorities and structures. Ideally, SCERTS instruction and support occur pervasively throughout the child's day, creating a model of care from which all providers and stakeholders function. A frequently noted benefit of the SCERTS model is that most interventions, including all of those mentioned in this chapter, can be used within its broad framework (Prizant et al., 2006).

The most rigorous evidence-based review of the SCERTS Model was published in 2014 (Wetherby et al., 2014). Researchers used randomized controlled trials to evaluate individual (i.e., two to three times weekly home and center treatment) and group (i.e., single weekly meetings) early social intervention for 82 toddlers with autism. Both treatment groups received intervention based upon the SCERTS framework. Children in the individual treatment group demonstrated greater gains with social communication skills (as measured by examiner evaluation and parent report) when compared to group treatment counterparts. Daily living and social skills improvements were also reported in those receiving individual SCERTS treatment (parent report).

In summary, the SCERTS Model has intuitive appeal for its flexibility, comprehensive nature and emerging evidence base. Although created to address the needs of children on the autism spectrum, this model is appropriate for other populations with CCN, especially those with severe intellectual disabilities. SCERTS also appears to meet the practitioner-friendly guidelines set forth in this chapter. One exception may be the lack of instructional structure and prescriptiveness for stakeholders, although it should be noted that this is also considered a strength of the model.

Augmentative and Alternative Communication   According to Beukelman and Mirenda (2013), AAC is an area of research, educational, and clinical practice that addresses temporary or permanent communication and related participation limitations. AAC is typically divided into aided (those external to the user) and unaided (those not external to the user) solutions, both of which have been central components of successful interventions for children with minimal verbal abilities.

Aided AAC solutions are illustrated in many of the approaches presented thus far in the chapter. For example, exchanging pictures (PECS) and using visual supports are AAC solutions. Others not highlighted include symbol displays on communication boards, computer tablets, and dedicated voice output communication aids (VOCA). For decades, aided AAC solutions have had broad appeal for those teaching minimally verbal children (Ogletree & Oren, 2006; Romski & Sevcik, 1996; Snell et al., 2010). Most recently, empirical data have supported this contention (Kasari et al., 2014).

Unaided AAC solutions have included vocalizations, gestures, and natural sign systems. Once again, the literature is replete with examples of unaided AAC solutions for individuals with CCN (Goods, Ishijima, Chang, & Kasari, 2013; Reichle, Ganz, Drager, & Parker-McGowan, 2016; Snell et al., 2010). In summary, interventions introducing unaided AAC have been successful with the promotion of social communication in children with complex communication needs (Shire, Kasari, Kaiser, & Fuller, 2016).

Clearly, aided and unaided AAC solutions have been used across the spectrum of structured interventions reviewed here and have garnered considerable empirical support. In fact, AAC devices (a subset of aided solutions) was designated as an "emerging" intervention by the NAC (2015), suggesting the existence of credible supportive research in this area. It is difficult to assess the practitioner friendliness of AAC solutions in that they vary widely and are used in a variety of interventions. One can at least assume that it is possible to introduce and use AAC in a manner that is "friendly" to all stakeholders.

ILLUSTRATIONS OF INTERVENTIONS FOR CHILDREN WHO ARE MINIMALLY VERBAL AND PRESENT WITH AUTISM SPECTRUM DISORDER

This chapter concludes with two cases that demonstrate common practice recommendations and challenges for children who are minimally verbal and on the autism spectrum. Abstract theoretical constructs specific to intervention are presented in an applied fashion as the possibilities afforded by structure and practitioner friendliness are explored. Cases address instruction specific to emergent communication and developmental/educational goals, and each is followed by a brief discussion.

Robert

Robert is a 6½-year-old child with autism. Prior to entering an elementary school program he was enrolled in an early intervention program. Robert was diagnosed with ASD at 16 months of age. He communicates with gestures and cries to regulate the behavior of others and to protest. Robert uses no words. He appears to comprehend simple requests if they are accompanied with gestures or other physical cues (e.g., objects and some photographs). Robert is easily agitated by changes in his routines and can become noncompliant as daily disruptions of his schedule occur.

Intervention Choice

Many, if not all, of the interventions presented thus far have specific applications for children with autism. In fact, the "gold standard" reviews for evidence-based interventions (i.e., the NAC [2015] and the NPDC [Wong et al., 2014]) used throughout this chapter feature studies addressing the needs of children on the spectrum. Accordingly, there are many possible intervention choices for Robert. For this case, the SCERTS model was chosen for its ability to introduce multiple interventions as a means of achieving communication, emotional, and functional developmental gains.

Case Illustration

The team-based SCERTS assessment for Robert revealed prelinguistic expressive communication abilities largely limited to gestures with contact and immature vocalizations used to request objects and actions and to protest. His receptive communication was more consistent with 15- to 18-month expectations, as he responded to simple speech accompanied by gestural cues and appeared to understand many object labels. Robert used behavioral outbursts (e.g., running away and hitting) to protest and escape. Outbursts typically occurred as routines were interrupted or when he was in noisy/busy environments. He also responded adversely to unexpected light touch. Robert's emotional state could quickly change from happiness and compliance to crying and dysregulation. Robert enjoyed stacking blocks and participated in routines that incorporated building. He also responded well to brief exposure to within- and across-task visual schedules utilizing photographs and objects. Robert was motivated by big hugs, movement opportunities, and time with blocks and puzzles. His family was excited to see Robert easily engaged by SCERTS examiners.

Robert's team-based goals in social communication included the symbolic expression of requests and protests. His goals addressing emotional regulation included the promotion of self- and other-regulated strategies to ease transitions and reduce behavioral outbursts. His transactional supports to address goals included photographs for communication exchange and visual schedules for within- and across-task transitions. Robert also enjoyed transactional supports like activity/strategy diaries (e.g., written collections of activities and suggestions to support Robert's participation) and weekly team meetings to create a comprehensive intervention effort that crossed stakeholders and settings.

Robert's interventions included many of the structured to limited structure treatments reviewed in this chapter. His team used aspects of ABA to understand and alter antecedent events contributing to Robert's behavioral outbursts. Some of these solutions included removing environmental triggers for behavior (e.g., noise), while others centered upon behavior replacement strategies that introduced equally powerful and more socially acceptable behavioral alternatives (e.g., AAC through picture exchange). Robert's team also applied semi-structured approaches like PRT and milieu teaching to address social communication goals within routines centered around highly motivating activities such as movement and block play. These treatments were used to introduce picture exchange for requesting and protesting. Finally, all stakeholders were encouraged to share, problem-solve, and teach through structured (staffing) and unstructured (daily diaries/news letters) communication channels. Robert's intervention was off to a collaborative start, but ultimate success would depend on team and stakeholder cohesiveness.

Clearly, Robert's case illustrates recommended practices. The question that remains relates to challenges associated with serving Robert. There are several, and three are mentioned here. First, successful implementation of the SCERTS model is predicated on efficient and collaborative practice. With so many involved in his care, it would seem that Robert's team is at risk for failure associated with communication and collaboration breakdowns. If these occur, the entire model is compromised. This is avoided through a commitment to careful planning. Second, monitoring and reporting change in Robert's communication and behavior will be difficult. Again, the plethora of care providers working across multiple settings could make Robert's treatment stagnate without quality data keeping that informs new goal selection and/or treatment modification. Finally, the flexibility associated with SCERTS in terms of intervention application may create a ripe context for professional dispute or bias. That is, an interventionist with a behavioral preference will need to be open to the possibility that interventions with less structure may be applied. This will require a mature provider who cares more for the child receiving her services than for the approach she may have championed over time.

Mary

Mary is a middle-school student identified as presenting classic autism at an early age. Her IEP identifies her primary disability as autism and she receives her educational services in a self-contained special-education public-school classroom. For the purpose of this case, Mary has both autism and a severe intellectual disability.

Intervention Choice

Mary's case illustrates that, for many children, aspects of several treatments can be combined to provide support through the day. With Mary, tangible symbols and eventually print were introduced through semi-structured to promote communication success and classroom instruction.

Case Illustration

Mary's case utilizes several semi-structured interventions and employs AAC. Mary's school day started with an interaction with the classroom aide around Mary's daily schedule calendar box. The calendar box contained six separated cubbies and a finished compartment. Each cubby contained a tangible symbol (part of an object) that represented an activity for the day. Additional objects or parts of objects were available to expand some activities.

An experience book (a book previously developed with Mary during a gardening experience, containing attached objects such as a baggie of dirt, a part of a plastic flowerpot, and the paper seed packet) was in Mary's first cubby and connected to her science activity. This book allowed conversation to: a) revolve around what was done in past science lessons specific to growing plants; and b) expand (e.g., presenting apples, peanut butter, and a plastic utensil) to include the production and consumption of healthy food. An additional blank experience book was available above Mary's calendar box for use in the next science lesson.

This sequence was repeated for Mary's major daily activities, including a functional math group, music class, lunch, shared reading time, and adapted physical education. All activities occurred within predictable routines, allowing for the instructional use of milieu teaching and PRT. Experience books were used with tangible symbols (AAC) for each daily activity, presenting new vocabulary and linking old and new experiences. Symbols were paired with raised three-dimensional print. Shared reading time focused on Mary's teacher reading with her through the presentation of tangible symbols, raised print, and speech amplified via an auditory trainer.

The use of the schedule box in Mary's day supported the left-to-right literacy sequencing, the anticipation of upcoming events, the reading of experience books, the introduction of new vocabulary, and emphasis on time concepts of past and future. The routine use of the calendar following a calendar conversation was highly scripted with a tangible symbol selected prior to beginning the task and returned to the finished box upon task completion. The access to her tangible symbols was critical to Mary's use of these tangible items as not only a receptive communication system but also within her expressive system. She was prompted during activities to make a choice between two possible tangible items. At lunch she was asked to choose between the juice box and water bottle to select her beverage choice (two objects in her lunch calendar cubby). Later in the day, Mary returned to her array of tangible symbols and selected the water bottle as a request for a drink break (something she did consistently and with no prompting). At this time, her teacher introduced a textured symbol, a card with a sandpaper feel, and the word "drink please" labeled at the top and bottom (words present for partners' benefit) that was paired with the drink choice to begin moving Mary's system from tangible to textured symbols. Mary went to the water bottle five times during a typical afternoon. Each time, she was presented with the textured symbol sandpaper card and then given the drink break. At the end of the day, all the items in the finished box were reviewed with Mary and placed back within her array of symbols. Clearly, Mary's familiarity with the water bottle as a requesting symbol made the bottle an excellent symbol for Mary's upcoming communication system— a textured/object board (AAC).

Mary's case illustrates several recommended practices, including the use of routines, scripting, specific interventions, and AAC in general. As with Robert's case, Mary's care will not proceed without challenges. First, successful implementation of a calendar box will require a keen understanding of Mary's symbol comprehension. This will only occur after rigorous assessment, including some trial-and-error diagnostic therapy. Second, once symbols are selected there must be a systematic effort to slowly introduce new symbols of graduated complexity, moving Mary toward more conventional symbol use. For concerns about both symbol use and development, Mary's team (especially her speech-language pathologist, special educator, psychologist, and visual impairment specialist) and all other stakeholders involved in her care will be invaluable resources. Third, Mary's care will necessitate a consistent eye to her sensory status. Again, her team (this time also including the audiologist) and stakeholders will need to address changes in Mary's sensory status that could impact treatment efforts. Finally, Mary's case, like most with children who present minimal verbal abilities, will require considerable stakeholder communication and planning. Without this in place, Mary will be at risk for stagnant and possibly ineffective treatment.

CONCLUSION

This chapter has proposed that interventions for children and youth with CCN share a host of evidence-based techniques and can be delivered in approaches across a continuum of therapeutic structure. Approaches that have emerged from the varied application of techniques differ in terms of their theoretical constructs and evidence base, offering providers considerable treatment choice.

For years, evidence base has been the central driver in intervention decision making for children and youth with CCN. This chapter has added another treatment dimension for consideration—practitioner friendliness. The idea of practitioner friendliness has been introduced noting critical variables for "friendliness," including stakeholder learnability, use across settings, effectiveness, efficiency, and social validity.

To conclude, the authors of this chapter support the idea that interventionists working with this special population of children and youth have many evidence-based and practitioner-friendly approaches at their disposal. Treatment choice in each individual case will necessitate a careful review of an individual's communication abilities and needs, as well as those of the stakeholders charged in her care. It is our hope that the ideas presented in this chapter will make treatment choices less complicated.

REFERENCES

Aslam, S., & Emmanuel, P. (2010). Formulating a researchable question: A critical step for facilitating good clinical research. *Indian Journal of Sexually Transmitted Diseases, 31*(1), 47–50. doi:10.4103/0253-7184.69003

Beukelman, D. R., & Mirenda, P. (2013). *Augmentative and alternative communication: Supporting children and youth with complex communication needs* (4th ed.). Baltimore: Paul H. Brookes Publishing Co.

Blank, M., & Milewski, J. (1981). Applying psycholinguistic concepts to the treatment of an autistic child. *Applied Psycholinguistics, 2*, 65–84.

Bondy, A., & Frost, L. (1993). Mands across the water: A report on the application of the picture-exchange communication system in Peru. *The Behavior Analyst, 16*, 123–128.

Bondy, A., & Frost, L. (1994). The Delaware autistic program. In S. Harris & J. Handleman (Eds.), *Preschool education programs for children with autism* (pp. 37–54). Austin, TX: PRO-ED.

Brady, N. C., Bruce, S., Goldman, A., Erickson, K., Mineo, B., Ogletree, B. T., . . . Wilkinson, K. (2016). Communication services and supports for individuals with severe disabilities: Guidance for assessment and intervention. *American Journal on Intellectual and Developmental Disabilities, 121*(2), 121–138. doi:10.1352/1944-7558-121.2.121

Carr, E. (1977). The motivation of some self-injurious behavior: A review of some hypotheses. *Psychological Bulletin, 84*(4), 800–816.

Carr, E., & Durand, V.M. (1985). Reducing behavior problems through functional communication training. *Journal of Applied Behavior Analysis, 18*, 111–126.

Casenhiser, D. M., Shanker, S. G., & Stieben, J. (2013). Learning through interaction in children with autism: Preliminary data from a social-communication-based intervention. *Autism, 17*(2), 228–249.

Charlop-Christy, M., Carpenter, M., Loc, L., LeBlanc, L., & Kellet, K. (2002). Using the Picture Exchange Communication System (PECS) with children with autism: Assessment of PECS acquisition, speech, social-communicative behavior and problem behavior. *Journal of Applied Behavior Analysis, 35*, 213–231.

Crozier, S., & Tincani, M. J. (2007). Effects of Social Stories on prosocial behavior on preschool children with autism spectrum disorders. *Journal of Autism and Developmental Disorders, 37*(9), 1803–1814.

Day, R. M., Powell, T. H., Dy-Lin, E. B., & Stowitschek, J. J. (1982). An evaluation of the effects of a social interaction training package on mentally handicapped preschool children. *Education and Training of the Mentally Retarded, 17*(2), 125–130.

Delprato, D. J. (2001). Comparisons of discrete-trial and normalized behavioral language intervention for young children with autism. *Journal of Autism and Developmental Disorders, 31*(3), 315–325.

Dettmer, S., Simpson, R. L., Myles, B. S., & Ganz, J. B. (2000). The use of visual supports to facilitate transitions of students with autism. *Focus on Autism and Other Developmental Disabilities, 15,* 163–169.

Dunlap, L. K., Dunlap. G., Koegel, L. K., & Koegel, R. L. (1991). Using self-monitoring to increase independence. *Teaching Exceptional Children, 2,* 17–22.

Eldevik, S., Hastings, R. P., Hughes, J. C., Jahr, E., Eikeseth, S., & Cross, S. (2010). Using participant data to extend the evidence base for intensive behavioral intervention for children with autism. *American Journal of Intellectual and Developmental Disabilities, 115*(5), 381–405.

Erickson, K., Hanser, G., Hatch, P., & Sanders, E. (2009). *Research-based practices for creating access to the general curriculum in reading and literacy for students with significant intellectual disabilities.* Chapel Hill, NC: Center for Literacy and Disability Studies.

Fey, M. E. (1986). *Language intervention with young children.* Boston: College-Hill; Little, Brown and Company.

Fey, M. E., Warren, S. F., Brady, N. C., Finestack, L. H., Bredin-Oja, S. L., Fairchild, M., & Yoder, P. (2006). Early effects of responsivity education/prelinguistic milieu teaching for children with developmental delays and their parents. *Journal of Speech, Language, and Hearing Research, 49,* 526–547.

Fey, M. E., Yoder, P. J., Warren, S. F., & Bredin-Oja, S. L. (2013). Is more better? Milieu communication teaching in toddlers with intellectual disabilities. *Journal of Speech, Language, Hearing, Research, 56*(2), 679–693.

Fiske, K. E., Cohen, A. P., Bamond, M. J., Delmolino, L., LaRue, R. H., & Sloman, K. N. (2014). The effects of magnitude-based differential reinforcement on the skill acquisition of children with autism. *Journal of Behavioral Education, 23*(4), 470–487.

Flippin, M., Reszka, S., & Watson, L. R. (2010). Effectiveness of the Picture Exchange Communication System (PECS) on language and speech of children with autism: A meta-analysis. *American Journal of Speech-Language Pathology, 19,* 178–195.

Foster, S. L., & Mash, E. J. (1999). Assessing social validity in clinical research: Issues and procedures. *Journal of Counseling and Clinical Psychology, 67,* 308–319.

Franco, J. H., Davis, B. L., & Davis J. L. (2013). Increasing social interaction using prelinguistic milieu teaching with nonverbal school-age children with autism. *American Journal of Speech Language Pathology, 22*(3), 489–502.

Ganz, J. B., Davis, L., Lund, E. M., Goodwyn, F. D., & Simpson, R. L. (2012). Meta-analysis of PECS with individuals with ASD: Investigation of targeted versus non-targeted outcomes, participant characteristics, and implementation phase. *Research in Developmental Disorders, 33,* 406–418. http://dx.doi.org/10.1016/j.ridd.2011.09.023

Ganz, J. B., & Simpson, R. L. (2004). Effects on communicative requesting and speech development of the Picture Exchange Communication System in children with characteristics of autism. *Journal of Autism and Developmental Disorders, 34,* 395–490.

Garfinkle, A. N., & Schwartz, I. S. (2002). Peer imitation: Increasing social interactions in children with autism and other developmental disabilities in inclusive preschool classrooms. *Topics in Early Childhood Special Education, 22*(1), 26–38.

Goods, K. S., Ishijima, E., Chang, Y. C., & Kasari, C. (2013). Preschool based JASPER intervention in minimally verbal children with autism: Pilot RCT. *Journal of Autism and Developmental Disorders, 43*(5), 1050–1056.

Gray, C., & Garand, J. (1993). Social Stories: Improving responses of students with autism with accurate social information. *Focus on Autistic Behavior, 8*(1), 1–10.

Greenspan, S. I. & Wieder, S. (2005) Can children with autism master the core deficits and become empathetic, creative, and reflective: A ten to fifteen year follow-up of a subgroup of children with autism spectrum disorders (ASD) who received a comprehensive Developmental, Individual-difference, Relationship-based (DIR) approach. *Journal of Developmental and Learning Disorders, 9,* 1–29.

Greenspan, S. I. (1979). Intelligence and adaptation: An integration of psychoanalytic and Piagetian developmental psychology. *Psychological Issues, 12*(3–4), 1–408.

Greenspan, S. I. (1989). *The development of the ego: Implications for personality theory, psychopathology, and the psychotherapeutic process.* New York, NY: International Universities Press.

Guess, D., Sailor, W., Rutherford, G., & Baer, D. M. (1968). An experimental analysis of linguistic development: The productive use of the plural morpheme. *Journal of Applied Behavior Analysis, 1,* 297–309.

Haring, T. G., & Breen, C. G. (1992). A peer mediated social network intervention to enhance the social integration of persons with moderate and severe disabilities. *Journal of Applied Behavior Analysis, 25*, 319–334.

Jeffree, D., Wheldall, K., & Mittler, P. (1973). Facilitating two-word utterances in two Down syndrome boys. *American Journal of Mental Deficiency, 78*(2), 117.

Jones, V. (2007). 'I Felt Like I Did Something Good'—The impact on mainstream pupils of a peer tutoring programme for children with autism. *British Journal of Special Education, 34*(1), 3–9.

Justice, L. (2010). When craft and science collide: Improving therapeutic practices through evidence-based innovations. *International Journal of Speech-Language Pathology, 12*(2), 79–86. doi:10.3109/17549500903373984

Kaiser, A. P., Hancock, T. B., & Nietfeld, J. P. (2000). The effects of parent-implemented enhanced milieu teaching on the social communication of children who have autism. [Special issue]. *Journal of Early Education and Development, 11*(4), 423–446.

Kaiser, A. P., Yoder, P. J., & Keetz, A. (1992). Evaluating milieu teaching. In S. F. Warren & J. Reichle (Eds.), *Causes and effects in communication and language intervention* (pp. 9–47). Baltimore: Paul H. Brookes Publishing Co.

Kasari, C., Kaiser, A., Goods, K., Nietfeld, J., Mathy, P., Landa, R., . . . Almirall, D. (2014). Communication interventions for minimally verbal children with autism: A sequential multiple assignment randomized trial. *Journal of the American Academy of Child and Adolescent Psychiatry, 53*(6), 635–646. doi:10.1016/j.jaac.2014.01.019

Koegel, L. K., Camarata, S. M., Valdez-Menchaca, M., & Koegel, R. L. (1997). Setting generalization of question-asking by children with autism. *American Journal on Mental Retardation, 102*(4), 346–357.

Koegel, L. K., Carter, C. M., & Koegel, R. L. (2003). Teaching children with autism self-initiations as a pivotal response. *Topics in Language Disorders, 23*(2), 134–145.

Koegel, L. K., Koegel, R. L., Shoshan, Y., & McNerney, E. (1999). Pivotal Response Intervention II: Preliminary long-term outcome data. *The Journal of The Association for Persons with Severe Handicaps, 24*(3),186–198. doi:10.2511/rpsd.24.3.186

Koegel, R. L., Koegel, L. K., & Surrat, A. (1992). Language intervention and disruptive behavior in preschool children with autism. *Journal of Autism and Developmental Disorders, 22*(2), 141–153.

Kohler, F. W., Strain, P. S., Hoyson, M., Davis, L., Donina, W. M., & Rapp, N. (1995). Using a group-oriented contingency to increase social interactions between children with autism and their peers: A preliminary analysis of corollary supportive behavior. *Behavior Modification, 19*, 10–32.

Kokina, A., & Kern, L. (2010). Social Story interventions for students with autism spectrum disorders: A meta-analysis. *Journal of Autism and Developmental Disorders, 40*, 812–826. doi:10.1007/s10803-009-0931-0

LeBlanc, L. A. (2010). Using video-based interventions with individuals with autism spectrum disorders: Introduction to the special issue. *Education and Treatment of Children, 33*(3), 333–337.

Lof, G. (2011). Science-based practice and the speech-language pathologist. *International Journal of Speech-Language Pathology, 13*(3), 189–196. doi:10.3109/17549507.2011.528801

Lovaas, O. I. (1987). Behavioral treatment and normal educational and intellectual functioning in young autistic children. *Journal of Consulting and Clinical Psychology, 55*(1), 3–9.

Lovaas, O. I., Koegel, R. L., Simmons, J. Q., & Stevens-Long, J. (1973). Some generalization and follow-up measures on autistic children in behavior therapy. *Journal of Applied Behavior Analysis, 6*, 131–166.

Lovaas, O. I., Schreibman, L., & Koegel, R. L. (1974). A behavior modification approach to the treatment of autistic children. *Journal of Autism and Childhood Schizophrenia, 4*, 111–129.

Makrygianni, M., & Reed, P. (2010). A meta-analytic review of the effectiveness of behavioral early intervention programs for children with Autistic Spectrum Disorders. *Research in Autism Spectrum Disorders, 4*(4), 577–593.

Mancil, G., Conroy, M., & Haydon, T. (2009). Effects of a modified milieu therapy intervention on the social communicative behaviors of young children with autism spectrum disorders. *Journal of Autism and Developmental Disorders, 39*(1), 149–163. doi:10.1007/s10803-008-0613-3

Matson, J. L., Sevin, J. A., Box, M. L., Francis, K. L., & Sevin, B. M. (1993). An evaluation of two methods for increasing self-initiated verbalizations in autistic children. *Journal of Applied Behavior Analysis, 26,* 389–398.

Mayo, N. E., Kaur, N., Barbic, S. P., Fiore, J., Barclay, R., Finch, L., . . . Lourenco, C. (2016). How have research questions and methods used in clinical trials published in clinical rehabilitation changed over the last 30 years? *Clinical Rehabilitation, 30*(9), 847–864. doi:10.1177/0269215516658939

McCleery, J. P., Elliott, N. A., Sampanis, D. S., & Stefanidou, C. A. (2013). Motor development and motor resonance difficulties in autism: Relevance to early intervention for language and communication skills. *Frontiers in Integrated Neuroscience, 24*(7), 30. doi:10.3389/fnint.2013.00030

McCurtin, A., & Roddam, H. (2012). Evidence-based practice: SLTs under siege or opportunity for growth? The use and nature of research evidence in the profession. *International. Journal of Language & Communication Disorders, 47*(1), 11–26.

McEachin, J. J., Smith, T., & Lovass, O. I. (1993). Long-term outcomes from children who received intensive early behavioral treatment. *American Journal on Mental Retardation, 97*(4), 359–372.

McEvoy, R. E., Loveland, K. A., & Landry, S. H. (1988). *The functions of immediate echolalia in autistic children: A developmental perspective. Journal of Autism and Developmental Disorders, 18*(4), 657–668.

McLean, J. E., & Snyder-McLean, L. (1988). Application of pragmatics to severely mentally retarded children and youth. In R. L. Schiefelbusch, & L. L. Lloyd (Ed.), *Language perspectives: Acquisition, retardation and intervention* (2nd ed., pp. 255–290). Austin, TX: Pro-Ed.

Meline, T. (2006). *Research in communication sciences and disorders: Methods, applications, evaluations.* Upper Saddle River, NJ: Pearson Education.

Mesibov, G. B., Shea, V., & Schopler, E. (with Adams, L., Burgess, S., Chapman, S. M., Merkler, E., Mosconi, M., Tanner, C., & Van Bourgondien, M. E.). (2005). *The TEACCH approach to autism spectrum disorders.* New York, NY: Springer.

Morrison, R. S., Sainato, D. M., Chaaban, B. D., & Endo, S. (2002). Increasing play skills of children with autism using activity schedules and correspondence training. *Journal of Early Intervention, 25,* 58–72.

National Autism Center (NAC). (2015). Findings and conclusions: National standards project, phase 2. Randolph, MA: Author.

Nevill, R. E., Lecavalier, L., & Stratis, E. A. (2016). Meta-analysis of parent-mediated interventions for children with autism spectrum disorder. *Autism, 22(2), 84–98.* doi:10.1177/1362361316677838

Odom, S. L., Boyd, B. A., Hall, L. J., & Hume, K. (2010). Evaluation of comprehensive treatment models for individuals with autism spectrum disorders. *Journal of Autism & Developmental Disorders, 40*(4), 425–436.

Odom, S. L., Hoyson, M., Jamieson, B., & Strain, P. S. (1985). Increasing handicapped preschoolers peer social interactions: Cross-setting and component analysis. *Journal of Applied Behavior Analysis, 18,* 3–16.

Ogletree, B.T. (2016a). Measuring communication and language skills in individuals with severe intellectual disabilities, In R. A. Sevcik & M. A. Romski (Eds.), *Communication interventions for individuals with severe disabilities: Exploring research challenges and opportunities* (pp. 281–299). Baltimore, MD: Paul H. Brookes Publishing Co.

Ogletree, B.T. (2016b). The communicative context of autism. In R. Simpson and B. Smith Myles (Eds.), *Educating children and youth with autism: Strategies for effective practice* (3rd ed., pp. 83–120). Austin, TX: Pro-Ed.

Ogletree, B.T., Bruce, S., Finch, A., & Fahey, R. (2011). Recommended communication-based interventions for individuals with severe intellectual disabilities. *Communication Disorders Quarterly, 32*(3), 164–175.

Ogletree, B. T., Davis, P., Hambrecht, G., and Wooten, E. (2012). The use of milieu training to promote picture exchange in a young child with autism: A pilot study. *Focus on Autism and Other Developmental Disabilities, 27*(2), 93–101.

Ogletree, B., Howell, A., & Carpenter, D. (2005). A procedure for socially valid goal setting. *Intervention in School and Clinic, 41*(2), 76–81.

Ogletree, B. T., & Oren, T. (1998). Structured yet functional: An alternative conceptualization of treatment for communication impairment in autism. *Focus on Autism and Other Developmental Disabilities, 13*(4), 228–233.

Ogletree, B., & Oren, T. (2001). Applications of ABA to communication training. *Focus on Autism and Other Developmental Disabilities, 16*(2), 102–109.

Ogletree, B. T., & Oren, T. (2006). *How to use augmentative and alternative communication with individuals with Autism Spectrum Disorders.* A series edited by Richard Simpson, Austin, TX: Pro-Ed.

Ogletree, B., Saddler, Y., & Bowers, L. (1995). Speech-language pathology. In B. Thyer & N. Kropf (Eds.), *Developmental disabilities: Handbook of interdisciplinary practice* (pp. 217–233). Cambridge, MA: Brookline Books.

Ogletree, B. T., Wetherby, A. M., & Westling, D. (1992). Profile of the prelinguistic intentional communicative abilities of children with profound mental retardation. *American Journal on Mental Retardation, 97*(2), 186–196.

Pajareya, K., & Nopmaneejumruslers, K. (2012). A one-year prospective follow-up study of a DIR/Floortime parent training intervention for pre-school children with Autistic Spectrum Disorders. *Journal of the Medical Association of Thailand, 95*(9), 1184–1193.

Parker-McGowan, Q., Chen, M., Reichle, J., Pandit, S., Johnson, L., & Kreibich, S. (2014). Describing treatment intensity in milieu teaching interventions for children with developmental disabilities: A review. *Language, Speech, and Hearing Services in Schools, 45*(4), 351–364.

Peters, A. (1977). Language learning strategies: Does the whole equal the sum of the parts? *Language, 53*, 560–573.

Peters-Scheffer, N., Didden, R., Korzilius, H., & Sturmey, P. (2011). A meta-analytic study on the effectiveness of comprehensive ABA-based early intervention programs for children with autism spectrum disorders. *Research in Autism Spectrum Disorders, 5*(1), 60–69.

Peterson, P., Carta, J., & Greenwood, C. (2005). Teaching milieu language skills to parents in multiple risk families. *Journal of Early Intervention, 27*, 94–109.

Prelock, P. A. (2006). *Autism spectrum disorders: Issues in assessment and intervention.* Austin, TX: Pro-Ed.

Prizant, B. M., & Duchan, J. F. (1981). The functions of immediate echolalia in autistic children. *Journal of Speech and Hearing Disorders, 46*, 241–249.

Prizant, B. M., & Rydell, P. J. (1984). An analysis of the functions of delayed echolalia in autistic children. *Journal of Speech and Hearing Research, 27*, 183–192.

Prizant, B. M., & Wetherby, A. M. (1998). Understanding the continuum of discrete-trial traditional behavioral to social-pragmatic, developmental approaches in communication enhancement for young children with ASD. *Seminars in Speech and Language, 19*, 329–353.

Prizant, B. M., Wetherby, A. M., Rubin, E., Laurent, A. C., & Rydell, P. J. (2006). *The SCERTS® Model.* Baltimore, MD: Paul H. Brookes Publishing Co.

Pyrczak, F. (2013). *Evaluating research in academic journals: A practical guide to realistic evaluation* (5th ed.). Glendale, CA: Pyrczak Publishing.

Quill, K. A. (1995). Visually cued instruction for children with autism and pervasive developmental disorders. *Focus on Autistic Behavior, 10*(3), 10–20.

Reichle, J., Ganz, J., Drager, K., & Parker-McGowan, Q. (2016). Augmentative and alternative communication applications for persons with ASD and complex communication needs. In *Prelinguistic and minimally verbal communicators on the autism spectrum.* (pp. 179–213). Springer Singapore. doi:10.1007/978-981-10-0713-2_9

Robey, R. R. (2004). Levels of evidence. *The ASHA Leader, 9*(5). doi:10.1044/leader. FTR2.09072004.5

Romski, M. A., & Sevcik, R. A. (1996). *Breaking the speech barrier: Language development through augmented means.* Baltimore, MD: Paul H. Brookes Publishing Co.

Rose, V., Trembath, D., Keen, D., & Paynter, J. (2016). The proportion of minimally verbal children with Autism Spectrum Disorder in a community-based early intervention programme. *Journal of Intellectual Disability Research, 60*(5), 464–477.

Rowland, C. M. (2009). Presymbolic communicators with autism spectrum disorders. In P. Mirenda & T. Iacono (Eds.), *Autism spectrum disorders and AAC* (pp. 51–81). Baltimore, MD: Paul H. Brookes Publishing Co.

Sansosti, F. J., Powell-Smith, K. A., & Kincaid, D. (2004). A research synthesis of Social Story interventions for children with autism spectrum disorders. *Focus on Autism and Other Developmental Disabilities, 19*(4), 194–204.

Searle, J.R. (1969). *Speech acts: An essay in the philosophy of language.* London: Cambridge University Press.

Sevcik, R. A., & Romski, M. (2016). *Communication interventions for individuals with severe disabilities: Exploring research challenges and opportunities.* Baltimore: Paul H. Brookes Publishing Co.

Shire, S., Kasari, C., Kaiser, A. P., & Fuller, E. (2016). Social communication interventions. In D. Keen, H. Meadan, N.C. Brady, & J. W. Halle (Eds.), *Prelinguistic and minimally verbal communicators on the autism spectrum* (pp. 149–178). Singapore: Springer.

Sigafoos, J., O'Reilly, M. F., Lancioni, G. E., Carnett, A., Bravo, A., Rojeski, L. & Halle, J. W. (2016). Functional assessment of problematic forms of prelinguistic behavior. In D. Keen, H. Meadan, N.C. Brady, & J.W. Halle (Eds.), *Prelinguistic and minimally verbal communicators on the autism spectrum* (pp. 212–145). Singapore: Springer.

Skinner, B. F. (1957). *Verbal behavior.* Englewood Cliffs, NJ: Prentice Hall.

Slocum, S. K., & Tiger, J. H. (2011). An assessment of the efficiency of and child preference for forward and backward chaining. *Journal of Applied Behavior Analysis, 44*(4), 793–805.

Smith, T. (2001). Discrete trial training in the treatment of autism. *Focus on Autism and Other Developmental Disabilities, 16,* 86–92.

Snell, M. E., Brady, N., McLean, L., Ogletree, B. T., Siegal, E., Sylvester, L., . . . Sevcik, R. (2010). Twenty years of communication intervention research with individuals who have severe intellectual and developmental disabilities. *American Journal on Intellectual and Developmental Disabilities, 115*(5), 364–380. doi:10.1352/1944-7558-115-5.364

Solomon, R., Van Egeren, L., Mahoney, G., Quon Huber, M., & Zimmerman, P. (2014). PLAY Project Home Consultation Intervention Program for Young Children with Autism Spectrum Disorders: A randomized controlled trial. *Journal of Developmental and Behavioral Pediatrics, 35*(8), 475–485.

Stahmer, A. C. (1995). Teaching symbolic play skills to children with autism using pivotal response treatment. *Journal of Autism and Developmental Disorders, 25,* 123–141.

Stevens-Long, J., & Rasmussen, M. (1974). The acquisition of simple and compound sentence structure in an autistic child. *Journal of Applied Behavior Analysis, 7*(3), 473–479.

Sulzer-Azaroff, B., Hoffman, A.O., Horton, C.B., Bondy, A., & Frost, L. (2009). The Picture Exchange Communication System (PECS): What do the data say? *Focus on Autism and Other Developmental Disabilities, 24*(2), 89–103.

Tager-Flusberg, H., & Kasari, C. (2013). Minimally-verbal school-aged children with autism spectrum disorder: The neglected end of the spectrum. *Autism Research, 6,* 468–478.

Virués-Ortega, J. (2010). Applied behavior analytic intervention for autism in early childhood: Meta-analysis, meta-regression and dose–response meta-analysis of multiple outcomes. *Clinical Psychology Review, 30,* 387–399.

Warren, S. F., Brady, N., Finestack, L. H., Bredin-Oja, S. L., Fairchild, M., Sokol, S., & Yoder, P. J. (2006). Early effects of responsivity education/prelinguistic milieu teaching for children with developmental delays and their parents. *Journal of Speech-Language-Hearing Research, 49,* 526–547.

Warren, Z., McPheeters, M. L., Sathe, N., Foss-Feig, J. H., Glasser, A., & Veenstra-VanderWeele, J. (2011). A systematic review of early intensive intervention for autism spectrum disorders. *Pediatrics, 127*(5). doi:10.1542/peds.2011–0426.

Weismer, E., & Kover, S. T. (2015). Preschool language variation, growth, and predictors in children on the autism spectrum. *Journal of Child Psychology and Psychiatry, 56*(12), 1327–1337. doi:10.1111/jcpp.12406

Wetherby, A. M., Guthrie, W., Woods, J., Schatschneider, C., Holland, R. D., Morgan, L., & Lord, C. (2014). Parent-implemented social intervention for toddlers with autism: An RCT. *Pediatrics,* originally published online November 3, 2014. doi:10.1542/peds.2014–0757

Wetherby, A. M., & Prizant, B. M. (Eds.). (2000). *Autism spectrum disorders: A developmental, transactional perspective.* Baltimore, MD: Paul H. Brookes Publishing Co.

Wetherby, A. M., Prizant, B. M., & Hutchinson, T. (1998). Communicative, social-affective, and symbolic profiles of young children with autism and pervasive developmental disorder. *American Journal of Speech-Language Pathology, 7,* 79–91.

Wieder, S., & Greenspan, S. I. (2003). Climbing the symbolic ladder in the DIR model through floor time/interactive play. *Autism, 7*(4), 425–435.

Wong, C., Odom, S. L., Hume, K., Cox, A. W., Fettig, A., Kucharczyk, S., . . . Schultz, T. R. (2013). *Evidence-based practices for children, youth, and young adults with Autism Spectrum Disorder.* Chapel Hill, NC: The University of North Carolina, Frank Porter Graham Child Development Institute, Autism Evidence-Based Practice Review Group.

Yoder, P., & Stone, W. L. (2006). A randomized comparison of the effect of two prelinguistic communication interventions on the acquisition of spoken communication in preschoolers with ASD. *Journal of Speech, Language, and Hearing Research, 49,* 698–711.

Yoder, P. J., & Warren, S. F. (2002). Effects of prelinguistic milieu teaching and parent responsivity education on dyads involving children with intellectual disabilities. *Journal of Speech, Language, Hearing Research, 45,* 1158–1174.

10

Evidence-Based Practices for Adolescents and Adults With Autism Spectrum Disorder and Complex Communication Needs

Erik W. Carter and Elizabeth E. Biggs

For many people, memories of their youth are often marked more by the relationships they developed than by the curricula they covered. Throughout middle and high school, interactions with friends, classmates, and other peers dominate the school day. Working together on a group project, conversing over lunch in the cafeteria, hanging out between classes, enjoying an extracurricular activity, attending a pep rally or school play, and traveling to and from school—these myriad points of social connection provide opportunities for adolescents to meet one another and enjoy time together. After graduation, relationships with peers reach into new community contexts. Gatherings with neighbors, social events with co-workers, fellowship with congregation members, involvement in affinity groups, connecting through social media, volunteering alongside others, and participation in other local activities—these experiences contribute to a network of relationships that can last throughout adulthood.

Such interactions and relationships are noteworthy not only for their prominence, but also for their impact. Scores of studies highlight the strong association between social relationships and quality of life indicators such as human flourishing (e.g., Allen & Bowles, 2012; Chu, Saucier, & Hafner, 2010; Demir, 2015; Rubin, Bukowski, & Laursen, 2009; Siedlecki, Salthouse, Oishi, & Jeswani, 2014). Such relationships can bring both enjoyment and deep satisfaction, provide much-needed social support and practical resources, expand access to valuable social capital, foster acquisition of new skills, contribute to a sense of belonging, and enhance one's quality of life. However, the converse also is true. Social scientists have confirmed what theologians have long affirmed—it is not good to be alone (e.g., Hawkley & Cacioppo, 2010; Holt-Lunstad, Smith, & Layton, 2010). Social isolation contributes to loneliness, depression, poor health outcomes, and a host of other potentially deleterious effects.

For adolescents and adults with autism spectrum disorder (ASD), these relationships are also of immense importance (Bogenschutz et al., 2015). Like anyone else, satisfying and supportive relationships contribute to the thriving of individuals with ASD who have complex communication needs (Carter, Bottema-Beutel, & Brock, 2014; Kersh, Corona, & Siperstein, 2013). The primary difference is that the interactions and relationships so essential to one's flourishing often require planned support and intervention. The purpose of this chapter is to provide guidance on enhancing the social and communication outcomes of adolescents and adults with ASD who experience complex communication needs (CCN). The chapter begins by highlighting the changing social context during secondary school and into adulthood. Then, reviews of descriptive studies provide a portrait of prevailing social and communication outcomes for adolescents and adults with ASD. Recognizing the importance of well-crafted interventions, research-based instructional strategies for fostering social connections are reviewed. Then, three promising intervention approaches are described—peer support arrangements, peer networks, and peer partner programs—that can be applied across contexts to promote social and communication outcomes for individuals with significant disabilities. The chapter concludes with recommendations for practice and research aimed at enhancing the social lives of individuals with CCN.

It is important to acknowledge that research involving adolescents and adults with ASD who have CCN is much more limited than research involving younger children (see reviews by Carter, Sisco, Chung, & Stanton-Chapman, 2010; Wong et al., 2014). The field's focus on early intervention and elementary education has not extended across the life span. Therefore, this chapter draws upon related literature involving youth and young adults with severe intellectual disability, as well as studies involving individuals across the entire autism spectrum. Also, there is an accent on enhancing social and communication outcomes within the context of peer relationships rather than within interactions with professionals. This emphasis is adopted because similar-age peers constitute people's primary interaction partners within school, work, and community settings. Moreover, providing opportunities for peers to meet, get to know, and develop relationships with this segment of their community holds significant potential to raise expectations, improve attitudes, and expand opportunities in the community (Carter, Biggs, & Blustein, 2016).

DYNAMIC CONTEXT OF ADOLESCENCE AND ADULTHOOD

As children enter adolescence and transition to adulthood, the contexts for social interaction shift substantially. These changes introduce new considerations and complexities that must be considered when designing interventions and support systems for students with ASD who have CCN (Carter, Common, et al., 2014).

Changing Locations

As students enter secondary school, the stability of settings and classmates that typically marks the elementary experience becomes much more fluid. For example, most high school students attend up to eight different classes each semester, encountering hundreds of different classmates and divergent teacher expectations across curricular areas (e.g., academics, related arts, electives, vocational). The introduction of extracurricular activities and transition programming brings adolescents into new school and community settings, each with their own social demands. After graduation, workplaces, college campuses, and community activities quickly become the primary locations in which young adults spend time in the company of others. The burgeoning use of new technologies (e.g., social networking, online communities) is also introducing ever-new avenues through which people meet one another, discover shared interests, exchange information, and make social plans. Each of these very diverse contexts introduces its own social norms and communication requirements that differ substantially from school, highlighting the importance of teaching contextually relevant skills in ways that support generalized use.

Changing Relationships

Throughout adolescence and into adulthood, the companionship of peers typically takes on increasing prominence and importance. For most adolescents, time spent in the company of peers quickly overshadows interactions with adults. Whereas the interactions of younger children tend to be more dyadic and supervised, adolescents must learn to navigate friendships, cliques, crowds, and intimate relationships that shift over time and often take place beyond the surveillance of adults (Rubin et al., 2009). New relationships are born more from shared interests and commonalities than mere proximity. After graduation, primary peers are no longer classmates but rather co-workers, neighbors, congregation members, and other community members (e.g., healthcare providers). The preeminence of peer relationships requires that professionals provide instruction and support that enables youth and adults with CCN to develop and maintain satisfying relationships with similar-age peers.

Changing Professional Involvement

The support needs of individuals with ASD and complex communication challenges are often substantial. Schools often rely extensively on individually assigned staff to support students with severe disabilities in classrooms, cafeterias, clubs, and other school activities. For example, the majority of states report employing more paraprofessionals than special educators (U.S. Department of Education, 2014), and job coaches are the dominant way of supporting integrated employment. Moreover, paraprofessionals regularly provide one-to-one instruction and spend substantial time, typically in close proximity, to the students they are supporting (Carter, O'Rourke, Sisco, & Pelsue, 2009; Giangreco & Broer, 2005). In contrast, for most individuals without disabilities, adolescence and early adulthood is a period marked by growing autonomy and a desire for independence. The near-constant presence of adults—in school or the workplace—can inadvertently limit opportunities for social interaction by making peers reluctant to initiate conversations or leading them to channel questions and comments through the adult rather than directly to the individual with ASD (Carter, Sisco, Brown, Brickham, & Al-Khabbaz, 2008). Steps should be taken to transition paraprofessionals, job coaches, and other staff from direct support roles to more facilitative roles that create social connections among individuals with ASD and their peers.

This shifting social landscape in adolescence and adulthood has several implications for intervention and support. First, interventions found effective for younger children with ASD cannot automatically be presumed to work for older individuals. For example, play-based interventions no longer fit the context of adolescence and early adulthood. The myriad differences in contexts and expectations may require refinement of these approaches, as well as exploration of new strategies. Second, the power of peers is important to harness relative to the design and delivery of interventions among adult adolescents and adults. Their capacity to provide individualized support in ways that enhance social outcomes is considerable. However, these peers need to be invited, prepared, supported, and encouraged for these new roles. Third, simple interventions are unlikely to be sufficient for promoting substantial improvements in the social lives of youth and adults with CCN. Multi-component interventions that attend to student, peer, professional, and environmental factors may hold the most promise for improving functional and socially valid outcomes (Carter, Bottema-Beutel, & Brock, 2014). Fourth, intentionality is imperative. Individuals with CCN are unlikely to develop the social skills and relationships so important to their thriving without sustained and strategic support. This last point that is explored next.

THE SOCIAL EXPERIENCES OF ADOLESCENTS AND ADULTS WITH ASD

Understanding the communication needs and social experiences of individuals with ASD has been the focus of considerable research. This section reviews recent descriptive studies addressing the social-related skills, interactions, and relationships of youth and adults with CCN. These findings highlight the necessity of individualized intervention to shift the current social landscape in meaningful ways.

Social and Communication Skills

Social and communication challenges are defining features of the ASD diagnosis (American Psychiatric Association, 2013). As students age, the deficits that lead to initial diagnosis generally persist. In their analyses of parent- and teacher-completed social skills assessments, Lyons, Huber, Carter, Chen, and Asmus (2016) found that a substantial proportion of high school students with autism and significant intellectual disability received below-average ratings across all social skill subdomains (e.g., communication, cooperation, assertion, empathy, engagement). Among high school students with disabilities who participate in the alternate assessment, as many as 10% still had no formal functional means of symbolic communication (Kleinert et al., 2015). Such portraits underscore the need for continued—rather than curtailed—instruction on critical social and communication skills during secondary school and beyond.

Social Interactions

The social-related challenges of students with ASD and other significant communication disabilities can combine with other barriers to limit their social interactions with peers. Chung, Carter, and Sisco (2012b) completed class-length observations of four middle-school students with ASD who used aided or unaided augmentative and alternative communication (AAC) to supplement existing communication. Within their general education classes, these students participated in any type of social interaction during just half (50.1%) of observation intervals. However, those interactions took place almost entirely with adults (e.g., paraprofessionals, special educators, general educators). When interactions involving classmates without disabilities did take place, students with ASD rarely initiated and were often passive in their roles. Carter and colleagues (2008) conducted 152 class-length observations of 23 middle- and high-school students with developmental disabilities enrolled in general education courses, almost half (*n* = 11) of whom had autism. Social interactions within these inclusive classrooms were relatively infrequent, involved a very narrow range of classmates, and focused on both academic and social topics. Moreover, no interactions at all took place among students with disabilities and their classmates during one quarter of all class periods.

Peer Relationships

The relationship networks of adolescents with ASD can vary widely (e.g., Kuo, Orsmond, Cohn, & Coster, 2013; Petrina, Carter, & Stephenson, 2014). Although some students have strong social connections, many others remain quite isolated. According to parents surveyed as part of the National Longitudinal Transition Study-2, 44% of youth with ASD (ages 13–17) never saw friends outside of school; 84% never or rarely received phone calls from friends; and 51% had not been invited to other youth's social activities during the past year (Wagner, Cadwallader, & Marder, 2003). In their study of quality of life among adolescents (ages 13–21) with autism and other developmental disabilities, Biggs and Carter (2016) found parent ratings to be lowest on items related to social support from friends and peer relationships. National Core Indicator (2011–2012) data indicate this isolation can extend into adulthood; more than two fifths (41%) of adults with autism receiving public services and supports were reported to have no friends or caring relationships with people other than paid staff and family members.

EFFECTIVE APPROACHES FOR ENHANCING SOCIAL COMMUNICATION OUTCOMES

Because of challenges using functional speech, adolescents and adults with ASD who have CCN benefit from using a multimodal approach to communication. A multimodal approach emphasizes the importance of different verbal and nonverbal means of communication—which is typical of how most people communicate. Everyone sends messages to others in a wide variety of forms or "modes," including speech, gestures, pictures, and written words. However, when functional verbal speech is limited, it is even more important to encourage and expand all communication modes that allow an individual to connect with others, share their ideas and interests, and express their wants and needs. AAC refers to all forms of communication used to either 1) replace speech as a means of communication or 2) augment (i.e., supplement) existing, but limited, speech. AAC includes a wide variety of different communication modes but is divided into two main categories—unaided and aided.

Unaided AAC includes communication modes other than speech that rely only on an individual's body and do not require other external equipment, materials, or devices. The most commonly used unaided AAC modes include vocalizations, gestures, facial expressions, and manual signing. Some of the earliest research investigating approaches to support the communication of individuals with ASD and CCN identified ways to teach participants to use manual signs (e.g., Remington & Clarke, 1983). Wendt (2009) conducted a systematic review of research related to the use of interventions involving manual signing for individuals with ASD and identified several different intervention strategies effective in teaching the acquisition and use of manual signs. Manual signs and other forms of unaided AAC can be appropriate and useful within a multimodal communication system for individuals with ASD. Because unaided AAC modes do not rely on an external device or tool that can be lost, left behind, or broken, they offer the advantages of portability and dependability. However, unaided AAC modes place considerable demands on communication partners to understand a message. Unfortunately, many unfamiliar and untrained communication partners may not be able to understand when an individual with ASD uses signs or idiosyncratic gestures (Mirenda, 2015).

Considerable effort also has been under way to understand the utility and effectiveness of aided AAC for individuals with ASD and CCN. Aided AAC includes various types of external tools or aids such as communication books, communication boards, and speech-generating devices (SGDs). Each of these different tools provides access to symbols that can be used to communicate. These symbols can come in a variety of forms including visual-graphic symbols (e.g., photographs, line-drawn pictures) and orthographic symbols (i.e., letters and words). The symbols are arranged on a communication aid, such as a board, book, or electronic device. Each symbol can be used to represent a single word, phrase, or a longer message. There is significant and growing evidence for the effective use of different types of aided AAC by individuals with ASD (e.g., Ganz et al., 2012; Wendt, 2009). However, there is much still to be learned about the use of aided AAC with this population, including the impact of different elements and characteristics of the communication aid in facilitating effective and utilitarian use. When encouraging the use of aided AAC, there are many different decisions that need to be made about the characteristics of the communication aid: What type of device? What type of symbols? How should symbols be organized? What vocabulary or communicative messages will be available? Each of these decisions is important and is best made using a team approach that takes into consideration the strengths and needs of the individual (Mirenda, 2015).

Educators, service providers, family members, and others who support the communication of adolescents and adults with ASD and CCN are faced with the task of identifying different maximally effective and functional communication modes—including speech, unaided AAC, and aided AAC. However, identifying promising communication modes, including the use of communication aids, is only the beginning of providing meaningful communication support. Various forms of AAC offer important means to supplement or replace the use of typical verbal speech to communicate. Yet, simply providing access to a communication aid is typically not sufficient to support communication and social interaction. For youth and adults with ASD and CCN, learning to communicate—including both with speech and with AAC—requires intentional support and instruction. A variety of instructional strategies have been identified as effective for improving the communication skills and social experiences of individuals with ASD who have CCN (e.g., Lang et al., 2014). This section highlights four research-based strategies: creating communication opportunities, modeling aided language, providing systematic communication support, and training communication partners. Table 10.1 shows examples of these research-based strategies, within peer support, peer network, and peer partner arrangements. These arrangements are discussed later in this chapter.

Table 10.1. Examples of research-based strategies within each intervention approach

Strategy	Intervention approach		
	Peer support arrangement	Peer network intervention	Peer partner program
Creating communication opportunities	Individualized plan outlines well-supported, shared experiences for an individual with ASD and peers within an academic or employment setting.	Social group around an individual with a disability promotes interaction during formal and informal meetings over time.	Programs provide group-based or one-to-one opportunities for shared activities and experiences among individuals with and without disabilities.
Providing systematic communication support	Peers can learn strategies to provide ongoing systematic communication support within the natural setting.	Peers and/or an adult facilitator (e.g., teacher, coach, paraprofessional, counselor) can embed the use of systematic communication support during the peer network meetings.	Peers can learn strategies to teach and encourage communication skills within the context of their interactions.
Modeling aided language	Peers can incorporate the use of aided AAC into their task-related and social interactions within the peer support arrangement.	Peer network members can use an aided AAC device when they interact with the individual with ASD during a shared, social activity.	Peers can model the use of aided AAC during their interactions.
Training communication partners	Peers receive information (e.g., background, interaction strategies, supports in the written plan) during an initial orientation meeting. Peers receiving ongoing support from a paraprofessional or teacher.	Peers learn about the goals for a network and specific interaction strategies during an initial meeting. Peers receive ongoing support from a facilitator.	Peers receive foundational background information and sometimes specific information about supporting interaction opportunities with individuals with disabilities.

CREATING COMMUNICATION OPPORTUNITIES

Adolescents and adults with ASD who have CCN are more likely to communicate with others when given both opportunity and support to do so. Creating communication opportunities involves engineering the environment and the individual's supports to promote interaction while reducing potential barriers. Too many adolescents and adults with ASD have few opportunities throughout the day for meaningful, positive interaction with others. For example, they may have little access to inclusive classes and extracurricular activities involving peers without disabilities (Kleinert et al., 2015; Morningstar, Kurth, & Johnson, 2017). Ensuring individuals with ASD are engaged in shared activities with others throughout their school and community settings is an important part of creating communication opportunities (Carter, Swedeen, & Kurkowski, 2008). Shared activities may include going to an athletic event, participating in a collaborative activity, playing a game, attending a club meeting, completing a service project, or joining a community group. When individuals with complex communication needs have not mastered the use of symbols to communicate, they may be limited to interacting primarily about things that are physically present (i.e., objects, materials, and people that are "here and now"; Rowland, 2009, p. 52). Therefore, shared activities and experiences are more likely to provide appropriate and meaningful communication opportunities when they involve motivating materials and other things that can be held and used during the interactions.

Another important aspect to creating communication opportunities involves embedding explicit strategies that encourage an individual to communicate into an individual's natural routines and activities. Educators, services providers, and others can structure an environment to promote interaction by offering choices, moving desired materials out of reach, asking questions, and interrupting preferred activities. For example, teachers, paraprofessionals, and parents have learned to create explicit opportunities for adolescents to communicate by using expectant delay when they noticed the individual's attention was directed to something he needed or wanted (Hamilton & Snell, 1993; Rodi & Hughes, 2000).

PROVIDING SYSTEMATIC COMMUNICATION SUPPORT

Another research-based strategy involves providing systematic prompting and support within ongoing communication opportunities. Historically, the earliest efforts to teach language to individuals with ASD were marked by highly structured interventions involving massed discrete trials in isolated settings (e.g., Lovaas, 1977). Although these approaches can improve verbal behavior and vocabulary within highly controlled intervention contexts, improvements in spontaneous communication and generalization can be limited. An effective alternative is to incorporate systematic promoting and support for communication within regular routines, sometimes called milieu teaching, incidental teaching, or naturalistic teaching (Collins, 2012). The day-to-day activities in which adolescents and young adults with ASD participate offer numerous opportunities to embed systematic support for communication and interaction. For example, paraprofessionals and peers can provide communication support during the normal ongoing activities and instruction in a classroom. Or, job coaches or co-workers can embed this type of support during vocational training and while on the job. Embedding systematic communication support inside of these types of natural environments may help emphasize and build functional communication, increase spontaneous communication, and help individuals generalize skills and interactions to diverse contexts and partners.

The typical steps to providing systematic communication support are listed next:

1. Identify the communication goal(s) and opportunities to communicate.

2. Use response prompting strategies to ensure individuals with ASD respond appropriately given an opportunity to communicate.

3. Reinforce communicative attempts.

4. Use fading prompts to build independence and spontaneity in communicating.

Response prompting strategies can include using time delay, expectant looking, questions, commands (e.g., "tell me what you want"), models, and physical prompting. These steps have been used successfully to teach specific functional communication skills to individuals with ASD across different communication goals and modes of communication. However, these procedures may be more applicable for teaching aided AAC use than speech because speech is less easily prompted, unless an individual has already established strong imitative speech (Lang et al., 2014). For example, Reichle and colleagues (2005) used systematic communication support to teach an adult with autism and intellectual disability to use a graphic symbol to request help during a vocational assembly task. Sigafoos and colleagues (2004) taught two young adults with ASD to use a voice-output SGD as a supplementary approach to requesting something by reaching. Hamilton and Snell (1993) embedded systematic communication support across home and school environments to teach the use of a communication book to an adolescent with ASD and intellectual disability.

MODELING AIDED LANGUAGE

The research-based strategy of modeling aided language is rooted in communication development theory. There is strong evidence the language input children receive (i.e., the quantity and quality of words spoken to children during their interactions) plays a central role in shaping their language development (e.g., Hart & Risley, 1995). Communication partners such as parents and educators can promote the acquisition of language by changing the amount and type of input they provide. Although much of the literature in this area specifically addresses young children learning to talk, there are important connections and implications for the language learning of adolescents and adults with ASD who are beginning communicators.

It is important to note that language input is a more complicated idea for adolescents learning to use aided AAC than for young children who are typically developing and are learning spoken language. Certainly adolescents and adults with ASD are different in many ways from young children, even though individuals in each group may be beginning communicators. One of these differences is related to the nature of communication input individuals in each group receive. Young children learning to speak will typically hear rich models of speech (Hart & Risley, 1995). However, individuals with ASD learning to use aided AAC are expected to use communication aids to interact, even though they may rarely see others communicate in this same way (Sennott, Light, & McNaughton, 2016). Adolescents and adults with ASD learning to use communication aids should be given many opportunities to watch and hear language models in the modes they are expected to produce expressively. This idea—to provide language models using both speech and aided AAC—has been referred to in a variety of ways, including augmented input (Romski & Sevcik, 1996) and aided language stimulation (Goossens, 1989). The central theory behind these approaches is similar: when communication partners use aided AAC as one of their own modes of communication within their natural, ongoing interactions, these aided language models can 1) help individuals with CCN build important connections between spoken words, graphic symbols, and their referents and 2) demonstrate that aided AAC is an encouraged mode of communication (Romski & Sevcik, 1996).

Modeling aided language involves communication partners integrating the use of aided AAC into their own ongoing, natural interactions with a beginning communicator. For example, a parent of an adolescent with ASD might say, "Tommy, let's go shopping to get some milk." To model aided language, the parent might point to graphic symbols *GO* and *MILK* on a communication board as they say each word within the context of the interaction. Or, a job coach for a young adult with ASD might say, "It's time for lunch" while pressing the symbols *TIME* and *LUNCH* on an SGD. In both examples, a communication partner incorporates his or her own use of aided AAC when interacting with the individual.

The body of literature on interventions involving modeling of aided language shows considerable promise for the effectiveness of this strategy in improving the communication skills of individuals with CCN (for reviews, see Biggs, Carter, & Gilson, in press; Sennott et al., 2016). However, the majority of this literature has focused on young children. Only a few studies have examined its effectiveness for adolescents and adults with ASD who have CCN. For example, in a longitudinal descriptive study, Romski and Sevcik (1996) evaluated the impact of the System for Augmenting Language (SAL) to improve the communication of 13 school-age children with developmental disabilities, including two adolescents with ASD. SAL involved 1) the use of an SGD, 2) individualized target vocabulary with visual-graphic symbols to represent them, 3) natural everyday environments that encourage communication, 4) modeling of aided language on the SGD by communication partners, and 5) ongoing monitoring and assessment. The communication performance of the two adolescents with ASD were comparable to the other 11 participants, including increases in the acquisition and use of graphic symbols to communicate with adults and peers over the 2-year period of data collection. In a separate longitudinal case study, Cafiero (2001) examined the impact of a teacher, speech-language pathologist, and paraprofessional providing aided language modeling for a 13-year-old with autism. When aided language was modeled using picture symbols on communication boards, the student increased the number of appropriately used symbols during communicative initiations.

TRAINING COMMUNICATION PARTNERS

Adolescents and adults with ASD who have CCN require communication partners who provide frequent communication opportunities, understand and interpret their communication behaviors, respond appropriately, and encourage interaction. Because communication is a two-way process, positive interactions depend not only on improving the communication skills of the individual with ASD but also the interaction skills of various communication partners (Carter, Bottema-Beutel, & Brock, 2014). However, communication partners often provide few communication opportunities and/or dominate interactions (Kent-Walsh & McNaughton, 2005). Peers, co-workers, community members, educators, health care providers, and family members may need training and support in positive interaction strategies to facilitate communication and serve as a bridge, rather than a barrier, to meaningful interaction with others. Several strategies can be taught to different people to encourage them to be responsive and effective communication partners, including maintaining appropriate proximity, using expectant delay (i.e., establish eye contact and wait and look with expectation for the individual to respond or initiate interaction), and responding to any and all communicative attempts (Downing & Chen, 2015).

PROMISING INTERVENTIONS

A number of recent literature reviews have focused on synthesizing interventions aimed at improving the social and communication outcomes of youth and young adults with ASD and/or with severe disabilities (Carter et al., 2010; Chung, Carter, & Sisco, 2012a; Hughes et al., 2013). Although there are many ways of organizing these research-based interventions, there are three primary categories: peer support arrangements, peer networks, and peer partner programs. Each offers a promising—yet distinctive—approach for addressing the social and communication needs of adolescents and adults with CCN.

PEER SUPPORT ARRANGEMENTS

Peer support arrangements involve equipping and supporting one or more peers to provide ongoing social, academic, and/or behavioral support to an individual with significant disabilities (Carter & Kennedy, 2006). Similar-age peers are recruited from within the same setting, participate in an initial training regarding their roles, provide individualized supports detailed in a written and rehearsed plan, and receive ongoing guidance and feedback from professionals (e.g., special educators, paraprofessionals, job coaches) as they work alongside their classmate or co-worker. These interventions are designed to increase communication opportunities and decrease reliance on adult-delivered supports by creating well-supported, shared activities. Socially, peers model age-appropriate communication and social skills, encourage contributions to ongoing discussions (both task- and social-related) in the setting, prompt use of a communication device, promote proximity and connections to peers, and diminish attitudinal barriers that may exist within the setting (Bandura, 1977; Carter, Biggs, & Blustein, 2016). Working closely with peers may increase the amount of individualized supports and promote increased corrective feedback and response opportunities students receive. In addition, involving peer confederates in this manner encourages use of activities and materials that align with what others in the setting are using (Carter & Kennedy, 2006). This structured partnership among peers typically lasts over time, throughout the semester or school year.

Within middle and high schools, peer support arrangements are commonly implemented within inclusive general education classes (e.g., Biggs, Carter, & Gustafson, 2017; Carter, Asmus, et al., 2016; Carter, Moss, Hoffman, Chung, & Sisco, 2011; Chung & Carter, 2013). In contrast to one-to-one paraprofessional support models, students with ASD who are part of peer-support arrangements are in a position to receive most (though certainly not all) of their assistance from their classmates. When writing an individualized peer support plan the educational team collaboratively outlines the various ways in which peers might provide different types of support (e.g., social, academic, other) across different class activities (e.g., arrival, large-group instruction, small-group activities, individual seatwork, other, departure). They then invite one to three peers without disabilities who could deliver these supports and who might benefit themselves from working alongside a classmate with severe disabilities. An initial orientation session—often led by the special educator or paraprofessional—addresses the specific information peers will need to be effective in their roles, including background about the classmate with whom they will work, strategies for enhancing communication outcomes, supports outlined in the written plan, and guidance on when and how to seek assistance (Carter, Cushing, & Kennedy, 2009). As students begin working together, paraprofessionals shift from a direct to indirect support role, strategically facilitating social and academic participation as students work together through much or all of the class period (Biggs et al., in press). Figure 10.1 shows a peer support plan for a student with CCN.

Within inclusive higher education programs, peer support arrangements can also be used to support enrollment in academic courses and other on-campus learning opportunities. More than 250 higher education programs now focus on supporting the inclusion of young adults with intellectual and developmental

Communication goals and targeted communicative functions

The student will
- Answer modified questions about class content given three symbols on a speech-generating device (SGD)
- Request help or assistance when needed to complete work
- Initiate greetings and use appropriate social amenities (e.g., Hello, Good-bye, How are you?)

How can peers be used as communication partners for these goals?

Peers can
- Review class content with their classmate and offer appropriate choices to answer academic questions using the SGD
- Encourage their classmate to request help and be available to respond to these requests
- Respond to their classmate's social initiations and encourage the student to greet and interact with others

When arriving or at the beginning of class
All students are entering the classroom and greeting others students, getting needed materials

Communication goal	The student could	Peers could	Teacher/ paraprofessional could	SGD vocabulary needed
Initiate greetings and use social amenities	• Greet peers and interact quietly • Gather needed materials • Listen and respond to the teacher during attendance	• Respond to greetings from their classmate • Encourage their classmate to initiate interactions with others • Be available to help gather materials, if asked	• Prompt and reinforce the student's initiations • Make sure the student has needed materials; if not, prompt him or her to ask for them	• Social greetings and responses • Help • Classroom materials

Figure 10.1.   Peer support plan for a student with complex communication needs.

During lectures and whole-group instruction
All students are listening to the teacher, taking notes, asking and answering teacher questions

Communication goal	The student could	Peers could	Teacher/ paraprofessional could	SGD vocabulary needed
Answer questions about class content Request help	• Listen to the teacher • Copy key words from peers' notes • Answer questions related to class content	• Redirect and encourage the student with positive feedback • Help with copying notes, if asked • Highlight choices of symbols on SGD when the student is asked a question	• Ask modified questions that can be answered with the SGD • Prompt student to ask for help with notes • Provide information and encouragement to peers for supporting the student	• Help • Content-related vocabulary

During small-group work
All students are working collaboratively to complete worksheets or other activities

Communication goal	The student could	Peers could	Teacher/ paraprofessional could	SGD vocabulary needed
Answer questions about class content Request help	• Participate in group activity • Ask peers for help	• Be sure the student can do part of the activity • Encourage with positive feedback • Provide communication opportunities by asking questions • Model vocabulary on SGD	• Ask modified questions that can be answered with the SGD • Prompt student to ask for help with activity • Give peers ideas for communication opportunities • Provide peers encouragement	• Help • Content-related vocabulary

Figure 10.1. *(continued)*

disabilities (see www.thinkcollege.net). The use of peer-mediated support models—both within and beyond the classroom—is considered a quality indicator of these innovative postsecondary programs (National Coordinating Center Accreditation Workgroup, 2016). Many higher education institutions rely on models that incorporate key elements of peer support arrangements (e.g., Griffin, Wendel, Day, & McMillan, 2016; Hafner, Moffatt, & Kisa, 2011). For example, peers might assist the student in working on his or her individualized learning plan, share ideas within a small-group project or with the entire class, or provide academic tutoring outside of class time. Given the capacity of college students to provide more advanced supports, the nature of the initial orientation training and the ongoing support provided to these peers is likely to differ from what is required in secondary schools.

Within the workplace, peer support arrangements are often delivered within the context of natural co-worker supports. A prominent approach for supporting integrated employment among adults with severe disabilities is through the provision of an external job coach. However, concerns have been raised about the ways in which this model might inadvertently limit social interactions and interdependent responsibilities on the job (Storey, 2003). In response to these concerns, one or more co-workers can be taught to assist the individual with a disability to understand the social and other norms within the setting, complete work-related tasks, and participate fully in the social milieu of the organization. For example, co-workers might support the individual with autism in navigating some of the complexities of social interactions specific to a workplace, such as learning new vocabulary specific to the employment sector; participating in fast-paced social and work-related interactions; using a variety of communication modes, including distance technologies (e.g., e-mail, texting) and social media; understanding the mix of formal and informal communication that takes place among co-workers; and conversing with a range of familiar (e.g., supervisors, co-workers) and unfamiliar (e.g., customers) communication partners (McNaughton & Chapple, 2013).

PEER NETWORK INTERVENTIONS

Peer network interventions involve establishing a cohesive social group that meets formally and informally over time to enhance the social skills and peer relationships of an individual with a significant disability (Carter et al., 2013; Haring & Breen, 1992). An educator, support provider, or other adult typically organizes and facilitates the formal meetings of the group but remains largely behind the scenes in encouraging and supporting participants to connect with one another throughout the week. After explaining the network with the individual with a severe disability and inviting his or her input on who should participate, the adult facilitator approaches potential peers. Three to six individuals—usually similar-age peers who have interests or experiences in common with the focus person—are invited to an initial orientation meeting. This orientation covers multiple topics, including 1) the primary goals of the network, 2) background and other information about the focus student, 3) the importance of confidentiality and respectful language, 4) expectations specific to the peer network and communication strategies relevant to the focus person, and 5) guidance on when to seek assistance from the facilitator. During weekly or biweekly network meetings, the adolescents or adults take part in a mutually enjoyable activity (e.g., interactive game, service project, meal), plan other times to connect with one another throughout the week (e.g., between classes, during breaks or lunch, after school or work), and identify ways to involve the focus person more fully in other aspects of school and community life. Over time, the involvement of the adult facilitator fades and peers take the lead in organizing network meetings and activities. Such networks expand the opportunities individuals with disabilities have to practice and receive natural feedback on social-communication skills within shared activities. These individualized approaches differ from peer support arrangements in their size, setting (i.e., beyond the classroom or workplace), and primary emphasis on social-related outcomes.

Peer network interventions have been evaluated extensively among high school students with ASD and/or intellectual disability, including those with CCN (e.g., Asmus et al., 2016; Gardner et al., 2014; Koegel et al., 2012). Peer network members are typically selected from among schoolmates who have overlapping schedules, shared interests, or other experiences in common. Within secondary schools, peer networks are typically organized by a special educator; however, they can be facilitated by any member of the school staff (e.g., coach, club leader, paraprofessional, school counselor). For example, Asmus and colleagues (2017) established peer networks for 47 high school students with severe disabilities (more than half of whom also had autism). These peer networks averaged five students and met an average of seven times throughout a single school semester. Adolescents with severe disabilities experienced significant increases in the number of extended social contacts they had and new friendships they developed. Similarly, Hochman, Carter, Bottema-Beutel, Harvey, and Gustafson (2015) established peer networks that met formally during school lunch periods for four students with ASD and identified peers. All the students with ASD experienced substantial increases in peer interactions and social engagement over the course of the semester.

Likewise, peer networks comprise an important avenue for fostering friendships and campus involvement within inclusive higher education programs. The breadth of activities that make up campus life typically leads college-level peer networks to adopt a somewhat broader focus or scope. For example, social networks can focus on shared meals, working out together, involvement in student organizations, participation in volunteer projects, or involvement in recreational activities (e.g., Culnane, Eisenman, & Murphy, 2016; Griffin, Mello, Glover, Carter, & Hodapp, 2016). Such social contexts are usually engaging and involve hands-on activities, making them ideal contexts for learning and practicing new social and communication skills. In addition, these supportive networks can have a positive impact on the attitudes, expectations, and self-perceptions of peers without disabilities who choose to become involved (Griffin et al., 2016; Rao & Petroff, 2011).

Peer networks can also be established in other community contexts. The establishment of "circles of friends" or "circles of support" have long been advocated as an avenue of creating social connections for adults with significant disabilities (Newton & Wilson, 2005; Perske, 1988). This variation on the peer network approach aims to engage a small group of individuals from the community in supporting an individual who is socially marginalized and facilitating problem solving together toward greater inclusion and belonging. For example, Amado (2013) outlines seven strategies that peer network facilitators can use to support relationships with others in the community and membership in larger community associations. Likewise, Preheim-Bartel, Burkholder, Christophel, and Guth (2015) described the ways in which peer network models can be carried out within faith communities to promote the social flourishing of members with disabilities. Such efforts to forge strong social ties are not without real challenges. For example, service providers must adeptly provide just enough assistance to foster social connections but do so in ways that are neither intrusive nor stifling (Lutfiyya, 1991). Moreover, care must be taken to ensure ongoing communication, transportation, and other supports remain available to the individuals with disabilities to sustain their involvement in valued relationships.

PEER PARTNER PROGRAMS

Peer partner programs are group-based, formal efforts to foster social relationship and peer interactions among individuals with and without significant disabilities

(Hughes & Carter, 2008). In contrast with the individualized approaches used within peer support arrangements and peer networks, peer partner programs focus on connecting groups of students within shared activities held during or beyond the school day. For example, some secondary schools offer course credit to peers without disabilities to free them up one period a day to spend time with students with significant disabilities in special education classrooms (Hughes et al., 2001). Other schools create inclusive social-oriented clubs that meet weekly or monthly for social, service, or project-based activities (e.g., Burns, Storey, & Certo, 1999; Dymond, Renzaglia, & Chun, 2008). On the college campus and in the community, programs typically focus on both group activities and one-to-one friendships and social mentoring relationships. Although these programs are referred to by a variety of names (e.g., peer buddy programs, peer partner clubs, Best Buddies), they all share in common the organizing of consistent interaction opportunities around shared activities, under the guidance of educators or staff. Unlike peer support arrangements and peer networks, rigorous evaluations of peer partner programs have not been conducted. However, descriptive studies confirm they are feasible, acceptable, and impactful approaches for creating social connections, reducing stigma, and encouraging relationships among students with and without significant disabilities (Carter & Pesko, 2008; Copeland et al., 2004).

These programs also provide a rich context for teaching communication skills and building social competence among individuals with complex communication needs. Numerous studies have examined how peers within these programs can be involved in teaching a broad range of relevant skills to students with significant disabilities. For example, Hunt and colleagues (1990, 1991) involved peers in teaching high-school students with disabilities to use communication books comprised of pictures depicting socially validated conversational topics with associated written labels, as well as to follow a specified conversational turn-taking structure. All students demonstrated increases in conversational turn-taking and conversational initiations; some also showed decreases in inappropriate interaction behaviors such as interrupting and perseverative statements. Hughes and colleagues (2000) examined the effects of teaching peers to provide instruction on self-prompted communication book training to high-school students with disabilities who had limited speech. All four students had increases in the conversation topics they discussed, had decreases in inappropriate interactions, and reported meeting their social goals.

IMPLICATIONS FOR PRACTICE AND RESEARCH

Satisfying social relationships and reliable communication are fundamental to flourishing throughout one's life. The instructional strategies and intervention approaches described in this chapter hold considerable promise for promoting positive social and communication outcomes amid the changing social landscape of adolescence and adulthood. First, the necessity of creating meaningful opportunities for communication and social connections has been a prominent theme throughout this chapter. Peer support arrangements, peer network interventions, and peer partner programs all establish regular contexts for students to meet and spend time with one another in sustained and satisfying ways. Although many individuals with ASD experience significant social and communication challenges, the paucity of well-supported opportunities to spend time with their peers continues to be the most prominent barrier to social relationships in many schools and communities (Feldman, Carter, Asmus, & Brock, 2016; Kleinert et al., 2015). Efforts to strengthen social and communicative competence are best addressed within the context of shared activities alongside one's peers.

Second, instructional strategies and intervention approaches should always be selected based on individualized needs and characteristics. Adolescents and adults with ASD and CCN represent a heterogeneous group of citizens with diverse needs, preferences, priorities, and participation preferences in their community. High-quality assessment must inform both the design and delivery of efforts to support the social and communication growth of these individuals (Bellini, Peters, Benner, & Hopf, 2007; Lyons et al., 2016). The need for a wider array of validated tools to assess the social and communication needs of youth and adults with complex communication needs remains pressing. Additional research is needed to identify additional processes and measures that interdisciplinary teams can draw upon to 1) identify skills that are most critical to full social participation in school, workplace, and community settings during and beyond the transition period and 2) evaluate the impact of social-focused interventions on multiple outcome levels (e.g., interactions, relationships, membership).

Third, it is important to solicit the perspectives of adolescents and adults on their social-related goals and the intervention approaches they would most prefer (Chu et al., 2010). The types of interactions and social experiences young people with disabilities value may differ from those often prioritized by educators and other specialists. Likewise, the intervention approaches used to support individuals with ASD should never inadvertently stigmatize or set them apart. Bottema-Beutel, Mullins, Harvey, Gustafson, and Carter (2016) found that youth and young adults with ASD were not uniform in their views on and preferences for seven different intervention components. Additional research is needed to explore how best to solicit such perspectives from individuals who experience difficulties expressing their viewpoints, as well as ways of engaging them in the selection of peer and professional facilitators.

Fourth, peers play a significant role in all of the intervention approaches described in this chapter. The confidence, competence, and commitment these peers possess will directly influence the social and communication outcomes individuals with CCN attain. Careful consideration should be given to how peers are selected, prepared, supported, and encouraged throughout their involvement. Although the avenues for involving peers have been described in prior studies, surprisingly little research has focused on the optimal ways of undertaking the steps of selecting, training, and supporting these participants relative to use of peer-mediated interventions and supports (Schaefer, Canella-Malone, & Carter, 2016). As future research is carried out with older individuals, more attention should be given to this core intervention component. Moreover, the impact of involvement on the outcomes of peers also warrants additional inquiry. Studies suggest younger peers benefit substantially from serving in socially supportive roles (e.g., Kamps et al., 1998). The extent to which similar benefits also accrue among fellow college students, co-workers, and other community members should be examined further (see Amado, Boice, Degrande, & Hutcheson, 2013; Griffin, Mello, et al., 2016).

Fifth, the ubiquity of social media and online communication should spur researchers to examine the supports and instruction needed to ensure individuals with ASD and CCN have access to these important avenues for peer interaction.

Although e-mail, texting, online communities, and social apps can create connections that transcend the boundaries of proximity and communication mode, these technological advances can also leave people with severe disabilities more disconnected if access is not supported. As a field, relatively little is known about how best to harness the promise of prevailing and emerging technologies to promote peer relationships.

CONCLUSION

From birth through retirement, social relationships remain an essential element of thriving and quality of life for individuals with and without disabilities. Yet, efforts to foster social connections and communicative competence often diminish as students with ASD make the transition from adolescence to adulthood. This chapter emphasized the need for sustained attention on the social lives of individuals with CCN. Through intentional planning, thoughtful supports, and reflective practices, educators and service providers can help the individuals they serve move from the margins to a place of full participation and belonging.

REFERENCES

Allen, K. A., & Bowles, T. (2012). Belonging as a guiding principle in the education of adolescents. *Australian Journal of Educational & Developmental Psychology, 12*, 108–119.

Amado, A. N. (2013). *Friends: Connecting people with disabilities and community members.* Minneapolis, MN: University of Minnesota, Institute on Community Integration.

Amado, A. N., Boice, C., Degrande, M., & Hutcheson, S. (2013). BeFrienders: Impact of a social ministry program on relationships for individuals with intellectual/developmental disabilities (I/DD). *Journal of Religion, Disability, and Health, 17*, 1–26. doi:10.1080/15228967.2013.752926

American Psychiatric Association. (2013). *Diagnostic and statistical manual of mental disorders* (5th ed.). Washington, DC: Author.

Asmus, J., Carter, E. W., Moss, C. K., Biggs, E. E., Bolt, D., Born, T. L., . . . Wier, K. (2017). Efficacy and social validity of peer network interventions for high school students with severe disabilities. *American Journal of Intellectual and Developmental Disabilities, 122*, 118–137. doi:10.1352/1944-7558-122.2.118

Asmus, J. A., Carter, E. W., Moss, C. K., Born, T. L., Vincent, L. B., Lloyd, B. P., & Chung, Y. (2016). Social outcomes and acceptability of two peer-mediated interventions for high school students with severe disabilities: A pilot study. *Inclusion, 4*, 194–214. doi:10.1352/2326-6988-4.4.195

Bandura, A. (1977). *Social learning theory.* Morristown, NJ: General Learning Press.

Bellini, S., Peters, J. K., Benner, L., & Hopf, A. (2007). A meta-analysis of school-based social skills interventions for children with autism spectrum disorders. *Remedial and Special Education, 28*, 153–162. doi:10.1177/07419325070280030401

Biggs, E. E., & Carter, E. W. (2016). Quality of life for transition-age youth with autism or intellectual disability. *Journal of Autism and Developmental Disorders, 46*, 190–204. doi:10.1007/s10803-015-2563-x

Biggs, E. E., Carter, E. W., & Gilson, C. B. (in press). Systematic review of interventions involving aided AAC modeling and their effectiveness for children with complex communication needs. *American Journal on Intellectual and Developmental Disabilities.*

Biggs, E. E., Carter, E. W., & Gustafson, J. R. (2017). Efficacy of collaborative planning and peer support arrangements to increase peer interaction and AAC use in inclusive classrooms. *American Journal of Intellectual and Developmental Disabilities, 122*, 25–48. doi:10.1352/1944-7558-122.1.25

Bogenschutz, M., Amado, A., Smith, C., Carter, E. W., Copeland, M., Dattilo, J., . . . Walker, P. (2015). National goals for social inclusion for people with IDD. *Inclusion, 3*, 211–218. doi:10.1352/2326-6988-3.4.211

Bottema-Beutel, K., Mullins, T., Harvey, M., Gustafson, J. R., & Carter, E. W. (2016). Avoiding the "brick wall of awkward": Perspectives of youth with autism spectrum disorder on socialization-focused intervention practices. *Autism, 20*, 196–206. doi:10.1177/1362361315574888

Burns, M., Storey, K., & Certo, N. J. (1999). Effect of service learning on attitudes toward students with severe disabilities. *Education and Training in Mental Retardation and Developmental Disabilities, 34*, 58–65.

Cafiero, J. M. (2001). The effect of an augmentative communication intervention on the communication, behavior, and academic program of an adolescent with autism. *Focus on Autism and Other Developmental Disabilities, 16*, 179–189. doi:10.1177/108835760101600306

Carter, E. W., Asmus, J., Moss, C. K., Amirault, K. A., Biggs, E. E., . . . Wier, K. (2016). Randomized evaluation of peer supports arrangements to support the inclusion of high school students with severe disabilities. *Exceptional Children, 82*, 209–233. doi:10.1177/0014402915598780

Carter, E. W., Asmus, J., Moss, C. K., Cooney, M. Weir, K., Vincent, L., . . . Fesperman, E. (2013). Peer network strategies to foster social connections among adolescents with and without severe disabilities. *TEACHING Exceptional Children, 46*(2), 51–59.

Carter, E. W., Biggs, E. E., & Blustein, C. L. (2016). Relationships matter: Addressing stigma among students with intellectual disability and their peers. In K. Scior & S. Werner (Eds.), *Intellectual disability and stigma: Stepping out from the margins* (pp. 149–164). London, UK: Palgrave McMillan.

Carter, E. W., Bottema-Beutel, K., & Brock, M. E. (2014). Social interactions and friendships. In M. Agran, F. Brown, C. Hughes, C. Quirk, & D. Ryndak (Eds.), *Equity and full participation for individuals with severe disabilities: A vision for the future* (pp. 197–216). Baltimore, MD: Paul H. Brookes Publishing Co.

Carter, E. W., Common, E. A., Sreckovic, M. A., Huber, H. B., Bottema-Beutel, K., Gustafson, J. R., Dykstra, J., & Hume, K. (2014). Promoting social competence and peer relationships for adolescents with ASD. *Remedial and Special Education, 35*, 27–37. doi:10.1177/0741932513514618

Carter, E. W., Cushing, L. S., & Kennedy, C. H. (2009). *Peer support strategies: Improving all students' social lives and learning.* Baltimore, MD: Paul H. Brookes Publishing Co.

Carter, E. W., & Kennedy, C. H. (2006). Promoting access to the general curriculum using peer support strategies. *Research and Practice for Persons with Severe Disabilities, 31*, 284–292. doi:10.1177/154079690603100402

Carter, E. W., Moss, C. K., Hoffman, A., Chung, Y., & Sisco, L. G. (2011). Efficacy and social validity of peer support arrangements for adolescents with disabilities. *Exceptional Children, 78*, 107–125. doi:10.1177/001440291107800107

Carter, E. W., O'Rourke, L., Sisco, L. G., & Pelsue, D. (2009). Knowledge, responsibilities, and training needs of paraprofessionals in elementary and secondary schools. *Remedial and Special Education, 30*, 344–349. doi:10.1177/0741932508324399

Carter, E. W., & Pesko, M. J. (2008). Social validity of peer interaction intervention strategies in high school classrooms: Effectiveness, feasibility, and actual use. *Exceptionality, 16*, 156–173. doi:10.1080/09362830802198427

Carter, E. W., Sisco, L. G., Brown, L., Brickham, D., & Al-Khabbaz, Z. A. (2008). Peer interactions and academic engagement of youth with developmental disabilities in inclusive middle and high school classrooms. *American Journal on Mental Retardation, 113*, 479–494. doi:10.1352/2008.113:479-494

Carter, E. W., Sisco, L. G., Chung, Y., & Stanton-Chapman, T. (2010). Peer interactions of students with intellectual disabilities and/or autism: A map of the intervention literature. *Research and Practice for Persons with Severe Disabilities, 35*, 63–79. doi:10.2511/rpsd.35.3-4.63

Carter, E. W., Swedeen, B., & Kurkowski, C. (2008). Friendship matters: Fostering social relationships in secondary schools. *TASH Connections, 34*(6), 9–12, 14.

Chu, P. S., Saucier, D. A., & Hafner, E. (2010). Meta-analysis of the relationships between social support and well-being in children and adolescents. *Journal of Social and Clinical Psychology, 29*, 624–645. doi:10.1521/jscp.2010.29.6.624

Chung, Y., & Carter, E. W. (2013). Promoting peer interactions in inclusive classrooms for students with speech-generating devices. *Research and Practice for Persons with Severe Disabilities, 32*, 94–109. doi:10.2511/027494813807714492

Chung, Y. Carter, E. W., & Sisco, L. G. (2012a). A systematic review of interventions to increase peer interactions for students with complex communication challenges. *Research and Practice for Persons with Severe Disabilities, 37,* 271–287. doi:10.2511/027494813805327304

Chung, Y., Carter, E. W., & Sisco, L. G. (2012b). Social interaction of students with severe disabilities who use augmentative and alternative communication in inclusive classrooms. *American Journal on Intellectual and Developmental Disabilities, 117,* 349–367. doi:10.1352/1944-7558-117.5.349

Collins, B. C. (2012). Using naturalistic language strategies. In B. C. Collins (Ed.), *Systematic instruction for students with moderate and severe disabilities* (pp. 87–101). Baltimore, MD: Paul H. Brookes Publishing Co.

Copeland, S. R., Hughes, C., Carter, E. W., Guth, C., Presley, J., Williams, C. R., & Fowler, S. E. (2004). Increasing access to general education: Perspectives of participants in a high school peer support program. *Remedial and Special Education, 26,* 342–352. doi:10.1177/07419325040250060201

Culnane, M., Eisenman, L. T., & Murphy, A. (2016). College peer mentoring and students with intellectual disability: Mentor's perspectives on relationship dynamics. *Inclusion, 4,* 257–269. doi:10.1352/2326-6988-4.4.257

Demir, M. (Ed.). (2015). *Friendship and happiness: Across the life-span and culture.* New York, NY: Springer.

Downing, J. E., & Chen, D. (2015). Beginning steps in communication intervention. In J. Downing, A. Hanreddy, & K. Peckham-Hardin (Eds.), *Teaching communication skills to students with severe disabilities* (pp. 107–136). Baltimore, MD: Paul H. Brookes Publishing Co.

Dymond, S. K., Renzaglia, A., & Chun, E. J. (2008). Inclusive high school service learning programs: Methods for and barriers to including students with disabilities. *Education and Training in Developmental Disabilities, 43,* 20–36.

Feldman, R., Carter, E. W., Asmus, J., & Brock, M. E. (2016). Presence, proximity, and peer interactions of adolescents with severe disabilities in general education classrooms. *Exceptional Children, 82,* 192–208. doi:10.1177/0014402915585481

Ganz, J., Earles-Vollrath, T., Heath, A., Parker, R., Rispoli, M., & Duran, J. (2012). A meta-analysis of single case research studies on aided augmentative and alternative communication systems for individuals with autism spectrum disorders. *Journal of Autism and Developmental Disorders, 42,* 60–74. doi:10.1007/s10803-011-1212-2

Gardner, K. F., Carter, E. W., Gustafson, J. R., Hochman, J. M., Harvey, M. N., . . . Fan, H. (2014). Effects of peer networks on the social interactions of students with autism spectrum disorders. *Research and Practice for Persons with Severe Disabilities, 39,* 100–118. doi:10.1177/1540796914544550

Giangreco, M. F., & Broer, S. M. (2005). Questionable utilization of paraprofessionals in inclusive schools: Are we addressing symptoms or causes. *Focus on Autism and Other Developmental Disabilities, 20,* 10–26. doi:10.1177/10883576050200010201

Goossens, C. (1989). Aided communication intervention before assessment: A case study of a child with cerebral palsy. *Augmentative and Alternative Communication, 5,* 14–26. doi:10.1080/07434618912331274926

Griffin, M. M., Mello, M. P., Glover, C. A., Carter, E. W., & Hodapp, R. (2016). Supporting students with intellectual disability in postsecondary education: The motivations and experiences of peer mentors. *Inclusion, 4,* 75–88. doi:10.1352/2326-6988-4.2.75

Griffin, M. M., Wendel, K. F., Day, T. L., & McMillan, E. (2016). Developing peer supports for college students with intellectual and developmental disabilities. *Journal of Postsecondary Education and Disability, 29,* 263–269.

Hafner, D., Moffatt, C., & Kisa, N. (2011). Cutting-Edge: Integrating students with intellectual and developmental disabilities into a 4-year liberal arts college. *Career Development for Exceptional Individuals, 34,* 18–30. doi:10.1177/0885728811401018

Hamilton, B. L., & Snell, M. E. (1993). Using the milieu approach to increase spontaneous communication book use across environments by an adolescent with autism. *Augmentative and Alternative Communication, 9,* 259–272. doi:10.1080/07434619312331276681

Haring, T. G., & Breen, C. G. (1992). A peer-mediated social network intervention to enhance the social integration of persons with moderate and severe disabilities. *Journal of Applied Behavior Analysis, 25,* 319–333. doi:10.1901/jaba.1992.25-319

Hart, B., & Risley, T. (1995). *Meaningful differences in the everyday experience of young American children*. Baltimore, MD: Paul H. Brookes Publishing Co.

Hawkley, L. C., & Cacioppo, J. T. (2010). Loneliness matters: A theoretical and empirical review of consequences and mechanisms. *Annals of Behavioral Medicine, 40,* 218–227. doi:10.1007/s12160-010-9210-8

Hochman, J. M., Carter, E. W., Bottema-Beutel, K., Harvey, M. N., & Gustafson, J. R. (2015). Efficacy of peer networks to increase social connections among high school students with and without autism. *Exceptional Children, 82,* 96–116. doi:10.1177/0014402915585482

Holt-Lunstad, J., Smith, T. B., & Layton, J. B. (2010). Social relationships and mortality risk: A meta-analytic review. *PLoS Med 7*(7), e1000316. doi:10.1371/ journal.pmed.1000316

Hughes, C., & Carter, E. W. (2008). *Peer buddy programs for successful secondary school inclusion*. Baltimore, MD: Paul H. Brookes Publishing Co.

Hughes, C., Copeland, S. R., Guth, C., Rung, L. L., Hwang, B., Kleeb, G., & Strong, M. (2001). General education students' perspectives on their involvement in a high school peer buddy program. *Education and Training in Mental Retardation and Developmental Disabilities, 36,* 343–356.

Hughes, C., Kaplan, L., Bernsetein, R., Boykin, M., Reilly, C., . . . Harvey, M. (2013). Increasing social interaction skills of secondary school students with autism and/or intellectual disability: A review of interventions. *Research and Practice for Persons with Severe Disabilities, 37,* 288–307. doi:10.2511/027494813805327214

Hughes, C., Rung, L. L., Wehmeyer, M. L., Agran, M., Copeland, S. R., & Hwang, B. (2000). Self-prompted communication book use to increase social interaction among high school students. *Journal of the Association for Persons with Severe Handicaps, 25,* 153–166. doi:10.2511/rpsd.25.3.153

Hunt, P., Alwell, M., & Goetz, L. (1991). Establishing conversational exchanges with family and friends: Moving from training to meaningful communication. *The Journal of Special Education, 25,* 305–319. doi:10.1177/002246699102500304

Hunt, P., Alwell, M., Goetz, L., & Sailor, W. (1990). Generalized effects of conversation skill training. *The Journal of the Association for Persons with Severe Handicaps, 15,* 250–260. doi:10.1177/154079699001500404

Kamps, D. M., Kravits, T., Lopez, A. G., Kemmerer, K., Potucek, J., & Harrell, L. G. (1998). What do the peers think? Social validity of peer-mediated programs. *Education & Treatment of Children, 21,* 107–134.

Kent-Walsh, J., & McNaughton, D. (2005). Communication partner instruction in AAC: Present practices and future directions. *Augmentative and Alternative Communication, 21,* 195–204. doi:10.1080/07434610400006646

Kersh, J., Corona, L., & Siperstein, G. (2013). Social well-being and friendship of people with intellectual disability. In M. Wehmeyer (Ed.), *The Oxford handbook of positive psychology and disability* (pp. 60–81). New York, NY: Oxford University Press.

Kleinert, H., Towles-Reeves, E., Quenemoen, R., Thurlow, M., Fluegge, L., Weseman, L., & Kerbel, A. (2015). Where students with the most significant cognitive disabilities are taught: Implications for general curriculum access. *Exceptional Children, 81,* 312–329. doi:10.1177/0014402914563697

Koegel, R. L., Fredeen, R., Kim, S., Danial, J., Rubinstein, D., & Koegel, L. (2012). Using perseverative interests to improve interactions between adolescents with autism and their typical peers in school settings. *Journal of Positive Behavior Interventions, 14,* 133–141. doi:10.1177/1098300712437043

Kuo, M. H., Orsmond, G. I., Cohn, E. S., & Coster, W. J. (2013). Friendship characteristics and activity patterns of adolescents with an autism spectrum disorder. *Autism, 17,* 481–500. doi:10.1177/1362361311416380

Lang, R., Sigafoos, J., van, D. M., Carnett, A., Green, V. A., Lancioni, G. E., & O'Reilly, M. F. (2014). Teaching functional communication to adults with autism spectrum disorders. In M. Tincani, & A. Bondy (Eds.), *Autism spectrum disorders in adolescents and adults: Evidence-based and promising interventions* (pp. 118–139). New York, NY: Guilford.

Lovaas, O. I. (1977). *The autistic child: Language development through behavior modification*. Oxford, England: Irvington.

Lutfiyya, Z. M. (1991). "A feeling of being connected': Friendships between people with and without learning difficulties. *Disability & Society, 6,* 233–245. doi:10.1080/02674649166780271

Lyons, G. L., Huber, H. B., Carter, E. W., Chen, R., & Asmus, J. A. (2016). Assessing the social skills and problem behaviors of adolescents with severe disabilities enrolled in general education classes. *American Journal on Intellectual and Developmental Disabilities, 121,* 327–345. doi:10.1352/1944-7558-121.4.327

McNaughton, D., & Chapple, D. (2013). AAC and communication in the workplace. *Perspectives on Augmentative and Alternative Communication, 22,* 30–36.

Mirenda, P. (2015). Considerations in developing and acquiring communication aids. In J. Downing, A. Hanreddy, & K. Peckham-Hardin (Eds.), *Teaching communication skills to students with severe disabilities* (pp. 137–162). Baltimore, MD: Paul H. Brookes Publishing Co.

Morningstar, M. E., Kurth, J. A., & Johnson, P. E. (2017). Examining national trends in educational placement for students with significant disabilities. *Remedial and Special Education, 38,* 3–12. doi:10.1177/0741932516678327

National Coordinating Center Accreditation Workgroup. (2016). *Report on model accreditation standards for higher education programs for students with intellectual disability: A path to education, employment, and community living.* Boston, MA: Institute for Community Inclusion.

Newton, C., & Wilson, D. (2005). *Creating circles of friends: A peer support and inclusion handbook.* Nottingham, UK: Inclusion Solutions.

Perske, R. (1988). *Circles of friends: People with disabilities and their friends enrich the lives of one another.* Nashville, TN: Abingdon.

Petrina, N., Carter, M., & Stephenson, J. (2014). The nature of friendship in children with autism spectrum disorders: A systematic review. *Research in Autism Spectrum Disorders, 8,* 111–126. doi:10.1016/j.rasd.2013.10.016

Preheim-Bartel, D., Burkholder, T. J., Christophel, L. A., & Guth, C. J. (2015). *Circles of love: Stories of congregations caring for people with disabilities.* Harrisonburg, VA: Herald Press.

Rao, S., & Petroff, J. (2011). 'He is more like us, looking for a person to date and eventually share his life with': Perspectives of undergraduate students on being a member of a 'circle of support'. *Disability and Society, 26,* 463–475. doi:10.1080/09687599.2011.567797

Reichle, J., McComas, J., Dahl, N., Solberg, G., Pierce, S., & Smith, D. (2005). Teaching an individual with severe intellectual delay to request assistance conditionally. *Educational Psychology, 25,* 275–286. doi:10.1080/0144341042000301201

Remington, B., & Clarke, S. (1983). Acquisition of expressive signing by autistic children: An evaluation of the relative effects of simultaneous communication and sign-alone training. *Journal of Applied Behavior Analysis, 16,* 315–328. doi:10.1901/jaba.1983.16-315

Rodi, M. S., & Hughes, C. (2000). Teaching communication book use to a high school student using a milieu approach. *Research and Practice for Persons with Severe Disabilities, 25,* 175–179. doi:10.2511/rpsd.25.3.175

Romski, M. A., & Sevcik, R. (1996). *Breaking the speech barrier: Language development through augmented means.* Baltimore, MD: Paul H. Brookes Publishing Co.

Rowland, C. M. (2009). Presymbolic communicators with autism spectrum disorders. In P. Mirenda & T. Iacono (Vol. Eds.) & D.R. Beukelman & J. Reichle (Series Eds.), *Autism spectrum disorders and AAC* (pp. 51–82). Baltimore, MD: Paul H. Brookes Publishing Co.

Rubin, K. H., Bukowski, W. M., & Laursen, B. (Eds.). (2009). *Handbook of peer interactions, relationships, and groups.* New York, NY: Guilford Press.

Schaefer, J. M., Canella-Malone, H. I., & Carter, E. W. (2016). The place of peers in peer-mediated interventions for students with intellectual disabilities. *Remedial and Special Education, 37,* 345–356. doi:10.1177/0741932516629220

Sennott, S. C., Light, J. C., & McNaughton, D. (2016). AAC modeling intervention research review. *Research and Practice for Persons with Severe Disabilities, 41,* 101–115. doi:10.1177/1540796916638822

Siedlecki, K. L., Salthouse, T. A., Oishi, S., & Jeswani, S. (2014). The relationship between social support and subjective well-being across age. *Social Indicators Research, 117,* 561–576. doi:10.1007/s11205-013-0361-4

Sigafoos, J., Drasgow, E., Halle, J., O'Reilly, M., Seely-York, S., Edrisinha, C., & Andrews, A. (2004). Teaching VOCA use as a communicative repair strategy. *Journal of Autism and Developmental Disorders, 34,* 411–422. doi:10.1023/B:JADD.0000037417.04356.9c

Storey, K. (2003). A review of research on natural support interventions in the workplace for people with disabilities. *International Journal of Rehabilitation Research, 26,* 79–84.

U.S. Department of Education. (2014). *Individuals with Disabilities Education Act data*. Washington, DC: Data Accountability Center.

Wagner, M., Cadwallader, T., & Marder, C. (2003). *Life outside the classroom for youth with disabilities*. Menlo Park, CA: SRI International.

Wendt, O. (2009). Research on the use of manual signs and graphic symbols in autism spectrum disorders: A systematic review. In P. Mirenda & T. Iacono (Vol. Eds.) & D.R. Beukelman & J. Reichle (Series Eds.), *Autism spectrum disorders and AAC* (pp. 83–139). Baltimore, MD: Paul H. Brookes Publishing Co.

Wong, C., Odom, S. L., Hume, K., Cox, A. W., Fettig, A., Kucharczyk, S., . . . Schultz, T. R. (2014). *Evidence-based practices for children, youth, and young adults with autism spectrum disorder*. Chapel Hill, NC: Frank Porter Graham Child Development Institute.

IV

Evidence-Based
Practices Implemented
in Natural Contexts

11

Naturalistic Developmental Behavioral Interventions for Young Children With Autism Spectrum Disorder and Complex Communication Needs

Kyle Sterrett and Connie Kasari

Autism interventions have expanded greatly since the early 2000s, both in number and in variety. However, nearly all (in one way or another) pay homage to Ivar Lovaas and his groundbreaking intervention study (1987) that found that 19 children receiving an intensive behaviorally based intervention (carried out for 40 hours per week over 2 years) improved significantly across cognitive and educational domains compared to 19 children receiving a less intense version of the same intervention. Lovaas, who developed discrete trial training over many years beginning in the 1960s, demonstrated in his 1987 study that intervention mattered for children's outcomes and, importantly, that children with autism spectrum disorder (ASD) could learn, with nearly half making dramatic change to nearly typical learning levels. From this early research on behaviorally based treatments the field of applied behavior analysis (ABA) became solidly associated with effective intervention for children with ASD (Cooper, Heron, & Heward, 1987). ABA techniques were widely accepted and quickly disseminated into clinical practice and research.

These methods have been largely assessed using single-case research designs, and although highly successful for many children in rates of initial learning, the research design also highlights the limitations of the method specifically related to maintenance and generalization of skills over short periods of time. This recognition, however, cannot all be attributed to method of intervention. It is likely that lack of maintenance or generalization may be related to selection of teaching target as well as teaching method. Method of teaching, selection of teaching targets, dose, and other factors may be important active ingredients of any intervention and to date remain largely unexplored (Kasari, 2002).

Despite a limited understanding of the active ingredients for ABA-based interventions, a number of modifications to ABA-based interventions began to emerge. Primarily these modifications sought to remedy limitations in maintenance and generalization by focusing on teaching approach. Incidental teaching was one such modification (Hart & Risley, 1982; McGee, Kranz, Mason & McClannahan, 1983). Incidental teaching is a set of procedures that use teaching principles similar to discrete trial training but manipulate the child's natural environment to reinforce the child's attention to adult-elicited cues by using a responsive adult partner to instruct, praise, and respond to the child (Hart & Risley, 1982). This manipulation of the natural environment was found to increase children's spontaneous speech in multiple settings (Hart & Risley, 1975). These early attempts to integrate more naturalistic principles into discrete teaching protocols were largely successful and paved the way for further research on the efficacy of such intervention models.

These same conclusions about the efficacy of modified behavioral interventions are supported by more recent research as well. A review found that while children have been shown to make considerable progress using discrete trial–training-based learning programs, around 20% make no gains and around 50% make some developmental gains but do not reach developmentally normed standards (Eldevik et al., 2010). In addition, much of the reported progress in these intervention trials are made in cognitive domains and not social communication, which is a core deficit of children with ASD (Howlin, Magiati, & Charman, 2009). Again, to remedy these limitations of more structured and discrete teaching techniques, a large body of literature has begun to emerge in support of so-called naturalistic developmental behavioral interventions (NDBIs; Schreibman et al., 2015). These interventions, a number of which will be described later in this chapter, meet the criteria of ABA-based interventions. They use aspects of operant conditioning; measurements are taken before, during, and throughout intervention; and they have socially significant goals (Schriebman et al., 2015). However, they also incorporate more "natural" teaching techniques such as using naturally occurring reinforcers, activities that are developmentally appropriate and preferred by the child, and lessons that take place in natural contexts (e.g., everyday routines in home or community).

Although many NDBIs developed from more structured ABA techniques, a separate and distinct treatment philosophy referred to as the developmental social-pragmatic model also emerged to address social communication deficits in children with ASD (Smith & Iadarola, 2015). The developmental social-pragmatic perspective on interventions is informed by the theory that social communication delays in children with autism stem from an inability to jointly engage in activities with social partners. As a result of this inability to jointly engage, there are a number of downstream effects on social communication development (Mundy & Crowson, 1997). The developmental social-pragmatic model and NDBIs are explored as philosophically different teaching approaches although they share many of the same principles; both are informed by naturalistic learning theories.

SOCIAL COMMUNICATION

One of the strengths of these NDBIs and the developmental social-pragmatic model is their focus on targeting social communication delays. Social communication delays are often the most intractable targets of intervention despite being the focus of a wide range of intervention attempts (see the next section for examples). This is particularly true of those children who may have complex communication needs (CCN). Despite theory-based intervention attempts and increased access to intensive early intervention programs, approximately 30–50% of children with ASD fail to develop phrase speech by school age (Tager-Flusberg & Kasari, 2013). The lack of speech development is a potent predictor of less positive outcomes later in life (Howlin, Goode, Hutton, & Rutter, 2004; McGovern & Sigman, 2005). As a result, development of social communication and language should continue to be a top target of intervention researchers.

For the purpose of this review, children with CCN show evidence of developmental delays in communication such as gestures (requesting or joint attention) and spoken language. Children with ASD and CCN generally fall into two categories: those who are considered to be minimally verbal and those who are preverbal (Tager-Flusberg & Kasari, 2013). Classification as minimally verbal generally refers to children who are school age (older than 5 years old) and who have little to no functional language. The other group are children who are preverbal. These children are often young (often 2–4 years old) and have language delays but will eventually go on to use functional language before they enter kindergarten. In discussing interventions targeting communication difficulties in young children with ASD, it is important to consider both groups as they often represent distinct populations and, as a result, need distinct interventions to target their heterogeneous needs.

MECHANISMS OF CHANGE

Often lost in the evaluation and discussion of interventions in ASD is that the overarching goal of each of these intervention packages is in some way to improve the quality of life of children and families. While the interventions to be discussed broadly fall within two general treatment philosophies (NDBIs and developmental social-pragmatic), the metrics they use to evaluate change vary widely. There is a growing literature discussing what are referred to as the active ingredients of intervention packages (Kasari, 2002). Active ingredients refer to the factors or mechanisms of change in the intervention—that is, what is driving the effect of a specific intervention package. There have been some empirical attempts to isolate active ingredients in ASD interventions (e.g., Gulsrud, Hellemann, Shire, & Kasari, 2015; Pickles et al., 2015). Although the active ingredients of most intervention packages have not been tested systematically, many treatment packages have hypothesized mechanisms of change based on their outcomes. There are two types of outcomes: 1) proximal, those that are directly related to the intervention procedures (e.g., teaching and measuring discrete social communicative gestures) and 2) distal, downstream intervention effects (e.g., language production). By looking at a study's proximal and distal outcome measures, one can determine the theorized mechanism of change (proximal outcome) and the downstream effects (distal outcome) of an intervention trial. It is clear that an intervention can succeed at a number of different levels; it can promote a proximal change, link a proximal change to a distal change, or do both. Each of the included studies will be evaluated in terms of their proximal and distal outcomes (empirically tested or theorized).

METHODOLOGICAL QUALITY OF
INCLUDED RANDOMIZED CONTROLLED TRIALS

Randomized controlled trials (RCT) are considered the gold standard methodology to evaluate the efficacy of intervention research (National Research Council, 2001). Although many interventions have been developed to target social communication in children with ASD using RCTs, positive results shown in randomized controlled designs do not necessarily qualify an intervention as evidenced-based. Within the RCT framework, studies can vary greatly in terms of methodological quality, and lack of sound methodology can cast doubt on significant findings or null effects. The studies that are discussed next were rated in terms of methodological quality based on the Cochrane criteria for judging risk of bias. For the purpose of this review, five potential sources of bias were evaluated: 1) random sequence generation, 2) blinding of outcome assessment, 3) incomplete outcome data, 4) selective reporting, and 5) group similarity at baseline (Higgins & Green, 2011). The results of these risk of bias assessments for each of the included studies are discussed and are summarized in Table 11.1. Single-case designs are important to the development and refinement of interventions and when well conducted provide preliminary evidence of efficacy. However, these designs can be difficult to evaluate due to issues surrounding publication bias (Sham & Smith, 2014), external validity, and the various methods used to evaluate effects (Lenz, 2013) and so are excluded from this review.

CHAPTER AIMS

The overarching goal of this chapter is to evaluate the evidence base for interventions targeting social communication development in children with ASD who have CCNs. Specifically, intervention studies were included that took place in natural contexts, included children younger than 10 years old, had a measure of social communication as an outcome, and were tested using a randomized controlled trial. A number of intervention programs are described, all of which have been evaluated in the context of RCTs. The development of these interventions and their theoretical underpinnings are discussed along with any preliminary evidence related to their efficacy. The strength of the evidence as well as the methodological quality of the trials are described and evaluated. Furthermore, a summary of intervention components for the treatments highlighted in the chapter is provided in Table 11.2.

OVERVIEW OF TREATMENTS

Naturalistic Developmental Behavioral Interventions

Early Achievements   Early Achievements is a developmentally based intervention that is targeted at increasing early social communication skills in toddlers with ASD. There are four overarching components to Early Achievements: developing interpersonal synchrony, social communication, and cognitive development, as well as understanding the optimal sequence of instruction (Landa, Holman, O'Neill, & Stuart, 2011). Early Achievements was developed based on research identifying the importance of socially driven interactions such as imitation and joint attention in developing symbolic understanding (Mundy, Sullivan, & Mastergeorge, 2009). This symbolic understanding is in turn linked to a number of

Table 11.1. Summary of risk of bias assessment

Authors	Intervention	Random sequence generation	Blinding outcome assessment	Incomplete outcome data	Reporting bias	Similarity at baseline
Casenhiser, Shanker, and Stieben (2011)	Floortime	low risk	low risk	high risk	high risk	low risk
Pajareya and Nopmaneejumruslers (2011)	Floortime	unclear	low risk	low risk	low risk	low risk
Solomon, Van Egeren, Mahoney, Huber, and Zimmerman (2014)	Floortime	low risk	low risk	high risk	high risk	high risk
Landa, Holman, O'Neill, and Stuart (2011)	EA	unclear	low risk	low risk	low risk	low risk
Roberts and Kaiser (2015)	EMT	low risk	high risk	high risk	low risk	low risk
Yoder and Stone (2006)	EMT	low risk	high risk	low risk	high risk	high risk[a]
Dawson et al. (2010)	ESDM	low risk	low risk	high risk	high risk	low risk
Rogers et al. (2012)	ESDM	low risk	unclear	high risk	high risk	high risk
Siller, Hutman, and Sigman, 2013	FPI	low risk	low risk	high risk[b]	low risk	low risk
Schertz, Odom, Baggett, and Sideris (2013)	JAML	unclear	mixed	low risk	low risk	low risk
Chang, Shire, Shih, Gelfand, and Kasari (2016)	JASPER	low risk	low risk	high risk	low risk	low risk
Kaale, Smith, and Sponheim (2012)	JASPER	low risk	low risk	low risk	low risk	high risk
Kasari, Freeman, and Paparella (2006)	JASPER	unclear	low risk	high risk	low risk	low risk
Kasari, Gulsrud, Wong, Kwon, and Locke (2010)	JASPER	low risk	low risk	low risk	low risk	low risk
Kasari, Kaiser, et al. (2014)	JASPER	low risk	low risk	high risk	low risk	low risk

(continued)

255

Table 11.1. *(continued)*

Authors	Intervention	Random sequence generation	Blinding outcome assessment	Incomplete outcome data	Reporting bias	Similarity at baseline
Kasari, Lawton, et al. (2014)	JASPER	low risk	low risk	low risk	low risk	low risk
Kasari, Siller, et al. (2014)	JASPER	low risk	low risk	high risk	low risk	low risk
Kasari, Gulsrud, Paparella, Hellemann, and Berry (2015)	JASPER	low risk	low risk	high risk	low risk	high risk
Lawton and Kasari (2012)	JASPER	low risk	low risk	low risk	high risk	high risk
Shire et al. (2016)	JASPER	low risk	low risk	low risk	low risk	low risk
Wong (2013)	JASPER	low risk	low risk	low risk	high risk	low risk
Carter et al., 2011	More than Words	low risk	low risk	high risk	low risk	low risk
Aldred, Green, and Adams (2004)	PACT	unclear	low risk	low risk	low risk	low risk
Green et al. (2010)	PACT	low risk	low risk	low risk[c]	low risk	high risk
Rahman et al. (2015)	PACT/PASS	low risk	low risk	high risk	low risk	low risk
Hardan et al. (2015)	PRT	low risk	low risk	low risk	low risk	low risk
Mohammadzaheri, Koegel, Rezaee, and Rafiee (2014)	PRT	unclear	mixed	low risk	low risk	low risk
Schreibman and Stahmer (2014)	PRT	unclear	high risk	high risk	low risk	low risk
Ingersoll (2010)	RIT	low risk	low risk	low risk	low risk	high risk
Wetherby et al. (2014)	SCERTS	low risk	low risk	high risk	high risk	low risk

Criteria based on the standards laid out in Higgins and Green (2011).

Key: EA, early achievements; EMT, enhanced milieu teaching; ESDM, Early Start Denver Model; FPI, Focused Playtime Intervention; JAML, Joint Attention Mediated Learning; JASPER, Joint Attention, Symbolic Play, Engagement, and Regulation; PACT, Preschool Autism Communication Trial; PRT, Pivotal Response Treatment; RIT, Reciprocal Imitation Training; SCERTS*, Social Communication, Emotion Regulation, and Transactional Support*.

[a] ADOS and object exchange entered as covariates in analysis.
[b] Evaluated withdrawn group, no difference.
[c] Missing data imputed.

positive outcomes such as language and broad social development (Toth, Munson, Meltzoff, & Dawson, 2006).

Early Achievements has been tested in one RCT of toddlers with ASD (Landa et al., 2011). This intervention took place in a classroom setting and also consisted of home-based parent training and education components. The two intervention groups were identical except the Interpersonal Synchrony group received supplementary lessons targeting imitation, joint attention, and affect sharing. Overall, although there was growth in both groups in terms of initiating joint attention and affect sharing over time as measured by the Communication and Symbolic Behavior Scales Developmental Profile™ (CSBS DP™; Wetherby & Prizant, 2002), there were no group differences. Only one component of the program was different between groups: *social imitation* (defined as imitating an adult model with eye contact, and tested in a direct instruction manner), which nearly doubled in the Interpersonal Synchrony group.

Early Start Denver Model   The Early Start Denver Model is a multidimensional intervention approach that seeks to integrate the elements of ABA with a focus on developing reciprocal relationships with communication partners. It is delivered in family's homes by both parents and trained therapists (Dawson et al., 2010). The Early Start Denver Model is targeted for children as young as 12 months.

The Early Start Denver Model was developed based on the Denver Model, which is a developmental intervention targeted at children 2–5 years old. A number of features of the Denver Model were incorporated into the Early Start Denver Model, such as the use of an interdisciplinary team to target a wide range of clinical goals including social communication. In addition, it incorporates the Denver Model's focus on child and parent engagement, functional object use and imitation, and lastly both verbal and nonverbal communication (Dawson et al., 2010, p. 15). This comprehensive model for early intervention places emphasis on developing imitation, joint attention, and social-orienting skills based on the associations between these skills and communication development (Dawson et al., 2004).

Two RCTs have been reported evaluating the efficacy of the Early Start Denver Model. The first RCT of the Early Start Denver Model comprehensive model was carried out by Dawson and colleagues (2010), with children 18–30 months old. The other consisted of a parent-mediated Early Start Denver Model approach for very young children ages 14– 24 months old (Rogers et al., 2012). The comparison group in both studies consisted of children receiving community-based interventions. The first trial found a moderately significant effect of treatment on children's receptive language at the 1-year assessment period, and at the 2-year assessment period treatment effects were found for both receptive and expressive language as well as adaptive communication. No treatment effects were seen in the parent-mediated intervention.

While other studies of the Early Start Denver Model have been completed, including in group settings carried out by therapists or teachers, these have generally been uncontrolled pre–post tests of treatment effectiveness (e.g., Vivanti et al., 2014). Thus, they are not reviewed here.

Enhanced Milieu Teaching   Enhanced milieu teaching (EMT) is a set of strategies meant to develop functional language and communication in children with ASD who have CCN. EMT has been researched in the context of single-case designs in children with ASD (Hancock & Kaiser, 2002; Kaiser, Hancock, & Nietfield, 2000). EMT is described as having four primary components: environmental arrangement, responsive interactions, language modeling, and milieu teaching. The intervention is designed to be carried out in the home throughout natural, daily routines such as hand washing or book reading.

EMT is framed as a developmental pragmatic communication intervention, which means that the adult in the interaction should facilitate and promote children's communicative initiations (Hancock & Kaiser, 2002). It is based on the early work of Hart and Risley (1975) related to incidental teaching in which language is taught by labeling and describing objects in the context of natural adult–child interactions. It also built on early studies finding that using environmental arrangement to promote communication (both physical arrangement and interactional arrangement) led to better language outcomes for children (Kaiser, Ostrosky, & Alpert, 1993). In addition, research on the importance of responsive interactions influenced the development of EMT (Weiss, 1981).

Two recent RCTs evaluated the effectiveness of EMT; however, neither were carried out with a sample of children with ASD. A third was of EMT blended with Joint Attention, Symbolic Play, Engagement, and Regulation (JASPER; described next) and so the effects of EMT cannot be isolated in that trial (Kasari, Kaiser, et al., 2014). The two non-ASD RCTs were tested in young children (2–5 years old) with intellectual disabilities and those at risk for language delays. The first trial consisted of a mixed parent- and therapist-implemented intervention (Roberts & Kaiser, 2015), and the second was a parent-mediated intervention (Kaiser & Roberts, 2013). As expected, the parents receiving the active training showed significantly higher EMT fidelity, which maintained over time; however, no effect on children's language was found on the observational, norm-referenced, or parent report measures. The second RCT found that parents in the treatment group were rated higher on EMT strategies, and the children had significantly higher receptive language. No effect was found for expressive language.

A small RCT with preschool children with ASD was tested using an adaption of Enhanced Milieu Teaching, responsive education/prelinguistic milieu teaching (RE/PMT; Yoder & Stone, 2006) compared to an intervention using visual symbols to improve requesting language (Picture Exchange Communication System [PECS]; Frost & Bondy, 2002). Children, 18 to 60 months of age, with ASD were recruited for the study. There was a main effect for the RE/PMT group in terms of object exchanges as predicted, but there was no main effect for requesting in the PECS group. Contrary to the researchers' hypotheses, children who entered the study with limited initiations of joint attention benefited significantly more from the PECS treatment, and those who were high on initiations of joint attention (greater than 7 initiation of joint attention acts at entry) benefited most from the RE/PMT.

Joint Attention, Symbolic Play, Engagement, and Regulation (JASPER)

JASPER is an intervention that systematically teaches joint engagement, play, social communication gestures, and language using naturalistic, developmental, and behavioral strategies (Kasari, Freeman, & Paparella, 2006). The primary components of the intervention include using environmental arrangement (e.g. motivating, developmentally appropriate toys, distraction-free environments, developmentally chosen targets), appropriate levels of prompting, nondirective speech when imitating and modeling language, and developmentally targeted play and joint attention (Gulsrud et al., 2015). The focus is on spontaneous rather than elicited or prompted outcomes.

First, the joint attention component of JASPER was developed based on a large body of research demonstrating the predictive nature of early joint attention gestures on positive language and social outcomes (Charman et al., 2003; Mundy, Sigman, & Kasari, 1990). The use of play as a context in which to teach early social skills was built both upon the importance of motivating contexts to skill acquisition, as well as the foundational importance of functional and symbolic play as it relates to building early positive social interactions with adults (Baron-Cohen, Lombardo & Tager-Flusberg, 2013; Charman et al., 2003). The last two pieces, engagement and regulation as targets of intervention, emerge from a body of literature showing that although effective social teaching often happens in the context of positive engagement (Tomasello & Todd, 1983), children with ASD often spend significantly less time jointly engaged, about 20% less time than their typically developing peers (Adamson, Deckner, & Bakeman, 2009). These early studies suggest that joint attention, joint engagement, and play should all be targets of intervention.

Many RCTs have tested the effectiveness of JASPER in improving early social communication skills. In a clinic-based setting, it was found to significantly increase children's initiations of and responses to joint attention. In addition, more flexible and symbolically complex play was shown from the intervention groups (Kasari et al., 2006). Two follow-up studies were conducted 1 and 5 years later and it was found that assignment into either treatment group was predictive of higher expressive language and vocabulary (Kasari, Paparella, Freeman, & Jahromi, 2008; Kasari, Gulsrud, Freeman, Paparella, & Hellemann, 2012).

This intervention approach was also tested in a pilot deployment trial where special education teachers were trained to carry out the intervention within their classrooms. Children, 36–72 months of age were recruited for the study (Wong, 2013). Treatment effects were observed for joint engagement, joint attention initiations and responses, as well as symbolic play.

Moving into more natural contexts, three more RCTs were conducted in which parents were trained to implement the intervention (Kasari, Gulsrud, Wong, Kwon, & Locke, 2010; Kasari, Lawton, et al., 2014; Kasari, Gulsrud, Paparella, Hellemann, & Berry, 2015). In each of these trials, children were found to increase significantly in their time spent jointly engaged with their caregivers as well as showing increases in diversity of types of play (except for the Kasari, Lawton, and colleagues [2014] trial, which found no increase in functional play type but improvements in symbolic play). Responsiveness to joint attention also showed positive gains; two trials (Kasari, Lawton, et al., 2014; Kasari et al., 2015) found increases in child-initiated joint attention.

JASPER was tested further in a number of deployment trials in which teachers in preschool classrooms implemented the intervention during their daily programs. (Lawton & Kasari, 2012). The children in the JASPER intervention group used significantly more joint attention and spent significantly more time jointly engaged. This teacher-implemented model was further tested and found comparable results (Chang, Shire, Shih, Gelfand, & Kasari, 2016; Kaale, Smith, & Sponheim, 2012). Children in the treatment group spent significantly more time in child-initiated joint engagement and had significantly greater initiations of joint attention, behavior regulation skills, and functional play. Significant differences on mental age and receptive language were found, but not on expressive language (Chang et al., 2016). These effects were found to maintain at the follow-up 12 months later in one trial (Kaale, Fagerland, Martinsen, & Smith, 2014).

Most recently, a 10-week RCT was conducted in early intervention programs in low resource neighborhoods with all intervention sessions carried out by teaching assistants (Shire et al., 2016). The teaching assistants underwent an initial in-person training program that was followed by remote support and one in-person booster session. Significant treatment effects that were maintained at follow-up were found for joint engagement, joint attention, and functional play.

A blended intervention of JASPER and EMT (JASP+EMT) was evaluated, combining elements of the two interventions into one comprehensive package (Kasari, Kaiser, et al., 2014). Children 5–8 years old were recruited for the study; all had at least 2 years of early interventions prior to entry and possessed fewer than 20 spontaneous words. The primary contrast was between children who received a speech-generating device (SGD) plus the behavioral intervention and those who received only the behavioral intervention. Those children who received an SGD were found to have significantly better spoken-language outcomes in terms of total spontaneous communication as well as commenting (i.e., joint attention) language. Overall, of the targeted social communication interventions, JASPER has been tested with the most children with ASD (580) across nine trials and with fairly consistent findings for social communication, play, and engagement outcomes.

Joint Attention Mediated Learning (JAML)   JAML has three primary intervention targets, the first is Focusing on Faces; this lesson is meant to help the children make more frequent looks toward caregivers' faces. The next step is referred to as Turn-Taking; the focus of these lessons are encouraging reciprocal play between the caregiver and the child. The last step, Joint Attention, is meant to combine the two prior lessons and help the child to engage in a triadic interaction between the object, the caregiver, and him- or herself. These skills are each taught in an ordered sequence until certain criteria are met, such as the demonstration of the skills across consecutive sessions (Schertz, Odom, Baggett, & Sideris, 2013). In one trial, mastery ranged from 2 to 6 months for all targets (Schertz & Odom, 2007).

JAML has been tested in single-case designs where positive results were seen on social communication targets (Schertz & Odom, 2007). Recently, Schertz, Odom, Baggett, and Sideris (2013) applied an RCT of parent-mediated JAML in a sample of toddlers. The primary outcome measure was the Precursors of Joint Attention Measure, which is an observational measure of the specific intervention targets (Focusing on Faces, Turn-Taking, Responding to Joint Attention, Initiating Joint Attention) that is coded from a parent–child interaction. It was developed specifically for the JAML intervention. Children were found to improve significantly on following faces and responding to joint attention scores coded from the observational measure but not the turn-taking or initiating joint attention scores. Group differences in favor of the JAML group were also found for receptive language as well as adaptive communication.

Pivotal Response Treatment (PRT)   PRT is an intervention that developed directly from more structured ABA approaches. It sought to remedy three main limitations of behavioral interventions, namely, to increase the speed with which target skills are acquired, help generalize those gains, and reduce disruptive and escape behaviors during teaching trials (Mohammadzaheri, Koegel, Rezaee, & Rafiee, 2014). PRT has been implemented by a number of different groups including clinicians (Schreibman & Stahmer, 2014), parents (Hardan et al., 2015), and teachers (Stahmer, Suhrheinrich, Reed, Bolduc, & Schreibman, 2010), typically in the context of one-to-one interactions between a child and adult.

One strategy used in PRT is establishing a direct relationship between the reinforcer and response (verbally requesting to open a jar to get the reward inside), which led to more rapid acquisition target skills (Koegel & Williams, 1980). Next, skills are taught within the context of child-preferred activities, which was found to be negatively correlated with social avoidant behaviors; that is, the children exhibited less escape and problem behaviors in a motivating context (Koegel, Dyer, & Bell, 1987). Last, teaching self-management, defined as the discrimination and self-initiating of appropriate social behavior, improved social skills and reduced disruptive behaviors (Koegel, Koegel, Harrower, & Carter, 1999).

Emerging from these foundational studies, PRT developed as a comprehensive treatment package that has been used to intervene on a number of different social communication targets. For example, some targets include imitative verbal language, speech intelligibility, and disruptive behaviors (Koegel, O'Dell, & Koegel, 1987; Koegel, Koegel & Surratt, 1992). These studies have either included primarily verbal participants or have been single-case designs.

To date there have been three RCTs of PRT targeting social communication skills in children with complex communication needs (Hardan et al., 2015; Mohammadzaheri et al., 2014; Schreibman & Stahmer, 2014). In the first trial (Schreibman & Stahmer, 2014), PRT was compared to PECS in a sample of preschool-age children. The goal of PRT in this intervention trial was to facilitate the development of functional verbal communication. No treatment differences were found in expressive language. However, there was a main effect of time with children in both conditions improving significantly over the course of the 6-month intervention. The largest increases were seen in parent-reported language use.

The second study (Mohammadzaheri et al., 2014) was an intervention trial that compared PRT to a structured ABA approach with older children (6–11 years old). The children had an average mean length of utterance of around 2.75, meaning that they were verbal yet still exhibited language delays. The primary differences between the PRT and the structured ABA intervention arms were that 1) the materials used in the PRT intervention were chosen by the child, 2) maintenance trials were interspersed with teaching trials in the PRT condition, 3) in the ABA group, reinforcers were not contingent to the target of the trials (although they were preferred objects and edibles), and 4) all responses were reinforced in the PRT group regardless of whether they were correct. The primary outcome was mean length of utterance but it is unclear from the reported results whether the PRT group made greater gains than the structured ABA approach. Both groups improved but it was not stated whether the difference between the groups at exit was statistically significant.

The last RCT of PRT was carried out by Hardan and colleagues (2015). Children with ASD, 24–60 months old, were recruited and randomized to a group PRT intervention or a psychoeducational control. Overall, it was found that children's frequency of utterances was significantly greater in the group PRT condition. This effect seems to be driven by imitative and nonverbally prompted utterances.

Reciprocal Imitation Training (RIT)   Multiple single-case designs were published in the development of RIT and later Project ImPACT (Improving Parents as Communication Teachers). Early research in typically developing children has shown that the ability to imitate emerges early in development (Meltzoff & Moore, 1977) and is important to a number of key social communication outcomes (Carpenter, Nagell, Tomasello, Butterworth, & Moore, 1998). In addition, imitation has been shown to be significantly impaired in children with ASD (Sigman & Ungerer, 1984), and also predictive of social communication development (Toth, Munson, Meltzoff, & Dawson, 2006). As a result, imitation has been an important target of intervention; RIT is one such intervention that has specifically targeted imitation. RIT consists of one-to-one lessons between a child and therapist. The sessions are centered around pairs of identical toys; the therapist imitates all of the child's behaviors with the toys as well as specific attempts at communication. If the child does not engage in any behaviors that can be imitated, the adult first models language and play acts and then physically prompts the child to imitate. The actions that the adult models include motor activities as well as play (Ingersoll, 2010).

A pilot RCT of RIT was conducted with children age 27–47 months old (Ingersoll, 2010). Children were randomized to either a 10-week RIT intervention that took place in a clinic setting or community-based treatment as usual. The RIT group was found to make significant improvements over the control group on both object and gestural communication. This was true of both spontaneous and elicited imitation. Effects were also seen in initiating joint attention and broad social and emotional development as reported by parents (Ingersoll, 2010; Ingersoll, 2012). However, imitation was not found to mediate these effects.

The next iteration of this intervention is Project ImPACT. It targets four social communication goals: 1) social engagement, 2) language, 3) imitation, and 4) play (Stadnick, Stahmer & Brookman-Frazee, 2015). Although single-case design and quasi-experimental studies have reported promising results, RCTs have yet to be reported (Ingersoll & Wainer, 2013; Stadnick et al., 2015).

Developmental Social-Pragmatic Interventions

Floortime   The Developmental, Individual-difference, Relationship-based (DIR) therapy, also known as Floortime, falls under the broader umbrella of developmental social-pragmatic interventions. Developmental social-pragmatic interventions are based on the idea that children should be taught functional skills in a developmentally appropriate order and that skills should not be targeted in isolation but rather in a broader social context (Casenhiser, Shanker, & Stieben, 2011). Floortime was developed based on the theory that there are six primary developmental stages, and that when one of these stages is interrupted developmental delays occur (refer to Greenspan, 1992). To date, these developmental stages have not been studied systematically. Floortime sessions consist of active play between the parent and child with feedback provided by an interventionist. The interventionist points out salient communicative moments to the parent and helps to interpret children's communicative intent and how to respond appropriately to that communication. The therapist also models the use of these responsive strategies with the child with the goal of increasing engagement and eventually children's initiations of social communication (Casenhiser et al., 2011).

In terms of empirical evidence, a RCT was carried out by Casenhiser and colleagues (2011) comparing a variation of Floortime to a no-treatment control in a sample of children 24–60 months old. They reported a marginally significant difference between the Floortime intervention group and the control on the Child Behavior Rating Scale total score as well as initiating joint attention. No group differences were found on standardized language assessments. This study was a preliminary analysis of an ongoing intervention trial introducing the potential for bias.

Another RCT testing the effectiveness of a variation of Floortime was conducted by Pajareya and Nopmaneejumruslers (2011). Children 2–6 years old were assigned to either a parent education group based on Floortime principles or a control group that received treatment as usual consisting of behaviorally based community interventions. Statistically significant differences in favor of the intervention group were found across measures of children's emotion regulation and autism severity.

Lastly, a parent-mediated Floortime-based intervention known as the Play and Language for Autistic Youngsters project was tested in a large sample of children (Solomon, Van Egeren, Mahoney, Huber, & Zimmerman, 2014). The intervention was long term, consisting of one 3-hour in-home consultation session per month for 12 months. These consultation sessions consisted of modeling, coaching, and video feedback. Treatment effects were found in diagnostic classification as measured by the Autism Diagnostic Observation Schedule-Generic as well as the quality of parent–child interactions in favor of the treatment group. No treatment effects were found on children's language.

Focused Playtime Intervention (FPI)   FPI is a family-centered, parent-mediated intervention that has four primary intervention goals: 1) to address the family's informational needs, 2) to use the family's home environment as the context for the intervention, 3) to have parents be active participants in the intervention, and 4) to encourage self-evaluation by caregivers (Siller, Hutman, & Sigman, 2013). The intervention is broadly based on the importance of responsive interactions and maternal synchronization on children's expressive language development (Baker, Messinger, Lyons, & Grantz, 2010; McDuffie & Yoder, 2010; Siller & Sigman, 2002). FPI sessions take place within the family's home and are centered around a standardized, developmentally appropriate set of toys. The first portion of the intervention session consists of active play between the child, parent, and therapist with opportunities for the parent to practice as well as observe the clinician's use of intervention strategies. The second half of the intervention consists of dyadic lessons on intervention strategies as well as video feedback from the play sessions (Siller et al., 2013).

FPI has been tested in the context of two RCTs for children with ASD. The first study compared the effects of FPI to a psychoeducational control (Siller et al., 2013). The outcomes of interest were ratings of responsive communication strategies from parents as well as children's engagement. No effect of group assignment was found, but gains in children's expressive language within the treatment group were moderated by baseline language, with children with low levels of expressive language benefiting most from treatment.

Another RCT was conducted with a sample of toddlers who were at high risk for ASD (Kasari, Siller, et al., 2014). The intervention group made significant improvements on parental responsiveness over the control, but these gains were not maintained at the follow-up period. Language and joint attention increased for both groups but there was no effect of treatment.

Hanen's More Than Words   Hanen's More Than Words Program is an intervention targeting communication development in children with ASD originally developed by Sussman (1999). It focuses on training parents in a number of critical areas such as 1) structuring everyday routines so that they are developmentally appropriate, 2) providing opportunities for children to communicate, and 3) appropriately responding to children's communication bids (Carter et al., 2011). The program consists of group sessions provided by a trained clinician providing a basis in the curricular content. Parents also receive supported one-to-one sessions with their child in the context of home and play routines. Last, video feedback on the use of their strategies during the sessions with their children was provided (Carter et al., 2011).

Hanen's More Than Words is based firmly in a social interactionist framework emphasizing the importance of mutual participation in social interactions between caregiver and children to develop language (Mahoney & Perales, 2003). Particularly important in the intervention procedures are a focus on the development of joint attention and pragmatic communication (Prizant & Meyer, 1993). The intervention was first tested in a series of case studies and a quasi-experimental study where it was found that parents increased in their responsiveness to children's communication and children showed increased vocabulary (Girolametto, Sussman, & Weitzman, 2007; McConachie, Randle, Hammal, & Le Couteur, 2005). Lastly, an RCT was conducted comparing Hanen's More Than Words to a no-treatment control (Carter et al., 2011). The primary outcome of parental responsivity did not reach statistical significance, nor did children's communication outcomes. Children with low object use at entry were found to improve on communicative gestures and intentional communication.

Preschool Autism Communication Trial   The Preschool Autism Communication Trial is a social communication intervention that targets parent's communication and responses to their children. This intervention is based on foundational studies that found that, as a consequence of delayed joint attention development (Mundy, Sigman, Ungerer & Sherman, 1986) as well as a lack of social pragmatic skills (Prizant & Wetherby, 1987), children with autism often fail to develop meaningful communication interactions with their parents. However, parents who were responsive to children's subtle communication attempts led to increased child-initiated communication as well as language (Jocelyn, Casiro, Beattie, Bow, & Kneisz, 1998). Parents start each session receiving introductory material about specific targets for the session. They then play with their child using developmentally appropriate toys, and the interaction is recorded. The parents are then given video feedback from the interventionist who identifies salient learning opportunities within the video and works on increasing parents' understanding of their child's communicative bids and what they can do to be receptive to those bids (Green et al., 2010).

In order to test these theories further, Aldred, Green, and Adams (2004) carried out a long-term (1-year) intervention trial. The goal of the intervention was to teach parents to replace adult-directed prompts with more responsive communication, a strategy meant to increase children's initiations and social involvement. Effects were found for children's total number of communicative acts as well as expressive language and quality of reciprocal social interactions.

The Preschool Autism Communication Trial was explored further in a large scale RCT of children with ASD who were 2–5 years old (Green et al., 2010). The study followed the same intervention procedures as the pilot trial. There was a nonsignificant effect on the primary outcome, autism severity, and on children's language. There were significant differences found in favor of the Preschool Autism Communication Trial group in terms of child communication initiations and to a lesser degree shared attention. Parent-rated measures of social communication and language showed significant effects in favor of the Preschool Autism Communication Trial group. At follow-up 6 years later, children in the intervention group saw decreased autism severity as well as more communicative initiations, but no group effects on language were seen (Pickles et al., 2016).

A mediation analysis evaluated both the direct and indirect effects of parents' behaviors on children's scores on the Autism Diagnostic Observation Schedule-Generic (Pickles et al., 2015). It was found that the scores were significantly mediated by parental synchrony as well as children's total initiations. This suggests that targeting parental behaviors through intervention is effective in improving core deficits of children with ASD.

The Preschool Autism Communication Trial intervention was further evaluated in a deployment trial in two countries: Pakistan and India. This iteration is referred to as PASS (Parent mediated intervention for Autism Spectrum Disorders in South Asia) and followed the same intervention principles as the original Preschool Autism Communication Trial (Rahman et al., 2015). As with the original trials, parents in the PASS group improved the quality of their interactions and children showed improved communication.

Social Communication, Emotional Regulation, and Transactional Support (SCERTS®)

The Social Communication, Emotional Regulation, and Transactional Support (SCERTS®) intervention model, like the Early Start Denver Model, is a multidisciplinary intervention model that is targeted at developing communication and broad socioemotional abilities (Prizant, Wetherby, Rubin, & Laurent, 2003). SCERTS focuses on targeting social communication in natural contexts and daily activities using transactional supports (Prizant, Wetherby, Rubin, Laurent, & Rydell, 2006). The SCERTS model is implemented in a classroom setting with a team of trained therapists in conjunction with the children's parents where they are taught through in-vivo modeling and explanation of the strategies used by the therapists (Prizant et al., 2006).

One quasi experimental trial evaluated the effectiveness of some components of the SCERTS curriculum in conjunction with a parent-mediated intervention called the Early Social Interaction (ESI) Project. ESI was developed based on seven primary recommendations that were made by the National Research Council (2001). These recommendations were that intervention should: 1) begin at the earliest signs of ASD, 2) take place for 5 hours per day, 5 days per week, 3) include systematic repetition of teaching trials, 4) include individualized adult attention, 5) include parent training, 6) include ongoing assessment and program evaluation, and 7) focus on key functional intervention targets such as social communication.

ESI was first tested using a quasi-experimental design (Wetherby & Woods, 2006). The intervention demonstrated positive effects on child social communication outcomes and was followed by an RCT across 2 sites comparing individual-to-group ESI. The individual ESI condition noted greater improvements over group ESI across children's broad social communication skills, adaptive functioning, as well as receptive language (Wetherby et al., 2014).

Table 11.2.   Brief summary of intervention components

Intervention	Context	Interventionist	Intervention components
Early Achievements	Classroom	Clinician/teacher	Developing interpersonal synchrony, social communication, and cognitive development through environmental supports and optimizing the sequence of instruction in a classroom context
Early Start Denver Model	Clinic and home	Clinicians and parents	Utilizing an interdisciplinary perspective; developing imitation, communication, and functional object use through child and parent engagement
Enhanced milieu teaching	Clinic and home	Clinicians and parents	Environmental arrangement, responsive interactions, language modeling, and milieu teaching (prompting for communication)
SCERTS	Classroom	Teacher	Transactional supports, environmental arrangement, accommodations, and modeling appropriate communicative skills in natural contexts
Floortime/DIR	Home	Parents and clinicians	Following children's attentional focus, taking advantage of salient communicative moments, interpreting children's communicative intent, and responding appropriately
Focused playtime	Home	Parents	Addressing families' informational needs, parental active participation, self-evaluation by caregivers, responsive communication, and developmentally appropriate play
More than Words	Home and Clinic	Parents and clinicians	Structuring everyday routines, providing natural communication opportunities, and responding to children's communication
Joint attention mediated learning	Clinic and home	Clinicians and parents	Focusing on faces, turn taking, and joint attention through structured parent–child interactions

Table 11.2.   *(continued)*

Intervention	Context	Interventionist	Intervention components
JASPER	Clinic, home, classroom	Clinicians, parents, and teachers	Environmental arrangement, appropriate levels of prompting, imitation and modeling of language using nondirective speech, developmentally targeted play, and communication targets
PACT	Clinic and home	Clinicians and parents	Video feedback, identifying salient communicative opportunities, and responding to children's communication
Pivotal Response Treatment	Clinic, home, and school	Clinicians and parents	Use of contingent reinforcers, teaching within preferred activities, and teaching self-management and initiations of appropriate communication
Reciprocal imitation training	Clinic	Clinicians	Modeling appropriate motor and play imitation and errorless learning through prompting

Key: SCERTS®, Social Communication Emotion Regulation, and Transactional Support®; Floortime/DIR, Developmental Individual-difference Relationship-based Floortime model; JASPER, Joint Attention Symbolic Play Engagement, and Regulation; PACT, Preschool Autism Communication Trial.

METHODOLOGICAL QUALITY OF THE INCLUDED TRIALS

A full summary of the risk of bias assessment can be found in Table 11.3. Important to note, out of the 32 articles that were reviewed, only four had low risk for bias across all of the criteria (Hardan et al., 2015; Kasari et al., 2010; Kasari, Lawton, et al., 2014; Shire et al., 2016). Although some issues may be out of the control of the researchers (e.g., some types of attrition), further steps must be taken to minimize potential bias in those domains that can be controlled such as blinding outcomes, proper randomization, and specifying primary and secondary outcomes a priori. By doing this, more confidence can be placed in the results generated by RCTs.

NATURALISTIC INTERVENTIONS ADDRESSING SOCIAL COMMUNICATION

The summary of articles provided previously represents a significant body of research conducted to evaluate the effects of interventions targeting social communicative delays in children with little to no language. As with the evaluation of the methodological quality of the included studies, the various interventions had mixed effects on children's social communication outcomes. Some showed positive effects on both proximal and distal outcomes whereas others had null findings across both. Indeed, with the limited findings of many of the trials it becomes critically important to weigh the cost and benefit of the interventions provided to children with little to no speech. As these interventions packages represent a significant investment of time and resources, it is important to be confident that they will benefit the children they serve.

Table 11.3. Summary of interventions targeting social communication in children with autism spectrum disorder (ASD) with complex communication needs.

Authors	Intervention	Approach	Age (months)	N=	Proximal SC outcome	Distal SC outcome	Primary measure(s)	Proximal effect (Cohen's d)	Distal effect (Cohen's d)
Landa et al., 2011	EA	NDBI	21-33	50	Imitation	IJA, play and language	CSBS-DP, MSEL	Imitation- 0.29	NS
Kaiser & Roberts, 2013	EMT	NDBI	30-54	77	Expressive language (observation)	Expressive and receptive language (standardized)	EVT, MCDI, NLS, PPVT	FU 6 and 12 month: MLU: .57, .6 NDW: .62, .46 (trained activity)	NS
Roberts & Kaiser, 2015	EMT	NDBI	24-42	97	Expressive and receptive language	Expressive and receptive vocabulary	PCX, PLS	Receptive language: d=.27, Expressive language: NS	Receptive vocab: .35, Expressive vocab: .38
Yoder & Stone, 2006	EMT	NDBI	18-60	36	Turn taking	Expressive language	ESCS, PCX	Turn taking: d , .82	Language: PECS: .5
Dawson et al., 2010	ESDM	NDBI	18-30	48	Communication and language	–	MSEL, VABS	MSEL: .62; VABS: .79	–
Rogers et al., 2012	ESDM	NDBI	14-24	98	Social and cognitive development	Expressive and receptive language	MCDI, MSEL, VABS	NS	NS
Wetherby et al., 2014	ESI/SCERTS	DSP	16-20	82	Social communication development and language	Adaptive behaviors and autism symptomology	ADOS, CSBS, MSEL, VABS	CSBS-Social Communication Hedge's g , .48, Receptive language: .58	ADOS SA Hedge's g , .15, VABS .59-68
Casenhiser, Shanker, and Stieben (2011)	Floortime	DSP	24-60	51	JA and JE	Language	CASL, CBRS, PLS	Att: .69, Inv: .87, Comp: .51, IJA: 1.02; Enj: .63	NS
Pajareya and Nopmaneejumruslers, 2011	Floortime	DSP	24-72	32	Emotion regulation and autism symptomology	–	CARS, FEAS, FEDQ	FEAS: d , .77, FEDQ: .9, CARS: .5	***

268

(continued)

Study	Intervention	Type	Age (months)	N	Social interaction / play outcome	ASD symptomology and language	Measures	Effect sizes	ADOS-g odds ratio
Solomon et al., 2014	Floortime	DSP	32–71	128	Quality of interactions and social development	ASD symptomology and language	ADOS-g, CBRS, FEAS, MBRS, MCDI, MSEL	MBRS: .62, CBRS: .54, FEAS: .48,	ADOS-g odds ratio: 2.39, MSEL: *NS*, MCDI: *NS*
Kasari, Siller, et al., 2014	FPI	DSP	15–31	66	IJA, RJA	Expressive and receptive language	ESCS, MSEL, PCX	*NS*	*NS*
Siller, Hutman, & Sigman, 2013	FPI	DSP	32–82	70	Expressive language	—	ESCS, MSEL	Expressive language: *NS* (Baseline expressive language moderates)	—
Carter et al., 2011	MTW	DSP	15–25	62	Intentional communication and gestures	—	ESCS, PCX, MSEL, VABS	All: *NS* (object use moderates)	—
Schertz, Odom, Baggett, and Sideris (2013)	JAML	NDBI	<30	23	JA	Communication	PJAM, MSEL, VABS	FF: 1.24, RJA: 1.39	MSEL Receptive: .34, VABS Communication: .59
Chang, Shire, Shih, Gelfand, and Kasari (2016)	JASPER	NDBI	36–60	66	JE, IJA, IBR, and play	Expressive and receptive language	ESCS, MSEL, SPA, TCX	Cohen's F: JE: .32, IJA: .32, IBR: .33, Functional Play: .31	Receptive language: *NG*, Expressive language: *NS*
Kaale, Smith, and Sponheim (2012)	JASPER	NDBI	24–60	61	JA and JE	JA (standardized)	ESCS, PCX, TCX	JE (MCX): .67, JA (TCX): .44	*NS*
Kasari, Freeman, and Paparella, (2006)/ Kasari, Paparella, Freeman, and Jahromi (2008)	JASPER	NDBI	36–48	58	IJA and JE	Language	ESCS, PCX, SPA	IJA: 1.01, JE: .83	.59
Kasari, Gulsrud, Wong, Kwon, and Locke (2010)	JASPER	NDBI	21–36	42	JA and JE	—	PCX	RJA: .74, functional play: .86, JE: .87	—

Table 11.3. *(continued)*

Authors	Intervention	Approach	Age (months)	N=	Proximal SC outcome	Distal SC outcome	Primary measure(s)	Proximal effect (Cohen's d)	Distal effect (Cohen's d)
Kasari, Kaiser, et al., 2014	JASPER	NDBI	60-96	61	Spontaneous language	–	NLS	TSCU: .62, TDWR: .29, TCOM: .44	–
Kasari, Lawton, et al., 2014	JASPER	NDBI	24-60	112	IJA, JE, and play	–	PCX	JE: .21, IJA: .14, Play: .30	–
Kasari, Gulsrud, Paparella, Hellemann, and Berry, 2015	JASPER	NDBI	22-36	86	JE	JA and play	PCX	JE (Cohen's f): .69	IJA: NS, Functional play: (Cohen's f) .06
Lawton & Kasari, 2012	JASPER	NDBI	36-60	16	JA and JE	JA (Standardized)	Class observation, ESCS, TCX	Class observation: JA: 1.85, TCX: SJE: 1.24, Object engagement: 1.41	NS
Shire et al., 2016	JASPER	NDBI	24-36	113	JE, JA, play (observation)	JA, IBR, play (standardized), CGI	SPACE, CGI, TCX	JE: .68, IJA: .24, IBR: .41, IJA Language: .34-.45, Functional play: .82	IJA (standardized): .39, CGI: .37-.48
Wong, 2013	JASPER	NDBI	36-72	33	JE, JA, play	JA and play (standardized)	Class observation, ESCS, SPA	JE: .41, RJA: .43, IJA: .21, Play: .51	RJA: 23
Aldred et al., 2004	PACT	DSP	29-60	28	Reciprocal interactions	Communication and language	ADOS, MCDI VABS	ADOS RSI: NG	MCDI comprehension: NS, Expressive:NG, VABS: NS

Study	Model	Age range	N	Outcome	Domain	Measures	Result 1	Result 2
Green et al., 2010	PACT	24–60	152	Child initiations and shared attention	Language	MCDI, PCX, PLS	Initiations: 48; Shared Attention, .32	NS
Rahman et al., 2015	PACT	24–108	65	Initiations and shared attention	Language and communication	PCX, VABS, CSBS, MCDI	Initiations: .99; SA: (-.7)	NS
Hardan et al., 2014	PRT	24–72	53	Frequency of verbal utterances	Language	MCDI, PCX, VABS	Frequency of utterances: .42	VABS Communication: .34, MCDI: NS
Mohammadzaheri. et al., 2014	PRT	60–121	30	MLU	Communication	CCC, Picture Labeling Task	Reported analysis unclear	Reported analysis unclear
Schreibman & Stahmer, 2014	PRT	20–48	39	Functional verbal language	–	EOWPVT, MSEL, MCDI	NS	–
Ingersoll, 2010	RIT	27–47	22	Imitation (elicited and spontaneous)	JA	ESCS, MIS	Elicited: .92; Spontaneous: 1.2	IJA: .97

Key: PACT, Pre-school Autism Communication Trial; DSP, developmental social-pragmatic model; ADOS, Autism Diagnostic Observation Scale; MCDI, MacArthur-Bates Communicative Development Inventories; VABS, Vineland Adaptive Behavior Scales; RSI, reciprocal social interactions; NS, non-significant; MTW, More Than Words; ESCS, Early Social Communication Scales; PCX, parent-child interaction; MSEL, Mullen Scales of Early Learning; JA, joint attention; JE, joint engagement; CASL, Comprehensive Assessment of Spoken Language; CBRS, Child Behavior Rating Scale; PLS, Preschool Language Scales; Att, attention to activity; Inv, involvement; Comp, compliance; IJA, initiating joint attention; Enj, enjoyment of interaction; JASPER, Joint Attention Symbolic Play Engagement and Regulation; NDBI, Naturalistic Developmental Behavioral Intervention; IBR, initiating behavior request; SPA, structured play assessment; TCX, teacher-child interaction; ESDM, Early Start Denver Model; PRT, Pivotal Response Treatment; RIT, reciprocal imitation training; MIS, Motor Imitation Scale; EMT, Enhanced Milieu Teaching; EVT, Expressive Vocabulary Test; NLS, natural language sample; PPVT, Peabody Picture Vocabulary Test; FU, follow-up; MLU, mean length of utterance; NDW, number of different word roots; TSCU, total social communicative utterances; TDWR, total different word roots; TCOM, total comments; FPI, Focused Playtime Intervention; EA, early achievements; CSBS DPTM, Communication and Symbolic Behavior Scales Developmental Profile™; SJE, supported joint engagement; CCC, Child Communication Checklist; CARS, Childhood Autism Rating Scale; Functional Emotional Assessment Scale; FEDQ, Functional Emotional Developmental Questionnaire; JAML, Joint Attention Mediated Learning; PJAM, Precursors of Joint Attention Measure; EOWPVT, Expressive One-Word Picture Vocabulary Test; CGI, clinical global impression; SPACE, Short Play and Communication Evaluation; ADOS-g, Autism Diagnostic Observation Schedule-generic; ESI, early social interactions; SCERTS®, Social-Communication, Emotional Regulation, and Transactional Support®; ADOS-SA, Standardized Autism Diagnostic Observation Schedule-Social Affective; PECS, Picture Exchange Communication System.

271

As can be seen in Table 11.1, many of the trials found no group differences on the primary outcomes (e.g., More Than Words, the Early Start Denver Model parent-mediated intervention, the Focused Playtime intervention, Pivotal Response Treatment, EMT). Others in Table 11.1 showed mixed or minimal effects. Ones with consistent and large effects, along with replications, include the Pre-school Autism Communication Trial and JASPER. What is needed in future studies is a better understanding of why some (but perhaps not other) interventions provide benefit. To this end, studies of the effective components of interventions must be better understood. One promising treatment mechanism was the adaptation of an intervention (JASPER; Kasari, Kaiser, et al., 2014) to be supplemented by access to an SGD. With the apparent success of this approach it would be valuable to consider how other effective interventions for children with complex communication needs could be augmented with the inclusion of an SGD or other AAC systems. The relative simplicity, cost efficiency, and ubiquity of these devices makes them a potentially powerful tool to intervene in natural contexts such as home and school. Future research is needed to address the effectiveness of this simple adaptation.

A WORD OF CAUTION

A brief search of several popular research databases (e.g., ERIC, psycINFO, Google Scholar) found more than 50 reviews of intervention trials for young children with ASD. This is significantly greater than the number of rigorously tested RCTs targeting social communication discussed in this chapter. Although synthesizing current data is important, researchers should strive to test innovative treatments and replicate others with promise using scientifically rigorous methodologies. In this way, effective interventions can be disseminated and utilized by clinicians, teachers, and parents—thereby putting more children with ASD on positive developmental courses.

CONCLUSION

This review discussed and evaluated a wide range of intervention approaches and philosophies, all of which to some degree took place in natural contexts. These interventions targeted many different types of social skills and broad developmental goals including joint attention, engagement, imitation, and spoken language. Many methodological limitations were found in the included studies; future research should pay particular care to carry out studies that are methodologically rigorous so that conclusions can be confidently drawn from the outcomes of intervention trials. Overall, a number of interventions were found to be successful in targeting social communication in children with delayed language. A majority of these trials targeted skills that were proximal to the intervention and so there should be a particular focus in future research on whether these proximal outcomes lead to positive downstream effects including children's quality of life, adaptive functioning, and educational attainment.

REFERENCES

Adamson, L. B., Deckner, D. F., & Bakeman, R. (2009). Early interests and joint engagement in typical development, autism, and Down syndrome. *Journal of Autism and Developmental Disorders, 40*(6), 665–676. doi:10.1007/s10803-009-0914-1

Aldred, C., Green, J., & Adams, C. (2004). A new social communication intervention for children with autism: Pilot randomised controlled treatment study suggesting effectiveness. *Journal of Child Psychology and Psychiatry, 45*(8), 1420–1430. doi:10.1111/j.1469-7610.2004.00338.x

Baker, J. K., Messinger, D. S., Lyons, K. K., & Grantz, C. J. (2010). A pilot study of maternal sensitivity in the context of emergent autism. *Journal of Autism and Developmental Disorders, 40*(8), 988–999.

Baron-Cohen, S., Lombardo, M., & Tager-Flusberg, H. (Eds.). (2013). *Understanding other minds: Perspectives from developmental social neuroscience.* Oxford, England: Oxford University Press.

Carpenter, M., Nagell, K., Tomasello, M., Butterworth, G., & Moore, C. (1998). Social cognition, joint attention, and communicative competence from 9 to 15 months of age. *Monographs of the Society for Research in Child Development, 63*(4), i–174. doi:10.2307/1166214

Carter, A. S., Messinger, D. S., Stone, W. L., Celimli, S., Nahmias, A. S., & Yoder, P. (2011). A randomized controlled trial of Hanen's 'More Than Words' in toddlers with early autism symptoms. *Journal of Child Psychology and Psychiatry, 52*(7), 741–752.

Casenhiser, D. M., Shanker, S. G., & Stieben, J. (2011). Learning through interaction in children with autism: Preliminary data from a social-communication-based intervention. *Autism, 17*(2), 220–241. https://doi.org/10.1177/1362361311422052

Chang, Y., Shire, S. Y., Shih, W., Gelfand, C., & Kasari, C. (2016). Preschool deployment of evidence-based social communication intervention: JASPER in the classroom. *Journal of Autism and Developmental Disorders, 46*(6), 2211–2223. doi:10.1007/s10803-016-2752-2

Charman, T., Baron-Cohen, S., Swettenham, J., Baird, G., Drew, A., & Cox, A. (2003). Predicting language outcome in infants with autism and pervasive developmental disorder. *International Journal of Language & Communication Disorders, 38*(3), 265–285. doi:10.1080/136820310000104830

Cooper, J. O, Heron, T. E, & Heward W. L. (1987). *Applied behavior analysis.* New York, NY: Macmillan.

Dawson, G., Rogers, S., Munson, J., Smith, M., Winter, J., Greenson, . . . J., Varley, J. (2010). Randomized, controlled trial of an intervention for toddlers with autism: The Early Start Denver Model. *Pediatrics, 125*(1). doi:10.1542/peds.2009-0958

Dawson, G., Toth, K., Abbott, R., Osterling, J., Munson, J., Estes, A., & Liaw, J. (2004). Early social attention impairments in autism: Social orienting, joint attention, and attention to distress. *Developmental Psychology, 40*(2), 271–283. https://doi.org/10.1037/0012-1649.40.2.271

Eldevik, S., Hastings, R. P., Hughes, J. C., Jahr, E., Eikeseth, S., & Cross, S. (2010). Using participant data to extend the evidence base for intensive behavioral intervention for children with autism. *American Journal on Intellectual and Developmental Disabilities, 115*(5), 381–405. doi:10.1352/1944-7558-115.5.381

Frost, L., & Bondy, A. (2002). *The Picture Exchange Communication System training manual.* New Castle, DE: Pyramid Educational Products.

Girolametto, L., Sussman, F., & Weitzman, E. (2007). Using case study methods to investigate the effects of interactive intervention for children with autism spectrum disorders. *Journal of Communication Disorders, 40*(6), 470–492.

Green, J., Charman, T., Mcconachie, H., Aldred, C., Slonims, V., Howlin, P., . . . Barrett, B. (2010). Parent-mediated communication-focused treatment in children with autism (PACT): A randomised controlled trial. *The Lancet, 375*(9732), 2152–2160. doi:10.1016/s0140-6736(10)60587-9

Greenspan, S. I. (1992). *Infancy and early childhood: The practice of clinical assessment and intervention with emotional and developmental challenges.* International Universities Press, Inc.

Gulsrud, A. C., Hellemann, G., Shire, S., & Kasari, C. (2015). Isolating active ingredients in a parent-mediated social communication intervention for toddlers with autism spectrum disorder. *Journal of Child Psychology and Psychiatry, 57*(5), 606–613. https://doi.org/10.1111/jcpp.12481

Hancock, T. B., & Kaiser, A. P. (2002). The effects of trainer-implemented enhanced milieu teaching on the social communication of children who have autism. *Topics in Early Childhood Special Education, 22*(1), 39–54.

Hardan, A. Y., Gengoux, G. W., Berquist, K. L., Libove, R. A., Ardel, C. M., Phillips, J., Minjarez, M. B., et al. (2015). A randomized controlled trial of pivotal response treatment group for parents of children with autism. *Journal of Child Psychology and Psychiatry, 56*(8), 884–892. doi:10.1111/jcpp.12354

Hart, B., & Risley, T. R. (1975). Incidental teaching of language in the preschool. *Journal of Applied Behavior Analysis, 8*(4), 411–420. https://doi.org/10.1901/jaba.1975.8-411

Hart, B., & Risley, T. R. (1982). *How to use incidental teaching for elaborating language*. Lawrence, KS: H & H Enterprises.

Higgins, J. P. T., & Green, S. (Eds.). (2011). *Cochrane handbook for systematic reviews of interventions* (Version 5.1.0). The Cochrane Collaboration. Available from www.handbook. cochrane.org.

Howlin, P., Goode, S., Hutton, J., & Rutter, M. (2004). Adult outcome for children with autism. *Journal of Child Psychology and Psychiatry, 45*(2), 212–229. doi:10.1111/j.1469-7610.2004.00215.x

Howlin, P., Magiati, I., & Charman, T. (2009). Systematic review of early intensive behavioral interventions for children with autism. *American Journal on Intellectual and Developmental Disabilities, 114*(1), 23. doi:10.1352/2009.114:23;nd41

Ingersoll, B. (2010). Brief report: Pilot randomized controlled trial of reciprocal imitation training for teaching elicited and spontaneous imitation to children with autism. *Journal of Autism and Developmental Disorders, 40*(9), 1154–1160. https://doi.org/10.1007/s10803-010-0966-2

Ingersoll, B. (2012). Brief report: Effect of a focused imitation intervention on social functioning in children with autism. *Journal of Autism and Developmental Disorders, 42*(8), 1768–1773. https://doi.org/10.1007/s10803-011-1423-6

Ingersoll, B., & Wainer, A. (2013). Initial efficacy of Project ImPACT: A parent-mediated social communication intervention for young children with ASD. *Journal of Autism and Developmental Disorders, 43*(12), 2943–2952.

Jocelyn, L. J., Casiro, O. G., Beattie, D., Bow, J., & Kneisz, J. (1998). Treatment of children with autism: A randomized controlled trial to evaluate a caregiver-based intervention program in community daycare centers. *Journal of Developmental and Behavioral Pediatrics, 19*(5), 326–334. doi:10.1097/00004703-199810000-00002

Kaale, A., Fagerland, M. W., Martinsen, E. W., & Smith, L. (2014). Preschool-based social communication treatment for children with autism: 12-month follow-up of a randomized trial. *Journal of the American Academy of Child & Adolescent Psychiatry, 53*(2), 188–198.

Kaale, A., Smith, L., & Sponheim, E. (2012). A randomized controlled trial of preschool-based joint attention intervention for children with autism. *Journal of Child Psychology and Psychiatry, 53*(1), 97–105.

Kaiser, A. P., Hancock, T. B., & Nietfeld, J. P. (2000). The effects of parent-implemented enhanced milieu teaching on the social communication of children who have autism [Special issue]. *Journal of Early Education and Development, 11*(4), 423–446.

Kaiser, A. P., & Roberts, M. Y. (2013). Parent-implemented enhanced milieu teaching with preschool children who have intellectual disabilities. *Journal of Speech, Language, and Hearing Research, 56*(1), 295–309. doi:10.1044/1092-4388(2012/11-0231)

Kaiser, A. P., Ostrosky, M. M., & Alpert, C. L. (1993). Training teachers to use environmental arrangement and milieu teaching with nonvocal preschool children. *Research and Practice for Persons with Severe Disabilities, 18*(3), 188–199. https://doi.org/10.1177/154079699301800305

Kasari, C. (2002). Assessing change in early intervention programs for children with autism. *Journal of Autism and Developmental Disorders, 32*(5), 447–461.

Kasari, C., Freeman, S., & Paparella, T. (2006). Joint attention and symbolic play in young children with autism: A randomized controlled intervention study. *Journal of Child Psychology and Psychiatry, 47*(6), 611–620. doi:10.1111/j.1469-7610.2005.01567.x

Kasari, C., Gulsrud, A., Freeman, S., Paparella, T., & Hellemann, G. (2012). Longitudinal follow-up of children with autism receiving targeted interventions on joint attention and play. *Journal of the American Academy of Child & Adolescent Psychiatry, 51*(5), 487–495.

Kasari, C., Gulsrud, A., Paparella, T., Hellemann, G., & Berry, K. (2015). Randomized comparative efficacy study of parent-mediated interventions for toddlers with autism. *Journal of Consulting and Clinical Psychology, 83*(3), 554–563. doi:10.1037/a0039080

Kasari, C., Gulsrud, A. C., Wong, C., Kwon, S., & Locke, J. (2010). Randomized controlled caregiver mediated joint engagement intervention for toddlers with autism. *Journal of Autism and Developmental Disorders, 40*(9), 1045–1056. doi:10.1007/s10803-010-0955-5.

Kasari, C., Kaiser, A., Goods, K., Nietfeld, J., Mathy, P., Landa, R., . . . Almirall, D. (2014). Communication interventions for minimally verbal children with autism: A Sequential multiple assignment randomized trial. *Journal of the American Academy of Child & Adolescent Psychiatry, 53*(6), 635–646. doi:10.1016/j.jaac.2014.01.019

Kasari, C., Lawton, K., Shih, W., Barker, T. V., Landa, R., Lord, C., . . . Senturk, D. (2014). Caregiver-mediated intervention for low-resourced preschoolers with autism: An RCT. *Pediatrics, 134*(1). doi:10.1542/peds.2013-3229

Kasari, C., Paparella, T., Freeman, S., & Jahromi, L. B. (2008). Language outcome in autism: Randomized comparison of joint attention and play interventions. *Journal of Consulting and Clinical Psychology, 76*(1), 125.

Kasari, C., Siller, M., Huynh, L. N., Shih, W., Swanson, M., Hellemann, G. S., . . . Sugar, C. (2014). Randomized controlled trial of parental responsiveness intervention for toddlers at high risk for autism. *Infant Behavior and Development, 37*(4), 711–721.

Koegel, R. L., Dyer, K., & Bell, L. K. (1987). The influence of child-preferred activities on autistic children's social behavior. *Journal of Applied Behavior Analysis, 20*(3), 243–252. https://doi.org/10.1901/jaba.1987.20-243

Koegel, L. K., Koegel, R. L., Harrower, J. K., & Carter, C. M. (1999). Pivotal Response Intervention I: Overview of approach. *Research and Practice for Persons with Severe Disabilities, 24*(3), 174–185. doi:10.2511/rpsd.24.3.174

Koegel, R. L., Koegel, L. K., & Surratt, A. (1992). Language intervention and disruptive behavior in preschool children with autism. *Journal of Autism and Developmental Disorders, 22*(2), 141–153.

Koegel, R. L., O'Dell, M. C., & Koegel, L. K. (1987). A natural language teaching paradigm for nonverbal autistic children. *Journal of Autism and Developmental Disorders, 17*(2), 187–200. doi:10.1007/bf01495055

Koegel, R. L., & Williams, J. A. (1980). Direct versus indirect response-reinforcer relationships in teaching autistic children. *Journal of Abnormal Child Psychology, 8*(4), 537–547. doi:10.1007/bf00916505

Landa, R. J., Holman, K. C., O'Neill, A. H., & Stuart, E. A. (2011). Intervention targeting development of socially synchronous engagement in toddlers with autism spectrum disorder: A randomized controlled trial. *Journal of Child Psychology and Psychiatry, 52*(1), 13–21.

Lawton, K., & Kasari, C. (2012). Teacher-implemented joint attention intervention: Pilot randomized controlled study for preschoolers with autism. *Journal of Consulting and Clinical Psychology, 80*(4), 687–693. https://doi.org/http://dx.doi.org/10.1037/a0028506

Lenz, A. S. (2013). Calculating effect size in single-case research: A comparison of nonoverlap methods. *Measurement and Evaluation in Counseling and Development, 46*(1), 64–73.

Lovaas, O. I. (1987). Behavioral treatment and normal educational and intellectual functioning in young autistic children. *Journal of Consulting and Clinical Psychology, 55*(1), 3–9. doi:10.1037/0022-006x.55.1.3

Mahoney, G., & Perales, F. (2003). Using relationship-focused intervention to enhance the social-emotional functioning of young children with autism spectrum disorders. *Topics in Early Childhood Special Education, 23*(2), 74–86. https://doi.org/10.1177/02711214030230020301

McConachie, H., Randle, V., Hammal, D., & Le Couteur, A. (2005). A controlled trial of a training course for parents of children with suspected autism spectrum disorder. *The Journal of Pediatrics, 147*(3), 335–340.

McDuffie, A., & Yoder, P. (2010). Types of parent verbal responsiveness that predict language in young children with autism spectrum disorder. *Journal of Speech, Language, and Hearing Research, 53*(4), 1026–1039.

McGee, G. G., Krantz, P. J., Mason, D., & Mcclannahan, L. E. (1983). A modified incidental-teaching procedure for autistic youth: Acquisition and generalization of receptive object labels. *Journal of Applied Behavior Analysis, 16*(3), 329–338. doi:10.1901/jaba.1983.16-329

McGovern, C. W., & Sigman, M. (2005). Continuity and change from early childhood to adolescence in autism. *Journal of Child Psychology and Psychiatry, 46*(4), 401–408. doi:10.1111/j.1469-7610.2004.00361.x

Meltzoff, A., & Moore, M. (1977). Imitation of facial and manual gestures by human neonates. *Science, 198*(4312), 75–78.

Mohammadzaheri, F., Koegel, L. K., Rezaee, M., & Rafiee, S. M. (2014). A randomized clinical trial comparison between pivotal response treatment (PRT) and structured applied behavior analysis (ABA) intervention for children with autism. *Journal of Autism and Developmental Disorders, 44*(11), 2769–2777.

Mundy, P., & Crowson, M. (1997). Joint attention and early social communication: Implications for research on intervention with autism. *Journal of Autism and Developmental disorders, 27*(6), 653–676.

Mundy, P., Sigman, M., & Kasari, C. (1990). A longitudinal study of joint attention and language development in autistic children. *Journal of Autism and Developmental Disorders, 20*(1), 115–128.

Mundy, P., Sigman, M., Ungerer, J., & Sherman, T. (1986). Defining the social deficits of autism: The contribution of non-verbal communication measures. *Journal of Child Psychology and Psychiatry, 27*(5), 657–669. doi:10.1111/j.1469-7610.1986.tb00190.x

Mundy, P., Sullivan, L., & Mastergeorge, A. M. (2009). A parallel and distributed-processing model of joint attention, social cognition and autism. *Autism research, 2*(1), 2–21.

National Research Council. (2001). *Educating children with autism.* Washington, DC: National Academies Press.

Pajareya, K., & Nopmaneejumruslers, K. (2011). A pilot randomized controlled trial of DIR/Floortime™ parent training intervention for pre-school children with autistic spectrum disorders. *Autism, 15*(5), 563–577. doi:10.1177/1362361310386502

Pickles, A., Harris, V., Green, J., Aldred, C., McConachie, H., Slonims, V., . . . Charman, T. (2015). Treatment mechanism in the MRC preschool autism communication trial: implications for study design and parent-focused therapy for children. *Journal of Child Psychology and Psychiatry, 56*(2), 162–170.

Pickles, A., Le Couteur, A., Leadbitter, K., Salomone, E., Cole-Fletcher, R., Tobin, H., . . . Green, J. (2016). Parent-mediated social communication therapy for young children with autism (PACT): Long-term follow-up of a randomised controlled trial. *The Lancet, 388*(10059), 2501–2509.

Prizant, B. M., & Meyer, E. C. (1993). Socioemotional aspects of language and social-communication disorders in young children and their families. *American Journal of Speech-Language Pathology, 2*(3), 56–71.

Prizant, B. M. & Wetherby, A. M. (1987). Communicative intent: A framework for understanding social-communicative behavior in autism. *Journal of the American Academy of Child Psychiatry, 26,* 472–479.

Prizant, B. M., Wetherby, A. M., Rubin, E., & Laurent, A. C. (2003). The SCERTS Model. *Infants & Young Children, 16*(4), 296–316. doi:10.1097/00001163-200310000-00004

Prizant, B. M., Wetherby, A. M., Rubin, E., Laurent, A. C., & Rydell, P. J. (2006). *The SCERTS® Model: A transactional, family-centered approach to enhancing communication and socioemotional abilities of children with autism spectrum disorder.* Baltimore, MD: Paul H. Brookes Publishing Co.

Rahman, A., Divan, G., Hamdani, S. U., Vajartkar, V., Minhas, A., Taylor, C., . . . Patel, V. (2015). Adapting an evidence-based intervention for autism spectrum disorder for scaling up in resource-constrained settings: The development of the PASS intervention in South Asia. *Global Health Action, 8*(1), 27278.

Roberts, M. Y., & Kaiser, A. P. (2015). Early intervention for toddlers with language delays: A randomized controlled trial. *Pediatrics, 135*(4), 686–693. doi:10.1542/peds.2014-2134

Rogers, S. J., Estes, A., Lord, C., Vismara, L., Winter, J., Fitzpatrick, A., . . . Dawson, G. (2012). Effects of a brief Early Start Denver Model (ESDM)–based parent intervention on toddlers at risk for autism spectrum disorders: A randomized controlled trial. *Journal of the American Academy of Child & Adolescent Psychiatry, 51*(10), 1052–1065. doi:10.1016/j.jaac.2012.08.003

Schertz, H. H., & Odom, S. L. (2007). Promoting joint attention in toddlers with autism: A parent-mediated developmental model. *Journal of Autism and Developmental Disorders, 37*(8), 1562–1575. doi:10.1007/s10803-006-0290-z

Schertz, H. H., Odom, S. L., Baggett, K. M., & Sideris, J. H. (2013). Effects of Joint Attention Mediated Learning for toddlers with autism spectrum disorders: An initial randomized controlled study. *Early Childhood Research Quarterly, 28*(2), 249–258. doi:10.1016/j.ecresq.2012.06.006

Schreibman, L., Dawson, G., Stahmer, A. C., Landa, R., Rogers, S. J., McGee, G., . . . Halladay, A. (2015). Naturalistic developmental behavioral interventions: Empirically validated treatments for autism spectrum disorder. *Journal of Autism and Developmental Disorders, 45*(8), 2411–2428. https://doi.org/10.1007/s10803-015-2407-8

Schreibman, L., & Stahmer, A. C. (2014). A randomized trial comparison of the effects of verbal and pictorial naturalistic communication strategies on spoken language for young children with autism. *Journal of Autism and Developmental Disorders, 44*(5), 1244–1251. doi:10.1007/s10803-013-1972-y

Sham, E., & Smith, T. (2014). Publication bias in studies of an applied behavior-analytic intervention: An initial analysis. *Journal of Applied Behavior Analysis, 47*(3), 663–678.

Shire, S. Y., Chang, Y. C., Shih, W., Bracaglia, S., Kodjoe, M., & Kasari, C. (2016). Hybrid implementation model of community-partnered early intervention for toddlers with autism: A randomized trial. *Journal of Child Psychology and Psychiatry.* doi:10.1111/jcpp.12672. [Epub ahead of print]

Sigman, M., & Ungerer, J. A. (1984). Cognitive and language skills in autistic, mentally retarded, and normal children. *Developmental Psychology, 20*(2), 293–302.

Siller, M., Hutman, T., & Sigman, M. (2013). A parent-mediated intervention to increase responsive parental behaviors and child communication in children with ASD: A randomized clinical trial. *Journal of Autism and Developmental Disorders, 43*(3), 540–555.

Siller, M., & Sigman, M. (2002). The behaviors of parents of children with autism predict the subsequent development of their children's communication. *Journal of Autism and Developmental Disorders, 32*(2), 77–89.

Smith, T., & Iadarola, S. (2015). Evidence base update for autism spectrum disorder. *Journal of Clinical Child & Adolescent Psychology, 44*(6), 897–922.

Solomon, R., Van Egeren, L. A., Mahoney, G., Huber, M. S. Q., & Zimmerman, P. (2014). PLAY project home consultation intervention program for young children with autism spectrum disorders: A randomized controlled trial. *Journal of Developmental and Behavioral Pediatrics, 35*(8), 475.

Stadnick, N. A., Stahmer, A., & Brookman-Frazee, L. (2015). Preliminary effectiveness of Project ImPACT: A parent-mediated intervention for children with autism spectrum disorder delivered in a community program. *Journal of Autism and Developmental Disorders, 45*(7), 2092–2104.

Stahmer, A. C., Suhrheinrich, J., Reed, S., Bolduc, C., & Schreibman, L. (2010). Pivotal response teaching in the classroom setting. *Preventing School Failure: Alternative Education for Children and Youth, 54*(4), 265–274.

Sussman, F. (1999). *More Than Words: The Hanen Program for parents of children with autism spectrum disorder,* Toronto, Ontario: The Hanen Centre.

Tager-Flusberg, H., & Kasari, C. (2013). Minimally verbal school-aged children with autism spectrum disorder: The neglected end of the spectrum. *Autism Research, 6*(6), 468–478.

Tomasello, M., & Todd, J. (1983). Joint attention and lexical acquisition style. *First Language, 4*(12), 197–211.

Toth, K., Munson, J., Meltzoff, A. N., & Dawson, G. (2006). Early predictors of communication development in young children with autism spectrum disorder: joint attention, imitation, and toy play. *Journal of Autism and Developmental Disorders, 36*(8), 993–1005. doi:10.1007/s10803-006-0137-7

Vivanti, G., Paynter, J., Duncan, E., Fothergill, H., Dissanayake, C., Rogers, S. J., & Victorian ASELCC Team. (2014). Effectiveness and feasibility of the Early Start Denver Model implemented in a group-based community childcare setting. *Journal of Autism and Developmental Disorders, 44*(12), 3140-3153.

Weiss, R. S. (1981). INREAL Intervention for Language Handicapped and Bilingual Children. *Journal of Early Intervention, 4*(1), 40–51. https://doi.org/10.1177/105381518100400106

Wetherby, A. M., & Prizant, B. M. (2002). *Communication and Symbolic Behavior Scales Developmental* Profile™ (CSBS DP™). Baltimore, MD: Paul H. Brookes Publishing Co.

Wetherby, A. M., & Woods, J. J. (2006). Early social interaction project for children with autism spectrum disorders beginning in the second year of life a preliminary study. *Topics in Early Childhood Special Education, 26*(2), 67–82.

Wetherby, A. M., Guthrie, W., Woods, J., Schatschneider, C., Holland, R. D., Morgan, L . . . Lord, C. (2014). Parent-implemented social intervention for toddlers with autism: an RCT. *Pediatrics, 134*(6), 1084–1093.

Wong, C. (2013). A play and joint attention intervention for teachers of young children with autism: A randomized controlled pilot study. *Autism, 17*(3), 340–357.

Yoder, P., & Stone, W. L. (2006). Randomized comparison of two communication interventions for preschoolers with autism spectrum disorders. *Journal of Consulting and Clinical Psychology, 74*(3), 426–435. doi:10.1037/0022-006x.74.3.426

12

Parent- and Peer-Mediated Interventions for Children With Autism Spectrum Disorder and Complex Communication Needs

Rose A. Mason and Stephanie Gerow

Children's language and communication development is directly related to the quantity and quality of communication they experience on a daily basis in natural environments (Landry, Smith, Swank, & Guttentag, 2008), with increased exposure yielding greater language acquisition. In addition, comprehension of language and the ability to interpret and respond appropriately to social nuances is improved when more language is directed toward them (Brady, Thiemann-Bourque, Fleming, & Matthews, 2013; Poll, 2011). For children with complex communication needs (CCN), including those with autism spectrum disorder (ASD), the need for language input is even greater to facilitate language acquisition and fluency. Unfortunately, children with significant language impairments such as those with ASD and minimal to no expressive communication typically received a decreased amount of language input from others (Poll, 2011) including parents and peers.

One means of addressing these barriers and increasing exposure to evidence-based practices (EBPs) for individuals with ASD is to teach individuals within the person's natural environment to implement interventions. Because there are not enough interventionists to provide the concentrated dosage of EBPs necessary for achieving optimal outcomes, training those within the natural environment will not only increase exposure to EBPs but will also increase opportunities for communicative initiations and responses with natural communicative partners (Trottier, Kamp, & Mirenda, 2011). Two obvious candidates are parents and peers because they are typically present daily within the natural environments of individuals with ASD. Both parent- and peer-mediated interventions are not separate, nuanced practices but rather delivery of EBP by the parent or peer serving as the mediator between the intervention and the focal child.

PEER-MEDIATED INSTRUCTION AND INTERVENTION

Most individuals with ASD desire positive social experiences and relationships. However, skill deficits including limited communication, poor eye contact, focus on stereotypic interests, and failure to engage in social reciprocity may preclude successful social attempts (Camargo et al., 2015; White, Scahill, Klin, Koenig, & Volkmar, 2007). Furthermore, social bids by individuals with ASD are likely to be overlooked or disregarded by peers as they likely do not understand ASD or have the skill set by which to navigate and successfully direct the social situation (Wolfberg, Dewitt, Young, & Nguyen, 2015). As a result, social attempts by individuals with ASD are likely to result in consequences such as negative responses, ignoring, and exclusion by peers, further decreasing the likelihood that they will make future social attempts (Choi, 2007; Wolfberg et al., 2015). This type of exchange leads to decreases in social opportunities, and thus decreases in communicative learning and development of social relationships, for individuals with ASD.

Considering this, peer-mediated instruction and interventions (PMIIs) are particularly advantageous as they capitalize on natural environments and trained peers to facilitate successful communication and socialization for individuals with ASD (Milley & Machalicek, 2012; White et al., 2007; Zagona & Mastergeorge, 2016). PMIIs are those interventions for which peers are taught to implement EBP (Coogle, Floyd, Hanline, & Kellner-Hiczewski, 2013; Zagona & Mastergeorge, 2016). PMII involves training the peers to engage socially with the focal child, initiate interactions, demonstrate the target skills, and provide necessary prompts and reinforcement for target behaviors (Zagona & Mastergeorge, 2016). During interaction, the interventionist assumes a facilitator role, prompting and guiding the peer when necessary, to provide prompts and reinforce communicative attempts by the focal child. Through implementation of PMIIs the learner with ASD improves targeted skills while the trained peer increases understanding of ASD and learns skills necessary to successfully engage and include the focal child (Wolfberg et al., 2015). Perhaps most important, PMII provides multiple occasions for individuals with ASD to socially connect with a responsive communicative partner and subsequently reap the social reinforcement from such interactions (Zagona & Mastergeorge, 2016).

Evidence Base for PMII

PMII has been identified as an EBP by both the National Professional Development Center for Autism Spectrum Disorders (Wong et al., 2015) and the National Autism Center (2015). The National Autism Center indicates that evidence supports the use of PMIIs, referred to as peer training packages, for improving learning readiness and communication skills as well as ameliorating challenging and incompatible behaviors such as stereotypy for children 3–14 years of age (National Autism Center, 2015). However, the National Professional Development Center indicates that evidence for the use of PMIIs is limited in the types of skills impacted and for what age ranges; PMII has been found to increase social skills for individuals with ASD ages 0–22 months, joint attention and play skills for children ages 0–14 months, and communication skills only for children ages 0–5 months (Chang & Locke, 2016; Wong et al., 2015).

Targeted Outcomes   The evidence base indicates PMII is effective for promoting acquisition and fluency of a variety of communication and social skills for individuals with ASD including social reciprocity and development of social relationships with peers (Stichter & Conroy, 2006; Whalon, Conroy, Martinez, & Werch, 2015). The most frequently targeted sociocommunicative skills are, broadly, initiations and responses (Watkins et al., 2015). Of the two skills, increasing social responding may have the most widespread impact as it is likely to increase the odds that peers will initiate social interactions (Choi, 2007; McGrath, Bosch, Sullivan, & Fuqua, 2003). In addition, PMII can be implemented to help teach individuals with ASD to remain actively engaged in socializations and conversations including through nonverbal communication, such as eye contact, nodding, and maintaining proximity (Zagona & Mastergeorge, 2016).

Participant Characteristics   In addition to effectiveness across skills, PMII is effective across ages, although the majority of evidence focuses on elementary-age children (Chang & Locke, 2016). In two recent reviews of the evidence base on PMII (Watkins et al., 2015; Zagona & Mastergeorge, 2016), the ages of participants across the included studies ranged from ages 3 to 21. PMII tends to incorporate typical social activities. For instance, Kalyva and Avramidis (2005) implemented a "circle of friends" intervention with young children ages 3–5, to increase initiations and responses. The intervention took place during the preschool's typical circle time activity and included preferred toys. In another study (Bambara, Cole, Kunsch, Tsai, & Ayad, 2016), the number and duration of communicative acts were increased for three high school students, ages 14–15 months, utilizing a multi-component PMII intervention that included the use of text cues and direct instruction. The intervention was implemented during the participants' regularly scheduled lunch, and the text cues included sentence prompts based on topics the participants had indicated they wanted to discuss. Prior to the initiation of the intervention, peers were directly taught strategies to increase conversations, initiations, and question asking (Bambara et al., 2016).

In addition to implementation of PMII across a variety of ages, PMII is also effective for individuals with ASD with a range of communication skills, from those with verbal communication in complete sentences to participants with minimal to no communication. For instance, PMII has been found to be effective in small-scale studies with both elementary-age children with little expressive language (Kamps et al., 2014) as well as adolescents with advanced speech skills (Bambara et al., 2016).

The evidence base also indicates PMII is effective for increasing communicative acts for individuals with minimal to no speech who utilize augmentative and alternative communication (AAC). PMIIs have been combined with AAC interventions during playtime for elementary students with CCN to individuals with ASD to initiate and respond to peers utilizing a speech-generating device (SGD; Trottier et al., 2011). Similarly, PMII have been combined with an intervention utilizing a Picture Exchange Communication System (PECS) to facilitate communicative acts during social activities for preschoolers with ASD and CCN (Thiemann-Bourque, Brady, McGuff, Stump, & Naylor, 2016). The research indicates that both peers and participants with ASD increase their communicative acts toward each other with implementation of PMIIs.

Intervention Components   As previously noted, PMIIs are a variation in the delivery of EBP in which peers are the delivery agent, serving as a mediator between the implementer and the target child. As such, PMII has been shown to be effective for a variety of EBP, the majority of which are grounded in applied behavior analysis (ABA). Most PMIIs include the educator training peers to implement a combination of strategies including direct instruction, prompting, and reinforcement with their friends with ASD (e.g., Banda, Hart, & Liu-Gitz, 2010; Corbett et al., 2014; Loftin, Odom, Lantz, 2008; Mason et al., 2014). Visual scripts, written or pictorial examples of initiations and responses, are also frequently incorporated into PMII (Ganz & Flores, 2008; Ganz et al., 2012; Kamps et al., 2014; Mason et al., 2014; Owen-DeSchryver, Carr, Calle, & Blakely-Smith, 2008). Pivotal Response Treatment (PRT), which is a behaviorally based EBP that is implemented across natural contexts and capitalizes on the motivation of individuals with ASD to increase prosocial communicative and behavioral responses, has also been implemented within a PMII framework (Harper, Symon, & Frea, 2008; Kuhn, Bodkin, Devlin, & Doggett, 2008; Pierce & Schreibman, 1995). PRT incorporates child interest(s) throughout the intervention, allowing the child to choose activities and to increase motivation (Koegel & Koegel, 2006). Attempts, or approximations, of target behaviors are reinforced (Koegel, Koegel, Vernon, & Brookman-Frazee, 2017). The use of PMII with PRT is compelling as both are conducive to promoting and supporting inclusion (Boudreau, Corkum, Meko, & Smith, 2015).

Implementation of PMII

Although PMII has been implemented in a variety of ways, particularly dependent on the targeted skills and the communicative needs of the individual with ASD, several key steps remain consistent throughout. Table 12.1 outlines key components for implementation of each step of PMII. These steps include: 1) choosing peers, 2) training peers and participants, and 3) implementing the intervention.

Choosing Peers   The first task to complete is identifying the peers that will participate in the intervention. As noted, the role of the peers in PMII is to provide opportunities to communicate including initiating and responding, exemplars of

Table 12.1.   Key components of peer-mediated instruction and intervention

Choosing peers	Training peers and participants	Delivering PMII
Highly skilled and socially competent communicators Well-liked by others Ongoing interest in the participant with ASD Agreeable to participating Strong record of attendance Good at following directions Close to the participant's age	Provide peers with information regarding characteristics of individuals with ASD and CCN. Decide whether to train peers and participants separately or together. Include instruction, modeling, role-play, and feedback. Focus for peers should be on strategies to elicit initiations and responses.	Facilitator chooses a variety of natural settings and materials including preferred and nonpreferred items. Facilitator sits at a distance from peer and participant. Facilitator provides prompts, feedback, and reinforcement to the peer. Facilitator limits interaction with the peer participant Facilitator intervenes directly with participant only when he/she is not responding to peer.

Key: PMII, peer-mediated instruction and intervention; ASD, autism spectrum disorder; CCN, complex communication needs.

effective communicative acts and social exchanges, and a social partner throughout multiple settings (Camargo et al, 2014; Chan et al., 2009). Thus, determining the number of peers to include and which peers will be most appropriate for the PMII is a crucial first step for implementation.

In terms of number of peers, PMII can be implemented with one peer (Laushey & Heflin, 2000) or a group of peers, sometimes referred to as peer networks (Kamps et al., 2014). With one peer, a buddy or tutor is trained and then appointed to remain with the individual with ASD during the chosen activity (DiSalvo & Oswald, 2002). Peer groups or networks, on the other hand, involve training multiple peers to mediate interventions. The purpose in such a configuration is to establish a system of peers for the individual with ASD with the expectation that he or she will have several communicative partners across settings (Kamps et al., 2015). Additionally, training several peers is likely to facilitate generalization and also provide an environment in which the trained peers are supporting and prompting one another to interact with the participant with ASD (Kamps et al., 2015).

Regardless of the peer configuration, the characteristics of the peers chosen are important to the success of PMII. As the goal of PMII interventions is to provide communicative opportunities and a model of good social and communication behaviors, peers recruited for participation in PMII need to be highly skilled and socially competent communicators (Watkins et al., 2015). It is also helpful if the peers have social capital, meaning they are generally well-liked by others outside of the PMII and others tend to be socially responsive to them (Chang & Locke, 2016; Locke, Rotheram-Fuller, and Kasari, 2012). Again, this is to support generalization and to serve as a model to others regarding how to interact with the individual with ASD. In addition, peers who seem to have an ongoing interest in the participant with ASD, including previous social attempts, and those that are agreeable to participation are appropriate choices for PMII (Boudreau et al., 2015; Locke et al., 2012). Milley and Machalicek (2012) also suggest that the peers have a record of attendance, follow directions well, and be close in age to the individual with ASD.

Peer and Participant Training   Once the peers have been chosen, the next step is training, including both the peers and participants with ASD. The first component of training is teaching the participating peers about ASD, including common characteristics, particularly as they relate to the participant with ASD and also regarding the use of AAC as relevant (DiSalvo & Oswald, 2002). Following this, training on the intervention for which the peers will serve as mediators can begin. Although training can follow several formats and is somewhat guided by the selected intervention, training will be most effective if it includes direct instruction, modeling, role-play, and feedback with reinforcement and error correction (Watkins et al., 2015). This can occur with either the peers alone or with both the peers and participant with ASD (Laugeson, Frankel, Gantman, Dillon, & Mogil, 2012). The focus of this training is typically providing the peers with strategies for delivering and eliciting initiations and responses, including use of AAC, as necessary. For instance, Thiemann-Bourque and colleagues (2016) trained peers, without the individual with ASD, to utilize and prompt use of the target participant's AAC system as a means for talking. In other studies, however, the peers and participants were taught together ways to initiate and respond to one another including the use of a visual cue card (Kamps et al., 2014; Mason et al., 2014).

Delivering the PMII   Once training has occurred, the intervention can begin with the peer delivering the strategies as trained while the adult facilitates the interactions as needed through the peer, minimizing any direct intervention with the participant with ASD (Milley & Machalicek, 2012). The facilitator should assume a background role, sitting at a distance from the group that allows for separation but also permits prompting and intervening when necessary. When interactions are not occurring, the facilitator provides prompts, feedback, and reinforcement directly to the peer (Owen-DeSchryver et al., 2008). Facilitators' interactions with the individual with ASD are limited and only occur after sufficient wait time in which the participant is unresponsive to the peer or challenging behavior occurs.

Setting and materials utilized for PMII moderate the impact of PMII on targeted skills. Research indicates implementation of PMII in natural contexts supports acquisition and maintenance (Camargo et al., 2014). Furthermore, implementing across a variety of settings will further increase the impact of PMII and likely support generalization (Harper et al., 2008; Mason et al., 2014; Owen-DeSchryver et al., 2008). Including a variety of materials (i.e. toys, games), necessary communication supports such as AAC, and potential activities, will provide more opportunities for requesting and interacting while increasing interest and motivation. Central to this is ensuring the materials include the target individual's preferred and nonpreferred items as mechanisms to entice interaction (Coogle, Floyd, (Coogle et al., 2013; Milley & Machalicek, 2012).

PMIIs Summary

In summary, clear evidence exists to support the use of PMII for individuals with ASD, including those with CCN (Boudreau et al., 2015; Chang & Locke, 2016; Wong et al., 2015). Involvement of peers not only increases opportunities for communication within natural settings but also serves as a catalyst for improved access to inclusive settings and positive social relationships.

PARENT-MEDIATED INTERVENTION

Communicative interactions with parents greatly affect children's language acquisition (Hart & Risley, 1999; Iovannone, Dunlap, Huber, & Kincaid, 2009). Young children often spend much more time with parents than they do professionals (e.g., teachers, specialists). Parents also interact with children in many settings and situations to which professionals typically do not have access. For example, in one day, a parent may interact with a child in the home, in the grocery store, and at a restaurant. It is unlikely that it would be feasible for an educator to interact with the child across each of these situations in one day. The child should have access to effective communication interventions in each of these settings. For these reasons, parent-mediated communication interventions are often a feasible method to increase the child's access to effective communication interventions (Matson et al., 2012; Symon, 2001); thus, practitioners should consider teaching parents of children with ASD to implement such interventions (Iovannone et al., 2009; Symon, 2001).

Evidence Base for Parent-Mediated Interventions

Reviews of the extant literature have identified parent-mediated interventions as an evidence-based practice for children with ASD (Wong et al., 2015; National

Autism Center, 2015). Currently, there is the most support for parent-mediated interventions for toddlers and children 6–11 years old (Schultz, 2013). Parent-mediated interventions have been used to address a number of social and communicative outcomes for children with ASD and CCN such as joint attention, play skills, and requesting (Schultz, 2013). For example, the parent-mediated PECS (Frost & Bondy, 2002) for children ages 2–3 years old with ASD and CCN has been shown to increase independent picture exchange requests (Park, Alber-Morgan, & Cannella-Malone, 2011). Studies like these consistently indicate that parent implementation of evidence-based interventions result in improved outcomes for children with ASD.

In addition, research has identified a number of secondary benefits related to teaching parents to implement interventions. One potential benefit of teaching parents to implement an intervention is that they may use that intervention in untrained situations (Hsieh, Wilder, & Abellon, 2011; Kashinath, Woods, & Goldstein, 2006; Stiebel, 1999) or teach other people who interact with the child to implement the intervention (e.g., grandparent, babysitter; Symon, 2005). For example, Symon (2005) taught three parents to implement PRT to improve spoken communication and appropriate behavior in three children with ASD. Parents were taught to implement the intervention using instructions, modeling, and feedback. The intervention resulted in increases in communication and appropriate behavior. In addition, parents were able to teach another adult who interacted with the child often to implement the intervention effectively. This study suggests that parents are able to train others to implement an intervention effectively, which may be especially useful in circumstances in which it is impractical to teach everyone who interacts with the child how to implement the intervention. However, there is a need for more research on which interventions parents can teach others to implement and which parent training strategies result in parents effectively teaching others to implement the intervention.

Teaching parents to implement interventions may also improve family functioning. For example, a parent-training program that consisted of two 2-hour seminars resulted in improvements in child behavior (Sofronoff, Jahnel, & Sanders, 2011). In addition, this program resulted in reductions in parent conflict and reductions in the use of dysfunctional parenting styles (Sofronoff et al., 2011). Another study indicated that parent training in AAC for three parents of children with ASD resulted in increases in child communication (Stiebel, 1999). In addition, teaching parents to promote communication resulted in parents feeling more confident that they can improve their children's communication (Stiebel, 1999). Together, these studies suggest that parent training may have positive impacts on the family in addition to those related to improvements in child behavior.

Implementing Parent-Mediated Interventions

Although there is evidence to support the efficacy of parent-mediated interventions for children with ASD and CCN, the extent to which these interventions improve communication depends on the intervention strategy and the parent training procedure. Therefore, it is important to carefully develop the intervention and training procedures. Generally, parent-mediated interventions include the following steps: 1) identifying a target outcome and collecting data on current performance, 2) developing an individualized intervention, 3) teaching the parent to implement the intervention, and 4) monitoring progress and making modifications.

Identifying the Target Outcome and Collecting Data on Current Performance

As a professional who works with parents, the first step in the consultation process is to identify a target outcome for the child. In the case of children with ASD who have CCN, communication is a frequent target outcome. Professionals should consider multiple sources when identifying the specific communication outcome that will be targeted. Consideration of any relevant assessment data, including observational data or data obtained from interviews with individuals who know the child well, is necessary to guide intervention development. These assessments help identify specific goals for intervention based on the child's current communication deficits and behavioral strengths. Chapter 2 of this book ("Autism-Focused Assessment and Program Planning," by Riccio and Prickett) provides detailed information regarding assessment of communication in individuals with ASD.

As a corollary to formal assessment data, it is important to consider parents' current priorities for their child's educational goals (Division for Early Childhood, 2014). Parents' implementation of interventions is dependent on their belief that the intervention will alter an important behavior. If targeted outcomes are not also priorities for the parent, the parent is unlikely to implement the intervention. On the other hand, if target outcomes are determined, based in part on the degree of importance for the parent, then the parent is more likely to be motivated to implement an intervention that will alter that behavior, even in the absence of professionals. Professionals can obtain information about parent priorities via parent report. This inclusion of parent opinion can help the practitioner tailor the outcome to family priorities, which may be different than the practitioner's due to a number of factors such as cultural, linguistic, educational, socioeconomic, or individual differences (Division for Early Childhood, 2014).

Once the target skill has been identified, professionals should develop an operational definition of the target behavior and a criterion for mastering the goal. The operational definition should describe an observable and measurable behavior. For example, the assessment data may indicate that Samantha has difficulty independently requesting. Samantha's mother indicates she would like Samantha to tell her what she wants to eat. This is valuable information, but the professional has not clearly described what will be measured and how it will be measured. Therefore, the professional needs to write a clear outcome in order to measure student progress. The following is an example of an outcome related to Samantha's requesting:

> Samantha will independently request three or more different preferred foods during snack time over three consecutive observations. An independent request is defined as choosing a picture card from an array of four, within arm's reach, and handing it to her mother, up to 5 feet away, without assistance.

This outcome describes a specific target response (choosing a card from an array of four and handing it to her mother within a particular distance). In addition, it describes a specific mastery criterion (three independent requests over three consecutive observations). Defining the target behavior clearly and specifying the mastery criterion will facilitate the progress monitoring process.

Prior to developing and implementing the intervention, the practitioner should collect data on the child's current performance on the outcome and current parent–child interactions (The IRIS Center, 2014). This will assist in the development of an individualized intervention, based on the child's current performance.

In addition, these data are necessary in order to adequately monitor child improvement following the intervention. The baseline data collected will be based on the specific outcome identified by the practitioner.

Developing an Individualized Intervention   Development of a specific target outcome will guide intervention decision making. When developing an intervention, the following should be considered: a) the research support for the intervention, b) parent preference for intervention components, and c) strengths and barriers to implementation in the child's environment. When available, practitioners should choose evidence-based interventions for children with ASD (Behavior Analyst Certification Board, 2012; Division for Early Childhood, 2014; Individuals with Disabilities Education Improvement Act of 2004, PL 108-446). Resources for identifying evidence-based interventions for children with ASD can be found in the references at the end of this chapter (National Autism Center; 2015; Wong et al., 2015). Specific examples of evidence-based interventions to improve communication outcomes for children with ASD include prompting procedures (e.g., modeling, scripts, and time delay), reinforcement, and functional communication training (Wong et al., 2015). Professionals should identify methods to incorporate those evidence-based interventions into typical family routines (Division for Early Childhood, 2014).

Consideration of parents' preferences will increase the likelihood that the intervention will be consistently implemented. For example, the parent can help decide the specific routine(s) in which he or she will implement the intervention and the frequency of implementation. In addition, the parent can help decide specific intervention procedures based on their preference. Prompting and reinforcement are both evidence-based interventions for improving communication outcomes in children with ASD (Wong et al., 2015). If the professional thinks that modeling and scripts are likely to be equally effective for the child, then the parent can help the professional decide which type of prompting procedure he or she would like to use. Incorporating parent preference will increase the likelihood that the parent is willing and able to implement the intervention. In addition, consideration of parent preference for certain intervention components helps increase the likelihood that the intervention will match the family's culture, especially in circumstances in which the family's culture differs from that of the practitioner's, and their individual needs.

Finally, relevant strengths and barriers present in the environment must be identified and addressed. Resources can include materials available in natural settings and contexts, such as the home (e.g., toys, materials related to adaptive skills, other individuals available to support the intervention). It is critical that professionals recommend interventions that do not require resources unavailable to the parent. For example, a teaching procedure that requires two adults to implement the strategy will not be possible if there is only one adult available to implement the intervention. Similarly, the practitioner should not assume that the parent has the resources available to create additional laminated picture cards if the practitioner recommends an exchange-based AAC system. For these reasons, it is important to identify the resources already available to the parent, or that the parent can easily obtain or produce. The professional should also encourage consistent and open communication with the parent about current resources the parent has to support the use of the intervention. For example, the child's grandparent may have spent time with the mother and child daily at the beginning of the intervention, but a recent change in employment status may affect the amount of time the grand-parent spends with the child.

Teaching the Parent to Implement the Intervention   When working with parents, it is important to use effective and explicit parent training strategies. Effective parent training strategies include some or all of the following components: a) written and verbal instructions, b) modeling, c) coaching and performance feedback, and d) goal setting or planning (Hsieh et al., 2011; Kaiser, Hancock, & Nietfeld, 2000; Kashinath et al., 2006; Schertz & Odom, 2007; Symon, 2005). Prior to training parents, make a task analysis of the steps required to implement the intervention. A task analysis includes a specific list of steps required to implement the intervention and will be utilized throughout parent training. The task analysis should be concise, clear, and free of professional jargon (e.g., consider using words such as "show" or "demonstrate" rather than "model").

The first step in any parent training strategy is to explain to the parent how to implement the intervention using written and/or verbal instructions (Hsieh et al., 2011; Kaiser et al., 2000; Kashinath et al., 2006; Schertz & Odom, 2007; Symon, 2005). In addition to the task analysis, consider including direct instruction on the purpose of the intervention and the specific outcome at the top of the document provided to the parent. Since the outcome is based on parent preference, reminding the parent of the purpose of the intervention will likely increase parent motivation to learn and implement the intervention. Written instructions should also include the parent-friendly task analysis of the steps to implement the intervention. Explain the intervention step by step to the parent. Ensure that the parent has the opportunity to ask questions as the intervention is explained. Finally, inclusion of a "helpful hints" or "don't forget" section on the instruction sheet may be useful (see Figure 12.1). This can include information that does not fit well in the step-by-step instructions but is critical for the intervention's efficacy. For example, child interest in the activity is critical for many communication interventions. The "helpful hints" section of the document can include information about monitoring child interest in the activity throughout the intervention. Following the written and verbal instructions, it is often helpful to demonstrate the intervention to the parent while describing the steps or following the written and verbal instructions (Hsieh et al., 2011; Kaiser et al., 2000; Kashinath et al., 2006; Symon, 2005; Tarbox, Wallace, & Tarbox, 2002). This modeling for the parent can be in person with the parent and the child or via a video model of the procedures.

Coaching and independent practice are effective strategies to improve the accuracy of parent implementation of interventions (Hsieh et al., 2011; Kaiser et al., 2000; Kashinath et al., 2006; Symon, 2005; Tarbox et al., 2002). Prior to implementing any of these procedures, the professional needs to have a method of monitoring the accuracy of parent implementation. This is often done using an implementation fidelity data sheet. The implementation fidelity data sheet needs to have the list of steps for implementing the intervention and space to mark the implementation as correct or incorrect for each item. It may be helpful to include space on the implementation fidelity sheet to record whether the professional coached the parent or not during the session (e.g., told them how to implement the intervention while they were implementing). This will help the professional assess the extent to which the parent can implement the intervention accurately and independently. The professional can use the implementation fidelity sheet throughout coaching, performance feedback, and independent practice sessions to monitor the accuracy

---

Sample Parent Instruction Sheet

Purpose: Increase Sam's ability to communicate his wants/needs

Outcome: Sam will independently request (using a one-word request) three or more times during 5 minutes of play in two consecutive visits

Routine: Playtime with dad

Materials needed: Preferred activities or toys

Steps

1. Follow Sam's lead. Play with an activity that he shows interest in.
2. Arrange the activity to encourage communication. If Sam is interested in playing with blocks, then give Sam a few blocks, but not all of the blocks.
3. If Sam indicates he wants more blocks (by pointing or reaching), say the name of the activity (e.g., "blocks")
4. If Sam doesn't repeat the word, try saying the word two more times. Wait about 5 seconds between each time you say the word.
5. If Sam says the word "blocks" at any point, give him the blocks. Repeat and expand on his language and provide praise (e.g., "Blocks, please. Awesome saying blocks!")

Don't Forget: This procedure will only work if Sam is interested in playing with the items or activities. Also, if Sam consistently does not communicate during these sessions, talk with your coach about his progress.

Figure 12.1.   Example of a parent instruction sheet.

of the parent's implementation and to identify steps that the parent consistently implements incorrectly, as applicable.

Coaching involves providing prompts or cues for implementation, instructions to change implementation as necessary, and praise for correct implementation (Kashinath et al., 2006; Olive, Lang, & Davis, 2008). During initial implementation of the intervention it is likely that the parent will require frequent coaching throughout the session. As the parent begins to demonstrate that he or she can implement the intervention, it is important to systematically fade prompts and coaching. Incorporating independent practice with performance feedback in the parent training is also helpful in decreasing the amount of coaching needed during implementation. This involves watching the parent implement the intervention independently, then providing feedback after the session. The feedback can include a) general comments about the overall intervention and interactions (e.g. "You both were having fun," "X used lots of words and responded well to you"), b) a description of correct implementation with modeling for steps implemented incorrectly, c) praise for steps implemented correctly, and d) opportunity for the parent to ask questions (Hsieh et al., 2011; Kaiser et al., 2000; Mouzakitis, Codding, & Tryon, 2015; Symon, 2005; Tarbox et al., 2002). When providing feedback, it is important to provide more praise and positive comments than correction to encourage and motivate the parent. Professionals can transition from coaching to independent practice with performance feedback in order to promote independent implementation and assess the parent's accuracy of implementation (e.g., Olive et al., 2008).

Planning and problem solving can be used to increase the likelihood that parents will implement the intervention across routines (Kashinath et al., 2006; Stiebel, 1999). Once the parent demonstrates that he or she is able to implement the intervention accurately and independently, it is important to incorporate strategies that will promote accurate implementation across multiple routines. The planning or problem-solving approach involves working with the parent to identify routines for implementation, specific procedures associated with that routine, and possible issues that might be associated with implementation in that routine (Kashinath et al., 2006; Stiebel, 1999). When implementing these procedures, it is important to continue to monitor the accuracy of parent implementation across the routines, albeit less frequently than during initial instruction. It is possible that some parents will implement the intervention accurately in one or more routines but not others. It may be necessary to implement training strategies such as coaching and performance feedback in additional routines to which the parent did generalize accurate implementation fidelity.

Monitoring Progress and Making Modifications   During parent training and implementation of the intervention, the practitioner should monitor both the child's performance and the parent's acquisition of accurate implementation. These data will provide valuable information about the efficacy of the intervention. Specifically, if the child's performance is not improving and the parent is not implementing the intervention accurately, the practitioner should provide additional parent training or work with the parent to make the intervention more feasible, rather than changing the intervention entirely (The IRIS Center, 2014). On the other hand, if the child is not improving and the parent is implementing the intervention accurately, the practitioner should consider modifying or changing the intervention (The IRIS Center, 2014). If the child is making progress toward the goal and the parent is implementing the intervention accurately, then the practitioner should recommend the continued use of the intervention or moving to the next goal, when appropriate. Once the child has mastered the first target skill, the outcome and intervention can be modified to address the next outcome.

While monitoring the child's progress, sharing information about the child's progress and any reasons for changing the intervention with the parent is important. Although, improvements in target outcomes may occur rapidly for some, it is important to remind the parent, and to remember as the professional, that change can take time. In many cases, significant improvements can require longer periods of time. It is important that the professional and parent do not abandon an effective intervention because the improvements are not rapid. However, it is also important that professionals do not continue to recommend an intervention that is ineffective. For this reason, professionals need to carefully monitor changes in performance and trends in performance throughout the intervention and make treatment decisions based on those changes. In addition, the method for measuring progress often needs to assess small, incremental improvements in behavior. For example, for some children, the practitioner may want to begin by monitoring the number of syllables or sounds the child produces rather than the number of words the child produces. Similarly, if utilizing AAC, begin with only one or two communication options before expanding to a full menu.

Future Research

Although this chapter has highlighted a number of studies in which parents implemented social and communication interventions for children with ASD, there are a number of areas in need of further investigation. Few studies have evaluated parent-implemented interventions to increase the use of AAC (Hong, Ganz, Neely, Gerow, & Ninci, 2016). In addition, the vast majority of studies on parent-mediated interventions involve researchers training parents to implement the intervention. There is a need for more research evaluating the efficacy of parent training delivered by the professionals who typically interact with parents (e.g., early intervention service providers, in-home parent trainers who work with school districts). Finally, a few studies have assessed parent generalization of accurate implementation of the intervention (e.g., Ingersol & Gergans, 2007; Kashinath et al., 2006). However, there is a need for more research needed on the variables and circumstances that promote generalization of parent implementation to novel situations.

Parent-Mediated Interventions Summary

Parent implementation can increase a child's access to effective interventions. When teaching parents to implement interventions, it is important to consider parent preference and to choose evidence-based interventions. Given the relative benefits of parent-mediated interventions, practitioners should include parents in the implementation of interventions for children with ASD and CCN, when possible.

CONCLUSION

Effectively addressing the needs of individuals with ASD and CCN requires intensive exposure to EBP. However, fulfilling this need is daunting given a lack of trained professionals and access to sufficient natural environments to support generalization and communicative opportunities. In addition, even with the presence of opportunities, if others do not understand how to respond to communicative attempts or initiate communication with individuals with ASD, efforts will go unreinforced and opportunities will be lost. As has been discussed throughout this chapter, training parents and peers to mediate the delivery of EBP will help support communication development and use across multiple communicative partners and contexts. Both parent-mediated and PMII are highly advantageous means of delivering effective EBP for addressing CCN in an inclusive and socially supportive manner.

REFERENCES

Bambara, L. M., Cole, C. L., Kunsch, C., Tsai, S., & Ayad, E. (2016). Peer-mediated intervention to improve the conversational skills of high school students with autism spectrum disorder. *Research in Autism Spectrum Disorders, 27*, 29–43.

Banda, E. R., Hart, S. L., & Liu-Gitz, L. (2010). Impact of training peers and children with autism on social skills during center time activities in inclusive classrooms. *Research in Autism Spectrum Disorders, 4*, 619–625.

Behavior Analyst Certification Board. (2012). *Behavior Analyst Certification Board Fourth Edition Task List.* Retrieved from: http://bacb.com/wp-content/uploads/2016/03/160101-BCBA-BCaBA-task-list-fourth-edition-english.pdf

Boudreau, A. M., Corkum, P., Meko, K., & Smith, I. M. (2015). Peer-mediated pivotal response treatment for young children with autism spectrum disorders: A systematic review. *Canadian Journal of School Psychology, 30*(3), 218–235.

Brady, N. K., Thiemann-Bourque, K., Fleming, K., & Matthews, K. (2013). Predicting language outcomes for children learning AAC: Child and environmental factors. *Journal of Speech, Language, and Hearing Research, 56*(5), 1595–1612.

Camargo, S. P. H., Rispoli, M., Ganz, J., Hong, E. R., Davis, H., & Mason, R. (2014). A review of the quality of behaviorally-based intervention research to improve social interaction skills of children with ASD in inclusive settings. *Journal of autism and developmental disorders, 44*(9), 2096–2116.

Chan, J. M., Lang, R., Rispoli, M., O'Reilly, M., Sigafoos, J., & Cole, H. (2009). Use of peer-mediated interventions in the treatment of autism spectrum disorders: A systematic review. *Research in Autism Spectrum Disorders, 3*(4), 876–889.

Chang, Y. C., & Locke, J. (2016). A systematic review of peer-mediated interventions for children with autism spectrum disorder. *Research in Autism Spectrum Disorders, 27*, 1–10.

Choi, S. (2007). Peer training methods for children and adolescents with autism: A review. *International Journal of Pedagogies and Learning, 3*(3), 92–100.

Coogle, C., Floyd, K., Hanline, M. F., & Kellner-Hiczewski, J. (2013). Strategies used in natural environments to promote communication development in young children at risk for autism spectrum disorder. *Young Exceptional Children, 16*(3), 11–23.

Corbett, B. A., Swainn, D. M., Coke, C., Simon, D., Newsom, C., Houchins-Juarez, N., . . . Song, Y. (2014). Improvement in social deficits in autism spectrum disorders using a theatre-based peer-mediated intervention. *Research in Autism Spectrum Disorders, 3*(4), 876–889.

DiSalvo, C. A., & Oswald, D. P. (2002). Peer-mediated interventions to increase the social interaction of children with autism consideration of peer expectancies. *Focus on Autism and Other Developmental Disabilities, 17*, 198–207.

Division for Early Childhood. (2014). *DEC recommended practices in early intervention/early childhood special education 2014.* Retrieved from http://www.dec-sped.org/recommended practices

Frost, M. S., & Bondy, A. (2002). *The picture exchange communication system training manual* (2nd ed.). Newark, DE: Pyramid Educational Consultants.

Ganz, J. B., & Flores, M. M. (2008). Effects of the use of visual strategies in play groups for children with autism spectrum disorders and their peers. *Journal of Autism and Developmental Disorders, 38*(5), 926–940.

Ganz, J. B., Heath, A. K., Lund, E. M., Camargo, S. P. H., Rispoli, M. J., Boles, M., & Plaisance, L. (2012). Effects of peer-mediated implementation of visual scripts in middle school. *Behavior Modification, 36*(3), 378–389.

Harper, C. B., Symon, J. B., & Frea, W. D. (2008). Recess is time-in: Using peers to improve social skills of children with autism. *Journal of Autism and Developmental Disorders, 38*, 815–826.

Hart, B., & Risley, T. R. (1999). *Children learning to talk in American Families.* Baltimore, MD: Paul H. Brookes Publishing Co.

Hong, E. R., Ganz, J. B., Neely, L., Gerow, S., & Ninci, J. (2016). A review of the quality of primary caregiver-implemented communication intervention research for children with ASD. *Research in Autism Spectrum Disorders, 25*, 122–136.

Hsieh, H.-H., Wilder, D. A., & Abellon, O. E. (2011). The effects of training on caregiver implementation of incidental teaching. *Journal of Applied Behavior Analysis, 44*, 199–203.

Individuals with Disabilities Education Improvement Act of 2004, PL 108-446, 20 U.S.C. §§ 1400 *et seq.*

Ingersoll, B., & Gergans, S. (2007). The effect of a parent-implemented imitation intervention on spontaneous imitation skills in young children with autism. *Research in Developmental Disabilities, 28*, 163–175.

Iovannone, R., Dunlap, G., Huber, H., & Kincaid, D. (2009). Effective educational practices for students with autism spectrum disorders. *Focus on Autism and Other Developmental Disabilities, 18*, 150–165.

The IRIS Center. (2014). *Evidence-based practices (part 3): Evaluating learner outcomes and fidelity.* Retrieved from http://iris.peabody.vanderbilt.edu/module/ebp_03/

Kaiser, A. P., Hancock, T. B., & Nietfeld, J. P. (2000). The effects of parent-implemented enhanced milieu teaching on the social communication of children who have autism. *Early Education & Development, 11*, 423–446.

Kalyva, E., & Avramidis, E. (2005). Improving communication between children with autism and their peers through the 'Circle of Friends': A small-scale intervention study. *Journal of Applied Research in Intellectual Disabilities, 18*, 253–261.

Kamps, D. M., Mason, R. A., Thiemann-Bourque, K., Feldmiller, S., Turcotte, A., & Miller, T. (2014). The use of peer networks to increase communicative acts of first grade students with autism spectrum disorders. *Focus on Autism and Other Developmental Disabilities, 29*(4), 230–245.

Kamps, D. M., Thiemann-Bourque, K., Heitzman-Powell, L., Schwartz, I., Rosenberg, N., Mason, R. A., & Cox, S. (2015). A comprehensive peer network intervention to improve social communication of children with autism spectrum disorders: A randomized trial in kindergarten and first grade. *Journal of Autism and Developmental Disorders, 45*(6), 1809–1824. doi:10.1007/s10803-014-2340-2

Kashinath, S., Woods, J., & Goldstein, H. (2006). Enhancing generalized teaching strategy use in daily routines by parents of children with autism. *Journal of Speech, Language, and Hearing Research, 49,* 466–485.

Koegel, R. L., & Koegel, L. K. (2006). *Pivotal response treatments for autism: Communication, social, and academic development.* Baltimore, MD: Paul H. Brookes Publishing Co.

Koegel, R. L., Koegel, L. K., Vernon, T. W., & Brookman-Frazee, L. I. (2017). Pivotal Response Treatment for Individuals with autism spectrum disorder. *Evidence-Based Psychotherapies for Children and Adolescents, 6*(14), 290.

Kuhn, L. R., Bodkin, A. E., Devlin, S. D., & Doggett, R. A. (2008). Using pivotal response training with peers in special education to facilitate play in two children with autism. *Education and Training in Developmental Disabilities, 43,* 37–45.

Landry, S. H., Smith, K. E., Swank, P. R., & Guttentag, C. (2008). A responsive parenting intervention: The optimal timing across early childhood for impacting maternal behaviors and child outcomes. *Developmental Psychology, 44*(5), 1335.

Laugeson, E. A., Frankel, F., Gantman, A., Dillon, A. R., & Mogil, C. (2012). Evidence-based social skills training for adolescents with autism spectrum disorders: The UCLA PEERS program. *Journal of Autism and Developmental Disorders, 42*(6), 1025–1036.

Laushey, K. M., & Heflin, L. J. (2000). Enhancing social skills of kindergarten children with autism through the training of multiple peers as tutors. *Journal of Autism and Developmental Disorders, 30*(3), 183–193.

Locke, J., Rotheram-Fuller, E., & Kasari, C. (2012). Exploring the social impact of being a typical peer model for included children with autism spectrum disorder. *Journal of Autism and Developmental Disorders, 42*(9), 1895–1905.

Loftin, R. L., Odom, S. L., & Lantz, J. F. (2008). Social interaction and repetitive motor behaviors. *Journal of Autism and Developmental Disorders 38*(6), 1124–1135.

Mason, R. A., Kamps, D., Turcotte, A., Cox, S., Feldmiller, S., & Miller, T. (2014). Peer mediation to increase communication and interaction at recess for students with autism spectrum disorders. *Research in Autism Spectrum Disorders, 8*(3), 333–344.

Matson, J. L., Turygin, N. C., Beighley, J., Rieske, R., Tureck, K., & Matson, M. L. (2012). Applied behavior analysis in autism spectrum disorders: Recent developments, strengths, and pitfalls. *Research in Autism Spectrum Disorders, 6,* 144–150.

McGrath, A. M., Bosch, S., Sullivan, C. L., & Fuqua, R. W. (2003). Training reciprocal social interactions between preschoolers and a child with autism. *Journal of Positive Behavior Interventions, 5*(1), 47–54.

Milley, A., & Machalicek, W. (2012). Decreasing students' reliance on adults: A strategic guide for teachers of students with autism spectrum disorders. *Intervention in School and Clinic, 48* (2), 67–75.

Mouzakitis, A., Codding, R. S., & Tryon, G. (2015). The effects of self-monitoring and performance feedback on the treatment integrity of behavior intervention plan implementation and generalization. *Journal of Positive Behavioral Interventions, 17,* 233–234.

National Autism Center. (2015). *Findings and conclusions: National standards project phase 2.* Randolph, MA: National Autism Center.

Olive, M. L., Lang, R. B., & Davis, T. N. (2008). An analysis of the effects of functional communication and a voice output communication aid for a child with autism spectrum disorder. *Research in Autism Spectrum Disorders, 2,* 223–236.

Owen-DeSchryver J. S., Carr, E. G., Calle, S. I., & Blakely-Smith, A. (2008). Promoting social interactions between students with autism spectrum disorders and their peers in inclusive school settings. *Focus on Autism and Other Developmental Disorders, 23,* 15–28.

Park, J. H., Alber-Morgan, S. R., & Cannella-Malone, H. (2011). Effects of mother-implemented Picture Exchange Communication System (PECS) training on independent communicative behaviors of young children with autism spectrum disorders. *Topics in Early Childhood Special Education, 31,* 37–47.

Pierce, K., & Schreibman, L. (1995). Increasing complex social behaviors in children with autism: Effects of peer-implemented pivotal response training. *Journal of Applied Behavior Analysis, 28,* 285–295.

Poll, G. H. (2011). Increasing the odds: Applying emergentist theory in language intervention. *Language, Speech, & Hearing Services in the Schools, 42*(4), 580–591.

Schertz, H. H., & Odom, S. L. (2007). Promoting joint attention in toddlers with autism: A parent-mediated development model. *Journal of Autism and Developmental Disorders, 37,* 1562–1575.

Schultz, T. R. (2013). *Parent-implemented intervention (PII) fact sheet.* Chapel Hill: The University of North Carolina, Frank Porter Graham Child Development Institute, The National Professional Development Center on Autism Spectrum Disorders.

Sofronoff, K., Jahnel, D., & Sanders, M. (2011). Stepping stones triple p seminars for parents of a child with a disability: A randomized controlled trial. *Research in Developmental Disabilities, 32,* 2253–2262.

Stichter, J. P., & Conroy, M. A. (2006). *How to teach social skills and plan for peer social interactions.* Austin, TX: Pro-Ed.

Stiebel, D. (1999). Promoting augmentative communication during daily routines: A parent problem-solving intervention. *Journal of Positive Behavior Interventions, 1,* 159–169.

Symon, J. B. (2001). Parent education for autism: Issues in providing service at a distance. *Journal of Positive Behavior Interventions, 3,* 160–174.

Symon, J. B. (2005). Expanding interventions for children with autism: Parents as trainers. *Journal of Positive Behavior Interventions, 7,* 159–173.

Tarbox, J., Wallace, M. D., & Tarbox, R. S. F. (2002). Successful generalized parent training and failed schedule thinning of response blocking for automatically maintained object mouthing. *Behavioral Interventions, 17,* 169–178.

Thiemann-Bourque, K., Brady, N., McGuff, S., Stump, K., & Naylor, A. (2016). Picture exchange communication system and pals: A peer-mediated augmentative and alternative communication intervention for minimally verbal preschoolers with autism. *Journal of Speech, Language, and Hearing Research, 59*(5), 1133–1145.

Trottier, N., Kamp, L., & Mirenda, P. (2011). Effects of peer-mediated instruction to teach use of speech-generating devices to students with autism in social game routines. *Augmentative and Alternative Communication, 27*(1), 26–39.

Watkins, L., O'Reilly, M., Kun, M., Gevarter, C., Lancioni, G. E., Sigafoos, J., & Lang, R. (2015). A review of peer-mediated social interaction interventions for students with autism in inclusive settings. *Journal of Autism and Developmental Disabilities, 45,* 1070–1083.

Whalon, K. J., Conroy, M. A., Martinez, J. R., & Werch, B. L. (2015). School-based peer-related social competence interventions for children with autism spectrum disorder: A meta-analysis and descriptive review of single case research design studies. *Journal of Autism and Developmental Disorders, 45*(6), 1513–1531.

White, S. W., Scahill, L., Klin, A., Koenig, K., & Volkmar, F. R. (2007). Educational placements and service use patterns of individuals with autism spectrum disorders. *Journal of Autism and Developmental Disorders, 37*(8), 1403–1412.

Wolfberg, P., DeWitt, M., Young, G. S., & Nguyen, T. (2015). Integrated play groups: Promoting symbolic play and social engagement with typical peers in children with ASD across settings. *Journal of Autism and Developmental Disorders, 45,* 830–845.

Wong, C., Odom, S. L., Hume, K. A., Cox, C. W., Fettig, A., Kurcharczyk, S., . . . Schultz, T. R. (2015). Evidence-based practices for children, youth, and young adults with autism spectrum disorder: A comprehensive review. *Journal of Autism and Developmental Disorders, 45*(7), 1951–1966.

Zagona, A. L., & Mastergeorge, A. M. (2016). An empirical review of peer-mediated interventions: Implications for young children with autism spectrum disorders. *Focus on Autism and Other Developmental Disabilities.* Advance online publication. doi:1088357616671295.

13

Visual and Environmental Supports for Learners With Autism Spectrum Disorder and Complex Communication Needs

Joanne M. Cafiero and Tabitha Jones-Wohleber

Visual and environmental supports have been used in the trenches of classrooms, therapy rooms, communities, and homes of individuals with autism spectrum disorder (ASD) and complex communication needs (CCN) for over 50 years. Visual supports are words, icons, pictures, logos, and objects that symbolically represent concepts, other objects, ideas, and locations, both in the concrete and the abstract. Many of these supports were created by practitioners and parents using ordinary materials and inspired by a desperate need to help those with ASD and CCN with limited or no speech. Thus, early stage use of visual supports was based on the "necessity is the mother of invention" principle.

Environmental supports are physical structures, equipment, and spatial arrangements that enhance the ability of the individual to function and participate effectively and independently within particular environments. Examples of environmental supports include quiet spaces, low sensory spaces, labeled areas, choice areas, and movement areas within a classroom, home, workplace, or community. Environmental supports can also address temporal structures and how a school or work day is organized (e.g., table-top activities alternating with gross motor activities). Often, visual supports are used to identify the tools, structures, and locations of the environmental supports. For example, icons can label a reading or math center, a box of preferred items, or a low-sensory quiet corner. This chapter addresses visual and environmental supports as part of evidence-based practices (EBPs).

Visual and environmental supports were originally based on practitioner trial and error, and these methods were disseminated through workshops and trainings before scientific data validated them. Practitioner expertise led the way in EBP and provided the stimulus for validating research. Empirical data can be a guide for practitioners seeking the most effective and efficient tools, but it is important to note that many of the cited research studies are short-term interventions that do not represent the long-term exposure required for learning a visual language system both for typical people and those with ASD and CCN. Some of the studies were conducted in clinical rather than natural environments. It is also important that the use of visual and environmental supports be scientifically validated in a way that does not just select a research question that is easy to measure (Light & McNaughton, 2016). These issues are critical in moving the field forward in identifying the most effective and socially valid interventions. Individuals are complex, and measuring skill acquisition in communicative input and output is also complex. Practitioners can best be informed by these three-pronged principles of good practice: clinical expertise, best available scientific evidence, and client and family input (American Speech-Language-Hearing Association, 2018).

A HISTORY OF VISUAL SUPPORTS

Early developments in visual and environmental supports recognized the importance of providing concrete cues help shape functional and communication skills in individuals with ASD and CNN. The evolution of practices that utilized cues to add information as well as structure and predictability to activities and environments, in tandem with the emergence of a myriad of practitioner-created and commercially available symbols systems, lay the foundation for tools now widely implemented to foster communication, participation, and understanding of expectations for individuals with ASD and CNN.

A Visual-Graphic Supports Timeline

The history of visual and environmental supports for people with ASD and CCN traces as far back as the mid-1960s with the development of the University of North Carolina TEACCH Autism Program (Schopler, Brehm, Kinsborne, & Reichler, 1971). The TEACCH program begins from the premise that autism is a culture; thus, specific tools, supports, and environmental adaptations reinforce the culturally based strengths and preferences of those with ASD and CCN while targeting their needs. The program thereby fosters the development of meaningful, engaging, and generalizable skill sets for participants. The environmental structures and adaptations of TEACCH, still thriving today, include symbolic visual and structural supports. The TEACCH work systems, designed for individuals across the lifespan, have been empirically validated and shown to lessen the challenges in ASD as well as increase independence, engagement, and overall well-being and quality of life (Mesibov & Shea, 2010). Principles of visual structuring are ubiquitous elements of high-quality and evidence-based educational programs. Many of the principles of the TEACCH® program are incorporated in the concept of Universal Design for Learning (UDL). UDL proposes that learning environments, tools, and strategies be structured and designed to accommodate and include all students and all learning styles, including, of course, students with ASD and CCN (CAST, 2016). In that respect, TEACCH® was a progressive and innovative program that paved the way for the universal implementation of visual and environmental supports.

The Evolution of Symbol Systems for Individuals with ASD and CCN

Visual supports for individuals with limited or no speech were developed and implemented from a belief that nonspeaking individuals with significant disabilities indeed had the right to communication and self-actualization. One of the earliest visual graphic language systems was developed by Charles Bliss (Blissymbolics International, 2016) for the purpose of disseminating a universal visual-graphic and semantic written language, independent of speech. The 5,000 symbols, initially called semantography, were inspired by Chinese written language and composed of 150–200 basic elements. These elements form 1,200 semantic characters that can be combined to create multi-character Bliss words. In 1971, Shirley McNaughton first used Bliss as a communication system primarily for children with physical disabilities (Blissymbolics International, 2016). Bliss and rebus symbols were the earliest documented visual symbols for language.

Other early stage visual support efforts are also worthy of mention. *Teaching Language with Pictures* (Giddan & Giddan, 1984) targeted communication through line drawings for students with ASD and CCN. Although used in a simple stimulus–response format, this methodology prompted symbolic communicative responses from many individuals for the very first time (Jane Giddan, personal communication, November 3, 2016). Tangible symbols, a currently unstandardized bank of tactile objects and representations of objects used to support learners with visual impairments, ASD, and CCN, is another example of an early-stage visual support strategy, used to this day. Finally, Blissymbols, simple line drawings used to support communicative input and output, served as a platform for later development of the widely used Picture Exchange Communication System (PECS) and the software package Boardmaker. Initially consisting of three large binders of symbols created and compiled by Roxie Mayer, a speech-language pathologist, to support her students, Boardmaker has evolved into a suite of software packages available in 44 languages. The symbols have become ubiquitous across AAC and special education communities. Although it was the first, several other well-developed symbol libraries have also emerged.

FEATURES AND FUNCTIONS OF VISUAL SUPPORTS

Characteristics of visual supports that influence the relevance and accessibility of those supports for individuals with ASD and CCN are varied and shaped by the individual's skills and needs. Factors such as iconicity, use of color, arrangement of symbols, and purpose affect decisions related to the selection and development of visual tools. Individual skills that influence both the selection and development as well as the use of visual tools include literacy skills, motor skills, and visual processing skills. Understanding the relationship between the features and functions of visual supports and an individuals' skills and needs is essential to developing and implementing effective tools.

Iconicity of Visual Supports

Iconicity refers to the relationship and resemblance between a symbol and its meaning, critical for individuals on the autism spectrum and with CCN because of their challenges with short-term memory, processing, and interfering sensory channels. Visual supports provide a static, predictable, inanimate cueing system with access automatically provided as long as it is needed. Difficulties with social interaction and anxiety are mitigated through the inanimate nature of visual supports; the supports become a buffer and a bridge between two communication partners.

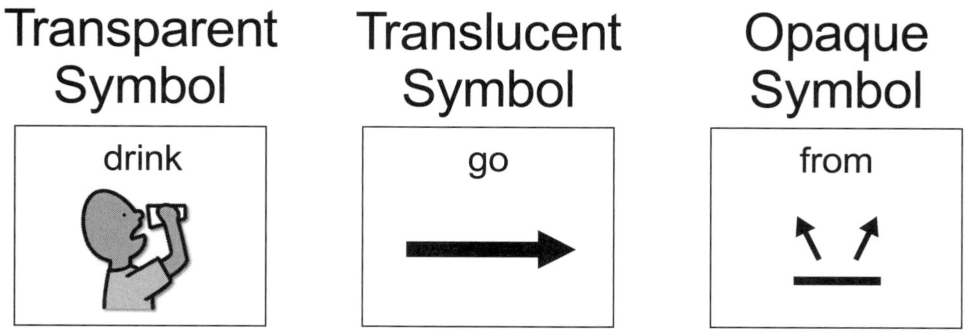

Transparent Symbol

drink

Translucent Symbol

go

Opaque Symbol

from

Figure 13.1. Examples of transparent, translucent, and iconic symbols. Created using Picture Communication Symbols ©1981–2016 by Mayer-Johnson LLC a Tobii Dynavox company. All Rights Reserved Worldwide. Used with permission. Boardmaker® is a trademark of Mayer-Johnson LLC.

Transparent symbols most clearly represent their referents whereas opaque symbols are more abstract and thus difficult to decipher for some learners because they have no clear-cut relationship to the referent. Translucent symbols are decipherable with additional information. See Figure 13.1 for examples of transparent, translucent, and opaque symbols in Picture Communication Symbols (PCS) format.

The iconicity of visual supports has been the subject of numerous research studies involving typical individuals as well as those with ASD and CCN. Iconicity is determined by the color, transparency, corresponding text, social content, and the cultural context of the symbol. In early studies with typical individuals, more transparent Rebus symbols were easier to learn than Blissymbolics (Ecklund & Reichle, 1987). Likewise, compared to other less iconic symbol systems it was found that individuals with significant disabilities learned the more transparent iconic picture systems more readily than Blissymbolics (Huriburt, Iwata & Green, 1982; Mirenda & Locke, 1989). Conversely, in a study of a PECS intervention, there was little or no difference in effectiveness between symbols of high and low transparency (Angermeier, Schlosser, Luiselli, Harrington, & Carter, 2008). There may also be a hierarchy of symbol transparency. Mirenda and Locke (1989) found that Blissymbols and text were the most difficult to understand whereas tangible objects the easiest.

Iconicity and Aided and Unaided Symbol Systems

Visual symbols can also be aided or unaided. An unaided symbol system, such as sign language or gestures, does not require any external tool with which to deliver the message. Aided symbols can be tangible symbol systems (objects or parts of objects), pictographs, ideographs, and photographs. What is critical is that the visual support be readily understandable or *transparent* for the intended user and, at the very least, learnable to the individual.

Aided systems require a tactile, tangible, visual tool such as line drawings, objects, or photographs. Unaided visual supports include gestures, facial expressions, and manual signs such as American Sign Language (ASL). Whereas some manual signs in ASL are iconic, such as DRINK and EAT, many are not. Manual signs are obviously more convenient, given that hands create the symbol, but they require more sophisticated fine motor skills than visual-graphic symbols. Important to note is that the speaking communication partner, as receiver, must understand ASL. Rotholz, Berkowitz, and Burberry (1989) found that when nonspeaking individuals with ASD/CCN used manual signs, their messages were less intelligible to speaking communication partners than when they used visual-graphic symbols. In a comparison study of requesting using either gestures or visual-graphic symbols, a child with Angelman syndrome produced more accurate requests using graphic modes (Martin, Reichle, Dimian & Chen, 2013). There may be a significant cognitive load to learning manual signs in addition to executing a complex motor act of signing. Motor planning and execution—the ability to identify, plan, and then execute a physical action—has recently been identified as a challenge for many individuals with ASD and CCN (Gowen & Hamilton, 2013).

When Standard Visual-Graphic Symbols Are Ineffective

For individuals most severely impacted by ASD and CCN, a boilerplate visual-graphic symbol system may not always be effective, even with long-term implementation. Features specific to symbols can also affect the rate at which they are learned and generalized. Stephenson (2007) found that color-coding symbol to referent, which adds another cue, improved speed and ease of picture recognition in individuals with CCN and severely limited verbal comprehension skills. Clustering symbols by color also improved the speed and accuracy of processing in individuals with ASD (Wilkinson & McIlvaine, 2013). In a study comparing grayscale to color on symbol acquisition and generalization, it was found that half of the preschool subjects with ASD successfully learned both symbol sets whereas the other half were more proficient with the grayscale (Hetzroni & Ne'eman, 2013).

Photographs are legitimate visual symbols and can be digitally manipulated for maximum iconicity. It was found that minimally verbal children and their ability-matched typical peers were able to successfully complete tasks with color photographs, black and white line drawings, and abstract pictures; however, both groups of children were more successful in the most iconic photographic condition. A transition intervention with photographs of contrasting (high and low) contextual complexity was implemented with 3 preschool children with ASD. Although both photographs were effective, the student with the most intense needs transitioned more independently and quickly with the contextually more complex photograph (Siegel & Lien, 2015).

Iconicity is affected not only by the visual features of the symbols but the cultural context within which they were developed (Huer, 2000). Some symbols are clearly culturally relevant (e.g., foods, customs, family structures) and therefore more iconic.

All of these factors may influence the user's *initial* response to the type of visual support and prompt the practitioner to explore in more detail the effect of color, transparency, text, and social and cultural features of the visual support. Nonetheless, it is important to keep in mind that exposure to an unfamiliar visual-graphic language system may not yield an immediate response from many individuals. What is required is a visually rich environment in which the speaking communicators are modeling and teaching communication while using the symbols consistently and over time.

Iconicity and Individual Processing Styles

Iconicity and transparency may also be affected by the particular processing strengths of the subjects in each of the aforementioned studies. Researchers noted that those students with better receptive language were more effective at a visual-processing experimental task (Hartley & Allen, 2015a, 2015b). Individuals with ASD and CCN did not perform picture recognition and matching tasks as well as their peers with functional language (Mirenda & Locke, 1989). Unfamiliarity with a symbol system as well as relying on verbal cues for identifying symbols may also affect the success of symbol use, questioning the premise of strong visual-processing skills, particularly in the ASD population (Tremblath, Vivante, Iocono, & Dissanayake, 2015). Romski and Sevcik (1996) theorize that spoken language may provide some of the scaffolding for recognizing and using visual symbols.

Visual Supports With Multiple Symbols

Although the use of multiple symbols infers an AAC device or complex communication display, simple visual supports can involve more than one symbol. When using more than one symbol as part of a visual support tool, both the graphic detail and the spatial orientation of the symbol on the visual tool are important factors to consider (Thistle & Wilkinson, 2013). A comparison study of icon learnability with typical adults found that training procedures using smaller symbols on consistent locations were more effective than procedures using large icons in random positions (Dukhovny & Zhou, 2016). This research, performed with typical individuals, may have relevance for those with ASD and CCN.

Visual Organizational Mode, Visual Input Mode, and Visual Expressive Mode

Shane and colleagues (2015) organized visual symbols by function: visual-organizational mode, visual-input or instructional mode, and visual-expressive mode. Visual-organizational supports individuals in negotiating environments, sequences and tasks; visual-input/instructional provides augmented input as communication and instructions; and visual-expressive is the actual use of the tool by the person with ASD and CCN to communicate. Visual-input/instructional is the processing of environmental and partner visual input; therefore, a more passive role is presumed; the person is looking, processing, and responding to the visual. Both the visual-expressive and visual-organizational involve more active participation of the individual; the individual with ASD and CCN is locating the symbols, engaging in self-management, or generating communicative output. This presumes a considerable cognitive load for the individual with ASD and CCN. In using a visual support for communicative output, the communicator must locate the symbol by attending to the task while engaging short-term memory and simultaneously screening out distractions (Thistle & Wilkinson, 2013). This automatically diverts and delays the symbol user from constructing and delivering the message to her communication partner or from self-prompting to manage a task. This highlights the importance of both being able to recognize and locate the symbol as efficiently and effectively as possible.

Text as Visual Symbols

Text is also a visual-graphic symbol system. It is ubiquitous in our environment and requires a minimum of support tools; therefore, it is reasonable to ask if and when text alone is the appropriate medium as the frontline symbol system for some individuals. In addition, there is a significant bank of anecdotal and scientific data on the incidence of hyperlexia, the spontaneous, unschooled ability to read words without *demonstrating* comprehension (Gregorenak et al., 2002) in both the speaking and nonspeaking ASD population. This may prompt practitioners to consider text as a primary symbol system.

It is common practice to pair symbols with text in visual support and AAC systems. Research has validated that the pairing of icon plus text systems does not appear to inhibit communicative input or output (Sennott, Light, & McNaughton, 2016; Cafiero, 2001; Romski & Sevcik, 1996). The addition of text enhances symbol meaning for the speaking communication partners, facilitating more effective aided input. For some nonspeaking individuals with ASD and CCN, however, there may be a hyper focus on text. Eye gaze and tracking studies have also considered the effect of the addition of text on visual attention to a symbol. In a comparison study of typical individuals with those on the autism spectrum, Nakano and colleagues (2010) found, when looking at captioned video, those with ASD looked significantly longer at the caption. It is unclear whether the focus was because of the inanimate nature of text or the actual processing of information. Astute observation of the individual and some good old-fashioned trial and error, especially when supported with data collection, can go a long way in making a determination as to whether text will be an effective option.

Literacy and Visual Supports

There is no question that literacy learning is intimately linked to communication. Sight word reading was successfully taught through the gradual fading of photo images on a text plus photo visual support (Birkan, McClannahan & Krantz, 2007). Another study used scripts and script fading to facilitate social interactions (Brown, Krantz, McClannahan, & Poulson, 2008). Emerging studies on systematic, research-based literacy opportunities and instruction for individuals with ASD and CCN are showing promise with moderate to significant gains in independently interacting with literacy artifacts as well as moving from emergent to conventional literacy skill levels in individuals with significant disabilities, including ASD and CCN (Hatch, 2009; Erickson, Clendon, Abraham, Roy, & Van der Karr, 2005; Koppenhaver, Erickson & Skotko, 2001).

It is important to distinguish that although the ultimate goal of communication may include literacy, there is always a critical and imminent need to provide effective, efficient iconic visual support systems to individuals with ASD and CCN, given the intensity of their social, self-management, and behavioral needs. For the vast majority of individuals in this population, text is the least iconic of physical symbolic systems (Mirenda & Locke, 1989). The implementation of a visual support system is the interactive (not drilled) juncture of context, symbol, and communication partners. The most iconic system for the individual should be the target visual support system for communicative input and output. Emergent and conventional literacy skills may be enhanced incidentally through text-symbol exposure and use. More formal literacy instruction can be implemented in concert with symbol support systems, through shared reading, and with systematic, research-based literacy instruction.

Feature Match: Visual Supports, ASD, and CCN

There is an important feature match between the learning styles and preferences of those with ASD and CCN and the characteristics of visual supports. The functioning of many individuals with ASD and CCN can be boosted through visual supports such as self-cueing, self-management tools, and pictorial task analyses. Multiple cue responding, the ability to process complex cues, is often another challenge for those with ASD and CCN. Visual supports can be as simple as a single highly transparent icon to several icons representing more complex ideas. Icons then, can be added or deleted to accommodate the current processing abilities of the individual, thereby adjusting the number of presented cues. Visual supports for both receptive and expressive communication address the growing body of research detailing difficulties with sensory processing and motor planning by providing a less complex mode than speech for self-cueing, communicating, and managing series of tasks. Table 13.1 summarizes the research on ASD and CCN that support the use of visual support systems.

VISUALLY AUGMENTED SPEECH

Each practitioner provides visual supports and access to those supports, which are compatible with the processing style of individual learners. More important, a visually augmented environment can sometimes segue into language development as the speaking communicators augment their speech by pointing to or highlighting the corresponding visual supports. Augmenting speech with visuals, generally referred to as augmentative and alternative communication (AAC), and also referred to as aided language stimulation (Goossens, Crain, & Elder, 1992), natural aided language (Cafiero, 2001), and aided language modeling (Sennott et al., 2016), has been empirically validated as increasing receptive and expressive language (see Chapter 4, "Overview of AAC for Individuals With Autism Spectrum Disorder and Complex Communication Needs," by Mirenda; Chapter 5, "Considerations in Implementing Aided Low-Tech AAC Systems for Individuals With Autism Spectrum Disorder and Complex Communication Needs," by Reichle et al., and Chapter 6, "High-Tech Aided AAC for Individuals With Autism Spectrum Disorder and Complex Communication Needs," by Caron & Holyfield).

The implementation of an AAC system is a dance between the speaking communicator and the communicator with CCN. Research suggests that comprehension appears to evolve over time and in response to the effectiveness of that dance. The augmentative and alternative communication system must also be part of the culture of the environment—embedded in every location, at the juncture of, and within every transition. An environment engineered for communication is not simply visual symbols as graffiti but a cue for practitioners to augment speech and model communication with visuals.

Table 13.1. Research and rationale for visual supports for individuals with autism spectrum disorder (ASD) and complex communication needs (CCN)

ASD and CCN	Evidence	Rationale for visual supports
Visual processing strengths	Kaldy, Giserman, Carter, and Blaser, 2016; Wilkinson and McIlvaine, 2013	Provides focus for engagement, communication, and self-management
Memory challenges and processing styles	Englund, Decker, Allen and Roberts, 2014; Goh and Peterson, 2012; Steele, Minshew, Luna, and Sweeney, 2007	Static, predictable nature allows reliance on recognition rather than memory and provides extended processing time.
Executive functioning challenges (e.g., self-management, initiating, maintaining and completing a task, managing transitions)	deVries and Geurts, 2015; Henry, Messer, and Nash, 2012; MacDuff, Krantz, and McClannahan, 1993; Semrud-Clikeman, Fine, Goldenning and Bledsoe, 2014; van den Bergh et al., 2014	Helps navigate routines for self-cueing, independence, and self-advocacy and also compensates for low inner speech
Social anxiety	Bellini, 2006; Davis et al, 2012; Factor, Condy, Farley, and Scarpa, 2016; Freeth, Bullock, and Milne, 2013; White, Bray, and Ollendick, 2012	Buffer and bridge between communication partners
Preference for inanimate objects	Bird, Press, and Richardson, 2011; Mongillo, Irwin, Whalen, Klaiman, Carter, and Schultz, 2008	Visual supports are static and inanimate.
Difficulty with multiple cues	Kelly, Leader, and Reed, 2015; Ploog, 2010; Rieth, Stahmer, Suhrheinrich, and Schreibman, 2015	Level of complexity can be controlled by systematically increasing or decreasing visual cues.
Difficulty with motor planning	Forti et al., 2013; Gowen and Hamilton, 2013; Stoit, van Shie, Slaats-Willemse, and Buitelaar, 2013	Pointing to, pulling, or moving a visual symbol is a simpler motor act than speech.
Problem behaviors	Brown and Mirenda, 2006; Mirenda, 1997; Vaughn and Horner, 1995	Use of visual supports in Functional Communication Training contexts affects immediate, sustained improvement in behavior. Contingency maps provide visual-graphic models of actions and consequences.
Prompt dependence	Hume and Odom, 2007; McClannahan and Krantz, 2010	Provides an external representation for self-cueing

Determining the Visual Support System

Systematic consideration of tools well-suited to meet a student's needs is appropriately addressed through the SETT Framework (Zabala, 2005). The SETT Framework helps teams gather and organize information to guide collaborative decisions about tools and strategies that foster the educational success of students with disabilities. The acronym SETT outlines a process by which specific focus is placed upon the

Student, Environment(s), Task(s) and Tool(s). This easy and effective framework emphasizes collaboration among team members to ensure all aspects of a student's needs. Strengths, interests, environment, and activities are considered when selecting tools and strategies to meet an individual's needs.

By highlighting both the characteristics of students as well as the environment and tasks that shape learning experiences, the SETT Framework brings to light the necessary considerations to select and customize learning tools, including visual supports, meaningfully. Important considerations in the decision-making process include ease and expediency of use and opportunities for meaningful and well-timed feedback. Additional considerations that influence the decision-making process may include the following: how the student physically accesses and/or manipulates her visual tools, symbol representation (e.g., photo, line drawing, word), balancing the logistics of ambulation or wheelchair use on portability, fine motor skills, vision skills, the need for cues or feedback, maintenance strategies, interfering behaviors such as mouthing or throwing items, the need for durability, and sensory needs that influence attention, self-regulation, and learning. Effectively implemented visual supports emphasize salient information about activities or the environment (Siegel & Lien, 2015) and are appropriately customized to direct attention and minimize opportunities for distracted behaviors and tangential interactions. For instance, a student who engages in self-stimulatory behavior by playing with small items such as cards, beads, or coins will likely be distracted by visual support tools with moveable pieces. Manipulating a picture schedule or other tool with removable hook and loop material such as Velcro pieces may be more distracting than beneficial. An alternative format, such as crossing off activities with a marker or manipulating a schedule on a wall (that is visible but out of reach from his work space), needs to be considered.

The case study at the end of this chapter describes use of the SETT Framework to engineer and structure the environment for a student with ASD and CCN. It is important, however, to be aware that a visual support system embedded into an environment functions as a second language, and as such, it must also be a common language among all communicators in that setting.

Tailoring Visual Supports: Attention, Motor Skills, and Sensory Needs

The SETT Framework can guide implementation of visual supports in two important ways: 1) by identifying the areas of need where implementation of visual supports may be beneficial, and 2) by identifying student characteristics that may influence access, customization, and individualization of visual supports, including the selection of materials, arrangement of targets, and determination of behaviors to interact with the visual tools.

The speaking communicators, practitioners, and peers have an active role in augmenting speech via the AAC system to provide information, alert transitions, guide self-monitoring, and model expressive communication opportunities. Individuals with ASD and CCN also have an active role. This consists of manipulating symbols (i.e., touching, pulling, or removing them from their "home") and presenting them to their communication partners as a message. For self-monitoring and communication, symbols are moved to locations representing active engagement or completion; becoming a metaphor for the process. Therefore, the tools and materials for an effective visual support system access are important.

Sensory Needs and Visual Support Systems: Practitioners' Perspectives

One's ability to maintain attention to task, demonstrate learning, and engage in self-regulatory behaviors are influenced by an individual's sensory needs and inputs (Case-Smith & Bryan, 1999). Factors such as processing visual, auditory, and tactile information can have an impact on one's ability to cognitively engage with information in the environment. A physiological need for tactile, kinesthetic, proprioceptive, or vestibular inputs and experiences during learning and activities that require engagement may influence the ability of individuals with ASD and CCN to attend, process, and engage with the visual materials, auditory information, and tactile supports available in the environment. Jane Ayres's work (1979) with sensory integration theory emphasizes the impact of sensory experiences and environmental inputs on the ability of one's body to function effectively within the environment to demonstrate learning as well as regulate emotions and behavior. In a systematic review of the literature reviewing the effectiveness of sensory integration, May-Benson & Koomar (2010) noted positive outcomes for short to moderate intervention-related durations when compared to no treatment in areas such as motor planning; socialization, attention, and behavioral regulation; reading-related skills; participation in active play; and achievement of individualized goals. However, others have found less promising evidence (Weitlauf, Sathe, McPheeters, & Warren, 2017). Although empirical evidence for sensory integration practices is limited, application of these principles may be useful for guiding and perhaps more important problem-solving the implementation of visual supports, environmental supports, as well as selection of learning materials. Holistic consideration of an individual's needs addresses not just instructional, self-management, organizational or readiness strategies but also the emotional and physical context in which visual tools, environmental supports, and learning are implemented.

In the context of using visual supports, proprioceptive input, for example, can be achieved by pushing completed task cards or tokens through the slot of a stiff or resistive material, such as the plastic lid of a container. This may be grounding for one student, evoking focus and calm readiness. For another student, the act of working a token through the slot may awaken the senses and increase alertness. The mechanical and access features of visual support systems should be designed to optimize an individual's sensorimotor and neurological perspectives as well as facilitate appropriate engagement with the tool.

Deciding the most appropriate attachment method for the visual supports is another example. Magnetic tape and Velcro are two common methods of attaching and detaching visual-graphic symbols from either their storage location or "symbol garage" or to the "in process" or "completion" location. Some practitioners report that the size of the Velcro is relevant. A larger piece of hook-and-loop Velcro will give more tactile, proprioceptive, and auditory input when being pulled off, compared to a smaller piece. For some individuals this kind of input may be so reinforcing as to override the utilitarian function of the visual support system—the pulling and peeling of the Velcro may interfere with functional implementation of the system (L. Burkhart, personal communication, November 10, 2016). Magnetic attachment systems do not provide as much tactile and proprioceptive input and may be a reasonable alternative. These important details are usually identified once the visual support system is in place; therefore, visual support systems are often works in progress, and practitioners need to be prepared to adapt and amend

Table 13.2.   Sensory channel considerations for customizing visual and environmental supports

Sensory channel	Customization considerations
Visual	Meaningful icons or graphics Pleasing visual arrangements Color for interest Color-coding for meaning Motivating icons such as favorite characters Interesting visual elements such as reflective tape, foam shapes, glitter, or other textures with various visual characteristics
Auditory	Verbal/auditory cues (paired with other sensory information) Transition chants, rings, or claps Rattles or clinks to indicate progress/achievement (dropping token in a cup)
Tactile	Real objects or partial objects Various textures to differentiate or extend information
Kinesthetic: coordinating one's body to perform tasks (i.e., DOING!)	Movement as a part of routines such as getting out of seat to sharpen pencil, pass out papers, or turn in work Working across a space that cannot be accessed from a sitting position, such as a countertop
Proprioceptive: awareness of one's body and body parts in space that can be achieved through pressure on and movement of joints and muscles	Use heavy duty Velcro Use ample amounts of Velcro relative to the size of moveable symbols Crumple paper to indicate task completion; write each step of a task on a separate piece of paper or sticky note Incorporate a "finished" position with resistance (e.g., push through a scored slot, open the container to put in, open snap or other fastener)
Vestibular: sensory input related to movement and balance	Wiggle seats Balance boards Sensory opportunities such as swinging or spinning to prepare the student for learning

systems as needed. See Table 13.2 for examples for customizing visual and environmental supports with consideration for sensory channels of individuals.

Practitioner-Tested Tools and Strategies: Environmental Supports

Although visual supports are often paired with environmental supports, a discussion of environmental supports as a separate factor in instructional design for individuals with ASD and CCN is warranted. Empirical data has not yet caught up with practitioner experience and expertise in strategies considered best practices in the area of environmental supports. Environmental supports encompass the science of ergonomics; that is, the designing of equipment, devices, and processes that fit the unique physical, emotional, and cognitive styles of a human being to optimize productivity by minimizing fatigue and discomfort (The American Heritage Dictionary of the English Language, 2017). Environmental supports are also a component of Universal Design for Learning (UDL). UDL is a framework to maximize teaching, learning, and engagement for all people based on scientific studies and insights on the cognitive, motor, and sensory features of how people actually learn. The three components of UDL are engagement, representation, and action and expression (CAST, 2016).

The environmental supports needed to encourage the student's full participation are shaped by space design, time schedules, lighting, equipment and furniture. Of course, a well-organized and clutter-free environment is also beneficial for all teachers and learners. Indeed, many adults have the option of designing their own work environments to accommodate their physical needs and information processing styles (Kluth, 2010). Unfortunately, often students do not have these options within their classrooms.

The following environmental supports are from the trenches of special education. These are practitioner-tested and primarily supported by common-sense and anecdotal reports.

Lighting and Sound

Kluth (2010) described accommodations that address sensitivities related to light and sound. Lighting can have an important effect on comfort and, therefore, learning. Some individuals with ASD are highly sensitive to light and to the low-grade buzzing of fluorescent lights. Some options include selective use of lighting, small lamps, and indirect lighting. Ambient noise can also be a distraction or even painful for an individual with ASD and CCN. Providing a "quiet corner," visually indicated with boundaries and pictures, can serve as a retreat for any student experiencing sound overload. A screened off space, study carrels, or a closet with floor pillows can also serve as places to minimize sensory input. Providing noise cancelling headphones can be a solution to sound sensitivity. Creating an environment for different sensory processing styles may minimize behavioral difficulties.

Seating and Learning Spaces

For some students with ASD and CCN, it is anecdotally reported that the wrap-around, one-piece desks are preferred. Providing other options such as loveseats, beach chairs, floor cushions, balance balls, bean bags, and chair-top wiggle cushions can provide variety and sensory input. Alternatively, some students may need the opportunity to stand. Lecterns and standing desks are gaining popularity with executives in helping to manage sitting fatigue, so why not provide that option for students (Kluth, 2010)?

The design of learning spaces should accommodate those who learn best while stationary as well as those who learn best by moving, and those who need some of both. Noisy, movement-friendly areas are as important as more reserved quiet seat-work areas. Some students with ASD and CCN like to pace. A rectangular pacing zone in a low-traffic area, such as across the back of the classroom, can be delineated by colored electrical tape (Kluth, 2010).

Temporal Supports

Temporal structures address how the practitioner organizes the activities of the day. Visual schedules provide the element of predictability. However, what is the appropriate proportion of learning while seated versus learning while moving? Many students with ASD and CCN have difficulty maintaining attention while seated at a desk for longer than several minutes. Alternating tabletop with gross-motor applications of curricular concepts can provide the sensory-motor input needed to extend attention beyond limited seated desk times. An example of a gross-motor application of a curricular concept would be requiring the student to move large, heavy labeled objects (such as laundry detergent containers filled with sand) with a number value as a math addition or subtraction activity.

Fidgets, small manipulatable objects that can give tactile and proprioceptive sensory-input to the user, garner strong practitioner favorability. Examples include squeeze toys, Koosh balls, play dough, or any favorite object as long as it enhances engagement. Fidgets are not just used as rewards; for some individuals they are essential for lowering anxiety and managing stress.

Slant boards are often recommended by occupational therapists to facilitate the correct position of the hand and wrist for handwriting. They also position materials for improved visual access per the Harmon Distance, the optimal angle and distance from the face and eyes for reading and writing (Cobb, 2012). As logic would follow, some practitioners report greater attention to instructional materials, including communication displays, when they are presented at an optimal angle relative to the individual's position. For students with complex sensorimotor needs, an upright position may be essential to ensure visual and motor access to visual supports and materials of instruction. It is incumbent upon the practitioner to consider factors related to positioning, access, and interaction opportunities for students who lack the physical autonomy to manage these dynamics of their own volition.

Implementing Visual and Environmental Supports

Visual and environmental supports function as input, output, and organizational tools. Although these are distinct categories, it is important to note all three functions are interdependent and mutually reinforcing and as such are part of an environment engineered for engagement and communication. Engineering the environment for communication was first detailed in 1992 by Goossens, Crain, and Elder in their landmark book, *Engineering the Preschool Environment for Interactive, Symbolic Communication*. This book originally targeted those with significant physical disabilities. It describes practical home, classroom, and therapeutic applications of the use of visual supports as an authentic second language. Results of this strategy were validated with students with significant physical disabilities (Goossens, 1984). In 1992, the effective use of visual supports in an engineered environment with an adolescent with ASD and CCN was demonstrated and showed increases in positive behaviors, engagement, and communicative output (Cafiero, 2001).

Environmental supports are implemented through visually labeling locations, objects, cues, and procedures within that environment. Temporal structures such as clocks, timers, notices, calendars, and schedules are in view. The ubiquitous presence of visual supports provides endless opportunities for speaking communicators to provide both verbal and visual input, for "heads-ups," clarifications, reminders, and information. Visual symbols can provide an advance notice of an activity, softening the effect of abrupt change for some with ASD and CCN. Providing advance notice has shown to decrease challenging behaviors (Schmit, Alper, Raschke, & Ryndak, 2000; Tustin, 1995). Visual closure systems, a tool and a method of removing the symbol from a completed scheduled activity, provides a concrete representation of the abstract concept of "finished." Applications of visual closure systems can be as simple as removing the symbol representing the completed activity, crossing it off with a pencil, or placing that symbol in a box or envelope so it is no longer visible.

Conventional Schedules and Activity Schedules

Visual schedules are the most common and effective supports in homes, classrooms, and workplaces for those with ASD and CCN. Visual schedules can be personal or general, and often individuals will have both. Visual schedules can be formatted horizontally from left to right as a precursor for literacy or vertically, reflective of a list. A visual closure system highlights the "in process" or completion of an activity.

Activity schedules are a series of pictures (e.g., symbols, photos) or words that cue an individual to perform a sequence of actions or tasks. It is the most empirically validated application of a visual support system (McClannahan & Krantz, 2010). Activity schedules can represent a sequence of activities throughout a day (between scheduled activities) or a series of steps for a particular task (within a scheduled activity). Figures 13.2–13.7 give examples of activity schedules. Activity schedules have been successfully implemented with children and adults most severely impacted by ASD and CCN. Activity schedules have facilitated independence and self-management that has generalized across activities, people, and environments

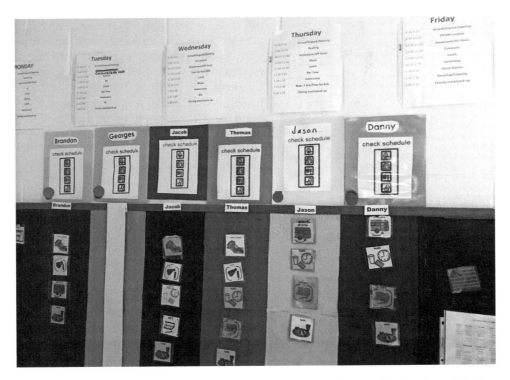

Figure 13.2. Individual student schedules of daily activities in a common classroom location. Created by Mary Kotrady (2016) using Picture Communication Symbols ©1981–2016 by Mayer-Johnson LLC a Tobii Dynavox company. All Rights Reserved Worldwide. Used with permission. Boardmaker® is a trademark of Mayer-Johnson LLC.

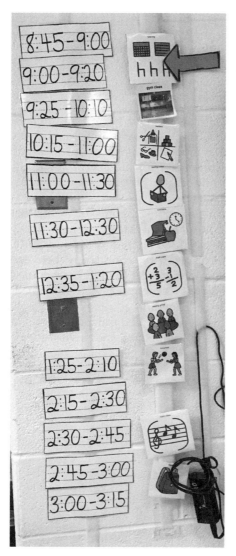

Figure 13.3. Classroom visual schedule. An orange arrow moves down the schedule indicating the current activity. Created by Amanda Keilholtz (2016) using Picture Communication Symbols ©1981-2016 by Mayer-Johnson LLC a Tobii Dynavox company. All Rights Reserved Worldwide. Used with permission. Boardmaker® is a trademark of Mayer-Johnson LLC.

(McClannahan & Krantz, 2010). The tools and materials for the implementation of an activity schedule vary and depend on the access needs of the individual. One common format is a small three-ring binder with the symbol or name of the activity on each page. The individual is prompted through a series of steps for utilizing the activity schedule book: opening the book/turning the page, pointing/looking at the symbol, obtaining the targeted activity, completing the activity, and putting it away. This receptive process is taught using most-to-least prompting with gestural rather than spoken input from the practitioner. Activity schedules have helped with transitions (Dooley, Wilczenski, & Torem, 2001), play skills (Hampshire, Butera, & Bellini, 2015), self-monitoring (Dunlap, Dunlap, Koegel, & Koegel, 1991), challenging behaviors (Krantz, MacDuff, & McClannahan, 1993), social skills (Parker & Kamps, 2011), and independence (Duttlinger, Ayres, Bevill-Davis, & Douglas, 2013). Other forms of activity schedules include visual task analyses, self-monitoring checklists, and social scripts with script fading. Activity schedules enable individuals with ASD and CCN to demonstrate long response chains, independently transition to other activities, and generalize those skills across environments without prompts or supports (MacDuff, Krantz, & McClannahan, 1993).

Visual supports for schedules are generally not faded because they provide the template and a foundation for inserting novel visuals and function much the way our personal and digital planners do. Other visual supports for specific task sequences may be given up spontaneously as the user learns the routine.

Visual Supports for Choice Making

Providing choices is an empirically validated strategy for those with ASD and CCN, relative to decreasing challenging behaviors and promoting self-determination, essential for living in the democratic society. Vaughn and Horner (1995) found that providing picture-based choices elicited fewer challenging behaviors than verbal options. Practitioners also reported that when an individual makes a choice that is not available, the speaking communicator can use visual supports to explain why, such as "later" or "first you must ___; then you can____." Practitioners report fewer challenging behaviors with this procedure. First–Then boards are widely employed for this purpose, as pictured in Figure 13.8. A task is visually represented; a reinforcer is then chosen from a menu of preferred choices, used at task completion. Visual choices can encompass multiple venues in an engineered environment, such as where to sit (e.g., blue chair or red chair) or with whom to sit (e.g., James or Kerry). These options give the individual both a sense of control and practice with using visuals for expressive communication and self-advocacy.

Visual choices can also be implemented within academic settings. Every Student Responds (EPR, Hopkins, 1979) is a strategy giving *all* students the option to respond in ways other than speech. The teacher may cue a group of students with a question and students can respond by selecting and displaying the correct response with a gesture or from a menu of visual choices on her desk.

Visual Supports Engineered with Flexibility

Behaviors often associated with autism can include rigidity, difficulties with transitions, difficulty maintaining attention to task, and starting and stopping an activity. For some students, implementation of simple, predictable visual supports alone are beneficial in mitigating the impacts of such behaviors. For other students it may be necessary to embed flexibility and otherwise design individualized programs to address specific behavioral needs. Creating flexible features within visual tools serves to create a clear and predictable plan for addressing exceptions to the routine; provide a tangible means to explain unanticipated changes in activities; and decrease transition time when the unexpected occurs, thereby increasing positive behavior during unpredictable events. For instance, a student who has difficulty transitioning to the next activity, when the current task

Figure 13.4. Personal schedule with picture and text. Color-coding is used to break the day into chunks. This facilitates ease of understanding of the activities of the day. Created using Picture Communication Symbols ©1981–2016 by Mayer-Johnson LLC a Tobii Dynavox company. All Rights Reserved Worldwide. Used with permission. Boardmaker® is a trademark of Mayer-Johnson LLC.

Figure 13.5.   Picture schedule on a ring. Cards are flipped on the ring as they are completed. This may be useful for individuals who require minimal visual clutter due to vision or processing needs. Created by Tabi Jones-Wohleber (2016) using Picture Communication Symbols ©1981–2016 by Mayer-Johnson LLC a Tobii Dynavox company. All Rights Reserved Worldwide. Used with permission. Boardmaker® is a trademark of Mayer-Johnson LLC.

is incomplete, may benefit from a "not yet finished" box, in addition to his "finished" box. This gives the student a clear structure for what to do with unfinished tasks, which may aid his ability to transition. Visual cues to "wait" or "listen" can be beneficial for helping students engage in turn taking or direct their attention toward their teacher during instruction. An individual may hold an "I'm waiting" cue while waiting or in between activities, often a difficulty for those with ASD and CCN.

Turn taking also requires flexibility and can be facilitated through a visual turn-taking template by flipping from "my turn" on one side to "I'm waiting" on the other as the roles reverse. Another strategy for creating flexibility may include using a self-monitoring clip to help a student maintain attention to task. The clip moves down a task analysis checklist and indicates "I'm working" on one side, and "I have a question/need help" on the other, prompting the student to self-monitor his ability to complete each task as he moves through the checklist. Having ready access to sticky notes or a small whiteboard allows "in the moment" visual input to adjust to dynamic environments and activities. Incorporating symbols such as "fire drill," "substitute teacher," or "special activity" into picture schedules can either prepare students in advance or inform them in the moment of unpredictable events by creating a concrete representation of unique events that may interfere with the familiar routine.

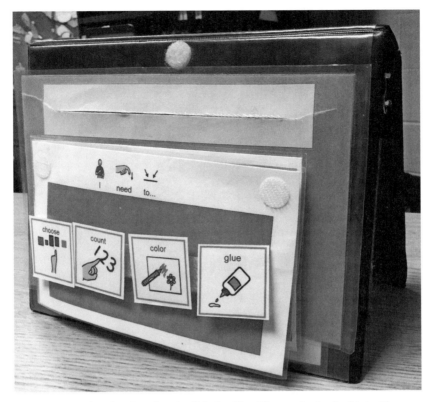

Figure 13.6. Task analysis board on the All-in-One Visual Support Book, a flexible tool for proving versatile input across an individual's environments. Created by Tabi Jones-Wohleber (2015) using Picture Communication Symbols ©1981–2016 by Mayer-Johnson LLC a Tobii Dynavox company. All Rights Reserved Worldwide. Used with permission. Boardmaker® is a trademark of Mayer-Johnson LLC.

Some students benefit from alternative means to demonstrate learning. For instance, a focus finder or flashlight may be used in lieu of pointing. These modalities frame or highlight a response and provide visual focus and can be used receptively or expressively. Figure 13.9 shows an example of a focus finder.

Timers for Enhancing Effectiveness of Visual Supports

Timers are another tool that can bolster the effectiveness of visual support tools and can be visual supports themselves. Benefits include supporting transitions, facilitating attention to task, providing opportunities to check in and review, and establishing expectations about how time will be spent. It is important to consider the individual and his or her environment when choosing a timer, specifically the type of feedback given when time expires. Simple kitchen timers typically have an auditory signal such as a ring or buzz. Sand timers and liquid motion timers are visual timers. Timers for individuals with sensory impairments may alert with lights and/or vibration. Timers with visual, auditory, and/or vibratory feedback are native to many mobile devices. Appropriate feedback considers the sensory needs and sensitivities of the individual as well as the context in which it will be used.

Figure 13.7. Visual instructions for an art project representing the finished product, steps of the task, and materials to be used. Created by Teresa Ismach (2016) using Picture Communication Symbols ©1981–2016 by Mayer-Johnson LLC a Tobii Dynavox company. All Rights Reserved Worldwide. Used with permission. Boardmaker® is a trademark of Mayer-Johnson LLC.

For example, an individual who uses a timer in the classroom for self-monitoring would likely benefit from visual or vibratory feedback so as not to disturb the class with an auditory interruption. Prudent implementation is warranted as the use of timers can be anxiety inducing for some individuals.

Priming

Priming is another strategy, generally implemented in conjunction with visuals, to help prepare individuals for an upcoming or novel experience. Priming tools can be picture or photo books or explanatory visual sequences that are rehearsed with an individual prior to the event.

Emotional Competence: Tools to Support the Language of Emotions

Emotional competence is one's ability to identify, respond to, and manage one's own and others' emotions for the purposes of making and maintaining friends,

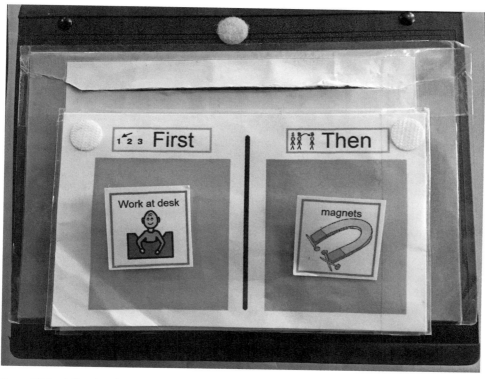

Figure 13.8. A first-then board, part of an All-in-One Visual Support Book. Created by Tabi Jones-Wohleber (2015) using Picture Communication Symbols ©1981–2016 by Mayer-Johnson LLC a Tobii Dynavox company. All Rights Reserved Worldwide. Used with permission. Boardmaker® is a trademark of Mayer-Johnson LLC.

academic success, and community integration (Na, Wilkinson, Karny, Blackstone, Stifter, 2016); this is often reduced to identification of emotion (e.g., "I feel mad") for students with ASD and CCN. Based on the components of emotional competence outlined by Saarni (1999), Na and colleagues proposed three steps for building emotional competence in students who use AAC: 1) provide and model language for a variety of emotions, 2) validate and discuss emotions, and 3) communicate about appropriate responses to emotions. Although the specific need to include the vocabulary of emotions on AAC devices was discussed, visual supports in the form of problem-solving cards or books or calm down kits are implemented by many practitioners as a useful scaffold for teaching this process of identifying, processing, and responding to emotions. These types of supports are found in quiet areas, "time-out" locations, and may be generic or customized to reflect the behaviors, needs, and experiences of specific individuals. Figure 13.10 illustrates an example of visual tools that support the process of understanding and processing emotions and appropriate behavior. Pairing such tools with an individual's AAC tool is imperative to provide ample opportunities to learn self-talk, a key skill for developing emotional competence, as well as for expressive communication. Teaching the language of emotions is not a behavior-management strategy to be used during times of heightened emotion. With a focus on the processing of emotions, an emphasis is placed on modeling the language of emotions across contexts,

Figure 13.9. A focus finder highlights information and provides an alternative means to demonstrate learning. Created using Picture Communication Symbols ©1981–2016 by Mayer-Johnson LLC a Tobii Dynavox company. All Rights Reserved Worldwide. Used with permission. Boardmaker® is a trademark of Mayer-Johnson LLC.

to describe self, others, and even storybook characters. As emotional beings, this approach to processing emotive events is worth exploring to help individuals understand and cope with the challenges of life.

Visual Supports for Managing Behaviors

Managing behaviors for students with ASD and CCN can be a difficult task for any practitioner. Receptive input to facilitate understanding of expectations can be provided through visual cues, scripts, and models. A ring of visual cues may be worn on a lanyard by school staff to discretely cue students to "sit" or "look." Positive behaviors can be reinforced by showing "good job." A widely utilized framework for objectively describing challenging situations are social narratives. These reflect appropriate responses to situations determined difficult for the student. One example is *Social Stories*, developed by Carol Gray (www.carolgraysocialstories.com). A flexible social script is pictured in Figure 13.11. Functional communication training is one of the most effective strategies for helping individuals understand and communicate about their emotional states: Visual support protocols are used to reduce or inhibit challenging behaviors by teaching communication skills, sometimes using AAC and visual supports that correspond to the function of the behavior (see Chapter 7, "Functional Communication Training for Durable Behavior Change" by McComas et al.).

Students who benefit from incentives to maintain positive behaviors may benefit from visual tools that provide a structure for self-monitoring their behaviors. These may include token reward boards or the Incredible 5-point Scale (Dunn Buron & Curtis, 2012), among others. When challenging behaviors do occur, students often require support to process the experience and debrief regarding their emotional experience. Calm-down kits or books, or customized social scripts, can facilitate this process.

Zack's Contingency Map

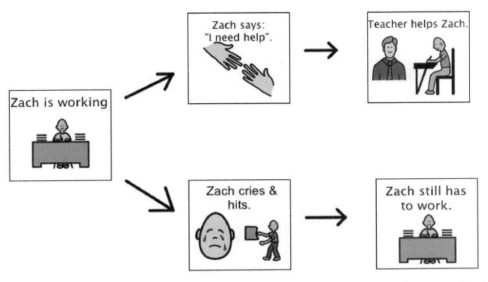

Figure 13.10.   A visual representation of actions and consequences. (Adapted by permission from content found in Brown, K. E. & Mirenda, P. [2006]. Contingency mapping: Use of a novel visual support strategy as an adjunct to functional equivalence training. *Journal of Positive Behavior Interventions, 8*[3], 155–164.)

Token systems utilizing concrete objects such as tokens, coins, and bingo markers, paired with visual cues, are effective tools for behavioral self-management. Token systems include visuals representing the task or expectation, the tokens for marking, and the reward for completion of the task. A simple token board could include a visual for "quiet voice," tokens, a target location for tokens, and a reinforcer visual. Individuals learn to use a token system through practitioner modeling or systematic fading of prompts using most-to-least or least-to-most prompting.

Reinforcer puzzles (Jennifer Waltrip, personal communication, May, 1997) are an example of a token system in which the image of the reinforcer is the token itself. When a token system is too abstract, a reinforcer puzzle may be more salient. The image, often with corresponding text, is cut into strips. Each letter of the word and section of the image is an individual strip. As the individual engages in the desired behaviors, a piece of the puzzle is constructed so that ultimately the reinforcer is earned when the image of the reinforcer is complete, as pictured in Figure 13.12.

Self-management and monitoring tools help individuals with CCN and ASD understanding their personal emotional states and those of others, as well as communicate that information by applying concrete representations to intangible emotions and behaviors. Whether due to simple unawareness or difficulty in attaching a linguistic tag to the feeling, these tools facilitate self-regulation, receptively and expressively. The Incredible 5-Point Scale is a numerical, graduated, 1–5-point tool that assigns a number to a variety of social-emotional situations, making their abstract quality more concrete (Dunn Buron & Curtis, 2012). Figure 13.13 is an

Figure 13.11. Something's Wrong social script. Choices are provided to identify emotions, causes, and solutions with moveable symbols. Pages stack to create a visual script of the situation. Created by Tabi Jones-Wohleber (2015) using Picture Communication Symbols ©1981–2016 by Mayer-Johnson LLC a Tobii Dynavox company. All Rights Reserved Worldwide. Used with permission. Boardmaker® is a trademark of Mayer-Johnson LLC.

example of the Incredible 5-Point Scale used to teach emotional states related to escalating behaviors.

Practitioners are wise to recognize that students who require behavioral support may require assistance in multiple forms to receptively understand expectations, demonstrate a measure of autonomy to self-regulate, as well as need tools to expressively process the event when emotive events or negative behaviors do occur. The essential purpose is to build self-awareness to foster greater self-advocacy.

TOOLS AND RESOURCES FOR CREATING AND CUSTOMIZING VISUAL SUPPORTS

A number of resources are available for practitioners and others implementing visual supports, including online image repositories and technology with visual supports built into applications or programs.

Figure 13.12.   Reinforcer puzzle for pretzels. (Source: Jennifer Waltrip, personal communication, May1997.)

Online Tools for Creating Visual Supports

A vast continuum of technology-based tools exists to gain access to, design, and customize visual materials to facilitate skill development, support task completion and attention to task, guide self-regulation, shape positive and productive behaviors, enhance social interactions, foster independence, improve comprehension of content, and increase communication skills and opportunities. Many online symbol libraries are available to generate static and interactive visual tools that incorporate picture symbols and/or photos. With some free and some paid options, there is wide variability in the types of symbols available, format options for accessing and arranging symbols, and customization features.

Digital and Mobile Technology and Visual Supports

Innovative mobile technologies have advanced access to visual supports in important and meaningful ways. Shane, Laubscher, Schlosser, Sorce, and Abramson (2012) discussed the broad-based benefits mobile technology has provided for individuals with ASD and other disabilities. Affordable, transportable, socially acceptable, and ubiquitous mobile technology tools have increased both access to and creation of visual content, instructional supports, and communication opportunities. Ongoing development of accessibility features that are native to mobile technology platforms continues to expand their universality. Highly relevant to individuals with ASD are interaction controls, such as scanning and custom gesture options, and guided access including use of passwords to limit unintended access to apps and customization tools within apps. In addition, built-in timers, clocks, and alerts

Figure 13.13. Incredible 5-point scale. (From Buron, K. D., & Curtis, M. [2012]. *The Incredible 5-Point Scale: Assisting students in understanding social interactions and controlling their emotional re-sponses.* Shawnee Mission, KS: AAPC Publishing [www.aapcpublishing.net]. Used with permission.)

provide feedback and self-monitoring cues often beneficial when used in tandem with other visual support tools, either low tech or high tech.

Sequencing symbols, photographs, or other picture representations for the purpose of creating schedules, task analysis checklists, or supporting literacy have widely been achieved using such commonly available tools such as Microsoft PowerPoint and a wide assortment of web sites. These tools can also now be created through features and apps available on mobile technologies. One simple example is putting photos in an album to create a sequence in the camera roll of iOS devices. A plethora of story creation apps are available to teach social skills, support literacy through visual supports with high-interest content, and engage students in writing tasks with a variety of feedback modalities. Most are sufficiently flexible to pair text and/or voice output with visual representations and often include the capability of embedding videos for instruction or reinforcement. It should be noted that the array of available apps is quickly changing and influenced by popularity, profitability, availability of tech support, and compatibility with operating system updates, among other factors (Farrall, 2016).

Maximizing the benefits of mobile technology by combining tools to customize learner experiences and expand access, the practice of app smashing is widely employed in special education classrooms. *App Smash*, a term coined by Greg Kulowiec in 2013, describes the process of transferring content created in one app to a second app for enhancement. Sometimes it is transferred to a third app and often the final product is published, shared, or stored in an alternative format. Apple, Android, and Windows-based platform tools support creation, use, and sharing of materials, including the following: photo and video editing and storage, export options to share resources across platforms, and options to convert content to alternative formats (e.g., JPEG to PDF). Mobile technologies lend themselves to creation of content to facilitate attention to task, self-regulation, independence, and communication with app smashing. Content created in one app may then be exported to file-sharing or storage apps such as Dropbox, iBooks, Google Drive, or e-mail.

Video Modeling

Mobile technology has also advanced the ease of implementation of well-documented EBPs such as video modeling and video self-modeling, which provide targeted and specific input or modeling of desired behaviors or expectations. Video modeling is a teaching tool in which a desired skill or behavior is shown, including from the learner's point of view and perspective. Video self-modeling is a video of the learner demonstrating the desired behavior. Video models are brief, just a few minutes long, which adds to the ease of use in light of current mobile technologies. Bellini and Akullian's (2007) meta-analysis of video modeling and video self-modeling interventions for children and adolescents with ASD asserts that video-modeling strategies facilitate skill acquisition and often result in maintenance of skills over time and transfer of skills to different communication partners and settings. The categories of skills taught with video modeling and video self-modeling included in the meta-analysis were social-communication skills, functional skills, and behavioral functioning. It is proposed that the effectiveness of video modeling and video self-modeling lies in Bandura's (1977) assertion that attention is necessary for modeling, and that modeling is only effective when the individual attends to the model. Over-selective attention to irrelevant stimuli in the environment, a trait often observed in individuals with ASD, is reduced in video modeling, by design and with editing. In addition, individuals with ASD are known to experience stress when interacting with others. In this connection, video viewing is not only a desired activity but requires minimal engagement with others for learning to occur.

Promising Practices

Video feedback, a strategy currently being used with good effect, involves app smashing. Annotation apps are used with productivity apps to create short videos that provide students meaningful feedback about writing tasks (Musselwhite & Hanser, 2016). For example, if a student writes "S S R P" in response to a picture of herself at the beach, a screenshot of the writing task and picture would be annotated using a video-recording feature. As the "Ss" are circled or highlighted, the audio recording attributes meaning and intent toward the letters written with statements such as "I see sun and sand. Sun and sand start with 'S'. Sun and sand definitely make me think of the beach." For some individuals, such feedback is informative and fosters a sense of accomplishment. The accessibility of such tools allows students to replay video feedback segments repeatedly creating increased input to facilitate learning.

Virtual reality has begun to emerge as a promising technology for improving social skills, cognition, and functioning in individuals with high-functioning autism (Kandalaft, Didehbani, Krawczyk, Allen, & Chapman, 2013). Cheng and Huang (2012) suggested that joint attention, a key element of learning, is enhanced by the immersion of virtual-reality experiences. Further advances in engagement-sensitive, virtual-reality technology may someday provide beneficial learning and engagement experiences for individuals with significant disabilities and complex communication disorders.

A Case Study

Joe is a third-grade student with ASD in a self-contained special education classroom with four other students with various disabilities. There is one teacher and two assistants in Joe's classroom. All of the students in Joe's class use some form of AAC. He uses a low-tech communication book to make requests, refuse, and respond. Joe rarely initiates, with the exception of approaching staff members for hugs. Although good-natured much of the time, Joe is difficult to engage and demonstrates challenging behaviors. Joe loves dinosaurs and the color green.

During instruction, Joe's materials are presented in an upright position on a black background to maximize his attention to learning materials. At times, Joe can be guided to participate in classroom activities, given visual prompts such as gestural cues, modeling, and ample repetition. He is highly responsive to routines. Although he will often look toward his teacher, he is not responsive to verbal instructions. At other times, Joe demonstrates impulsive behaviors such as throwing items placed in front of him. Materials of instruction and manipulatives are generally placed in sight but out of reach, are withheld, or are closely monitored by a staff member. When most resistant to participating in academic tasks, Joe cannot be directed to his seat and seeks out tight spaces between furniture to wedge his body. Joe frequently attempts to elope from loud environments such as music class and the cafeteria. He will not approach the auditorium during assemblies.

Joe's classroom is engineered with a class picture schedule on the wall, labels on many common objects, and a picture sequence for hand-washing routine above the sink. During instruction, language boards and individual picture symbols are provided. Joe's teacher created individual picture schedules for some students, as well as some first–then boards. She developed a token board for Joe and one other student. However, significant staff turnover during the first few months of the school year and impulsive behaviors from several students created challenges for presenting and managing the tools provided. Piles of visual supports were scattered throughout the classroom, with no one quite sure when to use which tool or with which student. Cards were inevitably misplaced. Quite simply, this teacher faced the very real challenge of managing myriad visual tools to support her learners, amid impulsive grabbing behaviors, limited table space, and frequent staff changes. In essence, the effectiveness of the visual schedules, task analysis boards, token boards, and first–then boards was trivialized by challenges that inhibited the teacher's ability to manage and maintain the supports needed to create a visually engineered environment for her students.

Now let's apply the SETT Framework to the decision-making process of determining appropriate visual and environmental supports for Joe in this classroom:

STUDENT: Joe

Strengths/Positive Behaviors: Affectionate/seeks hugs (proprioceptive input), communicates basic wants and needs using a low-tech communication book, responsive to routines, motivated by dinosaurs and the color green, beneficial presentation strategies include upright presentation and a contrasting black background.

Weaknesses/Areas of Need: Difficult to engage much of the time, requires significant prompting to participate, demonstrates sensory seeking and sensory avoidance challenging behaviors, impulsive behaviors make it difficult to engage with materials and manipulatives.

ENVIRONMENT:

School environments including Joe's classroom and other common spaces within the school. Joe requires visual supports that are compact, transportable, flexible, easy to use across environments, and easy for new staff to learn. Visual supports are used in tandem with aided communication tools.

TASKS:

Demonstrate cooperative engagement in classroom activities (with increasing independence).

Demonstrate learning and understanding during classroom lessons.

Participate in activities without demonstrating challenging behaviors related to sensory-seeking needs. (It is incumbent upon school staff to provide strategies and opportunities to ensure sensory needs are met.)

TOOLS:

To increase structure in this classroom to facilitate task completion and establish expectations in an easy-to-use format, an All-In-One Visual Support Tool was developed. A board that folded to include a first-then board on the front, a personal picture schedule in the middle, and a task analysis checklist on the back was mounted with a "finished" pocket to the front of a small 5.5- X 8-inch green binder. A token board was placed on the back of the binder. Carpet pages inside the binder stored symbols not in use.

To specifically address Joe's needs, a heavy-duty hook-and-loop fastener was used for his symbols, and frequent "squeezes" were incorporated into his schedule to ensure ample proprioceptive input. To foster increased attention during instruction, tasks were broken into small increments on the task analysis board, which he removed upon completion of each task. Although not immediately evident, over time it became clear that this process allowed Joe to more fully engage in instruction seemingly due to an increased understanding of what to expect from the activity and during the given time period. A small flashlight was also found to be beneficial for directing his attention to instructional tasks. Joe was also provided the following visual choices of activities to help him cope with noisy environments: staying outside the doorway of noisy environments to participate from a distance, wearing noise-cancelling headphones, or choosing a different activity. All of Joe's visual supports were stored on the carpet pages or in a zipper pouch in his binder. It traveled with him in a bag with his communication book throughout his school day.

As this scenario demonstrates, it is imperative to consider not only the visual supports that are needed but also the context in which visual supports will be implemented. Thoughtful design and flexible customization are necessary to ensure the use, management, and maintenance and transport of the tool, or more importantly combination of tools, that is a good fit for the environment and activities in which the student participates. An example of such a tool has been developed by Tabitha Jones-Wohleber and is available at www.PrAACticalAAC.org.

CONCLUSION

Development and implementation of visual and environmental supports is a fundamental consideration for providing individuals with ASD and CCN the organizational, receptive, and expressive modalities needed to engage meaningfully across environments and activities. Although such tools were initially borne out of necessity and experimentation, many of these practices have been validated through research that, in combination with evolving practitioner expertise, continues to guide EBPs related to their use.

The most commonly implemented visual supports include communication displays, visual schedules, and behavior management tools. These tools, and others, support interactions between individuals with ASD and CNN and their communication partner by creating an embedded language in the environment that builds understanding, fosters relationships, and promotes self-actualization. Technological innovations have been instrumental in expanding access to, and thereby use of, visual supports in environments in which individuals with ASD and CCN are supported. Such innovations continually shift the landscape for creating and presenting visually engineered environments, owing to increasingly ubiquitous access, ease of use, and interactive design.

Finally, the SETT Framework helps shape a thorough understanding of the needs and characteristics of an individual with ASD and CCN, as well as the environments in which the tools will be implemented for thoughtful development of visual and environmental supports to meet an individual's unique needs. Such supports foster understanding, cooperation, learning, engagement, and independence in a variety of ways. By creating an accessible environment, such supports allow individuals to gain autonomy, build relationships, and develop the sense of identity inherent in having an active role in the tasks and activities of one's life.

REFERENCES

American Speech-Language-Hearing Association. (2018). *Evidence-based practice (EBP)*. Retrieved from https://www.asha.org/Research/EBP.

Angermeier, K., Schlosser, R. W., Luiselli, J. K., Harrington, C., & Carter, B. (2008). Effects of iconicity on requesting with the picture exchange communication system in children with autism spectrum disorder. *Research in Autism Spectrum Disorders, 2,* 430–446.

Ayres, A. J. (1979). *Sensory integration and the child*. Los Angeles, CA: Western Psychological Services.

Bandura A. (1977). *Social learning theory*. Englewood Cliffs, NJ: Prentice Hall.

Bellini, S. (2006). The development of social anxiety in adolescents with autism spectrum disorders. *Focus on Autism and Other Developmental Disabilities, 21,* 138–145.

Bellini, S., & Akullian, J. (2007). A meta-analysis of video modeling and video self-modeling interventions for children and adolescents with autism spectrum disorders. *Exceptional Children, 73*(3), 264–287.

Bird, G., Press, C., & Richardson, D. C. (2011). The role of alexithymia in reduced eye-fixation in autism spectrum conditions. *Journal of Autism and Developmental Disorders, 41*(11), 1556–1564.

Birkan, B., McClannahan, L. E., & Krantz, P. J. (2007). Effects of superimposition and background fading on the sight-word reading of a boy with autism. *Research in Autism Spectrum Disorders, 1,* 117–125.

Blissymbolics International. (2016, October). *About Blissymbolics*. Retrieved from http://www. blissymbolics.org

Brown, J. L., Krantz, P. J., McClannahan, L. E., & Poulson, C. L. (2008). Using script fading to promote natural environment stimulus control of verbal interactions among youths with autism. *Research in Autism Spectrum Disorders, 2*(3), 480–497.

Brown, K. E., & Mirenda, P. (2006). Contingency mapping: Use of a novel visual support strategy as an adjunct to functional equivalence training. *Journal of Positive Behavior Interventions, 8*(3), 155–164.

Cafiero, J. M. (2001). The effect of an augmentative communication intervention on the communication, behavior and academic program of an adolescent with autism. *Focus on Autism and Other Developmental Disabilities, 16*(3), 179–189.

Case-Smith, J., & Bryan, T. (1999). The effects of occupational therapy with sensory integration emphasis on preschool-age children with autism. *The American Journal of Occupational Therapy, 53*(5), 489–497.

CAST. (2016, November). *About universal design for learning*. Retrieved from http://www.cast. org/our-work/about-udl.html#.WBzOtOErLEY

Cheng, Y., & Huang, R. (2012). Using virtual reality environment to improve joint attention associated with pervasive developmental disorder. *Research in Developmental Disabilities, 33*(6), 2141–2152.

Cobb, S. (n.d.) *Harmon revisited*. Brookfield, WI: The Vision Therapy Center. Retrieved July 27, 2012, from http://info.thevisiontherapycenter.com/Portals/91892/docs/Sarah%20Cobb%20 Harmon%20Revisited.pdf

Davis, T. E., III, Moree, B. N., Dempsey, T., Hess, J. A., Jenkins, W. S., Fodstad, J. C., & Matson, J. L. (2012). The effects of communication deficits on anxiety symptoms in infants and toddlers with autism spectrum disorders. *Behavior Therapy, 43*, 142–152.

deVries, M., & Geurts, H. (2015). Influence of autism traits and executive functioning on quality of life in children with autism spectrum disorder. *Journal of Autism and Developmental Disorder, 45*, 2734–2743.

Dooley, P., Wilczenski, F. L., & Torem, C. (2001). Using an activity schedule to smooth school transitions. *Journal of Positive Behavior Interventions, 3*, 57–61.

Drager, K. D. R., Postal, V., Carrolus, L., Castellano, M., Gagliano, C., & Glynn, J. (2006). The effect of aided language modeling on symbol comprehension and production in 2 preschoolers with autism. *American Journal of Speech Language Pathology, 15*(2), 112–125.

Dukhovny, E., & Zhou, Y. (2016). Effects of icon size and location on speed and accuracy of SGD access. *Augmentative and Alternative Communication*. doi:10.1080/07434618.2016.123 6835

Dunlap, L. K., Dunlap, G., Koegel, L. K., & Koegel, R. L. (1991). Using self-monitoring to increase independence. *Teaching Exceptional Children, 23*, 17–22.

Dunn Buron, K., & Curtis, M. (2012). *Incredible 5-Point Scale: The significantly improved and expanded second edition; Assisting students in understanding social interactions and controlling their emotional responses*. Shawnee Mission, KS: AAPC Publishing.

Duttlinger, C., Ayres, K. M., Bevill-Davis, A., & Douglas, K. H. (2013). The effect of a picture activity schedule for students with intellectual disability to complete a sequence of tasks following verbal direction. *Focus on Autism and Other Developmental Disabilities, 28*, 32–43.

Ecklund, S., & Reichle, J. (1987). A comparison, normal children's ability to recall symbols from two logo-graphic systems. *Language, Speech and Hearing Services in Schools, 18*, 34–40.

Englund, J. A., Decker, S. L., Allen, R. A., & Roberts, A. M. (2014). Common cognitive deficits in children with attention-deficit and hyperactivity disorder and autism: Working memory and visual-motor integration. *Journal of Psychoeducational Assessment, 32*, 95–106.

Ergonomic. (2017). In *The American Heritage Dictionary of the English Language*. Retrieved from https://ahdictionary.com/word/search.html?q=ergonomic

Erickson, K. A., Clendon, S., Abraham, L., Roy, V., & Van der Karr, H. (2005). Toward positive literacy outcomes for students with significant disabilities. *Assistive Technology Outcomes and Benefits, 2*(1), 45–54.

Factor, R. S., Condy, E. E., Farley, J. P., & Scarpa, A. (2016). Brief report: Insistence on sameness, anxiety and social motivation in children with autism spectrum disorder. *Journal of Autism and Developmental Disorders, 46*, 2548–2554.

Farrall, J. (2016). *What's up in Apple apps?* Pre-Conference Workshop at ISAAC Conference, Toronto, Canada.

Forti, S., Valli, A., Perego, P., Nobile, M., Crippa, A., & Molteni, M. (2011). Motor planning and control in autism: A kinematic analysis of preschool children. *Research in Autism Spectrum Disorders, 5*, 834–842.

Freeth, M., Bullock, T., & Milne, E. (2013). The distribution of and relationship between autistic traits and social anxiety in a UK student population. *The International Journal of Research and Practice, 17*, 571–581.

Giddan, N., & Giddan, J. (1984). *Teaching language with pictures.* Springfield, IL: Charles C. Thomas.

Goh, S., & Peterson, B. (2012). Imaging evidence for disturbances in multiple learning and memory systems in persons with autism spectrum disorders. *Developmental Medicine and Child Neurology, 54*, 208–213.

Goossens, C., Crain, S., & Elder, P. (1992). *Engineering the preschool environment for interactive, symbolic communication.* Birmingham, AL: Southeast Augmentative Communication Conference Publications.

Goossens, C.A. (1984). *The relative iconicity and learnability of verb referents differentially represented as manual signs. Blissymbolics and rebus symbols: An investigation with moderately retarded individuals.* (Doctoral dissertation, Purdue University, 1983). Dissertation Abstracts International, *45*, 809A.

Gowen, R., & Hamilton, A. (2013). Motor abilities in autism: A review using a computational context. *Journal of Autism and Developmental Disorders, 43*, 323–344.

Gregorenak, E. L., Klin, A., Pauls, D. L., Senft, R., Hooper, C., & Volkmar, F. (2002). A descriptive study of hyperlexia in a clinically referred sample of children with developmental delays. *Journal of Autism and Developmental Disorders, 32*(1), 3–12.

Hampshire, P. K., Butera, G. D., & Bellini, S. (2015). Self-management and parents as interventionists to improve homework independence in students with autism spectrum disorders. *Preventing School Failure, 60*(1), 22–34.

Hartley, C., & Allen, M. L. (2015a). Iconicity influences: How effectively minimally verbal children with autism and ability-matched typically developing children use pictures as symbols in a search task. *The International Journal of Research and Practice, 19*, 570–579.

Hartley, C., & Allen, M. L. (2015b). Symbolic understanding of pictures in low-functioning children with autism: The effects of iconicity and naming. *Journal of Autism and Developmental Disorders, 45*, 15–30.

Hatch, P. (2009). The effects of daily reading opportunities and teacher experience on adolescents with moderate to severe intellectual disability. *Pro Quest Dissertation Publishing*, 3352888.

Henry, L. A., Messer, D. J., & Nash, G. (2012). Executive functioning with specific language impairment. *Journal of Child Psychology and Psychiatry, 53*, 37–45.

Hetzroni, O. E., & Ne'eman, A. (2013). Facilitating children's ability to distinguish influence of colour on acquisition and generalisation of graphic symbols. *Journal of Intellectual Disability Research, 57*, 669–680.

Hopkins, C. J. (1979, November) Using every-pupil response techniques in reading instruction. *The Reading Teacher, 33*(2), 173–175.

Huriburt, B. I., Iwata, B. A., & Green, J. D. (1982). Nonvocal language acquisition in adolescents with severe physical disabilities: Blissymbolics versus iconic stimulus formats. *Journal of Applied Behavior Analysis, 15*, 241–258.

Huer, M. B. (2000). Examining perceptions of graphic symbols across cultures: Preliminary study of the pact of culture ethnicity. *Augmentative and Alternative Communication, 16*, 180–185.

Hume, K., & Odom, S. L. (2007). Effects of a work system on the work and play of children and individuals with autism. *Journal of Autism and Developmental Disorders, 37*, 1166–1180.

Jones-Wohleber, T. (2015). *How I do it: All-in-one visual support tool.* Available at http://praactical aac.org/praactical/how-i-do-it-the-all-in-one-visual-support-tool-by-tabi-jones-wohleber

Kaldy, Z., Giserman, I., Carter, A., & Blaser, E. (2016). The mechanisms underlying the ASD advantage in visual search. *Journal of Autism and Developmental Disorders, 46*, 1513–1527.

Kandalaft, M. R., Didehbani, N., Krawczyk, D. C., Allen, T. T., & Chapman, S. B. (2013). Virtual reality social cognition training for young adults with high-functioning autism. *Journal of Autism and Developmental Disorders, 43*(1), 34–44.

Kelly, M. P., Leader, G., & Reed, P. (2015). Stimulus overselectivity and extinction-induced recovery of performance as a product of intellectual impairment and autism severity. *Journal of Autism and Developmental Disorders, 45,* 3098–3106.

Kluth, P. (2010). *You're going to love this kid: Teaching students with autism in the inclusive classroom.* Baltimore, MD: Paul H. Brookes Publishing Co.

Koppenhaver, D. A., Erickson, K. A., & Skotko, B. G. (2001). Supporting communication of girls with Rett syndrome and their mothers in storybook reading. *International Journal of Disability, Development and Education, 48,* 396–410.

Krantz, P. J., MacDuff, M. T., & McClannahan, L. E. (1993). Programming participation in family activities for children with autism: Parents' use of photographic activity schedules. *Journal of Applied Behavior Analysis, 26,* 137–139.

Kulowiec, G. (2013). App Smashing: Part 1. *The History 2.0 Classroom.* Available at http://kulowiectech.blogspot.com/2013/02/app-smashing-part-i.html

Light, J., & McNaughton, D. (2016). *Designing AAC interventions and research to improve outcomes for individuals with complex communication needs.* Presented at ISAAC, Toronto, CA.

MacDuff, G. S., Krantz, P. J., & McClannahan, L. E. (1993). Teaching children with autism to use photographic activity schedules: Maintenance and generalization of complex response chains. *Journal of Applied Behavior Analysis, 26,* 89–97.

Martin, J. H., Reichle, J., Dimian, A., & Chen, M. (2013). Communication modality sampling for a toddler with Angelman syndrome. *Language Speech and Hearing in the Schools, 44,* 327–336.

May-Benson, T. A., & Koomar, J. A. (2010). Systematic review of the research evidence examining the effectiveness of interventions using a sensory integrative approach for children. *American Journal of Occupational Therapy, 64,* 403–414. doi:10.5014/ajot.2010.09071

McClannahan, L. E., & Krantz, P. J. (2010). *Activity schedules for children with autism: Teaching independent behavior.* Bethesda, MD: Woodbine.

Mesibov, G., & Shea, V. (2010). The TEACCH program in the era of evidence-based practice. *Journal of Autism and Developmental Disorders, 40,* 570–579.

Mirenda, P. (1997). Supporting individuals with challenging behavior through functional communication training and AAC: A research review. *Augmentative and Alternative Communication, 13,* 207–225.

Mirenda, P. & Locke, P. A. (1989). A comparison of symbol transparency in nonspeaking persons with intellectual disabilities. *Journal of Speech and Hearing Disorders, 54,* 131–140.

Mongillo, E. A., Irwin, J. R., Whalen, D. H., Klaiman, C., Carter, A. S., & Schultz, R. T. (2008). Audiovisual processing in children with and without autism spectrum disorders. *Journal of Autism and Developmental Disorders, 38,* 1349–1358.

Musselwhite, C., & Hanser, G. (2016). *Hands-on iPad video feedback: Make it informative and strategic! (and fun!!).* Presentation at Closing the Gap Conference, Minneapolis, Minnesota.

Na, J. Y., Wilkinson, K., Karny, M., Blackstone, S., & Stifter, C. (2016). A synthesis of relevant literature on the development of emotional competence: Implications for design of augmentative and alternative communication systems. *American Journal of Speech Language Pathology, 25*(3), 442–452.

Nakano, T., Tanaka, K., Endo, Y., Yamane, Y., Yamamoto, T., Nakano, Y., Ohta, H., Kato, N., & Kitazawa, S. (2010). Atypical eye gaze patterns in children and adults with autism spectrum disorder dissociated from developmental change in gaze behavior. *Proceedings of the Royal Society B.* doi:10.1098/rspb2010.0587, 2935–2943

Parker, D., & Kamps, D. (2011). Effects of task analysis and self-monitoring for children with autism in multiple social settings. *Focus on Autism and Other Developmental Disabilities, 26,* 131–142.

Ploog, B. O. (2010). Stimulus overselectivity four decades later: A review of the literature and its implications for current research in autism spectrum disorder. *Journal of Autism and Developmental Disorders, 40,* 1332–1349.

Rieth, S. R., Stahmer, A. C., Suhrheinrich, J., & Schreibman, L. (2015). Examining the prevalence of stimulus overselectivity in children with ASD. *Journal of Applied Behavior Analysis, 48,* 71–84.

Romski, M. A., & Sevcik, R. (1996). *Breaking the speech barrier: Language development through augmented means.* Baltimore: Paul H. Brookes Publishing Co.

Rotholz, D. A., Berkowitz, S. F., & Burberry, J. (1989). Functionality of two modes of communication in the community by students with developmental disabilities: A comparison of signing and communication books. *Research and Practice for Persons with Severe Disabilities, 14*, 227 –233.

Saarni, C. (1999). *The development of emotional competence.* New York, NY: Guilford Press.

Semrud-Clikeman, M., Fine, J., Goldenning, J., & Bledsoe, J. (2014). Comparison among children with autism spectrum disorder, nonverbal learning disorder and typically developing children on measures of executive functioning. *Journal of Autism and Developmental Disorders, 44*(2), 331–342.

Sennott, S., Light, J., & McNaughton, D. (2016). AAC modeling intervention research review. *Research and Practice for Persons with Severe Disabilities, 41*, 101–116.

Schmit, J. A., Alper, S., Raschke, D., & Ryndak, D. (2000). Effects of using a photographic cueing package during routine school transitions with a child who has autism. *Mental Retardation, 38*, 131–137.

Schopler, E., Brehm, S., Kinsborne, M., & Reichler, R. (1971). *Archives of General Psychiatry, 24*, 415–421. doi:10.1001/archpsyc.1971.01750110027005

Shane, H., Laubscher, E., Schlosser, R. W., Fadie, H. L., Sorce, J. F., Abramson, J. S., Flynn, S., & Corley, K. (2015). *Enhancing communication for individuals with autism: A guide to the visual immersion system.* Baltimore, MD: Paul H. Brookes Publishing Co.

Shane, H., Laubscher, E., Schlosser, R., Flynn, S., Sorce, J., & Abramson, J. (2012). Applying technology to visually support language and communication in individuals with autism spectrum disorders. *Journal of Autism & Developmental Disorders, 42*(6), 1228–1235.

Siegel, E., & Lien, S. (2015). Using photographs of contrasting contextual complexity to support classroom transitions for children with autism spectrum disorders. *Focus on Autism and Other Developmental Disabilities, 30*(2), 100–114.

Steele, D., Minshew, N. J., Luna, B., & Sweeney, J. A. (2007). Spatial working memory deficits in autism. *Journal of Autism and Developmental Disorders, 37*, 605–612.

Stephenson, J. (2007). The effect of color on the recognition and use of line drawings by children with severe intellectual disabilities. *Augmentative and Alternative Communication, 23*, 44–55.

Stoit, A. M. B., van Shie, H. T., Slaats-Willemse, D. I. E., & Buitelaar, J. K. (2013). Grasping motor impairments in autism: Not action planning but movement execution is deficient. *Journal of Autism and Developmental Disorders, 43*, 323–344.

Thistle, J. J., & Wilkinson, K. M. (2013). Working memory demands of aided augmentative and alternative communication for individuals with developmental disabilities. *Augmentative and Alternative Communication, 29*, 235–245.

Tremblath, D., Vivanti, G., Iocono, T., & Dissanayake, C. (2015). Accurate or assumed: Visual learning in children with autism spectrum disorders. *Journal of Autism and Developmental Disorders, 45*, 3276–3287.

Tustin, R. D. (1995). The effect of advance notice of activity transitions on stereotypic behaviors. *Journal of Applied Behavior Analysis, 28*, 91–92.

van den Bergh, S., Sanne, F. W. M., Scheeren, A. J., Begeer, S., Koot, H. M., & Guerts, H. M. (2014). Age related differences of executive functioning problems in everyday life of children and adolescents in the autism spectrum. *Journal of Autism and Developmental Disorders, 44*, 1959–1971.

Vaughn, B., & Horner, R. H. (1995). Identifying instructional tasks that occasion problem behaviors and assessing the effects of student versus teacher choice among these tasks. *Journal of Applied Behavior Analysis, 30*(2), 299–312.

Weitlauf, A. S., Sathe, N., McPheeters, M. L., & Warren, Z. E. (2017). Interventions targeting sensory challenges in autism spectrum disorder: A systematic review. *Pediatrics, 139*, e20170347. doi:10.1542/peds.2017-0347

White, S. W., Bray, B. B., Ollendick, T. H. (2012). Examining shared and unique aspects of social anxiety disorder and autism spectrum disorder using factor analysis. *Journal of Autism and Developmental Disorders, 42*, 874–884.

Wilkinson, K. M., & McIlvaine, W. J. (2013). Perceptual factors influence visual search for meaningful symbols in individuals with intellectual disabilities and Down syndrome or autism spectrum disorders. *American Journal on Intellectual and Developmental Disabilities, 118*(5), 353–364.

Zabala, J. S. (2005). *Using the SETT Framework to level the learning field for students with disabilities.* Retrieved from http://www.joyzabala.com/uploads/Zabala_SETT_Leveling_the_Learning_Field.pdf

14

Conclusions and Directions for Future Research

Jennifer B. Ganz and Richard L. Simpson

FUNDAMENTAL THEMES

Authors who wrote for this book, as well as other extant research literature contributors, agree on fundamental and structural themes linked to individuals with minimal or no functional speech. This chapter discusses those themes.

Communication Is Essential

First and foremost, there is unequivocal consensus that these individuals, including those diagnosed with autism spectrum disorder (ASD), must receive priority attention for amelioration of communication deficits. Communication is an essential human characteristic, and development of communicative assets is imperative. Unquestionably, without functional and utilitarian systems of communication, individuals with complex communication needs (CCN) will almost certainly achieve lesser life outcomes than they would with adequate interventions and supports to improve these deficits. Recognition and acknowledgment of communication as a core human trait and necessity is the first step toward ensuring all individuals with CCN receive appropriate programs, interventions, and instruction. Such affirmation acknowledges the vital and pivotal role of communication skills and that fully embracing and taking advantage of life's potential experiences and opportunities requires the ability to communicate.

This is not a novel concept. Throughout history, communication has been recognized as vital to human survival, development, and advancement (Jastrow, 1886). Given its crucial historical role, it logically follows that learning to communicate effectively is a basic human right that needs to be afforded every individual, regardless of situation, status, or circumstance, including the existence of a disability (Light & McNaughton, 2014). Decades ago, Skinner (1957) referenced the essential role of "verbal behavior," again acknowledging the unique and vital role of language-based interactions and shared expression. Of course, some children, adolescents, and adults with ASD and other disabilities develop little or no speech, hence augmentative and alternative forms of communication are required. These individuals confront significant challenges, yet they may thrive, succeed, and progress when provided tools that mitigate and circumvent limited or absent expressive and receptive language. Authors of the chapters in this book clearly support and advocate for the development of functional communication for all learners. In addition, they optimistically point to the significant outcomes that align with skill development. Authors strongly argue that special educators, speech-language pathologists, and other related professionals (e.g., behavior specialists, school psychologists) must commit the necessary time and energy needed to support the acquisition and functional use of communication skills in learners with disabilities who fail to develop functional, age-appropriate speech (Beukelman & Mirenda, 2013; Ganz, Davis, Lund, Goodwyn, & Simpson, 2012; McNaughton & Light, 2013). Finally, they bluntly observe that commitment and determination alone will not result in meaningful gains and authentically beneficial outcomes. Genuine communication gains among individuals with CCN occur when practitioners (in particular, educators, speech-language pathologists, and their related service colleagues) have the knowledge and skills needed to adequately assess communication; design, implement, and evaluate appropriate individualized programs; and combine this know-how with commitment and resolve.

Communication Is Complex

Chapter authors affirm what practitioners, parents, and other stakeholders have long observed among individuals with ASD and CCN. These individuals have complex, disparate, and highly idiosyncratic communication characteristics and needs. This fundamental second theme is prominently woven across the chapters. Plainly speaking, there are no universal solutions; and easy, simple, or one-size-fits-all fixes are unavailable! Mirenda (see Chapter 4, "Overview of AAC for Individuals With Autism Spectrum Disorder and Complex Communication Needs") sagely and succinctly observed that "a single AAC technique will *never* meet all of an individual's communication needs;" and that there is a need for "a combination of approaches, depending on the message and context." For sure, interventions and supports, including augmentative and alternative communication (AAC) methods, must be individually crafted and evaluated on an ongoing basis to address specific learner needs. Still, while clearly dispelling myths about the availability of easy and universal communication-deficit solutions, authors accentuate the capacity of learners to acquire and employ functional communication skills when provided individualized instruction and support.

In fact, researchers, practitioners, families, and others understand all too well the already significant challenges faced by individuals with disabilities become significantly more difficult when they lack functional communication skills. These are not just childhood and school-related issues. Living independently, establishing and maintaining reciprocal and satisfactory social relationships, accessing adequate health care, fully participating and taking advantage of available leisure opportunities, having suitable employment choices, and being wholly able to engage in myriad other activities that align with quality-of-life experiences are significantly reduced in the absence of a functional means of communication (Brown, Hatton & Emerson, 2013; Gerhardt, Macguire & Bloomer, 2016).

Communication and Evidence-Based Practices

A third broad-spectrum theme that chapter authors expressed is that communication deficits will not improve without the application of evidence-based interventions, and these methods must be applied with fidelity by knowledgeable professionals from multiple disciplines along with support of other stakeholders. Children with CCN who lack functional speech and conventional nonverbal communication and AAC instruction and systems will develop ways of communicating. However, in the absence of suitable instruction and interventions, these self-styled communication systems will be unconventional and limited in scope and shared understanding, and often linked to socially unacceptable initiations and responses (Carr & Durand, 1985; Plumb, Wetherby, Oetting, & Craig, 2013). Moreover, and perhaps most significantly, individuals who continue to use these self-developed tools may not acquire more adaptive and utilitarian communication assets on their own and merely as a function of time. Learners acquire enhanced communication repertoires when given suitable instruction (Ogletree, 2016; Prelock & McCauley, 2012). Supportive environments and structured experiences based on scientifically reinforced methods are salient elements of such programming, including coaching and response feedback and reinforcement; opportunities to use newly developed skills and assets in a variety of supported settings; natural setting generalization planning and instruction; parent and family program participation; and ongoing strategic backing of peers and encouraging peer allies (Chung, Carter, & Sisco, 2012; Symon, 2005; Whalon, Conroy, Martinez, & Werch, 2015).

Authors of this book added their voice to the chorus of others within the field in declaring that not all interventions and methods purported to be beneficial are in fact acceptable and useful. It is particularly critical that multidisciplinary practitioners (e.g., speech-language pathologists, educators, behavior analysts) select treatments, support methods, and interventions for learners with ASD that are evidence-based rather than those that are unproven or controversial, including those purported to assist learners with CCN (Foxx & Mulick, 2016). Unquestionably, there has been an unhealthy willingness among some professionals and parents to rely on unproven interventions and treatments. These so-called "novel strategies" and purported "cures" prey on the vulnerabilities of desperate parents and families and bode poorly relative to achieving positive outcomes with learners with CCN.

Reasonable, judicious, and scientifically minded professionals from multiple disciplines recognize the need for a range of evidence-based intervention approaches and methods for teaching communication skills, including AAC. Indeed, based on the idiosyncratic nature of communication and language deficits among individuals with CCN, in combination with the variety of settings and circumstances where programs will be implemented (e.g., classroom vs. clinic), variable tools will be required to achieve success. At the same time, discriminating and sagacious consumers and practitioners recognize the importance of using evidence-based and proven approaches. In general, evidence-based strategies and methods have been proven to consistently produce beneficial outcomes. These strategies have been validated based on established scientific research designs, clearly stated methodology and protocol, and proven evaluation methods (Odom et al., 2005). Minor terminology distinctions have been made, including between research-validated methods, scientifically supported methods, and evidence-based practices (EBPs) (Fixsen, Naoom, Blase, Friedman, & Wallace, 2005). However, each of these terms generally refers to interventions, strategies, and practices that have been shown to be effective based on scientifically objective and empirical proof. All told, consensus (and more important, factual empirical verification) is that learners are most likely to achieve the best outcomes when practitioners have available an assortment of intervention options. However, this variable menu assertion has a salient caveat: All approaches used with an individual with CCN must be evidence-based and scientifically verified.

Logical and common-sense thinking is increasingly leading practitioners and stakeholders to demand application and ongoing evaluation of EBPs and methods, including strategies that focus on developing communication skills. That there is a well-defined and unmistakable link between consistently and correctly using evidence-based interventions and supports and achieving the best school and post-school outcomes is compelling testimony for this reasoning (Cook, Tankersley, & Landrum, 2016; Simpson & Crutchfield, 2013). Yet, despite overwhelming evidence, supporting legislation, and availability of potentially effective tools and interventions, there continues to be a willingness among some stakeholders to bring into play unproven and nonscientific methods (Travers, Ayers, Simpson, & Crutchfield, 2016).

Understanding why some professionals and parents are willing to gamble on unproven intervention methods is a matter of opinion and conjecture. Clearly, multifaceted and complex factors are in play:

- Feelings of desperation and frustration that accompany recognition of the significant and seemingly overwhelming and pernicious nature of limited language development

- The perceived intractable nature of severe language and communication challenges

- The unknown etiology of some cases of limited or no expressive language development

- The effort involved and perceived modest progress associated with using some documented methods with individuals with CCN

- The seductive influence of advertisements and promotions for so-called novel approaches and exaggerated claims and undocumented declarations of "cures" and extraordinary benefits and outcomes

The quintessential example of such a sham method is facilitated communication (Ganz, Katsiyannis, & Morin, in press; Lilienfeld, Marshal, Todd, & Shane, 2014; Travers et al., 2016). Despite being exposed as a deceptive and bogus method years ago (Simpson & Myles, 1995; Wheeler, Jacobson, Paglieri, & Schwartz, 1993), facilitated communication continues to be used. This resilience and recent resurgence, at least in part, is a matter of deceptive rebranding (i.e., the term "facilitated communication" is now commonly referred to as rapid prompting), assisted and supported typing, typed communication, and similar terms (Todd, 2016; Travers, Tincani, & Lang, 2014).

Established and promising strategies were the subject of this book, hence facilitated communication and other unproven methods were not discussed in detail. Nevertheless, facilitated communication and other unproven methods are germane to this work. Practitioners and others, especially neophyte educators and related service personnel who are tasked with the challenging work of developing communication capacity and assets among learners with CCN, are exposed to a variety of competing intervention options. To say these front-line personnel routinely experience an avalanche of such material, at least some of which is hyped and unsubstantiated, is no exaggeration. Some of these methods have been shown to be efficacious and suitable for individuals with CCN, as is the case of strategies identified in this book. These methods have substance, a proven track record, and endorsements based on scientific vetting. We implore practitioners, parents and families, and other stakeholders to continue to seek up-to-date training and become better informed and more discerning consumers of AAC and other language and communication enhancement strategies, particularly as research regarding practices for individuals with ASD and CCN is rapidly expanding. We hope this book will assist in making this crusade a reality. Only when rank and file practitioners, parents and families, advocates, and other stakeholders are firmly committed and fully trained to use appropriate evidence-based approaches will individuals with CCN acquire functional communications skills.

FUTURE CHALLENGES AND RESEARCH THEMES

There is no question that the state of affairs relative to serving the needs of most children, adolescents, and adults with CCN requires additional development. In spite of recent advances in practices designed for this population, there is a significant research-to-practice gap. That is, there is a lag between research investigating the most efficacious practices and methods available to support and intervene with learners with CCN and implementation in classrooms, clinics, and programs. This book, primarily designed for practitioners and others who treat individuals with ASD and CCN, is intended to assist in ameliorating this problem by bridging the knowledge gap between AAC professionals and educational and behavioral professionals. That is, this volume aims to provide a bridge to educate practitioners and other stakeholders with regard to the evidence available across the disciplines of communication disorders, special education, and behavior analysis, while practitioners often receive training limited to their respective fields.

By its very nature this improvement process will be challenging and long term. Increasing the number of highly qualified professionals with knowledge, skills, and experiences in bringing evidence-based supports and intervention methods to the lives of individuals with significant communication impairments requires coordinated effort, including among front-line practitioners, higher-education personnel, preparation personnel, and researchers. In this connection, the authors briefly discuss several issues and challenges they think are logical and necessary matters for future inquiry.

Effectiveness and Individualized Intervention

First, although AAC and other interventions for people with ASD and CCN have been deemed to be evidence-based by some entities, this process has primarily been limited to general assessments of effectiveness. While broad-stroke evaluations of effectiveness are useful, further research may inform the field about unique and noteworthy variables, such as for whom and under what conditions specific interventions are more or less effective. That is, an intervention that is deemed to be generally effective may have a research base that focuses on subpopulations of people with ASD and CCN, or provides limited information on the characteristics population within the study. For example, much of the CCN research, across interventions for people with ASD, focuses on young, preschool or early-primary-age children. These interventions should be more thoroughly researched with adolescents and adults. Furthermore, the extant research literature by and large does not provide sufficient detail to determine whether a child has a CCN or the degree of the communication delays in the participants. This makes it difficult for parents and practitioners to assess whether identified interventions are well-matched for individual children and clients with ASD and CCN.

In order to address the need for adequate information to individualize treatment, research—such as a systematic literature review—must summarize the available primary research on interventions for people with ASD and CCN. These actions are needed to determine where the gaps are regarding age, concomitant diagnoses, communication level, context and setting, interventionists (e.g., natural communicative partners), components of interventions needed or not needed, and generalization and maintenance of outcome measures. Once such research is conducted and gaps are identified, primary research is needed to investigate questions related to those gaps (e.g., comparing effects with varied compilations of intervention components). For example, it is not clear if a slimmed-down version of an intervention package would be as effective as a more intensive intervention package for some individuals. Having such information could potentially yield time and cost savings that might be used for other instruction. Furthermore, for some individuals with challenging behaviors, functional communication training may be a necessary component to add to an AAC instructional package. A comprehensive meta-analysis is then needed to determine differential effects related to these items, based on an updated primary literature base. Relatedly, such work could better inform practitioners and other stakeholders about controversial and ineffective treatments, especially those methods with potential to result in harm or divert funds and time that could be dedicated to more effective interventions. Such work requires increased outreach efforts to ensure that accurate and practitioner-friendly and other accessible and comprehensible information is available to parents and practitioners.

Focusing on Naturalistic Interventions

Second, naturalistic intervention approaches need to be more thoroughly investigated, particularly regarding instruction to improve social and communication skills, which are necessary in almost every context. In particular, the impact of naturalistic communication interventions must be investigated related to determining what pivotal communication skills should be taught. Focusing on pivotal targets leads to increased opportunities for skill improvements, such as promoting learning of new vocabulary, expanding an individual's complexity of language and grammar used, and increasing learning across domains (e.g., literacy, behavior, academic subjects, social opportunities). The role of motivation in learning new communication and social skills also needs to be more thoroughly evaluated, specifically related to working with individuals with ASD and CCN. That is, tying instruction to an individual's preferred items, activities, and people perhaps may increase the efficiency and effectiveness of an intervention. Furthermore, consideration of motivating operations is likely and logically critical in teaching communication skills such as making requests and other initiations. For example, research may evaluate how to determine a child's current motivation to access a preferred object, such as his basketball, related to its degree of reinforcement value or satiation (e.g., how recently and how much he had played basketball). Furthermore, research is needed to investigate the likelihood that naturalistic instruction will increase the maintenance and generalization of skills and strategies across settings and individuals. Finally, critical components of specific interventions, such as behavioral and developmental strategies, need to be determined, specifically related to improved outcomes among individuals with ASD and CCN. This information would allow for development of a robust instructional protocol for improving communication skills for this population.

Training Communication Partners and Social Validity

Third, research is needed related to training natural communication partners to implement interventions or otherwise promote skills across multiple contexts. The social validity of a particular approach or communication mode is likely an important consideration in long-term acceptance and use of interventions by parents, practitioners, and peers. Social validity includes consideration of the key stakeholders related to the feasibility, acceptability, and preferences in implementation. This may involve application of strategies to gain or increase buy-in from natural communication partners, as well as individuals with ASD and CCN, by assessing preferences related to communication modalities, instructional dosage, targeted outcomes, and instructional contexts. Furthermore, research focused on increasing communication partners' fidelity of intervention implementation, generalization of implementation across new contexts, and maintenance of trained skills over time is needed. Finally, there is a significant need for research that will guide the efficient and effective means of training natural communication partners. Knowing how best to prepare responsive and supportive communication partners via instructional coaching, conjoint behavior consultation and other promising training strategies is a prerequisite to advancing this important process.

Evaluating the Use of Augmentative and Alternative Communication Among Individuals With Autism Spectrum Disorder and Complex Communication Needs

Fourth, given the ubiquitous nature of mobile technology, the use of these tools and devices must be evaluated relative to use with people with ASD and CCN. An ever-growing body of research can be found on the use of AAC with individuals with ASD and CCN; however, further research in needed to fine-tune the use of these AAC intervention components using high-tech mobile devices (Ganz, Morin, et al., 2017). Furthermore, as noted by Reichle, Simacek, and Parker-McGowan (see Chapter 5, "Considerations in Implementing Aided Low-Tech AAC Systems for Individuals With Autism Spectrum Disorder and Complex Communication Needs"), additional research is needed to evaluate features of technology-based display qualities (e.g., grid versus visual scene display, pictures versus written words), ease of navigating computer applications, as well as concrete-to-abstract consideration when selecting symbols to represent vocabulary. Furthermore, equitable access to technology should be evaluated and strengthened via future research. Finally, it is critical to note that any technology used will likely be under- or not utilized without explicit and high-quality instruction.

CONCLUSION

This last chapter, and this book, concludes with a call for improved preparation of personnel who serve learners with ASD and CCN, including research that will guide such instruction. The well-recognized need for high-quality personnel, including those with skills and knowledge required to effectively serve individuals with disabilities, is most publicly declared and publicized in relation to calls for educational reform. In the case of individuals with ASD and CCN this call notably extends to a wide range of age groups, including adults, and a variety of service providers (i.e., special educators, speech-language pathologists, behavior analysts) who serve these individuals.

Educators, speech-language pathologists, education-related service professionals and other school staff, clinical professionals, parents and families, and other stakeholders have the enormous responsibility of serving and advocating for individuals with ASD and CNN. This role requires significant knowledge and skills in designing, implementing, and monitoring AAC programs and other communication interventions and supports. When AAC is excluded from interventions and supports for individuals with ASD and CCN, this bodes poorly for optimal or even modest gains among individuals with significant communication needs. With one voice, authors who contributed to this book unambiguously commented on the poor outcomes that accrue when learners fail to receive appropriate and timely interventions and supports for significant communication impairments. There is general recognition of the necessity of adequately preparing personnel for roles in serving individuals with CCN; such preparation requires reliable, clarifying, and guiding research.

Relative to individuals with ASD and CCN, well-qualified personnel are those with a working knowledge of autism and CCN and the ability and experience to evaluate and put into operation evidence-based programs that specifically address communication needs, including AAC. There are currently available a variety of effective tools and methods for mitigating CCN and giving voice to individuals who lack conventional communication abilities. However, these tools and methods are not self-directing. They depend on knowledgeable, skilled, experienced, and dedicated personnel. Only when these tools are correctly applied in a timely manner with fidelity will they have optimal impact and lead to sustainable positive outcomes. Clearly, there is a pressing need for continuing high-quality research on how best to prepare educators and other professionals in the use of scientifically supported interventions and supports for individuals with CCN. Interventions that include parents and family members also facilitate the generalization and maintenance of learned skills; hence, guiding research on this topic is also needed.

In summary, there is strong reason for optimism relative to supports and programs that benefit individuals with CCN and their families. However, this positive outlook and hopeful outcomes for individuals with ASD will depend on the preparation and skills of teachers, speech-language pathologists, and other educational personnel and clinicians. This book will hopefully contribute to this process.

REFERENCES

Beukelman, D. R., & Mirenda, P. (2013). *Augmentative and alternative communication.* (4th ed.). Baltimore, MD: Paul H. Brookes Publishing Co.

Brown, I., Hatton, C., & Emerson, E. (2013). Quality of life indicators for individuals with intellectual disabilities: Extending current practice. *Intellectual and Developmental Disabilities, 51,* 316–332.

Carr, E. G., & Durand, V. M. (1985). Reducing behavior problems through functional communication training. *Journal of Applied Behavior Analysis, 18,* 111–126.

Chung, Y., Carter, E. W., & Sisco, L. G. (2012). A systematic review of interventions to increase peer interactions for students with complex communication challenges. Research and Practice for Persons with Severe Disabilities, 37, 271–287.

Cook, B., Tankersley, M., & Landrum, T. (2016). *Instructional practices with and without empirical validity.* United Kingdom: Emerald.

Fixsen, D. L., Naoom, S. F., Blase, K. A., Friedman, R. M., & Wallace, F. (2005). *Implementation research: A synthesis of the literature.* Tampa, FL: University of South Florida, Louis de la Parte Florida Mental Health Institute, The National Implementation Research Network (FMHI Publication #231).

Foxx, R. M., & Mulick, J. A. (2016). *Controversial therapies for autism and intellectual disabilities: Fad, fashion and science in professional practice.* New York, NY: Routledge.

Ganz, J. B., Davis, J., Lund, E., Goodwyn, F., & Simpson, R. L. (2012). Meta-analysis of PECS with individuals with ASD: Investigation of targeted versus non-targeted outcomes, participant characteristics, and implementation phase. *Research in Developmental Disabilities, 33,* 406–418.

Ganz, J. B., Katsiyannis, A., & Morin, K. (in press). Facilitated communication: The resurgence of a disproven treatment for individuals with autism. *Intervention in School and Clinic.* doi:10.1177/1053451217692564

Ganz, J. B., Morin, K., Foster, M. J., Vannest, K. J., Tosun, D. G., Gregori, E., & Gerow, S. (2017). High-technology augmentative and alternative communication for individuals with intellectual and developmental disabilities and complex communication needs: A meta-analysis. *Augmentative and Alternative Communication, 33,* 224-238. doi:10.1080/07434 618.2017.1373855.

Gerhardt, P., MacGuire, M., & Bloomer, H. (2016). Issues in quality of life and effective intervention with adults with ASD. In R. L. Simpson & B. S. Myles (Eds.), *Educating children and youth with autism: Strategies for effective practice* (pp. 83–120). Austin, TX: Pro-Ed.

Jastrow, J. (1886). The evolution of language. Science, 7, 555–557.

Light, J., & McNaughton, D. (2014). Communicative competence for individuals who require augmentative and alternative communication: A new definition for a new era of communication? *Augmentative and Alternative Communication, 30,* 1–18.

Lilienfeld, S. O., Marshall, J., Todd, J. T., & Shane, H. C. (2014). The persistence of fad interventions in the face of negative scientific evidence: Facilitated communication for autism as a case example. *Evidence-Based Communication Assessment and Intervention, 8,* 62–101.

McNaughton, D., & Light, J. (2013). The iPad and mobile technology revolution: Benefits and challenges for individuals who require augmentative and alternative communication. *Augmentative and Alternative Communication, 29,* 107–116.

Odom, S., Brantlinger, E. Gersten, R., Horner, R., Thompson, B., & Harris, K. (2005). Research in special education: Scientific methods and evidence-based practices. *Exceptional Children, 71,* 137–148.

Ogletree, B. (2016). The communicative context of autism. In R. L. Simpson & B. S. Myles (Eds.), *Educating children and youth with autism: Strategies for effective practice* (pp. 83–120). Austin, TX: Pro-Ed.

Plumb, A., Wetherby, A., Oetting, J., & Craig, E. (2013). Vocalization development in toddlers with autism spectrum disorders. *Journal of Speech, Language and Hearing Research, 56,* 721–734.

Prelock, P., & McCauley, R. (2012). *Treatment of autism spectrum disorders: Evidence-based intervention strategies for communication and social interaction.* Baltimore, MD: Paul H. Brookes Publishing Co.

Simpson, R., & Crutchfield, S. (2013). Effective educational practices for children and youth with autism spectrum disorders: Issues, recommendations for improving outcomes, and future trends. In B. Cook, M. Tankersley, & T. Landrum (Eds.), *Advances in learning and behavioral disabilities* (pp. 197–220). San Diego, CA: Emerald.

Simpson, R., & Myles, B. (1995). Effectiveness of facilitated communication with children and youth with autism. *Journal of Special Education, 28,* 424–439.

Skinner, B. F. (1957). *Verbal behavior.* Englewood Cliffs, NJ: Prentice Hall.

Symon, J. (2005). Expanding interventions for children with autism: Parents as trainers. *Journal of Positive Behavior Interventions, 7,* 159–173.

Todd, J. (2016). Old horses in new stables: Rapid prompting, facilitated communication, science, ethics, and the history of magic. In R. M. Foxx & J. A. Mulick (Eds.), *Controversial therapies for autism and intellectual disabilities* (2nd ed.). New York, NY: Routledge.

Travers, J., Ayers, K., Simpson, R., & Crutchfield, S. (2016). Fad, controversial, and pseudoscientific interventions. In R. Lang, T. Hancock, & N. Singh (Eds.), *Early intervention for young children with autism spectrum disorders* (pp. 257–292). New York, NY: Springer.

Travers, J. C., Tincani, M., & Lang, R. (2014). Facilitated communication denies people with disabilities their voice. *Research and Practice in Severe Disabilities, 39,* 195–202.

Whalon, K. J., Conroy, M. A., Martinez, J. R., & Werch, B. L. (2015). School-based peer-related social competence interventions for children with autism spectrum disorder: A meta-analysis and descriptive review of single case research design studies. Journal of Autism and Developmental Disorders, 45, 1513–1531. doi:10.1007/s10803-015-2373-1

Wheeler, D., Jacobson, J., Paglieri, R., & Schwartz, A. (1993). An experimental assessment of facilitated communication. *Mental Retardation, 31, 49–60.*

Index

Page numbers followed by *f* and *t* indicate figures and tables, respectively.